# HERON
# DERIVATION
## DICTIONARY

# HERON
# DERIVATION
# DICTIONARY

**A Quick Reference
for English Language
Derivations**

HERON
BOOKS

*Published by*
**Heron Books, Inc.**
20950 SW Rock Creek Road
Sheridan, OR 97378

heronbooks.com

Fifth Edition © 1995, 2023 Heron Books
All Rights Reserved

ISBN: 978-0-89739-346-1

2 June 2023

# Contents

# Introduction to the 5th Edition

This dictionary was originally created for middle and high school students learning the value of derivations in understanding words. Its 11,447 entries came from a comprehensive list of recommended books for teen readers, from *Old Yeller, A Wrinkle in Time* and *The Yearling* all the way up to Dickens' *David Copperfield,* Voltaire's *Candide* and Plato's *Republic.* As dictionaries for younger readers did not always include derivations or had overly sophisticated derivations, the *Heron Derivation Dictionary* filled a need.

Within a few years, the book's popularity was found to extend beyond teens, and this has remained true since the first edition was published in 1995.

This new edition retains all the original entries with some minor adjustments, while getting an overhaul in design and readability. The intention has always been to provide uncomplicated, easily assimilated derivations. That remains unchanged.

Whether you are a teen or a reader of any age, we hope you find this new edition useful. Our wish is simple: to enhance the pleasures available to those who enjoy a good read.

# Why This Dictionary?

This dictionary is all about beginnings.

A *derivation* is where something came from, its beginning. The wheelbarrow, we think, was created by a Chinese general almost 2000 years ago to carry military supplies. That's its derivation. Every object or idea has some kind of derivation. Words do too.

The word *muscle*, for example, has a derivation. Flex your upper arm and look at your biceps. What does it look like? Some Roman did this and gave birth to the word we now know as *muscle*, which meant "little mouse" in Latin, the language of the Ancient Romans.

More recently, the creators of Instagram needed a name for their photo-sharing app. They took the words "instant camera" and "telegram" and came up with the name: Instagram. Some word derivations are centuries old. Some are quite new.

Exploring the meanings of words is one of the great joys of learning. When learning about a word, you might also wonder:

Why do we say this word for that idea?

Where was it first used this way?

Why is it pronounced or spelled this way?

Does this word come from some other language?

Is it really old?

What was the word back then and what did it mean in that time and place?

*Virus,* for example, is another word that comes to us from Latin. From ancient records, one discovers the word was first used by some Roman roughly 2500 years ago. It meant "poison" or "slimy liquid." It was useful in describing certain things, so others started using it and soon it was part of the language. Over the centuries, the word *virus* has moved forward in time, making its way into English as we speak and write it today—which we call Modern English.

Here's another word story.

The English word *vinegar* began as the Latin words *vinum aigre*, "wine that is soured." *Vinum* meant "wine," *aigre* meant "sour." Later the French combined these into *vinaigre* to describe "sour wine." English speakers borrowed that word and changed it to *vinegar*. There are many types of vinegar today but making a red wine vinegar isn't hard: just open a bottle of red wine and leave it for several days. You might not like the taste, but you will have made vinegar.

This simple derivation can help you understand the word vinegar better. And that's why this dictionary was created:

To help you explore the beginnings of words,
their derivations.

# Reading Derivations

Every word listed in a dictionary is called an entry. This book has 11,480 entries, each with a derivation.

As you look at these derivations, you will find them short and to the point. Many derivations have fun and fascinating stories behind them, and there are books and websites that share these well. This dictionary just gives derivations, as simply as possible.

To help you understand how to read the derivations, let's look at a few sample entries.

> **bold** OLD ENGLISH *beald* brave.

Old English was the earliest form of English. The Old English word *beald* meant "brave." Over time, this word changed to become our Modern English word *bold*.

> **virus** LATIN poison, slimy liquid.

In this derivation, no Latin word is given. This is because the Latin word is the same as the modern English word. Compare this with the previous example, where the Old English word *beald*, being different from the modern word, is given.

> **grin** OLD ENGLISH *grennian*.

In this example, no meaning is given for the original Old English word. This is because the meaning hasn't changed.

> **peel** FRENCH *peler* take off, from LATIN *pilare* make bald, from *pilus* hair.

When a word has traveled through different languages, the derivation will often show this. In this case, the word came from Latin to French, then into English. First was the Latin word *pilus*, meaning "*hair*." Later someone used this to create the Latin word *pilare*, meaning "making something bald." The French changed the spelling and meaning a bit. From there it arrived to English as *peel*.

> **active** See **act**.

This means the derivation of the word "active" is essentially the same as the derivation of the word "act." By going to the entry "act," you will find a derivation that applies to both words.

> **act** Latin *agere* to do.

At the back of the book is a list of the languages included in the word derivations in this dictionary. Below some of these is a sub-list of related languages you may run into in other dictionaries. Whereas another dictionary might say "from French, from Old French," for simplicity this dictionary will just say "from French."

You will also find a world map. Noted on it, for the sake of orientation, are the locations where all the languages included in the derivations in this dictionary have been or are used. It shows locations only; it doesn't differentiate relative time periods.

Lastly, a full glossary is given in the back. It provides explanations of many different languages, including all of those referenced in this dictionary, as well as many often found in other dictionaries. This can help if you find yourself in a larger dictionary running into languages or other derivation-related terminology you aren't familiar with.

A quick glance at the map or glossary will usually provide you with all the information you need.

# A Brief History of English

## BEFORE ENGLISH WAS BORN

Though English is spoken today by millions of people around the world, it was born on an island called Britannia, later Britain.

Today Britain is the home of England, Scotland and Wales.

For hundreds of years this island was the home of a people called the Britons. Around 43 CE, however, as part of expanding their empire, the Romans invaded and took control of the island.

They introduced many changes, including the development of organized towns and proper roads for travelling between them. For nearly four hundred years they protected the island from further invasions, until the Roman Empire began to fall apart. By 410 CE, Britain was no longer protected by the power of the Roman army and its soldiers.

Soon invading tribes began arriving on Britain's shores. The largest of these were two tribes called the Angles and the Saxons, from parts of what we now call Denmark and Germany.

Marauding warriors and pirates, they seized land and wealth, making the island theirs.

The Britons retreated to Ireland and Wales and with them went the language that had been used in Britain for hundreds of years.

## THE BIRTH OF OLD ENGLISH
## Anglo-Saxon, 450 - 1100 CE

The Angles and Saxons spoke a completely different language than the Britons. They were a rougher people and their language sounded that way. Sometimes we refer to their language as *Anglo-Saxon*. They called it *Englisc,* and gradually it became the language spoken throughout Britain by both peasants and kings.

This was how English was born.

Old English (*old* meaning the first English spoken) is another name used for Anglo-Saxon. In this dictionary, all Anglo-Saxon words will simply be called *Old English.*

Many of the words we use today come directly from Old English, even simple words like *I, he, she, you, we, where, who* and *when.* Even the word *England* comes from "Angle-land."

It was a fairly simple but lively and descriptive language. It had a lot of short, punchy words, thousands of which we still use.

pig arrow friend MOON north GLOW cat

kiss break OWL

raven laugh RED queen year jump GHOST

BLOOD CHILD NAME dog

free ACORN FIGHT hook

SCAB MOTHER bruise

EARTH hand

heaven

# THE VIKING INFLUENCE
## Old Norse, 800 CE

About four hundred years after the Anglo-Saxon invasion, from the northernmost parts of Europe came new seafaring pirates and traders called Vikings. These new invaders, also called Norsemen, landed in the north of England.

They spoke a language we call *Old Norse.*

For the next 200 years there were continuous battles between the Anglo-Saxons and the Vikings. Naturally some Old Norse words got picked up and added into Old English.

Here are a few words that originally came from Old Norse.

skull
TRUST
ugly
WHIRL
SKIP
gang
fellow
sprint
sky
freckle
EGG
BERSERK
glitter
anger
troll
DIRT

Norway

Sweden

Vikings

Denmark

England

## THE FRENCH INFLUENCE
## Middle English, 1100—1500

Between Old English and Modern English (what we speak today) is a period of the language we call *Middle English*. What was different about Middle English?

It was the influence of the French language.

Previous invasions of England had come from the east and the north. This time it came from the south, from a portion of France still called Normandy. In 1066 a French Duke named William of Normandy led an invasion, and in the famous Battle of Hastings, his French army defeated the Anglo-Saxons.

William, known in history as William the Conqueror, became King of England. He spoke French and rewarded many of his French-speaking nobles with Anglo-Saxon land.

**England**

**Hastings**

**Normandy**

**France**

The Anglo-Saxon peasants resented William and his French-speaking aristocrats and never stopped speaking their own tongue. As a result, there came to be two words in use for many things, an English word and a French one: for examples, *cow* and *beef*, *ask* and *question*, *hide* and *conceal*.

Over time, the language became a mixture of Anglo-Saxon and French, what we now call Middle English.

Here are some of the words that came from French, all as a result of the Norman invasion and William taking over the throne.

peasant
PRINCE
government
continue
MAYOR
villain
dungeon
PURCHASE
prayer
tax
sir
commence
duke
SURRENDER

## THE GREEK AND LATIN INFLUENCE
### Modern English, 1500 – present day

The next major development of the English language came with the invention of the printing press in 1440. With increasing numbers of printed books available and being shared, many people in Europe began to discover the writings of the great Ancient Greek and Roman civilizations. Knowledge started to spread like wildfire. This time came to be known as the Renaissance, or "rebirth" (see derivation in this dictionary) of the ideas of Ancient Greece and Rome, ideas which had largely been lost in Europe for centuries.

With this dramatic change came new words. People learning to read and write ancient Greek and Latin found words they liked and brought them directly into English. Then they created even more new words by combining parts of Greek and Latin words.

Here are just a few examples of words that entered English at this time:

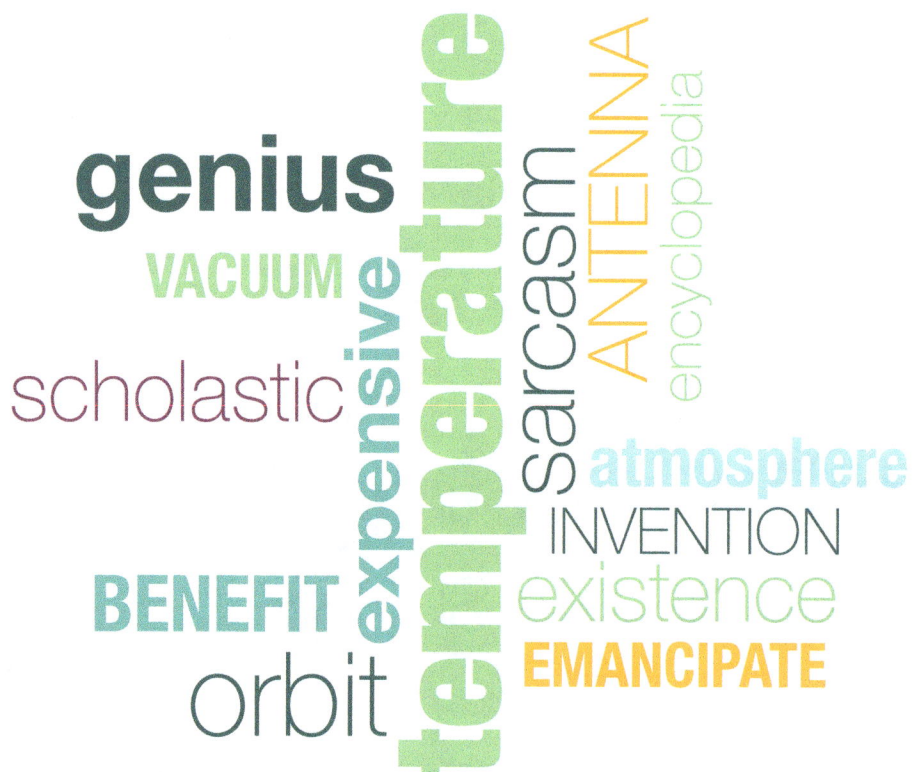

genius
temperature
VACUUM
expensive
sarcasm
ANTENNA
encyclopedia
scholastic
atmosphere
INVENTION
existence
BENEFIT
EMANCIPATE
orbit

## THE INFLUENCE OF LITERATURE
### Modern English

With the addition of so many new words during the Renaissance, English became more expressive and literature flowered. William Shakespeare (1564 – 1616) liked to invent colorful and expressive words, and through his plays and poems added over 200 of these to English. Believe it or not, this one man added the following words to the language, not to mention many others.

Amazingly, other writers added even more!

glow zany schoolboy amazement eyeball dewdrop fairyland WELL-READ DISGRACEFUL MOUNTAINEER domineering swagger cold-hearted

Here are a few more common words that came from literature:

**fragrance** ..................... from the poem *Paradise Lost*
*(scent, usually pleasant)* — by John Milton in 1667

butterfinger ................ from *The Pickwick Papers*
*(person who drops things)* — by Charles Dickens in 1836

MUNCHKIN ................. from *The Wonderful Wizard of Oz*
*(small, likable child)* — by L. Frank Baum in 1900

**nerd** ...................................... from *If I Ran the Zoo*
*(person who studies too* — by Dr Seuss in 1950
*much and lacks social skills)*

grok ......................................... from *Stranger in a Strange Land*
*(to understand deeply)* — by Robert Heinlein in 1961

There are thousands of words that settled into the language because a writer made them up. Readers liked the word, used it and it became part of English.

## THE INFLUENCE OF EXPLORATION AND TRADE
## Modern English

As English exploration and trade grew, merchants brought back not only goods but new words as well. Words like *cigar, tomato, chocolate, rodeo* and *tornado* came from Spain. Musical terms came from Italy along with words like *pizza, spaghetti, broccoli* and *balloon*. From Germany came words like *hamburger, pretzel* and *kindergarten*.

As English moved to America, Native American words found their way into the language. Many were names of places and geographical features, but also everyday words.

ALASKA jerky Mississippi CONNECTICUT raccoon moose chipmunk toboggan Chicago WYOMING hammock canoe OREGON COYOTE

With the world becoming more and more connected, English has acquired words from all over, like *burrito, igloo, leprechaun, boomerang, zombie, robot, mosquito, limousine, cashew* and *coconut*, to name just a few. And with the growth of technology and social media, more English words are being created all the time, words like *selfie, blog, screen time, smartphone, hashtag, e-bike*, and so many more.

## TODAY AND TOMORROW
### Modern English

English is now spoken by more than 25% of the world's population and is the language of international business and the internet. The development of Modern English will continue to be a fascinating story of growth and change—always reflecting the interests, activities, ideas and experiences of the people who speak it.

So, thanks to Native Americans, Shakespeare and Spaniards, you can now go find a *hammock*, relax and enjoy a *zany* book—with a delicious piece of dark *chocolate*.

# A SIMPLIFIED TIMELINE
## of the English Language

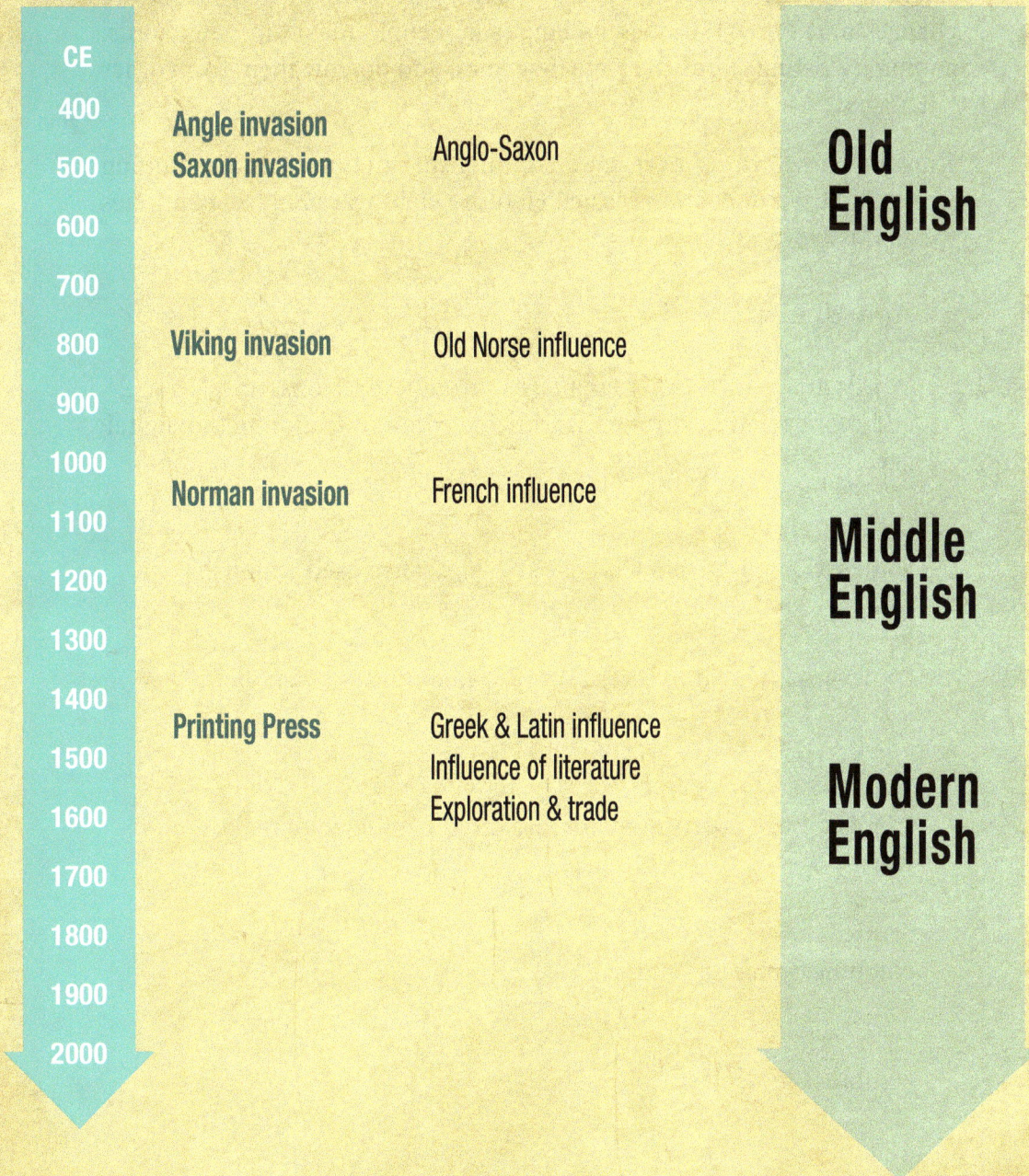

| CE | | | |
|---|---|---|---|
| 400 | Angle invasion | | |
| 500 | Saxon invasion | Anglo-Saxon | **Old English** |
| 600 | | | |
| 700 | | | |
| 800 | Viking invasion | Old Norse influence | |
| 900 | | | |
| 1000 | | | |
| 1100 | Norman invasion | French influence | |
| 1200 | | | **Middle English** |
| 1300 | | | |
| 1400 | Printing Press | Greek & Latin influence | |
| 1500 | | Influence of literature | **Modern English** |
| 1600 | | Exploration & trade | |
| 1700 | | | |
| 1800 | | | |
| 1900 | | | |
| 2000 | | | |

# How English Builds Its Vocabulary

The more you explore derivations, the more you realize how languages change over time.

English, like any other language, is a living, growing thing. As a culture changes and grows, so does its language. People make up new words, combine existing words to create new ones, and borrow them from other languages.

Knowing how words have entered English can make understanding words and their derivations easier. Here are eight ways English continues to build its vocabulary.

## 1. BORROWED

Words arrive from other languages through invasions, travel, trade, and more recently, through worldwide communication in the digital age.

**ketchup**
comes to English from Chinese *ke-tsiap,* sauce used with fish

**roster**
comes from Dutch *rooster,* a list or grid of duties for soldiers

## 2. COMBINED

Words, or even parts of words, are often combined to make a new word.

**applesauce**
combines *apple* and *sauce*

**livestream**
combines *live* and *stream*

## 3. EXPANDED

A prefix or suffix can be added to an existing word, expanding it and making a new word. English has thousands of words like this.

**rethink**
adds the prefix *re-* (again) to the word *think*

**merrily**
adds the suffix *-ly* (in a _____ way) to the word *merry*

## 4. SHORTENED

Words can be shortened, abbreviated or turned into acronyms (words formed from the first letters of a phrase).

**fridge**
is now a word for *refrigerator*

**vs**
is an abbreviation for *versus* and is now often used without a period

**BFF**
(best friends forever) is now a word found in most dictionaries

## 5. NEW DEFINITIONS

Often new words aren't new, they just have new definitions or find use as a different part of speech.

**surf**
is now something you can do on the internet as well as on ocean waves

**Google**
was the name of a company that then became a verb ("google it")

## 6. SOUND IMITATION

Many words are made by imitating a sound.

**hiss**
is a word describing a sound like that of a snake

**boom**
is a word describing the sound of an explosion

## 7. NAME STEALING

The most famous example of a word coming directly from a name is *sandwich,* from the name of its inventor, the Earl of Sandwich.

**diesel**
comes from the name of a German inventor, Rudolf Diesel

**granola**
was a brand name over a hundred years ago

## 8. INVENTION

Lastly, many words are just made up. Sometimes they become popular and part of the language. Sometimes they just die away. Often it's nearly impossible to find out who used it first.

**nifty, puzzle** and **gimmick**
are words invented by unknown people in history

Want to make up a word? Maybe you already have. If you can popularize it, it just might end up in a dictionary. And that's a word you will already know the derivation for!

# DERIVATIONS

# A

**a** OLD ENGLISH *an* one, an.

**a-**[1] OLD ENGLISH *an, on* in, on, at, out of.

**a-**[2] GREEK *a-, an-* not.

**aardvark** AFRIKAANS earth pig, from *aard* earth + *vark* pig.

**ab-** LATIN *ab-,* from, away, down.

**aback** OLD ENGLISH *onbæc.*

**abacus** LATIN counting board, from GREEK *abax*, probably from HEBREW *abaq* dust. The early abacus was a board covered with dust or sand, on which figures could be drawn and then brushed away.

**abalone** NATIVE AMERICAN *aulun.*

**abandon** FRENCH *mettre a bandon* put under someone else's power.

**abase** FRENCH *abaisser* to lower, from LATIN *ad-* to + *bassus* low.

**abash** FRENCH *abaiss*, from *esbahir*, from LATIN *ex-* out + *bahir* open wide.

**abate** FRENCH *abattre* beat down, from LATIN *ad-* to + *battuere* strike.

**abatis** FRENCH *abateis,* from LATIN *abateticius* throwing down.

**abattoir** See **abate.**

**abbey** FRENCH *abbaie* monastery (place where monks live), from LATIN *abbatissa*, office of an abbot.

**abbot** OLD ENGLISH *abbod*, from LATIN *abbas,* from GREEK, from Semitic *abba* father.

**abbreviate** LATIN *abbreviatus*, *ab-* from + *brevis* short.

**abdicate** LATIN *abdicare*, from *ab-* off + *dicare* to announce.

**abdomen** LATIN belly.

**abduct** LATIN *abductus*, from *ab-* away + *ducere* lead.

**aberrant** LATIN *aberrare*, from *ab-* from + *errare* wander.

**abet** FRENCH *abeter* to excite, from *a-* to + *beter* bait (tease).

**abeyance** FRENCH *abeance*, from *abauer*, from *a-* at + *bayer* gape (stare at with the mouth open).

**abhor** LATIN *abhorrere* shrink back from, from *ab-* away + *horrere* have the hair stand on end.

**abide** OLD ENGLISH *abidan*, from *a-* completely + *bidan* remain.

**ability** FRENCH *ablete*, from LATIN *habilis* easy to handle, from *habere* have.

**abject** LATIN *abjicere*, from *ab-* away + *jacere* throw.

25

**abjure** LATIN *abjurare*, from *ab-* away + *jurare* swear.

**able** FRENCH *ablete*, from LATIN *habilis* easy to handle, from *habere* have.

**-able** FRENCH, from LATIN *-abilis*.

**ablution** LATIN *abluere*, from *ab-* off + *luere* lave (wash away).

**abnegate** LATIN *abnegare*, from *ab-* away + *negare* deny.

**abnormal** FRENCH *anormal*, from LATIN *abnormis*, from *ab-* away + *norma* carpenter's square, rule.

**abode** See **abide**.

**abolish** FRENCH, from LATIN *abolotio*, from *abolere* destroy.

**abominate** LATIN *abominari* think of as a bad omen.

**aborigine** LATIN *ab-* from + *origine* the beginning.

**abort** LATIN *aboriri* miscarry.

**abound** FRENCH *abonder*, from LATIN *abundare* overflow, from *ab-* from + *unda* wave.

**about** OLD ENGLISH *abutan*, from *a-* to + *butan* outside.

**above** OLD ENGLISH *abufan*, from *a-* to + *bufan* above.

**abracadabra** LATIN.

**abrade** LATIN, from *abradere*, from *ab-* away + *radere* scrape.

**abreast** See a-[1] + **breast**.

**abridge** FRENCH *abregie*, from LATIN *abbreviare*, from *ab-* to + *errare* wander.

**abrogate** LATIN *abrogare* repeal, from *ab-* away + *rogare* propose.

**abrupt** LATIN *abrumpere*, from *ab-* away + *rumpere* break.

**abscess** LATIN *abscidere*, from *ab(s)-* from + *cedere* go.

**abscond** LATIN *abscondere*, from *ab(s)-* from + *condere* hide.

**absent** LATIN *abasense*, from *ab-* away + *esse* be.

**absolute** MIDDLE ENGLISH *absolut*, from LATIN *absolutus*, freed, acquitted, finished, from *absolvere*, set free, acquit. See **absolve**.

**absolution** MIDDLE ENGLISH from LATIN *absolutio*, from *absolvere*. See **absolve**.

**absolve** LATIN *absolvere* set free, acquit, from *ab-* from + *solvere* loosen.

**absorb** LATIN *absorbere*, from *ab-* from + *sorbere* drink.

**abstain** FRENCH *abstenir* refrain from, from LATIN *abstinere* withhold, from *ab-* from + *tenere* hold.

**abstinence** See **abstain**.

**abstract** LATIN *abstrahere* draw away from, from *ab-* away from + *trahere* draw.

**abstruse** LATIN *abstrudere*, from *ab-* away + *trudere* thrust.

**absurd** LATIN *absurdus* not to be heard of, from *ab-* away + *surdus* dull, deaf.

**abundance** FRENCH plenty, from LATIN *abundare* overflow, from *ab-* from + *unda* wave.

**abuse** FRENCH *abuser* misuse, from LATIN *abuti*, from *ab-* away + *uti* use.

**abut** FRENCH *aboter*, from LATIN *a-* to + *bout* end.

**abutment** See **abut** + **-ment**.

**abyss** LATIN *abyssus* bottomless pit, from GREEK *abussos*, from *a-* without + *byssos* bottom.

**acacia** LATIN, from GREEK *akakia* thorny tree.

**academy** FRENCH *academie*, from GREEK *akademia* a grove near Athens which became the place for Plato's (a famous Greek philosopher) Academy.

**acappella** ITALIAN singing in a chapel style, from LATIN *ad-* to + *capella* chapel.

**accede** LATIN *accedere*, from *ad-* to + *cedere* go.

**accelerate** LATIN *accelerare*, from *ad-* to + *celerare* hasten, from *celer* quick.

**accent** FRENCH proper speaking manner, from LATIN *ad-* to + *cantus* song added to speech.

**accept** LATIN *acceptare* receive, from *ad-* to + *capere* take.

**access** LATIN *accedere*, from *ad-* to + *cedere* go.

**accessory** LATIN *accedere*, from *ad-* to + *cedere* go.

**accident** LATIN *accidens* chance, from *ad-* to + *cadere* fall.

**acclaim** LATIN *acclamare* shout applause.

**accolade** FRENCH, from ITALIAN *accollare* to embrace, from LATIN *ad-* to + *collum* neck.

**accommodate** LATIN *accommodare* to fit with, from *ad-* to + *commodus* convenient.

**accompany** FRENCH *a-* to + *compaignon* comrade. See **companion**.

**accomplish** FRENCH *accomplier* to complete, from LATIN *ad-* to + *complere* complete.

**accord** FRENCH *accorder* to agree, from LATIN *ad-* to + *cor* heart.

**accordion** ITALIAN *accordare* be in tune.

**accost** FRENCH, from ITALIAN, from LATIN *accoster*, from *ad-* to + *costa* rib, side.

**account** FRENCH *acompter* to count up, from *a-* to + *conter* tell, from LATIN *computare*. See **compute**.

**accouter** FRENCH *acostrer*, from LATIN *ad-* to + *consuere* sew together.

**accretion** LATIN *accrescere*, from *ad-* to + *crescere* grow.

**accrue** FRENCH increase, from *accreistre*, from LATIN *accrescere*, from *ad-* to + *crescere* grow.

**accumulate** LATIN *accumulare*, from *ad-* to + *cumulare* pile up.

**accurate** LATIN *accurare*, from *ad-* to + *cura* care.

**accurse** OLD ENGLISH *cursian* curse.

**accuse** FRENCH *acuser*, from LATIN *accusare*, from *ad-* to + *causa* a cause.

**accustom** FRENCH *acostumer* become used to, from *à-* to + *costume* habit.

**ace** FRENCH *as*, from LATIN unit.

**acerbate** LATIN *acerbare* make harsh or bitter.

**acetonaemia** acetone + GREEK *(h)aimia* blood.

**acetone** LATIN *acetum* vinegar.

**acetylene** See acetone + -ene.

**ache** OLD ENGLISH *acan*.

**achieve** FRENCH *achever* complete, succeed, accomplish, from *à chef* at an end.

**acid** LATIN *acidus* sour.

**acknowledge** OLD ENGLISH *oncnawan* understand, recognize, from *on* regarding, about + *cnawan* recognize, understand.

**acme** GREEK *akme* a point, top.

**acne** LATIN, from GREEK *akme* point, top.

**acolyte** LATIN, from GREEK *akolouthos* follower.

**aconite** FRENCH *aconit*, from LATIN *aconitum*, from GREEK *akoniton*.

**acorn** OLD ENGLISH *æcern*.

**acoustic** FRENCH *acuostique*, from GREEK *akoustikos*, from *akouein* hear.

**acquaint** FRENCH *acointier*, from LATIN *adcognitare* to make known, from *ad-* to + *cognoscere* know.

**acquiesce** FRENCH, from LATIN *acquiescere*, from *ad-* to + *quiescere* to keep quiet, from *quies* rest.

**acquire** LATIN *acquirere* to get in addition, from *ad-* to + *quaere* seek.

**acquit** FRENCH *aqujiter* to set free, from LATIN *acquitare* to settle a claim, from *ad-* to + *quietare* quiet.

**acre** OLD ENGLISH *æcer* field.

**acrid** LATIN *acris* bitter.

**acriflavine** LATIN *acris* bitter + *flavis* yellow.

**acrimony** LATIN *acer* sharp.

**acrobat** FRENCH *acrobate*, from GREEK *akrobatos* walking on tiptoe, from *akros* high point + *bainen* go.

**acronym** GREEK *akros* at the end or top + *onyma* name.

**acropolis** GREEK *akropolis*, from *aktos* top + *polis* city.

**across** FRENCH *à croix* in the form of a cross.

**acrostic** FRENCH *acrostiche*, from GREEK *akrostichis*, from *akros* at the end + *stichos* line of poetry.

**act** LATIN *agere* do.

**actinobacillosis** LATIN *actinobacillus* a bacterium.

**action** FRENCH, from LATIN *agere* do.

**active** See act.

**actual** See act.

**actuary** LATIN *actuarius* clerk, from *actus*. See act.

**actuate** LATIN *actuatus*, from LATIN *actus*. See act.

**acumen** LATIN a point, from *acuere* sharpen.

**acupuncture** LATIN *acur* needle + *pungere* pierce.

**acute** LATIN *acuere* sharpen, from *acus* needle.

**-acy** FRENCH, from LATIN, from GREEK *-ateia* quality, condition.

**ad-** LATIN *ad-* to, at, toward.

**adage** FRENCH, from LATIN *adagium*, from *ad-* to + *aio* I say.

**adagio** ITALIAN *ad agio* at ease.

**adamant** FRENCH diamond, hardest metal, from GREEK *adamas*, from *a-* not + *daman* tame.

**adapt** FRENCH *adapter* to fit, from LATIN *adaptare*, from *ad-* to + *aptare* fit.

**add** LATIN *addere* add to, join, attach, from *ad-* to + *dare* give.

**addendum** LATIN that which is to be added, from *addere* add to. See **add**.

**adder** MIDDLE ENGLISH *nadder*, from OLD ENGLISH *nædre* snake.

**addict** LATIN *addicere*, from *ad-* to + *dicere* say.

**addle** OLD ENGLISH *adela* mud.

**address** FRENCH *a-* to + *dresser* direct, from LATIN *dirigere*. See **direct**.

**adduce** LATIN *adducere*, from *ad-* to + *ducere* lead.

**-ade** LATIN *-ata*.

**Adelphi** GREEK brothers.

**adenoids** GREEK *aden* gland + *eidos* form, shape.

**adept** LATIN *adeptus* a person skilled in alchemy, from having attained, from *adipisci* attain, from *ad-* to + *apisci* grasp.

**adequate** LATIN *adaequare*, from *ad-* to + *aequare* make equal.

**adhere** LATIN *adhaerere*, from *ad-* to + *haerere* stick.

**adieu** FRENCH, from LATIN *ad-* to + *Deus* God.

**adjacent** LATIN *adjacere* to be near, from *ad-* to + *jacere* lie still.

**adjective** LATIN *adjectivum* added word, from *ad-* to + *jacere* throw.

**adjourn** FRENCH *a* at + *jorn* day, from LATIN *diurnum* daily, from *dies* day.

**adjudge** LATIN *adjudicare*, from *ad-* to + *judicare* judge.

**adjudicate** See **adjudge**.

**adjust** LATIN *ad-* to + *justus* lawful, from *jus* law.

**adjutant** LATIN *adjuvare*, from *ad-* to + *juvare* help.

**administer** FRENCH *aministrer* to manage, from LATIN *administrare*, from *ad-* to + *ministrare* serve.

**admiral** FRENCH *amiral* officer of high rank, from ARABIC *amir-al-* commander of.

**admire** LATIN *admirari*, from *ad-* to + *mirari* wonder.

**admit** LATIN *admittere*, from *ad-* to + *mittere* send.

**admonish** FRENCH *amonester* to warn, from LATIN *admonere*, from *ad-* to + *monere* warn.

**ado** MIDDLE ENGLISH *at do* to do.

**adobe** SPANISH *adobe* brick that is dried by the sun instead of a fire, from ARABIC *at-tob* brick.

**adolescent** LATIN *adolescere*, from *ad-* to + *alecere* grow up, from *alere* feed.

**adopt** LATIN *adoptare*, from *ad-* to + *optare* choose.

**adore** FRENCH *adorare*, from *ad-* to + *orare* speak.

**adorn** FRENCH *adorner* to provide, from LATIN *adornare*, from *ad-* to + *ornare* decorate.

**adrenal** LATIN *ad-* + *renalis* of the kidneys, from *renes* kidneys.

**adroit** FRENCH *à droit* properly, from LATIN *ad-* to + *directus* straight.

**adult** LATIN *adultus*.

**advance** FRENCH *avancier* leave before someone, from LATIN *abante*, from *ad-* away + *ante* before.

**advantage** FRENCH *avant* before, from LATIN *ab ante* away before.

**advent** LATIN *adventus* arrival, from *advenire*, from *ad-* to + *venire* happen.

**adventure** FRENCH *aventure* chance, from LATIN *advenire*. See **advent**.

**adverb** LATIN *adverbium*, from *ad-* to + *verbum* word.

**adversary** FRENCH *aversier*, from LATIN *adversus*, from *ad-* to + *vertere* turn.

**adverse** FRENCH *advers* opposite, from LATIN *advertere*, from *ad-* to + *vertere* turn.

**advert** See **advertise**.

**advertise** FRENCH *advertir*, from LATIN *advertere*, from *ad-* to + *vertere* turn.

**advice** FRENCH *avis* opinion, from LATIN *ad-* to + *videre* look.

**advocate** FRENCH *avocat*, from LATIN *advocatus*, from *ad-* to + *vocare* call, from *vox* voice.

**adze (adz)** OLD ENGLISH *adesa*.

**aer-** GREEK *aer* air.

**aerator** See **aer-** + **-ate** + **-or**.

**aerial** LATIN *aerius* relating to air, from GREEK *aerios*.

**aerie** LATIN *aerea* nest of a bird, from FRENCH *aire*, from LATIN *area* open space.

**aero-** GREEK *aer* air.

**aerobic** FRENCH *aérobie*, coined 1863 by Louis Pasteur, from GREEK *aero-* air + *bios* life.

**aeronautics** GREEK *aer* air + *nautes* sailor.

**aesthetic** GREEK *aisthanesthai* perceive.

**affable** LATIN *affabilis*, from *ad-* to + *fari* speak.

**affair** FRENCH *afaire* concern, from *à faire* to be done, from LATIN *ad-* to + *facere* do, make.

**affect** LATIN *affectare* produce an effect upon, from *ad-* to + *facere* do, make.

**affiliate** LATIN *affiliare* to adopt, from *ad-* to + *filius* son.

**affinity** FRENCH *afinite*, from LATIN *affinis* near, from *ad-* to + *finis* end.

**affirm** FRENCH *afemer*, from LATIN *affirmare*, from *ad-* to + *firmare* make firm.

**affix** LATIN *affixare*, from *ad-* to + *figere* fasten.

**afflatus** LATIN *afflare* to blow on, from *ad-* to + *flare* blow.

**afflict** LATIN *affligere*, from *ad-* to + *flugere* strike.

**affluence** FRENCH, from LATIN *affluere*, from *ad-* to + *fluere* flow.

**afford** OLD ENGLISH *geforthian* accomplish.

**affray** FRENCH *esfraer* frighten, from LATIN *ex-* out of + GERMAN *frith* peace.

**affright** OLD ENGLISH *afyrht*.

**affront** FRENCH *afronter* hit in the face, from LATIN *ad frontem* to the face.

**Afghan** PASHTO *afghānī*, the people of Afghanistan.

**aficionado** SPANISH *aficionar*, from LATIN *affectio* warm feeling.

**afoot** See **a-**[1] + **foot**.

**afore** OLD ENGLISH *on foran*.

**afraid** MIDDLE ENGLISH *affraied*, from FRENCH *afrayer* frighten.

**afreet** ARABIC *'ifrit* evil demon or monster of Muslim mythology.

**aft** OLD ENGLISH *æftan*.

**after** OLD ENGLISH *æfter* behind in place or time.

**again** OLD ENGLISH *ongegn*, from *on-* toward + *gegn* direct.

**against** See **again**.

**agalactia** LATIN *agalaxia*, from GREEK *agalacia* not milk.

**agape** See **gape**.

**agate** FRENCH, from LATIN, from GREEK *achates*.

**agave** LATIN *Agave*, from GREEK *Agaue*, from *agauos* noble.

**age** FRENCH lifetime, from LATIN *aetas* time period.

**-age** FRENCH, from LATIN *aticum* belonging to.

**agent** LATIN *agere* do.

**agglomerate** LATIN *agglomerare*, from *ad-* to + *glomerare* form into a ball.

**aggrandize** FRENCH *agrandir*, from LATIN *ad-* to + *grandire* increase.

**aggravate** LATIN *aggravare*, from *ad-* to + *gravis* heavy.

**aggregate** LATIN *aggregare*, from *ad-* to + *gregare* herd.

**aggression** LATIN *aggressio* attack, from *aggredi* attack, from *ad-* to + *gradi* step.

**aggrieve** LATIN *aggravare*. See **aggravate**.

**aghast** MIDDLE ENGLISH *agasten* terrify, from OLD ENGLISH *gast* ghost.

**agile** FRENCH, from LATIN *agere* act.

**agitate** LATIN *agitare* move back and forth.

**aglet** FRENCH *aiguille*, from LATIN *acucula*, from *acus* needle.

**agnostic** GREEK *a-* not + *gignoskein* know.

**ago** MIDDLE ENGLISH *agon* go away, from OLD ENGLISH *agan*, from *a-* away + *gan* go.

**agog** FRENCH *a-* to + *gogue* joyful.

**agony** LATIN *agonia* great suffering, from GREEK *agonia* contest.

**agree** FRENCH *agreer* to please, from LATIN *ad-* to + *gratus* pleasing.

**agriculture** LATIN *agricultura*, from *ager* field, acre + *cultura* cultivate (farming of the land).

**ague** FRENCH sharp fever, from LATIN *acuta febris* sharp or severe fever.

**aid** FRENCH *aïder* to help, from LATIN *adjuvare*, from *ad-* to + *juvare* help.

**aide** FRENCH. See **aid**.

**ail** OLD ENGLISH *egle* harmful.

**aileron** FRENCH *aile*, from LATIN *ala* wing.

**aim** FRENCH *aesmer* to value, from LATIN *ad-* to + *aestimare* estimate.

**air** FRENCH, from LATIN *aer*, from GREEK *aer*.

**Airedale** the district of *Airedale* in West Riding, Yorkshire, England.

**aisle** FRENCH *ele* wing (of a building), from LATIN *ala* wing.

**akimbo** MIDDLE ENGLISH *in kenebowe*, in keen bow (at a sharp angle).

**-al** FRENCH, from LATIN *alis*.

**alabaster** FRENCH, from LATIN, perfume box made of alabaster, from GREEK *alabastos* vase of alabaster.

**alack** MIDDLE ENGLISH *ah, lack*, from *lack* loss, shame.

**alacrity** LATIN *alacritas* liveliness.

**alarm** FRENCH *alarme* warning of danger, from Italian *all'arme!* to arms! going back to LATIN *ad-* to + *ille* that + *arma* weapons.

**alas** FRENCH *a las* ah weary.

**albatross** SPANISH, from ARABIC *al qadus* water container, from GREEK *kados*, probably from HEBREW *kad* water jug.

**albino** SPANISH *albo* snow white, from LATIN *albus* white.

**album** LATIN blank tablet on which notices were written.

**albumen** LATIN *albumen* white of an egg, from *albus* white.

**alcalde** SPANISH, from ARABIC *al-qadi* the judge.

**alchemy** FRENCH *alcquimie*, from LATIN *alchimia*, from ARABIC *al-kimiya*, from GREEK *cheein* pour.

**alcohol** LATIN powder for decorating the eyelids, from ARABIC *al kuhl*.

**alcove** FRENCH, from SPANISH *alcoba*, from ARABIC *al* the + *qobbah* area that has an arched ceiling.

**alderman** OLD ENGLISH *eald* old + *man* man.

**ale** OLD ENGLISH *ealu*.

**alert** FRENCH *alerte* to arms, from ITALIAN *all'erta* on the watch.

**alfalfa** SPANISH, from ARABIC *al-fastasah*.

**algae** LATIN *alga* seaweed.

**algebra** ITALIAN, from ARABIC *al-jabr* put broken parts back together.

**alias** LATIN another.

**alibi** LATIN *allus ibi* elsewhere.

**alidade** FRENCH, from SPANISH *alidada*, from ARABIC *al'idadah* a ruler, index of an astrolabe.

**alien** FRENCH, from LATIN *alienus*, from *allus* other.

**alight**[1] (step down) MIDDLE ENGLISH *a-* out, off + *lihtan* get down.

**alight**[2] (having light) OLD ENGLISH *leoht* light.

**align** FRENCH *aligner*, from LATIN *ad-* to + *linea* line.

**alike** OLD ENGLISH *gelic*.

**aliment** LATIN *alimentum*, from *alere* nourish.

**alimentary** See **aliment** + **-ary**.

**alimony** LATIN *alimonia* support, from *alere* feed.

**alive** OLD ENGLISH *on life* having life.

**alkali** MIDDLE ENGLISH *alkaly*, from ARABIC *alqili* ashes, from *qalai* cook with fire.

**all** OLD ENGLISH *eall*.

**allay** OLD ENGLISH *alecgan*, from *a-* down + *lecgan* keep back.

**allege** LATIN *allegare*, from *ex-* out of + *litigare* sue.

**allegiance** FRENCH *a-* to + *ligeance*, from *liege*, from GERMAN *ledig* free.

**allegory** LATIN *allegoria*, from GREEK *allegoria*, from *allos* other + *agoreuelin* speak.

**allergy** GREEK *allos* other + *ergon* work.

**alleviate** LATIN *alleviare*, from *ad-* to + *levis* light.

**alley**[1] (walkway) FRENCH *alee* passage, from *aler* go, from LATIN *ambulare* walk.

**alley**[2] (marble) See **alabaster**.

**alliance** FRENCH *aliance* connection, from *alier*. See **ally**.

**alligator** SPANISH *el lagarto* the lizard.

**allocate** LATIN *allocatus* to allot, from *ad-* to + *locare* place.

**allot** FRENCH *aloter*, from *à* to + *loter* divide by lot (share).

**allow** FRENCH *alouer* grant, from LATIN *allocare* to allot, from *ad-* to + *locus* a place.

**alloy** FRENCH *aloi* standard, from *aloier* join, from LATIN *alligare*. See **ally**.

**allude** LATIN *alludere* to joke, from *ad-* to + *ludere* play.

**allure** FRENCH *alurer* attract, from *à* to + *lure* bait.

**ally** FRENCH *alier* bind to, from LATIN *alligare* join together, from *ad-* to + *ligare* bind.

**almanac** LATIN *almanach* diary, from GREEK *almenichiaka* calendar.

**almighty** OLD ENGLISH *eal* all + *mihtig* mighty.

**almond** FRENCH *almande*, from LATIN *amygdala*, from GREEK *amygdale*.

**almost** OLD ENGLISH *eallmæst*.

**alms** OLD ENGLISH *æmesse*, from LATIN *eleemosyna*, from GREEK *eleemosyne* pity.

**aloe** LATIN, from GREEK *alie*.

**aloft** OLD NORSE *a lopt* in the air.

**alone** MIDDLE ENGLISH *al one* all one.

**along** OLD ENGLISH *andlang*, from *and-* over against + *lang* long.

**aloof** probably from DUTCH *te leof* to windward (direction from which the wind is blowing).

**aloud** OLD ENGLISH *a-* on + *hlud*.

**alpaca** SPANISH *allpaca.*

**alphabet** LATIN a*lphabetum* the letters of a language, from GREEK *alphabeto,* from *alpha* A + *beta* B, the first two letters of the Greek alphabet.

**alpine** LATIN *alpinus.*

**also** OLD ENGLISH *ealswa* wholly so.

**altar** OLD ENGLISH, from LATIN *altaria* part of a holy table used to hold burnt offerings.

**altazimuth** See altitude + azimuth.

**alter** FRENCH *alterer* change, from LATIN *alterare,* from *alter* other.

**alternate** LATIN *alternare* do a thing by turns, from *alturnus* one after the other, from *alter* other.

**although** MIDDLE ENGLISH *al thogh.* See **all** + **though.**

**altimeter** See altitude + meter.

**altitude** LATIN *altus* high.

**altogether** See all + together.

**altruism** FRENCH *altruisme,* from ITALIAN *altrul* for or to others, from LATIN *alter* other.

**alulate** LATIN *ala* wing.

**alum** FRENCH, from LATIN *alumen.*

**aluminum** LATIN *aluminum,* from *alumen* alum (a special kind of salt).

**always** See all + way.

**amass** FRENCH, from LATIN *a-* to + *massare* pile up, from LATIN *massa* mass. See **mass.**

**amateur** FRENCH lover of something, from LATIN *amare* love.

**amaze** OLD ENGLISH *amasian* confuse completely.

**ambassador** FRENCH *ambassaduer,* from LATIN *ambactia* mission (special job), from *ambactus* servant.

**amber** FRENCH, from ARABIC *anbar* ambergris (gray amber).

**ambient** LATIN *ambire,* from *ambi-* around + *ire* go.

**ambiguous** LATIN *ambigere,* from *ambi-* around + *agere* act.

**ambition** LATIN *ambitio* going around (to get votes).

**amble** FRENCH *ambler* amble, from LATIN *ambulare* walk.

**ambrosia** LATIN *ambrosia* food of the gods, from GREEK *ambrotos,* from *a-* not + *brotos* mortal (can live forever).

**ambulance** FRENCH *hôpital ambulant* hospital on wheels.

**ambulate** LATIN *ambulare* walk.

**ambuscade** FRENCH *embuschier.* See **ambush.**

**ambush** FRENCH *embuschier* place in ambush, from LATIN *in-* in + *boscus* wood.

**ameliorate** FRENCH *améliorer,* from *a-* to + *meillor,* from LATIN *melior* better.

**amen** OLD ENGLISH, from LATIN, from GREEK, from HEBREW truth.

**amenable** FRENCH *a-* to + *mener* lead, from LATIN *minare* make animals move.

**amend** FRENCH *amender* make better, from LATIN *emendae* correct, from *ex-* out of + *menda* fault.

**America** *Amerigo* Vespucci (1454–1512), Italian explorer of South America.

**amethyst** LATIN *amethystus,* from GREEK *a-* not + *methystos* drunken, because it was believed that the stone could prevent drunkenness.

**amiable** FRENCH *amiable,* from LATIN *amicabilis,* from *amicus* friend.

**amicable** LATIN *amicabilis,* from *amicus* friend.

**amid** MIDDLE ENGLISH *on* at + *middan* middle.

**amigo** SPANISH friend, from LATIN *amicus*.

**amino** LATIN *am(monia)* + **ine**[1].

**amiss** OLD ENGLISH *an-* to + *missan* fail to hit.

**amity** FRENCH *amitié*, from LATIN *amicus* friend.

**ammonia** GREEK *ammoniac*, from *ammoniakon* temple of Ammon, near a certain type of salt deposit.

**amnesia** GREEK *amnesia*, from *a-* not + *mnasthai* remember.

**amnesty** LATIN, from GREEK *amnestia* forgetful. See **amnesia**.

**amoeba** LATIN, from GREEK *ameibein* change.

**amok** MALAY *amuk*.

**among** OLD ENGLISH *on gemang*, from *on-* in + *gemang* crowd.

**amorous** FRENCH, from LATIN *amorosus*, from *amor* love.

**amount** FRENCH *amonter* to amount to, from LATIN *ad-* to + *mons* mountain.

**ampersand** LATIN *and per se and* literally, "(the sign) & by itself is (the word) and."

**amphibian** GREEK *amphibios* living a double life, from *amphi* both + *bios* life.

**amphitheatre** LATIN, from GREEK *amphi-* both sides + *theatre* from FRENCH, from LATIN *theatrum* stage, from GREEK *theatron* place for seeing plays.

**ample** FRENCH full, from LATIN *amplus* large.

**amplify** FRENCH *amplifer* enlarge, from LATIN *amplificare*, from *amplus* ample + *facere* do, make.

**amplitude** LATIN *amplitudo*, from *amplus* large.

**amulet** FRENCH, from LATIN.

**amuse** FRENCH *amuser*, from *à* to + *muser* stare at.

**an** OLD ENGLISH *an*.

**-an** LATIN *–anus* belonging to.

**anachronism** FRENCH *anachronisme*, from LATIN *anachronismus*, from GREEK *anachronismos* a wrong time reference.

**anagram** FRENCH *anagramme*, from GREEK *ana* backwards + *gramma* letter, from *graphein* write.

**anal** LATIN *anus* a ring.

**analogy** GREEK *ana* according to + *logos* word.

**analysis** LATIN, from GREEK solution, from *ana-* up + *lyein* loose.

**anarchy** LATIN *anarchia*, from GREEK *an-* without + *archos* leader.

**anathema** LATIN, from GREEK thing devoted to evil, from *anatithenai* dedicate, from *ana-* up + *titheai* set.

**anatomy** FRENCH *anatomie* science of dissecting (learning about something by cutting it carefully into parts), from LATIN *anatomia* dissection, from GREEK *anatome*, from *ana-* up + *temnein* cut.

**-ance** FRENCH, from LATIN *-antia*.

**ancestor** FRENCH *ancestre* forefather, from LATIN *antecessor*, from *ante-* before + *cedere* go.

**anchor** OLD ENGLISH *ancor*, from LATIN *anchora*, from GREEK *ankyra* hook.

**anchovy** GREEK *aphye* small fish.

**ancient** FRENCH *ancien* old, from LATIN *ante* before.

**and** OLD ENGLISH *and*.

**andiron** FRENCH *andier*.

**anecdote** FRENCH, from GREEK *anekdota* things not published (such as gossip), from *an-* not + *ek-* out + *didonai* give.

**anemia** LATIN, from GREEK *an-* without + *haima* blood.

**anemometer** GREEK *anemos* wind + FRENCH *mètre,* from GREEK *metron* measure.

**anemone** LATIN, from GREEK *anemone* wind flower.

**anesthesia** GREEK *an-* without + *aisthesis* feeling.

**anew** OLD ENGLISH *of niowe* over again.

**angel** FRENCH *angele* holy messenger, from LATIN *angelus,* from GREEK *angelos* messenger.

**anger** OLD NORSE *angr* grief.

**angle** FRENCH *angle,* from LATIN *angulus* corner, from GREEK *ankylos* bent.

**Anglo-** LATIN *Anglus.*

**anguish** FRENCH *anguisse,* from LATIN *angustia* narrow.

**animal** LATIN living creature, from *anima* breath, life.

**animate** LATIN *animare* give life to, from *anima* breath, life.

**animosity** LATIN *animositas* spirit.

**anise** FRENCH *anis,* from LATIN *anesum,* from GREEK *aneson.*

**ankh** EGYPTIAN soul, life.

**ankle** OLD ENGLISH *ancleow.*

**anna** HINDI *ana.*

**annals** LATIN *annales libri* yearly books, from *annus* year.

**anneal** OLD ENGLISH *onælan* burn.

**annex** FRENCH, from LATIN *annectere,* from *ad-* to + *nectere* bind.

**annihilate** LATIN *annihilare,* from *ad-* to + *nihil* nothing.

**anniversary** LATIN *anniversarius,* from *annus* year + *vertere* turn.

**announce** FRENCH *anoncier,* from LATIN *ad-* to + *nuntiare* report, from *nuntius* messenger.

**annoy** FRENCH *anoier,* from LATIN *in odio habere* have in hate.

**annual** FRENCH *annuel,* from LATIN *annualis,* from LATIN *annus* year.

**annular** LATIN *anularis,* from *anulus,* from *anus* a ring.

**annulet** LATIN, from *anulus* a ring + FRENCH *-el,* from LATIN *-ellus.*

**anode** GREEK *ana-* up + *hodos* way.

**anodyne** LATIN, from GREEK *an-* without + *odyne* pain.

**anoint** FRENCH *enoindre,* from LATIN *inunguere,* from *in-* on + *ungere* smear with something greasy.

**anomalous** LATIN, from GREEK *an-* not + *homos* same.

**anonymous** GREEK *anonymos,* from *an-* without + *onyma* name.

**anorak** ESKIMO *anorak* heavy jacket.

**answer** OLD ENGLISH *andswaru* formal (sworn) statement in reply (to being accused of something), from *and-* in reply + *swerian* swear.

**ant** MIDDLE ENGLISH *amete,* from OLD ENGLISH *æmete.*

**-ant** LATIN *-antem* or *-entem.*

**antagonize** GREEK *antagonizesthai* struggle against, from *anti-* opposite + *agon* struggle.

**Antarctic** LATIN *antarcticus,* from GREEK *antarktikós,* from *ant-* against + *arktikos.* See **arctic.**

**ante-** LATIN before.

**antecedent** LATIN *antecedere* go before, from *ante-* before + *cedere* go.

**antediluvian** LATIN *ante-* before + *diluvium* flood.

**antelope** FRENCH, from LATIN, from GREEK *antholops* deer.

**antenna** LATIN horn, from long pole for a sail.

**anthem** OLD ENGLISH *antefn* verse of a song sung in response, from LATIN *antiphona*, from GREEK *antiphonos*, from *anti-* against + *phone* voice.

**anther** FRENCH *anthère*, from LATIN *anthera* medicine extracted from a flower, from GREEK *anthera*, from *antheros* flowery, from *anthos* flower.

**anthology** GREEK *anthologia* a gathering of flowers, from *anthos* flower + *legein* gather.

**anthracite** GREEK *anthrax*.

**anthrax** LATIN, from GREEK burning coal.

**anthropo-** GREEK *anthropos* man.

**anthropomorphism** GREEK *anthropos* man + *morphe* form, shape.

**anti-** GREEK against.

**antibiotic** LATIN *antibiosis*, from *anti-* against + GREEK *biosis* way of life, from *bios* life.

**antic** ITALIAN *antico* old, from LATIN *antiquus*. See **antique**.

**anticipate** LATIN *anticipare*, from *anti-* before + *capere* take.

**anticline** GREEK *anti-* against + *kleinen* incline.

**antidote** FRENCH, from LATIN *antidotum*, from GREEK *antidoton*, from *anti-* against + *didonai* give.

**antimony** LATIN *antimonium*.

**antipathy** LATIN, from GREEK *anti-* against + *pathein* feel.

**antique** FRENCH, from LATIN *antiquus* old, from *ante* before.

**antiseptic** GREEK *anti-* against + *sepein* make rotten or decayed.

**antithesis** GREEK *anti-* against + *tithenai* place.

**anus** LATIN *anus* a ring.

**anvil** OLD ENGLISH *anfilt*, from *an-* on + possible *filtan* beat.

**anxious** LATIN *anxius*, from *angere* choke.

**any** OLD ENGLISH *ænig* no matter which, at all.

**aorta** LATIN *aorta*, from GREEK *aorte*, from *aeirein* raise.

**apart** FRENCH *à part* aside, from LATIN *ad-* to + *pars* part.

**apartment** FRENCH *appartement*, from ITALIAN *appartamento* separation, from *parte* part.

**apathy** FRENCH *apathie*, from LATIN *apathia*, from GREEK *apatheia*, from *a-* without + *pathos* emotion.

**aperitif** FRENCH, from LATIN *apertus* open.

**aperture** LATIN *apertus* open.

**apex** LATIN a point.

**aphelion** LATIN, from GREEK, from *apo* away from + *helios* sun.

**aphesis** GREEK *apo-* from + *hienai* send, letting go.

**aphid** LATIN *aphides*, plural of **aphis**.

**aphis** Coined by Linnaeus, probably from GREEK *apheides* unsparing, lavishly bestowed.

**aphorism** FRENCH, from GREEK *aphorizein* divide, from *apo-* away + *horizein* go around.

**apiary** LATIN *apiarium*, from *apis* bee

**aplomb** FRENCH perpendicular, from *a-* to + *plomb* according to the plummet (weight).

**apocalypse** LATIN, from GREEK *apokalyptein* make known.

**apogee** FRENCH, from LATIN, from GREEK *apo-* from + *ge* earth.

**apology** LATIN *apologia* defense, from GREEK *apologia* speech in defense, from *apo-* from + *logos* speech.

**apophthegm** GREEK *apophthegma,* from *apo-* from + *phthengesthai* utter.

**apoplexy** FRENCH *apoplexie,* from LATIN *apoplexia,* from GREEK, from *apo-* down + *plessein* hit.

**apostle** OLD ENGLISH *apostol,* from LATIN *apostolus,* from GREEK *apostolos,* from *apo-* from + *stellein* send.

**apostrophe** FRENCH, from LATIN *apostrophus,* from GREEK *apostrophos,* from *apo-* from + *strephein* turn.

**apothecary** LATIN *apothecarius,* from *apotheca,* from GREEK *apotheke* storehouse, from *apo-* from + *tithenai* put.

**apothegm** See **apophthegm**.

**Appalachian** SPANISH *apalachen,* from NATIVE AMERICAN name for a particular village.

**appall** FRENCH *apallir,* from *a-* to + *palir* become pale, from LATIN *pallidus* pale.

**appaloosa** NATIVE AMERICAN *a palouse* after an American Indian tribe called the *Palouse*.

**apparatus** LATIN *ad-* to + *parare* prepare.

**apparel** FRENCH *apareiller* to clothe, from *a-* to + *pareiller* put like with like, from LATIN *ad-* to + *par* equal.

**apparent** LATIN *apparere*. See **appear**.

**apparition** FRENCH, from LATIN *apparere,* from *ad-* to + *parere* come into sight.

**appeal** FRENCH *apeler* to call, from LATIN *appellare* to call upon, from *ad-* to + *pellere* push.

**appear** FRENCH *aparoir* to show oneself, from LATIN *apparere,* from *ad-* to + *parere* come into sight.

**appease** FRENCH *apaiser* to pacify (calm), from *a* to + *pais* peace, from LATIN *pax.*

**appellation** LATIN *appellare*. See **appeal**.

**append** LATIN *appendere* to hang on, from *ad-* to + *pendere* hang.

**appendix** See append.

**appertain** FRENCH, from LATIN *appertinere,* from *ad-* to + *pertinere,* from *per-* hold thoroughly + *tenere.*

**appetite** FRENCH *apetit* desire, from LATIN *appetitus,* from *ad-* to + *petere* look for.

**applaud** LATIN *applaudere,* from *ad-* to + *plaudere* clap the hands.

**apple** OLD ENGLISH *æppel.*

**application** See apply.

**applique** See apply.

**apply** FRENCH *aplier,* from LATIN *applicare* to attach to, from *ad-* to + *plicare* fold.

**appoint** FRENCH *apointier* to arrange, from LATIN *ad-* to + *punctum* point.

**appose** FRENCH *aposer* set beside, from LATIN *apponere,* from *ad-* near + *ponere* put.

**appositive** LATIN *appositus,* from *ad-* near + *ponere* place.

**appraise** See praise.

**appreciate** LATIN *appretiare* to value at a price, from LATIN *ad-* to + *pretium* value, reward.

**apprehend** LATIN *apprehendere* to understand, from *ad-* to + *prehendere* take.

**apprentice** French *aprentis*, from Latin *apprehendere* to understand, from *ad-* to + *prehendere* take.

**approach** French *aprochier* to come near to, from Latin *a-* to + *prope* near.

**appropriate** Latin *appropriare*, from *ad-* to + *proprius* one's own.

**approve** French *aprover*, from Latin *approbare*, from *ad-* to + *probare* test, prove.

**approximate** Latin *approximatus* to come near to, from *ad-* to + *proximare* approach.

**apricot** French, from Arabic, from Latin *precoquere*, from *prae-* before + *coquere* cook.

**April** Middle English *Avril*, from French *avrill*, from Latin *aprilis*, possibly from Greek *Aphrodite*, goddess of love and beauty.

**apron** Middle English *a napron*, from French *naperon*, from *nape* a cloth, from Latin *mappa* napkin.

**apropos** French *à propos*, from Latin *ad-* to + *propositum* plan.

**apse** Latin *apsis*, from Greek *hapsis* loop, arch, from *haptein* fasten together (joining arcs to form a circle, especially in making a wheel).

**apsidiole** French *apsidiole* a small apse.

**apt** Latin *aptus* fitted.

**aptitude** Latin *aptitudo* fitness, from *aptus* fit, suited.

**apyrexia** Latin, from Greek *a-* not + *pyrexis* feverishness.

**aquarium** Latin *aqua* water.

**aquastat** Latin *aqua* water + *stata* still.

**aquatint** French *aquatinte*, from Latin *aqua tincta* dyed water, from *tingere* dye.

**aqueduct** Latin *aqua* water + *ducere* lead.

**arabesque** French, from Italian *Arabo* Arab, from Arabic *arab*, with reference to a particular Arabic design.

**Arabic** French, from Latin *Arabicus*.

**araneidan** Latin *aranea* spider.

**arbiter** Latin witness, from *ad-* to + *baetere* go.

**arbitrary** Latin *arbitrarius* uncertain, from *arbiter* judge (showing the uncertainty of judges' decisions).

**arbor** French *erber* place where grass or herbs are grown, from Latin *herba* grass, herb.

**arboreal** Latin *arboreus*. See **arbor**.

**arc** French, from Latin *arcus* a bow, arch.

**arcade** French arch, from Latin *arcus* bow, arch.

**arcane** Latin *arcanus* secret.

**arch** French *arche* chest, from Latin *arcus* bow, arch.

**-arch** Greek *archos* ruler.

**arch-** Latin *arch(i)-*, from Greek *arch(i)-*, from *archos* ruler.

**archaeology** Greek *archaios* ancient, from *arche* the beginning + *logos* word.

**archaic** Greek *archaikos* ancient.

**archetype** Latin *archetypum* original pattern, from Greek *archetypon*, from *archos* first + *typos* type.

**archie** the name *Archibald*.

**archipelago** Italian, from Greek *archi* chief + *pelagos* sea.

**architect** Latin, from Greek *archi-* chief + *tekton* carpenter.

**architrave** Italian *archi-* beginning, origin + *trave* beam, from Latin *trabem*.

**archive** FRENCH *archif*, from LATIN *archivum*, from GREEK *archeion* public building, from *arche* the beginning.

**arctic** FRENCH *artique*, from LATIN *articus*, from GREEK *arktos* northern.

**ardent** FRENCH *ardant* burning, from LATIN *ardens* burn.

**ardor** FRENCH, from LATIN *ardere* burn.

**arduous** LATIN *arduus* difficult.

**are** OLD ENGLISH *aron*.

**area** LATIN *area* open space.

**arecoline** PORTUGUESE *areca* palm tree + *-ine* like.

**arena** LATIN *arena* sandy place. Sand was used to cover the ground of large areas for sporting events in ancient Rome.

**areola** LATIN *areola* small area.

**argon** GREEK *a-* without + *ergon* work.

**argue** FRENCH *arguer* reason, from LATIN *arguere* prove, make clear.

**arid** LATIN *arere* be dry.

**arise** OLD ENGLISH *arisan*.

**aristocracy** FRENCH *aristocratie* rule of the nobly born, from GREEK *aristokaratia* rule of the best, from *aristos* best + *kratos* power.

**arithmetic** FRENCH *arismetrique*, from LATIN *arithmetica* science of numbers, from GREEK *arithmos* number.

**ark** OLD ENGLISH *earc*, from LATIN *arcere* enclose.

**armada** SPANISH *armar* provide with weapons, from LATIN *armare*, from *arma* weapons.

**armature** LATIN *armare* provide with weapons, from *arma* weapons.

**armistice** LATIN *arma* arms + *-stitium*, from *stare* stand.

**armor** See **armature**.

**army** FRENCH *armer* arm, from LATIN *armare*. See **armature**.

**arnica** LATIN.

**aroma** FRENCH *aromat*, from LATIN *aromata*, from GREEK sweet spice.

**around** See a-[1] + **round**.

**arouse** See a-[1] + **rise**.

**arrange** FRENCH *arengier* to put into order, from *à-* to + *rengier* put in order, from *renge* line, row.

**array** MIDDLE ENGLISH *arrayan* prepare, equip, from French *arreyer* arrange, equip, from *arredare* put in order.

**arrears** FRENCH *ariere* backward, from LATIN *ad-* to + *retro* behind.

**arrest** FRENCH *arester* to stay, from LATIN *ad-* to + *restare* stop.

**arrive** FRENCH *ariver* come to land, from LATIN *ad-* to + *ripa* shore.

**arrogant** LATIN *arrogare* claim for oneself, from *ad-* to + *rogare* ask.

**arrow** OLD ENGLISH *arwe*.

**arsenal** ITALIAN *arsenale* a dock, from ARABIC *dar sina a* wharf, workshop.

**arsenic** FRENCH, from LATIN, from GREEK *arsenikon* a yellow type of arsenic, from PERSIAN *zar* gold.

**arsenicum** LATIN *arsenicum* arsenic.

**arson** FRENCH, from LATIN *ardere* burn.

**art** MIDDLE ENGLISH, from FRENCH, from LATIN *ars*.

**artery** LATIN *arteria* this blood vessel, probably from GREEK *aeirein* raise.

**arthropod** LATIN *arthropoda*, from GREEK *arthron* joint + *podos* foot.

**artichoke** ITALIAN *articiocco*, from SPANISH *alcarchofa*, from ARABIC *al-harsuf*.

**article** FRENCH, from LATIN *articulus* division, from *artus* joint.

**articulate** LATIN *articulare* divide into joints, from *articulus* division, from *artus* joint.

**artifact** LATIN *ars* art + *factum* thing made.

**artificial** LATIN *artificium* work that requires great skill with the hands, from *ars* skill, art + *facere* do, make.

**artillery** FRENCH *artillerie*, from *artiller* protect from attack.

**artisan** FRENCH, from LATIN *ars* art.

**-ary** LATIN *-arius, -aria, -arium*.

**as**[1] (like, etc.) OLD ENGLISH *ealswa*.

**as**[2] (coin) LATIN *as* unit of weight

**ascend** LATIN *ascendere*, from *ad-* to + *scandere* climb.

**ascertain** FRENCH *acertener*, from LATIN *ad-* to + *certain* sure.

**ascetic** GREEK *askein* train the body.

**ascites** LATIN, from GREEK *askites* dropsy.

**ascot** a race course called Ascot Heath in Berkshire, England where such ties were fashionable.

**ascribe** LATIN *ascribere*, from *ad-* to + *scribere* write.

**asepsis** GREEK *a-* not + *sepein* make rotten.

**ash**[1] (grayish powder) OLD ENGLISH *æsce*.

**ash**[2] (tree) OLD ENGLISH *æsc*.

**ashamed** OLD ENGLISH *ascamian* feel shame.

**asinine** LATIN *asinus* ass.

**ask** OLD ENGLISH *ascian* to question.

**askance** MIDDLE ENGLISH *askoin*, from *a-* on + *skwyn*, from DUTCH *schuin* sideways.

**askew** See a-[1] + skew.

**asleep** FRENCH *on slaepe* in sleep.

**asp** LATIN *aspis*, from GREEK.

**asparagus** OLD ENGLISH *sparage*, from LATIN *sparagus*, from *asparagus*, from GREEK *asparagus*.

**aspect** LATIN *aspectus* look, from *ad-* to + *specere* look, behold.

**aspen** OLD ENGLISH *æspe*.

**asperity** LATIN *asper* rough, uneven.

**asphalt** LATIN *asphaltus*, from GREEK *asphaltos*, probably from *a-* not + *sphallein* cause to fall.

**asphodel** LATIN *asphodel*, from GREEK *asphodelos*.

**asphyxia** GREEK a stopping of the pulse, from *a-* not + *sphyzein* pulse.

**aspirant** See aspirate.

**aspirate** LATIN *aspirare*, from *ad-* to + *spirare* breathe.

**aspire** See aspirate.

**ass** OLD ENGLISH *assa*, from LATIN *asinus*.

**assail** FRENCH, from LATIN *assilire*, from *ad-* to + *salire* leap.

**assassin** FRENCH, from ARABIC *hashishiyyin* eaters of (the drug) hashish, Muslim suicide killers active at the time of the Christian Crusades.

**assault** FRENCH *asaut* attack, from LATIN *ad-* to + *saltus* leap.

**assay** FRENCH *essai* test, from LATIN *exagium*, from *ex-* out + *agere* act.

**assemble** FRENCH *assembler* to gather, from LATIN *ad-* to + *simul* together.

**assent** FRENCH *assetir*, from LATIN *assentire*, from *ad-* to + *sentire* feel.

**assert** LATIN *asserere,* from *ad-* to + *serere* join.

**assess** FRENCH *assesser* determine, tax, from LATIN *assessare,* from *assidere* to sit beside and help a judge, from *ad-* to + *sedere* sit.

**asset** FRENCH *assets,* from LATIN *ad-* toward + *satis* enough (to pay debts).

**assign** FRENCH, from LATIN *assignare* to give a share to, from *ad-* to + *signare* sign.

**assimilate** LATIN *assimilare,* from *ad-* to + *similare* make like.

**assist** FRENCH *assister* to help, from LATIN *assistere,* from *ad-* to + *stare* stand.

**associate** LATIN *associare* to join, from *ad-* to + *socius* companion.

**associative** See **associate**.

**assonance** FRENCH *assonance,* from LATIN *assonare* respond to, from *ad-* to + *sonare* sound.

**assort** FRENCH *assorter* to match, from LATIN *ad-* to + *sors* sort.

**assuage** FRENCH, from LATIN *ad-* to + *suavis* sweet.

**assume** LATIN *assumere,* from *ad-* to + *sumere* take.

**assure** FRENCH *aseürer* to make sure, from LATIN *assecurare,* from *ad-* to + *securus* sure.

**aster** LATIN, from GREEK *aster* star.

**asterisk** LATIN, from GREEK *aster* star.

**asteroid** GREEK *asteroeides* star-like, from *aster* star + *-eidos* form, shape.

**asthma** GREEK breathing hard.

**astigmatism** GREEK *a-* without + *stigma* a mark + *-ismos.*

**astonish** MIDDLE ENGLISH *astonen* stun, from FRENCH *estoner,* from LATIN *ex-* out + *tonare* thunder.

**astound** See **astonish**.

**astral** LATIN *astralis* relating to stars, from *astrum* star, from GREEK *astron.*

**astride** See *a-*[1] + **stride**.

**astro-** GREEK *aster* star.

**astrolabe** FRENCH, from LATIN, from GREEK *astron* star + *lambanein* take.

**astrology** FRENCH *astrologie,* from LATIN *astrologia* astronomy, from GREEK *astrologia,* from *astron* star + *-logia,* from *logos* word.

**astronaut** GREEK *astron* star + *nautes* sailor, from *naus* ship.

**astronomy** FRENCH *astronomie,* from LATIN *astronomia,* from GREEK *astron* star + *nomos* law.

**astute** LATIN *astus* craft.

**asylum** LATIN safe place, from GREEK *asylon,* from *a-* not, without + *style* right to take.

**at** OLD ENGLISH *æt.*

**atavism** FRENCH *atavisme,* from LATIN *atavus,* from *at-* beyond + *avus* grandfather.

**-ate** LATIN *-atus.*

**atheism** FRENCH *athéisme,* from GREEK *atheos,* from *a-* without + *theos* god.

**athlete** LATIN, from GREEK *athlos* contest + *athlon* prize.

**athwart** See *a-*[1] + **thwart**.

**-atic** FRENCH, from LATIN, from GREEK *atikos.*

**-ation** FRENCH, from LATIN *-tionis.*

**atlas** *Atlas,* one of the giants of Greek mythology, who was believed responsible for holding up the sky.

**atmosphere** LATIN *atmosphaera,* from GREEK *atmos* vapor + *sphaira* sphere.

**atoll** Maldive Islands, in the Indian Ocean.

**atom** LATIN *atomus* smallest bit, from GREEK *atomos* cannot be divided, from *a-* not + *temnein* divide, from the early belief that atoms could not be split.

**atone** MIDDLE ENGLISH *at-onen* at one as in "to be at one with", or in agreement with.

**atrium** LATIN.

**atrocious** LATIN *atrox* fierce, from *ater* black.

**atrophy** LATIN *atrophia* lack of food, from GREEK *a-* not + *trephein* feed.

**attach** FRENCH *attachier* to fasten, from *a-* to + GERMAN *takk* pointed thing.

**attack** FRENCH *attaquer,* from ITALIAN *attaccare* to join battle, from LATIN *ad-* to + GERMAN *takk* pointed thing.

**attain** FRENCH *ataindre* to reach, from LATIN *attingere,* from *ad-* to + *tangere* touch.

**attainder** See attain.

**attaint** See attain.

**attempt** FRENCH *atempter* to try, from LATIN *attemptare,* from *ad-* to + *temptare* try.

**attend** FRENCH *atendre* to wait, from LATIN *attendere,* from *ad-* to + *tendere* stretch.

**attenuate** LATIN *attenuare* to make thin, from *ad-* to + *tenuare,* from *tenuis* thin.

**attercop** OLD ENGLISH *attorcoppa* poison-head, from *ator* poison.

**attest** LATIN *attestari,* from *ad-* to + *testari* be a witness to.

**attic** FRENCH *attique* small, well-decorated room at the top of the house, following the style of Athens in ancient Greece, from LATIN *Atticus* having to do with Athens, from GREEK *Attikos.*

**attire** FRENCH *atirier* arrange, dress, from *a tire* in order.

**attitude** ITALIAN *attitudine* posture, from LATIN *aptitudo* fitness, from *aptus* fit, suited.

**attorney** FRENCH *atorné* one appointed, from *atorner,* from LATIN *ad-* to + *tornare* turn.

**attract** LATIN *attrahere,* from *ad-* to + *trahere* draw.

**attribute** LATIN *attribuere,* from *ad-* to + *tribuere* assign.

**attrition** LATIN *attritio,* from *ad-* to + *terere* rub.

**auburn** FRENCH *auborne,* from LATIN *alburnus,* from *albus* white, changed by MIDDLE ENGLISH *brun* brown.

**auction** LATIN *auctio* increase, from *augere.*

**audacity** LATIN *audax* bold.

**audience** FRENCH hearing, from LATIN *audire* hear.

**audit** LATIN *auditus* a hearing. In earlier times audits were done orally rather than in writing.

**audition** LATIN *auditio* hearing.

**auger** OLD ENGLISH *nafogar* drill for the nave (hub) of a wheel, from *nafu* nave or hub of a wheel + *gar* piercer.

**aught** MIDDLE ENGLISH, from OLD ENGLISH *awiht.*

**augment** LATIN *augmentare* grow.

**augur** LATIN priest at a fertility rite, from *augere* increase, enlarge, enrich.

**august** LATIN *augustus* majestic, magnificent, from *augere* increase, enlarge, enrich.

**August** OLD ENGLISH *August,* from LATIN *Augustus* title of the first Roman emperor, from *augustus* worthy of respect.

**aunt** LATIN *amita.*

**aura** LATIN, from GREEK *aer* air.

**aureole** LATIN *aureus* golden.

**auricle** LATIN *auris* ear.

**aurora** LATIN dawn.

**auroscope** LATIN *aurum* gold + GREEK *-skopion,* from *skopein* view, examine.

**auscultation** LATIN *auscultatio* listening + *-tion,* from FRENCH, from LATIN *-tionis.*

**auspicious** LATIN *auspicium* omen (sign of something to come).

**austere** LATIN *austerus* harsh, from GREEK *austeros,* from *avos* dry.

**Australia** LATIN *terra australis* southern land.

**author** FRENCH *autor* writer, creator, from LATIN *auctor* creator.

**authority** FRENCH *autorite* power, from LATIN *auctor* author, one in charge.

**auto-** GREEK *autos* self.

**autocrat** FRENCH *autocrate,* from GREEK *autokrates,* from *autos* self + *kratos* power.

**autograph** FRENCH *autographe* one's own signature, from LATIN *autographus* written with one's own hand, from GREEK *autographos,* from *autos* self + *graphein* write.

**automatic** GREEK *automatos* self acting.

**automaton** See automatic.

**automobile** See auto- + mobile.

**autonomous** GREEK *autonomia,* from *autos* self + *nomos* law.

**autopsy** LATIN *autopsia,* from GREEK seeing with one's own eyes, from *autos* self + *opsis* a sight.

**autumn** LATIN *autumnus.*

**auxiliary** LATIN *auxiliarius,* from *auxilium* aid.

**avail** FRENCH *valoir* be of value, from LATIN *valere* be strong.

**avalanche** FRENCH *avaler* descend, from *lavanche,* from LATIN, *labi* slip.

**avant-garde** FRENCH advance guard.

**avarice** FRENCH, from LATIN *avarus* greedy, from *avere* want.

**avenge** LATIN *a-* to + *vindicare* claim.

**avenue** FRENCH, from LATIN *advenire.* See **advent.**

**aver** FRENCH *averrer,* from LATIN *ad-* to + *verus* true.

**average** FRENCH *avarie,* from ITALIAN, from ARABIC *'awar* damaged goods. From the way payment for damage to goods on ships was figured out in the Middle Ages.

**averse** LATIN *avertere,* from *a-* from + *vertere* turn.

**avert** FRENCH *avertir,* from LATIN *avertere.* See **averse.**

**aviary** LATIN *avis* bird.

**aviation** FRENCH, from LATIN *avis* bird.

**avid** LATIN *avidus* greedy.

**avocado** SPANISH *aguacate.*

**avoid** FRENCH *esvuidier,* from *es-* out + *vuide* empty.

**avouch** FRENCH *avochier,* from LATIN *advocare,* from *ad-* to + *vocare* call, from *vox* voice.

**avow** FRENCH *avouer,* from LATIN *advocare,* from *ad-* to + *vocare* call.

**await** FRENCH, from LATIN *a-* to + *waitier* wait.

**awake** OLD ENGLISH *awacian* waken.

**award** FRENCH *eswarder* observe, from LATIN *ex-* from + *wardare* observe.

**aware** OLD ENGLISH *genær.*

**away** OLD ENGLISH *aweg.*

**awe** OLD NORSE *agi* be afraid.

**awful** MIDDLE ENGLISH *agheful,* from *aghe.* See **awe.**

**awkward** OLD NORSE *öfugr* turned the wrong way.

**awl** OLD NORSE *alr*.

**awning** nautical usage, perhaps from FRENCH *auvans*, from *auvent* a sloping roof.

**awry** See wry.

**ax (axe)** OLD ENGLISH *eax*.

**axial** LATIN *axis* axle, pivot + -*al* FRENCH, from LATIN *alis*.

**axillary** LATIN *axilla* armpit.

**axiom** LATIN *axioma* principle, from GREEK *axioma*.

**axis** LATIN *axis* axle, pivot.

**axle** OLD NORSE *oxull*.

**ayah** PORTUGUESE *aia* governess.

**aye** OLD NORSE *ei*.

**ayont** See beyond.

**azimuth** FRENCH *azimut*, from ARABIC *as-sumut* the ways.

**azure** FRENCH *azur*, from ARABIC *lazhuward* lapis lazuli, a deep blue color or stone.

# B

**baa** imitative.

**babble** imitative.

**babe** MIDDLE ENGLISH *baban*, probably a nursery word.

**babel** HEBREW *Babel* Babylon, an ancient city in SW Asia. According to an ancient story, the people there tried to build a tower to the sky and were stopped by God, who caused them to speak in different languages so they couldn't finish the tower.

**baboon** FRENCH *babuin* ape, fool, from *baboue* lip (of animals), from *bab* imitative.

**baby** MIDDLE ENGLISH *babi*. See **babe**.

**bachelor** FRENCH *bacheler* young man, from LATIN *baccalarius* young nobleman wishing to become a knight.

**back** OLD ENGLISH *bæc*.

**bacon** MIDDLE ENGLISH, from FRENCH *bacun* ham, lard strips.

**bacteria** LATIN, from GREEK *bakterion* stick. When bacteria were first seen under the microscope they looked like little sticks.

**bad** MIDDLE ENGLISH *badde* wicked.

**badge** MIDDLE ENGLISH *bage* the emblem.

**badger** origin uncertain.

**badinage** FRENCH *badiner* joke, from *badin* silly, from LATIN *badare* stare at with the mouth open.

**baffle** probably from SCOTTISH *bauchle* dishonor.

**bag** OLD NORSE *baggi* pack, bundle.

**bagatelle** FRENCH, from ITALIAN *bagatella*, from LATIN *baca* berry.

**bagel** GREEK *beugen* bend.

**baggage** FRENCH *bagage*, from LATIN *baga* chest.

**baguette** FRENCH, from ITALIAN *bacchetta*, from LATIN *baculum* a staff.

**bail**[1] (deposit) FRENCH *bail* custody, from *baillier* have in charge, from LATIN *bajulare* one who takes care of things.

**bail**[2] (remove water) FRENCH *baille* bucket, from LATIN *baca* trough (container for animals to drink from).

**baile** MIDDLE ENGLISH call to combat, from FRENCH *bailler* deliver blows.

**bailey** MIDDLE ENGLISH *baylle*, from FRENCH *baile*, from LATIN *bajulus* porter.

**bailiff** FRENCH *baillif*, from *bail* custody. See **bail**[1].

**bailiwick** FRENCH *bailiff,* from *bail* custody + MIDDLE ENGLISH *wik,* from OLD ENGLISH *wic* village.

**bairn** OLD ENGLISH *bearn.*

**bait** OLD NORSE *beita* cause to bite.

**baize** FRENCH *baie,* from LATIN *badius* brown.

**Bajan** *Barbadian,* a person who lives on the Caribbean island of Barbados.

**bake** OLD ENGLISH *bacan.*

**bakelite** L. H. *Baekeland* (1863-1944), its inventor + LATIN, from GREEK *ites.*

**balaclava** a Russian village. The cap was worn by soldiers in a 19th century battle there.

**balalaika** RUSSIAN.

**balance** FRENCH instrument used for weighing, from LATIN *bilanx* having two scales, from *bi-* two + *lanx* plate.

**balcony** ITALIAN *balcone,* from GERMAN *balcho* beam.

**baldric** MIDDLE ENGLISH *bauderik,* from FRENCH *baudrei,* from LATIN *balteus* belt.

**bale** FRENCH *balu.*

**baleful** OLD ENGLISH *bealu* evil + *-ful* complete.

**balk** OLD ENGLISH *balca* ridge.

**ball**[1] (sphere) OLD NORSE *böillr* globe.

**ball**[2] (dance) FRENCH *bal,* from *baler* dance, from LATIN *ballare,* from GREEK *ballizein.*

**ballad** FRENCH *balade* dancing song, from LATIN *ballare.*

**ballast** GERMAN, from DANISH *balrast,* from *bar* bare + *last* a load.

**ballet** FRENCH *ballet* little dance, from ITALIAN *balletto,* from *ballare* dance.

**balletomane** FRENCH. See **ballet** + **mania**.

**ballistic** LATIN, from GREEK *ballein* throw.

**balloon** ITALIAN *pallone* large ball, from *palla* ball.

**ballot** ITALIAN *ballotta* little ball, from the ancient Greek method of voting by using different colored balls to vote yes and no.

**ballotade** FRENCH *ballotte* small ball.

**bally** BRITISH, slang for *bloody.*

**ballybonkers** origin uncertain.

**balm** FRENCH *basme,* from LATIN *basamum* balsam (something that heals), from GREEK *balsamon.*

**balsam** OLD ENGLISH, from LATIN *basamum.* See **balm**.

**baluster** FRENCH *balustre,* from ITALIAN *balaustro* pillar. See **balustrade**.

**balustrade** FRENCH, from ITALIAN *balaustrata* provided with balusters, from *balaustro* pillar, from *balausta* flower of the wild pomegranate, from GREEK *balaustion.* Staircase uprights had double curves, like parts of the pomegranate flower.

**bambas** SPANISH sneakers.

**bamboo** PORTUGUESE *bambu,* probably from MALAY *samambu.*

**bamboozle** probably from an earlier beggar term invented in England about the 1700s.

**ban** OLD ENGLISH *bannan* summon, from FRENCH *ban* a public order.

**banal** FRENCH, belonging to common people. See **ban**.

**banco** SPANISH bank.

**band**[1] (group) FRENCH *bande* band, group.

**band**[2] (flat strip) FRENCH *bande* bond, tie.

**bandage** See **band**[2].

**bandana** HINDI *bandhnu* method of dyeing.

**bandit** ITALIAN *bandire* outlaw.

**bandoleer** FRENCH *bandoulière,* from SPANISH *bandolera,* from *banda* scarf.

**bane** OLD ENGLISH *bana* murderer.

**bang** OLD NORSE *banga* pound.

**bangle** HINDI *bangri* glass bracelet.

**banish** FRENCH *banir.* See **ban.**

**banister** alteration of **baluster.**

**bank**[1] (place to keep money) ITALIAN *banca* bench (of a banker).

**bank**[2] (shallow place) OLD NORSE *bakki.*

**bankrupt** ITALIAN *banca rotta* broken bench, from the Medieval custom of breaking the bench of a moneychanger (person who changes money for foreigners) who can't pay his bills, from LATIN *banca* bench + *rotta* broken, from *rumpere* break.

**banner** FRENCH *baniere* flag, from LATIN *bandum.*

**bannister** alteration of **baluster.**

**bannock** OLD ENGLISH *bannuc.*

**banquet** FRENCH, from ITALIAN *banchetto* little bench.

**banquette** FRENCH, from Norman *banque,* from DUTCH *bank* bench.

**bantam** *Bantam,* a place in South Asia, where the birds are thought to originate.

**banter** origin uncertain.

**baobab** LATIN *bahobab,* possibly from ARABIC *'abū hibāb* source of seeds.

**baptism** FRENCH *baptiser,* from LATIN *baptizare,* from GREEK *baptein* dip in water.

**bar**[1] (long narrow thing) FRENCH *barre,* from LATIN *barra* barrier.

**bar**[2] (unit of pressure) GREEK *baros* weight.

**bar mitzvah** HEBREW *bar* son of + *mitsva* commandment, from *tsiva* command.

**barb** FRENCH *barbe* beard, from LATIN *barba.*

**barbarous** LATIN *barbaricus* foreign, from GREEK *barbaros.*

**barbecue** SPANISH *barbacoa* used to describe a Native American style of cooking on a rack of wood, from NATIVE AMERICAN *barbakoa* wooden rack.

**barbel** FRENCH, from LATIN *barbus* the fish, from *barba* beard.

**barber** FRENCH *barbour,* from *barbe* beard, from LATIN *barba.*

**barberry** LATIN *barbers,* from ARABIC *barbaris.*

**barbican** FRENCH *barbicane,* from LATIN *barbacana,* from PERSIAN *barbar-kanah* house on a wall.

**bard** MIDDLE ENGLISH, from SCOTTISH *bard,* WELSH *bard* and IRISH *bardd.*

**bare** OLD ENGLISH *bær* without covering.

**bargain** FRENCH *bargaignier* haggle (argue about price or terms).

**barge** FRENCH flat boat, from LATIN *barca.*

**bark**[1] (tree covering) OLD NORSE *borkr.*

**bark**[2] (dog sound) OLD ENGLISH *beorcan.*

**barley** OLD ENGLISH *bere.*

**barlow** (knife) name of maker.

**barnacle** MIDDLE ENGLISH *barnakille* barnacle goose (a type of bird believed to hatch from barnacles), from LATIN *bernacula,* origin unknown.

**barometer** GREEK *baros* weight + *metron* measure.

**baron** FRENCH man, warrior.

**baroque** FRENCH, from PORTUGUESE *barroco* a pearl that is not perfect.

**barouche** GERMAN, from ITALIAN, from LATIN *birotus,* from *bi-* two + *rota* wheel.

**barrack** FRENCH *baraque* hut, from SPANISH *barraca* mud hut, from *barro* clay, from LATIN *barrum* clay.

**barracuda** SPANISH.

**barrage** FRENCH *tir de barrage* curtain of fire, from *barrage* barrier, from *barrer* bar, from FRENCH *barre.* See **bar**[1].

**barranca** SPANISH.

**barre** FRENCH bar.

**barrel** FRENCH *baril* cask.

**barren** FRENCH *baraigne* sterile (not able to reproduce).

**barrette** FRENCH *barre* bar.

**barricade** FRENCH barrier, from *barrique* barrel, from SPANISH *baril* cask.

**barrier** FRENCH, from *barre* rod. See **bar**[1].

**barrister** See **bar**[1].

**barrow**[1] (wheelbarrow) OLD ENGLISH *bearwe.*

**barrow**[2] (mound) OLD ENGLISH *beorg* hill.

**barter** FRENCH *barater,* from OLD NORSE *baratta* quarrel.

**bartizan** altered form of *brattice,* from MIDDLE ENGLISH *bretice,* from FRENCH *bretesche* wooden tower.

**basalt** LATIN *basaltes.*

**base**[1] (stand) LATIN *basis* foundation, from GREEK pedestal, base.

**base**[2] (low) FRENCH *base,* from LATIN *bassus* low, short.

**basement** LATIN *basis* foundation, from GREEK pedestal, base + FRENCH, from LATIN *-mentum.*

**bash** possibly from DANISH *baske* strike.

**basidium** LATIN *basis* foundation, from GREEK pedestal, base.

**basil** FRENCH *basile,* from LATIN *basilicum,* from GREEK *basilikon,* from *basileus* king.

**basin** FRENCH *bacin* bowl, from LATIN *bacca* water container.

**basis** LATIN *basis* foundation, from GREEK pedestal, base.

**basket** origin uncertain.

**Basque** FRENCH *basquine,* from SPANISH *vascon* the Basque region between Spain and France, from LATIN *Vasconia.*

**bass**[1] (low voice) MIDDLE ENGLISH *bas,* from LATIN *bassus* low.

**bass**[2] (fish) OLD ENGLISH *bærs.*

**bassinet** FRENCH *berceau* cradle.

**bassoon** FRENCH *basson,* from ITALIAN *bassone,* from *basso* low.

**bastard** FRENCH *fils de bast* child of the packsaddle and not from the marriage bed, meaning the child's parents were not married, from LATIN *bastum.*

**baste** FRENCH *bassiner* moisten, from *bassin* basin.

**bastille** FRENCH guarded fort, from *bastir* build.

**bastion** See **bastille**.

**bat**[1] (club) OLD ENGLISH *batt* club.

**bat**[2] (mammal) MIDDLE ENGLISH *bakke,* of SCANDINAVIAN origin.

**bat**[3] (blink) FRENCH *batire* beat.

**batch** MIDDLE ENGLISH *bacche* a baking.

**bate** See **abate**.

**bateau** FRENCH *batel,* from OLD ENGLISH *bat* boat.

**bath** OLD ENGLISH *bæth* liquid for bathing.

**bathetic** See **bathos**.

**bathos** GREEK depth.

**batiste** FRENCH *baptiste*, possibly from the use of similar cloths to wipe the heads of children after baptism.

**batling** See **bat**[1] + **-ling**.

**baton** FRENCH small stick, from *baston*, from LATIN *bastum* stick.

**battalion** FRENCH *battaillon*, from ITALIAN *battaglione*, from LATIN *battalia* battle, from *battuere* beat.

**batten** FRENCH *baton* small stick, from LATIN *bastum* stick.

**battenburg** the name of a town in Germany.

**batter** FRENCH *battre*, from LATIN *battuere* beat.

**battery** FRENCH *batterie* beat, from LATIN *battuere*.

**battle** FRENCH *bataille* a fight, from LATIN *battualia* exercises to help in fighting, from *battuere* beat.

**battledore** origin unknown, possibly from FRENCH *batedor* beater, from *batre* beat.

**bauble** MIDDLE ENGLISH *babel*, from FRENCH *baubel*, *belbel* toy, probably from LATIN *bellus* pretty.

**bauxite** FRENCH *Les Baux* a town in southeast France, where it is found.

**bavin** origin uncertain.

**bawdkin** FRENCH *baudekin*, from LATIN *baldakinus*, from *Bagdad* the city in Asia where the fabric was made.

**bawl** LATIN *baulare* bark, and possibly from OLD NORSE *baula* moo like a cow.

**bay**[1] (water) FRENCH *baie*, from LATIN.

**bay**[2] (color) FRENCH *bai*, from LATIN *badius*.

**bay**[3] (dog bark) FRENCH *abaiier*.

**bayonet** FRENCH *Bayonne* city in France where it was first made.

**bayou** FRENCH, from NATIVE AMERICAN *bayuk* river, creek.

**bazaar** PERSIAN *bazar* market.

**bazooka** a resemblance to a musical instrument invented and named that by an American comedian in the 1930s.

**be** OLD ENGLISH *beon*.

**be-** OLD ENGLISH *be-* about, near, by.

**beach** a dialect in Sussex, England, referring to pebbles made smooth by the waves, from OLD ENGLISH *bæce*, *bece* stream.

**beacon** OLD ENGLISH *beacen*.

**bead** MIDDLE ENGLISH *bede*, from OLD ENGLISH *gebed* prayer. In some religions beads are strung together and for each one a prayer is said.

**beadle** OLD ENGLISH *bydel*, from *beodan* bid, order.

**beagle** MIDDLE ENGLISH *begle*, possibly from FRENCH *beguele* noisy person.

**beak** FRENCH *bec* bird's bill, from LATIN *beccus*.

**beaker** OLD NORSE *bikarr*, from LATIN *bacar* wine glass.

**beam** OLD ENGLISH *bæm* piece of wood.

**bean** OLD ENGLISH.

**bear**[1] (carry) OLD ENGLISH *beran* carry, support.

**bear**[2] (mammal) OLD ENGLISH *bera*.

**beard** OLD ENGLISH.

**beat** OLD ENGLISH *beatan*.

**beatitude** FRENCH, from LATIN *beatitudo*, from *beatus* happy, blessed.

**beau** FRENCH fine, handsome, from LATIN *bellus* pretty.

**beauty** FRENCH *beaute*, from LATIN *bellus* beautiful.

**beaver**[1] (animal) MIDDLE ENGLISH *bever*, from OLD ENGLISH, from *beofor*.

**beaver**[2] (armor) MIDDLE ENGLISH *bavier*, from FRENCH *baviere* bib.

**because** MIDDLE ENGLISH *bi* by + FRENCH reason, from LATIN *causa*.

**beck**[1] (gesture) See **beckon**.

**beck**[2] (brook) MIDDLE ENGLISH *bek*, from OLD NORSE *bekkr* brook.

**beck**[3] (tool) OLD ENGLISH *becca* hook.

**beck**[4] (tub) possibly from DUTCH *bekken*, from German *becken* basin.

**beckon** MIDDLE ENGLISH *beknen*, from OLD ENGLISH *beacnian* make signs, from *beacen* beacon.

**become** OLD ENGLISH *becuman* happen.

**bed** OLD ENGLISH *bed* couch to sleep on.

**bedaub** See **be- + daub**.

**beech** OLD ENGLISH *bece*.

**beef** FRENCH *boef*, from LATIN *bovis* ox.

**been** See **be**.

**beep** imitative.

**beetle** MIDDLE ENGLISH *bital*, from OLD ENGLISH *bitela*, from *bitan* bite.

**befall** OLD ENGLISH *befeallan* fall.

**before** OLD ENGLISH *be-* by + *foran* before.

**beg** FRENCH *begger*, from *begard*, from DUTCH *beggaert*.

**beget** OLD ENGLISH *begitan* get.

**begin** OLD ENGLISH *beginnan* start.

**beguile** See **be- + guile**.

**behalf** OLD ENGLISH *be* by + *healf* half, side.

**behave** See **be- + have**.

**behemoth** LATIN *Behemoth* mythical animal, from HEBREW *b'hemoth* beast.

**behest** OLD ENGLISH *behæs*.

**behind** OLD ENGLISH *behindan*.

**beholden** OLD ENGLISH *bihealdan* hold.

**behoove** OLD ENGLISH *behofian* need.

**beige** FRENCH.

**bejabbers** AMERICAN slang, from *by Jesus*.

**belabor** See **be- + labor**.

**belabour** See **be- + labor**.

**belay** OLD ENGLISH *beleagan*.

**belch** OLD ENGLISH *bealcan*.

**beleaguer** DUTCH *belegeren* camp beside, from *be-* by + *leger* camp.

**belfry** FRENCH *berfrei*, from GERMAN *bercfrit* protecting tower, from *bergen* protect + *frid* peace. Originally a moveable tower used in attacks. It was later used as a watchtower (where one could keep a watch out for fire or enemies) which had an alarm bell to ring when something dangerous was sighted.

**belie** OLD ENGLISH *beleogan* deceive by lies.

**belief** MIDDLE ENGLISH *bileafe* faith, from OLD ENGLISH *geleafa* faith.

**bell** OLD ENGLISH *belle*.

**belladonna** ITALIAN *bella donna* fair lady, from the use of its juice in cosmetics.

**belle** FRENCH feminine of *beau* fine, handsome, from LATIN *bellus* pretty.

**belligerent** LATIN *belligerare* make war.

**bellow** OLD ENGLISH *bylgian* roar like a bull.

**bellows** See **belly**.

**belly** OLD ENGLISH *belig* bag.

**belong** MIDDLE ENGLISH *belongen* concern, from OLD ENGLISH *langian* want.

**below** See be- + low.

**belt** OLD ENGLISH, from LATIN *balteus*.

**bench** OLD ENGLISH *benc* long seat.

**bend** OLD ENGLISH *bendan* stretch a bow.

**beneath** OLD ENGLISH *be-* near + *neothan* down.

**benediction** LATIN *benedictionem*, from *benedicere* praise, from *bene* well + *dicere* speak.

**benefactor** LATIN *bene* well + *facere* do, make.

**benefit** MIDDLE ENGLISH *benfet*, from FRENCH, from LATIN *benefactum*, from *ben facere* do well.

**benevolence** FRENCH goodwill, from LATIN *benevolentia*, from *bene* well + *velle* wish.

**benign** FRENCH *benigne* kind, from LATIN *benignus*, from *bene* well + *genus* birth.

**benignant** See **benign**.

**benne** African *bene* the sesame plant.

**benzene** See **benzoin**.

**benzoin** FRENCH, from ITALIAN *benzoino*, from ARABIC *lubqan jawi* incense from Java, an island in South Asia.

**bequest** MIDDLE ENGLISH *biqueste*, from OLD ENGLISH *be-* by + *cwiss* saying.

**berate** OLD ENGLISH *be-* about, near, by + MIDDLE ENGLISH *raten* scold.

**bereave** OLD ENGLISH *befeafian*, from *be-* by + *reafian* rob.

**beret** FRENCH *beret* cap worn by Basque peasants, from *berret*, from LATIN *birrus* a hooded cloak.

**bergere** FRENCH shepherdess.

**berry** OLD ENGLISH *berie*.

**berserk** See **berserker**.

**berserker** OLD NORSE *berserkr* warrior clothed in bearskin, from *ber* bear + *serkr* coat.

**berth** probably from **bear**[1].

**bertha** feminine name, from GERMAN *berahta* bright one.

**beseech** OLD ENGLISH *besecan*.

**beset** OLD ENGLISH *besettan* set near.

**beside** OLD ENGLISH *besidan*.

**best** OLD ENGLISH *betst*.

**bestial** LATIN *bestia* beast.

**bestride** OLD ENGLISH *bestridan*.

**bet** probably from **abet**.

**bete noir** FRENCH black beast.

**betel** MIDDLE ENGLISH, from MALAY *vetilla*.

**betray** MIDDLE ENGLISH, from FRENCH *trair* hand over, from LATIN *tradere*.

**betroth** MIDDLE ENGLISH *be-* about + *treuthe*, from OLD ENGLISH *treowth* truth.

**better** OLD ENGLISH *betera* improved in health.

**between** OLD ENGLISH *betweonum*, from *be-* by + *tweon(um)* in pairs.

**betwixt** OLD ENGLISH *betwix*.

**bevel** probably from FRENCH *baivel*.

**beverage** FRENCH *bevre*, from LATIN *bibere* imbibe (drink).

**bevy** possibly from FRENCH *bevee* drink, as a gathering for that purpose.

**bewilder** OLD ENGLISH *be-* about, near, by + MIDDLE ENGLISH *wilder* get lost, probably from **wilderness**.

**bewuther** OLD ENGLISH *be-* about, near, by + OLD NORSE *kvidra* go back and forth.

**beyond** OLD ENGLISH *begeondan* farther on than.

**bezel** FRENCH *bisel* sloping edge.

**bezoar** SPANISH, from ARABIC *bazahr*, from PERSIAN *padzahr*, from *pad* expelling + *zahr* poison.

**bi-** LATIN *bi-* twice, doubly, two.

**bias** FRENCH *biais* slant.

**bib** LATIN *bibere* imbibe (drink).

**bibble** See **bib** + **-le**.

**Bible** LATIN, from GREEK *biblia* collection of writings, from *biblos* papyrus.

**bibliography** GREEK *bibliographia* the writing of books, from *biblion* little book + *graphein* write.

**biceps** LATIN *bi-* two + *caput* head.

**bicker** MIDDLE ENGLISH *bikeren*.

**bicorn** LATIN *bicornis*, from *bis* twice + *cornu* horn.

**bicycle** LATIN *bi-* two + GREEK *kyklos* wheel.

**bid** OLD ENGLISH *beodan* offer.

**biddy**[1] (hen) imitative.

**biddy**[2] (fussy old woman) form of *Bridget,* a female name. Figuratively related to **biddy**[1].

**bide** OLD ENGLISH *bidan* wait.

**bier** OLD ENGLISH *bær* a bed.

**bifurcate** LATIN *bi-* two + *furca* fork.

**big** MIDDLE ENGLISH *bigg,* origin uncertain.

**bigamy** LATIN *bigamus* twice married, from *bi-* two + GREEK *gamos* marriage.

**bigot** FRENCH, supposedly used to insult the Normans.

**bijou** FRENCH, from Breton *bizou* ring, from *biz* finger.

**bijouterie** See **bijou**.

**bilberry** OLD NORSE *bollr* ball + *ber* berry.

**bile** FRENCH, from LATIN *bilis*.

**bilge** See **bulge**.

**bilious** FRENCH *bilieux*, from LATIN *biliosus*, from *bilis* bile.

**bilk** first used in the game of Cribbage, possibly from **balk**.

**bill** FRENCH *bille*, from LATIN *billa* important paper with official stamp, from *bulla* knob (rounded part that sticks out).

**billet** FRENCH *bullete,* from LATIN *bulla* knob.

**billingsgate** *Billings,* the name of a gate in London. In the 17th century a fish market was located near the gate, and the speech there was abusive and foul.

**billion** See **bi-** + **million**.

**billow** OLD NORSE *bylgia* a wave.

**billycock** See **bully** + **cock**[2].

**bin** OLD ENGLISH manger, crib.

**binary** LATIN *bini* two together.

**bind** OLD ENGLISH *bindan* tie together.

**binge** BRITISH *binge* soak.

**binnacle** SPANISH *bitácula,* from LATIN *habitaculum* place to live.

**binocular** LATIN *bini* two together + *oculus* eye.

**bio-** GREEK *bios* life.

**biography** GREEK *biographia* a writing of lives, from *bios* life + *graphein* write.

**biology** See **bio-** + **-logy**.

**biome** GREEK *bios* life + *-oma* group.

**biped** LATIN *bipes* two-footer.

**bird** MIDDLE ENGLISH *brid*, from OLD ENGLISH *bridd* young bird.

**birth** OLD NORSE *byrth*.

**biscuit** FRENCH *pain bescoit* twice-baked bread (which stays preserved longer than single-baked bread), from *bis* twice + *cuit* cooked, from LATIN *coquere*.

**bisect** LATIN *bi-* two + *secare* cut.

**bishop** OLD ENGLISH *bisceop* church bishop, from LATIN *episcopus*, from GREEK *episkopos*, from *epi* on + *skopos* watcher.

**bismuth** GERMAN *wismut*.

**bisque** See **biscuit**.

**bit**[1] (bridle part) OLD ENGLISH *bite* bite.

**bit**[2] (small piece) OLD ENGLISH *bita* small piece bitten off.

**bit**[3] (for a drill) OLD ENGLISH *bite* bite.

**bite** OLD ENGLISH *bitan* cut into with the teeth.

**bitt** nautical, origin uncertain.

**bitter** OLD ENGLISH *biter* not sweet.

**bittern** FRENCH *butor*, probably from LATIN *butio*.

**bitts** See **bit**[1].

**bivouac** FRENCH, from GERMAN *biwacht*, from *bi-* by + *wacht* guard.

**bizarre** FRENCH, from ITALIAN *bizzaro* lively.

**black** OLD ENGLISH *blæc*.

**blackamoor** See **black** + **moor**[1].

**blackmail** OLD ENGLISH *blæc* black + SCOTTISH *male* rent, from OLD ENGLISH *mal* payment, from OLD NORSE agreement. Originally payment taken by dishonest clan chieftains from Scottish and English farmers who paid to not have their crops destroyed.

**bladder** OLD ENGLISH *blædre* sac in the body.

**blade** OLD ENGLISH *blæd* broad flat part of a tool.

**blame** FRENCH *blasmer* accuse, from LATIN *blasphemare* speak badly of.

**blanch** FRENCH *blanchir* whiten, from *blanc* white.

**blancmange** FRENCH *blanc* white + *manger* eat.

**bland** LATIN *blandus* soft.

**blank** FRENCH *blanc* white.

**blanket** FRENCH *blankete* white wool cloth, from *blanc* white.

**blare** MIDDLE ENGLISH *bleren* bellow (yell loudly).

**blasé** FRENCH *blaser*.

**blaspheme** FRENCH, from LATIN, from GREEK *blasphemein* speak evil of.

**blast** OLD ENGLISH *blæst* gust of wind.

**blatant** LATIN *baltier* babble (say quickly or foolishly).

**blather** OLD NORSE *blathra* talk in a foolish way.

**blaze** OLD ENGLISH *blæse* flame.

**bleach** OLD ENGLISH *blæcan*, from *blac* pale.

**bleak** OLD NORSE *bleikr* white.

**blear** OLD ENGLISH *blere* watery.

**bleat** OLD ENGLISH *blætan*.

**bleed** OLD ENGLISH *bledan* lose blood.

**blemish** FRENCH *blesmir* injure, origin uncertain.

**blend** OLD NORSE *blanda* mix.

**bless** OLD ENGLISH *bletsian* make holy with blood.

**blight** possibly from OLD NORSE *blikja* turn pale.

**blimp** perhaps from **limp,** not having a rigid frame.

**blind** OLD ENGLISH.

**blink** MIDDLE ENGLISH *blenchen.*

**blip** imitative.

**bliss** OLD ENGLISH *blithe.*

**blister** FRENCH *blestre* a swelling, from OLD NORSE *blastr.*

**blithe** OLD ENGLISH.

**blitzkrieg** GERMAN *blitz* lightning + *krieg* war.

**blizzard** a newspaper in Iowa that was the first to use the word to describe a heavy snowstorm in the late 1800s.

**bloat** MIDDLE ENGLISH *blote* soft, from OLD NORSE *blautr* soft.

**blob** imitative.

**block** FRENCH *bloc* log, from DUTCH *blok* a mass.

**blond** FRENCH fair, origin uncertain.

**blood** OLD ENGLISH *blod.*

**bloom** OLD NORSE *blom* flower.

**bloomers** Amelia J. *Bloomer* (1818–1894) who promoted them.

**blossom** OLD ENGLISH *blostma.*

**blot** perhaps from blend of **blemish** and **spot.**

**blotch** perhaps from blend of **blot** and **botch.**

**blouse** FRENCH the shirt, origin uncertain.

**blow**[1] (hit) MIDDLE ENGLISH *blaw.*

**blow**[2] (push air out) OLD ENGLISH *blawan* send air out.

**blubber** MIDDLE ENGLISH *blober* a bubble, probably imitative.

**blucher** name of a Prussian military officer.

**bludgeon** perhaps from FRENCH *bougeon,* from *bouge* a club.

**blue** MIDDLE ENGLISH *blewe,* from FRENCH *bleu,* related to GERMAN *blāo,* blue.

**bluestocking** mid-18th century London parties featuring intellectual discussions. Instead of full dress many who came wore simpler clothing, notably Benjamin Stillingfleet who wore blue-gray tradesman's stockings.

**bluff** possibly from DUTCH *bluffen* brag.

**blunder** OLD NORSE *blunda* shut the eyes.

**blunt** perhaps from OLD NORSE *blundra.* See **blunder.**

**blur** See **blear.**

**blush** OLD ENGLISH *blyscan* make red.

**bluster** GERMAN *blusteren* blow with strength.

**boa** LATIN.

**boar** OLD ENGLISH *bar.*

**board** OLD ENGLISH *bord* table.

**boast** FRENCH *bost* brag.

**boat** OLD ENGLISH *bat* small ship.

**boatswain** OLD ENGLISH *batswegan,* from *bat* small ship + *swegan,* from OLD NORSE *sveinn* boy.

**bob** MIDDLE ENGLISH *bobben* move up and down.

**bobbin** FRENCH *bobine.*

**bobbish** See **bob.**

**bobble** See **bob.**

**bobeche** FRENCH.

**bobolink** imitative of the bird's song.

**bode** OLD ENGLISH *bodian* announce.

**bodice**  See **body.**

**bodkin**  OLD ENGLISH *boydekin.*

**body**  OLD ENGLISH *bodig* physical form of man or animal.

**bog**  IRISH *bogach,* from *bog* soft.

**boggle**  SCOTTISH *bogle* ghost.

**bog-spavin**  See **bog** + **spavin.**

**bogus**  1827 name for a machine that copied money, possibly from WELSH *bwg* ghost.

**bogy**  possibly from WELSH *bwg* ghost.

**boil**  FRENCH *boillir* make bubbles, from LATIN *bulla* bubble.

**boisterous**  FRENCH *boisteus* rough.

**bold**  OLD ENGLISH *beald* brave.

**bole**  OLD NORSE *bolr.*

**boll**  OLD ENGLISH *bolla* bowl.

**bollard**  probably from **bole.**

**Bolshevik**  RUSSIAN *bolshevik* member of the majority, from *bolshe* greater.

**bolster**  OLD ENGLISH bed.

**bolt**  OLD ENGLISH arrow.

**bomb**  FRENCH *bombe,* from LATIN *bombus* a booming, from GREEK *bombos* deep hollow sound.

**bombard**  FRENCH *bombarder,* from *bombarde* cannon, from LATIN *bombarda* weapon for throwing stones, from *bombus.*  See **bomb.**

**bombast**  FRENCH, from LATIN *bombax* cotton, from GREEK *bombyx* silk.

**bombazine**  FRENCH, from LATIN *bambax.*  See bombast.

**bona fide**  LATIN *bona fides* good faith.

**bonanza**  SPANISH fair weather, from LATIN *bonus* good.

**bond**[1] (fasten)  MIDDLE ENGLISH.  See **band**[2].

**bond**[2] (slave)  MIDDLE ENGLISH.  See **bondage.**

**bondage**  OLD ENGLISH *bonda,* from OLD NORSE *bonde,* from *bua* live in a place.

**bone**  OLD ENGLISH *ban.*

**bonfire**  MIDDLE ENGLISH *bone fire* fires built outside for burning bones.

**bong**  imitative.

**bongo**[1] (antelope)  African name.

**bongo**[2] (drum)  SPANISH.

**bonhomie**  FRENCH *bonhomie,* from *bonhomme* good-natured man, from *bon* good + *homme* man.

**bonnet**  FRENCH *bonet* material used for hats.

**bonny**  SCOTTISH, probably ultimately from FRENCH *bon,* from LATIN *bonus* good.

**bonsai**  JAPANESE *bon* basin + *sai* plant.

**bonus**  LATIN good.

**boo**  imitative.

**booby**  probably from SPANISH *bobo* stupid.

**book**  OLD ENGLISH *boc* writing tablet.

**boom**  imitative.

**boon**  OLD NORSE *bon* a petition.

**boor**  DUTCH *boer,* from *gheboer* fellow traveler.

**boost**  AMERICAN, origin uncertain.

**boot**  FRENCH *bote.*

**booth**  OLD NORSE *buth* temporary place to be, from *bua* live in a place.

**booty**  FRENCH *butin,* from GERMAN *bute* share.

**booze**  DUTCH *buizen.*

**borage**  FRENCH, from LATIN *borrago* rough hair.

**border**  FRENCH *bordeüre* an edge.

**bore**[1] (hole) OLD ENGLISH *borian* make a hole.

**bore**[2] (wave) MIDDLE ENGLISH *bare*, from OLD NORSE *bara* a billow.

**bore**[3] (tiresome) possibly figurative, from **bore**[1] (on the idea of moving forward slowly, as in boring a hole).

**boreal** LATIN *borealis*, from GREEK mythological figure *Boreas*, god of the north wind.

**boreen** IRISH *bothar* a road + diminutive *-een*.

**born** See **bear**[1].

**borough** OLD ENGLISH *burg* town.

**borrow** OLD ENGLISH *borg* pledge.

**bosh** TURKISH *bosh* empty, worthless.

**bosom** OLD ENGLISH *bosm* breast.

**boss**[1] (in charge) DUTCH *baas* person in charge, master.

**boss**[2] (knob) MIDDLE ENGLISH & FRENCH *boce* hump, swelling.

**botanical** FRENCH *botanique* botany, from GREEK *botane* plant, herb.

**botch** MIDDLE ENGLISH *bocchen* mend.

**both** OLD NORSE *nathir* the two.

**bother** probably from IRISH *pother*.

**bottle** FRENCH *boteille* container having a neck, from LATIN *butticula*, from *buttis* wooden barrel for holding liquids.

**bottom** OLD ENGLISH *botm* lowest part.

**boudoir** FRENCH lady's private room, from *bouder* sulk, from a lady going to her boudoir when she was angry.

**bough** OLD ENGLISH *bog*.

**boulder** MIDDLE ENGLISH *bulder*, from *bulderstan* noisy stone (in a stream water roars around it).

**boulevard** FRENCH defensive wall, from DUTCH *bolwerc* bulwark (defensive wall).

**bounce** MIDDLE ENGLISH *bunsen* beat.

**bound** FRENCH *bodne* boundary, from LATIN *bodina* limit.

**boundary** LATIN *bunnarium*.

**bounty** FRENCH *bonte* goodness, from LATIN *bonitas*.

**bouquet** FRENCH bunch (as of flowers), from *bosc* forest.

**bourbon** *Bourbon* County, Kentucky, where it was first made.

**bourgeois** FRENCH, from LATIN *burgus* castle.

**bourne** FRENCH *boune*. See **bound**.

**bout** OLD ENGLISH *byht*.

**boutique** FRENCH, from GREEK *apotheke* place for storing things.

**bovine** LATIN *bovis* ox.

**bow**[1] (bend) OLD ENGLISH *bugan*.

**bow**[2] (weapon) OLD ENGLISH *boga*.

**bow**[3] (of a boat) probably from GERMAN *boog*.

**bowel** FRENCH *boel* intestine, from LATIN *botellus* sausage.

**bower** OLD ENGLISH *bur* a place to live.

**bowl** OLD ENGLISH *bolla* hollow container.

**bowsprit** probably GERMAN *bochspret*, from *boch* bow of a boat + *spret* pole.

**box** OLD ENGLISH container made of wood, from the box tree, from LATIN *buxus* box tree.

**boy** MIDDLE ENGLISH *boi*.

**boycott** Captain Charles *Boycott* (1832–1897) who was harassed by Irish farmers for his bad treatment of them.

**brace** FRENCH the two arms, from LATIN *bracchium* arm, from GREEK *brachion*.

**bracelet** FRENCH little arm, from LATIN *bracchium*. See **brace**.

**brachet** MIDDLE ENGLISH *braches*, from GERMAN *bracco*.

**brachiocephalic** LATIN *brachiocephalicus*, from GREEK *brachion* arm + *kephale* head.

**bracken** MIDDLE ENGLISH *bracken*, related to SWEDISH *broekne* fern.

**bracket** FRENCH *brague* the front flap of knee pants, from LATIN *braca*.

**brackish** DUTCH *brak* salt.

**bract** LATIN *bractea* thin metal plate.

**brad** OLD NORSE *broddr* a spike.

**brae** OLD NORSE *bra*.

**brag** MIDDLE ENGLISH *braggen*, origin unknown.

**braggadocio** brag (by adding an Italian ending). Invented by 16th century English writer Edmund Spenser.

**braid** OLD ENGLISH *bregdan* weave.

**brail** FRENCH *bracale* belt.

**Braille** Louis *Braille* (1809–1852) French teacher who invented it.

**brain** OLD ENGLISH *brægen* main part of the nervous system.

**brake**[1] (fern) MIDDLE ENGLISH. See **bracken**.

**brake**[2] (slow down) MIDDLE ENGLISH, from GERMAN, from *breken* break.

**brake**[3] (brushwood) GERMAN *brake* stumps.

**bramble** OLD ENGLISH *bræmel*, from *brom* broom.

**bran** FRENCH *bren*.

**branch** FRENCH *branche* bough, from LATIN *branca* paw, claw.

**brand** OLD ENGLISH *biernan* burn.

**brandish** FRENCH *brand* sword.

**brandy** DUTCH *brandewign*, from *branden* burn + *wign* wine, from LATIN *vinum*.

**brant** See **brand**.

**brass** OLD ENGLISH *bræs* melting together of copper and tin.

**brassiere** FRENCH, originally arm guard, from *bras* arm.

**bravado** SPANISH *bravada*, from *bravo* brave.

**brave** FRENCH, from ITALIAN *bravo* bold, wild, possibly from LATIN *rabidus* fierce.

**brawl** DUTCH *brallen* boast.

**brawn** FRENCH *braon* fleshy part.

**braxy** SCOTTISH, origin uncertain.

**bray** MIDDLE ENGLISH *braien*, from FRENCH *braire*, from LATIN *bragire* cry out.

**brazen** OLD ENGLISH *bræsen*, from *bræs* brass.

**brazier** FRENCH *braise* hot coals.

**breach** OLD ENGLISH *bryce* breaking.

**bread** OLD ENGLISH *bread* crumb.

**breadth** MIDDLE ENGLISH *bræde*, from OLD ENGLISH *brædu*, from *brad* broad.

**break** OLD ENGLISH *brecan* shatter.

**breakfast** See **break** + **fast**[2].

**breast** OLD ENGLISH *breost*.

**breath** OLD ENGLISH *bræth* air breathed out.

**breeches** OLD ENGLISH *brec* covering for the buttocks.

**breed** OLD ENGLISH *bredan* feed.

**breeze** SPANISH *briza* cold northeast wind.

**brethren** See **brother**.

**breviary** LATIN *brevairum*, from *brevis* brief.

**brevity** LATIN *brevis* brief.

**brew** OLD ENGLISH *breowan* make beer.

**bribe** FRENCH bit of bread given to a beggar, from *briber* beg.

**bric-à-brac** FRENCH *à bric et à brac* at random, any old way.

**brick** DUTCH *bricke*.

**bride** OLD ENGLISH *bryd*.

**bridegroom** OLD ENGLISH *brydguma* bride man.

**bridge** OLD ENGLISH *brycg* something built over a river or other waterway.

**bridle** OLD ENGLISH *bridel*.

**brief** FRENCH *bref*, from LATIN *brevis*.

**brier** OLD ENGLISH *brer*.

**brig** See **brigade**.

**brigade** FRENCH troop, from ITALIAN *brigare* fight.

**brigalow** AUSTRALIAN ABORIGINAL *buriagalah*.

**brigand** See **brigade**.

**brigantine** FRENCH *brigantin*, from ITALIAN *brigantino* pirate ship, from *brigante* robber. See **brigade**.

**bright** OLD ENGLISH *beorht* shining.

**brilliant** FRENCH *briller* shine, from LATIN *beryllus* beryl (a mineral).

**brim** MIDDLE ENGLISH *brimme* rim.

**brimstone** MIDDLE ENGLISH *brinston*, from *brinn* burn + *ston* stone.

**brindled** probably from MIDDLE ENGLISH *brended*, from *brinn* burn.

**brine** OLD ENGLISH *bryne* salt water.

**bring** OLD ENGLISH *bringan* cause to come.

**brink** MIDDLE ENGLISH *brink*, from GERMAN shore.

**briolette** FRENCH sparkle.

**briquette** FRENCH. See **brick**.

**brisk** FRENCH *brusque*.

**bristle** OLD ENGLISH *byrst* hog's hair.

**brittle** MIDDLE ENGLISH *britel* easily broken.

**broach** FRENCH *broche* stick used in roasting, from LATIN *brocca* pointed stick, from *broccus*.

**broad** OLD ENGLISH *brad* wide.

**brocade** ITALIAN *broccato* the material, from LATIN *broccus* sticking out like teeth.

**broccoli** ITALIAN *brocco* plant stalk.

**brochure** FRENCH a stitched work, from *brocher* stitch, from *broche* pointed tool, from LATIN *broccus* pointed teeth.

**brogue**[1] (dialect) probably from IRISH *barrog* hold (on the tongue).

**brogue**[2] (shoe) IRISH *brog* shoe.

**broil**[1] (cook) FRENCH *broiller* roast.

**broil**[2] (quarrel) FRENCH *brouiller* confuse.

**broker** FRENCH *brocour* seller of wine.

**bronchitis** GREEK *bronchos* windpipe.

**bronco** SPANISH rough.

**bronze** FRENCH, from ITALIAN *bronzo*.

**brooch** See **broach**.

**brood** OLD ENGLISH *brod* the young of an animal.

**brook** OLD ENGLISH *broc*.

**broom** OLD ENGLISH *brom*.

**brothel** MIDDLE ENGLISH miserable person, from OLD ENGLISH *breothan* go to ruin.

**brother** OLD ENGLISH *brothor*.

**brougham** BRITISH aristocrat Lord *Brougham* (1778–1868).

**brow** OLD ENGLISH *bru.*

**browse** FRENCH *broust* bud.

**bruise** OLD ENGLISH *brysan* crush.

**brumal** LATIN *brevima* shortest winter day.

**brunch** combination of **breakfast** + **lunch.**

**brunet(te)** FRENCH *brun,* from GERMAN brown.

**brunt** MIDDLE ENGLISH *bront* a hit or blow, of SCANDINAVIAN origin.

**brush** FRENCH *broce* bush, from LATIN *bruscia.*

**brusque** FRENCH harsh, from ITALIAN *brusco* sour, from LATIN *brucas* heather (a flower).

**brute** FRENCH *brut* rude, from LATIN *brutus* heavy, stupid.

**bryony** LATIN *bryonia,* from GREEK *bryein* swell.

**bubbe** probably from GERMAN *bube* boy or lad.

**bubble** DUTCH *bobble.*

**buccal** LATIN *bucca* cheek.

**buccaneer** FRENCH *boucanier* pirate, hunter, from *boucan,* a rack for cooking meat, from NATIVE AMERICAN *mukem* rack.

**buck** OLD ENGLISH *bucca* male goat.

**buckboard** See **buck** + **board,** probably from the bouncy ride.

**bucket** FRENCH *buket* pail, from OLD ENGLISH *buc* pitcher.

**buckle** FRENCH *boucle* metal ring, from LATIN *buccula* cheek strap of a helmet, from *bucca* cheek.

**buckram** FRENCH *boucassin* course, sticky linen, from *boquerant* a costly and delicate fabric, from LATIN *bucaranus.*

**buckwheat** DUTCH *boecweite* from *boec* beech (tree) + *weit* wheat, as the grains of buckwheat resemble beech tree nuts.

**bucolic** LATIN, from GREEK *boukolos* herdsman, from *bous* ox.

**bud** MIDDLE ENGLISH *budde.*

**Buddha** HINDI enlightened, from *budh* awake, know, related to SANSKRIT *bodhati* is awake, understands.

**buddy** possibly from BRITISH *butty* friend.

**budge** FRENCH *bouger* stir, from LATIN *bullire* boil.

**budget** FRENCH *bougette* little bag, from LATIN *bulga.* Originally meant a pouch or wallet.

**buff** MIDDLE ENGLISH *buffe leather,* from FRENCH *buffle* buffalo.

**buffalo** PORTUGUESE *bufalo* water buffalo, from LATIN *bufalus,* from *bubalus* wild ox, from GREEK *boubalos* buffalo.

**buffer** FRENCH *buffe* a blow.

**buffet** FRENCH bench.

**buffoon** ITALIAN *buffare* joke, puff (from medieval clowns making noise by puffing their cheeks and blowing out).

**bug** possibly from MIDDLE ENGLISH *bugge* something frightening, scarecrow.

**bugle** FRENCH *bugle* wild buffalo (the bugle horn is a musical instrument that had been made from the horn of an ox or buffalo), from LATIN *buculus* steer.

**build** OLD ENGLISH *bold* dwelling or house.

**bulb** LATIN *bulbus* root, onion, from GREEK *bolbos.*

**bulbul** ARABIC.

**bulge** FRENCH *boulge* leather bag, swelling, from *bougette* little bag, from LATIN *bulga.*

**bulk** OLD NORSE *bulki* heap.

**bull** OLD ENGLISH *bula* male of the cattle family.

**bullet** FRENCH *boule* ball, from LATIN *bulla* bubble or knob.

**bulletin** FRENCH *bulletin* ticket, from LATIN *bulla.*

**bullion** DUTCH, from FRENCH *billon* small coin, from *bille* stick.

**bullock** OLD ENGLISH *bullue,* from *bula* a steer.

**bully** DUTCH *boel* friend, later changed by the influence of the word *bull.* See **bull**.

**bullyrag** See **bully** + **rag**².

**bulrush** probably from OLD ENGLISH *bulla* + *rise* a small, grasslike plant.

**bulwark** DUTCH *bolwerc* bulwark (defensive wall), from *bole* flat piece of wood + *were* work.

**bum** GERMAN *bummler* tramp.

**bumbershoot** Slang combination of **umbrella** and **parachute**.

**bump** imitative.

**bumpkin** DUTCH *bommekijn* small cask (barrel for holding liquid).

**bumptious** possibly from **bump**.

**bun** probably from FRENCH *buigne* a swelling.

**bundle** MIDDLE ENGLISH *bundel* sheaf.

**bungalow** HINDI *bangla* low thatched house, from the *Bengal* region of India.

**bungle** imitative.

**bunker** SCOTTISH *bonkar* box.

**bunt** FRENCH *buter* strike.

**bunting** possibly from MIDDLE ENGLISH *bonting* cloth for sifting flour.

**buoy** FRENCH *boise* anchored floating marker.

**bur** MIDDLE ENGLISH *burre,* from SCANDINAVIAN.

**burble** imitative.

**burden** OLD ENGLISH *byrthen* load.

**bureau** FRENCH desk, from LATIN *burra* cloth.

**bureaucracy** FRENCH *bureaucratie,* from *bureau* desk, office + GREEK *-kratia* power, rule.

**burg** See **borough**.

**burgeon** FRENCH *burjon* bud.

**burgher** MIDDLE ENGLISH *burgh.* See **borough**.

**burglar** FRENCH *burgler* thief, from LATIN *burglator,* from *burgus.*

**burial** OLD ENGLISH *byrgels* tomb.

**burlap** probably from MIDDLE ENGLISH *borel* coarse cloth, from FRENCH *burel.*

**burlesque** FRENCH, from ITALIAN *burlesco* comical, from *burla* joke.

**burly** OLD ENGLISH *borlice* excellent.

**burn** OLD ENGLISH *bærnan.*

**burnish** FRENCH *burnir* polish, from *brun* brown.

**burr**¹ (prickle) See **bur**.

**burr**² (sound) imitative.

**burro** SPANISH, from LATIN *burricus* small horse.

**burrow** OLD ENGLISH *burg* town.

**burst** OLD ENGLISH *berstan* break.

**bury** OLD ENGLISH *byrgan.*

**bus** short for *omnibus,* from FRENCH, from LATIN bus for all.

**bush** MIDDLE ENGLISH.

**bushel** FRENCH *boissel* the measurement, from *boisse* one sixth of a bushel.

**business** OLD ENGLISH *bisignes.* See **busy**.

**buskin** probably from DUTCH *brosekin* small leather boot.

**bust**[1] (sculpture) FRENCH *buste,* from LATIN *bustum* tomb, which was often decorated with a bust of the dead.

**bust**[2] (break) See **burst**.

**bustard** LATIN *avis tarda* slow bird.

**buster** SPANISH *busté,* dialect form of *usted* you.

**bustle** OLD NORSE *buask* get ready.

**busy** OLD ENGLISH *bisig* be active.

**but** OLD ENGLISH *butan.*

**butane** butyl, from LATIN *butyrum* butter + *-ane* chemical suffix.

**butcher** FRENCH *bochier* seller of goat meat, from *boc* male goat.

**butt**[1] (end) possibly from FRENCH *bout* end, from OLD NORSE *butr* block of wood.

**butt**[2] (hit against) MIDDLE ENGLISH *buter,* from FRENCH *boter* push, shove.

**butte** FRENCH rising ground, from *but* goal.

**butter** OLD ENGLISH, from LATIN *butyrum,* from GREEK *boutyron,* from *bous* ox, cow + *tyros* cheese.

**buttock** OLD ENGLISH *buttuc* rump.

**button** FRENCH *boton* knob sewn to clothing, from *boter* bud.

**buttress** FRENCH *bouterez* supports.

**buy** OLD ENGLISH *byegan* purchase.

**buzz** imitative.

**by** OLD ENGLISH *be, bi.*

**bylaw** MIDDLE ENGLISH *bilage,* from OLD NORSE *bi-lagu* town law, from *bua* dwell + *lagu* law.

**byre** OLD ENGLISH *bur* hut.

# C

**cab** FRENCH *cabriolet* one-horse carriage, from ITALIAN *capriola* leap like a goat, from LATIN *caper* goat, because the carriage bounced like a goat leaping.

**cabal** FRENCH *cabale* plot, from LATIN *cabbala*, from HEBREW *qabbalah* lore, tradition, from *qibbel* receive.

**cabana** SPANISH *cabaña*, from LATIN *capanna* hut.

**cabane** earlier form of **cabin**.

**cabaret** FRENCH tavern, from LATIN *camera*. See **chamber**.

**cabbage** FRENCH *cabouche*, possibly from LATIN *caput* head.

**cabin** FRENCH *cabane* hut, from LATIN *capanna*.

**cabinet** FRENCH small room, from *cabine* gambling house.

**cable** FRENCH, from LATIN *capulum*, from *capere* take hold.

**cabochon** FRENCH *caboche* the head, from LATIN *caput* head.

**caboose** DUTCH *kabuys* ship's kitchen.

**cabriole** FRENCH *cabriole* a leap.

**cabriolet** See **cab**.

**cache** FRENCH *cacher* hiding place, from LATIN *coactare* force.

**cachet** FRENCH *cacher*. See **cache**.

**cackle** imitative.

**cacophony** LATIN, from GREEK *kakos* bad + *phone* voice.

**cactus** LATIN, from GREEK *kaktos* plant with prickly leaves.

**cad** probably from short for **cadet**.

**cadaver** LATIN probably from *cadere* fall.

**caddie** SCOTTISH for **cadet**.

**caddy** MALAY *catty*, a unit of weight (equal to a little more than a pound.)

**cadence** FRENCH, from LATIN *cadentia* falling (of dice), from LATIN *cadere* fall.

**cadet** FRENCH chief, from LATIN *caput* head.

**cadge** MIDDLE ENGLISH variation of **catch**.

**cadre** FRENCH, from ITALIAN *quadro* square, from LATIN *quadrus*.

**Caesar** LATIN *caedere* cut.

**café** FRENCH coffeehouse, from ITALIAN *caffé*. See **coffee**.

**cafeteria** SPANISH coffeehouse.

**caffeine** GERMAN, from ITALIAN *caffé*. See **coffee**.

**cag**[1] (keg)  OLD NORSE *kaggi* keg, cask.

**cag**[2] (stump)  OLD ENGLISH.

**cag**[3] (argument)  nautical slang.

**cage**  FRENCH, from LATIN *cavea.*

**cagged** (insulted)  See **cag**[3].

**cahoots**  FRENCH *cahute* hut.

**cairn**  early SCOTTISH *carn* heap of stones.

**caisson**  FRENCH ammunition wagon, from *caisse* chest, from LATIN *capsa* box.

**caitiff**  FRENCH *caitif* a captive, from LATIN *captivus.*

**cajole**  FRENCH *cajoler* chatter like a bird in a cage, from FRENCH *gaiole* cage, from LATIN *cavea.*

**cake**  OLD NORSE *kaka* small amount of baked dough.

**calabash**  SPANISH *calabaza,* possibly from ARABIC *aqr'ah yabisah* dry gourd (dried, hollowed out shell of some fruits, used for drinking from).

**calabozo**  SPANISH underground prison.

**calamity**  LATIN *calamitas* bad fortune.

**calandria**  SPANISH lark (bird).

**calcify**  LATIN *calx* lime + FRENCH *-fier,* from LATIN *ficare,* from *facere* do, make.

**calcine**  FRENCH, from LATIN *calcinare* heat.

**calcium**  LATIN *calx* lime, because it is found in lime.

**calculate**  LATIN *calculare* compute, from *calculus* small stone, as counting was done in ancient times with stones used as counters.

**calculus**  LATIN.  See **calculate**.

**caldron**  FRENCH, from LATIN *caldaria* warm bath, from *calidus* warm.

**calendar**  LATIN *kalendorium,* from *calendarium* account book, from *calendae* calends, the first day of the month in the ancient Roman calendar, when accounts were due for payment in ancient Rome.

**calender**  FRENCH *calendre,* from LATIN *calendar,* from *cylindrus.* See **cylinder**.

**calf**  OLD ENGLISH *cealf* and OLD NORSE *kalfr.*

**caliber**  GREEK *calibre* bore (inside tube) of a gun, from ARABIC *qalib* mold, from GREEK *kalopous* a form used by shoemakers to make shoes.

**calico**  *Calicut,* city in India where the cloth first came from.

**caliper**  See **caliber**.

**caliph**  FRENCH *calife,* from ARABIC *khalifa* successor.

**caliphate**  See **caliph** + **-ate**.

**calisthenics**  GREEK *kallos* beauty + *sthenos* strength.

**call**  OLD ENGLISH *ceallian* shout, from OLD NORSE *kalla.*

**calligraphy**  GREEK *kalligraphia* beautiful writing, from *kallos* beauty + *graphein* write.

**calliope**  LATIN, from GREEK *kallos* beauty + *ops* voice.

**callous**  LATIN *callosus* hard skinned.

**callow**  OLD ENGLISH *calu* bald.

**calm**  FRENCH *calme* quiet, from ITALIAN *calma* rest, from GREEK *kauma* heat of the sun when everyone rests.

**calomel**  FRENCH, from GREEK *kalos* beautiful + *melas* black.

**calorie**  FRENCH, from LATIN *calor* heat.

**calumny**  FRENCH *calomnie,* from LATIN *calumnia* accuse falsely.

**Calvary**  LATIN *calvaria* skull.

**calyx**  LATIN, from GREEK *kalyx.*

**cambium**  LATIN *cambiare* exchange.

**camboose**  variation of **caboose.**

**cambric**  *Cambrai* in France where the material was first made.

**camel**  FRENCH, from LATIN *cameilus,* from GREEK *kamelos,* from HEBREW *gamal.*

**camellia**  G. J. *Kamel* (1661–1706) Jesuit missionary to the Far East.

**cameo**  ITALIAN *cammeo,* from LATIN *camaeus.*

**camera**  shortened form of *camera obscura* (a darkened room with a small opening, an early means of replicating an image from the environment), literally dark chamber, from LATIN *camera* vault, room.

**camisole**  from FRENCH woman's jacket, from LATIN *camisa* shirt.

**camouflage**  FRENCH disguise.

**camp**  FRENCH field of battle, from ITALIAN *campo* field, from LATIN *campus.*

**campaign**  FRENCH *campagne* open country, military campaign, from LATIN *campania* open country, from *campus* field.  Early armies didn't like fighting in the cold of winter so they waited for warmer weather and open country.

**camphor**  FRENCH *camphre,* from LATIN *camfora,* from ARABIC *kafur,* from MALAY *kapur* camphor tree.

**campus**  LATIN field.

**can**[1] (able)  OLD ENGLISH *cunnan* know.

**can**[2] (container)  OLD ENGLISH *canne* a cup.

**canal**  LATIN *canalis* pipe, channel, from *canna* reed.

**canapé**  FRENCH for covered sofa, from the idea of covering toast or bread with something, from LATIN *canapeum* mosquito net, from GREEK *konops* mosquito.

**canard**  FRENCH hoax, from *vendre des canards a moitié* sell ducks by halves (a joke), deceive, from *caner* cackle (make a sound like a hen).

**canary**  *Canary* Islands, where the birds are native.

**can-can**  FRENCH *cancan,* from *canard* duck, because the dance looks somewhat like the walk of a duck.

**cancel**  MIDDLE ENGLISH *cancellen,* from FRENCH *cancellare* mark out by using a pattern of crossed strips, from LATIN erase, from *carcer* prison, because of the pattern of the bars.

**cancer**  LATIN, from GREEK *karkinos* crab, because the swollen blood vessels around some tumors look like the legs of a crab.

**candelabrum**  LATIN candlestick, from *candela* candle.

**candescent**  LATIN *candescere,* from *candere* glow.

**candid**  LATIN *candidus* white, shining.

**candidate**  LATIN *candidatus* person dressed in white, from *candidus* white.  In ancient Rome people seeking political office wore white togas, which stood for integrity.

**candle**  OLD ENGLISH *candel,* from LATIN *candela.*

**candor**  LATIN brightness, purity.

**candy**  FRENCH *sucre candi,* sugar that has been crystallized, from ARABIC *sukkar* sugar + *qandi* candied (coated with crystallized sugar).

**cane**  FRENCH *can(n)e* reed, from LATIN *canna,* from GREEK *kanna.*

**canikin**  diminutive of **can**[2].

**canine**  LATIN *canis* dog.

**canister**  LATIN *capistrum* basket made of reeds, from GREEK *kanna* reed.

**canker**  FRENCH *cancre,* from LATIN *cancer.*  See **cancer.**

**cannibal** SPANISH *canibal* a savage, from *galibi* strong men.

**cannikin** See **canikin.**

**cannon** FRENCH *canon* gun barrel, from LATIN *canna* reed. See **cane.**

**cannula** LATIN small reed or pipe.

**canny** OLD ENGLISH *cunnan* know.

**canoe** SPANISH *canoa,* from NATIVE AMERICAN *canaoua.*

**canon** OLD ENGLISH, from LATIN *canon,* from GREEK *kanon* rule.

**canopic** LATIN *Canopus* a town in ancient Egypt.

**canopy** LATIN *canapeum* mosquito net, from GREEK *konops* mosquito.

**cant**[1] (talk) LATIN *cantus* song, chant.

**cant**[2] (slant) MIDDLE ENGLISH *cant* corner, from LATIN *canthus* tire of a wheel.

**cantabile** ITALIAN, from LATIN *cantare* sing.

**cantaloupe** FRENCH, from ITALIAN *Cantalugo* town near Rome where the fruit was first grown in Europe.

**cantankerous** probably from MIDDLE ENGLISH *contek* argument.

**canteen** FRENCH *cantine,* from ITALIAN *cantina* cellar, from LATIN *cantus* corner.

**canter** short for Canterbury, a city in England that was a religious center in the 1300s. People rode their horses in the "Canterbury gallop" to get there.

**cantilever** See **cant**[2] + **lever.**

**cantilly** See **cant**[1].

**cantle** MIDDLE ENGLISH *cantel* corner, from FRENCH, from LATIN *cantellus,* from *canthus* tire of a wheel.

**canton** FRENCH, from ITALIAN, from LATIN *cantus* corner.

**cantor** LATIN singer.

**cantrev** WELSH *cant* hundred + *tref* town.

**cantrip** SCOTTISH.

**canula** See **cannula.**

**canvas** FRENCH *canevas* made of hemp (a plant that has a strong stem), from LATIN *cannabis* hemp, from GREEK *kannabis.*

**canvass** See **canvas.**

**canyon** SPANISH *cañón,* from LATIN *canna,* from GREEK *kanna* reed.

**cap** OLD ENGLISH *cæppe* hood, from LATIN *cappa* hood.

**capable** LATIN *capabilis* able, from *capere* take.

**capacious** LATIN *capere* take.

**capacity** LATIN *capacitas,* from *capere* take.

**caparison** FRENCH *caparasso* large hooded cloak, from LATIN *capa* hood.

**cape**[1] (garment) FRENCH, from Spanish *capa,* from LATIN *cappa* mantle, cloak.

**cape**[2] (land) LATIN *caput* headland, from *caput* head.

**caper** FRENCH *capriole* leap, from ITALIAN *capriola* leap (like a goat), from LATIN *caper* goat.

**capillary** LATIN *capillus* hair.

**capital**[1] (head) MIDDLE ENGLISH, from LATIN *capitalis* of the head, from *caput* head.

**capital**[2] (money) LATIN *capitale* stock, property, from *capitalis.* See **capital**[1].

**capitol** FRENCH *capitolie,* from LATIN *Capitolium* the religous house (temple) for the god Jupiter in ancient Rome.

**capitulate** LATIN *capitulatus* arrange under separate headings, from *caput* head.

**capo** short for ITALIAN *capotasto* chief key.

**capon** OLD ENGLISH, from LATIN *capo*.

**capote** FRENCH diminutive of **cape**[1].

**caprice** FRENCH, from ITALIAN *capriccio* whim (a sudden wish to do something without a reason).

**Capricorn** FRENCH *capricorne*, from LATIN *caper* goat + *cornu* horn.

**capriole** FRENCH leap, from ITALIAN *capriola* leap (like a goat), from LATIN *caper* goat.

**capsize** perhaps from SPANISH *capuzar* sink by the head, from *cabo* head.

**capstan** FRENCH *cabestan* something used for winding rope, from LATIN *capistrum*.

**capsule** FRENCH small container, from LATIN *capsa* box.

**captain** FRENCH *capitaine* commander of troops, from LATIN *capitaneus* chief, from *caput* head.

**caption** FRENCH, from LATIN *capere* take.

**captivate** LATIN *captivus* prisoner.

**captive** LATIN *captivus* prisoner.

**capture** FRENCH, from LATIN *capere* take.

**car** MIDDLE ENGLISH *carre* cart, from LATIN *carra*, a type of wheeled cart.

**carabineer** FRENCH *carabinier*.

**caracol** FRENCH *caracol*, *caracole*, from ITALIAN *caracollo* wheeling of a horse, from SPANISH *caracol* snail, spiral shell.

**carafe** FRENCH, from ITALIAN *caraffa*, from ARABIC *gharraf* drinking cup.

**carambola** PORTUGUESE, from HINDI *karanbal* a fruit tree.

**caramel** FRENCH *calamele*, from LATIN *calamella* sugar cane, from *canna* cane + *mellis* honey.

**carat** FRENCH, from GREEK *keration* the small seed of the carob tree, used as a weight in ancient times because the seeds are usually the same size and weight.

**caravan** FRENCH *caravoane*, from PERSIAN *karwan* company of travelers.

**carbine** FRENCH *carabin* mounted rifleman, possibly from LATIN *chadabula* engine for throwing stones, from GREEK *katabolh* destruction.

**carbohydrate** See **carbon** + **hydrate**.

**carbon** FRENCH, from LATIN *carbo* coal.

**carbuncle** MIDDLE ENGLISH, from FRENCH, from LATIN *carbunculus* a little coal.

**carcanet** FRENCH *carcan* iron collar on pillories, from LATIN *carcannum*.

**carcass** FRENCH *carcasse*.

**carcinoma** LATIN, from GREEK *karkinoma* cancer, from *karkinos* crab.

**card** FRENCH *carte* piece of stiff paper, from LATIN *charta* leaf of papyrus, from GREEK *chartes*.

**cardiac** FRENCH *cardiaque*, from LATIN *cardiacus* relating to the heart, from GREEK *kardia* heart.

**cardigan** the Earl of *Cardigan* (1797–1868), English general.

**cardinal** LATIN *cardinalis* chief, from *cardo* hinge (place where two things are joined), from the idea that when something is important other things hinge, or depend on it.

**cardio-** GREEK *kardia* heart.

**care** OLD ENGLISH *caru* trouble.

**careen** FRENCH *carener*, from ITALIAN *carenare*, from LATIN *carina* keel (steel or wood piece along the bottom of a boat).

**career** FRENCH *carrière* racecourse, from LATIN *carriara* street, from *carrus* wagon.

**caress** FRENCH *carasse,* from ITALIAN *carezza,* from LATIN *carus* dear.

**caret** LATIN something lacking.

**cargo** SPANISH load, from LATIN *carricare,* from *carrus* a wheeled cart.

**caricature** FRENCH picture that makes fun, from ITALIAN *caricare* load, from LATIN *carrus* wheeled cart. The picture was of a very overloaded wagon, and therefore making fun.

**caries** LATIN decay, from GREEK *ker* death.

**carillon** FRENCH chime, from LATIN *quaternio* group of four, from *quarter* four times, a group of four bells.

**carnage** FRENCH, from LATIN *caro* flesh.

**carnation** ITALIAN *carrigione* the color of one's skin.

**carnelian** LATIN *carneolus,* from *carnem* flesh, because of the flesh color.

**carnival** ITALIAN *carnevale* church holy day, from LATIN *carnelevarium* time during the religious year (Lent) when no meat is eaten, from *caro* meat + *levare* take away.

**carnivorous** LATIN *carnivorus,* from *caro* flesh + *vorare* devour, eat.

**carol** FRENCH *carole* dance, from GREEK *choraules* flute player playing with the chorus.

**carotene** LATIN *carota* carrot + *-enus,* from GREEK *-enos.*

**carouse** FRENCH *carous* all out, from GERMAN *garaus* drink.

**carp**[1] (fish) FRENCH *carpe,* from GERMAN *carpa.*

**carp**[2] (nag) OLD NORSE *karpa* brag.

**carpal** LATIN *carpalis,* from *carpus* wrist.

**carpenter** FRENCH *carpentier* worker in wood, from LATIN *carpentum* carriage.

**carpet** FRENCH *carpite,* from LATIN *carpita* woolen cloth, from *carpere* card (use a metal comb on cloth).

**carrack** MIDDLE ENGLISH, from FRENCH *carague,* from SPANISH *carraca,* from ARABIC *qurqur* merchant ship.

**carragheen** *Carragheen* near Waterford, Ireland.

**carriage** FRENCH *carier.* See **carry.**

**carrion** FRENCH, from LATIN *caro* flesh.

**carronade** *Carron,* Scotland, where it was first made.

**carrot** FRENCH *carotte,* from LATIN *carota,* from GREEK *karoton.*

**carry** FRENCH *carier* take in a vehicle, from LATIN *carricare* load, from *carrus* two-wheeled wagon.

**cart** OLD ENGLISH *cræt* chariot and OLD NORSE *kartr* a two-wheeled vehicle.

**cartage** See **cart** + **-age.**

**cartel** FRENCH, from ITALIAN *cartello* written challenge, from LATIN *c(h)arta* paper. See **card.**

**carter** See **cart** + **-er.**

**cartilage** FRENCH, from LATIN *cartilago.*

**carton** FRENCH board, from ITALIAN *cartone,* from *carta* paper, from LATIN *charta.*

**cartoon** FRENCH *carton,* from ITALIAN *cartone* sketch.

**cartridge** FRENCH *cartouche,* from ITALIAN *carta.* See **card.**

**carve** OLD ENGLISH *ceorfan* cut.

**carven** See **carve.**

**cascade** FRENCH waterfall, from LATIN *casus* a falling.

**case**[1] (event) FRENCH *cas* event, from LATIN *casus* chance, from *cadere* fall.

**case**[2] (box) LATIN *capsa* box, from *capere* take.

**cash** FRENCH *casse* money, from LATIN *capsa* box.

**cashew** FRENCH *acajou*, from NATIVE AMERICAN *acajoba*.

**casino** ITALIAN *case* house, from LATIN *casino* hut.

**cask** LATIN *quassare* shake hard.

**casserole** FRENCH *casse* bowl, from GREEK *kyathos*.

**cassette** FRENCH *casse* case. See **case**[2].

**cassia** MIDDLE ENGLISH, from LATIN, from GREEK *kasia* kind of cinnamon, from HEBREW *qesi'ah*.

**cassock** FRENCH *kazhaghand* jacket, from *kazh* silk.

**cast** OLD NORSE *kasta* throw.

**caste** FRENCH *casta* breed, from LATIN *castus* pure.

**caster** See **cast** + -**er**.

**castigate** LATIN *castigare* make clean, from *castus* pure.

**castle** FRENCH *castel*, from LATIN *castellum* fortress.

**castor**[1] (oil) FRENCH, from LATIN, from GREEK *kastor* beaver.

**castor**[2] (caster) See **cast**.

**castrate** LATIN *castrare* cut.

**casual** LATIN *casualis* chance, from *casus*.

**casualty** LATIN *casualitas*. See **casual**.

**cat** OLD ENGLISH.

**cataclysm** LATIN, from GREEK *kata*- down + *klyzein* wash.

**catacomb** LATIN *catacumba*, from *cata*, from GREEK *kata* by + *tumba* tomb.

**catalog** FRENCH *catalogue* list, from LATIN *catalogus*, from GREEK *katalogos* register.

**catalyst** GREEK *katalysis* breaking up into parts, from *kata*- down + *lyein* loose.

**catamaran** TAMIL *kattumaram*, wood tied together.

**catamount** MIDDLE ENGLISH *cat of the mountain*.

**catapult** LATIN, from GREEK *katapeltes*, from *kata*- down + *pallein* throw with force.

**cataract** LATIN *cataracta*, from GREEK *kataraktes*, from *kata*- down + *rhegnynai* break.

**catastrophe** GREEK *katastrophe* overturn, from *kata*- down + *strephein* turn.

**catch** FRENCH *cachier* hunt, from LATIN *captare* chase.

**catechism** LATIN *catechizare*, from GREEK *katechizein* teach, from *kata*- completely + *ecein* sound.

**category** LATIN class in logic, from GREEK *kategoria*.

**cater** FRENCH *acatour* buyer.

**caterpillar** OLD NORSE *catepilose*, from LATIN *catta pilosa* hairy cat.

**caterwaul** MIDDLE ENGLISH *caterwawen*, probably from DUTCH *kater* tomcat + *w(r)awlen* howl like a cat.

**cathedral** LATIN *ecclesia cathedralis* church having a bishop's (high official in the Catholic Church) seat, from *cathedra* chair.

**catholic** LATIN *catholicus* universal, from GREEK *katholikos*.

**catling** See **cat** + -**ling**.

**cattle** FRENCH *catel*, from LATIN *captale* property, from *caput* head.

**caucus** possibly from an 18th century political club called the *Caucus* club, from LATIN *caucus* drinking cup, from GREEK *kaukos.*

**caudal** LATIN *cauda* tail + FRENCH, from LATIN *alis.*

**cauldron** FRENCH *caudron,* from LATIN *caldaria,* from *cal(i)dus* hot.

**cauliflower** ITALIAN *cavolfiore,* from LATIN *caulis* cabbage.

**caulk** MIDDLE ENGLISH *cauken* walk, from FRENCH *cauguer,* from LATIN *calcare,* from *calx* a heel.

**cause** FRENCH reason, from LATIN *causa.*

**causeway** BRITISH *causey,* from LATIN *calx* limestone + OLD ENGLISH *weg* path.

**caustic** LATIN *causticus* eat or wear away, from GREEK *kastikos.*

**caution** LATIN *cautio* careful.

**cavalcade** FRENCH riding on a horse, from ITALIAN *cavalcata,* from LATIN *caballus* regular horse (not of particular quality or breeding).

**cavalier** FRENCH knight who rides a horse, from LATIN *caballarius* horseman, from *caballus* regular horse (not of particular quality or breeding).

**cavalry** FRENCH *cavalerie,* from ITALIAN *cavalieria.* See **cavalier.**

**cave** FRENCH den, from LATIN *cavare* make hollow.

**caveat** LATIN let him beware.

**cavil** FRENCH *caviller* make fun of, from LATIN *cavillari.*

**cavort** AMERICAN, originally *cauvaut,* probably from *ca-* + *vault* jump, leap.

**cay** SPANISH *cayo* barrier reef, from FRENCH *cay* sand bank, from LATIN *caium.*

**cease** FRENCH *cessar* stop, from LATIN *cessare.*

**cedar** FRENCH *cedre,* from LATIN *cedrus,* from GREEK *kedros.*

**cede** FRENCH, from LATIN *cedere* go.

**ceil** MIDDLE ENGLISH *celen,* from FRENCH *celer* conceal, from LATIN *celare,* probably influenced by *caelum* heaven.

**ceiling** See **ceil.**

**celandine** MIDDLE ENGLISH *celidoine,* from LATIN *celidonia,* from *chelidonia,* from GREEK *chelidon* a swallow, from an ancient story that swallows appeared at the time the flowers blossomed.

**celebrate** LATIN *celebrare* honor.

**celerity** FRENCH, from LATIN *celeritas,* from *celer* swift.

**celery** FRENCH *céleri,* from ITALIAN, from LATIN, from GREEK *selinon* parsley (green leafy edible plant).

**celestial** FRENCH *celestiel* heavenly, from LATIN *caelestis.*

**celibate** LATIN *caelebs* unmarried.

**cell** LATIN *cella* small room.

**cellar** MIDDLE ENGLISH *celer,* from FRENCH *celier,* from LATIN *cellarium* set of cells, food containers, from *cella* small room.

**cellophane** LATIN *cella* small room + GREEK *phainein* show.

**cellulose** FRENCH, from LATIN *cellula* small room for storing things, from *cella* small room.

**cement** FRENCH *ciment* mixture of stone and crushed bricks, from LATIN *caementum.*

**cemetery** LATIN *coemeterium,* from GREEK *koimeterion* burial ground.

**censor** LATIN critic.

**censure** LATIN *censura* opinion.

**cent** LATIN *centum* hundred.

**centaur** Latin *Centaurus*, from Greek *Kentauros*.

**centennial** Latin *centum* a hundred + *annus* year.

**center** Latin *centrum* middle point of a circle, from Greek *kentron*.

**centrifugal** Latin *centrifugus* fleeing from the center, from Latin *centrum* middle point + *fugere* flee. See **center**.

**centurion** See **century**.

**century** Latin *centuria*, from *centum* hundred.

**ceramic** Greek *keramos* potter's clay.

**cereal** Latin *cerealis* grain, from the Roman goddess of grain and agriculture, Ceres.

**cerebellum** Latin *cerebrum* the brain.

**ceremony** French *ceremonie* formal or holy procedure, from Latin *cerimonia*.

**cerise** French cherry.

**certain** French, from Latin *certus* sure.

**certificate** See **certify**.

**certify** French *certifier* make sure, from Latin *certificare*, from *certus* sure + *facere* do, make.

**certitude** French, from Latin *certitudo*.

**cerulean** Latin *caeruleus*, probably from *caelulum* like the sky, from *caelum* heaven.

**cession** French, from Latin *cedere* go.

**cestus** Latin *caestus*, from *caedere* strike, beat.

**chafe** French *chaufer* warm, from Latin *calefacere*, from *calere* be warm + *facere* do, make.

**chaff** Old English *ceaf*.

**chaffer** Old Norse *kapfor* trading journey.

**chagrin** French grief.

**chain** French *chaeine*, from Latin *catena*.

**chair** French *chaiere* seat, from Latin *cathedra*, from Greek *kathedra*.

**chaise** French seat. See **chair**.

**chalcedony** French *calcedoine*, from Latin *calcedonius*, from Greek *chalkedon* precious stone.

**chalet** French *chalé* herder's mountain hut, from *chaslet*, small farmhouse, from *chasel* farmhouse, from Latin *casa* house.

**chalice** French, from Latin *calix* a cup.

**chalk** Old English *cealc*, from Latin *calyx* kind of soft stone.

**challenge** French *chalenge* accusation, from Latin *calumnia* false accusation.

**challis** possibly from the English last name *Challis*.

**chamber** French *chambre* bedroom, from Latin *camera* arched ceiling, from Greek *kamara*, having an arched covering.

**chamberlain** Middle English *chaumberlein*, from French *chamberlenc*, from German *chamarling*, from Latin *camera* arched ceiling.

**chameleon** Latin *chamaeleon*, from Greek *chamai* dwarf + *leon* lion.

**chamois** French, from Latin *camox*.

**champ** imitative.

**champagne** the town of *Champagne* in northeast France, where the wine is made.

**champion** Middle English *champiun* person in combat, from French, from Latin *campio* fighter in the field, from *campus* field.

**chance** French *cheance* fall of the dice, from Latin *cadentia*, from *cadere* fall.

**chancellor** Middle English, from French *cancelier*, from Latin *cancellarius* an officer in a court of the Roman Empire.

**chancery** French *chancellerie*, from French *cancelier*. See **chancellor**.

**chandelier** FRENCH *chandelabre*, from LATIN *candelabrum*, from *candela* candle.

**chandler** FRENCH *chandelier* maker and seller of candles, from LATIN *candela* candle.

**change** FRENCH *changier* make different, from LATIN *cambiare* exchange.

**channel** FRENCH *chanel* canal, from LATIN *canalis*.

**chant** FRENCH *chanter* sing, from LATIN *cantare*.

**chanteuse** FRENCH.

**chanty** FRENCH *chanter* sing.

**chaos** LATIN empty space, from GREEK.

**chaparral** SPANISH *chaparro* evergreen oak.

**chapati** HINDI *chapati* unleavened bread.

**chapel** FRENCH *chapele*, from LATIN *cappella* cloak, from the cloak of a saint which was kept in a holy place for people to see.

**chaperone** FRENCH *chaperon* protector, from *chape* hood, from LATIN *cappa*.

**chaplain** FRENCH *chapelain*, from LATIN *cappella*. See **chapel**.

**chaps** MEXICAN *chaparejos*.

**chapter** FRENCH *chapitre* section of a book, from LATIN *capitulum*.

**char** OLD ENGLISH *cierr* time of working.

**charabanc** FRENCH car with bench.

**character** LATIN mark of quality, from GREEK *charakter* sharpen.

**charade** FRENCH a game, from *charra* chatter (speak quickly and foolishly).

**charcoal** MIDDLE ENGLISH *char cole,* probably from *charren* turn + *cole* coal.

**chard** FRENCH *carde*, from LATIN *carduus* thistle, artichoke.

**charge** FRENCH *charger* load, from LATIN *carricare* load a wagon, from *carrus* two-wheeled wagon.

**charisma** GREEK favor, gift of talent from the gods.

**charity** FRENCH *charité*, from LATIN *caritas* Christian love, from *carus* beloved.

**charlatan** FRENCH, from ITALIAN *ciarlatano*, from *ciarla* chat, prattle.

**charm** FRENCH *charme* magical song, from LATIN *carmen* song.

**chart** FRENCH *charte* map, from LATIN *charta* paper, from GREEK *chartes* sheets of papyrus.

**charter** FRENCH *chartre*, from LATIN *charta*. See **card**.

**chartreuse** FRENCH.

**chary** OLD ENGLISH *cearig* careful.

**chase** FRENCH *chacier* hunt, from LATIN *captare* try to catch.

**chasm** LATIN *chasma* opening, from GREEK.

**chassee** FRENCH *chassé* dance step.

**chassis** FRENCH frame, from LATIN *capsa* box.

**chaste** FRENCH, from LATIN *castus*.

**chasten** LATIN *castigare* punish.

**chat**[1] (talk) MIDDLE ENGLISH shortened form of **chatter**.

**chat**[2] (firewood) FRENCH *chats* cats, because of the soft roundness of the flowers of walnuts and willow.

**chateau** FRENCH, from LATIN *castellum* castle.

**chatelaine** FRENCH, from LATIN *castellum*. See **castle**.

**chattel** FRENCH *chatel*. See **cattle**.

**chatter** MIDDLE ENGLISH *chateren* twitter, gossip; of echoic origin.

**chauffeur** FRENCH *chauffer* one who stokes a fire, from LATIN *calefacere* make warm. (The first cars got their power from steam, so the French called the drivers chauffeurs.)

**chauvinism** FRENCH *chauvinisme*, from Nicolas *Chauvin*, a French soldier who was overly loyal to the emperor Napoleon I (1769–1821).

**chaw** See **chew**.

**cheap** OLD ENGLISH *ceap* bargain, from LATIN *caupo* one who trades.

**cheat**[1] (be unfair) MIDDLE ENGLISH *eschete*, from FRENCH *escheoir* get (fall to) one's share, from LATIN ex- out + *cadere* fall.

**cheat**[2] (low quality bread) possibly from **cheat**[1].

**check** FRENCH *eschec* loss (in the game of chess), from PERSIAN *shah* king (the most important chess piece).

**cheek** OLD ENGLISH *ceoke* jaw.

**cheer** FRENCH *chere* face, from LATIN *cara*, from GREEK *kara* face.

**chef** FRENCH *chef de cuisine* head (chief) cook, from LATIN *caput* head.

**chemise** MIDDLE ENGLISH, from FRENCH, from LATIN *camisia* shirt.

**chemist** FRENCH *chimiste*, from LATIN *chemista*.

**cherish** FRENCH *cher*, from LATIN *carus*.

**cheroot** FRENCH *cheroute*, from TAMIL *churuttu* roll of tobacco.

**cherry** FRENCH *cherise*, from LATIN, from GREEK *kerasos* cherry tree.

**cherub (cherubim)** HEBREW *k'rub* winged angel.

**chest** OLD ENGLISH *cest* box, from LATIN *cista*, from GREEK *kiste*.

**chestnut** MIDDLE ENGLISH *chesteine*, from FRENCH *chastaigne*, from LATIN *castanea*, from GREEK *kastaneia*.

**chevet** FRENCH *chevet* pillow.

**chevron** MIDDLE ENGLISH *cheveroun*, from FRENCH *chevron*, from LATIN *capra* goat.

**chew** MIDDLE ENGLISH *chewan*, from OLD ENGLISH *ceowan* bite.

**chic** FRENCH, from GERMAN *Schick* having good taste.

**chicory** MIDDLE ENGLISH *cicory*, from FRENCH *cicoree*, from LATIN *cichorium*, from GREEK *kichoreia*.

**chide (chidden)** OLD ENGLISH *cidan* quarrel.

**chief** FRENCH *chief, chef* leader, from LATIN *caput* head.

**chiffonier** FRENCH *chiffon*, from *chiffe* rag.

**chilblain** See **chill** + *blain*, from OLD ENGLISH *blegen* a sore.

**child** OLD ENGLISH *cild*.

**chili** SPANISH *chile* from NATIVE AMERICAN *chilli*.

**chill** MIDDLE ENGLISH *ciele* coldness, from *kal* be cold.

**chime** FRENCH *chimbe* cymbal, from LATIN *cymbalum*, from GREEK *kymbalon*.

**chimera** LATIN *chimaera*, from GREEK *chimaira* monster, originally a goat that has lived through one winter, from *cheima* winter.

**chimney** FRENCH *cheminee* fireplace, from LATIN *caminata*, from *caminus*, from GREEK *kaminos*.

**chin** OLD ENGLISH *cin*.

**chine** MIDDLE ENGLISH, from OLD ENGLISH *eschine*, from GERMAN *skina* small bone, shin bone.

**chink** MIDDLE ENGLISH *chine*.

**chinook** early NATIVE AMERICAN name *Tsinuk.*

**chinosol** GERMAN, from *china,* a variant spelling of *kina* or *quina.* See **quinine.**

**chip** OLD ENGLISH *cipp* log.

**chipmunk** NATIVE AMERICAN *atchitamon* squirrel.

**chirk** MIDDLE ENGLISH *chirken* creak, from OLD ENGLISH *circian* roar.

**chiropractic** GREEK *cheir* hand + *praktikos* practical.

**chirp** MIDDLE ENGLISH *chirpen,* from *chirken* twitter.

**chirrup** imitative.

**chisel** FRENCH, from LATIN *cisellus* cutting tool, from *caedere* cut.

**chiton** GREEK.

**chitterling** MIDDLE ENGLISH *chiterling* intestines, from GERMAN *kut* soft parts of the body.

**chivalry** FRENCH *chevalier* knight, from LATIN *caballarius* horseman, from *caballus* regular horse (not of particular quality or breeding).

**chloride** See **chloro-** + **-ide.**

**chlorine** See **chloro-** + **-ine**[1].

**chloro-** GREEK *chloros* pale green.

**chlorodyne** See **chloro-** + **anodyne.**

**chloroform** See **chloro-** + **formic acid.**

**chlorophyll** FRENCH *chlorophylle,* from GREEK *chloros* green + *phyllon* a leaf.

**chloroplast** GREEK *chloros* pale green + *-plast,* from GREEK *plastos* formed.

**chock** FRENCH *chouque* log.

**chocolate** FRENCH, from SPANISH, from NATIVE AMERICAN *chocolatl.*

**choice** FRENCH *choisir* choose.

**choir** FRENCH *cuer,* from LATIN *chorus* singers and dancers, from GREEK *choros.*

**choke** OLD ENGLISH *aceocian.*

**choler** FRENCH *colere,* from GREEK, from *chole* bile (stomach fluids that cause a bad taste in the mouth). The ancient Greeks thought bile caused anger.

**cholesterol** FRENCH *colere,* from GREEK, from *chole* bile (stomach fluids that cause a bad taste in the mouth) + GREEK *stereos* stiff.

**choline** See **choler** + **-ine**[1].

**choose** OLD ENGLISH *ceosan.*

**chop** MIDDLE ENGLISH *choppen,* probably from FRENCH *choper, coper* cut.

**chord** LATIN *chorda.* See **accord.**

**choreography** GREEK *choreia* dance + *-graphia* description, from *graphein* write.

**choriamb** LATIN *choriambus,* from GREEK *choriambos,* from *choreios* chorus + *iambos* forceful speech.

**choriambus** See **choriamb.**

**chorister** MIDDLE ENGLISH *querister,* from FRENCH *cuerister,* from LATIN *chorus* choir, from GREEK *choros.* See **chorus.**

**chorizo** SPANISH pork sausage.

**chortle** blend of **chuckle** and **snort,** invented by the English writer Lewis Carroll (1832–1898).

**chorus** LATIN, from GREEK *choros* a dance, chorus.

**chow** CHINESE *kaú* dog.

**Christ** OLD ENGLISH *Crist,* from LATIN *Christus,* from GREEK *Cristos,* translation of HEBREW *mashiah* Messiah (Jesus).

**chromatic** LATIN *chromaticus,* from GREEK *chroma* color.

**chrome** GREEK *chroma* color.

**chronic** LATIN *chronicus* time, from GREEK *chronos.*

**chronicle** MIDDLE ENGLISH *cronicle,* from FRENCH *chronique,* from LATIN *chronica,* from GREEK *chronos* time.

**chrono-** GREEK *chronos* time.

**chronology** See **chrono-** + **-logy.**

**chronoscope** See **chrono-** + **-scope.**

**chrysalis** LATIN *chrysallis,* from GREEK gold colored, from *chrysos* gold.

**chrysanthemum** LATIN, from GREEK *chrysos* gold + *anthemon* flower.

**chrysoprase** FRENCH *crisopace,* from LATIN *chrysoprasus,* from GREEK *chrysoprasos,* from *chrysos* gold + *prason* leek (a green vegetable).

**chuck** FRENCH *choquer* knock.

**chuckle** imitative.

**chug** imitative.

**chukka** HINDI *chakkar* circle.

**chum**[1] (bait) perhaps from SCOTTISH *chum* food.

**chum**[2] (friend) BRITISH slang for roommate.

**chunk** variant of **chuck.**

**chunter** imitative.

**chuppah** HEBREW *huppah* cover.

**church** OLD ENGLISH *circe* building for Christians to pray in, from GREEK *kyriakon* house of the Lord, from *kyrios* master, lord.

**churl** OLD ENGLISH *ceorl* peasant.

**churn** OLD ENGLISH *cyrin* container for making butter.

**chute** FRENCH fall, from LATIN *cadere.*

**cicada** LATIN.

**-cide** LATIN *caedere* kill.

**cider** FRENCH *cidre,* from LATIN *sicera,* from GREEK *sikera,* from HEBREW *shekar* strong drink.

**cigar** SPANISH *cigarro.*

**cigarette** diminutive of **cigar.**

**cilia** LATIN *cilia,* plural of *cilium,* an eyelid, eyelid-edge, eyelash.

**cinch** SPANISH *cincha* strap on a saddle, from LATIN *cingula* belt.

**cinder** OLD ENGLISH *sinder.*

**cinema** GREEK *kinema* motion.

**cinnamon** FRENCH *cinnamom,* from LATIN, from GREEK, from HEBREW *qinnamon.*

**cipher** FRENCH *cifre* zero, from ARABIC *çifr* empty.

**circle** LATIN *circulus,* from *circus* ring.

**circuit** MIDDLE ENGLISH, from FRENCH, from LATIN *circuitus* a going round, from *circumire,* from *circum* around + *ire* go.

**circulate** LATIN *circulari* form a circle.

**circum-** LATIN around.

**circumference** MIDDLE ENGLISH, from LATIN *circumferentia,* from *circum-* around + *ferre* carry.

**circumspect** MIDDLE ENGLISH, from LATIN *circumspectus,* from *circum-* around + *specere* look.

**circumstance** LATIN *circumstantia* surrounding condition, from *circum-* around + *stare* stand.

**circus** LATIN circle, from GREEK *kirkos.*

**cirque** FRENCH, from LATIN *circus* circle, from GREEK *kirkos.*

**cirrus** LATIN *cirrus* curl.

**cistern** FRENCH *cisterne,* from LATIN *cisterna* reservoir.

**citadel** ITALIAN *cittade* city, from LATIN *civitas* city, state.

**cite** FRENCH, from LATIN *citare* order to appear (before a judge), from *ciere* wake up.

**cithara** LATIN, from GREEK *kithara*.

**citizen** FRENCH *citeain* person in town, from *cite* city, from LATIN *civitas* city, state.

**citrate** See **citrus** + **-ate**.

**citrus** LATIN, from GREEK *kitron*.

**city** FRENCH *cité* large town, from LATIN *civis* citizen.

**civilize** FRENCH, from LATIN *civilis*, from *civis* citizen.

**clabber** IRISH *clabar*.

**claim** FRENCH *cla(i)mer* call out, from LATIN *clamare* call.

**clairvoyant** FRENCH *clairvoyance* having clear sight.

**clam** MIDDLE ENGLISH *clamp*, from OLD ENGLISH *clamm* grasp, bond.

**clamber** MIDDLE ENGLISH *clambren*.

**clammy** probably from OLD ENGLISH *clam* clay.

**clamor** FRENCH *clamour*, from LATIN *clamor* loud cry.

**clamp**[1] (hold together) DUTCH *klampe*.

**clamp**[2] (a pile or mound) DUTCH *klamp* heap.

**clan** MIDDLE ENGLISH, from SCOTTISH *clann* family, from IRISH *cland* offspring, from LATIN *planta* sprout.

**clandestine** LATIN *clandestinus*.

**clang** LATIN *clangere* sound again.

**clangor** LATIN *clangor* sound, noise.

**clank** See **clang**.

**clap** OLD ENGLISH *clæppan* beat.

**clapboard** GERMAN *klappholt* wood, from *klappen* fit together + *holt* wood.

**clapper** See **clap**.

**clapperdudgeon** See **clapper** + **dudgeon**.

**claret** MIDDLE ENGLISH, from FRENCH *vin claret* clear wine, from LATIN *clarus* clear.

**clarify** FRENCH *clarifier* make clear, from LATIN *clarificare*, from *carus* clear + *facere* do, make.

**clarinet** FRENCH *clarine* bell, from LATIN *clarus* clear.

**clarion** FRENCH *clairon*, from LATIN *clarlo*, from *clarus* clear.

**clash** imitative.

**clasp** MIDDLE ENGLISH *claspe*.

**class** FRENCH *classe*, from LATIN *classis* one of the six divisions of the Roman people, based on ownership of land and wealth.

**classic** LATIN *classicus* of the highest class, from *classis*. See **class**.

**classify** LATIN *classis*. See **class**.

**clatter** possibly from OLD ENGLISH *clatere* a rattle.

**clause** FRENCH, from LATIN *clausa* end of a sentence, from *claudere* close.

**clavicle** FRENCH *clavicule*, from LATIN *clavicula*, from *clavis* a key.

**clavier** FRENCH, from LATIN *claviarius* keyboard.

**claw** MIDDLE ENGLISH *claue*, from OLD ENGLISH *clawu*.

**claymore** SCOTTISH *claidheamhmor*, from *claidheamh* sword + *mor* great.

**clean** OLD ENGLISH *clæne* clear.

**clear** FRENCH *cler* pure, from LATIN *clarus* bright.

**cleat** OLD ENGLISH lump.

**cleave**[1] (divide) OLD ENGLISH *cleofan*.

**cleave**[2] (cling to) OLD ENGLISH *cleofian*.

**cleft** MIDDLE ENGLISH *clift*, from OLD ENGLISH *clyft*.

**clemency** MIDDLE ENGLISH *clemencie*, from LATIN *clemens* merciful.

**clement** LATIN *clemens* merciful.

**clench** OLD ENGLISH *(be)clencan* hold.

**clergy** FRENCH *clergie*, from LATIN *clericus*.

**clerk** OLD ENGLISH *clerc*, from LATIN *clericus* priest. During the Middle Ages, those who could read and write were mostly church people.

**clever** probably from NORWEGIAN *klöver* skillful.

**clew** OLD ENGLISH *cleowen* ball of thread. See **clue**.

**cliché** FRENCH, thin metal sheet used in 18th century printing, from the sound of a printing block dropped onto the still hot metal sheet. Later the word came to stand for something repeated in an identical way.

**click** imitative.

**client** LATIN *cliens* person dependent.

**cliff** OLD ENGLISH *clif*.

**climate** LATIN *clima* region, from GREEK *klima*.

**climax** LATIN, from GREEK *klimax* ladder.

**clinch** OLD ENGLISH *(be)clencan* hold.

**cling** OLD ENGLISH *clingan* shrink.

**clinic** LATIN *clinicus* treating patients who are in bed, from GREEK *kline* bed.

**clink** DUTCH *klinken*, imitative.

**clip** OLD NORSE *klippa* cut short.

**clipper** MIDDLE ENGLISH *clippen*. See **clip**.

**clipt** See **clip**.

**clique** FRENCH *cliquer* make a noise.

**cloak** FRENCH *cloche* bell, from LATIN *clocca*. The shape of a cloak is like a bell.

**cloche** FRENCH bell.

**clock** FRENCH *cloke*, from LATIN *clocca* bell. Many clocks had bells that rang when the hour came.

**clod** OLD ENGLISH.

**clodpole** See **clod** + GERMAN *poll* head.

**clog** MIDDLE ENGLISH *clogge* lump of wood.

**cloister** FRENCH *clostre* religious place to go for quiet, from LATIN *claustrum* enclosed place.

**close** FRENCH *clore* shut, from LATIN *claudere*.

**closet** FRENCH *clos*, from LATIN *claudere* close.

**closure** FRENCH, from LATIN *clausura*, from *claudere* close.

**clot** OLD ENGLISH *clott*.

**clothes** OLD ENGLISH *clathas*, from *clath* cloth.

**cloud** OLD ENGLISH *clud* mass of rock.

**clout** MIDDLE ENGLISH *cloule*, from OLD ENGLISH *clut* lump.

**clove**[1] (spice) MIDDLE ENGLISH *clowe*, from FRENCH *clou de girofle* nail of clove, from LATIN *clavus* nail, because of the shape.

**clove**[2] (slice of garlic) OLD ENGLISH *clufu* thing cloven.

**cloven** See **cleave**[1].

**clown** OLD NORSE *klunni* awkward person.

**club** OLD NORSE *clubba* thick stick.

**cluck** OLD ENGLISH *cloccian*.

**clue** OLD ENGLISH *cleowen* ball of thread. In an early legend a ball of thread was used to mark the way through a maze.

**clump** GERMAN *klumpe* shoe made from a piece of wood.

**clumsy** MIDDLE ENGLISH *clumsid* numb with cold, from OLD NORSE *klumsa* lockjaw (disease which causes the jaw to become stiff or tight).

**cluster** OLD ENGLISH *clyster* bunch.

**clutch**[1] MIDDLE ENGLISH *clucchan*, from OLD ENGLISH *clyccan*, bend the fingers, clench.

**clutch**[2]: (of eggs) MIDDLE ENGLISH *clucchen*, from OLD ENGLISH *clekken* create, from OLD NORSE *klekja* hatch.

**co-** LATIN *co-, com-* with.

**coach** FRENCH *coche*, from Hungarian *kocsi* the town of Kocs, where the coaches were made.

**coagulate** LATIN *coagulare*, from *co-* together + *agere* drive, make.

**coal** OLD ENGLISH *col* charcoal.

**coalesce** LATIN *coalescere*, from *co-* together + *alescere* grow up.

**coalition** LATIN *coalitio* meeting, from *coalescere*, from *co-* together + *alescere* grow up.

**coarse** See **course**.

**coast** FRENCH *coste* shore, from LATIN *costa* side.

**coat** MIDDLE ENGLISH, from French *cote*, origin unknown.

**coax** obsolete *coax, cokes* a fool.

**cob** OLD ENGLISH, used in several senses, most meaning "big," "rounded" or "head," but possibly of different origins.

**cobalt** GERMAN *kobold* goblin, from the belief that goblins put it in place of valuable silver in the mines.

**cobble** (paving stone) MIDDLE ENGLISH *cob* a rounded lump.

**cobbler** MIDDLE ENGLISH *cobelere*.

**cobra** PORTUGUESE *cobra (de capello)* serpent (with hood), from LATIN *colubra* a snake.

**cocciliana** LATIN *coccineus* scarlet + MODERN ENGLISH, from FRENCH *liana* twining plant.

**coccus** LATIN, from GREEK *kokkus* grain, seed, berry.

**coccyx** LATIN, from GREEK *kokkyx* cuckoo.

**cochlea** LATIN, from GREEK *kokhlias* snail, screw.

**cock**[1] (rooster) OLD ENGLISH *cocc* male bird.

**cock**[2] (tilt) OLD ENGLISH *cocc* male bird, from the way the bird tilts its head when it crows.

**cockatoo** DUTCH *kaketoe*, from MALAY *kakatua.*

**cockle** MIDDLE ENGLISH *cokel*, from FRENCH *coquille* shell, from LATIN *conchylium*, from GREEK *konchylion* shellfish.

**cockney** MIDDLE ENGLISH *cokenei* spoiled child, from *coken-ey* cock's egg.

**cocktail**[1] (shape) See **cock**[1] + **tail**.

**cocktail**[2] (drink) AMERICAN *cocktay*, from FRENCH *coquetier* egg-cup (first served in New Orleans in such cups).

**cocoa** SPANISH *cacao.*

**cod** OLD ENGLISH *codd* bag.

**coddle** LATIN *cal(i)dus* warm.

**code** FRENCH list of laws, from LATIN *codex* wooden tablet for writing.

**codger** probably from BRITISH *cadger* beggar.

**codicil** FRENCH *codicille*, from LATIN *codicillus* short writing.

**coefficient** See **co-** + **efficient**.

**coerce** LATIN *coercerce* shut in.

**coffee** ITALIAN *caffé,* from ARABIC *qahwah,* from an area in Africa called *Kaffa* where the coffee plant came from originally.

**coffer** MIDDLE ENGLISH, from FRENCH *cofre* a chest, from LATIN *cophinus* basket, from GREEK *kophinos.*

**coffin** FRENCH *cofin* chest, from LATIN *cophinus* basket, from GREEK *kophinos.*

**cog**[1] (tooth on a wheel) MIDDLE ENGLISH *cogge,* of SCANDINAVIAN origin.

**cog**[2] (ship) MIDDLE ENGLISH *cogge,* from FRENCH *cogue.*

**cogent** LATIN *cogere* force together.

**cognition** LATIN *cognoscere* knowledge, from *co-* together + *(g)noscere* know.

**cohere** LATIN *cohaerere,* from *co-* together + *haerere* stick.

**cohort** FRENCH *cohorte,* from LATIN *cohors* enclosed space or crowd.

**coigne (coynye)** IRISH *coinnemh.*

**coil** FRENCH *collir* collect, from LATIN *colligere.*

**coin** FRENCH, from LATIN *cuneus.*

**coincide** LATIN *coincidere* fall upon together, from *co-* together + *incidere* fall upon.

**colander** LATIN *colatorium,* from *colare* drain.

**cold** OLD ENGLISH *cald.*

**colic** MIDDLE ENGLISH *colik,* from FRENCH *colique,* from LATIN *colicus,* from GREEK *kolon* colon, from the area in the body that is affected.

**collaborate** LATIN *collaborare,* from *com-* with + *laborare* work.

**collage** FRENCH *colle* glue, from GREEK *kolla.*

**collapse** LATIN *collabi* fall in ruins.

**collar** FRENCH *colier* necklace, from LATIN *collum* neck.

**collaret** See **collar.**

**collate** LATIN *conferre,* from *com-* together + *ferre* bring.

**collateral** LATIN *collateralis,* from *com-* together + *lateralis* lateral (at the side).

**colleague** FRENCH *collègue,* from LATIN *collega,* from *com-* with + *legare* have help.

**collect** LATIN *colligere,* from *com-* together + *legere* gather.

**college** LATIN *collegium* association of persons.

**collet** FRENCH, from *col* neck, from LATIN *collum.*

**colloquy** LATIN *colloquium,* from *com-* together + *loqui* speak.

**collude** LATIN *com-* with + *ludere* play.

**collusion** See **collude.**

**cologne** FRENCH *Cologne,* from GERMAN *Köln,* city in Germany.

**colon** GREEK *kolon* clause.

**colonel** FRENCH *coronel,* from ITALIAN *colonna* military column, from LATIN *columna* column.

**colonnade** FRENCH, from ITALIAN, from LATIN *colomna* pillar.

**colony** LATIN *colonia* farm.

**color** MIDDLE ENGLISH, from FRENCH, from LATIN *colos* covering.

**colossus** LATIN huge statue, from GREEK *kolossos.*

**colter** See **coulter.**

**columbine** FRENCH *colombin,* from LATIN *columbina,* from *columbinus* like a dove.

**columel** LATIN *columella* small pillar.

**column** LATIN *columna* pillar.

**com-** LATIN *com-, cum-* with, together, very much.

**coma** LATIN, from GREEK *koma* deep sleep.

**comanche** SPANISH, from NATIVE AMERICAN *kimachi* stranger, other.

**comb** MIDDLE ENGLISH, from OLD ENGLISH *camb* toothed object.

**combat** FRENCH *combatre* fight, from LATIN *com-* with + *battuere* beat.

**combine** LATIN *combinare* unite, from *com-* with + *bini* two each.

**combustion** FRENCH, from LATIN *combusto*, from *comburere* burn up.

**come** OLD ENGLISH *cuman*.

**comedy** FRENCH *comedie* funny play, from LATIN *comoedia*, from GREEK *komoidia*, from *komos* party + *aeidein* sing. Ancient Greek comedies were festivals with singing.

**comet** OLD ENGLISH *cometa*, from LATIN, from GREEK *kome* hair.

**comfort** FRENCH *comforter* urge, from LATIN *comfortare* make stronger, from *com-* together + *fortis* strong.

**comic** MIDDLE ENGLISH *comice*, from LATIN *comicus*, from GREEK *komikos*.

**comma** LATIN, from GREEK *komma* that which is cut off, from *koptein* cut off.

**command** FRENCH *comander* order, from LATIN *commandare*, from *com-* together + *mandare* order.

**commemorate** LATIN *commemorare*, from *com-* much + *memorare* remind.

**commence** FRENCH, from LATIN *com-* together + *initiare* initiate (start).

**commend** LATIN *commendare*, from *com-* with + *mandare* command.

**commensurate** LATIN *com-* together + *mensura* a measure.

**comment** LATIN *commentum* invention, from *com-* together + *meminisse* remember.

**commerce** LATIN *commercium*, from *com-* together + *merx* merchandise.

**commiserate** LATIN *commiserari*, from *com-* with + *miserare* pity.

**commissar** See **commissary**.

**commissary** LATIN *commissarius*, from *commissus* entrusted.

**commission** FRENCH charge, from LATIN *commissio* contest. See **commit**.

**commissure** LATIN *commissura* joining.

**commit** LATIN *committere*, from *com-* together + *mittere* send.

**committee** FRENCH. See **commit**.

**commode** FRENCH, from LATIN *commodus* suitable, from *com-* together + *modus* measure.

**commodity** FRENCH *commodité* benefit, from LATIN *commoditatem* fitness, from *commodus*. See **commode**.

**common** FRENCH *comun* general, from LATIN *communis* shared by all, from *com-* together + *munia* public duties.

**commotion** LATIN *commotio*, from *com-* together + *movere* move.

**commune**[1] (talk with) FRENCH *comuner* share, from *comun*. See **common**.

**commune**[2] (place) FRENCH *commune*, from LATIN *communia* group sharing a common life, from *communis*. See **common**.

**communicate** LATIN *communicare* share.

**communion** FRENCH, from LATIN *communis*. See **common**.

**communism** FRENCH *communisme*, from *commun* general, from LATIN *communis*. See **common**.

**community** FRENCH *com(m)unete*, from LATIN *communitas*, from *communis*. See **common**.

**commutation** See **commute** + **-ation**.

**commute** LATIN *commutare* change, from *com-* with + *mutare* change.

**compact** MIDDLE ENGLISH, from LATIN *compactus*, from *compingere*, from *com-* together + *pangere* fasten, fix.

**companion** FRENCH, from LATIN *companio* friend who eats with one, from *com-* with + *panis* bread.

**company** FRENCH *compagnie* group of soldiers, from LATIN *companes* group of soldiers living and eating together, from *com-* with + *panis* bread.

**compare** FRENCH *comparer*, from LATIN *comparare*, from *com-* with + *par* equal.

**compartment** FRENCH *compartir*, from ITALIAN *compartimento*, from *compartire*, from *com-* very much + *partire* divide.

**compass** FRENCH *compas* measure, from LATIN *com-* together + *passus* step.

**compassion** FRENCH, from LATIN *compassio*, from *com-* with + *pati* suffer.

**compatible** FRENCH, from LATIN *compati* suffer with. See **compassion**.

**compel** LATIN *compellere*, from *com-* together + *pellere* drive.

**compendium** LATIN *compendium* a shortening, from *com-* together + *pendere* weigh.

**compensate** LATIN *compensare*, from *com-* with + *pensare* weigh.

**compete** LATIN *competere*, from *com-* together + *petere* seek.

**competent** See **compete**.

**compile** FRENCH, from LATIN *compilare*, from *com-* together + *pilare* make smaller.

**complacent** LATIN *complacere* be pleasing, from *com-* very much + *placere* please.

**complain** FRENCH *complaindre*, from LATIN *complangere*, from *com-* very much + *plangere* hit the chest.

**complaisance** See **complacent**.

**complement** LATIN *complementus*, from *complere*. See **complete**.

**complete** FRENCH, from LATIN *complere*, from *com-* very much + *plere* fill.

**complex** LATIN *complecti*, from *com-* with + *plectere* weave.

**compliment** FRENCH, from ITALIAN *complimento*, from LATIN *complere*. See **complete**.

**comply** FRENCH, from LATIN *complere*. See **complete**.

**component** LATIN *componere*. See **compose**.

**compose** FRENCH *composer*, from LATIN *componere*, from *com-* with + *poser* place.

**composite** See **compose**.

**compost** FRENCH, from LATIN *compositum*. See **compose**.

**compote** FRENCH. See **compose**.

**compound** FRENCH, from LATIN *componere*. See **compose**.

**comprehend** LATIN *comprehendere*, from *com-* with + *prehendere* take, seize.

**compulsion** MIDDLE ENGLISH, from LATIN *compulsio*, from *compellere*. See **compel**.

**compunction** LATIN *compunctio* pricking of the conscience, from *compungere*, from *com-* with + *pungere* prick.

**compute** LATIN *computare*, from *com-* with + *putare* figure out.

**comrade** FRENCH *comarade* roommate, from SPANISH *camarada*, from *camara* room, from LATIN *camera*.

**con**[1] (negation) LATIN *contra* against.

**con²** (study) Old English *cunnan* know, know how. See **can¹**.

**con³** (swindle) American *confidence man*, from scams in which the victim is persuaded to hand over money as a token of confidence.

**con⁴** (guide ships) French *conduire*, from Latin *conducere*. See **conduct**.

**con-** See **com-**.

**concatenate** Latin *concatenare* link together, from *com-* together + *catenare*, from *catena* a chain.

**concave** French, from Latin *concavus* hollow, from *com-* very much + *cavus* hollow.

**conceal** French *conceler* hide, from Latin *concelare*.

**concede** Latin *concedere* yield.

**conceit** Middle English *conceite*. See **conceive**.

**conceive** Latin *concipere* receive, from *com-* together + *capere* take.

**concentrate** French, from Latin *com-* together + *centrum* center.

**concentric** French *concentrique*, from Latin, from *com-* together + *centrum* center.

**conception** See **conceive**.

**concern** Latin *concernere* relate to, from *com-* together + *cernere* find out about.

**concert** French, from Italian, from Latin *concertare*, from *com-* with + *certare* strive (work for).

**concertina** See **concert** + **-ina**.

**conch** Middle English *conke*, from Latin *concha*, from Greek *konche*.

**conciliate** Latin *conciliare*, from *com-* with + *calare* call.

**concise** Latin *concidere*, from *com-* very much + *cadere* cut.

**conclave** French, from Latin a room that could be locked, from *com-* with + *clavis* a key.

**conclude** Latin *concludere*, from *com-* together + *claudere* shut.

**concoct** Latin *concoquere*, from *com-* together + *coquere* cook.

**concord** French *concorde*, from Latin *concordia*, from *concors* of the same mind, from *com-* together + *cors* heart.

**concrete** Latin *concrescere*, from *com-* together + *crescere* grow.

**concur** Latin *concurrere*, from *com-* together + *currere* run.

**concussion** Latin *concutere*, from *com-* together + *quatere* shake.

**condemn** Latin *condemnare*, from *com-* very much + *damnare* harm, condemn.

**condense** Latin *condensare*, from *com-* together + *densus* dense.

**condescend** Latin *condescendere*, from *com-* together + *descendere* descend.

**condiment** Latin *condimentum* a spice, from *condire* pickle (using something like vinegar to preserve food).

**condition** French *condicion*, from Latin *conditio* agreement, from *com-* together + *dicere* speak.

**condole** Latin *condolere*, from *com-* with + *dolere* be sad about.

**condone** Latin *condonare*, from *com-* very much + *donare* give.

**condor** Spanish, from Native American *cuntur* name for the bird.

**conduce** See **conduct**.

**conduct** Latin *conducere*, from *com-* together + *ducere* lead.

**conduit** See **conduct**.

**condyle** FRENCH, from LATIN *condylus,* from GREEK *kondylos* knuckle.

**cone** FRENCH *cône,* from LATIN *conus,* from GREEK *konos.*

**confabulate** LATIN *confabulare,* from *com-* together + *fabulari* converse.

**confection** LATIN *conficere,* from *com-* with + *facere* do, make.

**confederate** LATIN *confoederare* unite in a league (group), from *foedus* league.

**confer** LATIN *conferre,* from *com-* together + *ferre* bring.

**confess** LATIN *confiteri,* from *com-* together + *fateri* acknowledge.

**confetti** ITALIAN *confetto,* from LATIN *confectum,* small candy.

**confide** LATIN *confidere,* from *com-* very much + *fidere* trust.

**configure** LATIN *configurare,* from *con-* together + *figurare* shape.

**confine** FRENCH, from LATIN *confinum,* from *com-* with + *finis* end.

**confirm** FRENCH, from LATIN *confirmare,* from *com-* very much + *furmare* strengthen, from *firmus* firm.

**confiscate** LATIN *confiscare* put in a chest, from *com-* together + *fiscus* money chest, treasury.

**conflagation** LATIN *conflagrationem,* from *com-* very much + *flagrare* burn.

**conflict** LATIN *confligere,* from *com-* very much + *fligere* strike.

**conform** FRENCH *conformir,* from LATIN *conformare,* from *com-* together + *formare* form.

**confound** FRENCH *confondre* destroy, from LATIN *confundere,* from *com-* together + *fundere* pour.

**confront** LATIN *confrontare,* from *com-* together + *frons* forehead.

**confuse** MIDDLE ENGLISH *confusen,* from LATIN *confundere,* from *com-* together + *fundere* pour.

**confusticate** alteration of **confuse** or **confound.**

**conga** SPANISH *Congo* (a dance).

**congeal** FRENCH, from LATIN *congelare,* from *com-* together + *gelare* freeze.

**congenial** See **com-** + **genial.**

**conger** LATIN *conger* sea-eel, from GREEK *gongros.*

**congest** LATIN *congerere* pile up, from *com-* together + *gerere* carry.

**conglomerate** LATIN *conglomerare,* from *com-* together + *glomerare* gather into a ball, from *glomus* a ball.

**congratulate** LATIN *congratulari,* from *com-* together + *gratulari* wish joy, from *gratus* agree.

**congregate** LATIN *congregare* assemble, from *com-* together + *gregare* gather, from *congrex* flock.

**congress** LATIN *congredi,* from *com-* together + *gradi* walk, from *gradus* a step.

**congruent** LATIN *congruere* agree.

**congruous** See **congruent.**

**conifer** LATIN *conus* cone + *ferre* bring.

**conjecture** LATIN *conjectura,* from *com-* together + *jacere* throw.

**conjugate** LATIN *conjugare,* from *com-* together + *jugare* join, from *jugum* yoke.

**conjunction** FRENCH, from LATIN *conjungere,* from *com-* together + *jungere* join.

**conjure** FRENCH, from LATIN *conjurare,* from *com-* together + *jurare* swear.

**conker** See **conquer**.

**connect** LATIN *connectere*, from *com-* together + *nectere* tie together.

**connive** LATIN *conivere* wink.

**connoisseur** FRENCH, from LATIN *cognoscere*, from *co-* together + *(g)noscere* know.

**connote** LATIN *connotare*, from *com-* together + *notare* mark.

**conquer** FRENCH *conquerre* win, from LATIN *conquaerere*, from *com-* very much + *quaerere* look for.

**conquest** FRENCH *conqueste*, from LATIN *conquestus*, from *conquistus*.

**conscience** FRENCH awareness of good and evil, from LATIN *conscire*, from *com-* with + *scire* know.

**conscious** LATIN *conscius* aware. See **conscience**.

**consecrate** LATIN *consecrare*, from *com-* together + *sacrare* make holy, from *sacer* sacred.

**consecutive** FRENCH *consécutif*, from LATIN *consecutivus*, from *consequi*. See **consequence**.

**consensus** LATIN. See **consent**.

**consent** FRENCH *consentir* agree, from LATIN *com-* together + *sentire* feel.

**consequence** FRENCH, from LATIN *consequi*, from *com-* with + *sequi* follow.

**conservatory** See **conserve**.

**conserve** FRENCH *conserver* preserve, from LATIN *conservare*, from *com-* with + *servare* keep.

**consider** FRENCH *considerer* observe closely, from LATIN *considerare*, from *com-* with + *sidus* star.

**consign** LATIN *consignare* seal, from *com-* together + *signare*, from *signum* sign.

**consist** LATIN *consistere*, from *com-* together + *sistere* cause to stand, from *stare* stand.

**console** FRENCH *consoler* comfort, from LATIN *consolari*, from *com-* with + *solari* solace (comfort).

**consolidate** LATIN *consolidare*, from *com-* together + *solidare*, from *solidus* solid.

**consonance** LATIN *consonans* sound or letter, from *consonare*, from *com-* with + *sonare* sound.

**consort** FRENCH colleague, partner, wife, from LATIN *consortem* partner, neighbor, from *com-* with + *sors* a share.

**conspicuous** LATIN *conspicere* look at, from *com-* very much + *specere* see.

**conspire** FRENCH, from LATIN *conspirare*, from *com-* together + *spirare* breathe.

**constable** FRENCH *conestable* officer in charge of the stable, from LATIN *cones stabuli* "officer of the stable". The care of a king's horses was a very important matter.

**constant** FRENCH, from LATIN *constare*, from *com-* together + *stare* stand.

**constellation** MIDDLE ENGLISH *constellacion*, from FRENCH *constellation*, from LATIN *constellatus*, from *com-* with + *stellare* shine, from *stella* star.

**consternation** LATIN *consternare* make afraid.

**constituent** LATIN *constituere*. See **constitute**.

**constitute** LATIN *constituere*, from *com-* together + *statuere* cause to stand.

**constrain** MIDDLE ENGLISH *constreinen*, from FRENCH *constreindre*, from LATIN *constringere* bind together, from *com-* together + *stringere* pull tight.

**constrict** LATIN *constrictus*, from *constringere*. See **constrain**.

**construct** LATIN *constructus*, from *com-* with + *struere* pile up.

**construe** LATIN *construere*.  See **construct**.

**consul** LATIN *consulere*, from *con-* together + *salire* leap.

**consult** LATIN *consultare*.

**consume** LATIN *consumere*, from *com-* together + *sumere* take.

**consummate** LATIN *consummare*, from *com-* together + *summa* sum.

**contact** LATIN *contingere*, from *com-* together + *tangere* touch.

**contagion** LATIN *contagio* a touching, from *contingere*.  See **contact**.

**contain** FRENCH *contenir*, from LATIN *continere*, from *com-* together + *tenere* hold.

**contaminate** LATIN *contaminare* make unclean, from *contamen* contact, from *com-* together + *tangere* touch.

**contemplate** LATIN *contemplari* observe, from *com-* together + *templum* temple (religious building).  The ancient Roman priests watched in their temples for signs from the heavens.

**contemporary** LATIN *com-* with + *temporarius*, from *tempus* time.

**contempt** LATIN *contemnere*, from *com-* together + *temnere* scorn.

**contend** LATIN *contendere*, from *com-* together + *tendere* stretch.

**content** See **contain**.

**contest** LATIN *contestari*, from *com-* together + *testari* be a witness to, from *testis* witness.

**context** MIDDLE ENGLISH, from LATIN *contexere* weave together, from *com-* together + *texere* weave.

**contiguous** LATIN *contingere*.  See **contact**.

**continent**[1] (land) FRENCH, from LATIN *terra continens* continuous land, from *com-* with + *tenere* hold.

**continent**[2] (self-restraining) LATIN *continentem*, from *continere* hold together.  See **contain**.

**contingent** LATIN *contingere*.  See **contact**.

**continue** FRENCH *continuer* proceed, from LATIN *continuare* connect.  See **contain**.

**contort** LATIN *contorquere*, from *com-* very much + *torquere* twist.

**contour** FRENCH, from ITALIAN, from LATIN *contornare*, from *com-* very much + *tornare* turn.

**contra-** LATIN *contra-* against.

**contraband** SPANISH *contrabanda*, from ITALIAN *contrabando*, from LATIN *contra-* against + *bannum* law.

**contract** LATIN *contrahere*, from *com-* together + *trahere* draw.

**contradict** LATIN *contradicere* speak against, from *contra-* against + *dicere* say.

**contraption** origin unclear, perhaps based on **contrive**.

**contrary** FRENCH, from LATIN *contrarius*, from *contra-* against.

**contrast** FRENCH *constraster*, from LATIN *contra-* against + *stare* stand.

**contribute** LATIN *contribuere*, from *com-* with + *tribuere* pay out.

**contrite** FRENCH, from LATIN *conterere* grind, from *com-* together + *terere* wear out.

**contrive** FRENCH *controver* invent, from LATIN *con-* with + *tropus* manner of speech.

**control** FRENCH *contrerolle* copy kept of something to check it, from LATIN *contra-* against + *rotulus* little wheel.

**controversy** MIDDLE ENGLISH *controversie*, from LATIN *controversia*, from *contra-* against + *vertere* turn.

**contumely** FRENCH, from LATIN *contumelia*, from *com-* very much + *tumere* swell up.

**contuse** MIDDLE ENGLISH *contusan*, from LATIN *contundere*, from *com-* very much + *tundere* beat.

**conundrum** origin unknown.

**convalesce** LATIN *convalescere*, from *com-* very + *valescere* grow strong.

**convection** LATIN *convehere*, from *com-* together + *vehere* carry.

**convene** FRENCH, from LATIN *convenire*, from *com-* together + *venire* come.

**convenient** MIDDLE ENGLISH, from LATIN *convenire*. See convene.

**convent** FRENCH, from LATIN *convenire*. See convene.

**convention** LATIN *conventio* meeting. See convene.

**converge** LATIN *convergere*, from *com-* together + *vergere* turn.

**converse** FRENCH, from LATIN *convertere*, from *com-* with + *vertere* turn.

**convert** FRENCH *convertir* turn. See converse.

**convex** LATIN *convehere*, from *com-* together + *vehere* bring.

**convey** FRENCH *conveier*, from LATIN *com-* together + *via* way.

**convict** LATIN *convincere* prove. See convince.

**convince** LATIN *convincere*, from *com-* very + *vincere* conquer.

**convolute** LATIN *convolvere*, from *com-* together + *volvere* roll.

**convolve** See convolute.

**convolvulus** See convolute.

**convoy** FRENCH *convoier*, from LATIN *com-* with + *via* road.

**convulse** LATIN *convellere*, from *com-* together + *vellere* pluck (to pull).

**cony** FRENCH *conis*, from LATIN *cuniculus* rabbit.

**coo** imitative.

**cook** MIDDLE ENGLISH *cok*, from FRENCH *coc*, from LATIN *coquere* cook.

**cookie** probably from DUTCH *koekje*, from *coek* cake.

**cool** OLD ENGLISH *col*.

**coolie** HINDI *quli* hired servant.

**coop** MIDDLE ENGLISH *coupe*, from OLD ENGLISH *cype*, *cypa* basket, cask, probably from LATIN *cupa* tub, cask.

**cooper** MIDDLE ENGLISH, from LATIN *cuparius*, from *cupa* tub, cask.

**cooperate** LATIN *cooperari* work together, from *co-* together + *operari* work.

**coordinate** LATIN *coordinare*, from *co-* with + *ordinare* arrange, from *ordo* order.

**cope** FRENCH *couper* strike, from *colper*, from LATIN *colaphus*, from GREEK *kolaphos*.

**copious** LATIN *copiosus*, from *copia* abundant (more than enough).

**copper** OLD ENGLISH *copor*, from LATIN *cuprum*, from *aes Cyprium* metal of Cyprus, from GREEK *Kypros* Cyprus, place where copper was found in ancient times.

**copperas** MIDDLE ENGLISH and FRENCH *coperose*, from LATIN *aqua cuprosa* copper water.

**copse** MIDDLE ENGLISH *coppice*, from FRENCH *coupeiz* cut wood, from LATIN *colpare* strike, from *colpus* a blow. See cope.

**copy** FRENCH *copie*, from LATIN *copia* plenty.

**coquet** FRENCH *coqueter* flirt, from *coq* rooster.

**coquette**  See **coquet.**

**coquina**  SPANISH *coquina* shell-fish, from LATIN *concha* conch.

**coracle**  WELSH *corwg* leather-covered boat.

**coral**  FRENCH, from LATIN *coralium,* from GREEK *korallion.*

**coraline**  LATIN *corallina,* from *corallinus* coral-red.  See **coral.**

**corbel**  FRENCH *corb,* from LATIN *corvus* raven, from beaked shape.

**corchorus**  GREEK.

**cord**  FRENCH *corde,* from LATIN *chorda,* from GREEK *chorde* intestine.

**cordeling**  FRENCH *cordeler* twist.

**cordial**  LATIN *cordialis* relating to the heart, from *cor* heart.

**cordon**  FRENCH ribbon, from *corde.*  See **cord.**

**cordovan**  SPANISH *Cordoba* the city in Spain where the leather is manufactured.

**corduroy**  See **cord** + *duroy* a woolen fabric originating in England.  The French term *corde du roi* "cord of the king" referred to fabric used for king's hunting clothes.

**core**  FRENCH, probably from LATIN *cor* heart.

**coriander**  MIDDLE ENGLISH, from FRENCH, from LATIN *conriandrum,* from GREEK *koriandron.*

**cork**  SPANISH *alcorque,* from ARABIC *qurk,* from LATIN *cortex* bark of the cork oak tree.

**cormorant**  MIDDLE ENGLISH, from FRENCH *cormareng,* from *corp marenc,* from LATIN *corvus marinus,* from *corvus* raven + *marinus* marine.

**corn**  OLD ENGLISH grain with the seed still in.

**cornea**  MIDDLE ENGLISH, from LATIN *cornia tela* horny web, from the way the eye looks when it has a certain eye disease.

**corner**  FRENCH *cornere* angle, from LATIN *corneria,* from *cornu* point.

**cornet**  FRENCH little horn, from LATIN *cornu.*

**cornice**  FRENCH part of a wall, from ITALIAN *cornice,* from GREEK *koronis* something curved.

**cornpone**  See **corn** + NATIVE AMERICAN *pone* baked bread.

**cornucopia**  LATIN *cornu copia* horn of plenty, from Greek mythology.

**corolla**  LATIN crown, from GREEK *korone* wreath.

**corollary**  LATIN *corollarium* wreath of flowers given as a gift, from *corolla* little wreath.  See **crown.**

**corona**  See **crown.**

**coronary**  See **crown.**

**coronation**  See **crown.**

**coronet**  FRENCH *coronete,* from *corone,* from LATIN *corona* crown.

**corporal**[1] (soldier)  FRENCH, from LATIN *caporale,* from *capo* head.

**corporal**[2] (body)  LATIN *caporalis,* from *corpus* body.

**corporate**  LATIN *corporare* make into a body or group, from *corpus* body.

**corps**  See **corpse.**

**corpse**  FRENCH *corps* body, from LATIN *corpus.*

**corpulence**  FRENCH, from LATIN *corpulentia,* from *corpus* body.

**Corpus Christi**  LATIN body of Christ.

**corpuscle**  LATIN *corpuscuium,* from *corpus* body.

**corral**  SPANISH something closed or fenced in, from *corro* ring, from *correr,* from LATIN *currere* run.

**correct** LATIN *corrigere,* from *com-* together + *regere* lead straight.

**correlate** LATIN *correlatio,* from *com-* with + *referre,* from *re-* back + *ferre* bring.

**correspond** LATIN *correspondere* answer each other, from *com-* together + *respondere* answer.

**corridor** FRENCH passage, from ITALIAN *corridore* runner, from LATIN *currere* run.

**corrigible** FRENCH, from LATIN *corrigere.* See **correct.**

**corroborate** LATIN *corroborare* strengthen, from *com-* very much + *robur* oak, strength.

**corrode** LATIN *corrodere,* from *com-* very much + *rodere* gnaw.

**corrugate** LATIN *corrugare* wrinkle.

**corrupt** LATIN *corrumpere* ruin, from *com-* together + *rumpere* break to pieces.

**corsage** FRENCH chest, from *cors* body, from LATIN *corpus.*

**corsair** FRENCH *corsaire,* from ITALIAN *corsao,* from LATIN *cursus* course.

**corse** See **corpse.**

**corselet** See **corset.**

**corselette** See **corset.**

**corset** FRENCH little body, from *cors* body, from LATIN *corpus.*

**cortege** FRENCH, from ITALIAN *corteggio,* from LATIN *cohors* crowd.

**cortex** LATIN bark of a tree.

**cortisone** GREEK *cortiscosteron,* from *cortico* cortex (gray matter covering the brain).

**coruscate** LATIN *coruscus* shimmer.

**corvette** FRENCH, from LATIN *corbita navis* slow sailing ship, from *corbis* basket.

**corynebacterium** GREEK *koryne* club + LATIN, from GREEK *bakterion* stick. When bacteria were first seen under the microscope they looked like little sticks.

**cosmetic** GREEK *kosmetikos* skilled in arranging, from *kosmos* order, the world.

**cosmic** GREEK *kosmikos,* from *kosmos* order, the world.

**cosmography** See **cosmos** + **-graphy.**

**cosmonaut** RUSSIAN *kosmonaut,* from GREEK *kosmos* order, the world + *nautes* sailor.

**cosmopolitan** GREEK *kosmopolites* citizen of the world, from *kosmos* order, the world + *polites* citizen, from *polis* city.

**cosmos** GREEK *kosmos* order, the world.

**cossack** RUSSIAN *kozak.*

**cossus** LATIN the larvae of a moth found under tree bark.

**cost** FRENCH *co(u)ster,* from LATIN *constare,* from *com-* together + *stare* stand.

**coster** (hanging) FRENCH *costier* side, from LATIN *costera* is found.

**costume** FRENCH style of dress, from ITALIAN dress, from LATIN *consuetudo* custom, from *com-* very much + *sue* be used to.

**cot**[1] (bed) HINDI *khat.*

**cot**[2] (house) See **cottage.**

**cote** OLD ENGLISH, from OLD NORSE *kot.* See **cottage.**

**cotehardie** FRENCH *cote-hardie.*

**coterie** FRENCH organization of peasants, from *cotier* tenant of a cote. See **cottage.**

**cottage** FRENCH *cotage,* from *cote* hut, probably from OLD NORSE *kot* hut.

**cottier** FRENCH *cotier,* from *cota* cot. See **cottage.**

**cotton** FRENCH *coton*, from ARABIC *qutn*.

**couch** FRENCH *couche* place for lying down, from LATIN *collocare* place together, from *com-* together + *locare* place.

**couchant** FRENCH.

**cough** MIDDLE ENGLISH *coughen*, from GREEK *keuchen* grasp.

**coulter** OLD ENGLISH *culter*, from LATIN *culter* knife.

**council** FRENCH *concile* assembly, from LATIN *concilium*, from *com-* with + *calere* call.

**counsel** FRENCH *conseil* advice, from LATIN *consilium*.

**count**[1] (add up) FRENCH, from LATIN *computare*, from *com-* with + *putare* think.

**count**[2] (nobleman) FRENCH, from LATIN *comitis* companion, from *com-* with +*ire* go.

**countenance** FRENCH, from LATIN *continentia* bearing, from *continere* contain.

**counter-** LATIN *contra-* against.

**counter**[1] (opposite) FRENCH *contre* against, from LATIN *contra-*.

**counter**[2] (long table) FRENCH *counteour* counting table, from LATIN *computatorium* place for counting, from *computare*, from *com-* with + *putare* think.

**counterfeit** FRENCH *contrefaire* copy, from LATIN *contra-* against + *facere* do, make.

**countermand** FRENCH, from LATIN *contra-* against + *mandare* command.

**counterpoint**[1] (music) FRENCH *contrepoint*, from LATIN *cantus contrapunctus* song pointed against, from *contra-* against + *puncta* prick.

**counterpoint**[2] (stitching) FRENCH *cuilte contrepointe* quilt stitched through and through, from *coute pointe*, from LATIN *culcita puncta* quilted mattress, from *culcita* cushion + *puncta* prick.

**country** FRENCH *contree* area, from LATIN *contrata* landscape, from *contra-* against, that which is opposite one's view, or the landscape in front of you.

**county** FRENCH *conte* land ruled by a count, from LATIN *comes*.

**coup** FRENCH blow (hit), from LATIN *colpus*, from *colaphus*, from GREEK *kolaphos*.

**couple** FRENCH *co(u)ple* pair, from LATIN *copula* connection.

**coupon** FRENCH piece cut off, from *couper* cut, from *coup*.

**courage** FRENCH *corage* feelings, from LATIN *cor* heart.

**course** FRENCH *cours* a running, from LATIN *cursus* place for running.

**courser** See **course**.

**court** FRENCH *cort* royal court, from LATIN *cohors* company of soldiers.

**courteous** FRENCH *corteis*, from *cort*. See **court** + **-eous**.

**courtesan** FRENCH, from ITALIAN *cortigana* court lady, from *corte* court.

**courtesy** FRENCH *curteisie*, from *court*.

**courtier** possibly from FRENCH *cortoyer* be at court. See **court**.

**couscous** FRENCH, from ARABIC *kuskus*, from *kuskasa* hit or pound into small parts.

**cousin** FRENCH, from LATIN *consobrinus* child of a mother's sister.

**couture** FRENCH sewing, from LATIN *consuere*, from *com-* together + *suere* sew.

**cove**[1] (small bay) OLD ENGLISH *cofa* cave, cell.

**cove**[2] (person) BRITISH slang, possibly from GYPSY *cova* person, thing.

**covenant** FRENCH promise, from *covenir* agree, from LATIN *convenire*. See **convene**.

**cover** FRENCH *covir* hide, from LATIN *cooperire* cover entirely.

**covert** FRENCH *covrir* cover. See **cover**.

**covet** FRENCH *coveitier,* from LATIN *cupiditas* desire.

**covey** FRENCH *covee* flock of birds, from *cover* hatch, from LATIN *cubare* lie down.

**cow** OLD ENGLISH *cu.*

**coward** MIDDLE ENGLISH, from FRENCH *coart,* from *cove* tail, from LATIN *cauda.* A frightened animal puts its tail between its legs.

**cower** SCANDINAVIAN.

**cowl** OLD ENGLISH *cug(e)le* monk's hood, from LATIN *cucullus* hood.

**cowlick** See **cow** + **lick**, probably from the idea that the hair looks as if it had been licked by a cow.

**cowslip** OLD ENGLISH *cuslyppe*, from *cu* cow + *slyppe* slimy stuff.

**coxa** LATIN *coxa* hip.

**coxcomb** See **cock**[1] + **comb**.

**coxswain** MIDDLE ENGLISH *cok* ship's boat + OLD NORSE *sveinn* boy.

**coy** FRENCH, from LATIN *quietus* quiet.

**cozy** possibly from NORWEGIAN *koselig* snug.

**crab** OLD ENGLISH *crabba.*

**crack** OLD ENGLISH *cracian* make a sharp breaking sound.

**crackle** See **crack**.

**-cracy** FRENCH, from LATIN, from GREEK *-kratia,* from *kratos* rule.

**cradle** OLD ENGLISH *cradol.*

**craft** OLD ENGLISH skill.

**crag** MIDDLE ENGLISH, related to WELSH *craig* rock.

**crakow** *Crakow,* in Poland, from where the shoes originally came.

**cram** OLD ENGLISH *crammian* stuff.

**cramp** FRENCH *crampe.*

**crampon** French *crampoun* brace.

**crane** OLD ENGLISH *cran* the bird, from the way the machine looks like the long neck of a bird.

**cranium** LATIN, from GREEK *kranion.*

**crank** MIDDLE ENGLISH, from OLD ENGLISH *cranc* bent.

**cranny** FRENCH *cran,* from LATIN *crena* a notch (a V-shaped cut).

**crape** See **crepe**.

**crash** MIDDLE ENGLISH *crashen* smash, from FRENCH *crasir.*

**crass** LATIN *crassus* gross.

**cratch** MIDDLE ENGLISH *crecche,* from FRENCH *creche* manger.

**crate** LATIN *cratis* something made from wicker (wood strips woven together).

**crater** GREEK *krater.*

**cravat** FRENCH *cravate* necktie, from *Cravate* (French for "Croatian"). Croatians in the 17th century French army wore linen scarves.

**crave** OLD ENGLISH *crafian* demand.

**craven** FRENCH, from LATIN *crepare* creak.

**craw** MIDDLE ENGLISH *craue.*

**crawl** OLD NORSE *krafla.*

**crawfish** See **crayfish**.

**crayfish** MIDDLE ENGLISH *crevise,* from FRENCH *crevice,* from GERMAN *krebiz* crab.

**crayon** FRENCH pencil, from *craie* chalk, from LATIN *creta.*

**craze** MIDDLE ENGLISH *crasen* crack.

**creak** MIDDLE ENGLISH *creken.*

**cream** FRENCH *cresme* fatty part of milk, from LATIN *cramum,* from *chrisma* holy oil, from GREEK *chrisma* ointment (medicine for healing the skin).

**crease** MIDDLE ENGLISH *creste* crest, from FRENCH, from LATIN *crista.*

**create** LATIN *creare* make.

**creature** FRENCH animal, from LATIN *creature* thing created, from *creare* make.

**creche** FRENCH, from GERMAN *kiprra* crib.

**credence** FRENCH, from LATIN *credere.* See **creed.**

**credenza** ITALIAN, from LATIN *credentia* credence (originally a sideboard holding food to be tasted before serving).

**credible** LATIN *credere.* See **creed.**

**credit** FRENCH trust, from LATIN *creditum* loan, from *credere.* See **creed.**

**creed** OLD ENGLISH *creda* belief, from LATIN *credo* I believe, from *credere* trust.

**creek** MIDDLE ENGLISH *creke,* from OLD NORSE *kriki* a winding.

**creel** MIDDLE ENGLISH, originally SCOTTISH.

**creep** OLD ENGLISH *creopan.*

**creepie** See **creep.**

**cremate** LATIN *cremare.*

**crenel** FRENCH *crenel,* from *cren* notch.

**crenelate** See **crenel** + **-ate.**

**creosote** GREEK *kreas* flesh + *sozein* save.

**crepe** FRENCH *crépe,* from LATIN *crispus.*

**crepuscular** LATIN *crepusculum* twilight.

**crescendo** ITALIAN increase, from LATIN *crescere* grow.

**crescent** FRENCH *creissant* crescent of the moon, from LATIN *crescere* grow.

**crest** FRENCH, from LATIN *crista.*

**crevasse** FRENCH *crevace.* See **crevice.**

**crevice** FRENCH *crevace,* from *crever* split, from LATIN *crepare* crack.

**crew** FRENCH *creistre* grow, from LATIN *crescere.*

**crib** OLD ENGLISH *cribb* basket.

**cribbage** See **crib** + **-age.**

**cricket**[1] (insect) FRENCH *criquer* creak.

**cricket**[2] (game) FRENCH, probably from DUTCH *cricke* a stick.

**crime** FRENCH fault, from LATIN *crimen* offense.

**criminently** colloquial expression. See **crime.**

**crimp** GERMAN *krimpen* shrink.

**crimson** LATIN, from ARABIC *qirmiz.*

**cringe** OLD ENGLISH *cringan* fall in battle.

**crinkle** OLD ENGLISH *crincan.*

**crinoline** FRENCH hair cloth, from ITALIAN *crinolino,* from *crino* horsehair + *lino* thread, from LATIN *crinis* hair + *linum* flax.

**cripple** OLD ENGLISH *crypel* lame person.

**crisis** LATIN, from GREEK *krinein* separate.

**crisp** OLD ENGLISH curly, from LATIN *crispus.*

**criss-cross** MIDDLE ENGLISH *crist-crosse* Christ's cross.

**criterion** GREEK *krites* judge.

**critic** LATIN *criticus* able to judge, from GREEK *kritikos,* from *krites* judge.

**croak** OLD ENGLISH *cræcettan.*

**crochet** FRENCH little hook, of SCANDINAVIAN origin.

**crock** OLD ENGLISH *crocca* clay pot.

**crocodile** FRENCH, from LATIN, from GREEK *kiokodillos*.

**crocus** LATIN, from GREEK *krokos*.

**croissant** FRENCH crescent.

**croker** See **crocus**.

**crone** DUTCH *croonje* old sheep, from FRENCH *carogne* dead body of an animal, from LATIN *caro* flesh.

**crony** long-time friend, perhaps from GREEK *khronios* long-lasting, from *khronos* time.

**crook** OLD NORSE *krokr* hook.

**croon** DUTCH *cronen* growl.

**crop** OLD ENGLISH *cropp* ear of corn.

**croquet** FRENCH *crochet*, from *croc* hook.

**cross** OLD ENGLISH *cros*, from OLD NORSE *kross*, from LATIN *crux*.

**crotch** MIDDLE ENGLISH *crucche*. See **crutch**.

**crotchet** FRENCH *crochet*, from *croc* hook.

**crouch** FRENCH *crochir* become bent, from *croc* hook, of SCANDINAVIAN origin.

**croup**[1] (ill) imitative.

**croup**[2] (rump) FRENCH *croupe*.

**crow** OLD ENGLISH *crawa*.

**crowd** OLD ENGLISH *cruden* press.

**crown** FRENCH *corone* crown, from LATIN *corona* wreath, from GREEK *korone* curved object.

**crucial** FRENCH cross-shaped, from LATIN *crux* cross, from choosing a road at a crossroad.

**crucible** LATIN *crucibilum* night lamp used to light a holy cross, from *crux* cross.

**crucify** FRENCH *crucifier* nail to a cross, from LATIN *crucifigere*, from *crux* cross + *figere* fix.

**crude** LATIN *crudus* raw.

**cruel** FRENCH harsh, from LATIN *crudelis*.

**cruet** FRENCH, from LATIN *crudus* rough.

**cruise** DUTCH *kruisen* cross, from LATIN *crux* cross.

**cruller** DUTCH *krullen* curl.

**crumb** OLD ENGLISH *cruma* piece.

**crumpet** MIDDLE ENGLISH *crumplen*, from *crimplen* wrinkle.

**crumple** OLD ENGLISH *crump* bent, crooked.

**crunch** imitative.

**crupper** FRENCH *cropiere*, from *crope* rump.

**crusade** LATIN *cruciata*, from *cruciare* mark with the sign of a cross, from *crux* cross.

**crush** FRENCH *cruis(s)ir* break.

**crust** FRENCH *crouste*, from LATIN *crusta* shell.

**crustacean** LATIN *crusta* shell.

**crutch** OLD ENGLISH *crycc* staff.

**crux** LATIN cross.

**cry** FRENCH *crier* shout, from LATIN *quiritare* call for help from the *Quirites* (Roman citizens).

**crypt** LATIN *crypta* cave, from GREEK *kryptos* hidden.

**crystal** FRENCH *cristal*, from LATIN *crystallum* ice, from GREEK *krystallos*.

**cub** MIDDLE ENGLISH *cubbe* young fox.

**cube** LATIN *cubus* solid square, from GREEK *kybos*.

**cubicle** LATIN *cubiculum*, from *cubare* lie down.

**cubit** OLD ENGLISH, from LATIN *cubitum* the elbow.

**cuckoo** FRENCH *coucou cucu*. Imitative.

**cucumber** FRENCH, from LATIN *cucumis*.

**cuddle** possibly from MIDDLE ENGLISH *couthelen*, from *couth* someone known.

**cudgel** OLD ENGLISH *cycgel* club.

**cue**[1] (signal) possibly from the letter *Q*, for Latin *quando* meaning "when". The mark was found in the text of 16th century plays to show when the actor is to enter.

**cue**[2] (stick) FRENCH *queue*, from *coue*, from LATIN *cauda* tail.

**cuff** MIDDLE ENGLISH *cuffe* glove, from LATIN *cuphia* covering for the head.

**cuisine** FRENCH, from LATIN *coquina* kitchen, from *coquere* cook.

**cul-de-sac** FRENCH bottom of a sac, from LATIN *saccus* bag. See **sack**[1].

**culet**[1] (dues) FRENCH *cuillete*, from LATIN *collecta* collection of dues.

**culet**[2] (bottom) FRENCH *cul*, from LATIN *culus* anus.

**culinary** LATIN *culina* kitchen.

**cull** FRENCH *coillir* collect, from LATIN *colligere*.

**cullet** FRENCH *collet*, from *col* neck, from LATIN *collum*.

**culminate** LATIN *culminare*, from *culmen* peak.

**culotte** FRENCH *cul* rear end, from LATIN *culus*.

**culprit** FRENCH *culpable prit* guilty, ready, from LATIN *praesto* ready. From medieval law courts where the prosecutor said "Guilty—ready", which meant that he thought the accused was guilty and he was ready to prove it.

**cult** FRENCH *culte*, from LATIN *cultus* cultivation, worship, from *culere*. See **cultivate**.

**culter** See **coulter**.

**cultivate** LATIN *cultivare* prepare land for crops, from *culere* work land by plowing, etc.

**cultivator** See **cultivate**.

**culture** LATIN farming.

**culverin** FRENCH *couleuvre*, from LATIN *colubra* snake. Names of reptiles were frequently applied to early cannon.

**culvert** origin uncertain.

**cum** LATIN.

**cum laude** LATIN.

**cumber** FRENCH *encomber*, from *en-* in + *combre* something in the way.

**cumbrous** See **cumber** + -ous.

**cummerbund** HINDI *kamarband* male covering cloth for the lower abdomen.

**cumulate** LATIN *cumulare* heap up.

**cumulus** LATIN a heap.

**cuneiform** LATIN *cuneus* a wedge + FRENCH *forme* shape, from LATIN *forma*.

**cunning** MIDDLE ENGLISH knowing, from OLD ENGLISH *cunnan* know.

**cup** OLD ENGLISH *cuppa*, from LATIN *cupa* tub.

**cupola** ITALIAN dome (rounded roof), from LATIN *cupula* little cask (barrel for holding liquid), from *cupa* tub.

**cur** OLD NORSE *kurra* growl.

**curb** MIDDLE ENGLISH *courbe* bend, from FRENCH *courber*, from LATIN *curvare*.

**curd** MIDDLE ENGLISH *crud* any thickened liquid, probably from OLD ENGLISH *crudan* press.

**cure** FRENCH *curer* heal, from LATIN *curare*.

**curfew** FRENCH *coeverfu* cover fire, putting fires out at night, from *covrir* cover + *feu* fire. See **cover**.

**curiosity** LATIN *curiositas* desire for knowledge.

**curl** MIDDLE ENGLISH *curlen*, from *crulle* curly.

**curlew** FRENCH *corlieu*. Imitative.

**curlicue** See **curl** + **cue**[2].

**currant** FRENCH *raisins de Corauntz* raisins of Corinth.

**current** FRENCH *courre* run, from LATIN *currere*.

**curriculum** LATIN course of study.

**curry**[1] (brush) MIDDLE ENGLISH *curraien*, from FRENCH *correier* put in order.

**curry**[2] (sauce) TAMIL *kari*.

**curse** OLD ENGLISH *curs*.

**cursive** LATIN *cursivus* running, from *currere* run.

**cursory** LATIN *cursorius* quick in motion, from *cursor* runner.

**curt** LATIN *curius*.

**curtail** FRENCH *court* short, from LATIN *curtus* cut short.

**curtain** FRENCH, from LATIN *cortina* something (like a cloth) that is hanging around an enclosed place, from *cors* enclosed place.

**curtsy** See **courtesy**.

**curve** LATIN *curvus* bent.

**cushion** FRENCH *coissin*, from LATIN *coxa* hip.

**cusp** LATIN *cuspis* a point.

**custard** LATIN *crusta* crust.

**custody** LATIN *custodia* guard.

**custom** FRENCH *custume*, from LATIN *consuetudo* habit, from *com-* very much + *suere* be used to.

**cut** MIDDLE ENGLISH *cutten*, of SCANDINAVIAN origin.

**cute** See **acute**.

**cutlass** FRENCH *coutelas*, from LATIN *cultellus* little knife, from *culter* knife.

**cutler** FRENCH, from LATIN *culter* knife.

**cutlery** See **cutler** + -y[3].

**cutlet** See **cut** + **-let**.

**cwm** WELSH.

**-cy** FRENCH *–cie*, from LATIN *–cia*, from GREEK *-kia*.

**cyanide** GREEK *kyanos* blue + *-ide* use in names of simple chemical compounds.

**cycle** LATIN *cyclus*, from GREEK *kyklos* circle.

**cyclo-** GREEK *kyklos* circle.

**cyclone** GREEK *kyklon* moving in a circle, whirling around, from *kyklos* circle.

**cyclops** LATIN, from GREEK *kyklops* round-eyed.

**cyclorama** GREEK *kyklos* circle + *horama* sight, from *horan* see.

**cygnet** FRENCH *cynge*, from LATIN *cygnus* swan, from GREEK *kyknos*.

**cygnus** LATIN, from GREEK *kyknos*.

**cylinder** LATIN *cylindrus*, from GREEK *kylin dein* roll.

**cymbal** FRENCH, from LATIN *cymbalum*, from GREEK *kymble* hollow part of something used for eating or drinking.

**cynic** LATIN *cynicus* name for a group of Greek thinkers called the *Cynics*, from GREEK *kynikos* doglike, describing the bad temper thought to be shown by those thinkers.

**cypress** FRENCH, from LATIN *cupressus*, from GREEK *kyparissos*.

**cyst** LATIN *cystis*, from GREEK *kystis* pouch.

**cythara** See **cithara**.

**cytoplasm** GREEK *kytos* hollow, basket + *plasma* something molded.

**czar** RUSSIAN *tsar* emperor, from LATIN *Caesar* title used by Roman emperors.

# D

**dab** MIDDLE ENGLISH *dabben* strike.

**dabble** See **dab.**

**dad** child's word *dada.*

**dadder** See **dodder.**

**daddle** See **dodder.**

**daffodowndilly** See **daffodil.**

**daffodil** MIDDLE ENGLISH *affodill* asphodel, from LATIN *affodillus,* from *asphodelus,* from GREEK *asphodelos.*

**daft** MIDDLE ENGLISH *daffte* foolish, from OLD ENGLISH *gedæfte.*

**dagger** LATIN *daggarius.*

**dahlia** Anders *Dahl,* 18th century Swedish botanist.

**daily** OLD ENGLISH *dælic,* from *dæg* day.

**dainty** FRENCH *daintie* pleasure, from LATIN *dignitas* worth, from *dignus.*

**dairy** MIDDLE ENGLISH *deierie,* from OLD ENGLISH *dæge* female maker of bread.

**dais** FRENCH *deis* high table, from LATIN *discus* table, dish, from GREEK *diskos* round plate.

**daisy** OLD ENGLISH *dæges eage* day's eye.

**dale** OLD ENGLISH *dæl.*

**dally** FRENCH *dalier* talk.

**dam**[1] (hold water) GERMAN something built to hold back water.

**dam**[2] (lady) FRENCH *dame* lady.

**damage** FRENCH harm, from LATIN *damnum* loss.

**damask** MIDDLE ENGLISH *damaske,* from LATIN *Damascus,* city in the Middle East where the cloth, steel, etc. came, from, from GREEK *Damaskos,* from ARABIC *Dimashq.*

**dame** FRENCH lady, from LATIN *domina.*

**damn** FRENCH *damner* harm, from LATIN *damnare.*

**damosel** archaic or poetic for **damsel.**

**damp** GERMAN steam.

**damsel** FRENCH *dameisele,* from LATIN *domina* lady.

**damson** MIDDLE ENGLISH *damascene,* from LATIN *Prunum Damascenus* plum of Damascus. See **damask.**

**dance** FRENCH *danser.*

**dancette** LATIN *denticatus,* from *dens* tooth.

**dandelion** FRENCH *dent de lion* tooth of lion, from the pointed leaves, from LATIN *dens leonis.*

**dander** perhaps from SPANISH *redundar* overflow, from LATIN *redundare.*

**dandiprat**  perhaps from SCOTTISH, from *dandy* nickname for *Andrew* + *prat* prank, frolic.

**dandruff**  MIDDLE ENGLISH *dandruffe*, origin unknown, second part, from *huff, hurf* scab.

**dandy**  SCOTTISH nickname for *Andrew*.

**danger**  FRENCH *dangier* power, from LATIN *dominium* ownership, from *dominus* master.

**dangle**  SCANDINAVIAN.

**dapper**  possibly from DUTCH *dapper* moving lightly.

**dapple**  OLD NORSE *depill* a spot.

**dare**  OLD ENGLISH *durran*.

**dark**  OLD ENGLISH *deorc*.

**darling**  OLD ENGLISH *deorling* one dearly loved, from *deore* dear.

**darn**  FRENCH *darner* mend.

**dart**  FRENCH *dars* javelin, from LATIN *dardus*.

**dash**  SWEDISH *daska* slap.

**dastard**  MIDDLE ENGLISH, probably of SCANDINAVIAN origin.

**data**  LATIN things given, from *dare* give.

**date**  MIDDLE ENGLISH, from LATIN *dare* give. In ancient Rome, the first words of a letter were "I give this letter at Rome on (whatever the date was)".

**dative**  LATIN *dativus*, from *dare* give.

**dato**  SPANISH, from MALAY *datu* ruler.

**datum**  LATIN something given, from *dare* give.

**datura**  HINDI *dhatura* native name of the plant.

**daub**  FRENCH, from LATIN *dealbare* wash walls white, from *de-* entirely + *albus* white.

**daughter**  OLD ENGLISH *dohtor*.

**daunt**  FRENCH *danter* tame, from LATIN *domitare*.

**dauphin**  FRENCH the name *Dolphin*.

**davenport**  variously a couch, a desk or china, all from names of the makers.

**davit**  FRENCH diminutive of *David*.

**dawdle**  perhaps from early MODERN ENGLISH *daddle* walk unsteadily.

**dawn**  OLD ENGLISH *dagian* become day, from *dæg* day.

**day**  OLD ENGLISH *dæg*.

**daze**  OLD NORSE *dasast* become weary, from *dasi* tired.

**dazzle**  See **daze**.

**de-**  either LATIN *de-* from, away, down, entirely, or *dis-* apart, away.

**deacon**  OLD ENGLISH minister of the Christian Church, from LATIN *diaconus*, from GREEK *diadonos* servant.

**dead**  OLD ENGLISH *dead*.

**deaf**  OLD ENGLISH *deaf*.

**deal**  OLD ENGLISH *dælan* divide.

**dean**  FRENCH *deien* head of a church, from LATIN *decanus* leader of ten persons, from *decem* ten.

**dear**  OLD ENGLISH *deore* beloved.

**debase**  See **de-** + **abase**.

**debate**  FRENCH *debatre* argue, from LATIN *de-* down + *battuere* beat.

**debauch**  FRENCH *desbaucher* persuade to do something bad.

**debilitate**  LATIN *debilitare* weaken, from *debilis* weak.

**debit**  FRENCH, from LATIN *debitum* what is owing, from *debere*.  See **debt**.

**debonair** FRENCH *de bon aire* "of good breed".

**debouch** FRENCH *de-* away + *bouche* the mouth.

**debris** FRENCH *debrisier* break into pieces, from *de-* down + *brisier* break.

**debt** FRENCH, from LATIN *debere* owe, from *de-* from + *havere* have.

**debut** FRENCH *débuter* lead off, from *jouer de but* a first play, as in a game.

**decade** FRENCH, from LATIN *decas,* from GREEK *dekas* group of ten, from *deka* ten.

**decadence** FRENCH, from LATIN *decadentia,* from *de-* away + *cadere* fall (from what is good).

**decal** FRENCH *decalcomania,* from *de-* away + *calquer* copy + *manie* mania, fad.

**decanter** FRENCH, from LATIN *de-* from + *canthus* edge + OLD ENGLISH *-ere.*

**decapitate** FRENCH, from LATIN *decapitare,* from *de-* off + *caput* head.

**decay** FRENCH *decair* fall off, from LATIN *de-* away + *cadere* fall.

**decease** FRENCH, from LATIN *decedere,* from *de-* from + *cedere* go.

**deceit** FRENCH *deceite,* from *deceveir.* See **deceive.**

**deceive** FRENCH *deceveir,* from LATIN *decipere* capture, from *de-* from + *capere* take.

**December** FRENCH *Decembre,* from LATIN *December* name of the tenth month of the Roman calendar which started with March as the first month, from *decem* ten.

**decent** LATIN *decere* suitable.

**decibel** LATIN *decem* ten + *bel* after Alexander Graham *Bell.*

**decide** LATIN *decidere,* from *de-* off, from *caedere* cut.

**deciduous** LATIN *deciduus,* from *decidere* fall off, from *de-* down + *cadere* fall.

**decimal** LATIN *decimus* tenth.

**decimate** LATIN *decimare,* from *decem* ten. In ancient Rome, armies who revolted were punished by killing every tenth soldier in that army.

**decipher** See **de-** + **cipher.**

**decision** See **decide.**

**deck** DUTCH *dec* roof.

**declaim** LATIN *declamare,* from *de-* very much + *clamare* shout.

**declare** LATIN *declarare* make clear, from *de-* completely + *clarus* clear.

**declension** FRENCH, from LATIN *declinare.* See **decline.**

**decline** FRENCH *decliner* turn aside, from LATIN *declinare,* from *de-* from + *clinare* bend.

**declivity** LATIN *de-* down + *clivus* a slope.

**décor** FRENCH, from LATIN *decere* befit (be proper).

**decorate** LATIN *decorare,* from *decus* ornament.

**decorum** LATIN *decorus* proper.

**decoupage** FRENCH, from *decouper,* from *de-* out + *couper* cut.

**decoy** DUTCH *de kooi* the cage, from LATIN *cavea.*

**decrease** FRENCH *decreistre,* from LATIN *decrescere,* from *de-* from + *crescere* grow.

**decree** FRENCH, from LATIN *decretum,* from *de-* from + *cernere* decide.

**decrepit** FRENCH, from LATIN *de-* very much + *crepare* creak.

**decry** FRENCH *descrier* cry down, from LATIN *disquiritare.* See **de-** + **cry.**

**dedicate** LATIN *dedicare* declare, from *dicere* speak.

**deduce** LATIN *deducere,* from *de-* down + *ducere* lead.

**deed** OLD ENGLISH *dæd* act.

**deem** OLD ENGLISH *deman* judge.

**deep** OLD ENGLISH *deop.*

**deer** OLD ENGLISH *deor* animal, beast.

**deface** FRENCH *desfacier,* from LATIN *dis-* away + *facies* face.

**defame** FRENCH *diffamer,* from LATIN *diffamare,* from *dis-* away + *fama* reputation.

**default** FRENCH *defaute* lack, from LATIN *de-* from + *fallere* fail.

**defeat** FRENCH *desfaire,* from *dis-* from + *facere* do, make.

**defect** LATIN *deficere* failure, from *de-* from + *facere* do, make.

**defend** FRENCH *defendre* protect, from LATIN *defendere,* from *de-* away + *fendere* strike.

**defense** FRENCH, from LATIN *defendere.* See **defend.**

**defer** MIDDLE ENGLISH *differen,* from FRENCH *differer,* from LATIN *differre,* from *dis-* apart + *ferre* bring.

**defiant** FRENCH. See **defy.**

**deficit** FRENCH *déficit* shortage, from LATIN *deficere* be wanting. See **defect.**

**defile** FRENCH *defouler* walk on and make dirty, from OLD ENGLISH *fylan* dirty.

**define** MIDDLE ENGLISH *deffinen* state, explain the meaning of, from FRENCH *definer,* from LATIN *definire* limit, determine, define, from *de-* fully, completely + *finire* limit, mark the boundary of.

**definite** MIDDLE ENGLISH precise, established, from LATIN *definitus,* from *definire* mark the limits of.

**deflate** LATIN *de-* down + *in-* in + *flare* blow.

**deflect** LATIN *deflecter,* from *de-* from + *flectere* bend.

**deform** LATIN *deformare,* from *de-* from + *forme* form.

**defraud** FRENCH, from LATIN *defraudare,* from *de-* from + *fraus* fraud.

**defray** FRENCH, from LATIN *de-* entirely + *fraier* spend.

**deft** OLD ENGLISH *gedæfte* gentle.

**defunct** LATIN *defungi* finish, from *de-* from + *fungi* perform.

**defy** MIDDLE ENGLISH *defien,* from FRENCH *derier* lose faith in God, from LATIN *dis-* apart + *fidus* faithful.

**degenerate** LATIN *degenerare,* from *de-* down + *genus* race.

**degrade** FRENCH *degrader* take away the rank of, from LATIN *de-* down + *gradus* grade or rank.

**degree** FRENCH *defré* step, from LATIN *degradare,* from *de-* down + *gradus* grade or rank.

**deify** FRENCH *deifier* make a god of, from LATIN *deus* a god + *facere* make.

**deign** FRENCH *deignier* think worthy, from LATIN *dignari.*

**deism** FRENCH, from LATIN *deus* god.

**déjà vu** FRENCH already seen.

**deject** LATIN *dejicere,* from *de-* from + *jacere* throw.

**delaine** MODERN ENGLISH *muslin delaine,* from FRENCH *mousseline de laine* woolen muslin.

**delay** FRENCH *delaier*, from *de-* entirely + *laier* leave, from LATIN *laxare*.

**delectable** FRENCH, from LATIN *delectare*. See **delight**.

**delegate** LATIN *delegare*, from *de-* from + *legare* send.

**delete** LATIN *delere*, from *de-* from + *linere* smear.

**deliberate** LATIN *deliberare* weigh well, from *de-* completely + *libare* weigh, from *libra* scales.

**delicate** LATIN *delicatus* dainty. See **delight**.

**delicatessen** GERMAN *Delikatesse* very good food, from FRENCH, from LATIN *delicatus* very nice.

**delicious** FRENCH *delicieus* fine, from LATIN *deliciosus* pleasant, from *delicia*.

**delight** FRENCH *delitier* please, from LATIN *delectare*, from *de-* from + *lacere* cause to want.

**delineate** LATIN *delineare* sketch out, from *de-* down + *linea* line.

**delinquent** LATIN *delinquere*, from *de-* from + *linquere* leave.

**delirium** LATIN *delirum* madness, from going outside of the furrow (groove made during plowing), from *de-* from + *lira* line.

**deliver** FRENCH *delivrer* set free, from LATIN *deliberare*, from *de-* from + *liber* free.

**dell** OLD ENGLISH *del*.

**delphi** GREEK *delphis*, from *delphinos* dolphin, related to *delphys* womb.

**delude** LATIN *deludere*, from *de-* from + *ludere* play.

**deluge** FRENCH flood, from LATIN *diluvium*, from *dis-* off + *lavere* wash.

**deluxe** FRENCH *de luxe* of luxury, from LATIN *de-* of + *luxus* luxury.

**delve** OLD ENGLISH *delfan* dig.

**demagogue** GREEK *demagogos* popular leader, from *demos* people + *agogos* leader.

**demand** FRENCH *demander* ask, from LATIN *demandare*, from *de-* from + *mandare* trust.

**demarcation** SPANISH *linea de demarcacion*, from *de-* from + *marcar* mark. Originally the Line of Demarcation laid down by the Pope, dividing the New World between Spain and Portugal.

**demeanor** FRENCH, from LATIN *de-* from + *minari* threaten.

**dementia** LATIN madness, from *de-* down + *mens* mind.

**demerit** FRENCH, from LATIN *demereri* merit, from *de-* from + *mereri* deserve.

**demesne** FRENCH *demeine* belonging to a lord, from LATIN *dominum*.

**demi-** FRENCH, from LATIN *dimedius*, from *dimidus*, from *dis-* apart + *medius* middle.

**demiculverin** See **demi-** + **culverin**.

**demijohn** FRENCH *damejeanne* Lady Jane.

**demise** FRENCH *demettre* send away, from LATIN *dimittere*, from *de-* down + *mittere* send.

**demitasse** FRENCH *demi-* half + *tasse* a cup.

**democracy** FRENCH *democratie* popular government, from LATIN *democratia*, from GREEK *demokratia*, from *demos* people + *kratein* rule.

**demoiselle** FRENCH, from earlier *damoiselle*. See **damsel**.

**demolish** FRENCH *demolir*, from LATIN *demoliri*, from *de-* down + *moliri* build, from *moles* a mass.

**demon** LATIN *daemon* evil spirit, from spirit, from GREEK *daimon* fate.

**demonstrate** LATIN *demonstrare*, from *de-* from + *monstrare* show.

**demur** FRENCH *demourer* delay, from LATIN *demorari*, from *de-* from + *mora* delay.

**demure** MIDDLE ENGLISH *de-* entirely + FRENCH *mëur* ripe, from LATIN *maturus*.

**den** OLD ENGLISH *denn* home of a wild animal.

**denigrate** LATIN *denigrare* blacken, from *de-* entirely + *nigrare* make black, from *niger* black.

**denizen** FRENCH *deinzein* one living within, from *dein* within, from LATIN *de-* from + *intus* within.

**denominate** LATIN *denominare*, from *de-* entirely + *nominare*, from *nomen* name.

**denominator** See **denominate**.

**denote** LATIN *denotare*, from *de-* down + *notare* mark, from *nota* note.

**denouement** FRENCH *dé-* out + *nouer* tie, from LATIN **dis-** + *nodus* a knot.

**denounce** FRENCH *denouncier* announce, from LATIN *denuntiare*, from *de-* entirely + *nuntiare* announce.

**dense** LATIN *densus* thick.

**dent** MIDDLE ENGLISH. See **dint**.

**denticle** LATIN *denticulus*, from *dentem, dens* tooth.

**dentil** FRENCH *dentille*, from *dent* tooth, from LATIN *dens*.

**dentist** FRENCH *dentiste*, from *dent* tooth, from LATIN *dens*.

**denude** LATIN *denudare*, from *de-* off + *nudare* strip.

**deny** FRENCH *denoier* oppose, from LATIN *denegare*, from *de-* entirely + *negare* reject.

**deodorant** LATIN *de-* from + *odor* smell.

**depart** FRENCH *departir* divide, from LATIN *dis-* apart + *partire* divide.

**depend** FRENCH *dependre*, from LATIN *dependere*, from *de-* down + *pendere* hang.

**depict** LATIN *depingere*, from *de-* from + *pintere* paint.

**deplete** LATIN *deplere*, from *de-* from + *plere* fill.

**deplore** LATIN *deplorare*, from *de-* entirely + *plorare* cry.

**deploy** FRENCH *déployer* unfold, from LATIN *displicare*, from *dis-* apart + *plicare* fold.

**deport** FRENCH *deporter* send away, from LATIN *deportare*, from *de-* from + *portare* carry.

**depose** FRENCH *deposer* put down, from LATIN *de-* from + *pausare* halt.

**deposit** LATIN *deponer* put aside, from *de-* down + *ponere* put.

**depot** FRENCH warehouse, from LATIN *depositum* deposit (something put down). See **deposit**.

**deprave** LATIN *depravare*, from *de-* down + *pravus* wicked.

**deprecate** LATIN *deprecare*, from *de-* off + *precari* pray.

**depreciate** LATIN *depretiare*, from *de-* down + *pretium* price.

**depredation** LATIN *depraedari*, from *de-* entirely + *praedari* waste.

**depress** LATIN *deprimere*, from *de-* down + *premere* press.

**deprive** FRENCH *depriver*, from LATIN *de-* down + *privare* separate.

**depth** OLD ENGLISH *depthe*, from *deop*.

**depute** FRENCH *deputer*, from LATIN *deputare*, from *de-* down + *putare* make clean.

**deputy** See **depute**.

**derail** FRENCH *dérailler*. See **rail**.

**derailleur** FRENCH *dérailleur.* See **rail.**

**derange** FRENCH *deranger* change the arrangement of, from *des-* apart + *rengier* put in a row.

**derby** *Derby,* the name of a town in England, which is the site of an annual horse race.

**derelict** LATIN *derelinquere,* from *de-* entirely + *relinquere* relinquish (give up or abandon).

**deride** LATIN *deridere,* from *de-* down + *ridere* laugh.

**derive** FRENCH *deriver,* from LATIN *derivare,* from *de-* from + *rivus* stream.

**derrick** *Derrick,* the name of an early 17th century London hangman. First applied to the gallows, later to the crane.

**dervish** Middle East *darvesh* beggar.

**descant** FRENCH, from LATIN *dis-* apart + *cantus* song.

**descend** FRENCH *descendre,* from LATIN *de-* down + *scindere* climb.

**describe** LATIN *describere,* from *de-* from + *scribere* write.

**descry** FRENCH *descrier* announce, from *des-* from + *crier* cry, from LATIN *quiritare.*

**desecrate** MODERN ENGLISH *de-* do the opposite of + *(con)secrate.*

**desert** FRENCH, from LATIN *deserere,* from *de-* from + *serere* join.

**deserve** FRENCH *deservir,* from LATIN *deservire,* from *de-* entirely + *servire* serve.

**design** FRENCH *désigner* mark out, from LATIN *designare,* from *de-* out + *signum* a mark.

**desire** FRENCH *desirer,* from LATIN *desiderare* miss.

**desist** FRENCH, from LATIN *de-* from + *sistere* cause to stand, from *stare* stand.

**desk** LATIN *desca,* from LATIN *diskos* table, from LATIN *discus* dish, from GREEK *diskos* round plate.

**desolate** LATIN *desolare* abandon, from *de-* entirely + *solare* make lonely, from *solus* alone.

**despair** FRENCH *desperer* lose hope, from LATIN *desperare,* from *de-* away + *spes* hope.

**desperado** Old Spanish, from LATIN *desperare.* See **despair.**

**desperate** LATIN *desperare* lose hope. See **despair.**

**despise** FRENCH *despire* insult, from LATIN *despicere,* from *de-* down + *spicere* look.

**despite** FRENCH *despit* anger, from LATIN *despicere,* from *de-* down + *spicere* look.

**despoil** FRENCH, from LATIN *de-* entirely + *spoilare* spoil.

**despond** LATIN *despondere* give up, from *de-* from + *spondere* promise.

**despot** FRENCH chief lord, from GREEK *despotes* master.

**dessert** FRENCH *desservir* clear the table, from *des-* from + *servir,* from LATIN *servire* serve.

**destiny** FRENCH *destiner* fix, from LATIN *destinare* establish, from *de-* entirely + *stare* stand.

**destroy** FRENCH *destruire* ruin, from LATIN *destruere,* from *de* down + *struere* build.

**desultory** LATIN *desultor* one who jumps, from *desiltre,* from *de-* from + *salire* leap.

**detail** FRENCH *detailler* cut in pieces, from LATIN *de-* entirely + *talea* cutting.

**detain** LATIN *detinere,* from *de-* from + *tenere* hold.

**detect** LATIN *detegere,* from *de-* from + *tegere* cover.

**deter** LATIN *deterrere,* from *de-* from + *terrere* frighten.

**detergent** LATIN *detergere,* from *de-* off + *tergere* wipe.

**deteriorate** LATIN *deterior* worse.

**determine** FRENCH *determiner* make a decision about, from LATIN *determinare* limit, from *de-* entirely + *terminare* set bounds, from *terminus* an end.

**detest** FRENCH *detester,* from LATIN *detestari* curse somebody while calling a god to observe (witness) it, from *de-* entirely + *testis* witness.

**detonate** LATIN *detonare,* from *de-* from + *tonare* thunder.

**detour** FRENCH *détour,* from *détourner* turn away, from LATIN *dis-* apart + *tornare* turn. See **turn.**

**detract** LATIN *detrahere,* from *de-* from + *trahere* draw.

**detriment** LATIN *detrimentum,* from *deterere* damage, from *de-* off + *terere* rub.

**deuce** MIDDLE ENGLISH *dewes* two, from FRENCH *deus,* from LATIN *duo* two.

**deuterium** LATIN, from GREEK *deuteros* second.

**devastate** LATIN *devastare,* from *de-* entirely + *vastare* make empty, from *vastus* empty.

**develop** FRENCH *développer* unfold, from LATIN *dis-* apart + FRENCH *voloper* wrap.

**deviate** LATIN *deviare* go aside, from *de-* away + *via* way.

**device** FRENCH *devise* invention, from *deviser* divide. See **devise.**

**devil** OLD ENGLISH *deofol,* from LATIN *diabolus,* from GREEK *diabolos,* from *diaballein* make false statements about someone, from *dia-* across + *ballein* throw.

**devious** LATIN *devius,* from *de-* from + *via* road.

**devise** FRENCH *derviser* divide, from LATIN *dividere.*

**devoid** FRENCH *desvoidier,* from LATIN *dis-* apart + *vacare* be empty.

**devolve** LATIN *devolvere,* from *de-* down + *volvere* roll.

**devote** LATIN *devovere,* from *de-* from + *vovere* vow.

**devour** FRENCH *devorer* tear to pieces, from LATIN *devorare,* from *de-* entirely + *vorare* swallow.

**devout** FRENCH *devot,* from LATIN *devovere,* from *de-* from + *vovere* vow.

**dew** OLD ENGLISH *deaw.*

**dexter** LATIN on the right side, skillful.

**dextrose** See **dexter** + -ose[2].

**dharma** HINDI moral law, from SANSKRIT justice.

**dia-** GREEK *dia-* through, apart, across, around.

**diabetes** LATIN, from GREEK *diabainein* pass through (having to do with getting rid of body fluids), from *dia-* through + *bainein* go.

**diabolic** FRENCH *diabolique,* from LATIN *diabolicus,* from GREEK *diabolikos* devilish, from *diabolos.*

**diabolo** ITALIAN, from GREEK *diabolos* accuser, slanderer.

**diacritic** GREEK *diakritkios,* from *dia-* across + *krinein* separate.

**diadem** LATIN *diadema* royal wear for the head, from GREEK *diadema* band, from *dia-* around + *dien* bind.

**diagnosis** LATIN, from GREEK *diagnosis* see differences, from *dia-* between + *gignoskein* know.

**diagon** See **diagonal.**

**diagonal** LATIN *diagonalis* from one angle across to another angle, from GREEK *diagonios*, from *dia-* across + *gonia* angle, corner.

**diagram** LATIN *diagramma* scale, from GREEK figure that is marked with lines, from *dia-* across + *graphein* write.

**dial** LATIN *dialis* having to do with the day, from *dies* day.

**dialect** LATIN *dialectus*, from GREEK *dialektos* speech, from *dia-* between + *legein* talk.

**dialogue** FRENCH *dialoge*, from GREEK *dialogos*, from *dia-* between + *legein* talk.

**diameter** FRENCH *diametre* diameter of a circle, from GREEK *diametros*, from *dia-* through + *metron* measure.

**diamond** FRENCH *diamant*, from LATIN *diamas*, from *adamas*, from GREEK *a-* not + *daman* tame.

**diaper** FRENCH *dia(s)pre* fine cloth, from LATIN *diasprus*, from GREEK *diaspros* pure white.

**diaphanous** GREEK *diaphanes*, from *dia-* through + *phainein* show.

**diaphragm** LATIN *diaphragma*, from GREEK *dia-* through + *phragma* a fence.

**diary** LATIN *diarium* daily record, from *dies* day.

**diastolic** GREEK *diastole*, from *dia-* apart + *stellien* put.

**diatom** GREEK *diatomos* cut in two, from *diatemnein*, from *dia-* through + *temnein* cut.

**diatonic** FRENCH *diatonique*, from LATIN, from GREEK *diatonikos* stretched through, from *dia-* through + *teinein* stretch.

**diatribe** LATIN *diatriba*, from GREEK *diatribe* wearing away, from *dia-* through + *tribein* rub.

**dibble** MIDDLE ENGLISH *dibbel*, probably from *dibben* dip.

**dibs** *dibstone* part of a child's game.

**dice** MIDDLE ENGLISH *dis*. See **die**[2].

**dickcissel** imitative.

**dickens** probably from the name *Dick*.

**dicker** LATIN *dicker* set of ten pelts (skin and fur of animals). These were used for trading purposes.

**dictate** LATIN *dictare*, from *dicere* say.

**diction** LATIN *dicere* say.

**dictionary** LATIN *dictionarium* book of sayings, from *dicere* say.

**dictum** See diction.

**didactic** GREEK *didaktikos*, from *didaskein* teach.

**dido** (prank, caper) AMERICAN slang, origin uncertain.

**die**[1] (dead) OLD NORSE *deyja* cease to live.

**die**[2] (one dice) MIDDLE ENGLISH *de* one of a pair of dice, from FRENCH *de*, from LATIN *datum* something given, from *dare* give.

**diesel** Rudolf *Diesel* (1858–1913), German inventor.

**diet** MIDDLE ENGLISH *diete*, from FRENCH, from LATIN *diaeta*, from GREEK *diaita* way of living.

**differ** MIDDLE ENGLISH *differren* see differences, from FRENCH *different*, from LATIN *differe*, from *dis-* apart + *ferre* bring.

**difficulty** LATIN *difficultas* trouble, from *dis-* apart + *facilis* easy.

**diffident** LATIN *diffidere*, from *dis-* not + *fidere* trust.

**diffuse** LATIN *diffundere*, from *dis-* apart + *fundere* pour.

**dig** FRENCH *diguer*, from *digue* ditch, from DUTCH *dij*.

**digest** LATIN *digerere* separate, from *di-* apart + *gerere* carry on.

**digit** LATIN *digitus* finger, toe.

**dignify** FRENCH *dignifier* make worthy, from LATIN *dignificare*, from *dignus* worthy + *facere* do, make.

**dignitary** LATIN *dignitas* dignity.

**dignity** FRENCH *dignete*, from LATIN *dignus* worthy.

**digress** LATIN *digredi*, from *dis-* apart + *gradi* go.

**dike** OLD ENGLISH *diki*.

**dilapidated** LATIN *dilapidare* throw away, from *dis-* apart + *lapis* stone.

**dilate** LATIN *dilatare*, from *dis-* apart + *latus* wide.

**dilemma** LATIN, from GREEK *di-* two + *lemma* suggestion.

**dilettante** ITALIAN *dilettare*, from LATIN *delectare* delight.

**diligence** FRENCH speed, from LATIN *diligentia* carefulness, from *di-* apart + *legere* choose.

**dill** OLD ENGLISH *dile* dill, anise.

**dilute** LATIN *diluere* wash away, from *dis-* off + *luere*, from *lavare* wash.

**dim** OLD ENGLISH *dimm* dark.

**dime** FRENCH *disme*, from LATIN *decima* tenth part, from *decimus* tenth, from *decem* ten.

**dimension** FRENCH measure, from LATIN *dimensio*, from *dis-* off + *metiri* measure.

**diminish** LATIN *diminuere* make smaller.

**diminution** MIDDLE ENGLISH, from FRENCH, from LATIN *deminutio*.

**diminutive** FRENCH *diminutif* smallness, from LATIN *deminutivus*, from *deminuere* lessen.

**dimity** ITALIAN *dimito* coarse cotton, from LATIN *dimitum*, from GREEK *dimiton* double threaded.

**dimples** MIDDLE ENGLISH *dimpel*.

**din** OLD ENGLISH *dyne* noise.

**dine** FRENCH *disner* have dinner, from LATIN *dis-* away + *jejunium* fast (eating little or no food) or breaking a fast.

**ding** probably from OLD NORSE *dengja* hammer.

**dinghy** HINDI *dingi* small boat.

**dingy** BRITISH of unknown origin, possibly from OLD ENGLISH *dyncgig* dirty, dung-covered.

**dinner** FRENCH *dîner* dine. See **dine**.

**dinosaur** GREEK *deinos* terrible + *sauros* lizard.

**dint** OLD ENGLISH *dynt* a blow.

**diopter** FRENCH *dioptre*, from LATIN *dioptra*, from GREEK *dioptra* instrument for leveling, from *dia* through + *opsis* sight.

**dioptric** GREEK *dioptricos* having to do with the **diopter**.

**dip** OLD ENGLISH *dyppan*.

**diphtheria** LATIN, from FRENCH, from GREEK *diphthera* leather, from *dephein* tan hides, named so because of the hardness of the layer of tissue that develops in the air passages due to the disease.

**diploma** LATIN, from GREEK folded letter, from *diploos* double.

**dire** LATIN *dirus* terrible.

**direct** LATIN *directus* straight, from *dirigere* lay straight, from *dis-* apart + *regere* guide.

**directrix** LATIN *directrix*, from *director*. See **direct**.

**dirge** LATIN *dirige* direct, which happened to be the first word in a funeral song. Later came to mean any funeral song. See **direct**.

**dirk** SCOTTISH, origin uncertain, probably from the proper name.

**dirt** OLD NORSE *drit* waste, from the body.

**dis-** LATIN *dis-* apart, away, not, entirely.

**disaster** FRENCH *désastre,* from LATIN *dis-* apart + *astrum* star, from GREEK *astron,* from the ancient belief that the stars could cause bad fortune.

**disburse** FRENCH *desbourser* take money from a purse, from LATIN *dis-* apart + *bursa* purse. See **purse**.

**discard** FRENCH. See **dis-** + **card**.

**discern** FRENCH *discerner,* from LATIN *discernere,* from *dis-* apart + *cernere* separate.

**discharge** FRENCH *descharger* unload, from LATIN *dis-* from + *carrus* wagon.

**disciple** OLD ENGLISH *discipul,* from LATIN *discipulus,* from *discere* learn.

**discipline** FRENCH, from LATIN *discipulus.* See **disciple**.

**discombobulate** AMERICAN made up word, originally *discombobricate*.

**discomfit** FRENCH *desconfire* defeat, from LATIN *dis-* apart + *conficere* make happen.

**disconsolate** See **dis-** + **console**.

**discord** FRENCH *descorde* a quarrel, from LATIN *discordare,* from *dis-* apart + *cor* heart.

**discount** FRENCH *desconter,* from LATIN *dis-* apart + *computare* count.

**discourage** FRENCH *descourager,* from LATIN *dis-* apart + *cor* heart.

**discourse** FRENCH, from LATIN *dis-* from + *currere* run.

**discover** FRENCH *descovrir* uncover, from LATIN *discooperire,* from *dis-* apart + *cooperire* cover.

**discreet** MIDDLE ENGLISH *discret,* from LATIN *discretus.*

**discrepancy** FRENCH, from LATIN *discrepare* sound differently, from *dis-* from + *crepare* rattle.

**discriminate** LATIN *discriminare* divide, from *discernere.* See **discern**.

**discuss** LATIN *discutere,* from *dis-* apart + *quatere* shake.

**disdain** FRENCH *desdeignier* scorn, from LATIN *dis-* not + *dignari* think worthy.

**disease** FRENCH *desaise* sickness, from LATIN *dis-* apart + *aise* comfort.

**disgorge** FRENCH *desgorger,* from **dis-** + **gorge**.

**disgrace** FRENCH bad favor, from LATIN *dis-* apart + *gratia* favor.

**disgruntle** LATIN *dis-* apart + ancient *gruntle* grumble.

**disguise** FRENCH *desguisier,* from LATIN *dis-* apart + *guise* fashion.

**disgust** FRENCH *dis-* not + LATIN *gustus* taste.

**dish** OLD ENGLISH *disk.*

**dishabille** FRENCH *des-* not + *habiller* dress.

**dishevel** FRENCH *des-* apart + *cheval* hair, from LATIN *capillus.*

**dismal** MIDDLE ENGLISH, from FRENCH *dis mal* evil days (in the Middle Ages certain days were thought to be unlucky), from *dis mal,* from LATIN *dies mali,* from *dies* day + *malus* bad, evil.

**dismay** FRENCH *des-* entirely + *esmayer* take away the power.

**dismiss** LATIN *dimittere,* from *dis-* away + *mittere* send.

**disparage** FRENCH *desparagies* cause to marry beneath one's rank, from LATIN *dis-* apart + *parage* being equal in rank, from *par* equal.

**disparate** LATIN *disparare*, from *dis-* apart, not + *parare* make equal, from *par* equal.

**dispatch** SPANISH *despachar* send, from FRENCH *despeechier* set free, from LATIN *dis-* not + *impedicare* tangle up, from *pes* foot.

**dispel** LATIN *dispellere*, from *dis-* away + *pellere* drive.

**dispense** FRENCH *dispenser* give out, from LATIN *dispensare*, from *dis-* apart + *pendere* weigh.

**disperse** LATIN *dispergere*, from *dis-* out + *spargere* scatter.

**display** FRENCH *despleier* show, from LATIN *displicare*, from *displicare*, from *dis-* apart + *plicare* fold.

**disport** FRENCH *des-* not + *porter*, from LATIN *portare* carry.

**dispose** FRENCH *disposer* arrange, from LATIN *disponere*, from *dis-* apart + *ponere* place.

**dispute** FRENCH *desputer* quarrel, from LATIN *disputare*, from *dis-* apart + *putare* think.

**disrupt** LATIN *disrumpere*, from *dis-* apart + *rumpere* break.

**dissect** LATIN *dissecare*, from *dis-* apart + *secare* cut.

**dissemble** FRENCH *des-* not + *semble*, from LATIN *simulare* pretend.

**disseminate** LATIN *disseminare*, from *dis-* apart + *seminare* sow, from *semen* seed.

**dissent** LATIN *dissentire*, from *dis-* apart + *sentire* feel.

**dissipate** LATIN *dissipare*, from *dis-* apart + *supare* throw.

**dissociate** LATIN *dissoclare*, from *dis-* apart + *sociare* join, from *soclus* companion.

**dissolve** LATIN *dissolvere*, from *dis-* apart + *solvere* loosen.

**dissonance** LATIN *dissonare*, from *dis-* apart + *sonare* sound.

**dissuade** LATIN *dissuadere*, from *dis-* away + *suadere* get to do something.

**distaff** OLD ENGLISH *distæf*, from *dis-* flax (fiber) + *stæf* a staff.

**distance** LATIN *distare*, from *dis-* apart + *stare* stand.

**distemper** FRENCH, from LATIN *distemperare* disorder, from *dis-* apart + *temperare* mix in proportion.

**distill** FRENCH, from LATIN *destillare*, from *de-* down + *stillare* drip, from *stilla* a drop.

**distinct** LATIN *distinguere*, from *dis-* apart + *stinguere* prick.

**distinguish** LATIN *distinguere*.

**distort** LATIN *distorquere*, from *dis-* completely + *torquere* twist.

**distract** LATIN *distrahere*, from *dis-* apart + *trahere* draw.

**distress** FRENCH *distrece* bad fortune, from LATIN *distringuere*, from *dis-* apart + *stringere* pull tight.

**distribute** LATIN *distribuere*, from *dis-* apart + *tribuere* give shares.

**distributive** See **distribute** + -ive.

**district** FRENCH, from LATIN *districtus*, from *distringere*, from *dis-* apart + *stringere* stretch.

**disturb** LATIN *disturbare*, from *dis-* entirely + *turbare* put out of order, from *turba* a mob.

**ditch** OLD ENGLISH *dic*.

**divan** TURKISH *diwan*.

**dive** OLD ENGLISH *dyfan* dip.

**diverge** LATIN *divergere,* from *dis-* apart + *vergere* bend.

**diverse** LATIN *divertere,* from *dis-* apart + *vertere* turn.

**divert** FRENCH, from LATIN *divertere.* See **diverse.**

**divide** LATIN *dividere* separate.

**divine** FRENCH, from LATIN *divinus,* from *divus* a god.

**divorce** FRENCH, from LATIN *divortium,* from *divitere,* from *dis-* apart + *vertere* turn.

**divulge** LATIN *divulgare,* from *dis-* apart + *vulgare* make public, from *vulgus* the common people.

**dizzy** OLD ENGLISH *dysig* foolish.

**do** OLD ENGLISH *don.*

**docile** FRENCH, from LATIN *docilis,* from *docere* teach.

**dock** DUTCH *dicke* pier.

**doctor** LATIN teacher, from *docere* teach.

**doctrine** FRENCH teaching, from LATIN *doctrina,* from *doctor.* See **doctor.**

**document** FRENCH, from LATIN *documentum* example, lesson, from *docere* teach.

**dodder** MIDDLE ENGLISH *daderen.*

**dodge** possibly from SCOTTISH *did* jog.

**dodger** See **dodge.**

**dodo** PORTUGUESE *doudo* foolish.

**doff** MIDDLE ENGLISH *do off.*

**dog** OLD ENGLISH *docga.*

**doggerel** OLD ENGLISH.

**doggery** See **dog** + **-ery.**

**dogma** LATIN, from GREEK *dokein* think.

**doily** the name of a 17th century London shopkeeper.

**doit** DUTCH *duit* small coin.

**doldrums** OLD ENGLISH *dol* dull.

**dole** OLD ENGLISH *dal* portion.

**dolerite** FRENCH, from GREEK *doloros* deceitful.

**doll** nickname for Dorothy.

**dollar** GERMAN *daler,* from *thaler,* German silver coin, first made in the city of Joachims*thal* in the 16th century.

**dollop** MIDDLE ENGLISH *dallop* patch, tuft or clump of grass.

**dolorous** FRENCH *doloros,* from LATIN *dolorosus,* from *dolor* pain, grief.

**dolphin** FRENCH, from LATIN, from GREEK *delphis.*

**dolt** MIDDLE ENGLISH *dult,* from *dul* dull, from OLD ENGLISH *dol* stupid.

**-dom** OLD ENGLISH *dom.*

**domain** FRENCH *domaine* estate, from LATIN *dominus* master.

**dome** FRENCH, from LATIN, from GREEK *doma* housetop.

**domestic** LATIN *domesticus* having to do with a household, from *domus* house.

**domicile** FRENCH, from LATIN *domus* house.

**dominant** FRENCH ruling, from LATIN *dominari* rule.

**domineer** DUTCH *domineren* rule, from FRENCH *dominer,* from LATIN *dominari* rule.

**dominion** FRENCH rule, from LATIN *dominium* ownership.

**don**[1] (nobleman) SPANISH, from LATIN *dominus* master.

**don**[2] (put on) MIDDLE ENGLISH *do on.*

**donation**  FRENCH, from LATIN *donum* gift.

**donjon**  See **dungeon**.

**donkey**  possibly from the man's name *Duncan*.

**donne**  See **don**[1].

**donut**  See **dough** + **nut**.

**doom**  OLD ENGLISH *dom*.

**door**  OLD ENGLISH *dor* gate.

**dope**  DUTCH *doop* sauce, from *doopen* mix.

**dormant**  FRENCH *dormir* sleep, from LATIN *dormire*.

**dormer**  FRENCH, from LATIN *dormitorium*, from *dormire* sleep.

**dormitory**  LATIN *dormitorius*, from *dormire* sleep.

**dormouse**  MIDDLE ENGLISH, possibly from FRENCH *dormir* sleep + OLD ENGLISH *mus*. The rodent is inactive in winter.

**dorsal**  LATIN *dorsum* the back.

**dory**  Central America *dori* a type of canoe.

**dose**  FRENCH quantity, from LATIN *dosis*, from GREEK giving.

**doss**  FRENCH *dos*, from LATIN *dossum*, from *dorsum* back.

**dossier**  FRENCH 'bundle of papers', from *dos* back, because the shape of the bundle is somewhat like the shape of a back.  See **doss**.

**dot**  OLD ENGLISH *dotte* head of a boil.

**dotage**  See **dote**.

**dotard**  See **dote**.

**dote**  MIDDLE ENGLISH *doten*.

**dottle**  MIDDLE ENGLISH *dosel* a plug.

**double**  FRENCH, from LATIN *duplus* having two parts.

**doublet**  FRENCH something folded.

**doubt**  FRENCH, from LATIN *dubitare* hesitate.

**dough**  OLD ENGLISH *dag*.

**doughty**  OLD ENGLISH *dohtig* competent, good, valiant, from *dyhtig* strong.

**dour**  LATIN *durus* hard.

**douse**  MIDDLE ENGLISH strike, punch.

**dove**  MIDDLE ENGLISH *douve* pigeon, probably from OLD ENGLISH *dufe*.

**dovecote**  See **dove** + **cote**.

**dowager**  FRENCH *douagere*, from LATIN *dos* dowry, from *dare* give.

**dowdy**  MIDDLE ENGLISH *doude* unattractive woman.

**dowel**  MIDDLE ENGLISH *doule*.

**down**[1] (direction)  OLD ENGLISH *ofdune* downwards, from *dun* hill.

**down**[2] (feathers)  OLD NORSE *dunn*.

**down**[3] (grassy land)  OLD ENGLISH *dun* hill.

**dowry**  FRENCH *doaire*, from LATIN *dotarium*, from *dotare*, from *dos*, from *dare* give.

**doxology**  LATIN *doxologia*, from GREEK *doxa* praise + *-logia*, from *logos* word.

**doze**  MIDDLE ENGLISH *dosen*, from OLD NORSE *dusa* be quiet, rest, doze.

**drab**  FRENCH *drap* cloth, from the way undyed cloth looked, from LATIN *drappus*.

**drabble**  MIDDLE ENGLISH, from GERMAN *drabbeln* walk or splash in mud.

**drachm**  MIDDLE ENGLISH *dragme*, from FRENCH *dragme*, from LATIN *drachma*, from GREEK.  See **dram**.

**drachma**  LATIN, from GREEK *drachme* handful.  See **dram**.

**draft**  OLD NORSE *drattr* act of pulling.

**drag** OLD NORSE *draga*.

**dragon** FRENCH, from LATIN *draco* reptile monster, from GREEK *drakon*, from *derkesthai* see.

**drain** OLD ENGLISH *dreahnian*.

**drake** MIDDLE ENGLISH, from GERMAN *antrahho*.

**dram** FRENCH, from LATIN, from GREEK *drachme* handful, from *drassesthai* grab.

**drama** LATIN, from GREEK a deed, from *dran* do.

**drape** FRENCH *draper*, from *drap* cloth, from LATIN *drappus*.

**draw** OLD ENGLISH *dragan* drag.

**drawer** See **draw**.

**drawl** DUTCH *dralen* wait.

**dray** MIDDLE ENGLISH *dreye*, from OLD ENGLISH *dræge* something pulled.

**dread** MIDDLE ENGLISH *dreden* fear, from OLD ENGLISH *adrædon*.

**dream** OLD ENGLISH joy, music, from OLD NORSE *draumr* dream.

**dreary** OLD ENGLISH *dreorig* sad.

**dredge** probably from DUTCH *dregge* drag.

**dregs** OLD NORSE *dregg*.

**drench** OLD ENGLISH *drencan* make drink, from *drinken* drink.

**dress** FRENCH *drecier* arrange, from LATIN *dirigere*. See **direct**.

**dressage** FRENCH training.

**drey** See **dray**.

**dribbet** MIDDLE ENGLISH *driblet*. See **drip** + -let.

**drift** OLD NORSE snowdrift.

**drill** DUTCH *drillen* make a hole.

**drink** OLD ENGLISH *drincan*.

**drip** OLD ENGLISH *dryppan*.

**drive** OLD ENGLISH *drifan* push.

**drivel** OLD ENGLISH *dreflian* slobber.

**drizzle** MIDDLE ENGLISH *dresen* fall, from *dreosan*.

**drogue** possibly from SCANDINAVIAN.

**droll** FRENCH *drôle* funny, odd, from *drolle* merry man, from DUTCH funny little person.

**dromedary** FRENCH, from LATIN, from GREEK *dramein* run.

**dromond** FRENCH *dromon*, from LATIN *dromonen*, from GREEK *dromon* runner.

**drone**[1] (bee) OLD ENGLISH *dran* male bee.

**drone**[2] (sound) imitative.

**drool** OLD ENGLISH *dreflian* slobber.

**droop** OLD NORSE *drupa* hang the head.

**drop** OLD ENGLISH *dropa*.

**dropsical** See **dropsy**.

**dropsy** FRENCH, from LATIN, from GREEK *hydrops*, from *hydro* water.

**droshky** RUSSIAN *drogi* wagon.

**dross** OLD ENGLISH *dros*.

**drought** OLD ENGLISH *drugoth* dryness.

**drove** OLD ENGLISH *draf*.

**drown** OLD ENGLISH *druncnian* sink.

**drowse** OLD ENGLISH *drusan, drusian* sink.

**drowsy** See **drowse**.

**drudge** MIDDLE ENGLISH, from OLD ENGLISH *dreogan* work, suffer, endure.

**drug** FRENCH *drogue* medicine, from DUTCH *droog* dry.

**drugget** FRENCH *droguet*.

**druid** Latin *druides,* related to Irish *draiodh* sorcerer, magician.

**drum** Dutch *tromme.*

**druthers** combination of *I'd* and *rather.*

**dry** Old English *dryge.*

**dryad** Latin *dryas,* from Greek *drys* tree.

**dual** Latin *dualis* containing two, from *duo* two.

**dub** Old English *dubbian* strike.

**dubbin** See dub + -ing[1].

**dubious** Latin *dubiosus* doubtful, from *dubium* doubt.

**ducat** French, from Italian *ducato* coin with the image of a duke on it.

**duchess** French *duchesse* wife of a duke, from Latin *dux* leader.

**duct** Latin *ducere* lead.

**dudgeon** probably from French *en digeon* at the top of the dagger.

**due** French *devoir* owe, from Latin *debere.*

**duel** Latin *duellum,* from *bellum* war.

**duet** Italian, from Latin *duo* two.

**duff** See dough.

**duffel** Dutch the cloth, from *Duffel,* the town in Belgium where it was first made.

**duke** French *duc* lord, from Latin *dux* leader.

**dulce** Latin *dulcis* sweet.

**dulcet** French *doucet,* from Latin *dulcis* sweet.

**dulcimer (dulcimore)** French *doulce mer, doulcemele,* from Latin *dulce* sweet + *melos* song, from Greek *melos* melody.

**dull** Old English *dol* stupid.

**dumb** Old English *dumb* unable to speak.

**dumbfound** See dumb + confound.

**dump** Old Norse *dumpa* strike.

**dumpling** British *dump* damp, doughy + -ling.

**dun** Old English brownish black.

**dunce** John *Duns* Scotus, a 14th century religious scholar whose writings were at first popular but in the 16th century were made fun of.

**dune** Old English *dun.*

**dung** Old English *dung.*

**dungeon** French *donjon,* from Latin *dominio* tower, from *dominus* master.

**dunk** German *tunken* dip.

**dunlin** See dun + -ling.

**duo** Italian *duo* duet, from Latin *duo* two.

**dupe** French, from Latin *upupa* hoopoe (a stupid bird).

**duplicate** Latin *duplicare* double.

**durable** French, from Latin *durare* last, from *duras* hard.

**duration** Latin *duratio* hardness, from *durare* last, from *duras* hard.

**duress** French *duresce* hardness, from Latin *duritia.*

**dusk** Old English *dox* dark.

**dust**[1] (dirt) Old English.

**dust**[2] (form of do) Middle English *doest.*

**duty** French *duete* what is due, from *devoir* owe. See due.

**dwarf** Old English *dweorg.*

**dwell** Old Norse *dvelja* delay.

**dwindle** Old English *dwinan* dry up.

**dye** Old English *deag.*

**dyke** See **dike**.

**dynamic** FRENCH *dynamique* having energy, from GREEK *dynamikos* powerful, from *dynamis* power.

**dynamite** GREEK *dynamis* power.

**dynamo** *dynamoelectric machine,* from GREEK *dynamis* power + LATIN *electricus,* from *electrum* amber (a hard yellowish or brown material used to make jewelry), from GREEK *electron* because amber attracts other things to it when rubbed.

**dynasty** LATIN *dynastia* rule, from GREEK *dynasthai* be strong.

**dysentery** LATIN *dysenteria,* from GREEK *dysenteria,* from *dys* bad + *entera* intestines.

**dyspepsia** LATIN, from GREEK *dys-* bad + *pepsis* cooking, from *peptein* digest.

# E

**E coli** LATIN *E(scherichia) coli*, from T. *Escherich*, the German physician who discovered it in 1886 + *coli* of the colon.

**each** OLD ENGLISH *ælc*.

**eager** FRENCH *egre* keen, from LATIN *acer* sharp.

**eagle** FRENCH *aigle*, from LATIN *aquila*.

**ear** OLD ENGLISH *eare*.

**earl** OLD ENGLISH *eorl* warrior.

**early** OLD ENGLISH *ælice*.

**earn** OLD ENGLISH *earnian*.

**earnest** OLD ENGLISH *eornoste* serious.

**earth** OLD ENGLISH *eorthe* ground.

**ease** FRENCH *aise* comfort, from LATIN *adjacere* lie near.

**easel** DUTCH *ezel* little donkey, from LATIN *asinus*, because a donkey is used to support something.

**east** OLD ENGLISH.

**easy** FRENCH *aisier* put at ease, from *aise* comfort. See **ease**.

**eat** OLD ENGLISH *etan*.

**eaves** OLD ENGLISH *efes*.

**eavesdrop** OLD ENGLISH *efesdrypa* water that drips from the eaves (lower edge of a sloping roof), referring to someone standing under the eaves where rain could drip on them while trying to hear people talking inside the house.

**ebb** OLD ENGLISH *ebba*.

**ebony** LATIN *ebenus*, from GREEK *ebenos* from EGYPTIAN *hbny*.

**ebullient** LATIN *ebullire*, from *ex-* out + *bullire* boil.

**eccentric** MIDDLE ENGLISH *eccentrik*, from LATIN *eccentricus*, from *eccentros* out of the center, from GREEK *ekkentros*, from *ek-* out of + *kentron* center.

**Eccles** Name of a town in Lancashire, England.

**echelon** FRENCH rung of a ladder, from *échelle* ladder, from *eschelle*, from LATIN *scala*.

**echo** MIDDLE ENGLISH *ecco*, from LATIN *echo*, from GREEK.

**eclair** FRENCH lightning.

**eclectic** GREEK *eklegein*, from *ex-* out + *legein* pick.

**eclipse** FRENCH, from LATIN, from GREEK *ekleipsis* leaving out, from *ek-* out + *leipein* leave.

**eco-** GREEK *oikos* house, dwelling place.

**ecology** German *Ökologie,* from Greek *oikos* house + *-logia* study of.

**economy** Latin *oeconomia* management of a household, from Greek *oikonomos* manager, from *oikos* house + *nemein* manage.

**ecosystem** See eco- + **system.**

**ecstasy** French *extasie,* from Latin *ecstasis,* from Greek *ekstasis,* from *ek-* out + *histanai* place.

**eddy** Old Norse *itha* whirlpool.

**edelweiss** German *edel* noble + *weiss* white.

**edema** Middle English, from Greek *oidema,* from *oidein* swell, from *oidos* tumor, swelling.

**edge** Old English *ecg* sword.

**edifice** French, from Latin *aedificium* a building.

**edify** French *edifier* build, from Latin *aedificare.*

**edit** Latin *editio* bringing forth, from *ex-* out + *dare* give.

**edition** See **edit.**

**editor** See **edit.**

**educate** Latin *educare* train, from *ex-* out + *ducere* lead.

**-ee** French *-é.*

**eerie** Old English *earg* timid.

**efface** French *effacer* erase, from *esfacier,* from *es-* out + *face* appearance, from Latin *facies* face.

**effect** French, from Latin *effectus,* from *efficere* accomplish, from *ex-* out + *facere* do.

**effeminate** Latin *effeminare,* from *ex-* out + *femina* woman.

**efficacious** Latin *efficax,* from *efficere.* See **effect.**

**efficient** See **effect.**

**effigy** Latin *effigies* image.

**effloresce** Latin *efflorescere,* from *ex-* out + *florescere* blossom.

**effluent** Latin *effluentia,* from *effluere,* from *ex-* out + *fluere* flow.

**effort** French *esforcier* force, from Latin *ex-* out + *fortis* strong.

**effrontery** French, from Latin *effrons* shameless, from *ex-* from + *frons* forehead.

**effulgence** Latin *effulgentia,* from *effulgere,* from *ex-* out + *fulgere* shine.

**effuse** Latin *effundere,* from *ex-* out + *fundere* pour.

**efreet** Arabic *'ifrit* evil demon or monster of Muslim mythology.

**egg** Old Norse.

**eglantine** French *aigient,* from Latin *aculeus,* from *acus* a point.

**ego** Latin *ego* I.

**egregious** Latin *egregius* chosen from the herd, from *ex-* out of + *grex* herd.

**egress** Latin *egressus* a going out, from *ex-* out + *gradi* step.

**egret** French *aigrette,* from *aigron* a heron.

**eider** Old Norse *æthr.*

**either** Old English *æther* each of two.

**ejaculate** Latin *ejaculatus,* from *ejaculari,* from *ex-* out + *jaculari* throw, from *jaculum* javelin.

**eject** Latin *ejicere* throw out.

**eke** Old English *ecan* increase.

**ekename** See **eke** + **name.**

**elaborate** Latin *elaborare,* from *ex-* out + *laborare,* from *labor* labor.

**élan** French *élancer* dart.

**elapse**  LATIN *elabi,* from *ex-* out + *labi* glide.

**elastic**  LATIN *elasticus,* from GREEK *elaunein* drive.

**elastoplast**  BRITISH Trademark name for a band-aid, probably a combination of **elastic** + **plaster.**

**elate**  LATIN *elatus,* from *effere,* from *ex-* out + *ferre* bring.

**elbow**  OLD ENGLISH *elboga.*

**elder**  OLD ENGLISH *eldra* older.

**elect**  LATIN *eligere,* from *ex-* out + *legere* choose.

**electric**  LATIN *electricus,* from *electrum* amber (a hard yellowish or brown material used to make jewelry), from GREEK *electron* because amber attracts other things to it when rubbed.

**electroplate**  See **electric** + **plate.**

**electuary**  LATIN *electuarium* lick out.

**elegant**  LATIN *elegans,* from *ex-* out + *legare* choose.

**element**  LATIN *elementum* first principle.

**elementary**  See **element.**

**elephant**  FRENCH *oligant* ivory, from LATIN *elephantus,* from GREEK *elephas.*

**elevate**  LATIN *elevare,* from *ex-* out + *levare* lift.

**elevon**  See **elevate** + **aileron.**

**elicit**  LATIN *elicere,* from *ex-* out + *laedere* strike.

**eligible**  FRENCH qualified, from LATIN *eligibilis* preferred, from *eligere* choose.

**Elijah**  HEBREW *eliyahu* Jehovah is God.

**eliminate**  LATIN *eliminare* push out, from *ex-* out + *limen* threshold (bottom frame of a door).

**elite**  FRENCH select few, from *élire* choose, from LATIN *eligere.*

**elixir**  LATIN, from ARABIC *al-iksir* probably from GREEK *xerion* powder for drying out wounds, from *xeros* dry.

**ellipse**  LATIN *ellipsis,* from GREEK *elleipsis* fall short (of a perfect circle).

**ellipsis**  LATIN, from GREEK *elleipein.* See **ellipse.**

**elocution**  LATIN *elocutionem, elocutio,* from LATIN *eloqui* speak out.

**elongate**  LATIN *elongare* make last longer, from *ex-* out + *longus* long.

**elope**  FRENCH *aloper,* from OLD ENGLISH *a-* away + *hleapan* run.

**eloquent**  FRENCH, from LATIN *eloqui,* from *ex-* out + *loqui* speak.

**else**  OLD ENGLISH *elles.*

**elucidate**  LATIN *elucidare* give understanding to, from *ex-* out + *lucidus* clear, from *lux* light.

**elude**  LATIN *eludere* deceive, from *ex-* out + *ludere* play.

**em-**  See **en-.**

**emaciate**  LATIN *emaciare* make thin, from *ex-* out + *macies* thin.

**emanate**  LATIN *emanare,* from *ex-* out + *menare* flow.

**emancipate**  LATIN *emancipare* set free, from *ex-* away + *manus* hand + *capere* take, from the ancient Roman custom of the father taking the hand of his son and then letting go, which meant that the boy was released from the control of his parents.

**embalm**  FRENCH *embaumer.* See **en-** + **balm.**

**embarcadero**  SPANISH *embarcar,* from FRENCH *embarquer* put on a boat, from LATIN *in-* in + *barca* small boat.

**embargo**  SPANISH, from LATIN *in-* in + *barra* barrier.

**embark** FRENCH *embarquer* put on a boat, from LATIN *in-* in + *barca* small boat.

**embarrass** FRENCH *embarrasser* get in the way of, from LATIN *in-* in + *barra* bar. See **bar**[1].

**embassy** FRENCH *ambassee* errand, from LATIN *ambactus* servant.

**embellish** FRENCH *embellir* make beautiful, from LATIN *in-* in + *bellus* handsome.

**ember** OLD ENGLISH *æmerge*.

**embezzle** FRENCH *enbeseiller* destroy, from *en-* in + *besiler* destroy.

**emblem** LATIN *emblema* ornament, from *en-* in + *ballein* throw.

**embonpoint** FRENCH *en bon point* in good condition.

**emboucheur** FRENCH, from LATIN *in-* in + *bucca* the cheek.

**embrace** FRENCH *embracer* hug, from LATIN *in-* in + *brachium* arm, from GREEK *brachion* arm.

**embrasure** FRENCH opening of a window, from *embraser* widen.

**embrocate** LATIN, from GREEK *en-* in + *brechein* wet.

**embroider** FRENCH *en-* in + *brosder* design with needlework.

**embroil** FRENCH *embrouiller* confuse, from *en-* in + *brouillier* dirty.

**embryo** LATIN, from GREEK *embryon,* from *en-* in + *bryein* make larger.

**embryotomy** See **embryo** + *-tomy* cutting.

**emend** LATIN *emendare* correct, from *ex-* out + *mendum* a fault.

**emerge** LATIN *emergere* rise up, from *ex-* out of + *mergere* dip.

**emergency** See **emerge**.

**emeritus** LATIN *emereri,* from *ex-* out + *mereri* serve.

**emery** FRENCH *emeri,* from FRENCH *emmery,* from ITALIAN *smeriglo,* from GREEK *smyris* abrasive powder.

**-emia** GREEK *haima* blood.

**emigrate** LATIN *emigrare,* from *ex-* out + *migrare* move away from.

**eminence** LATIN *eminere* stand out.

**emir** FRENCH, from ARABIC *amir* commander.

**emissary** LATIN. See **emit**.

**emit** LATIN *emittere,* from *ex-* out + *mittere* send.

**emotion** FRENCH, from LATIN *emovere,* from *ex-* out + *movere* move.

**empathy** GREEK *empatheia,* from *en-* in + *pathos* feeling.

**emperor** FRENCH *emperere,* from LATIN *imperiator,* from *imperare* command, from *im-* in + *parare* put in order.

**emphasis** LATIN, from GREEK *en-* in + *phainein* show.

**empire** FRENCH, from LATIN *imperare*. See **emperor**.

**employ** FRENCH *employer* use, from LATIN *implicare,* from *in-* in + *plicare* fold.

**emporium** LATIN trading place, from GREEK *emporos* traveler + *poros* way.

**empty** OLD ENGLISH *æmtig*.

**emulate** LATIN *aemulari* try to equal.

**emulsion** LATIN *emulsio,* from *emulgere,* from *ex-* out + *mulgere* milk.

**-en** OLD ENGLISH.

**en-** GREEK in.

**enamel** FRENCH *enameler* decorate with enamel.

**enamor** FRENCH *en-* in + *amour,* from LATIN *amor* love.

**-ence** FRENCH, from LATIN *-entia.*

**enchant** FRENCH *enchanter,* from LATIN *incantare,* from *in-* in + *cantare* chant.

**enchilada** SPANISH *enchilar,* seasoned with chili.

**enclave** FRENCH piece of land closed in on all sides, from LATIN *inclavare* lock in, from *in-* in + *clavis* key.

**encore** FRENCH again.

**encounter** FRENCH, from LATIN *in-* in + *contra* against.

**encourage** FRENCH *encoragier* give courage to, from *en-* in + *corage* feelings.

**encroach** FRENCH *encrochier* take, from *en-* in + *croc* hook.

**encumber** FRENCH *encombrer* block up, from LATIN *in-* in + *cumbrus* barrier.

**encyclopedia** LATIN *encyclopaedia* a course of general education, from GREEK *enkyklios paideia* general education.

**end** OLD ENGLISH *ende.*

**endeavor** MIDDLE ENGLISH *endeveren* work at a duty, from *en-* in + *dever* duty, from FRENCH *devoir* owe, from LATIN *debere.*

**endemic** GREEK *endemos* native, from *en-* in + *demos* people.

**endive** FRENCH *endive,* from GREEK *entybon,* perhaps from EGYPTIAN *tybi* January, which is when the plant grows in Egypt.

**endo-** GREEK *endon* within, from *en-* in + *domos* house.

**endocardium** See **endo-** + GREEK *cardia* heart.

**endocrine** See **endo-** + GREEK *krinein* separate.

**endorse** MIDDLE ENGLISH *endossen* write on the back of, from FRENCH *endosser,* from LATIN *in-* in, on + *dorsum* back.

**endow** See **en-** + FRENCH *douer,* from LATIN *dotare* dowry.

**endure** FRENCH *endrer* make hard or strong, from LATIN *indurare,* from *in-* in + *durare* harden, from *duras* hard.

**-ene** LATIN *-enus,* from GREEK *-enos.*

**enema** LATIN, from GREEK *en-* in + *hienai* send.

**enemy** FRENCH *enemi* one who has hatred for another, from LATIN *inimicus* not friendly, from *in-* not + *amicus* friend.

**energy** LATIN *energia,* from GREEK *energeia,* from *en-* in + *ergon* work.

**enforce** FRENCH *enforcier* make stronger, from LATIN *in-* in + *fortis* strong.

**engage** FRENCH *engager* pledge, from *en-* in + *gage* pledge.

**engender** FRENCH *engendrer,* from LATIN *ingenerare,* from *in-* in + *generare* generate (produce).

**engine** FRENCH *engin* skill, from LATIN *ingenium* genius, from *in-* in + *gignere* produce.

**England** OLD ENGLISH *Engla land* the land of the Angles.

**engrail** MIDDLE ENGLISH *engrele,* from FRENCH *engresler,* from *en-* in + *gresle* hail shower, as though cut by hail in a shower.

**engrave** FRENCH *en-* in + *graver* cut into, from GREEK *graphien* write.

**engross** FRENCH *engrosser* write in large letters, from LATIN *in-* in + *grossus* thick.

**enhance** FRENCH *enhancer,* from *enhaucier* raise, from LATIN *in-* in + *altus* high.

**enigma** LATIN *aenigma* riddle, from GREEK *ainigma,* from *ainos* fable, riddle.

**enjoin** FRENCH *enjoindre* direct, from LATIN *injungere,* from *in-* in + *jungere* join.

**enjoy** FRENCH *enjoier* give joy to, from *en-* in + *joie* joy, from LATIN *gaudium* be glad.

**enmity** FRENCH *enemistie,* from LATIN *inimicus* unfriendly.

**ennui** FRENCH, from LATIN *in odio* in hatred.

**enormous** LATIN *enormis* huge, from *ex-* out of + *norma* pattern.

**enough** OLD ENGLISH *genog.*

**enrich** See **en-** + **rich.**

**enroll** FRENCH *enroller,* from *en-* make, put in + *rolle.* See **roll.**

**ensconce** LATIN *in-* in + probably FRENCH *sconce* hiding place.

**ensemble** FRENCH together, from LATIN *in-* in + *simul* at the same time.

**ensign** FRENCH *enseigne* sign, from LATIN *insigne* mark.

**ensue** FRENCH, from LATIN *insequi,* from *in-* in + *sequi* follow.

**ensure** FRENCH *enseurer* make sure.

**-ent** FRENCH *-ent,* LATIN *-ens.*

**entablature** ITALIAN *intavolatura,* from *intavolare,* from *in* in + *tavola* table.

**entail** MIDDLE ENGLISH *en-* in + *taile* agreement, from FRENCH *taillier* cut, from LATIN *talea.*

**enter** FRENCH *entrer,* from LATIN *intrare,* from *intra* within.

**enterprise** FRENCH *entreprise,* from LATIN *entreprendre,* from *inter-* among + *prehendere* take.

**entertain** FRENCH *entretenir* amuse, from LATIN *inter-* among + *tenere* hold.

**enthusiasm** GREEK *enthousiasmos,* from *enthous* inspired by a god, from *en-* in + *theos* god.

**entice** FRENCH *enticier* set on fire, excite, probably from LATIN *in-* in + *titio* firebrand (someone who stirs up trouble).

**entire** FRENCH *entier,* from LATIN *integer* whole.

**entitle** See **en-** + **title.**

**entity** LATIN *entitas* existence, from *ens* a thing, from *esse* be.

**entomology** GREEK *entoma* notched animals + *-logia,* from *logos* word.

**entourage** FRENCH *entourer* surround.

**entrails** FRENCH, from LATIN *intralia,* from *interaneus* internal, from *inter-* between.

**entrance** FRENCH *entirer* go into.

**entreat** FRENCH, from *en-* in + *traiter* treat.

**entrechat** FRENCH.

**entrecote** LATIN *inter-* between + *costa* rib.

**entree** FRENCH *entrer* enter.

**entrepreneur** FRENCH *entreprendre.* See **enterprise.**

**entry** FRENCH *entrer* enter.

**enumerate** LATIN *enumerare,* from *ex-* out + *numerare* count, from *numerus* a number.

**enunciate** LATIN *enuntiare,* from *ex-* out + *nuntius* messenger.

**envelop** FRENCH *enveloper* cover with something, from LATIN *in-* in + *volvere* roll.

**envelope** See **envelop.**

**environment** FRENCH *environner* surround, from *en-* in + *virer* turn around.

**envoy** FRENCH *envoyé* person sent, from LATIN *in viam* on the way.

**envy** FRENCH *envi,* from LATIN *invidere,* from *in-* upon + *videre* look.

**enzyme** GREEK *enzymos,* from *en-* in + *zyme* cause bread to rise.

**eon** GREEK *aion* an age.

**-eous** LATIN *-eus.*

**epaulet** FRENCH *épaule* shoulder, from LATIN *spatula* blade.

**épeé** FRENCH *espe,* from LATIN *spatha,* from GREEK *spathe* a broad flat sword.

**epergne** perhaps from FRENCH *épargne* saving, economy.

**epic** LATIN *epicus,* from GREEK *epilos,* from *epos* song, story.

**epi-** GREEK *epi-* upon, at, close upon (in space or time), on the occasion of, in addition.

**epicenter** See **epi-** + **center.**

**epidemic** FRENCH *épidemique* happening over a large area, from GREEK *epidemios,* from *epi-* among + *demos* people.

**epidermis** See **epi-** + GREEK *derma* skin.

**epidural** See **epi-** + LATIN *dural,* from *dura mater* + FRENCH, from LATIN *alis.*

**epiglottis** See **epi-** + GREEK *glottis.*

**epigram** FRENCH, from LATIN, from GREEK *epigramma,* from *epi-* upon + *graphein* write.

**epilogue** FRENCH, from GREEK *epilogos* conclusion, from *epi-* upon + *logos* word.

**episode** GREEK *epeisodios* following after the entrance, from *epi-* upon + *eis-* into + *hodos* a way.

**epistle** FRENCH letter, from LATIN *epitsola,* from GREEK *epistole* letter, from *epi-* to + *stellein* send.

**epitaph** LATIN *epitaphium,* from GREEK *epitaphion,* from *epi-* on + *taphos* tomb.

**epithet** LATIN *epitheton,* from GREEK *epitheton,* from *epi-* on + *tithenai* put.

**epitome** LATIN make shorter, from GREEK *epi-* upon + *tennein* cut.

**epoch** LATIN *epocha* measure of time, from GREEK *epoche,* from *epi-* upon + *eschein* have.

**equable** LATIN *aequare* make equal, from *aequus* equal.

**equal** LATIN *aequalis* even.

**equanimity** LATIN *aequanimitas,* from *aequus* even + *animus* mind.

**equator** LATIN *aequator,* from *aequare* make equal, from *aequus* even.

**equerry** FRENCH *ècurie* stable, from *escuerie* office of a squire (country gentleman who owns land), from LATIN *equus* horse.

**equilateral** LATIN *aequus* equal + *latus* side.

**equilibrium** LATIN *aequilibrium* level position, from *aequus* even + *libra* balance.

**equinox** FRENCH *equinoxe,* from LATIN *equinoxium,* from *aequinoctium* time of equal days and nights, from *aequus* even + *nox* night.

**equip** OLD NORSE *skipa* put enough men on a ship, from *skip* ship.

**equitation** LATIN *equitatio* riding, from *equus* horse.

**equity** FRENCH, from LATIN *aequitas* equality, from *aequus* equal.

**equivalent** LATIN *aequivalere* have equal power, from *aequus* even + *valere* be strong.

**equivocal** LATIN *aequus* even + *vocare* call.

**equivocate** LATIN *aequivocus* of a similar sound, from *adquus* equal + *vox* voice.

**-er** OLD ENGLISH *-ere.*

**era** LATIN *aera* counters (things used for counting), from *aes* brass (used for counters).

**erase** LATIN *eradere* scrape off, from *ex-* out + *radere* scrape, from the way the ancient Romans erased words written on a wax tablet by scraping off the wax.

**erect** LATIN *erigere* set up.

**ermine** FRENCH, probably from GERMAN *harmo* weasel.

**erode** LATIN *erodere* eat away at.

**err** FRENCH *errer* wander, from LATIN *errare*.

**errand** OLD ENGLISH *ærende* message.

**errant** FRENCH *errer* travel, from LATIN *iter* journey.

**erratic** LATIN *errare* wander.

**error** FRENCH *errour*, from LATIN *error*, from *errare* wander.

**erst** OLD ENGLISH *ærest*.

**erupt** LATIN *erumpere*, from *ex-* out + *rumpere* break.

**-ery** FRENCH *-erie*, from LATIN *-aria*.

**erysipelas** LATIN, from GREEK *erythros* red, from *pelas* skin.

**escape** FRENCH *escaper* get away, from LATIN *ex cappa* out of one's cape, from someone getting away by slipping out of his cape when it was grabbed.

**escarpment** FRENCH.

**escort** FRENCH *escorte* guide, from ITALIAN *scorgere* guide, from LATIN *ex-* out + *corrigere* make straight.

**escutcheon** FRENCH *escuchon*, from *escusson*, from LATIN *scutum* shield.

**esophagus** GREEK *oisophagos*, from *oisein* carry + *-phagos* eat.

**esoteric** GREEK *esoterikos* inner, from *eso* within.

**espadrille** FRENCH, from SPANISH *esparto* rope-soled shoe, from LATIN *spartum*, from GREEK *sparton* rope made of a fiber called *spartos*.

**espionage** FRENCH *espionnage* spying, from *espier* spy.

**espouse** FRENCH, from LATIN *sponsare*, from *sponsus*. See **spouse**.

**espresso** ITALIAN *caffè espresso* pressed-out coffee.

**-esque** ITALIAN *-esco*.

**esquicitos** SPANISH.

**esquire** FRENCH *escuier* squire (a knight's attendant), from LATIN *scutarius* one who holds a shield, from *scutum* shield.

**-ess** FRENCH, from LATIN *-issa*, from GREEK.

**essay** FRENCH *essai* trial, from LATIN *exagium*, from *exigere* weigh.

**essence** FRENCH being, from LATIN *essentia*, from *esse* be.

**establish** FRENCH *establir* decide, from LATIN *stabilire* make firm.

**estate** FRENCH *estat* condition, from LATIN *status*.

**esteem** FRENCH *estimer* figure the value of, from LATIN *aestimare* value.

**estimate** LATIN *aestimare* value.

**estrange** FRENCH *estrangier*, from LATIN *extraneare* treat as a stranger, from *extraneus* strange.

**estre** FRENCH being, condition.

**estrus** LATIN *oestrus*, from GREEK *oistros* strong emotion.

**estuary** LATIN *aestus* tide.

**-et** FRENCH.

**etch** DUTCH, from GERMAN *etzen* cause to eat.

**eternal** LATIN *aeternalis* everlasting, from *aeternus.*

**ether** LATIN, from GREEK *aithein* burn.

**ethereal** LATIN *aetherius.*

**ethical** LATIN *ethicus* moral, from GREEK *ethikos,* from *ethos* character.

**ethnic** LATIN, from GREEK *ethnikos* national, from *ethnos* nation.

**ethnology** See **ethnic** + **-logy**.

**ethylene** See **ether** + **-ene**.

**etiquette** FRENCH a ticket.

**-ette** FRENCH.

**ettin** OLD ENGLISH *eoten.*

**ettle** OLD NORSE *ætla* (also *etla, atla*) purpose.

**etude** FRENCH study.

**etymology** LATIN *etymologia* study of the origins of words, from GREEK *etymos* true + *-logia,* from *logos* word.

**eucalyptus** LATIN *eu-* good + GREEK *kalyptos* covered (from the covering of the buds), from *kalyptein* cover.

**eukaryote** LATIN *eukaryota,* from GREEK *eu-* good + *karyon* nut.

**eulogy** LATIN, from GREEK *eulogia* praise, from *eu-* well + *logia* speaking, from *legein* speak.

**eunuch** LATIN, from GREEK *eunouchos* bed guardian, from *eune* bed + *echein* keep.

**euphemism** GREEK *euphemismos,* from *eu* well + *pheme* speech.

**euphony** LATIN, from GREEK *eu-* well + *phone* voice.

**euthanasia** GREEK *eu-* well + *thanatos* death.

**evacuate** LATIN *evacuare* empty out, from *ex-* out + *vacuus* empty.

**evade** LATIN *evadere,* from *ex-* out + *vadere* go.

**evaluation** FRENCH *évaluer* estimate, from LATIN *ex-* out + *valere* be worth.

**evanesce** LATIN *evanescere,* from *ex-* out + *vanescere* disappear.

**evangel** FRENCH *evangile,* from LATIN *evangelium,* from GREEK *euangelion* good news, from *eu* well + *angelos* messenger.

**evaporate** LATIN *evaporature,* from *ex-* out + *vapor* steam.

**even** OLD ENGLISH *efen.*

**evening** OLD ENGLISH *æfnian.*

**event** LATIN *eventus,* from *ex-* out + *venir* come.

**eventual** LATIN *eventu(s)* event.

**ever** OLD ENGLISH *æfre.*

**every** OLD ENGLISH *æfreælc.*

**evict** LATIN *evincere,* from *ex-* totally + *vincere* conquer.

**evident** FRENCH, from LATIN *evidens* clear, from *ex-* out + *videre* see.

**evil** OLD ENGLISH *yfel* bad.

**evince** LATIN *evincere,* from *ex-* totally + *vincere* conquer.

**eviscerate** LATIN *eviscerare,* from *ex-* out + *viscera* internal organs.

**evoke** FRENCH, from LATIN *ex-* out + *vocare* call, from *vox* voice.

**evolution** See **evolve**.

**evolve** LATIN *evolvere,* from *ex-* out + *volvere* roll.

**ewe** OLD ENGLISH *eowu.*

**ewer** FRENCH *aiguier,* from LATIN *aquarius* having to do with water, from *aqua* water.

**ex-** LATIN *ex-* out, out of, away, upward, from, totally, without.

**exacerbate** LATIN *exacerbare* irritate, from *ex-* totally + *acerbus* harsh.

**exact** LATIN *exigere,* from *ex-* out + *agere* do, act.

**exaggerate** LATIN *exaggerare* pile or heap up, from *ex-* out + *agger* heap.

**exalt** FRENCH, from LATIN *exaltare,* from *ex-* out + *altus* high.

**examine** FRENCH *examiner* question, from LATIN *examin* weigh accurately.

**example** FRENCH *essample* pattern, from LATIN *exemplum,* from *ex-* out + *emere* buy.

**exasperate** LATIN *exasperare* make rough, from *ex-* totally + *asper* rough.

**excavate** LATIN *excavare* hollow out, from *ex-* out + *cavus* hollow.

**exceed** FRENCH *exceder,* from LATIN *excedere,* from *ex-* out + *cedere* go.

**excel** FRENCH, from LATIN *excellere,* from *ex-* out + *cellere* rise.

**excelsior** LATIN *excelsus* high, from *excellere* excel.

**except** FRENCH, from LATIN *exipere,* from *ex-* out + *capere* take.

**excerpt** LATIN *excerpere,* from *ex-* out + *carpere* pick.

**excess** FRENCH, from LATIN *excedere,* from *ex-* out + *cedere* go.

**exchange** FRENCH, from LATIN *excambiare.* See **ex-** + **change.**

**exchequer** FRENCH *eschekier* chessboard, from LATIN *scaccus.*

**excite** LATIN *excitare,* from *ex-* out + *ciere* call.

**exclaim** FRENCH, from LATIN *exclamare,* from *ex-* out + *clamare* shout.

**exclude** LATIN *excludere,* from *ex-* out + *claudere* close.

**excoriate** LATIN *excoriare,* from *ex-* off + *corium* skin.

**excrete** LATIN *excernere,* from *ex-* out + *cernere* separate.

**excruciate** LATIN *excruciare,* from *ex-* totally + *cruciare* crucify, from *crucis,* from *crux* cross.

**excursion** LATIN *excurrere,* from *ex-* out + *currere* run.

**excuse** FRENCH *excuser* cancel, from *ex-* from + *causa* cause.

**execute** FRENCH *execute* carry out, from LATIN *ex(s)ecutor,* from *ex(s)equi,* from *ex-* totally + *sequi* follow.

**executive** LATIN *ex(s)equi.* See **execute.**

**exemplary** FRENCH, from LATIN *exemplus* example.

**exemplify** LATIN *exemplificare* copy out, from *exemplum* an example + *facere* do, make.

**exempt** LATIN *eximere.* See **example.**

**exercise** FRENCH *exercice* practice, from LATIN *exercitium,* from *ex-* out + *arcere* enclose. Originally to turn a farm animal out of its pen.

**exert** LATIN *exserere* stretch out, from *ex-* out + *serere* join.

**exhale** FRENCH, from LATIN *exhalare,* from *ex-* out + *halare* breathe.

**exhaust** LATIN *exhaurire,* from *ex-* out + *haurire* draw.

**exhibit** LATIN *exhabere,* from *ex-* out + *habere* hold.

**exhilarate** LATIN *exhilarare* make glad, from *ex-* totally + GREEK *hilaros* happy.

**exhort** LATIN *exhortari,* from *ex-* out + *hortari* urge.

**exhume** LATIN *exhumare,* from *ex-* out + *humus* the ground.

**exile** FRENCH *exil* send away, from LATIN *ex(s) ilium.*

**exist** FRENCH, from LATIN *existere,* from *ex-* from + *sistere* make stand.

**exit** LATIN *exitus* going out.

**exo-** GREEK *exo* outside.

**exodus** LATIN, from GREEK *ex-* out + *hodos* way.

**exoduster** See **exodus.**

**exonerate** LATIN free from a burden, from *ex-* from + *onus* burden.

**exorbitant** LATIN *exorbitare,* from *ex-* out + *orbita* track, orbit.

**exosphere** See **exo-** + **sphere.**

**exotic** LATIN *exoticus* foreign, from GREEK *exotikos,* from *exo* outside.

**expand** LATIN *expandere,* from *ex-* out + *pandere* spread.

**expatiate** LATIN *ex-* out + *spatiari* walk about, from *spatium* space.

**expect** LATIN *ex(s)pectare,* from *ex-* out + *spectare* look.

**expectorate** LATIN *expectorare* force out of the breast, from *ex-* out + *pectus* breast.

**expedient** LATIN *expedire* free the feet, from *ex-* out + *pes* foot.

**expedite** See **expedient.**

**expedition** FRENCH, from LATIN *expedire* free the feet, from *ex-* out + *pes* foot.

**expel** LATIN *expellere,* from *ex-* out + *pellere* push.

**expend** LATIN *expendere,* from *ex-* out + *pendere* weigh.

**expense** LATIN *expensa* money to reduce costs, from *expendere* pay, from *ex-* out + *pendere* weigh.

**experience** FRENCH testing, from LATIN *experientia,* from *ex-* out of + *periculum* danger.

**experiment** FRENCH, from LATIN *experimentum,* from *experiri.* See **experience.**

**expert** FRENCH able, from LATIN *experiri* prove. See **experience.**

**expire** LATIN *ex(s)pirare,* from *ex-* out + *spirare* breathe.

**explain** LATIN *explanare,* from *ex-* out + *planare* make level, from *planus* level.

**explicate** LATIN *explicare,* from *ex-* out + *plicare* fold.

**explicit** LATIN *explicare.* See **explicate.**

**explode** LATIN *explodere* drive off the stage by clapping and making noise, from *ex-* out + *plaudere* applaud.

**exploit** FRENCH, from LATIN *explicare,* from *ex-* out + *plicare* fold.

**explore** LATIN *explorare* search out, from *ex-* out + *plorare* cry out.

**exponent** LATIN *exponere,* from *ex-* out + *ponere* put.

**export** LATIN *ex-* out + *portare* carry.

**expose** FRENCH *exposer* place in view, from LATIN *exponere,* from *ex-* out + *ponere* put.

**exposition** See **expose.**

**expostulate** LATIN *expostulare,* from *ex-* very much + *postulare* demand.

**expound** MIDDLE ENGLISH, from FRENCH *espondre,* from LATIN *exponere,* from *ex-* out + *ponere* put.

**express**  LATIN *exprimere* press out, from *ex-* out + *premere* press.

**expulsion**  See **expel**.

**expunge**  LATIN *expungere*, from *ex-* out + *pungere* prick.

**exquisite**  LATIN *exquirere* search out, from *ex-* out + *quaerere* ask.

**extant**  LATIN *ex(s)tare* exist, from *ex-* out + *stare* stand.

**extend**  LATIN *extendere*, from *ex-* out + *tendere* stretch.

**extensor**  LATIN, from *extendere*.  See **extend**.

**extenuate**  LATIN *extenuare*, from *ex-* out + *tenuare* make thin, from *tenuis* thin.

**exterior**  LATIN outward.

**exterminate**  LATIN *exterminare* drive out, from *ex-* out + *terminus* boundary.

**external**  LATIN *externus* on the outside.

**extinct**  LATIN *extinguere*, from *ex-* out + *stinguere* extinguish (kill).

**extinguish**  LATIN *extinguere*, from *ex-* out + *stinguere* extinguish.

**extirpate**  LATIN *ex(s)tirpare*, from *ex-* out + *stirps* root.

**extol**  LATIN *extollere*, from *ex-* upward + *tollere* raise.

**extra**  LATIN more than.

**extra-**  LATIN *exter(us)* beyond, outside, besides.

**extract**  LATIN *extrahere* draw out, from *ex-* out + *trahere* draw.

**extradition**  FRENCH, from LATIN *ex-* out + *traditio* surrender.

**extraneous**  LATIN *extraneus*, from *extra* more than.

**extraordinary**  LATIN *extra ordinem* out of the usual order.

**extrapolate**  LATIN *extra* more than + *inter* between + *polire* polish.

**extravagant**  LATIN *extravagari* wander outside the boundary, from *extra* beyond + *vagari* wander.

**extreme**  FRENCH, from LATIN *exterus* outward.

**extricate**  LATIN *extricare*, from *ex-* out + *tricae* difficulties.

**extroversion**  LATIN *extra-* more than + *versio* a turning.

**exuberence**  LATIN *exuberare*, from *ex-* totally + *uber* growing easily.

**exude**  LATIN *ex(s)udare*, from *ex-* out + *sudare* sweat.

**exult**  LATIN *ex(s)ultare*, from *ex-* out + *salire* leap.

**eye**  OLD ENGLISH *eage*.

**eyot**  MIDDLE ENGLISH *eyt* river island, from OLD ENGLISH *igeoo*.

**eyrie**  See **aerie**.

# F

**fable** FRENCH story, from LATIN *fabula*.

**fabric** FRENCH, from LATIN *fabrica* workshop, from *faber* a workman.

**fabulous** LATIN *fabulosus*, from *fabula* story.

**facade** FRENCH, from ITALIAN, from LATIN *facia* face.

**face** FRENCH, from LATIN *facies*.

**facet** FRENCH *facette*, from *face*. See **face**.

**facetious** FRENCH *facétie* joke, from LATIN *facetia*.

**facile** LATIN *facilis*, from *facere* do, make.

**facility** FRENCH, from LATIN *facilis*. See **facile**.

**facsimile** LATIN *fac simile* make similar.

**fact** LATIN *factum* something done, from *facere* do, make.

**factor** LATIN one who does, from *facere* do, make.

**factory** LATIN *factoria* place where things are made, from *factor* one who does, from *facere* do, make.

**factotum** LATIN *fac totum* do everything.

**faculty** FRENCH *faculte* ability, from LATIN *facultas*, from *facere* do, make.

**fade** FRENCH *fader*, from *fade* pale.

**fag** origin uncertain, probably from **flag**[4].

**fagot** FRENCH bundle of sticks, probably from GREEK *phakelos* bundle.

**Fahrenheit** G.D. *Fahrenheit*, 18th century German scientist.

**fail** FRENCH *faillir* be wanting, from LATIN *fallere* deceive.

**fain** OLD ENGLISH *fægen* glad.

**faint** FRENCH *feindre* copy, from LATIN *fingere* shape.

**fair** OLD ENGLISH *fæger* beautiful.

**faith** FRENCH *feit* trust, from LATIN *fides*.

**fake**[1] (pretend) probably from earlier *feague*, *feake*, from GERMAN *fegen* clean, sweep.

**fake**[2] (rope coil) nautical, origin uncertain.

**falcon** FRENCH, from LATIN *falconis*, from *falx* shaped like a sickle.

**fall** OLD ENGLISH *feallan* drop.

**fallacy** LATIN *fallacia*, from *fallere* deceive.

**fallible** LATIN *fallibilis* not honest, from *fallere* deceive.

**fallow** OLD ENGLISH *fealh*.

**false** FRENCH, from LATIN *fallere* deceive.

**falsetto** LATIN. See **false**.

**falter** MIDDLE ENGLISH *faltren*, probably from OLD NORSE *fultra(sk)*.

125

**fame** FRENCH, from LATIN *fama*.

**familiar** FRENCH *familier* closely acquainted, from LATIN *familia* household.

**family** LATIN *familia* household, from *famulus* servant.

**famish** FRENCH, from LATIN *fames* hunger.

**famous** LATIN *fama* fame.

**fan** OLD ENGLISH *fann*.

**fanatic** LATIN *fanaticus* encouraged by a god, from *fanum* temple.

**fancy** See fantasy.

**fandango** SPANISH.

**fang** OLD ENGLISH *fon*.

**fantasy** FRENCH, from LATIN, from GREEK *phantasia* appearance, from *phainein* show.

**fantoccini** ITALIAN, plural of *fantoccino*, diminutive of *fantoccio* puppet, from *fante* boy, servant.

**fantod** origin uncertain.

**far** OLD ENGLISH *feor(r)*.

**farandole** FRENCH, from ITALIAN *farandola*.

**farce** FRENCH humorous cause, from LATIN *facire* stuff, from comic routines "stuffed" between the acts of medieval religious plays.

**fardel**[1] (bundle) MIDDLE ENGLISH, from FRENCH, from ITALIAN *fardello*, from *fardo*, from ARABIC *fardah*, a camel's load.

**fardel**[2] (a fourth) MIDDLE ENGLISH, from OLD ENGLISH *feortha dæl* fourth part.

**fare** OLD ENGLISH *faran* go.

**farl** See fardel[2].

**farm** FRENCH *ferme*, from LATIN *firma* fixed payment, from *firmare* fix, from the original use of the word to mean a tax fixed on farmland, and later meaning the land itself.

**faro** FRENCH *pharaon* pharaoh, possibly because one of the cards used in the game formerly bore the picture of Pharaoh. See **pharaoh**.

**farrago** LATIN *farrago* medley, mix of grains for animal feed, from *far* corn.

**farrier** FRENCH, from LATIN *ferrum* iron.

**farrow** OLD ENGLISH *fearh* young pig.

**farther** MIDDLE ENGLISH *ferther*.

**farthing** OLD ENGLISH *foerthing*.

**farthingale** FRENCH *vergugalie,* from SPANISH *verdugo* tree shoot, from LATIN *viridis* green.

**fasces** LATIN *fascis* a bundle.

**fascia** LATIN a band, a sash.

**fascinate** LATIN *fascinare* charm.

**fascism** ITALIAN *Fascismo* Italian fascism, from *fascio* bundle, from *fasces* bundle of rounded sticks with an ax, the symbol in ancient Rome of authority.

**fashion** FRENCH *façon* appearance, from LATIN *factio* party.

**fast**[1] (swift) OLD ENGLISH *fæst* firm.

**fast**[2] (not eat) OLD ENGLISH *fæstan*.

**fastidious** LATIN *fastidiosus* full of disgust, from *fastidium* extreme dislike.

**fat** OLD ENGLISH *fætt*.

**fatal** LATIN *fatalis* deadly, from *fatum* destiny.

**fate** LATIN *fatum* destiny, what is spoken, from *fari* speak.

**father** OLD ENGLISH *fæder* male parent, God.

**fathom** OLD ENGLISH *fæthm* length of the arms when stretched out.

**fatigue** FRENCH *fatiguer* make tired, from LATIN *fatigare*.

**fatuous** LATIN *fatuus* foolish.

**faucet** MIDDLE ENGLISH, from FRENCH *fausset* stopper, perhaps from LATIN *faux* throat. A faucet was originally a screw which controlled the flow of liquid from a spigot.

**faugh** (exclamation) imitative.

**fault** FRENCH *faute* gap, from LATIN *fallere* lie to.

**faun** LATIN *Faunus* a Roman nature god.

**favor** FRENCH kindness, from LATIN goodwill.

**fealty** FRENCH *feauté*, from LATIN *fidelitas*, from *fides* faith.

**fear** OLD ENGLISH *fær* danger.

**feasible** FRENCH *faisible* can be done, from LATIN *facere* do, make.

**feast** FRENCH *feste* festival, from LATIN *festa*.

**feat** FRENCH, from LATIN *factum* something done. See **fact**.

**feather** OLD ENGLISH *fether*.

**feature** FRENCH *feture* form, from LATIN *factura*.

**February** LATIN *Februarius*, from *februarius mens* Roman month of purification, from *februm* way to purify (make clean).

**feces** LATIN *faeces*.

**feckless** SCOTTISH *feck* effect + OLD ENGLISH *-leas*.

**fecund** LATIN *fecundus* fruitful.

**federal** LATIN *foedus* a league.

**fedora** the name of a play and the title character, played by Sarah Bernhardt in 1882, in which she wore such a hat.

**fee** MIDDLE ENGLISH, from OLD ENGLISH *feoh* cattle, property, from OLD NORSE, from LATIN *pecus*, from GREEK *pokos*. In early days a person's wealth was based on the number of cattle owned.

**feeble** FRENCH *feble* lacking strength, from LATIN *flere* cry.

**feed** OLD ENGLISH *fedan*.

**feel** OLD ENGLISH *felan* touch.

**feign** FRENCH *feindre* copy, from LATIN *fingere* make.

**feint** FRENCH *feindre*. See **feign**.

**feisty** MIDDLE ENGLISH *fist* bodily gas escaping.

**felicity** FRENCH *felicite* happiness, from LATIN *felicitas*.

**feline** LATIN *felinus* having to do with a cat, from *felis* cat.

**fell**[1] (make fall) OLD ENGLISH *feallan*. See **fall**.

**fell**[2] (bad) FRENCH *fel* cruel, fierce, from LATIN *fello* villain. See **felon**[1].

**fellow** OLD ENGLISH *feolaga* partner, from OLD NORSE *felagi*, from *fe* cattle + *lag* putting property together for a common purpose.

**felon**[1] (criminal) FRENCH wicked person, from LATIN *fello*.

**felon**[2] (boil) LATIN *fel* gall, poison.

**felt** OLD ENGLISH.

**female** FRENCH *femelle*, from LATIN *femilla* young woman.

**feminine** FRENCH, from LATIN *femina*. See **female**.

**femur** LATIN.

**fence** MIDDLE ENGLISH *fens* defense.

**fend** See **defend**.

**fennel** OLD ENGLISH, from LATIN *feniculum*, from *femum* hay.

**ferment** FRENCH, from LATIN *fervere* boil.

**fern** OLD ENGLISH *fearn*.

**ferocious** LATIN *ferox* wild.

**ferret** FRENCH, from LATIN *fuor,* from *fur* thief.

**ferrule** FRENCH *virelle*, from LATIN *viriola* bracelet, spelling influenced by *ferrum* iron.

**ferry** OLD ENGLISH *ferian* carry.

**fertile** FRENCH, from LATIN *fertilis* have children.

**ferule** LATIN *ferula* rounded stick.

**fervent** LATIN *fervere* boil.

**fervid** LATIN *fervidus* burning.

**fervor** FRENCH, from LATIN *fervere* boil.

**fess** FRENCH, from LATIN *fascia* a band.

**fester** FRENCH *festre*, from LATIN *fistula* tube.

**festival** FRENCH *festival,* from LATIN *festum* feast.

**festoon** FRENCH *feston* wreath, from LATIN *festum* feast.

**fet** OLD ENGLISH *fetian* fetch.

**fetch** OLD ENGLISH *feccan* bring.

**fete** FRENCH *feste* festival.

**fetid** LATIN *f(o)etidus* stink.

**fetish** FRENCH *fétiche* something that has magical power, from PORTUGUESE *fetiço* charm, from LATIN *facticus* art.

**fetlock** MIDDLE ENGLISH *fitlok,* from DUTCH.

**fetter** OLD ENGLISH *fot* foot.

**fettle** MIDDLE ENGLISH *fetlen* make ready, probably from OLD ENGLISH *fetel* belt.

**feud**[1] (quarrel) FRENCH *faide*, from GERMAN *gahida* quarrel.

**feud**[2] (feudal land) LATIN *feodum,* from GERMAN *feho* cattle + *od* wealth.

**fever** OLD ENGLISH *fefor*, from LATIN *febris*.

**few** OLD ENGLISH *feawe*.

**fewter** FRENCH *feutre*, from LATIN *filtrum* felt lining.

**fey** OLD ENGLISH *fæge* fated.

**fiancé** FRENCH *fiancer,* from *fidus* faithful.

**fiasco** ITALIAN bottle. "Make a bottle" was a saying that carried the meaning "fail in a performance," or "pull off a complete flop." The reason for the saying is unknown.

**fib** MIDDLE ENGLISH, origin uncertain, perhaps from fable.

**fiber** FRENCH, from LATIN *fibra*.

**fibula** LATIN a clasp.

**-fic** FRENCH *fique*, from LATIN *ficus*, from *facere* do, make.

**fichu** FRENCH.

**fickle** OLD ENGLISH *ficol*.

**fiction** FRENCH, from LATIN *fictio* a making.

**fiddle** OLD ENGLISH *fithele*.

**fidelity** FRENCH, from LATIN *fidelitas* faithfulness, from *fides* faith.

**fidget** MIDDLE ENGLISH *fiken* fidget, hasten, from OLD NORSE *fikjask* desire eagerly.

**fie** imitative.

**fief** FRENCH *fief*, from *fieu* fee.

**field** OLD ENGLISH *feld* open land.

**fiend** OLD ENGLISH *feond* enemy, devil.

**fierce** FRENCH *f(i)ers* wild, from LATIN *ferus*.

**fiesta** SPANISH.

**fife** GERMAN *Pfeife* pipe, from LATIN *pipare* sound like a bird.

**fig** FRENCH, from LATIN *ficus*.

**fight** OLD ENGLISH *feohtan* struggle.

**figment** LATIN *figmentum* something made.

**figure** FRENCH form, from LATIN *figura* thing made.

**filament** LATIN *filamentum,* from *filum* thread.

**filbert** the feast day of Saint *Philbert,* which occurred during the harvest of the nuts.

**filch** MIDDLE ENGLISH *filchen.*

**file** MIDDLE ENGLISH *filen,* from FRENCH *filer* to string papers on a thread, from LATIN *filum* thread.

**filial** LATIN *fillus* son, *filla* daughter.

**filibuster** SPANISH *filibustero,* from DUTCH *vrijbulter* pirate. See **freebooter.** In the middle of the 19th century bands of adventurers were organized in the U.S. to go to Central America (where they were called *filibusteros*) to create problems for governments. The word came to be in use in American politics to give the idea that a filibuster created problems for the government.

**filigree** FRENCH, from ITALIAN, from LATIN *filum* a thread + *granum* grain.

**fill** OLD ENGLISH *fyllan.*

**fillet** FRENCH *fil,* from LATIN *filum.*

**fillip** imitative.

**film** OLD ENGLISH *filmen* thin layer.

**filter** FRENCH, from LATIN *filtrum* strainer.

**filth** OLD ENGLISH *fylth* rotten.

**filtration** See **filter.**

**fin** OLD ENGLISH *finn.*

**final** LATIN *finalis,* from *finis* end.

**finale** ITALIAN.

**finance** FRENCH payment, from *finer* pay, from LATIN *finire* end.

**finca** SPANISH *fincar* ranch.

**finch** OLD ENGLISH *finc.*

**find** OLD ENGLISH *findan.*

**fine**[1] (superior) FRENCH, from LATIN *finis* end.

**fine**[2] (payment) FRENCH *fin* exact, from LATIN *finis* end.

**finesse** FRENCH delicate, from *fin.* See **fine**[1].

**finger** OLD ENGLISH.

**finish** FRENCH *finir,* from LATIN *finire* end.

**finite** LATIN *finire* end.

**fiord** OLD NORSE *fjörthr.*

**fir** OLD ENGLISH *fyrh.*

**fire** OLD ENGLISH *fyr.*

**firk** OLD ENGLISH *fercian.*

**firkin** DUTCH *vierdel* a fourth.

**firm** FRENCH *ferme* strong, from LATIN *firmus.*

**firmament** LATIN *firmamentum,* from *firmare* make strong, from *firmus* firm.

**first** OLD ENGLISH *fyrst.*

**fiscal** FRENCH, from LATIN *fiscalis,* from *fiscus* money basket.

**fish** OLD ENGLISH *fisc.*

**fission** LATIN *fissio* split by force.

**fit** MIDDLE ENGLISH *fitten,* from OLD NORSE *fitja* knit.

**fix** LATIN *figere* fasten.

**fixture** LATIN *fixtura,* from *fixus,* from *figere* fasten.

**fizz** imitative.

**fjord** See **fiord.**

**flabbergast** probably from **flabby** + **aghast.**

**flabby** See **flap.**

**flaccid** LATIN *flaccus* flabby.

**flag**[1] (banner) MIDDLE ENGLISH *flagge*, probably from OLD NORSE *flogra* wave or flap quickly.

**flag**[2] (paving) OLD NORSE *flaga* stone slab.

**flag**[3] (wild iris) MIDDLE ENGLISH *flagge*. See **flag**[1].

**flag**[4] (droop) MIDDLE ENGLISH *flakken, flacken* flap, flutter, probably from OLD NORSE *flakka* flicker, flutter.

**flagellum** LATIN *flagellum* whip, scourge.

**flagon** FRENCH *flascon* bottle, from LATIN *flasco*.

**flagrant** LATIN *flagrare* burn.

**flail** FRENCH *flaiel*, from LATIN *flagellum* whip.

**flair** FRENCH sense of smell, from LATIN *fragrare* smell sweet.

**flake** OLD NORSE *flackna* flake off.

**flamboyant** FRENCH *flamboyer* flame, from LATIN *flamma*.

**flame** FRENCH *flamme* blaze, from LATIN *flamma*.

**flamenco** SPANISH gypsy-like.

**flamingo** SPANISH *flamengo* flame-colored.

**flange** perhaps from FRENCH *flanche* flank, side.

**flank** FRENCH *flanc* side.

**flannel** WELSH *gwlanen*, from *gwlan* wool.

**flap** MIDDLE ENGLISH *flappe*, probably imitative.

**flare** MIDDLE ENGLISH spread out hair, origin uncertain.

**flash** MIDDLE ENGLISH *flaschen* splash.

**flask** FRENCH *flasque* container for gunpowder, from LATIN *flasca* wine bottle.

**flat** OLD NORSE *flatr* level.

**flatter** FRENCH *flater* calm.

**flaunt** possibly from NORWEGIAN *flanta* show off.

**flautist** ITALIAN *flautista*, from *flauto* flute.

**flavor** FRENCH *flaur* odor, from LATIN *flare* blow.

**flaw** See **flake**.

**flax** OLD ENGLISH *fleax*.

**flay** OLD ENGLISH *flean*.

**fleam** MIDDLE ENGLISH *fleme*, from LATIN *phlebotomus*, from GREEK *phlebotomon*, from *phlebos* vein + *tomos* piece cut off.

**fleck** OLD NORSE *flekkr*.

**flection** See **flexion**.

**fledge** OLD ENGLISH *flycge* having feathers.

**flee** OLD ENGLISH *fleon*.

**fleece** OLD ENGLISH *fleos*.

**fleet** OLD ENGLISH *fleotan* float.

**flesh** OLD ENGLISH *flæsc*.

**flet** OLD ENGLISH *flett* flat.

**fleur-de-lis** FRENCH *fleur* flower + *de* of + *lis* lily.

**flewsey** MODERN ENGLISH *flue* fluff.

**flex** LATIN *flectere* bend.

**flexion** LATIN *flexionem* bend.

**flicker** MIDDLE ENGLISH *flikeren*, from OLD ENGLISH *flicorian* flutter.

**flight** OLD ENGLISH *flyht*, from *fleotgan*.

**flimsy** origin uncertain, perhaps from **film**.

**flinch** FRENCH *flenchir* bend.

**flinders** SCANDINAVIAN *flindra* splinter.

**fling** MIDDLE ENGLISH *flingen* rush, from OLD NORSE *flengja* whip.

**flint** OLD ENGLISH *flint* rock.

**flip** imitative.

**flirt** possibly from FRENCH *fleureter* move from flower to flower, from *fleur* flower, from LATIN *flos*.

**flit** OLD NORSE *flytia* carry.

**flivver** origin uncertain.

**float** OLD ENGLISH *flotian*.

**flock**[1] (group) OLD ENGLISH *flocc*.

**flock**[2] (wool) FRENCH *floc* lock of wool.

**floe** probably from NORSE *flo* layer, slab, from *flo*.

**flog** possibly from LATIN *flagellare* whip.

**flood** OLD ENGLISH *flod*.

**floor** OLD ENGLISH *flor* bottom of a room.

**flop** See **flap**.

**florid** LATIN *floridus* full of flowers, from *flos* flower.

**florin** MIDDLE ENGLISH, from FRENCH, from LATIN *florem*, from *flos* flower.

**floss** FRENCH *floche*, from *floc*, from LATIN *floccus* tuft of wool.

**flotilla** SPANISH *flota* fleet.

**flotsam** FRENCH, from DUTCH *vloten* float.

**flounce**[1] (body movement) MIDDLE ENGLISH, imitative origin, possibly related to NORSE *flunsa* hurry.

**flounce**[2] (ruffle) MIDDLE ENGLISH *frounce* pleat, wrinkle, fold, from FRENCH *fronce* wrinkle.

**flounder**[1] (motion) perhaps from **founder**, influenced by DUTCH *flodderen* flop about.

**flounder**[2] (fish) FRENCH *floundre*, from *flondre*, from OLD NORSE *flydhra*.

**flour** FRENCH *fleur de farine* flower (the best part of) the meal.

**flourish** FRENCH *florir* blossom, from LATIN *flos* flower.

**flout** MIDDLE ENGLISH *flouten* play the flute, from FRENCH *flauter*, from *fleute*. See **flute**.

**flow** OLD ENGLISH *flowan*.

**flower** MIDDLE ENGLISH *flour*, from FRENCH *flor*, from LATIN *florem*.

**flub** AMERICAN, origin uncertain.

**fluctuate** LATIN *fluctuare*, from *fluctus* wave.

**flue** possibly from FRENCH *fluie* a flowing.

**fluent** LATIN *fluere* flow.

**fluff** FRENCH *velu* shaggy, from LATIN *villus* shaggy hair.

**fluid** LATIN *fluidus* flowing.

**fluke**[1] (fish, parasite) OLD ENGLISH *floc* flatfish.

**fluke**[2] (luck) origin unknown, originally a lucky shot at billiards.

**fluke**[3] (anchor) possibly from resemblance to the fish. See **fluke**[1].

**flume** FRENCH, from LATIN *flumen* river, from *fluere* flow.

**flummox** BRITISH, origin uncertain.

**flunk** AMERICAN slang, origin uncertain.

**flunky** See **flank**.

**fluorescence** LATIN *fluere* flow + *escens* ending.

**flurry** See **flutter** + **hurry**.

**flush** blend of **flash** and MIDDLE ENGLISH *flusschen* fly up suddenly.

**fluster** probably from SCANDINAVIAN.

**flute** FRENCH *flaute*, possible imitative.

**flutter** OLD ENGLISH *flotorian* flap the wings.

**flux** LATIN *fluxus* flowing.

**fly** OLD ENGLISH *fleoge.*

**foal** OLD ENGLISH *fola.*

**foam** OLD ENGLISH *fam.*

**foc'sle** See **forecastle.**

**focus** LATIN floor of a fireplace, because this was the center of the home.

**fodder** OLD ENGLISH *foda* food.

**foe** OLD ENGLISH *fah.*

**fog** probably from SCANDINAVIAN.

**foible** weak point of a sword blade, from FRENCH *foible* weak, from *fieble* feeble.

**foil** MIDDLE ENGLISH *foilen* trample on, from FRENCH *fouler,* from LATIN *fullo* person who prepares woolen cloth.

**foist** probably from DUTCH *vuisten* take in the hand, as in concealing loaded dice in one's hand so as to cheat by switching them, from *vuist* fist.

**fold** OLD ENGLISH *fealdan.*

**foliage** FRENCH, from LATIN *follum,* from *foliatus* leafy.

**folio** LATIN *folium* leaf.

**folk** OLD ENGLISH *fole* people.

**follicle** LATIN *folliculus* little bag, from *follis* bellows, inflated ball.

**follow** OLD ENGLISH *folgian.*

**folly** FRENCH *folie* foolishness, from *fol* fool, from LATIN *follis* windbag.

**foment** LATIN *fomentare* help the body by putting wet heat on painful places, from *fomentum* keep warm.

**fond** MIDDLE ENGLISH *fonne* a fool.

**fondle** See **fond.**

**fondue** FRENCH, from *fondre* melt.

**font**[1] (bowl) OLD ENGLISH, from LATIN *fons* fountain.

**font**[2] (printing) FRENCH *fonte,* from *fondre.*

**food** OLD ENGLISH *foda.*

**fool** FRENCH *fol* foolish person, from LATIN *follis* windbag (person who talks a lot but doesn't say anything important).

**foot** OLD ENGLISH *fot.*

**footling** See **foot** + **-ling.**

**fop** MIDDLE ENGLISH *foppe* a fool, from DUTCH *foppen* fool, from GERMAN *foppen.*

**for** OLD ENGLISH.

**for-** OLD ENGLISH.

**forage** FRENCH *fourage,* from *forre* food for cattle, sheep, etc.

**foray** FRENCH *forrer* forage.

**forbid** OLD ENGLISH *forbeodan.*

**force** FRENCH strength, from LATIN *fortis* strong.

**forceps** LATIN, from *formus* hot + *capere* take, from a tool used by a blacksmith to grasp hot things.

**ford** OLD ENGLISH shallow place.

**fore** OLD ENGLISH before.

**fore-** OLD ENGLISH.

**forebode** OLD ENGLISH.

**forecastle** See **fore** + **castle.**

**foreclose** FRENCH *forclore* shut out, from LATIN *foris* outside + *claudere* shut.

**foreign** MIDDLE ENGLISH *foreyne* outside, from FRENCH *forain,* from LATIN *foris.*

**forelock** See **fore** + **lock**[2].

**forensic** LATIN *forensis* public, from *forum* marketplace.

**foresee** OLD ENGLISH *foreseon*.

**forest** FRENCH, from LATIN *forestis* wood not fenced in, from *foris* outside.

**forestall** MIDDLE ENGLISH *forestallen* prevent from going forward, from OLD ENGLISH *foresteall*.

**forfeit** FRENCH *forfaire* act beyond the law, from LATIN *foris* outside + *facere* do.

**forfend** See **for-** + **fend**.

**forge** MIDDLE ENGLISH, from FRENCH, from LATIN *fabrica* workshop, from *faber* worker.

**forget** OLD ENGLISH *forgitan*.

**forgive** OLD ENGLISH *forgifan* give.

**forgo** OLD ENGLISH *forgan* pass over.

**fork** OLD ENGLISH *forca*, from LATIN *furca*.

**forlorn** OLD ENGLISH *forleosan* lose.

**form** FRENCH *forme* shape, from LATIN *forma*.

**-form** See **form**.

**formal** LATIN *formalis* relating to form, from *forma* shape.

**formaldehyde** MODERN ENGLISH **formic acid** + *aldehyde*, from *al(cohol)* + *dehyd(rogenated)*, alcohol without hydrogen.

**Formalin** See **formaldehyde** + **-ine** (trademark name for a solution of formaldehyde in water).

**format** FRENCH, from GERMAN, from LATIN *formare* shape.

**former** MIDDLE ENGLISH *formere* first, from OLD ENGLISH *forma*.

**formic acid** LATIN *formica* ant (the acid was obtained from red ants).

**formidable** FRENCH, from LATIN *formidare* be afraid of.

**formula** LATIN small pattern, from *forma* shape.

**forsake** OLD ENGLISH *for-* away + *sacan* work for.

**forswear** OLD ENGLISH *forswerian* swear falsely.

**fort** FRENCH, from LATIN *fortis*.

**forth** OLD ENGLISH.

**fortify** FRENCH *fortifier*, from LATIN *fortis* strong + *facere* do, make.

**fortitude** LATIN *fortis* strong.

**fortnight** OLD ENGLISH fourteen nights.

**fortuitous** LATIN *fortuitus*, from *fors* chance.

**fortune** FRENCH chance, from LATIN *fortuna* luck.

**forum** LATIN area out of doors.

**forward** OLD ENGLISH *foreweard*.

**fossil** LATIN *fodere* dig.

**foster** OLD ENGLISH *fostrian* feed.

**foul** OLD ENGLISH *ful* rotten.

**found**[1] (past tense of find) MIDDLE ENGLISH, from OLD ENGLISH *funden*.

**found**[2] (establish) MIDDLE ENGLISH *founden*, from FRENCH *fonder*, from LATIN *fundus* base.

**found**[3] (melt metal) FRENCH *fondre* pour out, melt, mix together, from *fondre*, from LATIN *fundere* melt, cast, pour out.

**founder** FRENCH *fondrer* sink, from LATIN *fundus* base.

**foundling** MIDDLE ENGLISH *fundeling*, from *fundan*. See **find** + **-ling**.

**fount** See **fountain**, influenced by FRENCH *font* fount.

**fountain** FRENCH *fontaine* water, from LATIN *fontana*, from *fons*.

**fourchette** FRENCH *fourchette*, from *fourche*. See **fork**.

**fowl** OLD ENGLISH *fugol* bird.

**foyer** FRENCH hearth (floor of a fireplace), from LATIN *focus*. Theatres in early times had hearths in their entrance halls.

**fracas** FRENCH *fracasser* break in small bits, from LATIN *frangere* break + *quassare* shake.

**fraction** LATIN *frangere* break.

**fractious** See **fraction**.

**fracture** LATIN *fractura*.

**fragile** FRENCH, from LATIN *fragilis*, from *frangere* break.

**fragment** LATIN *fragmentum* a piece.

**fragrant** LATIN *fragrare* give out a sweet smell.

**frail** FRENCH *fraile* weak, from LATIN *fragilis* easily broken.

**fraise** FRENCH, from *fraiser* ruffle.

**frame** OLD ENGLISH *framian* be helpful.

**franchise** FRENCH freedom, from *franc* free. See **frank**.

**frank** FRENCH *franc* free, from LATIN *francus* a Frank. The Frankish tribe had conquered the territory the Romans called Gaul and renamed it France. Only the ruling Franks were free men.

**frantic** FRENCH *frenetique*, from LATIN *phreneticus* mad, from GREEK *phrenetikos*, from *phren* mind.

**fraternal** FRENCH *fraternite*, from LATIN *frater* brother.

**fraud** FRENCH *fraude*, from LATIN *fraus* dishonesty.

**fraught** DUTCH *vracht* a load (for a ship).

**fray** FRENCH, from LATIN *fricare* rub.

**frazzle** possibly from GERMAN *faselen*, from OLD ENGLISH *fæs*.

**freak** possibly from OLD ENGLISH *grician* dance.

**freckle** OLD NORSE *freknur* small spots of the skin.

**free** OLD ENGLISH *fri*.

**freebooter** DUTCH *vrijbuiter*, from *vrijbuit* plunder, from *vrij* free + *buit* booty, from *buiten* exchange or plunder, from *buten*.

**freeze** OLD ENGLISH *freosan*.

**freight** DUTCH *vracht* a load (for a ship).

**frenzy** FRENCH *frenesie*, from LATIN *phrenesis*. See **frantic**.

**frequent** FRENCH, from LATIN *frequens* crowded.

**fresco** ITALIAN fresh, from GERMAN *frisc*.

**fresh** OLD ENGLISH *fersc* not salted.

**fret** OLD ENGLISH *fretan* eat up.

**friar** FRENCH *frere* brother, from LATIN *frater*.

**fribble** imitative.

**fricassee** FRENCH *fricasser* cut up and fry.

**friction** LATIN *fricare* rub.

**Friday** OLD NORSE *Friedaeg* Frigg's (the Norse goddess of love) + *tag* day.

**friend** OLD ENGLISH *freond*.

**frieze** FRENCH, from LATIN *frisium* embroidered cloth.

**frigate** FRENCH, from ITALIAN *fregata*.

**fright** OLD ENGLISH *fyrhto* terror.

**frigid** LATIN *fiigidus* cold.

**frijole** SPANISH.

**frill** MIDDLE ENGLISH, origin uncertain.

**fringe** FRENCH *frenge* border of cloth threads that hang, from LATIN *fimbriae* threads.

**frippery** FRENCH *frepe* a rag.

**frisado** SPANISH.

**frisk** FRENCH *frisque* lively, from GERMAN *frisc.*

**frisson** FRENCH, from LATIN *frictionem,* from *frictio* shiver.

**fritter** possibly from FRENCH *fraiture* a breaking, from LATIN *fractura.*

**frivolous** LATIN *frivolus.*

**frizz** FRENCH *friser* curl, from LATIN *frigere* fry, because fried meat can curl at the ends.

**frizzle** MIDDLE ENGLISH curl hair. See **frizz.**

**frock** FRENCH *froc* hood.

**frog** OLD ENGLISH *frogga.*

**frolic** DUTCH *vrolijk* merry, from *vro* glad.

**from** OLD ENGLISH.

**front** LATIN *frons* forehead.

**frontier** FRENCH *frontiere* border of a country, from LATIN *frons* forehead.

**frost** OLD ENGLISH *froesan* freeze.

**froth** OLD NORSE *frotha* foam.

**frown** MIDDLE ENGLISH *frounen,* from FRENCH *fro(i)gnier,* from *frogne* angry look, grimace.

**frowsty** MIDDLE ENGLISH smelly, origin uncertain.

**fructify** FRENCH, from LATIN *fructificare,* from *fructus* enjoy.

**fructose** LATIN *fructus* fruit + chemical suffix *-ose.*

**frugal** LATIN *frugalis* fit for food, from *frux* fruit.

**fruit** FRENCH *fruit,* from LATIN *fructus.*

**frustrate** LATIN *frustrari* disappoint, from *frustra* without success.

**frustum** LATIN a piece.

**fry** MIDDLE ENGLISH *frien,* from FRENCH *frire* cook in a frying pan with fat, from LATIN *frigere* fry.

**fuddle** MIDDLE ENGLISH get drunk, origin uncertain.

**fudge** MIDDLE ENGLISH *fadge* make suit, fit, origin uncertain.

**fuel** FRENCH *fouaille,* from LATIN *focale,* from *focus* floor of a fireplace.

**fugitive** FRENCH *fugitif* fleeing, from LATIN *fugere* flee.

**-ful** OLD ENGLISH complete.

**fulcrum** LATIN.

**fulfill** OLD ENGLISH *fullfyllan* fill full.

**full** OLD ENGLISH.

**fuller** OLD ENGLISH.

**fulminate** LATIN *fulminare* thunder.

**fulsome** See **full** + **some.**

**fumble** DUTCH *fommelen.*

**fume** FRENCH *fum* smoke, from LATIN *fumus.*

**fumigate** LATIN *fumigare,* from *fumus* smoke + *agere* make.

**fun** MIDDLE ENGLISH *fonne* a fool.

**function** LATIN *functio* performance.

**fund** LATIN *fundus* bottom.

**fundamental** MIDDLE ENGLISH, from LATIN *fundamentalis* of the foundation, from *fundamentum* foundation, from *fundus* bottom.

**funeral** LATIN *funeralia,* from *funus* death.

**fungus** LATIN mushroom, from GREEK *spongos* sponge.

**funicular** LATIN *funiculum,* from *funis* a rope.

**funnel** LATIN *fundibulum,* from *infundibulum,* from *in-* in + *fundere* pour.

**fur** FRENCH *fuerre* a knife case.

**furbelow** FRENCH *falbala.*

**furbish** FRENCH *forbir* polish.

**furious** FRENCH *furieux* rage, from LATIN *furiosus,* from *furia.*

**furl** FRENCH *ferlier* tie up, from *ferm* firm + *lier* tie.

**furlong** OLD ENGLISH *furh* a furrow + *lang* long.

**furlough** DUTCH *verlof.*

**furnace** FRENCH *fornais* large oven, from LATIN *fornax* oven.

**furnish** FRENCH *fornir* supply.

**furniture** FRENCH *fourniture,* from *fournir.* See **furnish.**

**furor** FRENCH *fureur,* from LATIN *furor.*

**furrow** OLD ENGLISH *furh.*

**further** OLD ENGLISH *furthra* before.

**furtive** LATIN *furtivus* stolen, from *fur* thief.

**fury** FRENCH, from LATIN *furia furere* rage.

**furze** OLD ENGLISH *fyrs.*

**fuse** ITALIAN *fuso* shaft, from LATIN *fusus.*

**fuselage** FRENCH *fuselé* tapered, spindle-shaped.

**fusiform** LATIN *fusus* spindle + FRENCH *forme* shape, from LATIN *forma.*

**fusillade** FRENCH *fustiller* shoot.

**fuss** imitative.

**fusty** FRENCH *fuste* smell, from *fust* tree trunk, from LATIN *fustis* stick.

**futile** LATIN *futilis* worthless.

**futtock** nautical. See **foot** + **hook.**

**future** FRENCH *futur,* from LATIN *futurus* about to be, from *esse* be.

**fuzz** MIDDLE ENGLISH *fusse.*

**-fy (-ify, -efy)** FRENCH *-fier,* from LATIN *ficare,* from *facere* do, make.

# G

**gab** FRENCH *gabba* make fun of.

**gabble** See **gab** + **-le**.

**gable** FRENCH, from OLD NORSE *gafl.*

**gad** possibly from OLD ENGLISH *gædeling* companion.

**gadget** from *gadjet* sailors' slang for any small mechanical thing or part of a ship, perhaps from FRENCH *gâchette* catchpiece of a mechanism, from *gâche* staple of a lock.

**gadroon** FRENCH *godron*, from *godet* cup without handle, from DUTCH *kodde* log.

**gaff** FRENCH *gaffe*, from *gaf* boat hook.

**gaffe** FRENCH *gaffe* clumsy remark. See **gaff.**

**gaffer** See **grandfather** or **godfather.**

**gag** imitative.

**gage** FRENCH *pledge.*

**gaggle** MIDDLE ENGLISH *gagelen* cackle.

**gain** FRENCH *gaigner* win.

**gainsay** OLD ENGLISH *gegn* against + *secgan* say.

**gait** OLD NORSE *gata* path.

**gaiter** FRENCH *guêtre.*

**gala** ITALIAN, from FRENCH *gale* enjoyment.

**galaxy** FRENCH *galaxie*, from LATIN *galaxias*, from GREEK *gala* milk.

**gale** MIDDLE ENGLISH *gaile* wind, origin uncertain.

**galingale** FRENCH *galingal*, from ARABIC *khalanjan.*

**galipot** FRENCH possibly from *garipot* pine tree.

**gall**[1] (swelling) MIDDLE ENGLISH *galle*, from OLD ENGLISH *gealla*, from LATIN *galla*, lump on a plant.

**gall**[2] (bile) OLD ENGLISH *galla.*

**gall**[3] (on a tree) FRENCH *galle*, from LATIN *galla* the oak-apple.

**gall bladder** See **gall**[2] + **bladder.**

**gallant** FRENCH *galant* brave, from *gale* pleasure.

**galleass (galliass)** FRENCH *galeace*, from ITALIAN *galeaza.*

**galleon** SPANISH *galeón*, from LATIN *galea.* See **galley.**

**gallery** FRENCH *galerie* long room, from LATIN *galeria.*

**galley** MIDDLE ENGLISH, from FRENCH *galie* large ship, from LATIN *galea*, from GREEK.

**galley-west** BRITISH *colleywesson* awry, of unknown origin.

**gallipot** possibly from pottery that was brought in galleys (ships from the Mediterranean).

**gallon** FRENCH *galon,* from LATIN *galo* jug.

**gallop** FRENCH *galoper.*

**gallows** MIDDLE ENGLISH *galwe,* from OLD ENGLISH *galga.*

**gallus** See **gallows.**

**galore** IRISH *goleor* be enough.

**galoshes** FRENCH *galoche,* probably from *gallicula* small shoe.

**galumph** blend of *gallop* and *triumph,* coined by Lewis Carroll.

**galvanism** FRENCH, from ITALIAN, from Luigi *Galvani* (1737–1798), Italian physicist.

**gambit** FRENCH, from SPANISH *gambito* tripping, from ITALIAN, from LATIN *gamba,* from GREEK *kampe* a joint.

**gamble** MIDDLE ENGLISH *gamenen,* from OLD ENGLISH *gamenian* play.

**gambol** FRENCH, from ITALIAN *gambata* a kick.

**gambrel** possibly from FRENCH *gamberel.*

**game** OLD ENGLISH *gamen* sport.

**gammer** See **godmother.**

**gammon** FRENCH *gambe.*

**gamut** LATIN *gamma ut,* from *gamma* the name of the last note of medieval music + *ut* another name for the first note.

**gander** OLD ENGLISH *gandra.*

**gang** OLD NORSE *gangr* a going.

**gangling** possibly from SCOTTISH *gangrel* wandering beggar, from MIDDLE ENGLISH.

**ganglion** GREEK *ganglion* tumor.

**gangrene** LATIN *gangraena,* from GREEK *gangriana* eat away at something.

**gannet** OLD ENGLISH *ganot.*

**gantry** FRENCH, from LATIN *canterius* beast of burden, from GREEK *kanthon.*

**gap** OLD NORSE *gap.*

**gape** OLD NORSE *gapa.*

**gar** See **garfish.**

**garage** FRENCH *garer* guard.

**garantizados** SPANISH.

**garb** FRENCH *garbe* good fashion, from ITALIAN *garbo* grace.

**garbage** MIDDLE ENGLISH *garbage* intestines of birds.

**garble** ITALIAN *garbellare* sift, from ARABIC *gharbala,* from LATIN *cribrum* sieve.

**garden** FRENCH *gardin.*

**garderobe** FRENCH *garderobe,* from *garder* keep, guard + *robe* robe.

**garfish** MIDDLE ENGLISH *gare* spear + *fish* fish.

**gargantuan** a book about a huge king titled *Gargantua and Pantagruel* written in 1535 by the French writer François Rabelais, based on an early French legend about a kindly giant.

**garget** FRENCH *gargate, garguette* throat.

**gargle** FRENCH *gargouiller* make a bubbling sound, from *gargate* throat.

**gargoyle** FRENCH *gargouiller.* See **gargle.**

**garibaldi** Giuseppe *Garibaldi* (1807–1882), Italian patriot.

**garland** FRENCH *garlande.*

**garment** FRENCH *garnement* robe, from *garnir* protect.

**garner** FRENCH *gernier* place to store grain, from LATIN *granarium.*

**garnet** FRENCH, from LATIN *granatus* pomegranate.

**garnish** FRENCH *garnir* protect.

**garret** FRENCH *garite* tall tower for guards, from *garir* defend.

**garrison** FRENCH *garison,* from *garir* defend.

**garrote** SPANISH a stick used to wind a cord or rope, from FRENCH.

**garrulous** LATIN *garrire* talk quickly.

**garter** FRENCH *garet* the back of the knee.

**garth** MIDDLE ENGLISH, from OLD NORSE *garthr* farmyard.

**gas** DUTCH, from GREEK *chaos* empty space.

**gash** FRENCH *garser,* from LATIN *charaxare* scratch, from GREEK *charassein.*

**gasket** ENGLISH *caskette* small rope used to secure a furled sail, origin uncertain.

**gaskin** probably short for *galligaskins* loose fitting pants, from FRENCH *garguesque,* from ITALIAN *grechesca* Greek (as in Greek breeches).

**gasp** OLD NORSE *geispa* yawn.

**gaster** GREEK stomach.

**gastric** See **gaster.**

**gastronomy** FRENCH *gastronomie,* from GREEK *gaster* stomach + *nemein* regulate, from *nomos* rule.

**gate** OLD ENGLISH *geat.*

**gather** OLD ENGLISH *gaderian* bring together, from *geador* together.

**gauche** FRENCH left, from *gauchir* turn aside.

**gaudy** MIDDLE ENGLISH *gaude,* from LATIN *gaudere* enjoy.

**gauge** FRENCH.

**gaum** possibly from OLD ENGLISH *guma.*

**gaunt** MIDDLE ENGLISH, from FRENCH *gant,* origin uncertain, perhaps from SCANDINAVIAN.

**gauntlet** MIDDLE ENGLISH, from FRENCH *gantelet* armored glove, from *gant* glove.

**gauze** FRENCH *gaze* thin cloth, which is supposed to first have come from Gaza, a city near the Mediterranean Sea.

**gavel** SCOTTISH *gable* a tool.

**gawk** OLD ENGLISH *ga(gol)* foolish person.

**gay** FRENCH *gai* merry.

**gaze** MIDDLE ENGLISH, of NORSE origin.

**gazebo** origin uncertain, perhaps with some humor based on the word *gaze.*

**gazelle** FRENCH *gazel.*

**gazette** FRENCH newspaper, from ITALIAN *gazetta* coin worth little, also the price of a newspaper in Venice, Italy in the 16th century, from LATIN *gaza* wealth, from GREEK treasure.

**gazogene** FRENCH *gazogène,* from *gaz* gas + *-gène.* See **-gen.**

**gear** OLD NORSE *gervi* equipment.

**gebel** ARABIC *jebel* mountain.

**geezer** FRENCH, from GERMAN *wisa* manner.

**gefüllte fish** YIDDISH, from GERMAN *gefüllt* filled, stuffed, from *fullen* fill.

**geisha** JAPANESE.

**gel** See **gelatin.**

**gelatin** FRENCH *gélatine,* from ITALIAN *gelatina* jelly, from LATIN *gelare* freeze.

**geld** OLD NORSE *gelda* unable to reproduce.

**gem** FRENCH *gemme* jewel, from LATIN *gemma.*

**Gemini** LATIN *gemini* twins (plural of *geminus* twin).

**-gen** FRENCH *gène,* from GREEK *genes* born.

**gendarme** FRENCH, from LATIN *gens* a people + *de* of + *arma* arms.

**gender** FRENCH *gendre* sort, from GREEK *genus.*

**gene** GERMAN *gen*, from GREEK *genos* race.

**general** FRENCH universal, from LATIN *generalis*, from *genus* kind, type.

**generate** LATIN *generare*, from *genus* race.

**generic** LATIN *genus* kind, type.

**generous** LATIN *generosus* noble birth, from *genus* kind, type.

**genesis** LATIN creation, from GREEK.

**genial** LATIN *genialis* pleasant, from *genius* guardian spirit.

**genie** FRENCH (in FRENCH version of Arabian Nights, for ARABIC *jinni, jinn* spirit), from LATIN genius.

**genitive** FRENCH, from LATIN *casus genitivus* case of origin.

**genius** LATIN guardian spirit.

**genre** FRENCH kind, from LATIN *genus* kind.

**genteel** FRENCH *gentil* noble birth, from LATIN *gentilis* same family (clan), from *gens* clan.

**gentian** FRENCH, from LATIN *gentiana*.

**gentile** LATIN *gentilis* of the same clan (group of families), from *gens* clan.

**gentle** FRENCH *gentil* noble birth, from LATIN *gentilis*. See **gentile**.

**gentry** FRENCH *genterise* rank, from *gentil* noble birth. See **gentle**.

**genuflect** LATIN *genu* the knee.

**genuine** LATIN *genuinus* natural.

**genus** LATIN kind, type.

**geo-** GREEK *gaia, ge* the earth.

**geodesy** GREEK *ge* the earth + *dalien* divide.

**geography** LATIN *geographia*, from GREEK *geographia* writing about the earth, from geo- + -graphy.

**geology** LATIN *geologia*, from GREEK geo- + -logy.

**geometry** FRENCH *geometrie*, from LATIN *geometria*, from GREEK *gaia, ge* the earth + *-metria* measurement.

**geranium** LATIN, from GREEK *geranion* bill of a crane, because the seed looks like it has a beak.

**gerbil** FRENCH *gerbille*, from *gerbo*.

**germ** LATIN *germinare* bud, from *germen* bud.

**gesticulate** LATIN *gesticulari* make gestures, from *gerere* carry on.

**gesture** LATIN *gestura* behavior, perform, from *gerere* carry on.

**get** OLD NORSE *geta*.

**gewgaw** MIDDLE ENGLISH *giuegoue, gugaw*.

**geyser** Icelandic *Geysir* name of a hot spring in Iceland, from OLD NORSE *geysa* gush.

**ghastly** OLD ENGLISH *gastlic* ghostly, from *gast* ghost.

**ghetto** perhaps from ITALIAN *getto* foundry, from *gettare* pour, from LATIN *jactare* throw. *Ghèto,* a part of Venice, Italy, was set aside in 1516 for Jews to live in. Before that time the area was a foundry (a place where metal is melted and poured into molds for making things).

**ghost** OLD ENGLISH *gast*.

**ghoul** ARABIC *ghul* demon.

**giant** FRENCH *geant*, from LATIN *gigas* a huge creature from mythology, from GREEK *gigas*.

**gibber** imitative.

**gibbet** FRENCH *gibet*, from *gibe* club.

**gibbous** LATIN *gibbosus*, from *gibba* a hump.

**gibe** FRENCH *giber* handle roughly.

**giddy** OLD ENGLISH *gidig* foolish.

**gift** OLD NORSE *gipt.*

**gig** MIDDLE ENGLISH *gigge, ghyg* spinning top (in *whyrlegyg*), also *giglet* giddy girl, from OLD NORSE *geiga* turn sideways.

**gigantic** LATIN *gigas.* See **giant**.

**giggle** imitative.

**gild** MIDDLE ENGLISH *gilden,* from OLD ENGLISH *gyldan* cover with a layer of gold.

**gill**[1] (fish) MIDDLE ENGLISH *gile,* from OLD NORSE *giolnar* gills.

**gill**[2] (glen) MIDDLE ENGLISH, from OLD NORSE *gil* a deep glen.

**gill**[3] (measure) MIDDLE ENGLISH, from FRENCH *gille* a wine measure, from LATIN *gillo* earthenware jar.

**gilt**[1] (gold) See **gild**.

**gilt**[2] (sow) OLD NORSE *gylt-r* young sow.

**gimcrack** MIDDLE ENGLISH *gibbecrak* an ornament.

**gimlet** FRENCH, from DUTCH *wimmel* tool.

**gimmick** AMERICAN, origin uncertain.

**gimp**[1] (limp) AMERICAN slang, origin uncertain.

**gimp**[2] (cord) DUTCH, origin uncertain.

**gin**[1] (machine) MIDDLE ENGLISH, from FRENCH *engin* machine, from LATIN *ingenium* skill.

**gin**[2] (drink) FRENCH *genvre* juniper tree, from LATIN *juniperus* from an alcoholic drink that was flavored with juniper berries.

**ginger** OLD ENGLISH *gingifer* the plant.

**gingham** MALAY *ginggang* striped cloth.

**gingivitis** LATIN *gingiva* gums + -itis.

**giraffe** FRENCH, from ITALIAN *giraffa,* from ARABIC *zarafa.*

**gird** OLD ENGLISH *gyrdan* surround.

**girdle** OLD ENGLISH *gyrdel* belt worn around the waist.

**girl** MIDDLE ENGLISH *girle* youngster (child).

**girt** OLD ENGLISH *gyrdan* surround.

**girth** OLD NORSE *gjörth* hoop.

**gist** FRENCH.

**gittern** FRENCH *guiterne,* from SPANISH *guittarra* guitar.

**give** OLD ENGLISH *giefan.*

**gizzard** FRENCH *gisier,* from LATIN *gigeria* cooked insides of poultry.

**glacier** FRENCH *glace* ice, from LATIN *glacies.*

**glad** OLD ENGLISH *glæd* cheerful.

**glade** MIDDLE ENGLISH *glade, glode,* from OLD NORSE *gladr* bright.

**gladiator** LATIN swordsman, from *gladius* sword.

**gladius** LATIN.

**glamour** SCOTTISH *gramarye* magic.

**glance** FRENCH *glacier* slip, from LATIN *glaciare* turn into ice.

**gland** FRENCH *glande,* from LATIN *glandual* gland of the throat.

**glare** GERMAN *glaren.*

**glass** OLD ENGLISH *glæs.*

**glaze** MIDDLE ENGLISH *glasen* make a glass surface, from OLD ENGLISH *glæs* glass.

**gleam** OLD ENGLISH *glæm* brightness.

**glean** FRENCH *glener,* from LATIN *glennare.*

**glede** OLD ENGLISH *glida.*

**glee** OLD ENGLISH *gleo* joy.

**glen** WELSH *glyn.*

**glib** DUTCH *globberig* slippery.

**glide** OLD ENGLISH *glidan* slide.

**glimmer** OLD ENGLISH *glæm*.

**glimpse** MIDDLE ENGLISH *glimsen* glow, from OLD ENGLISH *glæm* brightness.

**glint** possibly from SWEDISH *glinta* slip.

**glisten** OLD ENGLISH *glisnian*.

**glitter** OLD NORSE *glitra* sparkle.

**glitzy** probably from GERMAN *glitzern* glitter.

**gloaming** OLD ENGLISH *glow* twilight.

**gloat** OLD NORSE *glotta*.

**glob** possibly from a blend of **blob** and **gob**.

**globe** LATIN *globus* ball.

**glockenspiel** GERMAN *glocke* a bell + *spiel* play.

**glom** SCOTTISH.

**gloom** MIDDLE ENGLISH *gloumen*, possibly from OLD ENGLISH *glumian*.

**glop** possibly from **glue** + **slop**.

**glory** FRENCH *glorie*, from LATIN *gloria* honor, praise.

**gloss**[1] (shine) SCANDINAVIAN, from GERMAN *glos*.

**gloss**[2] (explanation) MIDDLE ENGLISH *glose*, from FRENCH *glosa*, from LATIN *glossa* word needing explanation, from GREEK *glossa* language.

**glossary** See **gloss**[2].

**glottis** GREEK *glotta*, from *glossa* tongue.

**glove** OLD ENGLISH *glof*.

**glow** OLD ENGLISH *glowan* shine.

**glucose** FRENCH *glucose*, from GREEK *gleukos* sweet wine, from *glyks* sweet.

**glue** FRENCH *glu*, from LATIN *glus*, from *gluten*.

**glum** MIDDLE ENGLISH *glomen*. See **gloom**.

**glut** FRENCH *gloutir* gulp down, from LATIN *gluttire*.

**gluten** LATIN glue.

**glutton** FRENCH *glouton* greedy eater, from LATIN *glutto*.

**gnarled** MIDDLE ENGLISH *knur* a knot.

**gnash** MIDDLE ENGLISH *gnasten*, from OLD NORSE *gnasten*.

**gnat** OLD ENGLISH *gnæt*.

**gnaw** OLD ENGLISH *gnagan*.

**gnome** FRENCH, from GREEK *gnome* thought.

**gnomon** LATIN, from GREEK *gignoskein* know.

**go** OLD ENGLISH *gan*.

**goad** OLD ENGLISH *gad*.

**goal** MIDDLE ENGLISH *gol* limit.

**goat** OLD ENGLISH *gat*.

**gob** FRENCH *gobe* lump.

**gobble** MIDDLE ENGLISH *gobben* drink with greed.

**goblet** MIDDLE ENGLISH, from FRENCH *gobelet* cup.

**goblin** FRENCH *gobelin*, from LATIN *gobelinus*, perhaps from *cabalus*, from GREEK *kobalos* sprite.

**god** OLD ENGLISH.

**godfather** See **god** + **father**.

**godmother** See **god** + **mother**.

**goggle** MIDDLE ENGLISH *gogelen*.

**goiter** FRENCH *goitron* throat, from LATIN *guttur*.

**gold** OLD ENGLISH.

**golf** possibly from SCOTTISH *gowf* strike.

**golliwog** name of a doll in an illustrated series of children's books written in the early part of the 20th century.

**gombeen** IRISH *gaimbín*, from LATIN *cambium* exchange.

**-gon** GREEK *gonia* an angle.

**gondola** ITALIAN *gondola*, from *gondula*.

**gong** MALAY probably imitative of the sound.

**good** OLD ENGLISH *god* excellent.

**good-bye** *God be with you* or *ye*.

**goodness** OLD ENGLISH *godnes* kindness.

**goof** FRENCH *goffe* stupid, from ITALIAN *goffo*.

**goose** OLD ENGLISH *gos*.

**gore**[1] (blood) OLD ENGLISH *gor* dirt.

**gore**[2] (pierce the skin) MIDDLE ENGLISH *goren*, from *gore* spear, from OLD ENGLISH *gar*.

**gorge** FRENCH throat, from LATIN *gurges* whirlpool.

**gorilla** GREEK *gorillai* tribe of hairy people, possibly from an African name.

**gorse** MIDDLE ENGLISH *gorst*, similar to LATIN *hordeum* barley.

**gosling** MIDDLE ENGLISH *goslynge*. See **goose** + **-ling**.

**gospel** OLD ENGLISH *godspel* teachings of Jesus, the Gospel, from *god* good + *spel* news.

**gossamer** MIDDLE ENGLISH *gosesomer* goose summer, the time in the fall when the geese are in season.

**gossip** OLD ENGLISH *godsibb* godparent (person who agrees to be responsible for the religious training of another's child), from *god* God + *sibb* relative.

**Gothic** LATIN, from GREEK *gothoi*.

**gouge** FRENCH, from LATIN *gubia*.

**goulash** HUNGARIAN *gulyashus*, from *gulyas* herdsman + *hus* meat. Originally beef or lamb soup made by herdsmen while pasturing.

**gour** HINDI *gaur* large ox.

**gourd** FRENCH, from LATIN *cucurbita*.

**gourmet** FRENCH winetaster.

**gout** FRENCH *goute*, from LATIN *gutta* drop, because in medieval times it was thought that drops of fluids in the body affected the places where two bones are joined (joints).

**govern** FRENCH *governor* rule, from LATIN *gubernare*, from GREEK *kybernan*.

**gown** FRENCH *goune* long coat, from LATIN *gumma* fur.

**grab** MIDDLE ENGLISH *grabben* hold firmly, probably from GERMAN.

**grace** FRENCH, from LATIN *gratia* favor, charm.

**grade** LATIN *gradus* step.

**-grade** LATIN *gradi* walk.

**gradely** MIDDLE ENGLISH *greithlic*, from OLD NORSE *griethligr*.

**gradient** LATIN *gradi* walk.

**gradual** LATIN *gradualis* by degrees, from *gradus* step.

**graduate** LATIN *graduari* take an academic degree, from *gradus* step.

**graft** MIDDLE ENGLISH *graffe*, from FRENCH *grafe*, from LATIN *graphium* pointed pencil, from GREEK *graphein* write.

**grail** FRENCH *graal*, from LATIN *gradalis* cup.

**grain** FRENCH, from LATIN *granum* seed.

**gram** FRENCH, from LATIN, from GREEK *gramma* small weight.

**-gram** GREEK *gramma* small weight.

**grammar** MIDDLE ENGLISH *gramarye,* from FRENCH *grammaire,* from LATIN *grammatica,* from GREEK *grammatike tekhne* art of letters, from *gramma* letter, from *graphein* draw or write.

**grampus** MIDDLE ENGLISH *grapays,* from FRENCH *graspeis,* from LATIN *crassus piscis,* from *crassus* fat + *piscis* fish.

**granary** LATIN *granum* grain.

**grand** FRENCH great, from LATIN *grandis* large.

**grandfather** See **grand** + **father.**

**grandiloquent** LATIN *grandiloquus,* from *grandis* great + *loqui* speak.

**grandiose** FRENCH, from ITALIAN *grandioso,* from *grande* great, from LATIN *grandis.*

**grandmother** See **grand** + **mother.**

**grange** FRENCH barn, from LATIN *granum* seed.

**granite** ITALIAN *granito* grained, from LATIN *granum* grain.

**granola** See **grain** + **-ola.**

**grant** FRENCH *granter* promise, from LATIN *credere* believe.

**granule** LATIN *granulum,* from *granum* grain.

**grape** FRENCH bunch of grapes, from *graper* gather with a hook.

**grapeshot** See **grape** + *shot.* See **shoot.**

**-graph** GREEK *graphos.*

**graphic** LATIN *graphicus* relating to drawing, from GREEK *graphikos,* from *graphein* write, draw.

**-graphy** GREEK *-graphia* description, from *graphein* write.

**grapnel** MIDDLE ENGLISH, from FRENCH *grapin* hook.

**grapple** FRENCH *grape* hook.

**grasp** MIDDLE ENGLISH *graspen,* from OLD ENGLISH *gegræppian.*

**grate**[1] (grind) FRENCH *grater.*

**grate**[2] (frame) LATIN *cratis* crate.

**grateful** LATIN *gratus* pleasing + **-ful.**

**gratify** LATIN *gratificari* please, from *gratus* pleasing + *facere* do, make.

**gratis** LATIN *gratia* a favor.

**gratitude** FRENCH, from LATIN *gratus* pleasing.

**gratuitous** LATIN *gratuitus* free.

**grave**[1] (burial) OLD ENGLISH *græf.*

**grave**[2] (important) FRENCH, from LATIN *gravis.*

**gravel** FRENCH *gravelem,* from *greve* stony or pebbly shore.

**gravity** LATIN *gravitas* weight.

**gravy** MIDDLE ENGLISH *grave* spiced sauce, from LATIN *granatus* having many grains, from *granum* seed, from gravies seasoned with the grains of spices.

**gray** OLD ENGLISH *græg.*

**graze** MIDDLE ENGLISH *grasen,* from OLD ENGLISH *grasian,* from *græs* grass.

**grease** FRENCH *graisse* animal fat, from LATIN *crassus* fat.

**great** OLD ENGLISH *great* large.

**grebe** FRENCH.

**greedy** OLD ENGLISH *grædig.*

**green** OLD ENGLISH *grene, groeni,* related to *growan* grow.

**greengage** See **green** + Gage (the surname).

**greensward** See **green** + from OLD ENGLISH *sweard* a skin.

**greet** OLD ENGLISH *gretan.*

**gregarious** LATIN *grex* flock.

**gremlin** MODERN ENGLISH, British Royal Air Force slang, origin unknown, possibly from IRISH *gruaimin* bad-tempered little fellow.

**grenade** FRENCH small bomb, from LATIN *granum* seed, because a grenade looks like a pomegranate, a fruit with many seeds.

**grid** See **gridiron**.

**griddle** FRENCH *gridil* grate. See **gridiron**.

**gridiron** MIDDLE ENGLISH *gredire* griddle, from FRENCH *gridil* grate.

**grieve** FRENCH *grever* burden, from LATIN *gravare*.

**griffin** FRENCH *griffon,* from LATIN *gryphus,* from GREEK *grypos* curved, because of the curved beak.

**grill** FRENCH *gril,* from LATIN *craticula*.

**grille** FRENCH, from LATIN *graticula*.

**grim** OLD ENGLISH fierce.

**grimace** FRENCH *grimuche*.

**grimalkin** probably from OLD ENGLISH *græg* + *malkin* short form of the name *Matilda* or *Maud*.

**grime** possibly from OLD ENGLISH *grima* mask.

**grin** OLD ENGLISH *grennian*.

**grind** OLD ENGLISH *grindan* make into small parts.

**grip** OLD ENGLISH *gripe*.

**gripe** OLD ENGLISH *gripan* take.

**grisly** OLD ENGLISH *grislic*.

**grist** OLD ENGLISH.

**grit** OLD ENGLISH *greot*.

**grizzle** FRENCH *gris* gray.

**groan** OLD ENGLISH *granian*.

**groat** DUTCH *grote*.

**grocer** FRENCH *grossier* person who sells goods in large amounts, from LATIN *grossarius,* from *grossus* great.

**grog** "Old *Grog*", nickname for English Admiral Edward Vernon (1684–1757), because he wore a *grogram* (special kind of coat made of silk and wool).

**groin** probably from OLD ENGLISH *grynde*.

**groom** MIDDLE ENGLISH *grom* boy.

**groove** DUTCH *groeve* channel.

**grope** OLD ENGLISH *grapian* touch.

**gross** FRENCH *gros* thick, from LATIN *grossus*.

**grotesque** FRENCH fanciful, from ITALIAN *pittura grottesca* cave painting, from *grotta* cave, from paintings found on the basement walls of Roman ruins. See **grotto**.

**grotto** ITALIAN, from LATIN *grupta,* from *crypta* burial place, from GREEK *krypte* hidden.

**grouch** MIDDLE ENGLISH *grucchen.* See **grudge**.

**ground** OLD ENGLISH *grund* bottom.

**groundsel** OLD ENGLISH, possibly *gund* pus + *swelgan* swallow, from its use in healing.

**group** FRENCH *groupe,* from ITALIAN *groppo* knot.

**grouse** MIDDLE ENGLISH *grows,* origin unknown.

**grove** OLD ENGLISH *graf*.

**grovel** OLD NORSE *agrufu* face downward.

**grow** OLD ENGLISH *growan*.

**grub** MIDDLE ENGLISH *grubben*.

**grudge** FRENCH *groucier* grumble.

**gruel** FRENCH *gru* oatmeal.

**gruesome** SCOTTISH *grue* be terrified.

**gruff** DUTCH *grof* heavy.

145

**grumble** probably from Dutch *grommelen*.

**grunge** possibly from **grime** + **sludge**.

**grunt** Old English *grunnettan* make a sound like a pig.

**guano** Spanish *huanu* droppings.

**guarantee** See **guaranty**.

**guaranty** French *guarantie*, from *garant* protection.

**guard** French *garder* protect.

**guava** Spanish *guayaba*.

**gudgeon** French, from Latin *gobio*, from Greek *kobios*.

**guerrilla** Spanish *guerilla*, from *guerra* war, from German *werra* quarrel.

**guess** probably from Dutch *gessen*.

**guest** Old Norse *gestr* visitor.

**guffaw** imitative.

**guide** French *guider* lead.

**guild** Old Norse *gildi* payment.

**guilder** Middle English, from Dutch *gulden florijn* golden florin (gold coin of medieval France).

**guile** French.

**guillotine** the French physician Joseph I. *Guillotin* (1738–1814), who recommended its use during the French Revolution.

**guilt** Old English *gylt* crime.

**guimp** See **gimp**[2].

**guinea** the country of *Guinea* in Africa.

**guinea pig** probably from *Guinea-men*, ships that traveled between England, Africa, and South America, in which the animals were first brought to England.

**guise** French way.

**guitar** French *guitare*, from Spanish *guitarra*, from Arabic *qitara* instrument with strings, from Greek *kithara* type of lyre (small harp used by the ancient Greeks).

**gulch** imitative.

**gules** French *goules*, from Latin *gulae*.

**gulf** French *golfe* bay, from Italian *golgo*, from Greek *lokpos*.

**gull**[1] (bird) Middle English, related to Welsh *gwylan* gull.

**gull**[2] (silly person) probably from Middle English *golle* silly person.

**gullet** French *goulet*, from Latin *gula* throat.

**gullible** See **gull**[2].

**gully**[1] (channel) Middle English *golet* water channel, probably from French *goulet*, from Latin *gula* throat.

**gully**[2] (knife) origin uncertain, perhaps related to **gullet**.

**gulp** Dutch *gulpen*.

**gum** Middle English *gomme*, from French *gomme* sticky liquid from some trees, from Latin *gummi*, from Greek *kommi* from Egyptian *kemai*.

**gumption** Scottish common sense, shrewdness, possibly from Middle English *gome* attention, heed, from Old Norse *gaumr* heed.

**gun** Old Norse *Gunnhildr* female name, from *gunnr* war + *hildr* battle, from the Scandinavian habit of giving their weapons female names.

**gunnel** (gunwale) Middle English *gonne walle*, from **gun** + *wale* plank. Originally a platform on the deck of a ship to support the mounted guns.

**gunny** (sack) Hindi *goni* coarse fabric, from Sanskrit *goni* sack.

**gurgle** imitative.

**gurry** MIDDLE ENGLISH diarrhoea (later applied to fish remains and to a wheelbarrow used to haul them).

**guru** HINDI *guru* teacher.

**gush** imitative.

**gusset** FRENCH *gouchet, gousset.*

**gust** OLD NORSE *gustr.*

**gusto** ITALIAN taste, from LATIN *gustus.*

**gut** OLD ENGLISH *guttas* intestines.

**gutter** FRENCH *goutiere* channel, from *goute* drop, from LATIN *gutta.*

**guttural** LATIN *guttur* throat.

**guy**[1] (person) *Guy* Fawkes (1570–1606), leader of the Gunpowder Plot attempt to blow up the British Parliament building in 1605.

**guy**[2] (line) FRENCH *guie* a guide, from *guier.*

**gymkhana** HINDI *gend-khana* ball-house, the name given to a racquet court.

**gymnasium** LATIN athletic school, from GREEK *gymnasion,* from *gymnos* naked, because ancient Greek athletes exercised naked.

**gyp** See gypsy.

**gypsum** LATIN *gypsum,* from GREEK *gypsos* chalk.

**gypsy** MIDDLE ENGLISH *gypcian* Egyptian, because it was mistakenly thought that Gypsies came from Egypt.

**gyrate** LATIN *gyrare,* from *gyrus* circle, from GREEK *gyros.*

**gyrfalcon** FRENCH *girfaucon,* from GERMAN *gir* hawk.

# H

**ha** imitative.

**haberdasher** probably from FRENCH *hapertas* kind of cloth.

**habergeon** FRENCH *haubergeon,* from *hauberc* medieval coat of armor. See **hauberk**.

**habit** FRENCH, from LATIN *habitus* condition, from *habere* have.

**habitat** LATIN *habitare,* from *habere* have.

**habituate** LATIN *habitus.* See **habit**.

**hack**[1] (chop) OLD ENGLISH *haccian* cut.

**hack**[2] (horse) See **hackney**.

**hackamore** probably from SPANISH *jaquima* halter.

**hackle** MIDDLE ENGLISH *hechele,* from *hackle* bird feathers, from OLD ENGLISH *hacele.*

**hackney** MIDDLE ENGLISH *hakene* hackney horse, from *Hackney,* a town in England once famous for its horses. These horses were often worn out, from being overused.

**had** See **have**.

**haddock** MIDDLE ENGLISH, origin uncertain.

**hafod** WELSH summer house.

**haft** OLD ENGLISH *hæft.*

**hag** OLD ENGLISH *hægtesse* witch.

**haggard** FRENCH *hagard* not tamed.

**haggle** possibly from SCANDINAVIAN.

**hail**[1] (greet) MIDDLE ENGLISH *hailen* greet, from OLD NORSE *heill* well.

**hail**[2] (ice) MIDDLE ENGLISH *haile,* from OLD ENGLISH *hægel.*

**hair** OLD ENGLISH *hær.*

**halberd** GERMAN *helmbarie,* from *helm* handle + *barte* an ax.

**halcyon** MIDDLE ENGLISH *alcioun,* from LATIN *alycon* kingfisher (bird), from GREEK *(h)alkyon.* According to Greek mythology, *Alkyone,* the daughter of the god of the winds, threw herself into the sea when she learned her husband was dead. She was changed into a kingfisher. She built a floating nest on the sea, and whenever she laid eggs the sea was always calm at that place.

**hale**[1] (healthy) OLD ENGLISH *hal.* See **heal**.

**hale**[2] (summon) FRENCH *haler* pull, haul.

**half** OLD ENGLISH *h(e)alf.*

**hall** OLD ENGLISH *heall* large roofed place.

**hallah** HEBREW.

**hallelujah** LATIN *alleluja,* from GREEK *hallelouia,* from HEBREW *halelu* praise + *ya* God.

**hallmark** a *mark* first put on gold or silver items in the 1300s at the Goldsmith's *Hall* in London to show quality or purity.

**hallo** FRENCH *hola,* from *ho* ahoy + *la* there.

**hallow** OLD ENGLISH *halgian.*

**hallucinate** LATIN *(h)allucinari* wander in the mind.

**halo** LATIN *halos* circle of light around the sun or moon, from GREEK *halos* circle or disk.

**halogen** GREEK *hals, halo-* salt + *-gen* produce, because a salt is formed in reactions of these elements with metal.

**halt** GERMAN *halten* hold.

**halter** OLD ENGLISH *hælfter.*

**halyard** MIDDLE ENGLISH *halier,* from *halen* pull.

**ham** OLD ENGLISH *hamm.*

**hamburger** the German town of *Hamburg,* where hamburgers were first known to be made.

**hame** DUTCH horse collar.

**hamlet** FRENCH *hamel* village, from GERMAN *hamm* enclosed area.

**hammer** OLD ENGLISH *hamor.*

**hammock** SPANISH *hamaca,* origin uncertain.

**hamper**[1] (get in the way) MIDDLE ENGLISH *hamperen* surround.

**hamper**[2] (large basket) FRENCH *hanap* a cup.

**hand** OLD ENGLISH.

**handicap** MODERN ENGLISH *hand in cap,* a game where two players would put their hands (holding money) into a cap.

**handiwork** OLD ENGLISH *handgeweorc.*

**handkerchief** See **hand** + **kerchief.**

**handle** OLD ENGLISH *hand* hand.

**handsome** MIDDLE ENGLISH *handsom* easy to handle, ready at hand.

**handy** See **hand.**

**hang** OLD ENGLISH *hangian.*

**hangar** FRENCH *hangar* shed, from *hanghart,* from LATIN *angarium* shed in which horses are shod.

**hanger**[1] (something hanging) See **hang.**

**hanger**[2] (woods) OLD ENGLISH *hangra.*

**hank** OLD NORSE *hankar.*

**hanker** probably from DUTCH *hankeren* want.

**hansom** Joseph A. *Hansom* (1803–1882), Englishman who designed the cab.

**hap** OLD NORSE *happ* good luck.

**haphazard** See **hap** + **hazard.**

**hapless** See **hap** + **-less.**

**happen** MIDDLE ENGLISH *happenen,* from OLD NORSE *happ* good luck.

**happy** OLD NORSE *happ* good luck.

**harangue** MIDDLE ENGLISH speech, from LATIN *harenga* speech made at a meeting.

**harass** FRENCH *harasser,* from *harer* set a dog to chase, from *hare* the hunting cry to urge the dog to chase.

**harbinger** FRENCH *herberge* temporary place to stay, from the idea of the person who went ahead of an army to find shelter.

**harbor** OLD ENGLISH *herebeorg* place to stay, from *here* army + *beorg* protection.

**hard** OLD ENGLISH *heard* solid.

**hardy** FRENCH *hardi* bold.

**hare** OLD ENGLISH *hara.*

**harem** ARABIC *haram* women's rooms, from *harama* forbidden, because men were forbidden to enter.

**haricot** FRENCH possibly from *harigoter* tear into scraps.

**hark** MIDDLE ENGLISH *herkien,* possibly from OLD ENGLISH *heorcnian.*

**harlequin** ITALIAN, from FRENCH *Herlequin,* a devil in medieval legend.

**harm** OLD ENGLISH *hearm.*

**harmonium** GREEK *harmonion.*

**harmony** LATIN *harmonia* agreement of sounds, from GREEK *harmonia,* from *harmos* fitting.

**harness** FRENCH *harneis* armor, from OLD NORSE.

**harp** OLD ENGLISH *hearpe.*

**harpoon** DUTCH, from FRENCH *harper* claw, from OLD NORSE *harpa* squeeze.

**harpsichord** FRENCH *harpechorde* harp string, from LATIN *harpichordium,* from *harpa* harp + *chorda* string.

**harpy** FRENCH, from LATIN, from GREEK *harpazien* seize.

**harridan** FRENCH *haridelle* worn-out horse.

**harrow** probably from OLD NORSE *harfr.*

**harry** OLD ENGLISH *hergian* make raids, from *here* army.

**harsh** MIDDLE ENGLISH *harsk,* from DANISH bad smell or taste.

**hart** OLD ENGLISH *heorot.*

**hartebeest** AFRIKAANS, from DUTCH *harte* hart (deer) + *beest* beast.

**harum-scarum** probably from **harry** + **scare** + **them.**

**harvest** OLD ENGLISH *hærfest* season for gathering crops.

**has** See **have.**

**hash** FRENCH *hacher* chop with heavy blows, from *hache* ax.

**hasp** FRENCH *haepse.*

**hassock** OLD ENGLISH *hassue* grass that is not smooth. Hassocks were originally made from such grass.

**haste** MIDDLE ENGLISH, from OLD ENGLISH speed.

**hastilude** LATIN *hastiludus,* from *hasta* spear + *ludus* play.

**hat** OLD ENGLISH *hætt.*

**hatch**[1] (egg) MIDDLE ENGLISH *hacchen.*

**hatch**[2] (door) OLD ENGLISH *hæcc* a grate.

**hatchet** FRENCH *hatchette,* from *hache* ax.

**hate** OLD ENGLISH *hatian.*

**hathi** HINDI, from SANSKRIT *hastin* elephant, from *hasta* elephant's trunk.

**hauberk** FRENCH *hausberc* neck protector, from FRANKISH *hals* the neck + *bergan* protect.

**haughty** FRENCH *haut* high, from LATIN *altus.*

**haul** FRENCH *haler* pull, from DUTCH *halen* get.

**haunch** FRENCH *hanche* hip.

**haunt** FRENCH *hanter* be at a place often.

**hauteur** FRENCH *haut* high, proud, from LATIN *altus.*

**have** OLD ENGLISH *habban.*

**haven** OLD ENGLISH *hæfen* harbor, from OLD NORSE *höfn.*

**haversack** FRENCH, from GERMAN *habersack* sack of oats.

**havoc** FRENCH *havot* take by force.

**haw** OLD ENGLISH *haga* enclosure, hedge.

**hawk** OLD ENGLISH *hafoc.*

**hawser** FRENCH *hauceor,* from *halcier* pull up, from LATIN *altus* high.

**hawthorn** OLD ENGLISH *haga* hedge + *thorn.*

**hay** OLD ENGLISH *hieg.*

**hayron** MIDDLE ENGLISH *heiroun,* from FRENCH *hairon,* from LATIN *hagironem* heron.

**hazard** MIDDLE ENGLISH, from FRENCH *hasard* dice game, from ARABIC *yasara* playing at dice.

**haze**[1] (mist) See **hazy.**

**haze**[2] (harass) OLD ENGLISH *haser* annoy.

**hazy** probably from OLD ENGLISH *hasu* like dusk.

**he** OLD ENGLISH *he.*

**head** OLD ENGLISH *heafod.*

**headlong** MIDDLE ENGLISH *hedlong.*

**heal** OLD ENGLISH *hælan* make whole.

**health** OLD ENGLISH *hælth* being well in body or mind.

**heap** OLD ENGLISH.

**hearse** MIDDLE ENGLISH frame for holding many candles over a coffin, from FRENCH *herse* large rake, from LATIN *hirpex* harrow (a large rake used to prepare ground for planting), from *hirpus* wolf (from the long teeth on the harrow).

**heart** MIDDLE ENGLISH *herte,* from OLD ENGLISH *heorte.*

**hearth** OLD ENGLISH *heorth.*

**heat** OLD ENGLISH *hætu* great warmth.

**heath** OLD ENGLISH *hæth.*

**heathen** OLD ENGLISH *hæthen* person who lives on a heath (land that is empty), from *hæth* heath. Originally, people who lived in areas away from the city.

**heather** MIDDLE ENGLISH *haddyr.*

**heave** OLD ENGLISH *hebban* lift.

**heaven** OLD ENGLISH *heofon.*

**heavy** OLD ENGLISH *hefig.*

**Hebrew** OLD ENGLISH, from HEBREW *'ibhri* one from across (the river).

**hecatomb** LATIN, from GREEK *hecaton* a hundred + *bous* ox.

**heckle** MIDDLE ENGLISH *hechele.* See **hackle.**

**hectic** LATIN *hectica* continuous, from GREEK *hektikos,* from *hexis* condition of the body.

**hecto-** FRENCH, from GREEK *hekaton* a hundred.

**hector** GREEK *Hector,* a Trojan hero killed by Achilles.

**heddle** OLD ENGLISH, small cords on a loom, origin uncertain.

**heder** HEBREW *hedher* chamber.

**hedge** OLD ENGLISH *hecg.*

**hedonism** GREEK *hedone* pleasure + *ismos.*

**heed** OLD ENGLISH *heden.*

**heel**[1] (of foot) OLD ENGLISH *hela.*

**heel**[2] (a boat) MIDDLE ENGLISH *hield,* from OLD ENGLISH *hyldan* incline.

**heeled** (provided) AMERICAN slang. See **heel**[1]. Originally said of a gamecock furnished with a metal spur.

**heft** See **heave.**

**hegemony** GREEK *hegemon* leader.

**height** OLD ENGLISH *heihthu.*

**heinous** FRENCH *haineus,* from *haine* hate.

**heir** FRENCH, from LATIN *heres.*

**heirloom** See **heir** + **loom**[1].

**heist** See **hoist.**

**helicopter** FRENCH *héicoptèr,* from GREEK *helix* spiral + *pteron* wing.

**helio-** LATIN, from GREEK *helios* sun.

**heliostat** LATIN *heliostata,* from **helio-** + GREEK *statos* standing.

**heliotrope** FRENCH, from LATIN *heliotropium,* from GREEK *heliotropion,* from *helios* sun + *tropos* turn.

**helium** LATIN, from GREEK *helios* sun, because it was first discovered in the sun.

**helix** LATIN, from GREEK spiral, from *helissein* turn around.

**hell** OLD ENGLISH hidden place.

**hello** GERMAN *hala* fetch, especially in calling for a ferryman.

**helm** OLD ENGLISH *helma* position of guidance, control.

**helmet** FRENCH.

**help** OLD ENGLISH *helpan.*

**helter-skelter** imitative of the sound of children's running feet.

**helve** OLD ENGLISH *helfe.*

**hem** MIDDLE ENGLISH, from OLD ENGLISH border of a piece of cloth.

**hemisphere** LATIN *hemisphaerium* a half globe, from GREEK *hemisphairion,* from *hemi* half + *sphaira* ball, sphere.

**hemlock** OLD ENGLISH *hymlic.*

**hemorrhage** FRENCH *hémorrhagie,* from LATIN *haemorrhagia* dangerous bleeding, from GREEK *haimorrhagia,* from *haima* blood + *rhegnynai* to burst.

**hemp** OLD ENGLISH *hænep.*

**hen** OLD ENGLISH *henn.*

**henbane** See **hen** + **bane.**

**hence** MIDDLE ENGLISH *hennes* away, from OLD ENGLISH *heonan.*

**henchman** OLD ENGLISH *hengst* horse + *-man* possibly meaning "groom".

**hennin** FRENCH.

**hepatic** LATIN *hepaticus,* from GREEK *hepatikos,* from *hepar* the liver.

**hepta-** GREEK seven.

**heptarchy** See **hepta-** + **-arch.**

**her** OLD ENGLISH *hire.*

**herald** FRENCH *herau(l)t* royal officer.

**herb** FRENCH, from LATIN *herba.*

**herd** OLD ENGLISH *heord.*

**here** OLD ENGLISH *her.*

**heredity** FRENCH, from LATIN *hereditas,* from *heres* heir.

**heresy** FRENCH *heresie,* from LATIN *haeresis,* from GREEK *hairesis* choice.

**heritage** FRENCH inheritance, from *heriter* inherit, from LATIN *hereditare,* from *heres* heir.

**hermit** FRENCH *(h)ermite,* from LATIN *(h)ememita,* from GREEK *eremites* person who lives in a desert, from *dremia* desert.

**hernia** LATIN.

**hero** LATIN *heros* man born from a god, from GREEK.

**heron** FRENCH *hairon.*

**herring** OLD ENGLISH *hering.*

**herringbone** See **herring** + **bone.**

**hesitate** LATIN *haesitare* stick fast, from *haerere* stick.

**hew** OLD ENGLISH *heawan* strike.

**hex** GERMAN *Hexe* witch.

**hexamine** GREEK *hex-* six + *amine*. See **amino-**.

**hey** MIDDLE ENGLISH *hei*.

**hiatus** LATIN *giatus* gap.

**hibernate** LATIN *hibernare*, from *hibernus* wintry.

**hiccup** imitative.

**hick** *Hick*, early nickname for Richard.

**hide**[1] (conceal) OLD ENGLISH *hydan*.

**hide**[2] (animal skin) OLD ENGLISH *hid*.

**hideous** FRENCH *hideus*, from *hide* terror.

**hierarchy** LATIN *hierarchia* rule of a priest, from GREEK *hierarchia*, from *hieros* sacred + *archein* rule.

**hieroglyphic** FRENCH, from LATIN, from GREEK *heros* sacred + *glyphein* carve.

**high** OLD ENGLISH *heah*.

**hijack** AMERICAN *high(way)* + *jacker* one who holds up.

**hike** See **hitch**.

**hilarity** FRENCH *hilarité*, from LATIN *hilaritas*, from GREEK *hilaros* merry.

**hill** OLD ENGLISH *hyll*.

**hillock** MIDDLE ENGLISH small hill, from OLD ENGLISH *hyll* + *-ock* small.

**hilt** OLD ENGLISH.

**him** OLD ENGLISH.

**Himalayan** SANSKRIT *himalayah*, from *hima* snow + *alaya* abode.

**hind** OLD ENGLISH *hindan*.

**hinder** OLD ENGLISH *hindrian*.

**hinge** MIDDLE ENGLISH *hengen* hang.

**hint** OLD ENGLISH *hentan* take.

**hip** OLD ENGLISH *hype*.

**hippo-** GREEK *hippos* a horse.

**hippodrome** See **hippo-** + GREEK *dromos* a course.

**hippogriff** See **hippo-** + **griffin**.

**hippopotamus** See **hippo-** + GREEK *ptoamos* river.

**hire** OLD ENGLISH *hyr* payment for the use of something.

**his** OLD ENGLISH.

**hiss** imitative.

**history** LATIN *historia* story of past events, from GREEK *historia*, from *histor* learned.

**hit** OLD ENGLISH *hittan*.

**hitch** MIDDLE ENGLISH *hicchen* move jerkily.

**hithe** See **hythe**.

**hither** OLD ENGLISH *hinder*.

**hive** OLD ENGLISH *huf*.

**hoard** OLD ENGLISH *hord* treasure.

**hoarhound** MIDDLE ENGLISH *horhowne*, from OLD ENGLISH *hare hune*, from *har* hoar, hoary + *hune* name of a plant.

**hoarse** OLD ENGLISH *has*.

**hoax** See **hocus-pocus**.

**hob**[1] (ledge) possible variation of **hub**.

**hob**[2] (goblin) old form of *Robin*, an elf in English folk tales.

**hobbit** stories by J.R.R. Tolkein, 20th century English writer.

**hobble** MIDDLE ENGLISH *hobelen*, from DUTCH *hobbelen* jolt.

**hobby** MIDDLE ENGLISH *hobyn* small horse, possibly from DUTCH *hobben* move back and forth.

**hobnob** OLD ENGLISH *habban* have + *nabban* not to have.

**hoboy** FRENCH *hautbois* high wood.

**hock**[1] (leg joint) MIDDLE ENGLISH *hockshin*, from OLD ENGLISH *hoh-sinu* heel sinew.

**hock**[2] (pawn) DUTCH *hok* jail, pen, doghouse.

**hockey** FRENCH *hoquet* bent stick, from *hoc* hook.

**hocus-pocus** LATIN rhyming words used by jugglers and magicians.

**hodge-podge** FRENCH *hochepot*, from *hocher* shake + *pot* pot.

**hoe** FRENCH *houe*, from GERMAN *houwan*.

**hog** OLD ENGLISH *hogg*.

**hoist** DUTCH *hyssen* raise up.

**hoity-toity** rhyme based on obsolete *hoit* lively play.

**hold** OLD ENGLISH *h(e)aldan* keep.

**hole** OLD ENGLISH *hol*.

**holiday** OLD ENGLISH *haligdæg* holy day.

**holler** FRENCH *hola*, from *ho* ahoy + *la* there.

**hollow** OLD ENGLISH *holh* hole.

**holo-** FRENCH, from LATIN, from GREEK *holos* whole.

**holocaust** MIDDLE ENGLISH, from FRENCH *holocauste*, from LATIN *holocaustum* whole burnt offering or sacrifice, from GREEK *holokauston*, from *holos* whole + *kaiston* burnt.

**holus-bolus** humerous Latin-sounding term meaning whole bolus (lump of earth).

**holy** OLD ENGLISH *halig* sacred.

**holystone** See **holy** + **stone**, perhaps because sailors knelt as if in prayer while using it to scrub decks.

**homage** FRENCH duty owed to a lord, from *hom* man, from LATIN *homo* man.

**homburg** *Homburg* the town in Germany where the hat originated.

**home** OLD ENGLISH *ham*.

**homeopathy** GERMAN *Homöopathie*, from GREEK *homoios* same + *-patheia* effect.

**homicide** FRENCH, from LATIN *homicidium*, from *homo* man + *-cidium*, from *caedere* kill.

**homily** LATIN *homilia* sermon, from GREEK *homilia* instruction.

**hominy** NATIVE AMERICAN *rockahominy* something ground.

**homogeneous** LATIN *homogeneus* of the same kind, from GREEK *homogenes*, from *homos* same + *genos* kind, race.

**homonym** LATIN *homonymum*, from GREEK *homonymos* having the same name.

**honcho** JAPANESE *hancho* leader, from *han* group + *cho* chief.

**hone** OLD ENGLISH *han* a stone.

**honest** FRENCH, from LATIN *honestus* having honor.

**honey** OLD ENGLISH *hunig*.

**honeymoon** MIDDLE ENGLISH *hony moone*, referring to the sweetness of the first month of a marriage.

**honky-tonk** AMERICAN *honk-a-tonk*, origin uncertain.

**honor** FRENCH, from LATIN dignity.

**hood** OLD ENGLISH *hod* covering for the head and neck.

**-hood** OLD ENGLISH *had* order, condition, rank.

**hoodlum** probably from GERMAN *hudilump* miserable person.

**hoof** OLD ENGLISH *hof*.

**hook** OLD ENGLISH *hoc* bent piece of metal.

**hookah** ARABIC *huqqah* pipe for smoking.

**hooky** possibly from MIDDLE ENGLISH *hook it* escape.

**hooligan** possibly from the Irish family name *Hooligan*.

**hoop** OLD ENGLISH *hop*.

**hoosegow** SPANISH *juzgado* court of justice, from LATIN *judex* judge.

**hoot** imitative.

**hop** MIDDLE ENGLISH *hoppen*, from OLD ENGLISH *hoppian* leap.

**hope** OLD ENGLISH *hopa* trust.

**hopscotch** OLD ENGLISH *hoppian* leap + *scotch* line.

**hora** HEBREW *hōrāh*, from ROMANIAN *horă*.

**horde** FRENCH pack, from TURKISH *ordu* camp.

**horehound** OLD ENGLISH *harhune*.

**horizon** FRENCH, from LATIN, from GREEK *horos* limit.

**hormone** GREEK *hormon* that which sets in motion.

**horn** OLD ENGLISH highest part of the body.

**hornet** OLD ENGLISH *hyrnetu, hurnitu* large wasp, beetle.

**hornswoggle** AMERICAN, origin unknown.

**horoscope** FRENCH, from LATIN *horoscopus*, from GREEK *horoskopos*, from *hora* hour (of birth) + *skopos* watcher.

**horrible** FRENCH, from LATIN *horribilis*, from *horrere* tremble.

**horror** LATIN *horridus* frightful.

**hors d'oeuvre** FRENCH *hors d'oeuvre*, from *hors*, from *fors* outside + *de-* from + *oeuvre* work.

**horse** OLD ENGLISH *hors*.

**horticulture** LATIN *hortus* garden + *cultura* cultivate (grow).

**hosanna** LATIN *hosamma*, from GREEK *hosanna*, from HEBREW *hoshia na* save now, we pray.

**hose** OLD ENGLISH *hosa* clothes for the leg.

**hospitable** FRENCH, from LATIN *hospes* host.

**hospital** FRENCH place for persons in need, from LATIN *hospitale* guest room, from *hospes* guest.

**host**[1] (person) MIDDLE ENGLISH *hoste*, from FRENCH innkeeper, from LATIN *hospes* guest.

**host**[2] (large number) MIDDLE ENGLISH *host*, from FRENCH *host* army, from LATIN *hostis*, from enemy.

**hostage** FRENCH *(h)ostage*, from LATIN *obses*. See **host**[2].

**hostel** MIDDLE ENGLISH, from FRENCH, from LATIN *hospitale* guest room.

**hostile** LATIN *hostis* enemy.

**hostler** MIDDLE ENGLISH *hosteler* innkeeper, from FRENCH *hostelier*.

**hot** OLD ENGLISH *hat*.

**hotel** FRENCH inn, from *hostel*, from LATIN *hospitale* guest room, from *hospes* guest.

**hound** OLD ENGLISH *hund*.

**houppelande** FRENCH.

**hour** MIDDLE ENGLISH, from FRENCH *hore*, from LATIN *hora*, from GREEK *hora* time.

**house** OLD ENGLISH *hus*.

**hovel** MIDDLE ENGLISH roofed passage, vent for smoke, origin uncertain.

**hover** MIDDLE ENGLISH *hoveren* stay in the air.

**how**[1] (what way) OLD ENGLISH *hu*.

**how**[2] (hollow) SCOTTISH *howe*, from MIDDLE ENGLISH *holl* valley.

**howdah** P<small>ERSIAN</small> *haudah.*

**howl** M<small>IDDLE</small> E<small>NGLISH</small> *houlen.*

**hoyden** D<small>UTCH</small> *heiden* uncivilized person.

**huarache** S<small>PANISH</small>, from N<small>ATIVE</small> A<small>MERICAN</small> *kwarachi.*

**hub** M<small>IDDLE</small> E<small>NGLISH</small>, perhaps from *hubbe* lump.

**hubbub** of uncertain origin, perhaps I<small>RISH</small>, from *abu* a battle cry.

**hubris** G<small>REEK</small> *hubris* outrage.

**huddle** possibly from M<small>IDDLE</small> E<small>NGLISH</small> *hoderen* cover up.

**hue** M<small>IDDLE</small> E<small>NGLISH</small> *hewe,* from O<small>LD</small> E<small>NGLISH</small> *heow* shape.

**huff** imitative.

**hug** probably from O<small>LD</small> N<small>ORSE</small> *hugga* comfort.

**huge** F<small>RENCH</small> *ahuge.*

**hulk** O<small>LD</small> E<small>NGLISH</small> *hulc,* possibly from L<small>ATIN</small> *hulcus,* from G<small>REEK</small> *holkas* trading ship.

**hull** O<small>LD</small> E<small>NGLISH</small> *hulu* shell of a seed.

**hullabaloo** imitative.

**hum** imitative.

**human** L<small>ATIN</small> *humanus,* from *homo* man.

**humanity** F<small>RENCH</small> *humanite* human nature, from L<small>ATIN</small> *humanitas.*

**humble** F<small>RENCH</small>, from L<small>ATIN</small> *humilis* low, from *humus* ground.

**humbug** B<small>RITISH</small> slang, origin uncertain.

**humdinger** possibly from **hum** + **ding.**

**humdrum** imitative rhyme.

**humid** L<small>ATIN</small> *(h)umidus.*

**humiliate** L<small>ATIN</small> *humiliare,* from *humilis.* See **humble.**

**humility** F<small>RENCH</small> *humilite,* from L<small>ATIN</small> *humilitas* lowness.

**hummock** M<small>IDDLE</small> E<small>NGLISH</small>, nautical term, origin uncertain.

**humor** M<small>IDDLE</small> E<small>NGLISH</small> juice of an animal or plant, from F<small>RENCH</small>, from L<small>ATIN</small> *umor* body fluid.

**hump** G<small>ERMAN</small> *humpe* thick piece.

**hunch** M<small>IDDLE</small> E<small>NGLISH</small> push, thrust, origin unknown.

**hundred** O<small>LD</small> E<small>NGLISH</small>.

**hunger** O<small>LD</small> E<small>NGLISH</small> *hungor.*

**hunk** D<small>UTCH</small> *hunke.*

**hunker** probably from O<small>LD</small> N<small>ORSE</small> *hokra* creep.

**hunt** O<small>LD</small> E<small>NGLISH</small> *huntian.*

**hurdle** O<small>LD</small> E<small>NGLISH</small> *hyrdel* movable frame used as a fence.

**hurl** M<small>IDDLE</small> E<small>NGLISH</small> *hurlen,* from G<small>ERMAN</small> *hurreln* toss.

**hurly-burly** earlier *hurling and burling,* rhyme based on **hurl.**

**hurrah** G<small>ERMAN</small> *hurra* cheer.

**hurricane** S<small>PANISH</small> *huracán* violent storm, from N<small>ATIVE</small> A<small>MERICAN</small> *hurakan* name of an evil spirit.

**hurry** possibly from M<small>IDDLE</small> E<small>NGLISH</small> *horyed* rushed, from G<small>ERMAN</small> *hurren* move quickly.

**hurt** F<small>RENCH</small> *hurter* strike.

**hurtle** M<small>IDDLE</small> E<small>NGLISH</small> *hurten.* See **hurt.**

**husband** O<small>LD</small> E<small>NGLISH</small> *husbonda* master of a house, from O<small>LD</small> N<small>ORSE</small> *husbondi.*

**hush** M<small>IDDLE</small> E<small>NGLISH</small> *huscht* quiet.

**husk** D<small>UTCH</small> *husken* little house, from *huus* house.

**hussar** HUNGARIAN *huszár* army horseman, from LATIN *cursarius* pirate, from *cursus* rob, from *corsus* course.

**hustle** DUTCH *hutslen* shake.

**hutch** FRENCH *huche* chest, from LATIN *hutica.*

**huzza, huzzah** originally a sailor's shout.

**hyacinth** GREEK *hyakinthos.*

**hybrid** LATIN *hybrida.*

**hydrate** FRENCH, coined by French chemist Joseph-Louis Proust, from GREEK *hydor* water.

**hydraulic** LATIN *hydraulicus* water engine, from GREEK *hydor* water + *aulos* pipe. The Greeks had a kind of pipe organ played by using water.

**hydro-** GREEK *hydor* water.

**hydrogen** FRENCH *hydrogène,* from GREEK *hydor* water + *gennan* produce, because water is produced when hydrogen is burned.

**hydroponic** GREEK *hydro-* water + *-ponic,* from *ponein,* from *ponos* labor.

**hydrostatic** See **hydro-** + **static.**

**hygiene** FRENCH, from GREEK *hygies* health.

**hyla** GREEK *hyle* wood.

**hymn** LATIN *hymnus* song of praise, from GREEK *hymnos.*

**hype** AMERICAN. See **hyperbole.**

**hyper** See **hyper-** + **active.**

**hyper-** GREEK above, over, beyond.

**hyperactive** See **hyper-** + **active.**

**hyperbola** See **hyperbole.**

**hyperbole** LATIN, from GREEK, from *hyperballein* throw over or beyond, from *hyper-* beyond + *bol-*, from *ballein* throw.

**hypertrophy** See **hyper-** + **-trophy.**

**hyphen** LATIN, from GREEK together, from *hypo-* under + *heis* one.

**hypnotic** LATIN *hypnoticus,* from GREEK *hypnotikos,* from *hypnos* sleep.

**hypo-** GREEK under, below.

**hypochondria** LATIN belly, from GREEK *hypo* under + *chondros* part of the breastbone, from an early belief that depression came from that part of the body.

**hypocrisy** FRENCH *hypocrisis* pretending, from GREEK *hypokrites,* from *hypo-* under + *krinesthai* argue.

**hypodermic** GREEK *hypo-* under + *derma* the skin.

**hypothesis** GREEK foundation, from *hypo-* under + *tithenai* place.

**hyssop** OLD ENGLISH *ysope,* from Latin *hyssopus,* from GREEK *hyssopos* a plant of Palestine, used in Jewish purification rites, from HEBREW *ezobh.*

**hysteria** LATIN, from GREEK.

**hythe** OLD ENGLISH *hyth* a river-landing.

**I** OLD ENGLISH *ic.*

**-ia** LATIN, from GREEK.

**-ial** LATIN *-ialis.*

**-ian** LATIN *-ianus.*

**-ibility** LATIN *-ibilitas.*

**-ic** FRENCH *-ique,* from LATIN *-icus,* from GREEK *-ikos.*

**-ical** LATIN *-icus.*

**ice** OLD ENGLISH *is.*

**icicle** OLD ENGLISH *is* ice + *gicel* piece of ice.

**icon** LATIN image, from GREEK *eikon.*

**iconoclast** LATIN *iconoclastes,* from GREEK *eikon* image + *klastes* breaker.

**ichor** GREEK, origin unknown.

**-ide** use in names of simple chemical compounds. See **oxide.**

**idea** LATIN model, from GREEK form, model.

**ideal** LATIN *idealis,* from *idea.* See **idea.**

**identical** LATIN *identicus.* See **identity.**

**identity** LATIN *identitas* sameness, from LATIN *idem* the same.

**ideology** GREEK *idea* form, model + *-logia,* from *logos* word.

**ides** FRENCH, from LATIN *idus.*

**idiom** LATIN *idioma,* from GREEK *idios* one's own.

**idiosyncrasy** GREEK *idio-* one's own + *synkrasis* mixture, from *syn-* together + *kerannynai* mix.

**idiot** MIDDLE ENGLISH *idiote,* from FRENCH, from LATIN *idiota* ignorant person, from GREEK private person, from *idios* one's own. A Greek private person (one without professional knowledge) could not work for the government because they were thought to be ill-informed.

**idle** OLD ENGLISH *idel* useless.

**idol** FRENCH, from LATIN *idollum* image, from GREEK *eidolon.*

**idyll** LATIN *idyllium,* from GREEK *eidyllion* little picture, from *eidos* picture.

**if** OLD ENGLISH *gif.*

**igloo** ESKIMO for house, dwelling.

**igneous** LATIN *igneus* of fire, fiery, from *ignis* fire.

**ignite** LATIN *ignire* set on fire, from *ignis* fire.

**ignoble** FRENCH, from LATIN *ignobilis* unknown, from *in-* not + *gnobilis* of noble birth.

**ignominy** FRENCH, from LATIN *ignomina,* from *in-* not + *nomen* name.

**ignorant** FRENCH, from LATIN *ignorare.* See **ignore.**

**ignore** FRENCH, from LATIN *ignorare,* from *in-* not + *gnarus* knowing.

**iguana** SPANISH *iuana.*

**il-** See **in-**[1], **in-**[2]. Used when the root word starts with the letter *l.*

**-ile** FRENCH *-il, -ile,* from LATIN *-ilis.*

**ilk** OLD ENGLISH *ilca* same.

**ill** OLD NORSE *illr* bad.

**illimitable** See **il-** + **limit** + **-able.**

**illuminate** LATIN *illuminare* cause to have light, from *in-* in + *lumen* light.

**illusion** FRENCH, from LATIN *illusio* deceive.

**illustrate** LATIN *illustrare* light up.

**illustrious** LATIN *illustris* bright.

**im-** See **in-**[1], **in-**[2]. Used when the root starts with *m.*

**image** FRENCH statue, from LATIN *imago.*

**imagine** FRENCH *imaginer* form in the mind, from LATIN *imaginari* imagination.

**imbecile** FRENCH weak, without support, from *in-* not + *bacillus* little staff.

**imbibe** LATIN *imbibere,* from *in-* in + *bibere* drink.

**imbue** LATIN *imbuere* stain.

**imitate** LATIN *imitari* copy.

**immaculate** LATIN *in-* not + *maculare* soil, from *macual* a spot.

**immediate** LATIN *immediatus,* from *in-* not + *medius* middle.

**immense** LATIN *immensus,* from *in-* in + *metiri* measure.

**immerse** LATIN *immergere,* from *in-* into + *mergere* dip.

**immigrate** LATIN *immigrare,* from *in-* in + *migrare* move from place to place.

**imminent** LATIN *imminere* threaten.

**immolate** LATIN *immolare* sprinkle grain on a sacrificial victim, from *in-* in, on + *mola* meal (grain).

**immune** LATIN *immunis* exempt, from *in-* without + *munia* duties.

**imp** OLD ENGLISH *impa* young plant, from LATIN *impotus* graft (putting a bud from one plant onto a cut made in another so there is one plant from two), from GREEK *emphytos.* In the 15th century the word meant to repair the wing of a falcon. Later it came to mean putting wings on a person, such as a small demon or wicked spirit.

**impact** LATIN *impingere,* from *in-* in + *pangere* drive in.

**impair** FRENCH *empeirer,* from LATIN *in-* in + *pejor* worse.

**impala** AFRICAN.

**impale** LATIN *in-* in, on + *palus* stake.

**impart** LATIN *impartire* share with, from *in-* in + *pars* share.

**impasse** FRENCH *in-* not + *passer* go across. See **pass.**

**impeach** FRENCH *empe(s)cher* get in the way of, from LATIN *impedicare* be in difficulty, from *in-* in, on + *pedicare* chain wound around the feet of criminals, from *pes* foot.

**impeccable** LATIN *impeccabilis,* from *in-* not + *peccare* sin.

**impecunious** LATIN *in-* not + *pecuniosus* rich, wealthy, from *pecunia* money.

**impede** LATIN *impedire* put chains on prisoners, from *in-* in + *pes* foot.

**impediment** LATIN *impedimentem.* See **impede.**

**impel** LATIN *impellere,* from *in-* on + *pellere* drive.

**impend** LATIN *impendere,* from *in-* in, on + *pendere* hang.

**imperative** LATIN *imperativus,* from *imperatum* command.

**imperial** LATIN *imperialis,* from *imperium* rule.

**imperious** LATIN *imperium* rule.

**impersonate** LATIN *in-* in + *persona* mask.

**impetuous** FRENCH, from LATIN *impetus.* See **impetus**.

**impetus** LATIN *impetere* attack, from *in-* in + *petere* rush at.

**impinge** LATIN *impingere,* from *in-* in + *pangere* strike.

**implement** LATIN *implementum* a filling up, from *implere,* from *in-* in + *plere* fill.

**implicate** LATIN *implicatus,* from *implicare* involve. See **imply**.

**implicit** LATIN *implicitus,* from *implicare* involve. See **imply**.

**implore** LATIN *implorare* beg, from *in-* very much + *plorare* cry out.

**imply** FRENCH *emplier* involve, from LATIN *implicare* involve, from *in-* in + *plicare* fold.

**import** LATIN *importare,* from *in-* in + *portare* carry.

**important** FRENCH, from LATIN *importare* be of weight, from carry in. See **import**.

**importune** FRENCH, from LATIN *importunus* causing trouble, from *in-* not + *(op)portunus* before the port, from *potrus* resting place.

**impose** FRENCH *imposer* put on, from LATIN *imponere,* from *in-* in + *ponere* place.

**impostor** LATIN *imponere* place on. See **impose**.

**impotent** LATIN *impotens* powerless, from *in-* not + *posse* be able.

**impoverish** FRENCH *empoverir* make poor, from LATIN *in-* in + *pauper* poor.

**imprecate** LATIN *imprecari* call down, from *in-* on + *precari* pray.

**impregnable** FRENCH *imprenable,* from LATIN *in-* not + *prenable,* from *prendere* take.

**impress** MIDDLE ENGLISH *impressen,* from LATIN *imprimere,* from *in-* in + *premere* press.

**imprint** FRENCH, from LATIN *imprimere,* from *in-* on + *premere* press.

**impromptu** FRENCH not prepared, from LATIN *in promptu* in readiness.

**improve** FRENCH *emprower* benefit, from *em-* in + *prou* a benefit, from LATIN *prodesse* be of advantage.

**improvise** ITALIAN *improvissare,* from LATIN *improvisus* not foreseen, from *in-* not + *providere* see ahead.

**impudent** LATIN *impudens,* from *in-* not + *pudere* feel shame.

**impugn** LATIN *impugnare,* from *in-* against + *pugnare* fight.

**impulse** LATIN *impulsus.* See **impel**.

**impute** LATIN *imputare* charge, from *in-* to + *putare* think, estimate.

**in** OLD ENGLISH.

**in-**[1] (not, without) LATIN *in-* not.

**in-**[2] (in) LATIN *in-* in, into, on, toward, against.

**-ina** LATIN.

**inane** LATIN *inanis* empty.

**inaugurate** LATIN *inaugurare* look for guidance, from omens (sign of something to come) before acting. See **augur**.

**incandescent** LATIN *incandescere* become hot, from *in-* in + *candescere,* from *candere* glow.

**incantation** LATIN *incantatio* enchantment, from *incantare,* from *in-* in + *cantare* chant.

**incapable** LATIN *incapabilis,* from *in-* not + *capabilis* able to hold.

**incarcerate** LATIN *incarcerare,* from *in-* in + *carcer* prison.

**incarnate** LATIN *incarnare,* from *in-* in + *caro* flesh.

**incendiary** LATIN *incendiarius* causing a fire, from *incendium* fire. See **incense.**

**incense** MIDDLE ENGLISH *encens,* from FRENCH, from LATIN *incensum,* from *incendere* set on fire, from *in-* in + *candere* glow.

**incentive** LATIN *incentivus* set the tune, from *incinere* sound, from *in-* in + *canere,* from *cantus* song.

**incessant** LATIN *in-* not + *cessare* cease.

**inch** OLD ENGLISH *ynce,* from LATIN *uncia* a twelfth part.

**inchoate** LATIN *inchohare* begin, harness, from *in-* in + *cohum* a strap that ties two parts of a plow together.

**incident** LATIN *incidere* happen, from *in-* on + *cadere* fall.

**incinerate** LATIN *incinerare* turn into ashes, from *in-* in + *cinis* ashes.

**incipient** LATIN *incipere,* from *in-* on + *capere* take.

**incise** FRENCH *inciser,* from LATIN *incidere,* from *in-* into + *caedere* cut.

**incisor** LATIN *incisor* that which cuts into, from *incisus.* See **incision.**

**incision** FRENCH, from LATIN *incisionem,* from *incidere,* from *in-* into + *-cidere* cut.

**incite** LATIN *incitare,* from *in-* in + *citare* excite.

**inclement** LATIN *inclemens* harsh, from *in-* not + *clementem* mild.

**incline** FRENCH *incliner,* from LATIN *inclinare,* from *in-* on + *clinere* lean.

**include** LATIN *includere,* from *in-* in + *claudere* close.

**incognito** ITALIAN unknown, from LATIN *incognitus,* from *in-* not + *cognoscere* know.

**incommode** FRENCH, from LATIN *incommodus* inconvenient, from *in-* not + *commodus* convenient.

**incontinent** FRENCH, from LATIN *incontinentem,* from *in-* not + *continentem,* from *continere* hold together.

**incorporate** LATIN *incorporatus,* from *incorporare,* from *in-* in + *corpus* body.

**increase** FRENCH *encrestre* grow, from LATIN *increscere,* from *in-* in + *crescere* grow.

**increment** LATIN *incrementum* increase.

**incriminate** LATIN *incriminare* accuse, from *in-* against + *crimen* charge.

**incubate** LATIN *incubare,* from *in-* on + *cubare* lie.

**incubus** LATIN nightmare, that which lies on one, from *incubare* lie on.

**inculcate** LATIN *inculcare* walk on with the heel, from *in-* in + *calx* heel.

**inculpate** LATIN *inculpare* blame, from *in-* on + *culpa* blame.

**incumbent** LATIN *incumbere* obtain, from *in-* on + *combere* lie down.

**incur** LATIN *incurrere,* from *in-* in + *currere* run.

**indefatigable** FRENCH, from LATIN *in-* not + *defatigare* tire out.

**indelible** LATIN *indelebilis,* from *in-* not + *delere* destroy.

**indemnify** LATIN *indemnis* not hurt, from *in-* not + *demnum* harm.

**indent** MIDDLE ENGLISH *indenten*, from FRENCH *endenter*, from LATIN *indentare* provide with teeth, make a V-cut in an edge, from *in-* in + *dens* tooth.

**indenture** MIDDLE ENGLISH *endenture,* from LATIN *indenture.* See **indent.** Copies of documents had jagged edges for identification.

**index** LATIN. See **indicate.**

**Indian** LATIN *Indianus,* from *India* India. When Columbus got to America he thought he had discovered India.

**indicate** LATIN *indicare* show, from *in-* in + *dicare* declare.

**indict** LATIN *indictare* accuse, from *in-* in + *dictare,* from *dicere* say.

**indigenous** LATIN *indigena,* from *indu* in + *gignere* be born.

**indigent** FRENCH, from LATIN *indigere* be in need, from *indu* in + *egere* need.

**indignant** LATIN *indignari* think not worthy, from *in-* not + *dignus* worthy.

**indigo** SPANISH, from LATIN *indicum,* from GREEK *Indikos* Indian, from *India.*

**indite** FRENCH *enditer* write down, from LATIN *in-* in + *dictare.*

**individual** MIDDLE ENGLISH, from LATIN *individualis,* from *individuus,* from *in-* not + *dividere* divide.

**indolent** LATIN *indolens* painless, from *in-* not + *dolere* feel pain.

**indomitable** LATIN *in-* not + *domare* tame.

**induce** LATIN *inducere,* from *in-* in + *ducere* lead.

**indulge** LATIN *indulgere* be kind to.

**indurate** LATIN *induratus,* from *indurare* make hard, from *in-* not + *durus* hard. See **endure.**

**industry** FRENCH *industrie* work, from LATIN *industria,* from *industrius* active.

**-ine**[1] (like) FRENCH, from LATIN *-inus.*

**-ine**[2] (feminine nouns) LATIN, from GREEK *-ine.*

**inebriate** LATIN *inebriare,* from *in-* thoroughly + *ebrius* drunk.

**ineffable** LATIN *ineffabilis,* from *in-* not + *ex-* out + *fari* speak.

**inept** LATIN *ineptus,* from *in-* not + *aptis* fit.

**inert** LATIN *in-* not + *ars* art.

**inevitable** LATIN *in-* not + *evitabilis* avoidable.

**inexorable** LATIN *inexorabilis,* from *in-* not + *exorare* change the mind by pleading, from *ex-* out + *orare* pray.

**inexplicable** LATIN *inexplicabilis,* from *in-* not + *explicabilis,* from *explicare,* from *ex-* out of + *plicare* fold.

**infamy** LATIN *infamia* bad reputation.

**infant** MIDDLE ENGLISH *infaunt,* from FRENCH *enfant,* from LATIN *infans* without speech, from *in-* not + *fari* speak.

**infantry** FRENCH *infanterie,* from ITALIAN *infanteria,* from *infante* child, foot soldier, from LATIN *infans* baby.

**infatuate** LATIN *infatuare* make a fool of, from *in-* in + *fatus* foolish.

**infect** LATIN *infecere* stain, from *in-* in + *facere* do, make.

**infer** LATIN *inferre,* from *in-* in + *ferre* bring.

**inferior** LATIN *inferior,* from *inferus* low.

**infernal** LATIN *infernalis* relating to the underworld, from *inferus* low.

**inferno** ITALIAN *inferno,* from LATIN *infernus* lying beneath, from *inferus* low.

**infest** LATIN *infestare* attack.

**infidel** LATIN *infidelis*, from FRENCH, from LATIN *in-* not + *fidelis* faithful.

**infinite** LATIN *infinite*. See **in-**[1] + **finite**.

**infinitesimal** LATIN *infinitus* infinite.

**infinitive** LATIN *infinitus* indefinite, from *in-* not + *finitius* definite.

**inflate** LATIN *inflare*, from *in-* in + *flare* blow.

**inflect** LATIN *inflectere*, from *in-* in + *flectere* bend.

**inflict** LATIN *infligere*, from *in-* against + *fligere* strike.

**influence** FRENCH power flowing, from the stars, from LATIN *influentia*, from *influere*, from *in-* in + *fluere* flow, from the belief that forces flowing from the stars affect human life.

**influenza** ITALIAN influence, from LATIN *influentia*. See **influence**.

**inform** FRENCH *enformer* give shape or form to, from LATIN *informare*, from *in-* in + *forma* shape, pattern.

**infrared** LATIN *infra-* below + OLD ENGLISH *read*.

**infringe** LATIN *infringere*, from *in-* in + *frangere* break.

**infuriate** LATIN *infuriare*, from *in-* in + *furia* rage.

**infuse** LATIN *infundere*, from *in-* in + *fundere* pour.

**-ing**[1] (action name) OLD ENGLISH *-ing, -ung*. Attached to verbs to mean their action, result, product, material, etc.

**-ing**[2] (going on) OLD ENGLISH *-ende*.

**ingenious** LATIN *ingenosus* smart, from *ingenium* talent, from *in-* in + *gignere* produce.

**ingénue** FRENCH, from LATIN *ingenuus*. See **ingenuous**.

**ingenuous** LATIN *ingenuus*, from *in-* in + *gignere* produce.

**ingest** LATIN *ingerere*, from *in-* into + *gerere* carry.

**inglenook** SCOTTISH *aingeal* fire + MIDDLE ENGLISH *nok*, from SCANDINAVIAN.

**ingot** OLD ENGLISH *in-* in + *goten* poured, from *geotan* pour.

**ingrate** FRENCH, from LATIN *in-* not + *gratis* grateful.

**ingratiate** LATIN *in-* in + *gratia* favor.

**ingredient** LATIN *ingredi* begin.

**inhabit** LATIN *inhabitare*, from *in-* in + *habitare* dwell, from *habitus*. See **habit**.

**inhale** LATIN *inhalare*, from *in-* in + *halare* breathe.

**inherent** LATIN *inhaerere*, from *in-* in + *haerere* stick.

**inherit** FRENCH *enheriter*, from LATIN *inhereditare*, from *in-* in + *heres* heir.

**inhibit** LATIN *inhibere* hinder, from *in-* in + *habere* hold.

**inimical** LATIN *inimicalis* like an enemy, from *inimicus* enemy.

**iniquity** FRENCH, from LATIN *iniquus* unequal, from *in-* in + *aequus* equal.

**initial** LATIN *initium*, from *in-* in + *ire* go.

**initiate** LATIN *initare*. See **initial**.

**inject** LATIN *injicere*, from *in-* in + *jacere* throw.

**injunctive** LATIN *injungere*. See **enjoin** + **-ive**.

**injury** LATIN *injuria*, from *in-* not + *jus* right.

**ink** FRENCH *enque*, from LATIN, from GREEK *enkauston* red ink, from *enkalein* burnt in.

**inn** OLD ENGLISH.

**innate** Latin *innasci*, from *in-* in + *nasci* be born.

**inning** Old English *innung* a getting in.

**innocent** Latin *innocens*, from *in-* not + *nocere* do wrong to.

**innocuous** Latin *in-* not + *nocuus* harmful, from *nocere* harm.

**innovate** Latin *innovare*, from *in-* in + *novare* change.

**innuendo** Latin *innuere* nod to, from the use of a nod to suggest something without speaking.

**inoculate** Middle English *enoculaten*, from Latin *incoulare* graft (putting part of a plant onto a cut made in another to make a better plant, from the parts of two), from *in-* in + *oculus* eye, bud. The idea of putting a germ into the body to make the body well is similar to grafting part of a plant to another to make a better plant.

**inordinate** Latin *inordinatus*, from *in-* not + *ordo* order.

**inositol** Greek *inos-* muscle + Latin, from Greek *ites* + the *-ol* ending of alcohol.

**inquest** French *enqueste*, from Latin *inquirere* search for. See **inquire**.

**inquire** French, from Latin *inquirere*, from *in-* into + *quaerere* search.

**inquisitive** See inquire.

**inscribe** Latin *inscribere*, from *in-* in + *scribere* write.

**inscrutable** Latin *inscrutabilis*, from *in-* not + *scrutari* examine.

**insect** Latin *insectum* notched, from *in-* into + *secare* cut. Refers to the insect body having different parts.

**inseminate** Latin *inseminare*, from *in-* in + *seminare* sow, from *semen* seed.

**insert** Latin *inserere*, from *in-* in + *serere* join.

**insidious** Latin *insidiosus*, from *insidiae* plot, from *in-* in + *sedere* sit.

**insignia** Latin *insigne*, from *in-* in + *signum* a mark.

**insinuate** Latin *insinare* bring in by winding or turning, from *in-* in + *sinus* curve, hollow.

**insipid** French, from Latin *in-* not + *sapere* taste.

**insist** Latin *insistere*, from *in-* in + *sistere* stand.

**insolate** Latin *insolare* expose to the sun, from *in-* in + *sol* the sun.

**insolent** Latin *insolens*, from *in-* not + *solere* used to.

**insomnia** Latin *in-* without + *somnus* sleep.

**inspect** Latin *inspicere*, from *in-* at + *specere* look.

**inspire** Latin *inspirare*, from *in-* in + *spirare* breathe.

**install** Latin *installare*, from *in-* in + *stallum* seat.

**instance** French, from Latin *instantia* being present.

**instant** Latin *instare*, from *in-* upon + *stare* stand.

**instigate** Latin *instigare* cause action.

**instill** French, from Latin *instillare*, from *in-* in + *stilla* a drop.

**instinct** Latin *instinctus* impulse, from *instinguere* cause to move forward.

**institute** Latin *instituere*, from *in-* in + *statuere* establish.

**instruct** Latin *instruere*, from *in-* in + *struere* pile up.

**instrument** FRENCH, from LATIN *instuere.* See **instruct.**

**insula** LATIN island.

**insular** See **insulate.**

**insulate** LATIN *insulatus,* from *insula* island.

**insult** LATIN *insultare,* from *in-* on + *saltare,* from *salir* leap.

**insurance** See **ensure.**

**insurgent** LATIN *insurgere,* from *in-* upon + *sugere* rise.

**insurrection** FRENCH, from LATIN *insurgere,* from *in-* upon + *sugere* rise.

**intact** LATIN *in-* not + *tangere* touch.

**intaglio** ITALIAN *in-* in + *tagliare* cut, from LATIN *taliare* split.

**integer** LATIN whole.

**integral** See **integer.**

**integrate** LATIN *integrare* make whole.

**integrity** LATIN *integritas.* See **integer.**

**intellect** LATIN *intellegere* understand, from *inter-* between + *legere* choose.

**intelligence** FRENCH, from LATIN *intelligere.* See **intellect.**

**intelligible** LATIN *intelligere.* See **intellect.**

**intend** MIDDLE ENGLISH, from LATIN *intendere,* from *in-* at + *tendere* stretch.

**intense** LATIN *intensus* stretch out. See **intend.**

**inter** FRENCH, from LATIN *in-* in + *terra* earth.

**inter-** LATIN *inter-* among, between.

**intercede** LATIN *intercedere,* from *inter-* between + *cedere* go.

**intercept** LATIN *intercipere,* from *inter-* between + *capere* take.

**interchange** FRENCH *entrechangier* change, from LATIN *inter-* between + *cambiare.* See **change.**

**interdict** FRENCH, from LATIN *interdictum* prohibit, from *inter-* between + *dicere* speak.

**interest** LATIN of importance, from *inter-* between + *esse* be.

**interfere** FRENCH *entreferir* hit each other, from LATIN *entre-* between + *ferire* hit.

**interim** LATIN in the meantime, from *inter-* between.

**interior** FRENCH, from LATIN *inter-* between.

**interject** LATIN *interjicere,* from *inter-* between + *jacere* throw.

**interlard** FRENCH *entrelarder,* from *entre* between + *larder* lard, from FRENCH *lard* bacon fat.

**interlocutor** LATIN *inter-* between + *loqui* talk.

**interlude** LATIN *interludium* type of comic skit between mystery plays of the Middle Ages, from *inter-* between + *ludus* play.

**intermediate** LATIN *inter-* between + *medius* middle.

**intermit** LATIN *intermittere,* from *inter-* between + *mittere* send.

**intern** FRENCH *interne* internal, from LATIN *internus.*

**internal** LATIN *internus* internal.

**interpolate** LATIN *inter-* between + *polire* polish.

**interpose** FRENCH, from LATIN *inter-* between + *ponere* put.

**interpret** FRENCH, from LATIN *interpretari* explain.

**interrogate** LATIN *interrogare* question, from *inter-* between + *rogare* ask.

**interrupt** LATIN *interrumpere* break off, from *inter-* between + *rumpere* break.

**intersect** LATIN *intersecare* cut apart, from *inter-* between + *secare* cut.

**intersperse** LATIN *interspergere,* from *inter-* among + *spargere* scatter.

**interval** LATIN *intervallum* space between, from *inter-* between + *vallum* defense, wall.

**intervene** LATIN *intervenire* come between, from *inter-* between + *venire* come.

**interview** FRENCH *entrevue* meeting, from *entrevoir* see, from LATIN *inter-* between + *videre* see.

**intestine** LATIN *intestinus* internal, from *intus* within.

**intimate**[1] (close) FRENCH *intime* inward, from LATIN *intimus* farthest in.

**intimate**[2] (hint) LATIN *intimare* make known.

**intimidate** LATIN *intimidare,* from *in-* in + *timidus* afraid.

**into** See in-[1] + **to.**

**intone** FRENCH, from LATIN. See in-[2] + **tone.**

**intoxicate** LATIN *intoxicare* poison, from *in-* in + *toxicus* poison. See **toxic.**

**intransigent** FRENCH *intransigeant,* from SPANISH *intransigente,* from LATIN *in-* not + *transigere* come to agreement.

**intrepid** LATIN *intrepidus,* from *in-* not + *trepidus* alarmed.

**intricate** LATIN *intricare* tangle up, from *in-* in + *tricae* confusion.

**intrigue** FRENCH, from ITALIAN, from LATIN *intricare.* See **intricate.**

**intrinsic** FRENCH, from LATIN *intrinsecus* inward, from LATIN *intra-* within + *secus* close.

**intro-** LATIN into, within, inward.

**introduce** LATIN *introducere,* from *intro-* within + *ducere* lead.

**introvert** LATIN *intro-* to the inside + *vertere* turn.

**intrude** LATIN *intrudere,* from *in-* not + *trudere* force in.

**intuition** LATIN *intuitio* looking into, from *intueri,* from *in-* in + *tueri* look at.

**inundate** LATIN *inundare,* from *in-* upon + *unda* wave.

**inure** MIDDLE ENGLISH *in* in + *ure* practice, work, from FRENCH *ovre,* from LATIN *opera* a work.

**invade** LATIN *invadere,* from *in-* in + *vadere* go.

**invalid** FRENCH *invalide* make unable, from LATIN *invalidus* not well, from *in-* not + *validus* strong.

**invect** See **invective.**

**invective** FRENCH, from LATIN *invectus,* from *invehi.* See **inveigh.**

**inveigh** LATIN *invehi* attack with words, from *invehere* attack, from *in-* in + *vehere* carry.

**inveigle** FRENCH *aveugler* blind, from LATIN *ab-* from + *oculus* an eye.

**invent** LATIN *invenire,* from *in-* on + *venire* come.

**inventory** LATIN *inventorium* list, from *invenire* find. See **invent.**

**invert** LATIN *invertere,* from *in-* to + *vertere* turn.

**invest** LATIN *investire,* from *in-* in + *vestire* clothe, from *vestis* clothing.

**investigate** LATIN *investigare* trace out, from *vestigum* a track.

**invidious** LATIN *invidiosus,* from *invidia* envy.

**invigorate** See **vigor.**

**invite** LATIN *invitare* entertain.

**invoke** LATIN *invocare*, from *in-* on + *vocare* call.

**involve** LATIN *involvere* cover, from *in-* in + *volvere* roll.

**iodine** FRENCH *iode*, from GREEK *iodes* violet-colored.

**iodoform** LATIN *iodum* iodine + *formyl* formic acid.

**ion** GREEK *ienai* go.

**-ion** GREEK.

**iota** GREEK the name of the smallest Greek letter.

**ipecacuanha** PORTUGUESE.

**ir-** See in-¹, in-².

**irascible** FRENCH, from LATIN *irascibilis,* from *irascit* become angry.

**irate** LATIN *ira* anger.

**ire** FRENCH, from LATIN *ira* anger.

**iridescent** LATIN *iris* rainbow. See **iris**.

**iris** MIDDLE ENGLISH, from LATIN rainbow, from GREEK.

**irk** MIDDLE ENGLISH *irken* be tired of.

**iron** MIDDLE ENGLISH *iren*, from OLD ENGLISH.

**ironmonger** See **iron** + **monger**.

**irony** LATIN *ironia* hide one's feelings while speaking, from GREEK *eironeia*, from *einein* speak.

**irradiate** LATIN *irradiare* send out rays.

**irrational** See **ir-** + **rational**.

**irrigate** LATIN *irrigare*, from *ir-* in + *rigare* make wet.

**irritate** LATIN *irritare* excite.

**irrupt** LATIN *irrumpere*, from *ir-* into + *rumpere* break.

**is** OLD ENGLISH.

**-ish** OLD ENGLISH *-isc*.

**isinglass** probably from DUTCH *huizen* sturgeon (type of fish) + *blas* bladder.

**Islam** ARABIC *islam* submission (to the will of God).

**island** MIDDLE ENGLISH, from OLD ENGLISH *igland* piece of land surrounded by water.

**-ism** GREEK *-ismos*.

**iso-** GREEK *isos* equal.

**isobar** GREEK *isos* equal + *baros* weight, from *barys* heavy.

**isolate** ITALIAN *isolato* separated, from *isola* island, from LATIN *insula*.

**isometric** GREEK *isos* equal + *metron* a measure.

**isosceles** LATIN having two legs, from GREEK *isoskeles,* from *isos* equal + *skelos* leg.

**isotherm** GREEK *isos* equal + *therme* heat, from *thermos* hot.

**Israel** HEBREW *y isra'el* "God strives" also "he who wrestles with God".

**issue** FRENCH way out, from *issir* go out, from LATIN *exire*, from *ex-* out + *ire* go.

**-ist** FRENCH, from LATIN, from GREEK *-istes*.

**it** OLD ENGLISH *hit*.

**italic** LATIN *italicus* Italian. The first use of the type style was in an Italian edition of the work of Virgil (an early Roman poet).

**itch** OLD ENGLISH *giccan*.

**-ite** LATIN, from GREEK *ites*.

**item** LATIN *ita* so, thus.

**itinerant** LATIN *itinerari* travel, from *iter* walk.

**itinerary** Latin *itinerarium* report of a journey, from *iter* walk.

**-ition** French *-ition* or Latin *-itio*.

**-itis** Latin, from Greek inflammation.

**its** See **it**.

**-ity** French *-ite*, from Latin *-itas*.

**-ive** French *-if*, from Latin *-ivus*.

**ivory** Middle English *ivorie*, from Latin *eboreus* made of ivory, from *ebur* ivory, from Egyptian *ebou* elephant.

**-ize** French, from Latin, from Greek *-izein*.

# J

**jab** MIDDLE ENGLISH *jobben* peck.

**jabber** imitative.

**jabot** FRENCH, gizzard, unknown origin.

**jack** FRENCH, from LATIN *Jacobus* Jacob.

**jackal** TURKISH *çakal*, from PERSIAN *shaghal*, from SANSKRIT *srgala* the howler.

**jackanapes** apparently from "*Jack an ape*" a monkey.

**jackdaw** common name of the daw (bird).

**jacket** FRENCH *jaquette* sleeveless coat, from SPANISH *jaco* coat, from ARABIC *shakk*.

**jade**[1] (gem) SPANISH *piedra de ijada* stone of the side, because it was thought that jade could cure pains in the side.

**jade**[2] (horse) OLD NORSE *jalda* a mare.

**jaeger** GERMAN *jäger* one who hunts.

**jag**[1] (sharp point) MIDDLE ENGLISH *jagge*.

**jag**[2] (active time) AMERICAN a quantity, a lot, from MODERN ENGLISH load of hay or wood.

**jail** FRENCH *gaole* prison, from LATIN *gabiola* cage, from *cavea*.

**jake** probably from the name Jake.

**jalap** FRENCH, from SPANISH *jalapa* the plant, from *Jalapa*, Mexican town where the plant was first used.

**jalopy** origin uncertain, perhaps from *Jalapa*, Mexico, where many U.S. used cars went.

**jam** MODERN ENGLISH, origin uncertain.

**jamb** FRENCH *jambe* leg, from LATIN *gamba* leg, from GREEK *kampe* bend.

**jangle** FRENCH *jangler* chatter.

**janitor** LATIN doorkeeper, from *janua* door, from *Janus* Roman god of gates.

**January** MIDDLE ENGLISH *Janyuere* first month of the ancient Roman year, from LATIN the god *Janus*, god of gates and beginnings.

**japonica** LATIN *japonicus* having to do with Japan.

**jar**[1] (container) MIDDLE ENGLISH *jarre*, from FRENCH, from SPANISH *jarra*, from ARABIC large earthen container for keeping water.

**jar**[2] (shake) MIDDLE ENGLISH, imitative, representing a harsh vibratory sound.

**jargon** FRENCH chatter.

**jaundice** FRENCH *jaune* yellow, from LATIN *galbinus* greenish yellow, from *galbus* yellow.

**jaunty** FRENCH *gentil* pleasing, from nobly born, from LATIN *gens* race.

**javelin** FRENCH *javeline* long, thin dart.

**jaw** FRENCH *jawe*, from *joe* cheek.

**jay** FRENCH *gal*, from LATIN *gaius* a jay.

**jazz** AMERICAN, origin uncertain, possibly a style of ragtime dancing.

**jealous** FRENCH *jalous,* from LATIN *zelosus,* from GREEK *zelos.*

**jeameses** *James* the name of a footman, and therefore his costume.

**jeep** U.S. Army *G.P.* (general purpose).

**jeer** possibly from OLD ENGLISH *cegan* call out.

**jehoshaphat** biblical name.

**jelly** FRENCH *gelee* frost, from LATIN *gelare* freeze.

**jennet** FRENCH, from SPANISH *jinete* horseman, from ARABIC *Zenata* a tribe.

**jenny** the name *Jane.*

**jeopardy** MIDDLE ENGLISH *jeuparti,* from FRENCH *je parti* even chance, from LATIN *jocus* game + *partire* divide.

**jerfalcon** See **gyrfalcon.**

**jerk** imitative.

**jerkin** MIDDLE ENGLISH, origin uncertain.

**jersey** the British island *Jersey,* where the cloth and the cow originally came from.

**jess** FRENCH *ges* throw, from LATIN *jactus* metal mold.

**jest** FRENCH *geste* tale, from LATIN *gerere* perform.

**Jesuit** LATIN *Jesusta,* from **Jesus** + **-ite.**

**Jesus** LATIN *Iesus,* from GREEK *Iesous,* from HEBREW *hesha'a* help of Jehovah.

**jet** FRENCH *jeter* throw, from LATIN *facere.*

**jetsam** MIDDLE ENGLISH *jetteson.* See **jettison.**

**jettison** FRENCH *getaison* throw, from LATIN *jactionem,* from *jectare* toss about.

**jetty** FRENCH *jetée.* See **jet.**

**jewel** FRENCH *jouel* gem, from LATIN *jocus* game.

**jib** DANISH *gibbe* jibe.

**jibe** DUTCH *gijpen.*

**jig** MIDDLE ENGLISH, possibly from FRENCH *giguer* dance, from *gigue* a fiddle.

**jigger** (to damn) probably from some sense of **jig.**

**jiggle** See **jig.**

**jilt** a made-up begger term in England about 1640.

**jimson weed** originally *Jamestown weed* after *Jamestown* Colony, an early English settlement in North America, where it was first found.

**jingle** imitative.

**jinrikisha** JAPANESE *jin* a man + *riki* power + *sha* carriage.

**jinx** LATIN *iynx,* from GREEK *iynx* the wryneck, a bird used in black magic.

**job** MIDDLE ENGLISH, origin uncertain.

**jobberknoll** MIDDLE ENGLISH *jobard* fool + *noll,* from OLD ENGLISH *knol* head.

**jockey** SCOTTISH *Jock,* nickname for John.

**jocular** LATIN *joculus* little joke, from *jocus* game.

**jodhpur** *Jodhpur* former state in India.

**jog** MIDDLE ENGLISH *joggen* urge on.

**johnnycake** possibly from *journey cake.*

**join** FRENCH *joindre* connect, from LATIN *jungere* join.

**joint** FRENCH, from LATIN *jungere* join.

**joist** FRENCH *giste* a bed, from LATIN *jacere* rest.

**joke** LATIN *jocus* game.

**jolly** FRENCH *jolif* festive, perhaps from OLD NORSE *jol* feast.

**jolt** MIDDLE ENGLISH combination of *jot* to jolt and *joll* to bump.

**jonquil** FRENCH, from SPANISH *junquillo*, from LATIN *juncus* grasslike plant.

**joree** imitative.

**jorum** possibly from Biblical *Joram* who "brought with him vessels of silver, and vessels of gold, and vessels of brass."

**josh** AMERICAN, probably from the name *Josh*, from *Joshua*.

**joss** PORTUGUESE *deos*, from LATIN *deus* a god.

**jostle** See **joust**.

**jot** LATIN *iota* the smallest letter, from GREEK letter.

**jour** FRENCH, from LATIN *diurnus*, from *dies* day.

**journal** FRENCH daily, from *journal*, from LATIN *diurnalis*, from *dies* day.

**journey** FRENCH *journee* day, from LATIN *dies*.

**journeyman** MIDDLE ENGLISH *journee* day's work + *man*.

**joust** FRENCH *jouste*, from *jouster* meet, from LATIN *iuxtare*, from *iuxta* near.

**jovial** FRENCH, from ITALIAN *joviale*, from LATIN *Jovialis* of Jupiter, from *Jovius* Jupiter, Roman god of the sky. From the idea that people were affected by the planets. The planet Jupiter was thought to be the source of joy and happiness.

**jowl** OLD ENGLISH *ceafl* jaw.

**joy** FRENCH *joie*, from LATIN *gaudium*.

**jubilant** LATIN *jubilare* shout with joy.

**jubilee** FRENCH *jubile*, from LATIN *jubilaeus* year of jubilee, from GREEK *iobelos*, from HEBREW *yovel* ram's horn, which was blown on the year of the jubilee.

**judge** FRENCH *juge*, from LATIN *judex* juror, from *jus* law + *dicere* say.

**judicious** FRENCH *judicieus*, from LATIN *judicium* judgment.

**jug** nickname for the girl's name *Joan*, which a jug was jokingly called.

**juggernaut** HINDI *jagat* world + *natha* lord.

**juggle** FRENCH *jogler*, from LATIN *joculari* joke.

**jugular** LATIN *jugularis*, from *jugulum* collarbone, from *jugum* yoke (a wooden frame that fits around the necks of oxen to join them together for use in pulling wagons, etc.).

**juice** FRENCH *jus* sauce, from LATIN *jus*.

**jujube** FRENCH, from LATIN *zizyphum*, from GREEK *zizyphon*.

**julep** FRENCH, from ARABIC *gul* rose + *ab* water.

**July** MIDDLE ENGLISH *Julie*, from FRENCH *Julie*, from LATIN *Julius*, from the Roman leader Julius Caesar, who was born in this month.

**jumble** possibly from a combination of **jump** and **tumble**.

**jumby** AFRICAN *zumbi* evil spirit.

**jump** GERMAN *gumpen*.

**jumper** MODERN ENGLISH *jump* short coat, from FRENCH *jupe* skirt, from ARABIC *jubbah* loose outer garment.

**junco** SPANISH *junco* reed, bush.

**junction** LATIN *junctio* a joining.

**June** FRENCH, from LATIN *Junius* the name of the goddess *Juno*, protector of women and marriage.

**jungle** HINDI *jangal* forest.

**junior** LATIN *juvenis* young.

**juniper** LATIN *juniperus.*

**junk**[1] (boat) SPANISH and PORTUGUESE *junco.*

**junk**[2] (trash) PORTUGUESE *junco* a reed, from LATIN *juncus.*

**junket** LATIN *juncus* a grasslike plant.

**junta** SPANISH *junta* council, meeting, from LATIN *juncta* joint, from *juncta*, from *jungere* join.

**jupe** FRENCH *jube,* from ARABIC *aljuba.*

**Jupiter** LATIN *Iupeter.*

**Jurassic** FRENCH *Jurassique,* from the *Jura* Mountains between France and Switzerland where fossils of the period were found.

**jurisdiction** FRENCH, from LATIN *jurisdictio,* from *jus* law + *dicere* say.

**jurisprudence** LATIN *jurisprudentia,* from *juris* of right, of law + *prudentia* knowledge, a foreseeing.

**jury** FRENCH *juree* oath, from *jurer* swear, from LATIN *jurare.*

**just** MIDDLE ENGLISH, from FRENCH right, from LATIN *justus,* from *jus* law.

**justaucorps** FRENCH *juste* fitting closely + *au corps* to the body

**justice** See **just.**

**justify** FRENCH *justifier* prove the innocence of, from LATIN *justus* fair + *facere* do, make.

**jut** origin uncertain.

**jute** HINDI *jhuto* matted hair.

**juvenile** LATIN *juvenilis,* from *juvenis* young.

**juxtapose** FRENCH *juxta,* from LATIN near.

# K

**ka** EGYPTIAN.

**kaiser** LATIN *Caeser*.

**kajawah** PERSIAN.

**kale** SCOTTISH, from *cole* cabbage, from MIDDLE ENGLISH *cawul*.

**kaleidoscope** GREEK *kalos* beautiful + *eidos* form + *skopen* examine.

**kangaroo** AUSTRALIAN ABORIGINAL.

**kaolin** FRENCH, from CHINESE *kao-ling* name of the place where it is found.

**karate** JAPANESE *kara* empty + *te* hand.

**karma** SANSKRIT *karman* fate.

**katydid** imitative.

**kayak** ESKIMO.

**kedge** MIDDLE ENGLISH *caggen* fasten.

**keel**[1] (central bottom boat frame piece) MIDDLE ENGLISH *kele*, from OLD NORSE *kjölr*.

**keel**[2] (flat bottomed ship) MIDDLE ENGLISH *kele*, from DUTCH *kiel* boat.

**keel**[3] (stir) MIDDLE ENGLISH *kelen*, from OLD ENGLISH *celan*, from *col* cool.

**keel**[4] (red stain) IRISH *cil*.

**keen**[1] (sharp) MIDDLE ENGLISH *kene,* from OLD ENGLISH *cene* wise.

**keen**[2] (wailing) IRISH *caoinim* I wail.

**keep** OLD ENGLISH *cepan*.

**keg** OLD NORSE *kaggi*.

**kelp** MIDDLE ENGLISH *culp*.

**ken** OLD ENGLISH *cennan* make known.

**kennel** FRENCH *chenil*, from LATIN *canis* dog.

**kerchief** FRENCH *couvrechief* cover the head, from *couvrir* cover + *chef* head, from LATIN *caput*.

**kernel** OLD ENGLISH *cyrnel*.

**kerosene** GREEK *keros* wax, because a wax is used in making it.

**kersey** possibly from the village of Kersey in Suffolk, England.

**kestrel** FRENCH *cresserelle*.

**ketch** MIDDLE ENGLISH *cacchen* catch.

**ketchup** CHINESE *ke-tsiap* sauce used with fish.

**kettle** OLD NORSE *ketill*, from LATIN *catillus* small bowl.

**key**[1] (for lock) MIDDLE ENGLISH *keye*, from OLD ENGLISH *cæg*.

**key**[2] (island) SPANISH *cayo*.

**khaki** HINDI *khak* dust.

**kibbutz** HEBREW.

**kick** MIDDLE ENGLISH *kiken,* origin uncertain.

**kid** OLD NORSE *kith* young goat.

**kidney** MIDDLE ENGLISH *kidenere,* possibly from OLD ENGLISH *cwith* womb + *ey* egg, because of the likeness in shape.

**kike** possibly from *-ki* or *-ky,* endings on the names of Eastern European Jews who came to the U.S. in the early 1900s.

**Kilkenny** the name of an Irish town.

**kill** MIDDLE ENGLISH *killen,* possibly from OLD ENGLISH *cwellan.*

**kiln** OLD ENGLISH *cylene* oven, from LATIN *culina* kitchen.

**kilo-** FRENCH, from GREEK *chillioi* thousand.

**kilt** MIDDLE ENGLISH *kilten,* probably of SCANDINAVIAN origin.

**kimono** JAPANESE.

**kimquat** See **kumquat.**

**kin** OLD ENGLISH *cynn* family.

**-kin** MIDDLE ENGLISH, from DUTCH suffix meaning "little."

**kind** MIDDLE ENGLISH *kynde,* from OLD ENGLISH *gecynde* natural.

**kindergarten** GERMAN *kind* child + *garten* garden.

**kindle** MIDDLE ENGLISH *kindlen,* from OLD NORSE *kynda* light a fire.

**kindred** OLD ENGLISH *cynn* family + *ræden* condition.

**kine** OLD ENGLISH *cyna.*

**kinesthesia** GREEK *kinein* move + *aisthesis* sensation.

**kinetic** GREEK *kinetikos* moving, from *kinetos* moved, from *kinein* move.

**king** OLD ENGLISH *cyning* male ruler.

**kingdom** OLD ENGLISH *cyningdom.*

**kink** DUTCH twist in a rope.

**kiosk** FRENCH *kiosque,* from PERSIAN *kushk* palace, villa.

**kip**[1] (hides) MIDDLE ENGLISH *kyppe,* from DUTCH *kijp* hides.

**kip**[2] (bed) DANISH *kippe* alehouse.

**kip**[3] (money) THAI.

**kip**[4] (weight) *kilopound.* See **kilo-** + **pound**[2].

**kipper** OLD ENGLISH *cypera* male salmon, perhaps from *coper,* copper metal, by similarity of color.

**kiss** OLD ENGLISH *cyssan.*

**kissel** RUSSIAN *kisel.*

**kit** DUTCH *kitte* large wooden bowl.

**kitchen** OLD ENGLISH *cycene,* from LATIN *coquina,* from *coquere* cook.

**kite** OLD ENGLISH *cyta.*

**kith** OLD ENGLISH *cyththu* relationship.

**kithe (kythe)** MIDDLE ENGLISH *kithen,* from OLD ENGLISH *cythan* make known.

**kittel** YIDDISH *kitl.*

**kiver** See **cover.**

**kiwi** MAORI.

**klaxon** trademark for a kind of loud horn.

**knack** MIDDLE ENGLISH *knak* sharp hit.

**knave** OLD ENGLISH *cnafa* boy, servant.

**knead** OLD ENGLISH *cnedan.*

**knee** OLD ENGLISH *cneow.*

**kneel** OLD ENGLISH *cneowlian,* from *cneow* knee.

**knell** OLD ENGLISH *cnyllan* ring a bell.

**knickerbocker** the pen name used by Washington Irving to publish his *History of New York.*

**knickers** See **knickerbocker**, by resemblance to short trousers worn by Dutchmen pictured in Washington Irving's *History of New York.*

**knife** OLD ENGLISH *cnif.*

**knight** OLD ENGLISH *cniht* boy.

**knit** OLD ENGLISH *cnyttan* tie by knotting.

**knob** MIDDLE ENGLISH *knobe.*

**knock** OLD ENGLISH *cnocian* hit hard.

**knoll**[1] (hilltop) OLD ENGLISH *cnoll.*

**knoll**[2] (bell sound) See **knell**.

**knot** OLD ENGLISH *cnotta.*

**know** OLD ENGLISH *cnawan* recognize, identify, understand as a truth or fact.

**knowledge** See **know**.

**knuckle** GERMAN *knokel* little bone.

**knurl** probably from MIDDLE ENGLISH *knur* a knot.

**kobold** GERMAN *kobold, kobolt.*

**kow-tow** CHINESE *k'o-t'ou* knock head.

**kremlin** FRENCH, from RUSSIAN *kreml.*

**krone** GERMAN *krone* crown.

**krypton** LATIN, from GREEK, from *kryptos* hidden.

**kudos** GREEK *kydos* glory.

**kudu** AFRICAN *koedoe.*

**kugel** YIDDISH, from GERMAN *kugel, kugele* ball, globe.

**kumquat** CHINESE *kamkwat*, from *kam* golden + *kwat* orange.

# L

**labboard**  See **larboard**.

**label**  FRENCH ribbon.

**labor**  FRENCH *labour* trouble, from LATIN *labor* work, pain.

**laboratory**  LATIN *laboraterium* workshop, from *laborare* work.

**laburnum**  LATIN.

**labyrinth**  LATIN *labyrinthos* maze, from GREEK *labyrinthos*.

**lac**  HINDI *lakh*, from SANSKRIT *laksa*.

**lace**  FRENCH *las* knotted rope, from LATIN *laqueus*.

**lacerate**  LATIN *lacerare*, from *lacer* hurt badly.

**lachrymose**  LATIN *lacrima* teary-eyed.

**lack**  possibly from DUTCH *lac*.

**lackadaisical**  MODERN ENGLISH *lackadaisy*, from *lack-a-day*, from *alack the day*.

**lackey**  FRENCH *laquais* footman (man who helps in the house), from TURKISH *ulak* man who carried messages.

**laconic**  LATIN *Laconicus*, the ancient country Laconia (*Lakonikos* in Greek), near Greece, where a race of people called the Spartans lived.  The Spartans used few words to express themselves.

**lacquer**  FRENCH, from PORTUGUESE *laca* gummy substance.

**lactic**  LATIN *lactis*, from *lac* milk.

**ladder**  OLD ENGLISH *hlæder* frame with steps.

**lade**  OLD ENGLISH *hladan* load up, heap.

**laden**  OLD ENGLISH *hladan* load up, heap.

**ladle**  OLD ENGLISH *hlædel*, from *hladan*, load up, heap.

**lady**  OLD ENGLISH *hlæfdige* loaf-kneader (mistress of the house who kneads bread).

**lag**  possibly from DUTCH *lakke* go slowly.

**lagoon**  ITALIAN *laguna* pool, from LATIN *lacuna* pond.

**lair**  OLD ENGLISH *leger* bed.

**lake**  FRENCH *lac* pond, from LATIN *lacus* large body of water.

**lam**  OLD NORSE *lemja* lame.

**lamb**  OLD ENGLISH.

**lambent**  LATIN *lambentem*, from *lambere* lick.

**lame**  OLD ENGLISH *lama* not able in body.

**lament**  FRENCH, from LATIN *lamentari* make a long sound of grief or pain.

**laminate**  LATIN *laminare* thin piece.

**laminitis** LATIN *lamina* thin piece of metal or wood + -itis.

**lamp** FRENCH *lampe* something that lights, from LATIN *lampas* torch, from GREEK *lampas*.

**lampoon** FRENCH *lampons* let us drink (part of a drinking song).

**lamprey** FRENCH *lampreie,* from LATIN *lampreda.*

**lance** MIDDLE ENGLISH, from FRENCH spear, from LATIN *lancea* light spear.

**lancet** FRENCH *lancette* small lance.

**land** OLD ENGLISH *land* solid piece of Earth.

**landau** the German town *Landau* where the carriage was originally made.

**landscape** DUTCH *landschap* painting of land scene, from *land* land + -*schap* shape.

**lane** OLD ENGLISH.

**langouste** FRENCH.

**language** FRENCH *langage,* from *langue* tongue, from LATIN *lingua* tongue, speech.

**languid** FRENCH *languide,* from LATIN *languidus,* from *languere* be faint or listless from lack of energy.

**languish** FRENCH *languir* grieve, become ill, from LATIN *languere* be faint or listless from lack of energy.

**lank** OLD ENGLISH *hlanc.*

**lantern** FRENCH *lanterne* box with clear sides that contains a light, from LATIN *lanterna* lamp, from GREEK *lampein* shine.

**lanthorn** See **lantern**.

**lanyard** FRENCH *laniere,* from *lasne* noose.

**lap** OLD ENGLISH *lapian* take up liquid with the tongue.

**lapel** OLD ENGLISH *læppa* part of clothing.

**lapstrake** MODERN ENGLISH (shipbuilding) *lap* overlap + *strake* line of planking.

**lapis lazuli** LATIN *lapis* a stone + *lazulus* azure (sky blue color).

**laporotomy** GREEK remove part of the intestine.

**lapse** LATIN *lapsus* fall.

**larboard** OLD ENGLISH *hladan* bring up water + *bord* table.

**larceny** FRENCH, from LATIN *latrocinari* rob, from *latro* robber.

**lard** FRENCH bacon fat, from LATIN *lardum.*

**larder** FRENCH tub in which bacon is kept, from *lard* bacon. See **lard**.

**large** FRENCH, from LATIN *largus* having more than enough.

**largess** FRENCH *largesse,* from LATIN *largus* more than enough.

**lariat** SPANISH *la reata* the rope.

**lark**[1] (bird) OLD ENGLISH *lawerce.*

**lark**[2] (play) OLD NORSE *leika* play.

**larva** LATIN *ghost.*

**larynx** GREEK.

**lasagna** ITALIAN, from LATIN *lasanum,* from GREEK *lasanon* a pot.

**lascar** HINDI *lashkar,* from ARABIC *al-askar* army.

**lascivious** LATIN *lasciviosus,* from *lascivia.*

**lash**[1] (whip) MIDDLE ENGLISH *lassche.*

**lash**[2] (bind) MIDDLE ENGLISH *lashen,* from FRENCH *lachier,* from *lacier* lace.

**lashings** IRISH plenty.

**lass** MIDDLE ENGLISH *lasse,* probably from OLD NORSE.

**lassitude** LATIN *lassitudo.*

**lasso** SPANISH *lazo*, from LATIN *laqueus*.

**last**[1] (slowest) MIDDLE ENGLISH *laste*, from OLD ENGLISH *latost*, from *læt*.

**last**[2] (continue) OLD ENGLISH *læstan*.

**latch** OLD ENGLISH *læccan* take.

**late** OLD ENGLISH *læt* slow.

**lateen** FRENCH *voile latine*, Latin sail.

**latent** LATIN *latere* hidden.

**lateral** LATIN *lateralis*, from *latus* side.

**lath** OLD ENGLISH *lætt* narrow piece of wood used in building.

**lathe** probably from DUTCH *lade*, from *drejelad* supporting framework.

**lather** OLD ENGLISH *leathor*.

**latitude** FRENCH, from LATIN *latitudo*, from *latus* wide.

**latke** RUSSIAN *latka* pastry.

**latrine** LATIN *latrina*, from *lavatrina* washbasin, washroom, from *lavatus*, from *lavare* wash + *-trina* workplace.

**latter** OLD ENGLISH *lætra* slower, from *læt* slow.

**lattice** FRENCH *lattis*, from GERMAN *latte* a lath (narrow strip of wood used in building lattices, etc.).

**laud** FRENCH, from LATIN *laudes*, from *laus* praise.

**laudanum** LATIN variation of *ladanum* used by a 16th century Swiss physician to name a remedy based on opium.

**laugh** OLD ENGLISH *hlæhhan*.

**launch** FRENCH *lancher*, from *lancier* throw, from *lance* spear. See **lance**.

**laund** FRENCH *launde* wooded ground, from early IRISH *lann*. See **land**.

**launder** MIDDLE ENGLISH one who washes clothes, from FRENCH *lavandier*, from LATIN *lavanda* things to be washed, from *lavare* wash.

**laureate** MIDDLE ENGLISH, from LATIN *laureatus* crown with flowers, from *laurea corona* laurel (type of flower) crown, because of the ancient Roman custom of honoring poets, athletes and other heroes by crowning them with a laurel wreath.

**laurel** FRENCH, from LATIN *laurus*.

**lava** ITALIAN *lave*, from LATIN *labes* a fall, from *labi* slide.

**lavabo** LATIN *lavare* wash.

**lavage** FRENCH, from *laver* wash.

**lavatory** LATIN *lavatorium* place for washing, from *lavare* wash.

**lavender** FRENCH, from LATIN *lavandria*, from *lavare* wash. The plant was used to scent washed fabrics and as a bath perfume.

**lavish** FRENCH *lavasse* rain, from *laver* wash, from LATIN *lavare* wash.

**law** MIDDLE ENGLISH *lawe*, from OLD ENGLISH *lagu* body of rules, from OLD NORSE *lag* a law, something laid down and fixed or set.

**lax** LATIN *laxus* loose.

**lay**[1] (hire) OLD NORSE *leiga* hire.

**lay**[2] (law term) FRENCH *lie*, from ITALIAN *legge*, from LATIN *lex* law.

**lay**[3] (put down) OLD ENGLISH *lecgan*.

**lay**[4] (poem) FRENCH *lai*.

**lazy** MIDDLE ENGLISH *laysy*, origin uncertain.

**-le** MIDDLE ENGLISH *-el*, from OLD ENGLISH *-ol*.

**leach** OLD ENGLISH *leccan* moisten. See **leak**.

**lead**[1] (to guide) OLD ENGLISH *lædan*.

**lead**[2] (metal) OLD ENGLISH.

**leaf** OLD ENGLISH.

**league** FRENCH *ligue,* from ITALIAN *liga,* from LATIN *ligare* bind.

**leak** OLD NORSE *leka* drip.

**lean**[1] (bend) OLD ENGLISH *hleonian* bend.

**lean**[2] (thin) OLD ENGLISH *hlæne* thin.

**leap** OLD ENGLISH *hleapan* jump.

**learn** OLD ENGLISH *leornian* get knowledge.

**lease** FRENCH, from LATIN *laxare* loosen.

**leash** FRENCH, from LATIN *laxus* lax.

**least** OLD ENGLISH *læst* smallest.

**leather** OLD ENGLISH *lether.*

**leave** OLD ENGLISH *læfan* allow to remain.

**leaven** FRENCH *levain,* from LATIN *levamen* rising.

**lecithin** FRENCH *lécithine,* from GREEK *lethikos* yolk of an egg.

**lectern** FRENCH *letrun* reading desk, from LATIN *lectrum,* from *legere* read.

**lecture** LATIN *lectura* a reading, from *legere* read.

**lede** OLD ENGLISH *leod* people.

**ledge** probably from MIDDLE ENGLISH *leggen.*

**ledger** MIDDLE ENGLISH *legger* record book, from OLD ENGLISH *lecgan* place.

**leduc** FRENCH the duke.

**lee** OLD ENGLISH *hleo* protection.

**leech** OLD ENGLISH *læce.*

**leek** OLD ENGLISH *leac.*

**leer** OLD ENGLISH *hleor* face.

**left** MIDDLE ENGLISH *lift* left side, from OLD ENGLISH *lyft* weak.

**legacy** FRENCH *legacie* office of an official, from LATIN *legare* choose someone for an official job.

**legal** FRENCH, from LATIN *legalis* having to do with the law, from *lex* law.

**legate** FRENCH, from LATIN *legare,* from *lex* law.

**legend** FRENCH *legende* a writing, from LATIN *legenda* thing to be read, from *legere* read.

**legerdemain** FRENCH *leger de main* light of hand.

**legible** LATIN *legibilis,* from *legere* read.

**legion** FRENCH Roman body of soldiers, from LATIN *legio,* from *legere* choose.

**legislation** LATIN *legislationem* bringing of a law, from *legis,* from *lex* law + *lationem* bringing.

**legitimate** LATIN *legitimare* make lawful, from *legitimus* lawful.

**legume** FRENCH, from LATIN *legumen,* from *legere* gather.

**leisure** FRENCH *leisir* free time, from LATIN *licere* be allowed.

**lemon** FRENCH, from ARABIC *laimun.*

**lend** OLD ENGLISH *lænan.*

**length** OLD ENGLISH *lengthu.*

**lenient** LATIN *lenire* soften, from *lenis* soft.

**lens** LATIN lentil, because the shape of a glass lens looks like a lentil seed.

**-lent** LATIN *-lentus.*

**lenticular** LATIN *lenticularis,* from *lenticula,* from *lens* lentil. See **lens.**

**leopard** FRENCH, from LATIN, from GREEK *leopardos,* from *leon* lion + *pardos* panther.

**leotard** J. *Léotard,* 19th century tightrope walker.

**leper** FRENCH *lepre,* from LATIN *lepra,* from GREEK *lepros* rough, having scales, from *lepein* peel.

**leprechaun** IRISH *lupracan* very small body, from *lu* little + *corpan* small body, from LATIN *corpus* body.

**leprosy** See **leper**.

**lesion** FRENCH, from LATIN *laesio*, from *laedere* harm.

**less** OLD ENGLISH *læsa* smaller.

**-less** OLD ENGLISH *-leas*.

**lesson** FRENCH *leçon* lecture, from LATIN *lectio* a reading.

**lest** OLD ENGLISH *thy læs the* by the less that.

**let** OLD ENGLISH *lætan* allow.

**-let** FRENCH *-el*, from LATIN *-ellus*.

**lethal** LATIN *lethalis*, from *letum* death.

**lethargy** LATIN *lethargia* sleepiness, from GREEK *lethargia*, from *lethargos*, from *lethe* forgetful + *argos* not busy, from *a-* not + *ergon* work.

**letter** FRENCH *lettre* letter of the alphabet, from LATIN *littera*.

**lettuce** FRENCH, from LATIN *lactuca*, from *lac* milk, from its milky juice.

**leukemia** GREEK *leukos* white + *haima* blood.

**levee** FRENCH *lever* raise.

**level** FRENCH *livel* carpenter's level (tool that tells if a surface is level), from LATIN *libella* balance.

**lever** FRENCH *levier* crowbar (tool that helps to get a box lid open), from *lever* raise, from LATIN *levare*.

**leverat** FRENCH *levre*, from LATIN *lepus* hare.

**leviathan** LATIN *leviathon* sea monster.

**levity** LATIN *levitas* lightness. See **light**[2].

**levy** See **lever**.

**lexicon** GREEK *lexikon*, from *lexis* a word, from *legein* speak.

**liable** FRENCH *lier* bind, from LATIN *ligare*.

**liaison** FRENCH *liason*, from LATIN *ligare* bind.

**liana** MODERN ENGLISH, from FRENCH *liane*.

**libation** LATIN *libatio* liquid poured out as an offering to a god.

**libel** LATIN *libellus* little book. In ancient Rome little books were written and sent around for the purpose of damaging reputations.

**liberal** FRENCH, from LATIN *liberalis* free man, from *liber* free.

**liberate** LATIN *libarare* set free.

**liberty** FRENCH *liberte* freedom, from LATIN *liberatas*.

**libido** LATIN, from *libere* to please.

**library** FRENCH *librairie* collection of books, from LATIN *librarius*, from *liber* book.

**lice** plural of **louse**.

**license** FRENCH granting permission to do something, from LATIN *licentia*.

**lichee** CHINESE *li-chih*.

**lichen** LATIN, from GREEK, probably from *leichein* lick.

**licit** LATIN *licere* be permitted.

**lick** OLD ENGLISH *liccian*.

**licorice** FRENCH, from LATIN *liquiritia*, from GREEK *glykys* sweet + *rhiza* root.

**lie** OLD ENGLISH *leogan* make a false statement.

**lief** OLD ENGLISH *leof* dear.

**liege** probably from FRENCH *liege* person owned by a lord, from LATIN *laetus* serf.

**lieutenant** FRENCH *lieu* place + *tenant* holding, from LATIN *tenere* hold.

**life** OLD ENGLISH *lif* time from birth to death.

**lift** OLD NORSE *lypia* raise.

**ligament** LATIN *ligamentum* band, tie, from *ligare* bind.

**ligature** FRENCH, from LATIN *ligatura* a band, from *ligatus*, from *ligare* bind.

**light**[1] (brightness) OLD ENGLISH *leht*, from *leoht*.

**light**[2] (weight) OLD ENGLISH *leoht*.

**light**[3] (dismount) OLD ENGLISH *lihtan*.

**lightning** OLD ENGLISH *lightnen* lighten (make bright).

**lignite** LATIN *lignum* wood + GREEK *ites*.

**like** OLD ENGLISH *(ge)lic* similar.

**lilac** FRENCH, from ARABIC *nilac* bluish.

**lilt** MIDDLE ENGLISH *lulte*.

**limb** OLD ENGLISH *lim*.

**limber** MIDDLE ENGLISH, origin uncertain.

**limbo** LATIN border.

**limerick** *Limerick*, Ireland, place where at parties the same song would be sung after each person who came up with a nonsense verse.

**limit** FRENCH *limiter*, from LATIN *limes* boundary.

**limousine** FRENCH coat worn by people in *Limousin*, France, where a horse-drawn car was built.

**limp** OLD ENGLISH *limpan* have happen to one.

**limpet** OLD ENGLISH, from LATIN *lempreda*.

**limpid** FRENCH *limpide*, from LATIN *limpidus*, from *limpa* water.

**limpsy** See limp.

**linchpin** possibly from MIDDLE ENGLISH *lynspin*, from OLD ENGLISH *lynis* axle pin.

**line** OLD ENGLISH *line* rope, from LATIN *linea* linen thread.

**lineament** LATIN *lineamentum*, from *lineare* make a straight line.

**linen** OLD ENGLISH.

**-ling** OLD ENGLISH.

**linger** MIDDLE ENGLISH *lengeren* wait, from OLD ENGLISH *lengan* cause to wait longer than needed.

**lingo** probably from LATIN *lingua* tongue.

**linguist** LATIN *lingua* tongue.

**liniment** LATIN *linimentum*, from *linire* spread.

**linimentum** LATIN. See liniment.

**link** OLD NORSE *hlekkr* chain.

**linnet** FRENCH *linette*, from *lin* flax, because the bird eats the seeds of the flax plant.

**linoleum** LATIN *linum* flax + *oleum* oil.

**linseed** OLD ENGLISH.

**linsey-woolsey** MIDDLE ENGLISH *lin* flax + *wolle* wool.

**linstock** DUTCH *lontstok*, from *lont* wooden match + *stok* stick.

**lintel** FRENCH *lintel*, from LATIN *limes* boundary.

**lion** FRENCH, from LATIN *leonis*, from GREEK *leon*.

**lip** OLD ENGLISH *lippa*.

**lipoma** LATIN, from GREEK *lipos* fat + *-oma* tumor.

**lipoprotein** GREEK *lipos* fat + GERMAN, from FRENCH, from GREEK *proteios* primary, from *protos* first.

**lipper** nautical usage, related to **lip** or **lap**.

**liquid** FRENCH, from LATIN *liquidere*.

**liquidate** LATIN *liquidare*.

**liquor** FRENCH *licor,* from LATIN *liquor.*

**lisp** MIDDLE ENGLISH *lispen,* from OLD ENGLISH *wlisp.*

**list**[1] (items) MIDDLE ENGLISH *liste,* from OLD ENGLISH *liste* border.

**list**[2] (lean) MIDDLE ENGLISH *listen,* from OLD ENGLISH *lystan* desire.

**list**[3] (listen) MIDDLE ENGLISH *listen,* from OLD ENGLISH *hlystan,* from *hlyst* hearing.

**listen** OLD ENGLISH *hlysnan.*

**litany** FRENCH *litanie,* from LATIN *litania* form of prayer, from GREEK *litaneia* prayer.

**liter** FRENCH *litre,* from LATIN, from GREEK *litra* a pound.

**literal** LATIN *litteralis* relating to a letter, from *littera.* See **literate.**

**literate** LATIN *littera* a letter of the alphabet.

**literature** FRENCH, from LATIN *litteratura* learning, from *littera.* See **literate.**

**lithe** OLD ENGLISH soft, mild.

**lithium** GREEK *lithos* stone.

**litho-** GREEK *lithos* stone.

**litigate** LATIN *litigare* argue, from *lit* quarrel + *agere* go.

**litter** FRENCH *litiere* bed, from LATIN *lectus* bed.

**little** OLD ENGLISH *lytel.*

**liturgy** LATIN *liturgia,* from GREEK *leitourgia* public service, from *leos* people + *ergon* work.

**live** OLD ENGLISH *lifian* have life.

**lively** OLD ENGLISH *liflic.*

**liver** OLD ENGLISH *lifer.*

**livery** FRENCH *livree* gift of clothes to a servant, from *livrer* deliver, from LATIN *liberare* set free.

**livid** FRENCH, from LATIN *lividus* blueish. Early use of the word described someone pale with anger, then came to mean someone red-faced with anger.

**livre** FRENCH money, from LATIN *libra* scales for weighing.

**lizard** FRENCH *lesard,* from LATIN *laceria.*

**load** OLD ENGLISH *lad* journey.

**loaf** OLD ENGLISH *hlaf.*

**loam** OLD ENGLISH *lam.*

**loan** OLD NORSE *lan.*

**loath** OLD ENGLISH *lath* hostile.

**loathe** OLD ENGLISH *lath* hateful.

**lob**[1] (toss) MIDDLE ENGLISH *lobbe* heavy

**lob**[2] (spider) OLD ENGLISH *lobbe.*

**lobby** FRENCH *loge* small house, from LATIN *lobia* covered area.

**lobe** LATIN *lobos,* from GREEK.

**lobscouse** DANISH *lobskous.*

**lobster** OLD ENGLISH *loppestre,* corruption of LATIN *locusta* lobster, locust (influenced by OLD ENGLISH *loppe,* a variant of *lobbe,* spider).

**local** FRENCH, from LATIN *localis* relating to a place, from *locus* place.

**locate** LATIN *locare* place.

**lock**[1] (fasten) OLD ENGLISH *loc* bolt, fastening, enclosure.

**lock**[2] (hair) OLD ENGLISH *locc.*

**loco** SPANISH insane, origin uncertain.

**loco-** LATIN *locus* a place.

**locomotive** See **loco-** + **motion.**

**locus** LATIN *locus* place.

**locust** LATIN *locusta.*

**lode** OLD ENGLISH *lad* way.

**lodestone** MIDDLE ENGLISH, from OLD NORSE *leith* way + OLD ENGLISH *stan*.

**lodge** FRENCH *loge* small house, from LATIN *lobia* covered area.

**loft** OLD NORSE *lopt* upper room.

**log** MIDDLE ENGLISH *logge,* probably from OLD NORSE *lag* tree cut down.

**logarithm** LATIN *logarithmus* ratio-number, from GREEK *logos* proportion, ratio, word + *arithmos* number.

**logic** LATIN *logica* art of reasoning, from GREEK *logike,* from *logos* word, reason.

**logistics** FRENCH *logistique,* from *logis* lodging, from *loger* lodge, from *loge* small house.

**logo** GREEK *logogram* sign for a word, from *logos* word + *gram* written.

**-logy** GREEK *-logia,* from *logos* word.

**loin** FRENCH *loigne,* from LATIN *lumbus.*

**loiter** possibly from DUTCH *loteren* delay.

**loll** DUTCH *lollen.*

**lollop** See **loll.**

**lone** See **alone.**

**lonely** See **alone.**

**long**[1] (distance) OLD ENGLISH *lang* not short.

**long**[2] (want) OLD ENGLISH *langian.*

**longevity** LATIN *longus* long + *aevum* age.

**longitude** LATIN *longitudo* length.

**longshore** See **along** + **shore.**

**look** OLD ENGLISH *locian.*

**loom**[1] (machine) MIDDLE ENGLISH *lome,* from OLD ENGLISH *loma* tool.

**loom**[2] (appear large) SCANDINAVIAN.

**loon** MIDDLE ENGLISH *loom* diving bird.

**loony** See **lunatic.** (Also, from the wild cry of the **loon.**)

**loop** OLD NORSE *hlaup* leap.

**loose** OLD NORSE *lauss* free.

**loot** HINDI *lut,* from SANSKRIT *lota* stolen property.

**lop** MIDDLE ENGLISH *loppen,* from OLD ENGLISH *loppian.*

**lope** OLD NORSE *hiaupa* lead.

**loquacious** LATIN *loquax,* from *loqui* speak.

**lord** OLD ENGLISH *hlaford,* from *hlaf* loaf + *weard* keeper, from master of a household with dependents who eat his bread.

**lore** OLD ENGLISH *lar* teaching.

**lorgnette** FRENCH *lorgner* squint + *-ette.*

**lorry** BRITISH railroad usage, probably from *lurry* pull.

**lose** OLD ENGLISH *losian* escape.

**loss** possibly from OLD ENGLISH *los* ruin.

**lot** OLD ENGLISH *hlot* share, what is used as a playing piece in a game of chance.

**lotion** LATIN *lotio* washing.

**lottery** FRENCH, from DUTCH *lot* lot.

**lotus** LATIN plant, from GREEK *lotos.*

**loud** OLD ENGLISH *hlud.*

**lounge** SCOTTISH, origin uncertain.

**louse** OLD ENGLISH *lus.*

**lout** MIDDLE ENGLISH *lutien* stay hidden.

**louver** MIDDLE ENGLISH *luver,* from FRENCH *lover.*

**love** OLD ENGLISH *lufu.*

**low** OLD NORSE *lagr.*

**lox** YIDDISH *laks,* from GERMAN *lachs* salmon.

**loyal** French, from Latin *legalis* relating to the law, from *lex* law.

**lozenge** Middle English rhombus, from French *losenge,* diamond-shaped.

**lubber** Middle English *lobbe* heavy, from German *lobbe* hanging lump of flesh.

**lubricate** Latin *lubricare* make slippery.

**lucid** Latin *lucidus* bright.

**luck** Dutch *luc* good fortune.

**lucrative** Latin *lucrum* gain.

**ludicrous** Latin *ludicrus* playful, from *ludus* play.

**lug** Middle English *luggen,* probably of Scandinavian origin.

**luggage** See **lug** + **-age.**

**lugubrious** Latin *lugubris* very sad.

**lukewarm** Middle English *lukewarme* (slightly warm, tepid), origin uncertain.

**lulav** Hebrew *lulabh* branch.

**lull** Middle English *lullen* origin imitative.

**lullaby** Middle English *lullai* cradlesong words + *-by* as in *bye-bye.*

**lullian** 13th century philosopher Raymund *Lull.*

**lumber** Middle English *lomeren.*

**luminary** French, from Latin *luminarium,* from *lumen* light.

**lump** Middle English *lumpe.*

**lunar** Latin *luna* moon.

**lunatic** Middle English *lunatik,* from French *lunatique,* from Latin *lunaticus* moonstruck, from *luna* moon, from a belief that insanity is related to or caused by the phases of the moon.

**lunch** See **luncheon.**

**luncheon** Middle English *nonechenche* light mid-day meal, from *none* noon + *schench* drink, from Old English *scenc,* from *scencan* pour out.

**lung** Old English *lungen.*

**lunge** French *allonger* lengthen, from Latin *ad-* to + *longus* extended.

**lupine** Latin *lupis* wolf, origin uncertain for name of plant.

**lurch** nautical *lee-larch* sudden roll to leeward, perhaps from French *lacher* let go, from Latin *laxus* loose.

**lure** French *loirre.*

**lurid** Latin *luridus* pale yellow.

**lurk** Middle English *lurken,* from *lurne* frown.

**luscious** Middle English *lucius.* See **delicious.**

**luster** French *lustre* bright, from Italian *lustro,* from Latin *lustrare.*

**lute** French *lut,* from Arabic *al`ud* the wood.

**luxury** French, from Latin *luxeria* too much.

**-ly** Old English *-lic.*

**lye** Old English *leag.*

**lymph** French *lymphe,* from Latin *lympha* clear water.

**lymphosarcoma** See **lymph** + Greek *sarkoma* fleshy.

**lynch** *Lynch's law,* possibly from Charles *Lynch,* 1736–86, a Virginia planter who organized bands of patriots to punish people who supported the British during the American Revolution.

**lynx** Greek.

**lyre** Latin, from Greek *lyra.*

**lyric** Latin *lyricus* relating to the lyre, an early stringed instrument.

# M

**macabre** FRENCH *danse macabre* dance of death.

**macadam** J. L. *McAdam* (1756–1836) Scottish engineer.

**macaroni** ITALIAN *maccaroni*.

**macaroon** FRENCH *macaron*, from ITALIAN *maccarone*.

**mace**[1] (club) MIDDLE ENGLISH, from FRENCH large hammer, from LATIN *matteola*.

**mace**[2] (spice) MIDDLE ENGLISH, from FRENCH *macis*, from LATIN *macir* red spice from India, from GREEK *makir*.

**machete** SPANISH *macho* hammer, from LATIN *marculus* small hammer.

**machine** FRENCH engine, from LATIN *machina*, from GREEK *machos* something built in a skillful way.

**macho** SPANISH male, from LATIN *masculus*. See **masculine**.

**mackeral** FRENCH *makerel*.

**mackinaw** *Mackinac* Island, a small island in the area between Lake Michigan and Lake Huron.

**mackintosh** C. *Macintosh* (1766–1843), Scottish inventor.

**macramé** FRENCH, from ITALIAN, from TURKISH *makrama* towel, from ARABIC·*miqrama* embroidered cloth (cloth decorated using needle and thread).

**macro-** GREEK *makros* long.

**mad** OLD ENGLISH *(ge)mæded* drive mad.

**madam** FRENCH *ma dame* my lady, from LATIN *mea* my + *domina* lady.

**madras** *Madras*, India, where it was first made.

**madrigal** ITALIAN *madrigale*, from LATIN *mandra* pastoral song.

**maelstrom** DUTCH name of a well-known whirlpool off the coast of Norway that was reputed to destroy everything that came near it, from *maalen* whirl, grind + *stroom* stream.

**maestro** ITALIAN *maesta* master, from LATIN *magister*.

**magazine** FRENCH *magasin* store, from ITALIAN *magazzino*, from ARABIC *makhzan* storehouse. In the 16th century *"Magazine"* was used in the titles of books, to give the idea that the book was a "storehouse of knowledge".

**maggot** MIDDLE ENGLISH *magot*, from OLD ENGLISH *matha*, from OLD NORSE *mathkr*.

**magic** FRENCH *magique*, from LATIN *magice*, from GREEK *magikos* of the Magi.

**magistrate** LATIN *magistratus* public person, from *magister* master.

**magma** MIDDLE ENGLISH dregs, from LATIN dregs of an ointment, from GREEK ointment.

**magnanimous** LATIN *magnanimus* high-minded (having high ideals), from *magnus* great + *animus* mind.

**magnate** LATIN *magnas* great man, from *magnus* great.

**magnesium** LATIN *magnesia*, from GREEK *Magnesia*, region in Thessaly.

**magnet** MIDDLE ENGLISH *magnete*, from LATIN *magnetum* lodestone, from GREEK *ho Magnes lithos* the Magnesian stone, from *Magnesia*, source of magnetized ore.

**magnificent** FRENCH *magnificient* grand, from LATIN *magnificus* noble, from *magnus* great + *facere* do, make.

**magnify** FRENCH *magnifier*, from LATIN *magnificare*, from *magnus* great + *facere* do, make.

**magnitude** LATIN *magnitudo* greatness.

**magnolia** P. *Magnoll* (1638–1715) French botanist.

**magpie** *Mag* short for Margaret + *pie* earlier name of the bird.

**maharajah** HINDI *maharaja* great king, from *maha* great + *raja* king.

**mahogany** SPANISH *mahogani*.

**mahout** HINDI *mahaut, mahawat*.

**maiden** OLD ENGLISH *mægden*.

**mail**[1] (postal) MIDDLE ENGLISH *male* bag, from FRENCH, from GERMAN *malhe*, from *malaha* wallet, bag.

**mail**[2] (armor) FRENCH *maille*, from LATIN *macula* net.

**maim** FRENCH *mahaignier* wound.

**main** OLD ENGLISH *mægen* strength.

**maintain** MIDDLE ENGLISH, from FRENCH *maintenir*, from LATIN *manu tenere* hold in one's hand, from *manus* hand + *tenere* hold.

**maize** SPANISH *maíz* Indian corn.

**majesty** FRENCH *majeste*, from LATIN *majestas* authority, from *major* greater. See **major**.

**major** LATIN greater, from *magnus* great.

**majordomo** SPANISH or ITALIAN, from LATIN *major* greater + *domus* house.

**majority** FRENCH *majorité*, from LATIN *major* greater. See **major**.

**make** OLD ENGLISH *macian* produce.

**mal-** FRENCH badly, from LATIN *male*.

**malachite** LATIN *molochitis*, from GREEK *molochitis lithos* mallow stone, from *molokhe* mallow.

**malady** FRENCH *maladie* sickness, from *malade*, from LATIN *male habitus* badly kept.

**malaise** FRENCH *mal* bad + *aise* ease.

**malapert** FRENCH *mal apert* ill-skilled, from *mal-* badly + *apert* skillful, from *espert*, from LATIN *expertus*. See **expert**.

**malaria** ITALIAN *mala aria* bad air, because it was once thought that bad air from swamps caused the disease, from LATIN *malus* bad + *aer* air.

**male** FRENCH *ma(s)le* manly, from LATIN *mas* male.

**malefactor** LATIN person who does evil, from *maleficus* wicked, from *male* evil + *facere* do, make.

**malevolent** LATIN *malevolens* jealous, from *male* evil + *velle* wish.

**malfeasance** LATIN *malus* evil + *facere* do, make.

**malice** FRENCH wickedness, from LATIN *molus* bad.

**malign** LATIN *malignare*, from *malignus* wicked.

**malinger** FRENCH *malingre* sickly, from *mal* bad + *heingre* tired look, from being ill.

**mall** MODERN ENGLISH, from *The Mall* in London, a broad, tree-lined promenade, formerly used for a game called *pall-mall* played with a ball and a mallet, from FRENCH *pallemaille*, from ITALIAN *pallamaglio*, from *palla* ball + *malleus* mallet.

**mallender** FRENCH *malandre*, from LATIN *malandria*.

**mallet** FRENCH *maillet*, from *mail* hammer, from LATIN *malleus*.

**malodorous** See **mal- + odor + -ous**.

**malt** OLD ENGLISH *mealt* barley or other grain used for making beer or a similar drink.

**mammal** LATIN *mammalia*, from *mamma* breast.

**mammee** SPANISH *mamey*.

**mammoth** RUSSIAN *mamont*, from *mamma* earth, because mammoths were thought to dig in the earth.

**man** OLD ENGLISH *mann*.

**manacle** FRENCH, from LATIN *manicula* little hand, from *manus* hand.

**manage** ITALIAN *maneggiare* handle, from *mano* hand, from LATIN *manus*.

**manchet** MIDDLE ENGLISH, origin uncertain.

**mandarin**[1] (Chinese official) PORTUGUESE *mandarim*, from MALAY *mantri*, from HINDI, from SANSKRIT, from *mantrin* counsellor, from *mantra* counsel.

**mandarin**[2] (fruit) **mandarin**[1], from the similarity of color to the yellow silk robes worn by Chinese officials.

**mandate** LATIN *mandatum* order, from *manus* hand + *dare* give.

**mandible** FRENCH, from LATIN *mandibula* jaw, from *mandere* chew.

**mandolin** FRENCH *mandoline*, from ITALIAN *mandolino*, from LATIN, from GREEK *pandoura* a kind of stringed instrument.

**mane** MIDDLE ENGLISH, from OLD ENGLISH *manu*.

**maneuver** FRENCH *manoeuvre* manual labor, from *manuevre*, from LATIN *manu operare* work by hand, from *manu* hand + *operare* work.

**mange** FRENCH *mangeue* an itch, from LATIN *manducare* eat.

**mangel-wurzel** GERMAN *mangold* beet + *wurzel* root.

**manger** MIDDLE ENGLISH, from FRENCH *mangeure*, from *mangier* eat, from LATIN *manducare*, from *mandere* chew.

**mangle** FRENCH *mehaigner* injure greatly.

**mania** LATIN, from GREEK *mania* madness.

**manicure** FRENCH, from LATIN *manus* hand + *cura* care.

**manifest** FRENCH, from LATIN *manifestus* struck by the hand.

**manifold** OLD ENGLISH *manigfeald* various.

**manikin** DUTCH *manneken* little man, from *man* man.

**manipulate** See **manipulation**.

**manipulation** FRENCH clever trick, from LATIN *manipulus* handful.

**manna** LATIN, from GREEK, from ARABIC, from HEBREW *man*.

**manner** FRENCH *manere* way of behaving, from LATIN *manuarius* of the hand, from *manus* hand.

**manometer** GREEK *manos* thin + FRENCH *mètre,* from GREEK *metron* measure.

**manor** FRENCH *manoir* live in, from LATIN *manere* remain.

**mansard** FRENCH *mansarde,* from *toit à la mansarde,* from architect Nicholas François *Mansart.*

**mansion** FRENCH *manse,* from LATIN *mansio* a dwelling.

**manta** SPANISH *manta* blanket (wrap or cloak), from LATIN *mantellum* cloak.

**manteau** See **mantle.**

**manticore** MIDDLE ENGLISH, from LATIN *manticora,* from GREEK *mantikhoros,* possibly from a PERSIAN word meaning "maneater."

**mantis** GREEK prophet.

**mantle** FRENCH *mantel* cloak, from LATIN *mantellum.*

**manual** MIDDLE ENGLISH *manuel,* from FRENCH, from LATIN *manus* a hand.

**manufacture** FRENCH, from LATIN *manufactura* work done by hand, from *manufactura,* from *manus* a hand + *facere* do, make.

**manumit** LATIN *manumittere,* from *manus* a hand + *mittere* send.

**manure** FRENCH *manouvrer* work with the hands.

**manuscript** LATIN *manuscriptum* something written by hand, from *manu scriptus* written by hand, from *manu* hand + *scriptus* written, from *scribere* write.

**many** OLD ENGLISH *manig.*

**manzanita** SPANISH *manzana* apple.

**map** LATIN *mappa mundi* map of the world, from *mappa.*

**mar** OLD ENGLISH *merran* hinder.

**maraca** PORTUGUESE.

**marae** MAORI, cleared space, free of trees.

**marathon** the legend of an ancient Greek soldier's run (approximately 26 miles), from the city of *Marathon* to Athens, to announce a military victory at Marathon.

**marauder** FRENCH steal, from *maurad* person who wanders, from *maraud* tomcat.

**marble** FRENCH *marbre* the stone, from LATIN *marmor,* from GREEK *marmaros* white shiny stone.

**marcel** *Marcel* Grateau, early 20th century French hairdresser.

**march**[1] (measured walk) FRENCH *marcher,* from *marchier* trample.

**March**[2] (month) MIDDLE ENGLISH *marche,* from FRENCH *marz,* from LATIN *Martius* month of Mars (the god of war).

**march**[3] (boundary) FRENCH *marche.*

**mard** See **mar.**

**mare** OLD ENGLISH *mere* horse.

**margarine** FRENCH, from GREEK *margaron* pearl.

**margin** LATIN *margo* border.

**marina** ITALIAN or SPANISH seashore, from LATIN *marinus,* from *mare* sea.

**marinade** FRENCH *marin* relating to the sea, from LATIN *marinus.* See **marine.**

**marinate** ITALIAN *marinare* pickle.

**marine** MIDDLE ENGLISH *maryne,* from FRENCH *marin,* from LATIN *marinus,* from *mare* sea.

**marionette** FRENCH *Marion,* from *Mary* the mother of Jesus, probably from the "little Mary" in an early religious puppet play.

**maritime** FRENCH, from LATIN *maritimus*, from *mare* sea + *-timus*, from *intimus* inmost or *ultimus* last, here indicating association with.

**marjoram** FRENCH, probably from LATIN *amaracus*, from GREEK *amarakos*.

**mark** OLD ENGLISH *mearc* boundary.

**market** FRENCH trade, from LATIN *mercatus*, from *merx* merchandise (things that are bought and sold).

**marlin** See **marlinspike**, by similarity of shape of its snout to the ropeworking tool.

**marline** DUTCH *marlijne*, from *marren* tie + *lijn* line. See **line**.

**marlinspike** DUTCH *marlijn* small cord, from *marlen* fasten or secure (a sail), probably from *maren* tie, moor + **spike**.

**marmalade** FRENCH *marmelade*, from LATIN, from GREEK *melimelon*, from *meli* honey + *melon* apple.

**marmite** FRENCH pot or kettle.

**marmot** FRENCH *marmottiane* probably from LATIN *mus montanus* mountain mouse.

**maroon**[1] (abandon) MODERN ENGLISH *maron* fugitive black slave in West Indies jungle, from FRENCH *marron*, possibly from SPANISH *cimmaron* wild, untamed, from *cimarra* thicket.

**maroon**[2] (dark red) FRENCH *marron* chestnut.

**marplot** See **mar** + **plot**.

**marque** ITALIAN *marca* a mark.

**marquee** FRENCH *marquise* banner over an officer's tent.

**marriage** FRENCH *mariage*, from *marier* marry. See **marry**.

**marrow** OLD ENGLISH *mearh*.

**marry** MIDDLE ENGLISH *marien*, from FRENCH *marier*, from LATIN *maritare* marry, from *maritus* husband.

**Mars** LATIN.

**marsh** OLD ENGLISH *merisc*.

**marshal** FRENCH *mareschal* person in charge, from GERMAN *marah* horse + *scalc* servant. The medieval marshal's job was to provide good war horses for soldiers to ride.

**marsupium** LATIN, from GREEK *marsypion*, from *marsypos* pouch, purse.

**martello tower** Cape *Martella* in the Mediterranean, which was taken by the British in 1794.

**marten** FRENCH *martrine*.

**martial** MIDDLE ENGLISH *martialle*, from LATIN *martialis* relating to Mars, the Roman god of war.

**martinet** Gen. J. *Martinet*, 17th century French drillmaster.

**martingale** FRENCH, probably from SPANISH *amlariaga* rein, from ARABIC.

**martlet** FRENCH *martelet*, from *martinet* marten (like a weasel).

**martyr** OLD ENGLISH, from LATIN, from GREEK a witness.

**marvel** FRENCH *merveille* wonder, from LATIN *mirabilia* wonderful things, from *marari* wonder.

**mascara** SPANISH mask, possibly from ARABIC *maskharah* person in costume.

**mascot** FRENCH *mascotte*, from *masco* magician.

**masculine** LATIN *mansulinus* male, from *masculus*, from *mas* male.

**mash** OLD ENGLISH *mascewyrt* crushed grain used in making beer or other such liquids.

193

**mask** FRENCH *masque*, from ITALIAN *maschera*, possibly from ARABIC *maskharah* person in costume.

**masochism** Leopold von Sacher-*Masoch*, 1836–95, Austrian writer who first described it.

**mason** FRENCH *masson*, from LATIN *matio*.

**masque** See **mask**.

**masquerade** FRENCH *mascarade* group of masked persons, from ITALIAN *mascherata*, from *maschera* masked person. See **mask**.

**Mass** OLD ENGLISH *mæsse*, from LATIN *missa*, from *mittere* send, dismiss.

**mass** LATIN *masse*, from GREEK *maza* barley cake.

**massacre** FRENCH *macacre* mess.

**massage** FRENCH *masser*, from ARABIC *mass* touch.

**mast** OLD ENGLISH *mæst*.

**mastaba** ARABIC.

**master** MIDDLE ENGLISH *maistre*, from OLD ENGLISH *magister* teacher, from LATIN *magister*, from *magnus* great.

**masticate** LATIN *masticare* chew, from GREEK *mastichan*, from *mastax* a mouth.

**mastiff** FRENCH *mestif*, from *mastin*, from LATIN *mansuetus* tame.

**mastitis** GREEK *mastos* the breast + -itis.

**mastoid** GREEK *mastoeides*, from *mastos* breast + *eidos* form.

**mat**[1] (floor covering) MIDDLE ENGLISH *matte*, from OLD ENGLISH, from LATIN *matta*.

**mat**[2] (frame) FRENCH faded.

**match**[1] (wood) MIDDLE ENGLISH *macche* wick of a candle, from FRENCH *mesche*, from LATIN *myxa*.

**match**[2] (pair) OLD ENGLISH *mæcca*, from *gemæcca* companion, from *macian* make.

**mate** DUTCH *gemate*.

**materia** LATIN.

**material** LATIN *materialis*, from *materia* wood.

**maternal** LATIN *maternus*, from *mater* mother.

**mathematics** LATIN *mathematica*, from GREEK *mathematike*, from *mathema* something learned.

**mathetic** GREEK *mathetikos*.

**matinee** FRENCH *matin* morning, from LATIN *Matuta* ancient Roman goddess of dawn.

**matins** FRENCH morning prayer, from *matin* morning, from LATIN *Matuta* ancient Roman goddess of dawn.

**matriarch** LATIN *mater* mother + GREEK *archos* ruler.

**matriculate** LATIN *matriculare* enroll, from *matricula* list.

**matrix** LATIN womb, from *mater* mother.

**matron** FRENCH *matrone* married woman, from LATIN *matrona*, from *mater* mother.

**matte** FRENCH faded.

**matter** MIDDLE ENGLISH *matiere*, from FRENCH, from LATIN *materia*.

**mattock** OLD ENGLISH *mattuc*.

**mattress** FRENCH *materas* blanket to lie on, from ARABIC *matrah* cushion.

**mature** LATIN ripe.

**matzoh** HEBREW *matsa*.

**maudlin** *Maudlin* an early English name, from MIDDLE ENGLISH *Maudelen,* from LATIN *Magdalene,* from GREEK *Madalene* Mary Magdalene, woman in the Bible who cried because of her sins.

**maul** FRENCH *mail* hammer, from LATIN *malleus.*

**mauna** (must not) SCOTTISH.

**mauve** FRENCH mallow (plant), from LATIN *malva.*

**maven** HEBREW *mevin.*

**maverick** Samuel A. *Maverick,* 1803–70, Texan who decided not to brand his calves because his ranch was on an island.

**maxilla** LATIN upper jaw, from *mala* jaw, cheekbone.

**maxillary** See **maxilla** + **-ary.**

**maxim** FRENCH *maxime,* from LATIN *maxima,* from *maximus* greatest. See **maximum.**

**maximum** LATIN *maximus* greatest, from *magnus* great.

**May** FRENCH *Mai,* from LATIN *Maias* month of Maia, Roman earth goddess.

**mayhap** See **may** + **happen.**

**mayhaw** See **may** + **hawthorn.**

**mayhem** FRENCH *mahaym* injury, from *mahaignier* injure.

**mayonnaise** FRENCH *mayonaisse,* from *Mahón,* chief town of Minorca (Spanish island), which was captured by the French in 1756. The sauce is said to have been named in honor of this event.

**mayor** FRENCH *maire,* from LATIN *major* greater.

**maze** OLD ENGLISH *amasian* great surprise.

**mead** MIDDLE ENGLISH *mede,* from OLD ENGLISH *me(o)du.*

**meadow** OLD ENGLISH *mæd* land used for growing hay.

**meager** FRENCH *maigre* thin, from LATIN *macer.*

**meal** MIDDLE ENGLISH *meel* mealtime, from OLD ENGLISH *mæl,* from LATIN *metiri* measure.

**mean**[1] (intend) MIDDLE ENGLISH *menen,* from OLD ENGLISH *mænan.*

**mean**[2] (middle) MIDDLE ENGLISH *mene,* from FRENCH *meien,* from LATIN *medianus.*

**mean**[3] (not kind) MIDDLE ENGLISH *mene* common, from OLD ENGLISH *mæne.*

**meander** LATIN *maeander* winding pattern, from GREEK *maiandros,* from *Maiandros* the name of a winding river in Asia.

**measles** DUTCH *masel.*

**measure** FRENCH *mesure* measure, from LATIN *mensura.*

**mecca** ARABIC.

**mechanic** LATIN *mechanicus,* from GREEK *mechanikos,* from *mechane* a machine.

**meconium** LATIN, from GREEK *mekonion,* from *mekon* poppy (flower).

**medal** FRENCH *médaille,* from ITALIAN *medaglia,* from LATIN *metallum* metal.

**medallion** FRENCH *médaillon* large medal, from ITALIAN *medaglione,* from *medaglia* medal. See **medal.**

**meddle** FRENCH *medler* mix, from LATIN *miscere.*

**medial** LATIN *medialis* middle, from *medius.*

**median** LATIN *medianus* middle, from *medius.*

**mediate** LATIN *mediare* divide in the middle, from *medius* middle.

**medic** LATIN *medicus* physician.

**medica** MIDDLE ENGLISH *medice,* from LATIN *medica,* from GREEK, from *medike poa* Median grass, a kind of clover from Media.

**medical** FRENCH, from LATIN *medicus* physician.

**medicate** LATIN *medicari* heal.

**medicine** FRENCH *medecine,* from LATIN *medicina* healing art.

**medieval** LATIN *medius* middle + *aevum* age.

**mediocre** FRENCH, from LATIN *mediocris* halfway up a mountain, from *medius* middle + *ocris* a peak.

**meditate** LATIN *meditari* think about.

**Mediterranean** LATIN *mare Mediterranean* Mediterranean Sea.

**medium** LATIN the middle.

**medley** FRENCH *medlee* mixture, from LATIN *miscere.*

**meech** FRENCH *muchier* hide.

**meek** MIDDLE ENGLISH *meke,* from OLD NORSE *mjukr* gentle.

**meet** OLD ENGLISH *metan* find.

**mega-** GREEK *megas* great.

**megalomania** FRENCH *mégalomanie,* from GREEK, from *megalou + mania.* See **mega- + mania.**

**megaron** GREEK hall.

**meiosis** LATIN, from GREEK *meioun* make smaller.

**melagris** GREEK a type of bird.

**melancholy** FRENCH *melancolie* gloomy, from LATIN *melancholia,* from GREEK *melas* black + *chole* bad taste.

**Meleager** GREEK *Meleagros* one of the Argonauts.

**melee** FRENCH *méler* mix, from *mesler,* from LATIN *miscere.*

**mellay** FRENCH *mellée.* See **melee.**

**mellifluous** LATIN *mellifluus* flowing with honey, from *mel* honey + *fluere* flow.

**mellow** OLD ENGLISH *melu* flour.

**melodeon** melody, made up by the inventor of the musical instrument.

**melodrama** FRENCH *mélodrame,* from GREEK *melos* song + *drama* play, from the early dramas that included songs.

**melody** LATIN *melodia* song, from GREEK *melos* song + *aiden* sing.

**melon** FRENCH, from LATIN, from GREEK *melopepon.*

**melt** OLD ENGLISH *meltan.*

**member** FRENCH *membre* arm or leg, from LATIN *membrum.*

**membrane** MIDDLE ENGLISH, from LATIN *membrana.* See **member.**

**membrillo** SPANISH.

**memento** LATIN remember.

**memoir** FRENCH *mémoire* record, account, from LATIN *memoria* account of history.

**memorandum** MIDDLE ENGLISH, from LATIN *memorandus,* from *memorare* have in mind.

**memory** FRENCH *memorie,* from LATIN *memoria,* from *memor* mindful.

**menace** FRENCH threat, from LATIN *minacia.*

**menagerie** FRENCH place for keeping animals of the house, from *ménage* having to do with the home, from LATIN *mansio* place to live in.

**mend** MIDDLE ENGLISH *menden* shortened from *amenden.* See **amend.**

**mendacious** LATIN *mendax* lying.

**menial** MIDDLE ENGLISH *meineal* servant, from *meine(e)* having to do with the house, from LATIN *mansio* home.

**menopause** GREEK *men* month + *pausis* a stopping.

**menses** LATIN *mensis* month.

**menstruate** LATIN *menstruare,* from *mensis* month.

**mensuration** LATIN *mensuratio* measuring, from *mensura.* See **measure**.

**-ment** FRENCH, from LATIN *-mentum*.

**mental** FRENCH, from LATIN *mentalis,* from *mens* mind.

**mention** FRENCH, from LATIN *mentio*.

**menu** FRENCH small, from LATIN *minutus*.

**mezzanine** FRENCH, from ITALIAN *mezzanino,* from *mezzano* middle, from LATIN *medianus* of the middle, from *medius*.

**mercantile** FRENCH, from ITALIAN, from LATIN *mercari* merchant.

**mercenary** LATIN *mercenarius* hired for pay, from *merces* reward.

**mercer** FRENCH *mercier* trader, from LATIN *merx*.

**merchandise** FRENCH *marchaundise,* from *marchaunt.* See **merchant**.

**merchant** FRENCH *marcheant* trader, from LATIN *mercari* trade.

**mercury** LATIN *Mercurius*.

**mercy** FRENCH *merci* thanks, from LATIN *merces* reward.

**mere**[1] (only) LATIN *merus* not mixed.

**mere**[2] (lake) OLD ENGLISH.

**merge** LATIN *mergere* dip.

**meridian** FRENCH *meridien,* from LATIN *meridianus* midday, from *meridies*.

**meridienne** FRENCH. See **meridian**.

**meringue** FRENCH.

**merit** FRENCH, from LATIN *meritum* value, from *merere* earn.

**merlon** FRENCH, from ITALIAN *merlone,* from *merlo* battlement.

**merry** OLD ENGLISH *myrge* pleasant.

**mesa** SPANISH table, from LATIN *mensa*.

**mesalliance** FRENCH *mésalliance,* from *mes-* bad + *alliance.* See **alliance**.

**mesh** DUTCH *maesche* net.

**mesmerism** F. A. *Mesmer* (1734–1815), Austrian physician who developed a system of treatment through hypnotism.

**mesquite** SPANISH *mesquite,* from NATIVE AMERICAN *mizquitl*.

**mess** FRENCH *mes* course (part of a meal served at one time), from LATIN *missus,* from *mittere* send.

**message** FRENCH, from LATIN *mittere* send.

**Messiah** LATIN, from GREEK *Messias,* from HEBREW *mashiah* anointed.

**meta-** GREEK *meta* in the midst of, among, with, after.

**metabolism** GREEK *metabole* change, from *meta* beyond + *ballein* throw.

**metacarpus** LATIN, from *metacarpium,* from GREEK *metakarpion,* from *meta* between + *karpos* wrist.

**metal** LATIN *metallum,* from GREEK *metallon*.

**metallurgy** LATIN, from GREEK *metallon* metal, mine + *ergon* work.

**metamorphosis** LATIN, from GREEK change, from *meta* over + *morphe* form.

**metaphor** LATIN *metaphora,* from GREEK *metaphora,* from *meta* over + *pherein* carry.

**metatarsus** GREEK *meta-* after + *tarsus* sole of the foot.

**metathesis** LATIN, from GREEK *metathesis*, from *metatithenai* transpose, from *meta-* change + *tithenai* place.

**mete** OLD ENGLISH *metan* measure.

**meteor** LATIN *meteorum*, from GREEK *meteoron* thing in the air, from *meta* beyond + *eora* in the air.

**meter** FRENCH *mètre*, from GREEK *metron* measure.

**methane** See **methyl** + **-ane**.

**method** FRENCH *methode*, from LATIN *methodus*, from GREEK *methodos* system.

**methyl** FRENCH, from GREEK *methy* wine + *hyle* wood.

**methylcellulose** See **methyl** + **cellulose**.

**methylene** FRENCH *méthylène*. See **methyl**.

**meticulous** LATIN *meticulosus* full of fear, from *metus* fear.

**métier** FRENCH, from LATIN *ministerium*.

**metric** See **meter**.

**metronome** GREEK *metron* measure + *nomos* rule.

**metropolis** LATIN mother city, from GREEK *meter* mother + *polis* city.

**mettle** variation of **metal**.

**mew**[1] (cage) FRENCH *muer*, from LATIN *mutare* change.

**mew**[2] (cat sound) imitative.

**mews** See **mew**[1].

**mezuzah** HEBREW door post.

**mezzo** ITALIAN middle, from LATIN *medius*.

**miasma** LATIN, from GREEK *miainein* make dirty or not pure.

**mica** LATIN *micare* shine.

**Mick** shortened form of the name Michael.

**mickle** MIDDLE ENGLISH *mikel*, from OLD ENGLISH *micel*.

**micro-** GREEK *mikros* small.

**microbe** FRENCH, from GREEK *mikros* small + *bios* life.

**microscope** See **micro-** + **-scope**.

**mid-** OLD ENGLISH *midde* middle.

**midday** OLD ENGLISH *middæg* noon.

**middle** OLD ENGLISH *middel*.

**middy** See **midshipman**.

**midge** OLD ENGLISH *mycg* gnat.

**midget** MODERN ENGLISH **midge** + *-et* little sand fly.

**midriff** OLD ENGLISH *midhrif*, from *midd* middle + *hrif* belly.

**midshipman** See **mid-** + **ship** + **man**.

**midst** MIDDLE ENGLISH *middes* middle, from OLD ENGLISH *on midden* in the middle.

**midwife** MIDDLE ENGLISH *midwif*, from OLD ENGLISH *mid* with + *wif* woman.

**mien** FRENCH *mine* look.

**might** MIDDLE ENGLISH *myghte* power, from OLD ENGLISH *might*.

**migraine** FRENCH, from LATIN *hemicrania* pain on one side of the head, from GREEK *hemikrania*, from *hemi* half + *kranion* skull.

**migrate** LATIN *migrare*.

**milch** OLD ENGLISH *milce*.

**mild** OLD ENGLISH *milde* kind.

**mildew** MIDDLE ENGLISH *mildeau* honeydew (from aphids), from OLD ENGLISH *meledeaw*. First used to describe the fungus in 14th century, from similarity of appearance.

**mile** OLD ENGLISH *mil*, from LATIN *milia* Roman unit of measure, 1,000 paces.

**milieu** FRENCH middle place, from LATIN *medius* middle + *locus* place.

**militant** LATIN *militare* serve as a soldier.

**military** LATIN *militaris*, from *miles* soldier.

**milk** OLD ENGLISH *meolc*.

**mill** MIDDLE ENGLISH *melle*, from OLD ENGLISH *mylen*, from LATIN *mola* millstone (flat stones that grind grain).

**millennium** LATIN *mille* thousand + *annus* year.

**millet** FRENCH *mil*, from LATIN *millum* millet.

**milli-** LATIN *mille* thousand.

**milliliter** See **milli-** + **liter**.

**milliner** *Milan*, Italy, a city famous for its cloth, hats, gloves, etc.

**million** FRENCH, from ITALIAN *millione*, from *mille* thousand, from LATIN.

**mime** LATIN *mimus* actor, from GREEK *mimos*.

**mimic** LATIN *mimicus*, from GREEK *mimikos*, from *mimos* actor.

**miminy-piminy** imitative.

**minaret** FRENCH minarete, from ITALIAN *minaretto*, from ARABIC *manara* lighthouse, from *nar* fire, light.

**mince** FRENCH *mincier* cut into small pieces, from LATIN *minutia*.

**mind** OLD ENGLISH *gemynd* memory.

**mine** MIDDLE ENGLISH, from FRENCH, mine, tunnel, ore.

**mineral** FRENCH *miniere*, from *miner*. See **mine**.

**mingle** MIDDLE ENGLISH *menglen* join, from OLD ENGLISH *mengan* mix.

**miniature** ITALIAN small picture, from LATIN *miniare* paint red, from *minium* red lead (soft metal). In the Middle Ages texts of books were hand printed in black ink. Red ink was used for titles, headings and decorations, which were small pictures.

**minimum** LATIN *minimus* smallest.

**minion** FRENCH *mignon* pretty.

**minister** FRENCH *ministre* servant, from LATIN *minister*, from *minor* minor.

**ministry** LATIN *minium* service.

**mink** SCANDINAVIAN.

**minnow** OLD ENGLISH *myne*.

**minor** LATIN *minor* less.

**minotaur** GREEK *minotauros*, from *Minos*, king of Crete + *tauros* bull.

**minstrel** FRENCH *menestrel* servant, from LATIN *ministerialis*, from *ministerium* service.

**mint**[1] (plant) MIDDLE ENGLISH *mynte*, from OLD ENGLISH *minte*, from LATIN *menta*, *mentha*, from GREEK *minthe* herb.

**mint**[2] (money) OLD ENGLISH *mynet* coin, from LATIN *moneta*, from *Moneta*, name of a goddess in whose temple in Rome money was coined.

**minuet** FRENCH *menu* small, from LATIN *minutus*, from the small steps of this dance.

**minus** LATIN *minor* less.

**minute** LATIN *minutus* small.

**minx** MIDDLE ENGLISH *mynx* pet dog.

**miracle** FRENCH, from LATIN *miraculum* wonderful thing, from *mirus* wonderful.

**mirage** FRENCH *mirer* look at, from LATIN *mirare* see, from *mirari* wonder at.

**mire** OLD NORSE *myrr* swamp.

**mirror** FRENCH *mirour*, from LATIN *mirare* see, from *mirari* wonder at.

**mirth** OLD ENGLISH *myrgth*.

**mis-** OLD ENGLISH *mis-* and FRENCH *mes-* badly, wrongly.

**misanthrope** GREEK *misanthropos* hating mankind, from *misein* hate + *anthropos* man.

**miscellaneous** LATIN *miscellaneus* mixed, from *miscellus*.

**mischief** FRENCH *meschief* damage, from *meschever*, from *mes-* wrong + *chief* head.

**miscreant** FRENCH *mescroire* not believe, from *mes-* wrong + LATIN *credere* believe.

**miser** LATIN.

**miserable** FRENCH, from LATIN *miserabilis*, from *miser*.

**misfeasance** FRENCH *mesfaisance*, from *mesfaire* do wrong, from *mes-* wrong + LATIN *facere* do, make.

**misnomer** FRENCH *mesnommer* name incorrectly, from *mes-* wrong + LATIN *nominare* name.

**miss** OLD ENGLISH *missan*.

**missal** LATIN *missa* Mass.

**missile** LATIN *mittere* send, throw.

**mission** LATIN *missio* a sending.

**Mississippi** FRENCH *Messipi*, from NATIVE AMERICAN *Missi-ziibi* Big River.

**missive** FRENCH, from LATIN *mittere* send.

**mistake** OLD NORSE *mistaka* take by mistake.

**mistress** MIDDLE ENGLISH *maistresse*, from FRENCH *maistresse*, from *maistre* chief. See **master** + **-ess**.

**mite** OLD ENGLISH.

**miter** MIDDLE ENGLISH *mitre*, from FRENCH, from LATIN *mitra*, from GREEK *mitra* headband.

**mitigate** LATIN *mitigare* make soft.

**mitochondrion** GREEK *mitos* a thread + *chondrion* a small cartilage (the tough tissue that forms a part of the skeleton).

**mitten** FRENCH *mitaine*.

**mix** LATIN *mixcere*.

**mizzen** FRENCH *misaine*, from ITALIAN, from LATIN *medianus*. See **median**.

**mnemonic** GREEK *mnemonikos*, from *mneme* memory.

**moan** possibly from OLD ENGLISH *mænan* complain.

**moat** FRENCH *mote* mound.

**mob** LATIN *mobile vulgus* movable crowd.

**mobcap** DUTCH *mop* woman's cap + OLD ENGLISH *cæppe* hood, from LATIN *cappa*.

**mobile** LATIN *mobilis*, from *movere* move.

**moccasin** NATIVE AMERICAN.

**mock** FRENCH *mocquier*.

**mode** LATIN *modus* manner, measure.

**model** FRENCH *modelle* pattern, from ITALIAN *modello*, from LATIN *modulus*, from *modus* manner, measure.

**moderate** LATIN *moderari* control.

**modern** LATIN *modernus* of the present, from *modo* just now, from *modus* manner, measure.

**modest** LATIN *modestus*, from *modus* manner, measure.

**modify** FRENCH *modifier* change, from LATIN *modificare* control, from *modus* measure + *facere* to do, make.

**modulate** LATIN *modulari*, from *modus* manner, measure.

**module** FRENCH, from LATIN *modus* manner, measure.

**moider** possibly from **muddle**.

**moiety** FRENCH *moitie*, from LATIN *medietas* half.

**moil** FRENCH *moillier* moisten, from LATIN *mollis* soft.

**moist** FRENCH *moiste* wet, from LATIN *mucidus* moldy, from *mucus* slime. Probably influenced by LATIN *musteus* fresh, new, from *museum* new wine.

**moke**[1] (net) OLD ENGLISH *max* net.

**moke**[2] (donkey) BRITISH slang, origin unknown.

**moke**[3] (fog) BRITISH, origin unknown.

**molar** MIDDLE ENGLISH, from LATIN *molaris dens* grinding tooth, from *mola*. See **mill**.

**molasses** LATIN *mel* honey.

**mold**[1] (form) MIDDLE ENGLISH *molde*, from FRENCH *modle*, from LATIN *modus* measure.

**mold**[2] (growth) MIDDLE ENGLISH *mold*.

**mole**[1] (animal) MIDDLE ENGLISH *mouldwarp* earth-thrower, from OLD ENGLISH *molde* earth + *weorpan* throw away.

**mole**[2] (skin spot) OLD ENGLISH *mal* spot, mark.

**mole**[3] (harbor wall) FRENCH *môle* breakwater, from LATIN *moles* barrier.

**molecule** FRENCH, from LATIN *molecula*, from *mole* mass.

**molest** FRENCH *molester*, from LATIN *molestus* troublesome, from *moles* a burden.

**moletta** See **mulatto**.

**mollify** FRENCH *mollifier*, from LATIN *mollificare* soften, from *mollis* soft + *facere* do, make.

**mollusk** FRENCH *mollusque*, from LATIN *mollis* soft + *facere* do, make.

**molt** MIDDLE ENGLISH *mouten*, from OLD ENGLISH, from LATIN *mutare* change.

**molten** See **melt**.

**moment** LATIN *momentum*, from *movere* move.

**mon** JAPANESE family crest.

**monarch** LATIN *monarcha* only ruler, from GREEK *monarches*, from *monos* alone + *archein* rule.

**monastery** LATIN *monasterium*, from GREEK *monasterion*, from *monazein* live alone, from *monos* alone.

**Monday** MIDDLE ENGLISH, from OLD ENGLISH *Monandæg* moon's day, from LATIN *lunae dies*.

**money** FRENCH *moneie* coin, from LATIN *moneta* place for making money. See **mint**[2].

**monger** OLD ENGLISH *mangere* dealer, from LATIN *mango*.

**mongoose** HINDI *mungus*.

**mongrel** OLD ENGLISH *mengan* mixture.

**monitor** LATIN *monitor* advisor, from *monere* warn.

**monk** OLD ENGLISH *munuc*, from LATIN, from GREEK *monos* alone.

**monkey** GERMAN *Moneke*, from a medieval story about animals.

**mono-** GREEK *monos* one, single, alone.

**monocle** FRENCH, from LATIN *monoculus* one-eyed, from GREEK *monos* single + LATIN *oculus* eye.

**monody** LATIN, from GREEK *monodidia*, from *monos* single + *aeiden* song.

**monogamy** FRENCH, from LATIN *monogamia*, from GREEK *monos* single, alone + *gamos* marriage.

**monogram** LATIN, from GREEK *monos* single + *gramma* letter.

**monolith** FRENCH, from LATIN *monolithus* made of one stone, from GREEK *monolithos*, from *monos* single, alone + *lithos* stone.

**monologue** FRENCH, from GREEK *monologos* speaking alone, from *monos* single + *logos* word.

**monomachy** FRENCH *monomachie*, from LATIN *monomachia*, from GREEK *monomaxia*, from *mono* single + *maxia* fight.

**monopoly** LATIN *monopolium*, from GREEK *monopolion*, from *monos* single, alone + *polein* sell.

**monotonous** LATIN, from GREEK *monotonia*, from *monos* single + *tonos* sound.

**monsieur** FRENCH *mon* my + *sieur* lord.

**monsoon** DUTCH *monssoen*, from PORTUGUESE *monçao*, from ARABIC *mausim* season.

**monster** FRENCH *monstre*, from LATIN *monstrum*, from *monere* warn.

**montage** FRENCH *monter* put together. See **mount**.

**Montgolfier** FRENCH name of the brothers J. M. and J. E. *Montgolfier* who invented the hot air balloon.

**month** OLD ENGLISH *monath*.

**monument** LATIN *monumentum*, from *monere* warn.

**mood** OLD ENGLISH *mod* mind.

**moon** MIDDLE ENGLISH *mone*, from OLD ENGLISH *mona*.

**Moor** FRENCH *More*, from LATIN *Morus*, from *Maurus*, from GREEK *Mauros* inhabitant of Mauritania.

**moor**[1] (dock a ship) MIDDLE ENGLISH, possibly from GERMAN *moren* tie.

**moor**[2] (land) MIDDLE ENGLISH *more*, from OLD ENGLISH *mor*.

**moot** OLD ENGLISH *mot* meeting.

**mop** MIDDLE ENGLISH *mappe*, from FRENCH *mappe* napkin, from LATIN *mappa*.

**mope** possibly from DUTCH *mopen*.

**mopoke** imitative.

**moppet** MIDDLE ENGLISH *moppe* rag doll.

**moraine** FRENCH.

**moral** LATIN *moralis* relating to manners, from *mos* custom.

**morale** FRENCH *moral*, from LATIN *moralis*. See **moral**.

**morass** DUTCH *moeras* marsh, from FRENCH *mareis*.

**moray** LATIN *muraena* kind of fish, from GREEK *myraina*.

**morbid** LATIN *morbidus* sick, from *morbus* disease.

**more** OLD ENGLISH *mara*.

**morganatic** FRENCH *morgenatique* morning gift, from LATIN *matrimonium ad morganaticam* marriage of the morning, probably from GERMAN *morgan geba* morning gift. From the custom of the husband giving a wife of lower rank a gift the morning after their marriage.

**morgue** FRENCH, originally a building in Paris where bodies were kept awaiting identification.

**morning** MIDDLE ENGLISH *morwening*, from *morwen*, from OLD ENGLISH *morgen*.

**moron** GREEK *moros* foolish.

**morose** LATIN *morosus* bad tempered, from *mos* manner.

**morphine** LATIN *Morpheus* the god of dreams.

**morrow** OLD ENGLISH *morwe*, from *morgen* morning.

**morsel** FRENCH *mors*, from LATIN *morsum* a bite.

**mort**[1] (death) FRENCH *mort*, from LATIN *mortuum* dead.

**mort**[2] (quantity) BRITISH, origin uncertain.

**mortal** FRENCH, from LATIN *mortalis*, from *mors* death.

**mortar** FRENCH *mortier* cement, from LATIN *mortarium* bowl for mixing or pounding.

**mortgage** FRENCH *mort* dead + *gage* pledge.

**mortify** FRENCH *mortifier* put to death, from LATIN *mortificare* kill, from *mors* death + *facere* do, make.

**mortuary** LATIN *mortuarius*, from *mortuus* dead.

**mosaic** FRENCH *mosaïque*, from ITALIAN *mosaico*, from LATIN *mosaicus*, from *musivum*, from *Musa*. See **muse**[2].

**mosque** FRENCH *mosquée*, from ITALIAN, from SPANISH, from ARABIC *masjid* place of worship, from *sajada* pray.

**mosquito** SPANISH *mosca* fly, from LATIN *musca*.

**most** OLD ENGLISH *mast*.

**-most** OLD ENGLISH *-mest*.

**mote** OLD ENGLISH *mot*.

**motel** combination of **motor** + **hotel**.

**moth** OLD ENGLISH *moththe*.

**mother** OLD ENGLISH *modor*.

**motif** FRENCH theme, from LATIN *motivum* something that causes an action. See **motive**.

**motile** LATIN *motus*, from *movere* move.

**motion** LATIN *motio* movement.

**motive** FRENCH *motif*, from LATIN *motivum* something that causes an action, from *motivus* moving, from *movere* set in motion.

**motley** MIDDLE ENGLISH, from FRENCH *motteley*, probably from OLD ENGLISH *mot* speck.

**motor** LATIN mover, from *movere* move.

**mottle** See **motley**.

**motto** ITALIAN a saying, from LATIN *muttum* word, from *muttire* mutter.

**mouflon** FRENCH, from LATIN *mufron*.

**moulage** FRENCH *moul(er)* mold.

**mould** BRITISH spelling for mold. See **mold**[1] and **mold**[2].

**moulinet** FRENCH *moulin* mill.

**moult** See **molt**.

**mound** possibly from DUTCH *mond* protection.

**mount** FRENCH *monter* go up, from LATIN *mons* mountain, high hill.

**mountain** FRENCH *montaigne* high hill, from LATIN *monanus*, from *mons*.

**mountebank** ITALIAN *montabanco* climb on the bench (to speak in front of an audience), from *montare* climb + *in* on + *banco* bench.

**mourn** OLD ENGLISH *murnan* feel sadness.

**mouse** OLD ENGLISH *mus*.

**mousse** FRENCH froth, from LATIN *mulsa*, from *mulsum* honey wine.

**mouth** OLD ENGLISH *muth*.

**move** FRENCH *mover*, from LATIN *movere* put in motion.

**mow** OLD ENGLISH *muga* cut down crops.

**much** OLD ENGLISH *mycel*.

**mucilage** FRENCH *mucilago* stale juice, from LATIN *mucere* be moldy.

**muck** OLD NORSE *myki* manure.

**mucous** LATIN *mucus*.

**mud** MIDDLE ENGLISH *mudde*, from GERMAN *mudde*.

**muddle** See **mud**.

**muezzin** ARABIC *mu'adhdhin*, from *adhana* announce.

**muff** DUTCH *mof* covering for the hands, from *moffel* thick glove, from LATIN *muffula*.

**muffin** MODERN ENGLISH *moofin*, possibly from GERMAN *muffen*.

**muffle** FRENCH *enmoufler* wrap up, from *moufle*, from LATIN *muffula* thick glove.

**mug** probably from SCANDINAVIAN.

**mulatto** SPANISH *mulato*, from *mulo* mule (whose mother is a horse and whose father is a donkey), from LATIN *mulus*.

**mulberry** OLD ENGLISH *morberie*, from LATIN *morum* mulberry.

**mulch** MIDDLE ENGLISH *molsh* soft, moist, from OLD ENGLISH *melsc*, *milisc* mellow, sweet.

**mule** OLD ENGLISH *mul*, from LATIN *mulus*.

**mullein** FRENCH *moleine*, from LATIN *mollis* soft.

**mullet** FRENCH *mulet*, from LATIN *mullus*.

**mulligatawny** TAMIL *miakutannil* a spicy soup, from *milaku* pepper + *tanni* water.

**multifarious** LATIN *multifarius*, from *multifariam*, from *multi-* many + *-fariam* parts.

**multiple** FRENCH, from LATIN *multiplus*, from *multus* many + *plex* fold.

**multiply** FRENCH *multiplier*, from LATIN *multiplicare*. See **multiple**.

**multitude** FRENCH, from LATIN *multitudo* a great number.

**mum** FRENCH *momer*, from *momo* imitative.

**mumble** MIDDLE ENGLISH *momelen*, from *mom* unclear sound.

**mumblety-peg** *mumble the peg*. Formerly the loser of the game had to pull a peg out of the ground with his teeth.

**mummy** FRENCH *momie*, from Latin *mumia*, from ARABIC *mumiyah* embalmed body.

**mumps** GERMAN *mimpfeln* mumble while eating.

**mundane** FRENCH, from LATIN *mundus* world.

**municipal** LATIN *municipalis*, from *munia* official duties + *capere* take.

**munificent** LATIN *munificens*, from *munus* gift + *facere* do, make.

**munitions** FRENCH *munition*, from LATIN *munitio* defense.

**muntin** FRENCH *montant* an upright blow or thrust.

**mural** FRENCH relating to a wall, from LATIN *muralis*, from *murus* wall.

**murder** OLD ENGLISH *morthor*.

**murky** OLD NORSE *myrkr* dark.

**murmur** FRENCH imitative.

**murrey** FRENCH *moré*, from LATIN *moratus*, from *morum* mulberry.

**muscle** LATIN *musculus* little mouse, from *mus* mouse, because some muscles look like a mouse when they are in use.

**muse**[1] (think about) FRENCH *muser*, dream, wonder, idle about.

**muse**[2] (inspiration) LATIN *Musa*, from GREEK *Mousa* any of the nine Greek goddesses of art, literature and science.

**museum** LATIN, from GREEK *mouseion* shrine (place of worship), from *Mousa*.  See **muse**[2].

**mush** See **mash**.

**mushroom** FRENCH *moisseron*, from LATIN *mussirio*.

**music** LATIN *musica*, from GREEK *mousike*, any art guided by the Muses, especially music, from *Mousa*.  See **muse**[2].

**musicale** shortened form of FRENCH *soirée musicale* musical evening.

**musk** MIDDLE ENGLISH, from FRENCH *musc*, from LATIN *muscus*, from GREEK *moskhos*, from PERSIAN *mushk*, from SANSKRIT *muska* testicle, from *mus* mouse.

**musket** FRENCH *mousquet*, from ITALIAN *moschetto* originally meant arrow of a bow, from LATIN *musca* fly.

**muslin** FRENCH *mousseline*, from ITALIAN *mussolino*, from *Mosul* city in Iraq where it was first produced.

**mussel** OLD ENGLISH *muscle*, from LATIN *musculus*.

**must** OLD ENGLISH *moste*.

**mustache** FRENCH *moustache*, from ITALIAN *mostaccio*, from GREEK *mystax* upper lip.

**mustachio** SPANISH *mostacho* or ITALIAN *mostaccio*.

**mustang** SPANISH *mestengo* animal that strays, from *mesta* roundup of stray animals, from LATIN *mixta* mixed.  Originally applied to stray animals that got mixed with a herd.

**mustard** FRENCH *moustarde*, from LATIN *mustum* new wine.

**muster** FRENCH *monstrer* show, from LATIN *monstrare*.

**musty** possibly from **moist**.

**mutation** FRENCH *mutacion*, from LATIN *mutatio* change.

**mute**[1] (silent) FRENCH *muet*, from *mut, mo*, from LATIN *mutus* silent, dumb.

**mute**[2] (bird dropping) FRENCH *émeut*.

**mutilate** LATIN *mutilare* maim (hurt a body part so badly that it can no longer be used).

**mutiny** FRENCH *mutin*, from *muete* revolt, from LATIN *movere* move.

**mutter** MIDDLE ENGLISH *moteren*.

**mutton** FRENCH *moton* a ram, from LATIN *multo* sheep.

**mutual** FRENCH *mutuel*, from LATIN *mutuus*.

**mux** See **muck**.

**muzzle** FRENCH *musel*, from *muse* snout (the nose and jaws of some animals).

**my** OLD ENGLISH *min*.

**myopia** LATIN, from GREEK *myein* shut + *ops* eye.

**myriad** GREEK *myrias* ten thousand, from *myrios* countless.

**myrrh** FRENCH *mirre*, from LATIN *murra*, from GREEK *myrrha*, from ARABIC *murr*.

**myrtle** FRENCH *myrtille*, from LATIN *myrtus*, from GREEK *myrtos*.

**mystery** LATIN *mysterium* secret worship, from GREEK *mysterion*, from *myein* close lips and eyes.

**mystic** LATIN, from GREEK *mystikos*, from *mystes* initiate.

**myth** LATIN *mythos* fable, from GREEK.

**mythology** LATIN *mythologia*, from GREEK legend, from *mythos* fable + *logos* word.

**nab** probably from Danish *nappe* grab.

**nabob** Arabic *nâ'ib* governor.

**nacelle** French *nacelle*, from Latin *naucella*, from *navis* a ship.

**nadir** French, from Latin, from Arabic *nazir* opposite to the zenith (point in the sky directly overhead).

**naffy** British *NAAFI* for N(avy), A(rmy), and A(ir) F(orce) I(nstitutes) (military canteen service).

**nag**[1] (horse) Middle English *nagge* small riding horse, origin uncertain.

**nag**[2] (annoy) Old Norse *gnaga* eat at bit by bit.

**naiad** French, from Latin, from Greek *naein* flow.

**nail** Old English *nægel*.

**nainsook** Hindi *nain* the eye + *sukh* pleasure.

**naive** French *naïf* natural, from Latin *nativus*.

**naked** Old English *nacod* bare.

**namby-pamby** nickname given the poet *Ambrose* Phillips (1674–1749) by more skilled poets of the time who thought his poems childish and silly.

**name** Old English *nama*.

**nankeen** *Nanking* in China, from where the cloth was first exported.

**nanny** baby talk for *Anna*, a woman's name.

**nap** Old English *hnappian*.

**nape** Middle English.

**napery** French *naperie*, from *nape*.

**napkin** French *nappe* linen.

**narcissus** Latin, from Greek *narkissos*, from *narke* numbness. From a Greek myth about *Narcissus*, who fell in love with his reflection in a pool of water, and could do nothing else but look at it. He wasted away and died and his body turned into the flower called narcissus.

**narcotic** French *narcotique*, from Greek *narkotikos*, from *narke* numbness.

**narrate** Latin *narrare* tell.

**narrow** Old English *nearu*.

**nasal** French, from Latin *nasus* nose.

**nasty** possibly from Dutch *nestig* dirty.

**nation** French, from Latin *natio* people.

**native** French, from Latin *nativus* born.

**natron** French, from Spanish, from Arabic *natrun*, from Greek *nitron*.

**natty** See neat.

**natural** French, from Latin *naturalis* by birth.

**nature** French, from Latin *natura* course of things, from *nasci* be born.

**naturopathy** nature + -pathy a particular system of treatment.

**naught** OLD ENGLISH *nawiht* nothing, from *na* no + *wiht* person.

**naughty** MIDDLE ENGLISH *naught* wicked act.

**nausea** LATIN seasickness, from GREEK *nausie*, from *naus* ship.

**nautical** LATIN, from GREEK *nautes* sailor, from *naus* ship.

**nave** MIDDLE ENGLISH *navis*, from LATIN ship.

**navette** FRENCH little boat, from LATIN *naveta*, from *navis* ship.

**navigate** LATIN *navigare* sail, from *navis* ship + *agere* drive.

**navy** FRENCH *navie* ships, from LATIN *navis* ship.

**nay** OLD NORSE *nei* no, from *ne* not + *ei* ever.

**near** OLD ENGLISH.

**neat** FRENCH *net* clean, from LATIN *nitidus* shining.

**neatherd** See **neat** + **herd**.

**nebula** LATIN cloud.

**necessary** LATIN *necessarious*, from *necesse*, from *ne-* not + *cedere* go.

**neck** OLD ENGLISH *hnecca*.

**necromancy** FRENCH *nygromancie*, from LATIN *nigromantia*, from LATIN *necromantia*, from GREEK *nekros* dead body + *manteia*, from *mantis* prophet.

**nectar** LATIN drink of the gods, from GREEK *nektar*.

**nectarine** See **nectar** + -ine[1].

**need** OLD ENGLISH *nied*.

**needle** OLD ENGLISH *ned*.

**nefarious** LATIN *nefus* crime, from *ne-* not + *fas* lawful.

**negation** FRENCH, from LATIN *negare* deny.

**neglect** LATIN *negligere*, from *neg-* not + *legere* gather.

**negligee** FRENCH *négliger* neglect.

**negligent** FRENCH, from LATIN *negligere*. See **neglect**.

**negotiate** LATIN *negotiari*, from *negotium* business, from *nec-* not + *otium* ease.

**Negro** FRENCH *negre*, from SPANISH *negro* black, from LATIN *nigrum* dark, black (applied to the sky, to skin color, etc.)

**Negus** AMHARIC *n'gus* king, from *nagasha* he ruled.

**neighbor** OLD ENGLISH *neahgebur* farmer.

**neither** OLD ENGLISH *na-hwæther* nor whether.

**neo-** GREEK *neos* new.

**neon** GREEK *neon*, from *neos* new.

**neoprene** GREEK *neos* new + *(chloro)prene* a colorless liquid.

**nephew** FRENCH *nevue*, from LATIN *nepos*.

**nephritis** LATIN, from GREEK, from *nephros* kidney + -itis inflammation.

**ne plus ultra** LATIN no more beyond.

**nepotism** FRENCH *népotisme*, from ITALIAN *nepotismo*, from *nepote* nephew, from LATIN *nepos*. Originally, privileges granted to "nephews" (actually sons) of Catholic popes.

**Neptune** LATIN *Neptunus* the Roman god of the sea.

**nerve** LATIN *nervus* strength.

**nesh** OLD ENGLISH *hnesce*.

**-ness** OLD ENGLISH *-nes(s)*.

**nestle** OLD ENGLISH *nestlian* bird's nest.

**net** OLD ENGLISH *net* mesh.

**nettle** OLD ENGLISH *netele.*

**network** See **net** + **work.**

**neuro-** GREEK *neuro-*, from *neuron* nerve (originally sinew, tendon, cord, bowstring).

**neurocranium** See **neuro-** + **cranium.**

**neuron** GREEK nerve.

**neurosis** GREEK nerve + LATIN *-osis* abnormal condition.

**neuter** FRENCH, from LATIN *neiture* neither, from *ne-* not + *uter* either.

**neutral** FRENCH, from LATIN *neutralis*, from *neuter*, from *ne-* not + *uter* either.

**never** OLD ENGLISH *næfre* at no time, from *ne-* not + *æfre* always.

**new** OLD ENGLISH *niwe.*

**newel** FRENCH, from LATIN *nucalis* like a nut, from *nux* nut.

**newfangled** MIDDLE ENGLISH *newefangel*, from OLD ENGLISH *niwe* new + *fon* take.

**newt** MIDDLE ENGLISH *an eute*, from OLD ENGLISH *efeta.*

**nexamine** LATIN *nex* binding + *amine* protein.

**next** OLD ENGLISH *nehst.*

**nexus** LATIN binding together.

**niagara** NATIVE AMERICAN town name.

**nibble** probably from GERMAN *nibbelen.*

**nibblish** See **nibble.**

**nice** MIDDLE ENGLISH stupid, from FRENCH, from LATIN *nescius* ignorant, from *nescire*, from *ne-* not + *scire* know.

**niche** FRENCH corner, from LATIN *nidus* nest.

**nick** possibly from OLD NORSE *hnykla* wrinkle.

**nickel** SWEDISH, from GERMAN *kupfernickel* false copper (copper-colored but containing no copper), from *kupfer* copper + *nickel* devil.

**nicker** imitative.

**nickname** OLD ENGLISH *eaca* addition + *nama* name.

**nicotiana** See **nicotine.**

**nicotine** Jean *Nicot* (1530–1600), who introduced tobacco into France.

**nictate (nictitate)** LATIN *nictitare*, from *nictare* wink.

**niece** FRENCH *n(i)ece*, from LATIN *neptis.*

**niggard** MIDDLE ENGLISH *nygart*, origin uncertain.

**niggle** probably from NORWEGIAN *nigla.*

**nigh** OLD ENGLISH *neah.*

**night** OLD ENGLISH *niht.*

**nightingale** OLD ENGLISH *nihtegale*, from *niht* night + *galan* sing.

**nightmare** MIDDLE ENGLISH *niht* night + *mare* demon.

**nihilism** LATIN *nihil* nothing + GREEK *-ismos.*

**nimble** MIDDLE ENGLISH *nymel* quick, from OLD ENGLISH *niman* take.

**nimbus** LATIN.

**nincompoop** earlier *nicompoop*, origin unknown.

**nip** MIDDLE ENGLISH *nippen* pinch, from GERMAN or OLD NORSE *hnippa.*

**nipple** MIDDLE ENGLISH *nyppell*, *neble*, from OLD ENGLISH *neb* bill, beak, snout.

**nirvana** SANSKRIT *nirvana* extinction, disappearance.

**niter** FRENCH *nitre*, from LATIN *nitrum*, from GREEK *nitron.*

**nitric** French *nitrique*. See **niter**.

**nitrogen** French *nitrogène*, from Greek *nitron*.

**nit-wit** German *nit*, from *nicht* not + Old English *wit* understanding.

**nix** German *nichts* nothing.

**no** Old English *ne a* not ever.

**nob** Scottish *knabb*.

**noble** French upper classes, from Latin *nobilis* famous.

**nock** Dutch *nocke* notch.

**nocturne** French, from Latin *nocturnus* relating to night.

**nod** Middle English *nodden*.

**noddle** Middle English *nodle*.

**node** Latin *nodus* knot.

**nodule** Latin *nodus* knot.

**noggin** Middle English small cup, mug, possibly from *nog* strong ale.

**noise** Middle English clamor, shouting, from French *noise* uproar, brawl; apparently from Latin *nausea* annoyance.

**nomad** Latin *nomas* wanderer, from Greek *nomos* pasture.

**nombril** French the navel.

**nomenclature** Latin *nomenclatura* call by name, from *nomen* name + *calare* call.

**nominal** Latin *nominalis*, from *nomen* name.

**nominate** Latin *nominare* name, from *nomen* name.

**nominative** French *nominatif*, from Latin *nominativus* pertaining to naming, from *nominare*. See **nominate**.

**non-** Latin not.

**non sequitur** Latin *non-* not + *sequor* follow.

**nonchalant** French, from Latin *non-* not + *calene* be warm.

**nondescript** Latin *non-* not + *describere*, from *de-* down + *scribere* write.

**none** Old English *nan*.

**nonpareil** French, from Latin *non-* not + *pareil* equal, from *par*.

**nonplus** Latin *non-* not + *plus* more.

**noodle**[1] (dough) German *Nudel*.

**noodle**[2] (head) Middle English *nodle*.

**nook** Middle English *nok*, from Scandinavian.

**noon** Old English *non* ninth hour after sunrise, from Latin *nona hora* ninth hour (about 3 PM). The change to noon meaning midday occurred during the 14th century.

**noose** Latin *nodus*.

**nor** Middle English *nother* neither.

**norm** Latin *norma* carpenter's tool.

**normal** Latin *normalis*, from *norma* rule, pattern.

**north** Old English.

**nose** Old English *nosu*.

**nostalgia** Latin, from Greek *nostos* return home + *algos* pain.

**nostril** Old English *nosthyrl*, from *nosu* nose + *thyrel* hole.

**nostrum** Modern English, from Latin *nostrum remedium* our remedy, from *noster* ours. Originally, medicines offered by people who made their own mixtures.

**not** Old English *ne*.

**notable** Latin *notabilis*, from *notare* note.

**notary** Latin *notare* note.

**notation** Latin *notatio*, from *notare* note.

**notch**  FRENCH *oche* nick.

**note**  LATIN *nota* sign.

**nothing**  OLD ENGLISH *na thing*.

**notice**  FRENCH, from LATIN *notitia*.  See **note**.

**notify**  FRENCH *notifier* make known, from LATIN *notus* known + *facere* do, make.

**notion**  LATIN *notio* idea, from *noscere* come to know.

**notorious**  LATIN well-known, from *notus* known.

**nought**  OLD ENGLISH *nowiht*.

**noun**  FRENCH name, from LATIN *nomen*.

**nourish**  FRENCH *norir* bring up, from LATIN *nutrire*.

**nova**  LATIN *nova stella* new star, from *novus* new.

**noveau**  FRENCH *novel* new, from LATIN *novellus*. See **novel**.

**novel**  FRENCH new, from LATIN *novellus,* from *novus* new.

**November**  LATIN *November* ninth month of the early Roman calendar, which started with March as the first month, from *novem* nine.

**novena**  LATIN *novem* nine.

**novice**  FRENCH, from LATIN *novicius,* from *novus* new.

**novocaine**  LATIN *novus* new + *-caine*, from *cocaine* (used as a local anesthetic).

**now**  OLD ENGLISH *nu*.

**noxious**  LATIN *noxa* harm.

**nozzle**  See **nose**.

**nuance**  FRENCH *nuer* shade, from *nue* cloud, from LATIN *nubes*.

**nub**  GERMAN *knubbe* knob.

**nubbin**  GERMAN *knubbe* knob.

**nubia**  LATIN *nubes* cloud.

**nubile**  LATIN *nubilis*, from *nubere* marry.

**nucleus**  LATIN a kernel.

**nudge**  possibly from NORWEGIAN *nyggia* push.

**nugatory**  LATIN *nugatorius* worthless, futile, from *nugator* trifler, from *nugae* jests, trifles.

**nugget**  origin unknown, possibly from BRITISH *nug* lump.

**nuisance**  FRENCH *nuire*, from LATIN *nocere* annoy.

**null**  FRENCH, from LATIN *nullus* not any, from *ne-* not + *ullus* any.

**nullify**  LATIN *nullificare,* from *nullus* not any + *facere* do, make.

**numb**  MIDDLE ENGLISH *nimen* take, from OLD ENGLISH *niman*.

**number**  FRENCH *nombre* unit, from *numerus*.

**numeral**  LATIN *numeralis*, from *numerus* unit.

**numerator**  LATIN *numerare* count.

**numerous**  LATIN *numerus* a number.

**numinous**  LATIN *numen* divine approval (expressed by nodding the head), from *nuere* nod.

**nun**  OLD ENGLISH *nunne*, from LATIN *nonna*.

**nuptial**  LATIN *nuptiae* marriage, from *nubere* marry.

**nurse**  FRENCH *nurrice* one who nurses a baby, from LATIN *nutrire* nourish.

**nurture**  FRENCH, from LATIN *nutrire* nourish.

**nut**  OLD ENGLISH *hnutu*.

**nutgall**  See **nut** + **gall**[3].

**nutmeg**  MIDDLE ENGLISH *notemygge*, from FRENCH *noiz muscade* musky (strong odor) nut.

**nutrition**  LATIN *nutritio,* from *nutrire* feed.

**nux vomica** Latin *nux* nut + *vomere* vomit.

**nuzzle** Old English *nosu.*

**nylon** made-up word.

**nymph** French, from Latin *nympha,* from Greek *nymphe.*

**nystagmus** Latin *nystagmos* drowsiness, from Greek *nystazein* be sleepy.

# O

-o[1] (combining) GREEK usage, in combinations such as Anglo-Saxon (where *Angle + -o* makes the combining form *Anglo*).

-o[2] (ending) MODERN ENGLISH slang usage, as in wino, weirdo, combo.

**o'clock** MIDDLE ENGLISH *of the clock*.

**oaf** OLD NORSE *alfr* elf, from an early idea that babies not beautiful or normal had been put there by an elf.

**oak** OLD ENGLISH *ac*.

**oasis** LATIN, from GREEK, from EGYPTIAN word for "fertile place in the desert".

**oath** OLD ENGLISH *ath* promise to God to do something, or that what one says is true.

**ob-** LATIN toward, against, over, opposite, entirely.

**obbligato** ITALIAN obliged, from LATIN.

**obdurate** LATIN *odburare*, from *ob-* very much + *burare* make hard.

**obedient** FRENCH, from LATIN *obedire* serve. See **obey**.

**obeisance** FRENCH *obeissance*, from *obeir* obey, from LATIN *obedire* serve. See **obey**.

**obese** LATIN *obesus* fat, from *obedere* eat.

**obey** FRENCH *obeïr*, from LATIN *obedire* serve, from *ob-* to + *audire* hear.

**obfuscate** LATIN *obfuscare* darken, from *ob-* toward, against + *fuscus* dark.

**obituary** LATIN *obituarius*, from *obitus* death, from *ob-* toward + *ire* go.

**object** LATIN *objectus* something thrown in the way, from *objicere*, from *ob-* against + *jacere* throw.

**objective** LATIN *objectivus*, from *objectus*. See **object**.

**oblation** LATIN *oblatio* offering, from *offere*, from *ob-* toward + *ferre* bring.

**obligate** LATIN *obligare* bind. See **oblige**.

**oblige** FRENCH *obliger* bind, from LATIN *obligare*, from *ob-* toward + *ligare* bind.

**oblique** LATIN *obliiquus* slanting, from *ob-* toward + *liquis* slanted.

**obliterate** LATIN *oblitarare* erase, from *ob-* over + *littera* letter.

**oblivion** LATIN *obliviosus*, from *oblivisci* forget.

**oblong** LATIN *oblongus* long, from *ob-* toward + *longus* long.

**obnoxious** LATIN *obnoxius*, from *ob-* against + *noxa* injury.

**oboe** ITALIAN, from FRENCH *hautbois*, from *haut* high + *bois* wood.

**obscene** LATIN *obscenus* very bad.

**obscure** FRENCH *obscur* dark, from LATIN *obscurus,* from *ob-* over + *scurus* covered.

**obsequious** LATIN *obsequium,* from *ob-* to + *sequi* follow.

**observe** FRENCH *observer* examine, from LATIN *observare* watch, from *ob-* over + *servare* keep.

**obsess** LATIN *obsidere* sit at, from *ob-* toward + *sedere* sit.

**obsolete** LATIN *obsolescere,* from *ob-* opposite + *solere* be used to.

**obstacle** FRENCH *o(b)stacle,* from LATIN *obstaculum,* from *obstare* stand in the way, from *ob-* against + *stare* stand.

**obstetrics** LATIN *obstetricus* relating to a midwife (woman whose work is helping to deliver babies), from *obstetrix* midwife, she who stands by, from *ob-* against + *stare* stand.

**obstinate** LATIN *obstinare* continue trying, from *ob-* toward + *stare* stand.

**obstreperous** LATIN *obstreperous* clamorous, from *obstrepere* oppose noisily, from *ob-* against + *strepere* make a noise.

**obstruct** LATIN *obstruere* block, from *ob-* against + *struere* pile up.

**obtain** FRENCH *obtenir* get, from LATIN *obtinere* take hold of, from *ob-* entirely + *tenere* hold.

**obtrude** LATIN *obtrudere* push with force against, from *ob-* against + *trudere* push.

**obtuse** LATIN *obtundere* beat against, from *ob-* against + *tundere* strike.

**obverse** LATIN *obvertere* turn against, from *ob-* against + *vertere* turn.

**obviate** LATIN *obviare* prevent, from *ob-* against + *via* way.

**obvious** LATIN *obvius* at hand, from *ob-* toward + *via* way.

**occasion** LATIN *occasio* opportunity, from *ob-* toward + *cadere* fall.

**occipital** FRENCH, from LATIN *ob-* toward + *caput* head.

**Occitan** FRENCH.

**occlude** LATIN *occludere,* from *ob-* to + *claudere* close.

**occult** LATIN *occulere,* from *ob-* to + *celere* cover up.

**occupy** FRENCH *occuper* to take, from LATIN *occupare,* from *ob-* to + *capere* take.

**occur** LATIN *occurrere,* from *ob-* towards + *currere* run.

**ocean** FRENCH, from LATIN *oceanus,* from GREEK *okeanos.*

**ocellus** LATIN *oculus* eye.

**ocher** LATIN, from GREEK *ochros* pale yellow.

**octa-** GREEK *okto* eight.

**octagon** See **octa-** + GREEK *gonia* angle.

**octave** LATIN *octava,* from *octo* eight.

**October** LATIN *October* eighth month of the early Roman calendar, which started with March as the first month, from *octo* eight.

**octopus** GREEK *okto* eight + *pous* a foot.

**odd** OLD NORSE *oddi* triangle, third.

**oddments** See **odd** + **-ment**.

**ode** FRENCH, from LATIN song, from GREEK *oide.*

**odious** FRENCH *odieus,* from LATIN *odiosus,* from *odium* hatred.

**odor** FRENCH *odeur* smell, from LATIN *odor.*

**odyssey** the ancient GREEK poem which told about the adventures of *Odysseus* on his way home from war.

**oedematous** See **edema** + **-ous**.

**of** OLD ENGLISH.

**off** OLD ENGLISH.

**offal** MIDDLE ENGLISH *ofall* off-fall.

**offence** See **offend**.

**offend** FRENCH *offendre* hurt, from LATIN *offendere*, from *ob-* against + *fendere* hit.

**offense** See **offend**.

**offer** OLD ENGLISH *offrian* sacrifice, from LATIN *offerre* bring before, from *ob-* toward + *ferre* bring.

**office** FRENCH duty, from LATIN *officium*, from *opificium*, from *opus* work + *facere* do, make.

**official** See **office**.

**officiate** See **office**.

**offshoot** See **off** + **shoot**.

**ogle** probably from GERMAN *oegeln*, from *oog* the eye.

**ogre** FRENCH giant, from LATIN *Orcus* Roman god of the lower world.

**ohm** G.S. *Ohm* (1789–1854) German scientist.

**-oid** GREEK *eidos* form, shape.

**oil** FRENCH *huile*, from LATIN *oleum* olive oil, from GREEK *elaion*.

**Ojibwa** NATIVE AMERICAN *O'chepe'wag* plaited shoes, describing their moccasins. Also spelled *Ojibway*.

**OK** abbreviation of "oll korrect", AMERICAN folk spelling of "all correct".

**okra** AFRICAN *nkrumah*.

**-ol** the *-ol* ending of **alcohol**.

**-ola** AMERICAN, probably originally in *pianola*.

**old** OLD ENGLISH *ald* of the past.

**oleander** LATIN.

**olfactory** LATIN *olfacere* smell, from *olere* have a smell + *facere* do, make.

**oligarchy** GREEK *oligarchia* government by a few, from *oligos* few + *archein* rule.

**oliphant** See **elephant**.

**olive** FRENCH, from LATIN *oliva*, from GREEK *elaia*.

**-ology** GREEK *-ologia* has to do with.

**ombudsman** SWEDISH *ombud* deputy + *man* man.

**omelet** FRENCH *omelette*, from LATIN *lamella* thin plate.

**omen** LATIN.

**ominous** LATIN *ominosus*, from *omen* omen.

**omit** LATIN *omittere*, from *ob-* very much + *mittere* let go, send.

**omnibus** FRENCH, from LATIN for all, from *omni* all, because the transportation was for the use of all classes of people.

**omnipotent** LATIN *ominipotens*, from *omnis* all + *potens* powerful.

**omnivorous** LATIN *omnivorus*, from *omnis* all + *vorare* eat in a greedy way.

**on** OLD ENGLISH.

**once** MIDDLE ENGLISH *ones*.

**one** OLD ENGLISH *an*.

**onerous** LATIN *onerosus*, from *onus* burden.

**onion** FRENCH, from LATIN *unio* unity, a single onion, even though it has many layers.

**only** OLD ENGLISH *anlic*.

**onomatopeia** LATIN, from GREEK *onomatopoiia*, from *onomatos* name + *poiein* make.

**onslaught** DUTCH *annslag*, from *slagen* strike.

215

**ontology** LATIN *ontologia*, from GREEK *ontos* being + *-logia* study of.

**onus** LATIN.

**onyx** FRENCH, from LATIN, from GREEK nail.

**ooze** OLD ENGLISH *wos* sap.

**opal** LATIN, from GREEK *spallios*, from *upala* precious stone.

**opaque** LATIN *opacus* shady.

**open** OLD ENGLISH.

**opera** ITALIAN *opera in musica* work set to music, from LATIN *opera* a work.

**operate** LATIN *operari* work, from *opus* work.

**opiate** LATIN *opiatus* bringing sleep, from *opium*. See **opium**.

**opinion** FRENCH belief, from LATIN *opinio*.

**opium** LATIN, from GREEK *opion*, from *opos* vegetable juice.

**opponent** LATIN *opponere*, from *ob-* against + *ponere* set.

**opportune** LATIN *opportunus* toward the harbor, from *ob-* toward + *portus* harbor, referring to the helpful winds in the harbor.

**oppose** FRENCH *opposer*, from LATIN *opponere*. See **opponent**.

**oppress** FRENCH *oppresser*, from LATIN *oppressare*, from *opprimere*, from *ob-* against + *premere* press.

**opprobrium** LATIN *opprobare* blame, from *ob-* against + *probrum* a disgrace.

**opt** FRENCH *opter* choose + LATIN *optare*.

**opthalmic** GREEK *ophthalmos* eye

**opthalmoscope** See **opthalmic** + **-scope**.

**optic** FRENCH *optique*, from LATIN, from GREEK *optikos*.

**optimism** FRENCH *optimisme*, from LATIN *optimum* the best.

**optimum** LATIN *optimus* best, from *ops* riches.

**option** FRENCH, from LATIN *optio* choice, from *optare* wish.

**opulent** LATIN *opulentus* rich, from *ops*.

**opus** LATIN work.

**or** OLD ENGLISH *oththe* other.

**-or** FRENCH, from LATIN.

**oracle** FRENCH, from LATIN *orare* speak, pray.

**oral** LATIN *oris*, from *os* mouth.

**orange** FRENCH *orenge*, from ARABIC *nāranj*, from PERSIAN *nāranga*.

**orangutan** MALAY *orang* man + *hutan* forest.

**oration** LATIN *oratio* speech.

**oratory** LATIN *oratoria*.

**orb** LATIN *orbis* circle.

**orbit** FRENCH, from LATIN *orbita* path, from *orbis* circle.

**orc** OLD ENGLISH *orcthyrs*, *orcneas* ogre, from LATIN *Orcus* hell.

**orca** MIDDLE ENGLISH *orc*, *ork* large whale, from FRENCH *orque* sea monster, from LATIN *orca*, a kind of whale.

**orchard** OLD ENGLISH *ortgeard*, from LATIN *hortus* a garden + OLD ENGLISH *geard* yard.

**orchestra** LATIN, from GREEK place in the Greek theatre where the chorus danced, from *orcheisthai* dance.

**ordain** FRENCH *ordeiner*, from LATIN *ordinare* set in order.

**ordeal** OLD ENGLISH *ordel* judgment. From an ancient method of deciding guilt or innocence in which the accused person had to do a dangerous action. If he didn't get hurt, the gods had found him innocent.

**order** FRENCH *ordre,* from LATIN *ordo.*

**ordinal** LATIN *ordinalis,* from *ordo* straight row.

**ordinance** FRENCH *ordenance* rule, from LATIN *ordinare* set in order, from *ordo* straight row.

**ordinary** FRENCH, from LATIN *ordinarius* regular, from *ordo* order.

**ore** OLD ENGLISH *ar.*

**oregano** SPANISH, from LATIN *origanus,* from GREEK *oreiganon,* from *oros* mountain + *ganos* brightness, ornament.

**organ** LATIN *organum* musical instrument, from GREEK *organon* tool.

**organdy** FRENCH *organdi,* origin uncertain.

**organize** LATIN *organizare* arrange, from *organum.* See **organ.**

**orgy** FRENCH, from LATIN, from GREEK *orgia* secret ceremony.

**orient** FRENCH east, from LATIN *oriens* rising sun, east, from *oriri* rise.

**orienteering** SWEDISH *orientering.* See **orient.**

**orifice** FRENCH, from LATIN *orificium* opening, from *or,* from *os* mouth + *facere* do, make.

**origin** LATIN *origo* beginning.

**Orkney** OLD NORSE *Orkney-jar* Seal Islands, from *orkn* seal.

**ornament** FRENCH *ornement,* from LATIN *ornamentum* decoration.

**ornate** LATIN *ornare* decorate.

**ornery** contraction of **ordinary.**

**orphan** LATIN *orphanus,* from GREEK *orphanos.*

**orrery** Charles Boyle, Earl of *Orrery* (1676–1731), for whom one was made.

**ortho-** GREEK *orthos* straight.

**orthodontics** GREEK *orthos* straight + *odontos* tooth + FRENCH *-ique,* from LATIN *-icus,* from GREEK *-ikos.*

**orthodox** LATIN *orthodoxus* having the right faith, from GREEK *orthodoxos,* from *orthos* right + *doxa* opinion, from *dokein* think.

**orthography** See **ortho-** + **-graphy.**

**oscillate** LATIN *oscillare* swing.

**-ose**[1] (full of) LATIN *-osus.*

**-ose**[2] (chemical) FRENCH, originally in *glucose.*

**osier** FRENCH, from LATIN *auseria.*

**osmosis** LATIN, from GREEK *osmos* force into.

**ossicone** LATIN.

**ostensible** FRENCH open, from LATIN *ostendere* to show, from *obs-* against + *tendere* stretch.

**ostentation** LATIN *ostendere.* See **ostensible.**

**osteopathy** GREEK *osteon* bone + *-pathy,* from *pathos* suffering, disease, feeling.

**ostler** See **hostler.**

**ostracize** GREEK *ostrakízein* order away from a group by voting on it. Pieces of broken pots were used as voting pieces, from *oístrakon* shards (pieces of broken pots).

**ostrich** FRENCH, from LATIN *ans* bird + *struthio* ostrich, from GREEK *strouthos.*

**otoscope** GREEK *oto-* ear + ITALIAN *scopo* target, from GREEK *skopos.*

**otter** OLD ENGLISH *oter.*

**ottoman** FRENCH, from ITALIAN *Ottomano,* from ARABIC *Uthmani,* from *Uthman* founder of the empire.

**ounce** FRENCH *once* unit of weight, from LATIN *uncia* one of twelve.

**-ous** LATIN *-osus* full of.

**ousel** OLD ENGLISH *osle.*

**oust** FRENCH *oster,* from LATIN *obstare* get in the way, from *obs-* against + *stare* stand.

**out** OLD ENGLISH *ut.*

**outlaw** OLD ENGLISH *utlaga* one put outside of the law, from OLD NORSE *utlagr* sent away from the group.

**outrage** FRENCH, from LATIN *ultra* beyond.

**oval** LATIN *ovalis,* from *ovum* egg.

**ovary** LATIN *ovum* egg.

**ovation** LATIN *ovatio* celebration honoring a general who won.

**over-** OLD ENGLISH *ofer-* too much, above.

**overt** FRENCH *ovrir* open, from LATIN *aperire.*

**overture** FRENCH opening, from LATIN *apertura.*

**overwhelm** See over- + whelm.

**ovipositor** LATIN *ovum* egg + *positor* one who places, from *ponere* place.

**ovule** FRENCH *ovule,* from LATIN *ovulum* small egg, from *ovum* egg.

**ovum** LATIN egg.

**owe** OLD ENGLISH *agan* have to pay.

**owl** OLD ENGLISH *ule.*

**own** OLD ENGLISH *agan.*

**ox** OLD ENGLISH *oxa.*

**oxide** FRENCH *ox(ygène)* + *-ide,* from *acide* acid. See **oxygen.**

**oxygen** FRENCH *oxygène,* from GREEK *oxys* acid + *-genes* produced, from the idea that oxygen was essential in the formation of acids.

**oyster** FRENCH *oistre,* from LATIN *ostrea, ostreum* oyster, from GREEK *ostreon.* Related to GREEK *ostrakon* hard shell and *osteon* bone.

**ozone** GERMAN *Ozon* the gas, from GREEK *ozon* smelling, from *ozein* smell.

# P

**pace** FRENCH *pas* step, from LATIN *passus*.

**pacific** FRENCH *pacifique*, from LATIN *pacificus* peaceful. See **pacify**.

**pacify** FRENCH *pacefier*, from LATIN *pacificare* make peace, from *pax* peace + *facere* do, make.

**pack** DUTCH and GERMAN *pak* bundle.

**pact** FRENCH, from LATIN *pactum*, from *pax* peace.

**pad** MIDDLE ENGLISH bundle of straw to lie on.

**paddle** MIDDLE ENGLISH *padell* small spade, from LATIN *padela* perhaps from *patella* pan, plate.

**paddock** OLD ENGLISH *pearruc*.

**paddy** MALAY *padi*.

**padlock** MIDDLE ENGLISH *pad* (meaning uncertain) + *lokke* lock.

**padre** LATIN *pater* father.

**paduasoy** FRENCH *pou de soie* pelt of silk.

**paean** LATIN, from GREEK *paian* song to Apollo (who is also called *Paian*).

**pagan** LATIN *paganus* villager, from *pagus* village.

**page**[1] (book) FRENCH, from LATIN *pagina* page for writing.

**page**[2] (boy) FRENCH young boy, from GREEK *paidion*, from *pais* child.

**pageant** LATIN *pagina* scene of a play, from *pagina* page for writing.

**pagoda** PORTUGUESE *pagode*, from PERSIAN *butkadah*, from *but* idol + *kadah* house.

**pail** OLD ENGLISH *pægel* small measure, from LATIN *pagella*, from *pagina* page for writing.

**pain** FRENCH *peine* punishment, from LATIN *poena*, from GREEK *poine*.

**paint** FRENCH *peindre* color, from LATIN *pingere*.

**painter**[1] (artist) See **paint**.

**painter**[2] (rope) FRENCH, from LATIN *pendere* hang.

**paiocke** Shakespeare's *Hamlet*, a variation of peacock.

**pair** FRENCH *paire* a set of two, from LATIN *par* equal.

**paisley** the city in Scotland where it was first made.

**pajama** HINDI, probably from PERSIAN *paejamah*, from *pae* leg + *jamah* clothing.

**pajock** possibly from **peacock**.

**pal** GYPSY *phal* brother, friend, comrade.

**palace** FRENCH *palais* royal house, from LATIN *palatium*, from *Palatium* Palatine Hill in Rome, hill where the first very beautiful royal palace was built.

**palanquin** PORTUGUESE *palanquim*, from MALAY *palangki*, from SANSKRIT *palyanka* couch, bed, from *pari* around + *ancati* it bends, curves.

**palate** LATIN *palatum* roof of the mouth.

**palatinate** See **palatine**.

**palatine** FRENCH, from LATIN *palatium* palace.

**palaver** PORTUGUESE *palavra* work, from LATIN *parabola* comparison, parable (short story that teaches a moral lesson), from GREEK *parabole*. See **parable**.

**pale**[1] (little color) FRENCH not having color, from LATIN *pallidus*.

**pale**[2] (stake) FRENCH, from LATIN *palus* stake.

**paleo-** GREEK *palaio-* old, ancient, from *palai* long ago, far back.

**paleoscincus** See **paleo-** + LATIN *scincus*, from GREEK *skinkos* lizard.

**palestra** FRENCH *palestre*, from LATIN *palaestra*, from GREEK *palaistra* wrestling school, from *palaiein* wrestle + *-tra* place.

**palette** FRENCH, from LATIN *pala* tool for digging.

**palfrey** FRENCH *palefrei*, from LATIN *palafredus*, from *paraveredus* extra horse, from GREEK *para* beside + LATIN *verdus* post horse (provided for travelers).

**palimsest** LATIN *palimpsestus*, from GREEK *palimpsestos* scraped again, from *palin* again + *psen* rub smooth.

**palindrome** GREEK *palin* again + *dramein* run.

**palisade** FRENCH *palissade*, from LATIN *palus* stake.

**pall**[1] (covering) OLD ENGLISH *pæll* robe, from LATIN *pallium* covering.

**pall**[2] (boring) from **appall**.

**pallet** FRENCH *paillete* straw, from LATIN *palea*.

**palliate** LATIN *palliatus* covered with a cloak, from *pallium* cloak.

**pallid** LATIN *pallidus*.

**pallor** LATIN.

**palm** FRENCH *paume* inner part of the hand, from LATIN *palma*.

**palmar** LATIN *palmaris*.

**palmette** See **palm** + **-ette**.

**palmetto** SPANISH *palmito*, from *palma*, from LATIN palm.

**palomino** SPANISH coloring of a dove, from LATIN *palumbes* dove.

**palpable** LATIN *palpabilis* can be touched, from *palpare* touch.

**palpitate** LATIN *palpitare* beat rapidly.

**palsy** FRENCH *paralysie*, from LATIN *paralysis*, from GREEK nerves not working properly.

**paltry** probably from GERMAN *palte* rag.

**pamper** MIDDLE ENGLISH *pamperen*, from DUTCH *pameren*.

**pamphlet** LATIN *panfletus* little book, from FRENCH *Pamphilet* a medieval Latin poem that was first published in a small booklet of a few pages.

**pan** OLD ENGLISH *panne*.

**pan-** GREEK *pas* all, every.

**panache** FRENCH, from LATIN *penna* feather.

**pancreas** LATIN, from GREEK *pankreas*, from *pan-* all + *kreas* flesh, because it has no bone.

**pandemic** GREEK *pandemos*, from *pan-* all + *demos* the people.

**pandemonium** LATIN, from GREEK *pan-* all + *daimon* demon, invented by the English poet John Milton (1608–1674) as the name for the capital of hell.

**pander** GREEK *Pandarus* a character in a medieval legend who was the communicating person between a girl and a man who were separated.

**pandowdy** AMERICAN, origin uncertain.

**pane** FRENCH *pan* piece, from LATIN *pannus* piece of cloth.

**panegyric** FRENCH *panegryique*, from LATIN *panegyricus*, from GREEK *panegyris* public meeting, from *pan-* all + *ageirein* bring together.

**panel** FRENCH piece, from LATIN *pannus* piece of cloth.

**pang** MIDDLE ENGLISH, origin uncertain.

**pangolin** MALAY *peng-goling* roller, from *goling* roll. The animal curls into a ball.

**panic** FRENCH *panique* sudden fear, from GREEK *Panikos* relating to Pan, god of forests and shepherds, who was said to scare people when he showed up unexpectedly.

**pannier** FRENCH *panier* basket, from LATIN *panarium* breadbasket, from *panis* bread.

**pannikin** See **pan** + DUTCH *kin* little.

**panoply** GREEK *panoplia* armor, from *pan-* all + *hopla* arms.

**panorama** GREEK *pan-* all + *horama* view.

**pant**[1] (quick breath) probably from FRENCH *pantaisier* gasp, from GREEK *phantasia* imagination, nightmare.

**pant**[2] (clothes) See **pantaloon**.

**pantaloon** FRENCH, from *Pantalone* character in a 16th century Italian comic play who wore tight pants, from ITALIAN *Pantaleone* name of a 4th century saint.

**pantelette** See **pantaloon**.

**pantheon** LATIN *Pantheon* Roman temple, from GREEK *pantheios* common to all the gods, from *pan-* all + *theos* a god.

**panther** FRENCH, from LATIN, from GREEK.

**pantler (panter)** MIDDLE ENGLISH *paneter*, from LATIN *panetarius* baker. See **pantry**.

**pantograph** FRENCH *pantographe*, from GREEK *pant* all + *graphe* write.

**pantomime** LATIN *pantomimus*, from GREEK *pantomimos* actor (imitator of all), from *panto-* all + *mimos* imitator.

**pantry** FRENCH *paneterie* place where bread is kept, from LATIN *panetaria*, from *panis* bread.

**papa** FRENCH, from LATIN, originally a child's word.

**papaw** See **pawpaw**.

**papaya** SPANISH.

**paper** FRENCH *papier*, from LATIN *papyrus* paper made from papyrus, from GREEK *papyros* the plant.

**papillae** LATIN nipples.

**papilloma** LATIN *papula* pimple.

**papist** LATIN *papista*, from *papa*. See **pope**.

**papoose** NATIVE AMERICAN *papoos*.

**papyrus** LATIN, from GREEK.

**par** LATIN equal.

**para-** GREEK beside, beyond, aside from.

**parable** FRENCH, from LATIN, from GREEK *parabole* comparison, from *para-* beside + *ballein* throw.

**parabola** GREEK *parabole*. See **parable**.

**parachute** FRENCH *para-* guarding against + *chute* fall.

**parade**  FRENCH display, from SPANISH *parada,* from LATIN *parare* make ready.

**paradigm**  LATIN *paradigma* example, from GREEK *paradeigma,* from *para-* beside + *deigma* example.

**paradise**  FRENCH, from LATIN *paradisus* heaven, from GREEK *paradeisos* a garden.

**paradisiacal**  See **paradise** + GREEK *-iacal* like.

**paradox**  LATIN *paradoxum* something unexpected, from GREEK *paradoxos,* from *para-* beyond + *doxa* opinion, from *dokein* think.

**paraffin**  GERMAN wax, from LATIN *parum* too little + *affinis* having to do with, because things don't stick to it well.

**paragon**  ITALIAN *paragone* standard of value, from GREEK *para-* beside + *akone* whetstone (stone used for sharpening).

**paragraph**  LATIN *paragraphus,* from GREEK *paragraphos,* from *para-* beside + *graphein* write.

**parakeet**  SPANISH *perquito.*

**parallax**  GREEK *parallaxis,* from *para-* beyond + *allassein* change.

**parallel**  FRENCH, from LATIN *parallelus,* from GREEK *parallelos,* from *para-* side by side + *alleos* one another.

**parallelogram**  FRENCH *parallélogramme,* from LATIN *parallelogrammum,* from GREEK *parallelogrammon,* from *parallelos* parallel + *graphein* write.

**paralysis**  LATIN, from GREEK *paralyein* loosen at the side, from *para-* beside + *lyein* loose.

**parameter**  GREEK *para-* beside + *metron* measure.

**paramount**  FRENCH *par amont* at the top, from LATIN *per-* beyond + *admontem* uphill.

**paramour**  FRENCH *par amour* with love.

**paranoia**  LATIN, from GREEK *para-* beside + *nous* the mind.

**parapet**  ITALIAN *parapetto* chest-high wall, from *para-* against + *petto* chest, from LATIN *pectus.*

**paraphernalia**  LATIN things a bride brings to her marriage in addition to her dowry, from GREEK *parapherna,* from *para-* beside + *pherne* dowry.  See **dowry.**

**paraphrase**  FRENCH, from LATIN *paraphrasis,* from GREEK *paraphrasis,* from *para-* beyond + *phrazein* tell.

**paraplegia**  LATIN, from GREEK *paraplegia* paralysis of one side of the body, from *para-* beside + *plege* paralysis.

**parasite**  LATIN *parasitus* one who lives off another, from GREEK *parasitos* one who eats at the table of another, from *para-* beside + *sitos* food, from ancient Greek and Roman men who offered praise and kind words in return for food or support.

**parasol**  FRENCH, from ITALIAN *parasole,* from *parare* guard against + *sole* sun, from LATIN *sol.*

**paratyphoid**  See **para-** + **typhoid.**

**parboil**  FRENCH *par* through + *boullir* boil.

**parcel**  FRENCH *parcelle* small part, from LATIN *pars.*

**parch**  MIDDLE ENGLISH, possibly from *perchen, perishen* perish.

**parcheesi**  HINDI *pachisi,* from *pachis* twenty-five (highest throw of the dice), from SANSKRIT *panca* five + *vinsati* twenty.

**parchment**  FRENCH *parchemin* skin, from LATIN *pergamina,* from GREEK *Pergamon* city where parchment was first made.

**pardon**  FRENCH *pardonner* forgive, from LATIN *perdonare,* from *per-* through + *donare* give.

**pare**  FRENCH *parer* trim, from LATIN *parare* make ready.

**parent** French, from Latin *parens* father or mother.

**parenthesis** Latin something put in, from Greek *para-* beside + *entithenai* put in.

**parfait** French perfect.

**parfleche** French *parer* deflect + *fleche* arrow.

**pariah** Tamil *paraiyan* drummer, member of a low caste (rank) whose duty it is to beat drums at festivals, from *parai* drum.

**parietal** Latin *parietalis*, from *paries* wall.

**parimutuel** French a mutual bet.

**parish** French *paroisse* religious area, from Latin *parchia*, from Greek *paroilia*, from *para-* beside + *oikos* house.

**parity** Latin *paritas*, from *par* equal.

**park** French *par*, from Latin *parricus*.

**parka** Russian.

**parkin** perhaps from proper name *Perkin* or *Parkin*.

**parlance** French *parler* speak.

**parlay** French *paroli*, from Italian *paro* equal, from Latin *par* equal.

**parley** French *parlee* conversation, from *parler* speak, from Latin *parabolare*, from *parabola*. See **parable**.

**parliament** French *parlement* conference, from *parler* speak. See **parable**.

**parlor** French *parleor* place for conversation, from *parler* speak. See **parable**.

**parochial** French, from Latin *parochia* parish. See **parish**.

**parody** French, from Latin, from Greek *paroidia*, from *para-* beside + *oide* song.

**parole** French promise, from Latin *parabola* story with a moral, from Greek *parabole*. See **parable**.

**paroxysm** French, from Latin, from Greek *para-* beyond + *oxynein* sharpen, from *oxys* sharp.

**parquet** French *parc* a park.

**parrot** French *perrot*.

**parry** French *parer* defend, from Latin *parare* make ready.

**parse** Latin *pars orationis* part of speech.

**parsley** possibly from German *petarsile*, from Latin *petrosilium*.

**parsnip** Middle English *nepe* turnip.

**parson** French *persone*, from Latin *persona* priest. See **person**.

**part** Latin *pars* share.

**partake** Middle English part taking, from Latin *participatio* participation.

**partial** French, from Latin *partialis*, from *pars* share.

**participate** Latin *participare* share in, from *pars* share + *capere* take.

**participle** French *participe*, from Latin *participium* sharing, from *pars* share + *capere* take.

**particle** Latin *particula* small part, from *pars* share.

**particular** French *particuler* special, from Latin *particularis* small part, from *particula*. See **particle**.

**partisan** French, from Italian *partigiano* partner, from *parte* part, from Latin *pars* share.

**partition** French *particion*, from Latin *partitionem*, from *partire* part (divide).

**partner** French *parçoner* one who shares, from Latin *partionarius*, from *partitio* sharing.

**partridge** French *perdriz*, from Latin *perdix*, from Greek.

**parturition**  LATIN, from *parturire* be in labor, from *parere* bear.

**party**  FRENCH *partie* side, from *partir* divide, from LATIN *pars* share.

**parvenu**  FRENCH *parvenir* arrive, from LATIN *pervenire.*

**pasque-flower**  FRENCH *passefleur*, from *passer* a step + *fleur* flower, from *pasque* Easter.

**pass**  FRENCH *passer* go across, from LATIN *passus* step.

**passage**  FRENCH *passage* going across, from *passer* move on.  See **pass**.

**passel**  variant of **parcel**.

**passenger**  FRENCH.  See **passage**.

**passion**  FRENCH suffering, from LATIN *passio*, from *pati* suffer.

**passive**  LATIN *passivus* able to suffer.

**passport**  FRENCH *passeport*, from *passer* move + *port* harbor.

**paste**  GREEK *pasta* barley cereal.

**pastel**  FRENCH crayon, from ITALIAN *pastello*, from LATIN *pastellus*, from GREEK *pasta* barley cereal.

**pastern**  MIDDLE ENGLISH shackle for an animal, from FRENCH *pasturon*, from LATIN *pastor*.  See **pastor**.

**pasteurize**  Louis *Pasteur* (1822–1895), French scientist who discovered the process.

**pastiche**  FRENCH, from ITALIAN *pasticcio* mixture, from LATIN *pasta* dough.  See **paste**.

**pastor**  LATIN shepherd, from *pascere* feed.

**pastoral**  LATIN *pastoralis* relating to shepherds, from *pastor*.  See **pastor**.

**pastry**  FRENCH *paste* dough, from LATIN *pasta*, from GREEK *pasta* barley cereal + FRENCH *erie* place of business, from LATIN *arius*.

**pasture**  FRENCH food, from LATIN *pastura*, from *pascere* feed.

**pasty**  See **paste**.

**pat**  imitative.

**pat-a-cake**  the first words of a nursery rhyme, said or chanted to accompany the action of patting or gently clapping together a child's hands.

**patch**  FRENCH *pieche*, from *piece* part of a whole.  See **piece**.

**pate**  (top of head)  perhaps from FRENCH *patene* or LATIN *patena*, both from *patina* pan, dish.

**patella**  LATIN *patella* pan, kneecap, from *patina* pan.

**patent**  FRENCH, from LATIN *patere* lie open, because the paper of the patent was open for the public to see.

**patera**  LATIN *patera*, from *patere* be open.

**paternal**  LATIN *paternalis*, from *pater* father.

**path**  OLD ENGLISH *pæth*.

**pathetic**  LATIN *patheticus*, from GREEK *pathetkios* able to experience emotion, from *pathein* suffer, from *pathos* suffering.

**pathogenic**  FRENCH *pathogénique*, from GREEK *pathos* disease + FRENCH *génique* producing.

**pathos**  GREEK suffering, emotion.

**-pathy**  See **pathos**.

**patient**  FRENCH one who is waiting to get medical care, from LATIN *pati* suffer.

**patio**  SPANISH.

**patriarch**  FRENCH *patriarche*, from LATIN *patriarcha* father of a tribe, from GREEK *patriarches*, from *pater* father + *archein* rule.

**patrician**  LATIN *patricius* noble, from *pater* father.

**patrimony** FRENCH *patrimoine* inheritance, from LATIN *pater* father.

**patriot** FRENCH *patriote*, from LATIN *patriota* persons of the same country, from GREEK *patriotes*.

**patrol** FRENCH *patrouiller* paddle in mud, because guards often had to walk back and forth in mud, from *patte* paw.

**patron** FRENCH protector, from LATIN *patronus*, from *pater* father.

**patsy** ITALIAN *pazzo* crazy person.

**patten** FRENCH *patin* clog.

**patter**[1] (tapping) imitative.

**patter**[2] (fast or easy talk) MIDDLE ENGLISH *pater* mumble prayers rapidly, from LATIN *pater noster* the prayer "Our Father," which priests recited rapidly.

**pattern** See **patron**, from the idea of the father setting a good example for the child to copy.

**patty** FRENCH *pâté* pastry, from *pastee* pie, from *paste* dough. See **paste**.

**paucity** FRENCH, from LATIN *paucus* few.

**paunch** FRENCH *panche* belly, from LATIN *pantex*.

**pauper** LATIN poor person.

**pause** FRENCH, from LATIN *pausa* stop, from GREEK *pausis*.

**pave** FRENCH *paver* cover ground with stones, from LATIN *pavire* hit with force.

**pavilion** MIDDLE ENGLISH, from FRENCH *paveillun* tent, from LATIN *papilio* butterfly, because the tents looked somewhat like a butterfly.

**paw** FRENCH *poue*.

**pawky** SCOTTISH dialect, origin unknown.

**pawn** FRENCH *pan* promise.

**pawpaw** probably from **papaya**.

**pax** MIDDLE ENGLISH, from LATIN peace.

**pay** FRENCH *paier*, from LATIN *paccare* make peace, from *pax* peace.

**pea** MIDDLE ENGLISH *pese*, from OLD ENGLISH.

**peace** FRENCH *pais*, from LATIN *pax*.

**peach** FRENCH *pesche*, from LATIN *pessica*, from *persicum malum*, Persian apple.

**peacock** MIDDLE ENGLISH *poucock*, from *po*, from OLD ENGLISH *pawa* peafowl + MIDDLE ENGLISH *coc*. See **cock**[1].

**peak** GERMAN *pek* pike.

**peal** MIDDLE ENGLISH *pele*, from *apele* appeal.

**pearl** FRENCH *perle*, from LATIN *perna* a sea animal that sometimes contains pearls.

**peart** See **pert**.

**peasant** FRENCH *pais* country, from LATIN *pagus* village.

**pease** MIDDLE ENGLISH *paisen*, from FRENCH *paiser*, from *pais*. See **peace**.

**peat** MIDDLE ENGLISH *pete*, from LATIN *peta*.

**pebble** FRENCH *papolstan* pebble stone.

**peccary** NATIVE AMERICAN *pakira*.

**peck** MIDDLE ENGLISH *picken* pierce.

**pectoral** LATIN *pectoris*, from *pectus* breast.

**peculiar** LATIN *peculiaris* one's own.

**pecuniary** LATIN *pecunia* money.

**pedagogue** FRENCH, from LATIN *paedagogus* name for slaves who helped boys get to school, from GREEK *paidagogos*, from *pais* boy + *agogos* leader.

**pedal** LATIN *pedalis*, from *pes* foot.

**pedant** ITALIAN *pedante* teacher.

**peddle** See **peddler**.

**peddler** MIDDLE ENGLISH *peoddere, peddere,* origin uncertain.

**pedestal** FRENCH *piédestal* support, from ITALIAN *piedistallo* support, from *pie* foot, from LATIN *pes* + *di* of + *stallo* a rest.

**pedestrian** LATIN *pedester,* from *pes* foot + LATIN *-ianus.*

**pedi-** LATIN *pes, pedem* foot.

**pediatrics** GREEK *pais* child + *iatreia* medical help.

**pedicab** See **pedi-** + **cab.**

**pedicel** LATIN *pedicellus* little foot.

**pedigree** FRENCH *pie de grue* foot of a crane (type of bird with long feet). Some charts that show the family tree have connecting lines that look like the foot of a crane.

**pediment** MODERN ENGLISH alteration of *periment, peremint,* origin uncertain.

**pedlar** BRITISH spelling of **peddler.**

**peedoodle** probably a made-up word.

**peel**[1] (fruit skin) OLD ENGLISH *pilian* and FRENCH *pillier* take off, from LATIN *pilare* make bald, from *pilus* hair.

**peel**[2] (baker's shovel) MIDDLE ENGLISH, from FRENCH *pele,* from LATIN *pala* spade, shovel.

**peel**[3] (stake) MIDDLE ENGLISH *pel, pele,* from FRENCH *pel, piel* stake, from LATIN *palus.*

**peep**[1] (sound) imitative.

**peep**[2] (look) MIDDLE ENGLISH *pepe.*

**peer**[1] (equal) FRENCH *per* of equal rank, from LATIN *par* equal.

**peer**[2] (look) short for **appear.**

**peevish** MIDDLE ENGLISH *peyvsh.*

**peg** probably from DUTCH *pegge* little wooden pin for attaching.

**pejorative** LATIN *pejorare* make worse, from *pejor* worse.

**pelerine** FRENCH *pèlerin* a pilgrim, from LATIN *peregrinus* foreign.

**pelican** LATIN *pelicanus,* from GREEK *pelekan,* from *pelekys* ax, from the way the pelican's bill looks.

**pellet** FRENCH *pelote* small ball, from LATIN *pila* ball.

**pell-mell** FRENCH *pêle-mêle* mix, from *pesle-mesle,* from *mesler* mix.

**pellucid** LATIN *pellucidus,* from *per-* through + *lucere* shine.

**pelt**[1] (strike) LATIN *pillare* drive.

**pelt**[2] (animal skin) FRENCH *pelterie,* from *pel* skin, from LATIN *pellis.*

**peltry**[1] (skins) See **pelt**[2].

**peltry**[2] (trash) See **paltry.**

**pelvis** LATIN a basin.

**pemmican** NATIVE AMERICAN *pemikkan* fat meat, from *pimiy* fat.

**pen**[1] (writing tool) FRENCH *penne,* from LATIN *penna* feather, because the earliest pens were made from feathers.

**pen**[2] (yard) OLD ENGLISH *penn.*

**penal** LATIN *poena* punishment, from GREEK *poine* penalty.

**penalty** LATIN *poenalitas* punishment, from *poenalis.*

**penance** FRENCH *peneance,* from LATIN *paenitentia* feel sorry for doing wrong.

**pence** BRITISH penny.

**penchant** FRENCH *pencher* lean, from LATIN *pendere* hang.

**pencil** FRENCH *pincel* painter's brush, which looked like a little tail, from LATIN *penis* tail.

**pendant** FRENCH *pendre* hang, from LATIN *pendere* hang.

**pendulum** LATIN *pendere* hang.

**penetrate** LATIN *penetrare* enter.

**penguin** probably from WELSH *pen gwyn* white head.

**penicillin** LATIN *penicillus* painter's brush, because the mold looks like that. See **pencil**.

**peninsula** LATIN *paeninsula*, from *paene* almost + *insula* island.

**penis** LATIN tail.

**penitence** FRENCH, from LATIN *paenitentia*. See **penance**.

**pennant** FRENCH *penne*, from LATIN *penna* a feather and FRENCH *penon* flag.

**penny** OLD ENGLISH *pening*.

**pension** FRENCH payment, from LATIN *pensio*.

**pensive** FRENCH *pensif*, from *penser* think, from LATIN *pensare* think about.

**pent** MIDDLE ENGLISH, from *penned*. See **pen**[2].

**penta-** GREEK, from *pente* five.

**pentaprism** See **penta-** + **prism**.

**penteconter** GREEK *penthkonthr*, from *pentekonta* fifty.

**penthouse** MIDDLE ENGLISH *pendize*, from FRENCH *pentiz*, from *apentis* attached building, from LATIN *appendicium*, from *appendere* hang.

**penult** LATIN *paenultima syllaba* last syllable but one, from *paene* almost + *ultimus* last.

**penumbra** LATIN *paene* almost + *umbra* shadow.

**penury** LATIN *penuria* want.

**peon** SPANISH foot soldier, from LATIN *pedo*, from *pes* foot.

**peony** OLD ENGLISH *peonie*, from LATIN *poenia*, from GREEK *palon* name given to Apollo, god of medicine, because of the flower's former medicinal use.

**people** FRENCH *pueple*, from LATIN *popularis*.

**pep** See **pepper**.

**peplos** GREEK.

**pepper** OLD ENGLISH *pipor*, from LATIN *piper*, from GREEK *peperi*.

**per** LATIN *per-* through, by.

**per-** LATIN *per-* through, by.

**per capita** LATIN *per capita* by heads.

**perambulate** LATIN *perambulare*, from *per-* through + *ambulare* walk.

**percale** FRENCH.

**perceive** FRENCH *percevoir*, from LATIN *percipere*, from *per-* through + *capere* take.

**percent** LATIN *per centum* for every hundred.

**perception** See **perceive**.

**perch**[1] (bird rest) from FRENCH *perche*, from LATIN *pertica* measuring rod.

**perch**[2] (fish) FRENCH *perche*, from LATIN *perca*, from GREEK *perke*.

**perchloride** See **per-** + **chlorine**.

**percolate** LATIN *percolare*, from *per-* through + *colare* strain.

**percussion** LATIN *percutere* strike.

**perdition** MIDDLE ENGLISH, from FRENCH *perdiciun*, from LATIN *perdere*, from *per-* thoroughly + *dare* give.

**peregrinate** LATIN *peregrinari*, from *peregrinus* traveling.

**peregrine** LATIN *peregrinus* traveling.

**peremptory** LATIN *peremptorius*, from *per-* thoroughly + *emere* take.

**perennial** LATIN *perennis*, from *per-* through + *annus* year.

**perfect** MIDDLE ENGLISH *parfit*, from FRENCH, from LATIN *perficere*, from *per-* completely + *facere* do, make.

**perfidy** FRENCH *perfidie*, from LATIN *perfidia*, from *per-* through + *fides* faith.

**perforate** LATIN *perforare*, from *per-* through + *forare* bore (make a hole by drilling).

**perforce** FRENCH *par force* by force, from LATIN *per-* by + **force**.

**perform** FRENCH *parformer* do, from *parfournir*, from LATIN *per-* through + *fournir* get done.

**perfume** FRENCH *parfumer*, from ITALIAN, from LATIN *per-* through + *funare* smoke.

**perfunctory** LATIN *perfunctorius*, from *per-* thoroughly + *fungi* perform.

**pergola** ITALIAN arbor, from LATIN *pergula* protecting cover.

**perhaps** See **per** + **hap**.

**peri** PERSIAN *pari* a beautiful female being descended from bad angels.

**peridot** FRENCH.

**perihelion** GREEK *peri* near + *helios* sun.

**peril** FRENCH danger, from LATIN *periculum*.

**period** FRENCH, from LATIN *periodus* sentence, from GREEK *periodos*.

**periodontal** GREEK *peri-* around + *odon* (*odontos*) tooth.

**periphery** FRENCH, from LATIN *peripheria*, from GREEK *periphereia*, from *peri-* around + *pherein* carry.

**periscope** GREEK *peri-* around + *skopein* examine.

**perish** FRENCH *perir* die, from LATIN *perire*.

**peristyle** FRENCH, from LATIN, from GREEK *peri-* around + *stylos* a column.

**peritoneum** GREEK *peritonaion* abdominal membrane, from *peri-* around + *teinein* stretch.

**periwinkle**[1] (plant) MIDDLE ENGLISH *parvink*, from OLD ENGLISH *perwince*, from LATIN *pervinca*, from *pervincire* entwine, bind, from *per-* thoroughly + *vincire* bind, fetter.

**periwinkle**[2] (snail) OLD ENGLISH *pinewincle*, from *pine* mussel, probably from LATIN *pina*, from GREEK *pine* + OLD ENGLISH *wincel* corner.

**perjure** FRENCH *parjurer*, from LATIN *perjurare*, from *per-* through + *jurare* swear.

**perk** FRENCH *perquer*, from LATIN *pertica* pole.

**permanent** FRENCH, from LATIN *permanere*, from *per-* through + *manere* remain.

**permeate** LATIN *permeare*, from *per-* through + *meare* glide.

**permit** LATIN *permittere*, from *per-* through + *mittere* send.

**permutate** LATIN *permutare*, from *per-* through + *mutare* change.

**pernicious** FRENCH *pernicieux*, from LATIN *pernicies*, from *per-* thoroughly + *necare* kill, from *nex* death.

**peronall** FRENCH *perron*, from LATIN *petra* stone.

**peroxide** See **per-** + **oxide**.

**perpendicular** FRENCH, from LATIN *perpendicularis* vertical, from *perpendere* balance carefully, from *per-* thoroughly + *pendere* hang.

**perpetrate** LATIN *perpetrare*, from *per-* thoroughly + *patrare* bring about.

**perpetual** FRENCH *perpetuel*, from LATIN *perpetuus* constant.

**perplex** FRENCH, from LATIN *perplexus* confused, from *per-* through + *plectere* twist.

**perquisite** LATIN *perquisitum*, from *perquirere*, from *per-* thoroughly + *quaerere* try to get.

**persecute** FRENCH *persecuter*, from LATIN *persequi*, from *per-* through + *sequi* follow.

**persevere** FRENCH *perseverer*, from LATIN *perseverare*, from *per-* thoroughly + *severus* severe.

**persiflage** FRENCH *persifler* make fun of.

**persimmon** NATIVE AMERICAN.

**persist** FRENCH, from LATIN *persistere*, from *per-* through + *sistere* make stand, from *stare* stand.

**person** FRENCH *persone* human being, from LATIN *persona*, from actor's mask.

**personate** LATIN *personatus*, from *persona* actor's mask.

**personnel** FRENCH.

**perspective** LATIN *perspicere*, from *per-* through + *specere* look.

**Perspex** LATIN *perspicere* look through, from *per* through + *specere* look (at).

**perspicacious** LATIN *perspicax*, from *perspicere*, from *per* through + *specere* look.

**perspicacity** FRENCH *perspicacité*, from LATIN *perspicacitas* discernment, from *perspicax* sharp-sighted, from *perspicere* look through.

**perspire** FRENCH, from LATIN *perspirare*, from *per-* through + *spirare* breathe.

**persuade** LATIN *persuadere*, from *per-* thoroughly + *suadere* urge.

**pert** FRENCH *aspert* able, from LATIN *expertus* experienced.

**pertain** FRENCH *partenir* belong, from LATIN *pertinere*, from *per-* thoroughly + *tenere* hold.

**pertinent** FRENCH, from LATIN *pertinere* belong.

**perturb** FRENCH, from LATIN *perturbare*, from *per-* thoroughly + *turbare* disturb.

**peruse** MIDDLE ENGLISH *perusen* use up, from LATIN *per-* thoroughly + MIDDLE ENGLISH *usen* use.

**pervade** LATIN *pervadere*, from *per-* through + *vadere* to go.

**perverse** FRENCH, from LATIN *pervertere* turn about.

**pervert** See **perverse**.

**peso** SPANISH, from LATIN *pendere* weigh.

**pessary** MIDDLE ENGLISH *pessarie*, from LATIN *pessarium*, from GREEK *pessarion*, from *pessos* oval stone.

**pessimism** FRENCH, from LATIN *pessimus* worst.

**pest** FRENCH *peste*, from LATIN *pestis* plague (deadly disease that spreads quickly).

**pester** FRENCH *empestrer* hobble (tie a horse's legs to keep it in one place), from LATIN *pastorum*, from *pastus* pasture.

**pestilent** LATIN *pestis* plague.

**pestle** FRENCH *pestel*, from LATIN *pistillum*, from *pinsere* pound.

**pet** SCOTTISH, of uncertain origin.

**petal** LATIN, from GREEK *petalos* spread out.

**peter** (dwindle) AMERICAN miners' slang, origin uncertain.

**petiole** LATIN *petiolus*, from *pes* foot.

**petit** FRENCH.

**petition** FRENCH *peticiun*, from LATIN *petitio*, from *petere* ask.

**petrel** possibly from LATIN *petrus*.

**petrify** FRENCH *pétrifier* turn into stone, from LATIN *petra* rock, from GREEK *petra* + LATIN *facere* do, make.

**petro-** GREEK *petra* a rock, or *petros* a stone.

**petroglyph** See petro- + GREEK *glyph*e carving.

**petroleum** LATIN rock oil, from *petra* rock, from GREEK *petra* + *oleum* oil.

**petticoat** FRENCH *petit* (small) + *cote* (coat), because it was originally a short coat for men worn under armor.

**pettifogger** MODERN ENGLISH *pettifactor*, from petty + factor.

**petty** FRENCH *petit* small.

**petulant** LATIN *petulans*, from *petere* attack.

**pew** FRENCH *pule*, from LATIN *podium* balcony, from GREEK *podion*, from *pous* foot.

**pewter** FRENCH *peutre* tin.

**phaeton** Greek myth of *Phaeton,* son of Helios (god of the sun) who tried to drive the chariot of the sun across the sky.

**phalanx** LATIN, from GREEK line of battle.

**phantasm** FRENCH, from LATIN, from GREEK *phantasma*, from *phantazein* show.

**phantom** FRENCH *fanto(s)me* ghost, from LATIN *phantasma*, from GREEK *phantazein* show.

**pharaoh** EGYPTIAN *pr-'o* great house.

**pharmacy** FRENCH *pharmacie*, from LATIN, from GREEK *pharmakon* drug.

**pharyngeal** See pharynx + -al.

**pharyngitis** See pharynx + -itis.

**pharynx** GREEK, from *pharyngos* windpipe, throat.

**phase** LATIN *phasis*, from GREEK *phainesthai* appear.

**pheasant** FRENCH *fesaunt*, from LATIN *phasiana*, from GREEK *phasianos*, from *Phasis* a river in eastern Asia where the bird was observed.

**phenomenon** LATIN *phaenomenon* appearance, from GREEK *phainesthai* appear.

**philander** GREEK *philos* loving + *andros*, from *aner* man.

**philanthropy** LATIN, from GREEK *philein* love + *anthropos* man.

**philharmonic** FRENCH *philharmonique* loving music, from ITALIAN, from GREEK *philos* loving + *harmonia* harmony.

**philodendron** GREEK, from *philodendros*, from *philo-* loving + *dendron* tree.

**philology** FRENCH, from LATIN, from GREEK *philologia* love of literature, from *philein* love + *logos* word, thought.

**philomath** GREEK *filos* friend, loving + *math* learn

**philopena** perhaps from GREEK *philo* a friend + LATIN *poena* penalty.

**philosophy** LATIN *philosphia* study of wisdom, from GREEK *philosophia*, from *philos* loving + *sophos* wise.

**philter** FRENCH *philtre*, from LATIN *philtrum*, from GREEK *philtron* love-charm, from *philein* love.

**phlegm** FRENCH *flemme*, from LATIN *phlegma* swelling, from GREEK *phlegein* burn.

**phloem** GERMAN, from GREEK *phloos* bark.

**phobia** LATIN, from GREEK *phobos* fear.

**phoenix** OLD ENGLISH *fenix*, from LATIN *phoenix*, from GREEK *phoinix*.

**phoneme** GREEK *phonema*, from *phonein*, from *phone* sound, voice.

**phonetic** LATIN *phoneticus*, from GREEK *phonetikos*, from *phone* sound.

**phonic** GREEK *phone* sound.

**phony** BRITISH *fawney* a ring said to be gold that wasn't, from IRISH *fainne* ring.

**phosphorus** LATIN *Phosphorus* morning star, from GREEK, from *phos* light + *pherein* carry.

**photo-** GREEK *phos* light.

**photography** See photo- + -graphy.

**photovoltaic** See photo- + volt + -ic.

**phrase** LATIN *phrasis*, from GREEK *phrasis* speech.

**phrenology** GREEK *phren* mind + *-logia*, from *logos* word.

**phycology** GREEK *phykos* seaweed +*-logia*, from *logos* word.

**phylactery** LATIN *phylacterium* charm, from GREEK *phylakterion*.

**phylum** LATIN, from GREEK *phylon* class.

**physic** MIDDLE ENGLISH art of healing, from FRENCH *fisike*, from LATIN *physica* study of nature, from GREEK *physis* nature, from *phyein* bring forth, produce, make grow.

**physical** MIDDLE ENGLISH, from LATIN *physicalis* of nature, natural, from *physica*. See **physic**.

**physiology** GREEK *physis* nature + *-logia*, from *logos* word.

**pianoforte** ITALIAN *piano* soft + *forte* loud, from LATIN *fortis* strong, because the piano can play loud and soft.

**piazza** ITALIAN, from LATIN *platea* courtyard, broad street, from GREEK *plateia* broad.

**pick** FRENCH *piquer* pierce.

**picket** FRENCH *piquet* pointed stake.

**pickle** DUTCH *pekel*.

**picnic** probably from FRENCH *pique* pick + *nique* a little bit.

**pictograph** LATIN *pictus* painted + GREEK *graphos*.

**picture** LATIN *pingere* paint.

**picturesque** FRENCH *pittoresque*, from ITALIAN *pittoresco* pictorial, from *pittore* painter, from LATIN *pictorem*.

**picul** MALAY *pikul* the heaviest load a man can carry on his back.

**piddle** MIDDLE ENGLISH *peddle*, work in a trifling way, origin uncertain.

**pie** OLD ENGLISH *pye*.

**piece** FRENCH, from LATIN *pecia* broken part.

**pied** MIDDLE ENGLISH *pie* magpie (bird), from LATIN *pica*, from *picus* woodpecker (in reference to the bird's black and white plumage).

**piedmont** ITALIAN *Piemonte* region in northern Italy, from *piede* foot + *monte* mountain.

**pier** LATIN *pera*, from *peira* stone.

**pierce** FRENCH *perc(i)er* make a hole, from LATIN *pertundere*, from *per-* through + *tundere* strike.

**piety** FRENCH *piete* good conduct, from LATIN *pietas*.

**pig** MIDDLE ENGLISH *pigge*.

**pigeon** FRENCH *pijon* young bird, from LATIN *pipio*, from *pipire* chirp.

**piggin** perhaps from MIDDLE ENGLISH *pig*, earthenware pot, origin uncertain.

**pigment** LATIN *pigmentum*, from *pingere* paint.

**pike**[1] (pick) OLD ENGLISH *pic* a pickax.

**pike**[2] (spear) FRENCH *pique*, from *pic* sharp point or spike.

**pike**[3] (highway) See **turnpike**.

**pike**[4] (fish) from **pike**[2], from its long, pointed jaw.

**pilau** PERSIAN *pilaw.*

**pile**[1] (heap) LATIN *pila* stone barrier.

**pile**[2] (cloth nap) FRENCH *pyle,* from LATIN *pilus* hair.

**pile**[3] (big stake) OLD ENGLISH *pil,* from LATIN *pilum* heavy javelin.

**pileate** LATIN *pileus* cap.

**pilfer** FRENCH *pelfrer,* from *pelfre* booty (things taken in a robbery).

**pilgrim** FRENCH *pelerin,* from LATIN *peregrinus* foreign.

**pillage** FRENCH *piller* rob.

**pillar** FRENCH *piler,* from LATIN *pilare,* from *pila.*

**pillion** LATIN *pellis* a skin.

**pillory** FRENCH *pilori.*

**pillow** OLD ENGLISH *pyle.*

**pilot** FRENCH *pilote,* from ITALIAN *pilota,* from GREEK *pedon* rudder for steering a boat.

**pimpernel** FRENCH, from LATIN *piper* pepper.

**pimple** OLD ENGLISH *pypel.*

**pin** OLD ENGLISH *pinn.*

**pinafore** MODERN ENGLISH *pin + afore* on the front (it was originally pinned to a dress front).

**pince-nez** FRENCH nose-pincher.

**pincers** FRENCH *pinecure,* from *pincier* pinch.

**pinch** FRENCH *pincier.*

**pindar** DUTCH *piendel,* from AFRICAN *mpinda* peanut.

**pindling** AMERICAN, perhaps from *piddling.* See **piddle.**

**pine**[1] (tree) OLD ENGLISH *pin,* from LATIN *pinus.*

**pine**[2] (want) OLD ENGLISH *pinian* torment, from LATIN *poena,* from GREEK *poine.*

**pineal** FRENCH *pinéal,* from LATIN *pinea* pine cone, from *pinus* pine tree.

**pinion**[1] (feather) FRENCH *pignon,* from LATIN *penna* wing.

**pinion**[2] (small gear) FRENCH *pignon,* from crenellation, battlement, from LATIN *pinna.*

**pink**[1] (color) MIDDLE ENGLISH *pink* plant name, possibly from DUTCH *pink* small.

**pink**[2] (cut) MIDDLE ENGLISH *pink* pierce, stab, make holes in.

**pinnace** FRENCH, from SPANISH, from LATIN *pinus* pine.

**pinnacle** MIDDLE ENGLISH *pinacle,* from FRENCH, from LATIN *pinnaculum,* from *pinna* feather.

**piñon** SPANISH, from LATIN *pinus* pine.

**pint** FRENCH, from LATIN *pinta,* probably originally a painted spot marking the level in a measure.

**pinto** SPANISH, from LATIN *pingere* paint.

**pioneer** FRENCH *pionnier,* from *peon* foot soldier, from LATIN *pedo,* from *pes* foot.

**pious** LATIN *pius.*

**pip** MIDDLE ENGLISH *pipin* seed of a fleshy fruit, from FRENCH *pepin.*

**pipe** OLD ENGLISH, from OLD NORSE *pipa,* from LATIN *pipare* chirp.

**piquant** See **pique.**

**pique** FRENCH *piquer* prick.

**piranha** PORTUGUESE *piranah,* from NATIVE AMERICAN *pira nya,* from *pira'ya* scissors.

**pirate** LATIN, from GREEK *peirates,* from *peiran* attack.

**pirogue** FRENCH, from SPANISH *piragua.*

**pirouette** FRENCH spinning top.

**Pisces** LATIN *piscis* fish.

**pistachio** ITALIAN *pistacchio,* from LATIN *pistacium* pistachio nut, from GREEK *pistakion,* from *pistake* pistachio tree, from PERSIAN *pista.*

**pistil** FRENCH, from LATIN *pistillum.*

**pistol** FRENCH *pistole* short firearm, of uncertain origin.

**piston** FRENCH, from ITALIAN *pistare* pound, from LATIN *pinsere.*

**pit** OLD ENGLISH *pytt,* from LATIN *puteus* a well.

**pita** Modern GREEK *petta* bread.

**pitch**[1] (throw) MIDDLE ENGLISH *picchen.*

**pitch**[2] (tar) OLD ENGLISH *pic,* from LATIN *pix.*

**pith** OLD ENGLISH *pitha* necessary part.

**piton** FRENCH a spike.

**pittance** FRENCH *pitance* allowance of food, from LATIN *pietas* religious works and duties.

**pituitary** LATIN *pituitarius* mucous, from *pituita* phlegm, mucus.

**pity** FRENCH *pite,* from LATIN *pietas* good conduct, kindness.

**pivot** FRENCH hinge.

**pizza** ITALIAN pie.

**placard** FRENCH poster, from *plaquer* stick on, from DUTCH *placken* a piece.

**placate** LATIN *placare.*

**place** MIDDLE ENGLISH, from OLD ENGLISH place, open space, from LATIN *platea* wide street, from GREEK *plateia hodos* flat, level road.

**placebo** LATIN I shall please.

**placenta** LATIN a cake, from GREEK *plax* a flat object.

**placid** LATIN *placidus.*

**placket**[1] (plan, map) probably from FRENCH *plaquette* tablet, from *plaque* thin plate.

**placket**[2] (clothing) probably from MIDDLE ENGLISH *placard,* armor breastplate, perhaps related to **pocket.**

**plagiarism** LATIN *plagiarius* kidnapper.

**plague** FRENCH, from LATIN *plaga,* from GREEK *plege* bad fortune.

**plaid** SCOTTISH *plaide* blanket.

**plain** FRENCH flat, from LATIN *planus.*

**plaintiff** FRENCH *plaintif.* See **plaintive.**

**plaintive** FRENCH *plaintif* complaining, from LATIN *planctus.*

**plait** FRENCH *pleit,* from LATIN *plicare* fold.

**plan** FRENCH ground plan, from LATIN *planus* flat.

**planchette** FRENCH small board, from *planche* plank.

**plane** LATIN *planum* level surface.

**planet** MIDDLE ENGLISH, from FRENCH *planete,* from LATIN *planeta,* from GREEK *planetes* wanderer.

**planetarium** See **planet** + LATIN *-arium* a place for.

**plank** FRENCH *planke* board, from LATIN *planca.*

**plankton** GERMAN, from GREEK *planktos* wandering, from *plazesthai* wander.

**plant** OLD ENGLISH *plante,* from LATIN *planta.*

**plantain** SPANISH *pla(n)tano* plane tree, from LATIN *platanus* plane.

**plantation** LATIN *plantare* plant.

PLAQUE

**plaque** FRENCH, from DUTCH *plake* disk (something thin, flat and round).

**plash** OLD ENGLISH *plæsc* pool of water, puddle.

**plasma** LATIN image, from GREEK. See **plastic**.

**plaster** OLD ENGLISH, from LATIN *implastrum*, from GREEK *emplastron*, from *emplassein* cover with something sticky.

**plastic** LATIN *plasticus* forming, from GREEK *plastikos*, from *plassein* form.

**plasticine** See **plastic** + -**ine**[1].

**plastron** FRENCH, from ITALIAN *piastra* thin plate of metal.

**plate** FRENCH *plat* flat, from GREEK *platys*.

**plateau** FRENCH *plat* flat. See **plate**.

**platen** MIDDLE ENGLISH *plateine*, from FRENCH *platine* metal plate, from *plat* flat.

**platform** FRENCH *plateforme*, from *plat* flat + *forme* form.

**platinum** SPANISH *plata* silver, from FRENCH *plate* something flat. See **plate**.

**platitude** FRENCH *plat* flat. See **plate**.

**Platonic** MIDDLE ENGLISH, from LATIN *Platonicus*, from GREEK *Platonikos*, from *Platon* Plato (429-347 B.C.), Greek philosopher.

**platoon** FRENCH *peloton* a ball, group, from *pelote* small ball, from LATIN *pila* ball.

**platter** FRENCH *plater* dish, from *plat* flat. See **plate**.

**platypus** LATIN, from GREEK *platypous* flat-footed, from *platys* broad, flat + *pous* foot.

**plaudit** LATIN *plaudere* applaud.

**plausible** LATIN *plausibilis* deserving applause, from *plaudere* applaud.

**play** OLD ENGLISH *pleg(i)an*.

**plaza** SPANISH, town square or gathering place, from LATIN *platea*, wide street.

**plea** FRENCH *plaid* discussion, from LATIN *placitum* opinion, from *placere* be pleasing.

**pleasant** FRENCH *plaisir* be agreeable. See **please**.

**please** FRENCH *plaisir* be agreeable, from LATIN *placere* be pleasing.

**plebian** LATIN *plebs* common people.

**plebiscite** FRENCH *plébiscite*, from LATIN *plebiscitum* a decree or resolution of the people, from *plebis* the common people + *scitum* decree, from *scire* know.

**plectrum** LATIN, from GREEK *plektron* thing to strike with, from *plek-*, from *plessein* strike.

**pledge** MIDDLE ENGLISH *plegge* bail, a guarantee, from FRENCH *plege*, from Latin *plebere*, from *pleo* fulfill.

**pledget** origin uncertain, possibly from MIDDLE ENGLISH *plug*, from DUTCH *plagge* patch of cloth.

**plenitude** FRENCH, from LATIN *plenus* full.

**plenty** FRENCH *plente*, from LATIN *plentas*, from *plenus* full.

**plenum** LATIN *plenum spatium* full space, from *plenus* complete, full.

**plethora** LATIN, from GREEK *plethos* fullness.

**plew** FRENCH *poil* hair.

**pliable** FRENCH *plier* bend, from LATIN *plicare* fold.

**plight** FRENCH *pleit* a fold, condition.

**plinth** FRENCH *plinthe*, from LATIN *plinthus*, from GREEK *plinthos* brick, squared stone.

**plod** imitative.

**plop** imitative.

**plot** OLD ENGLISH piece of ground.

234

**plouter** Scottish, origin uncertain.

**plover** French *plover,* from *plovier,* from Latin *plovarius,* from *pluvia* rain.

**plow** Middle English *ploh,* from Old English *plog,* from Old Norse *plogr.*

**pluck** Old English *pluccian* pull off.

**plug** Dutch *plugge* wooden peg.

**plum** Old English *plume.*

**plumage** French, from Latin *pluma* feather.

**plumb** French *plomb,* from Latin *plumbum* lead (heavy, soft metal).

**plume** French, from Latin *pluma* feather.

**plummet** French *plommet.* See **plumb.**

**plump**[1] (rounded) Dutch *plomp* not pointed.

**plump**[2] (drop) imitative.

**plunder** German baggage.

**plunge** French *plongier* sink, from Latin *plumbum.* See **plumb.**

**plunk** imitative.

**plural** Latin *pluralis,* from *plus* more.

**plus** Latin *plus* more.

**plush** French *peluche,* from Latin *pilus* hair.

**plutocracy** Greek *ploutokratia,* from *ploutos* wealth + *-kratia* rule, from *kratos* rule, power.

**plutonic** Greek *Pluto* Greek god of the underworld.

**ply** See **apply.**

**pneumatic** Latin, from Greek *pneuma* breath.

**pneumonia** Latin, from Greek *pneumon* lung, from *pnein* breathe.

**poach**[1] (cook egg) French *pochier* put in a bag, from *poche* pocket.

**poach**[2] (steal) French *pocher,* from *pochier* walk on.

**pocket** French *pokete* little bag, from *poke* bag.

**pod** Middle English *podware, codware,* from Old English *cod* husk of seeded plants.

**podiatry** Greek *pous* foot + *iatreia* art of healing.

**podium** Latin, from Greek *podion,* from *pous* foot.

**poem** French, from Latin *poema,* from Greek *poiema,* from *poiein* make.

**poesimeter** apparently an invented word.

**pogrom** Russian destruction.

**poignant** French *poindre* prick, from Latin *pungere.*

**poinsettia** Joel R. *Poinsett* U.S. ambassador to Mexico, who brought the plant to the attention of botanists.

**point** French mark, from Latin *pungere* prick.

**poise** French *poiser* weigh, from Latin *pensare.*

**poison** French, from Latin *potio.*

**poke**[1] (action) Dutch *poken.*

**poke**[2] (sack) French *poke,* from *poche* pocket, purse.

**poke**[3] (tobacco) Native American *puck* smoke.

**poker**[1] (card game) possibly from German *poche,* from *pochen* brag.

**poker**[2] (metal rod) See **poke**[1].

**Polaris** Latin *stella polaris* pole star.

**pole**[1] (long stick) Old English *pal* stake (stick for putting in the ground), from Latin *pallus.*

**pole**[2] (earth axis) Latin *polus* end of an axis, from Greek *polos* axis.

**polemic** French, from Greek *polemos* war.

**police** FRENCH, from LATIN *politia* government, the state, from GREEK *politeia*, from *polis* city.

**policy** FRENCH *policie* government, from LATIN *politia*. See **police**.

**polio** LATIN *poliomyelitis*, from GREEK *polios* gray + *myelos* marrow (the soft tissue inside bones).

**polish** FRENCH *polir* make smooth, from LATIN *polire*.

**polite** LATIN *polire* make smooth.

**politic** FRENCH *politique* political, from LATIN *politicus* state, from GREEK *politikos*, from *polis* city.

**polka** SLAVIC *Polka*, name for the dance, literal meaning "Polish woman."

**poll** MIDDLE ENGLISH *pol(le)* head, from the idea of counting heads, from DUTCH.

**pollard** See **poll** + *-ard* in reference to the coin having a head on it.

**pollen** LATIN dust.

**polliwog** MIDDLE ENGLISH *polwygle*, from *pol* head + *wiglen* wiggle.

**pollock** SCOTTISH *podlok*.

**pollute** LATIN *polluere*.

**polo** CHINESE *pulu* ball.

**polonaise** FRENCH *danse polonais* a Polish dance, from *Pologne* Poland, from LATIN Polonia.

**polonium** LATIN *Polonia* Poland, by the Polish scientist Marie Curie who co-discovered it.

**poltergeist** GERMAN *poltern* make a noise + *Geist* ghost.

**poltroon** FRENCH *poultron* rascal, coward, from ITALIAN *poltrone* lazy fellow, coward.

**poly-** GREEK *polys* much, many.

**polychrome** FRENCH of many colors, from GREEK *polys* many + *chroma* color.

**polyethylene** See poly- + GREEK *aithein* burn + LATIN *-enus*, from GREEK *-enos*.

**polygamy** GREEK *polygamia*, from *polys* many + *gamos* marriage.

**polymer** GREEK *polymeres*, from *polys* many + *meros* part.

**polyp** FRENCH *polype*, from LATIN *polypus* octopus, from GREEK *polypous* many-footed, from *polys* many + *pous* foot.

**polyphony** GREEK *polyphonia*, from *polys* many + *phone* sound.

**pomade** FRENCH, from ITALIAN *pomata*, from LATIN *pomum* fruit.

**pome** FRENCH *pome* apple.

**pomegranate** See pome + FRENCH *granade*, from LATIN *granatum* having seeds.

**pomelé** See **pomely**.

**pomelo** See **pome**.

**pomely** FRENCH *pomelé* marked with round spots, from *pomel* little apple.

**pommel** FRENCH *pomel* rounded part on the handle of a sword, from LATIN *pomum* apple.

**pomp** LATIN *pompa*, from GREEK *pompe*.

**pompadour** Madame *Pompadour* (1721–1764), a friend of one of the kings of France, she made the style popular.

**pompous** LATIN *pomposus*, from *pompa*. See **pomp**.

**poncho** SPANISH *pontho* woolen cloth.

**pond** MIDDLE ENGLISH, from OLD ENGLISH *pund*.

**ponder** FRENCH, from LATIN *ponderare* weigh, from *pondus* a weight.

**ponderous** LATIN *ponderosus* heavy, from *pondus* a weight.

**pone** NATIVE AMERICAN.

**pontiff** FRENCH *pontif* high priest in ancient Rome, from LATIN *pontifex*, from *pons* bridge + *facere* do, make.

**pontificate** LATIN *pontifex*, from *pons* bridge + *facere* do, make.

**pontoon** FRENCH *ponton* low flat boat, from LATIN *pons* bridge.

**pony** FRENCH *poulenet*, from LATIN *pullus* young animal.

**poodle** GERMAN *Pudel*, from *pudeln* splash in water. The dogs were originally used to find and bring back water birds shot by hunters.

**pooka** IRISH *puca*, from OLD ENGLISH *puki*.

**pool**[1] (water) OLD ENGLISH *pol* small body of water.

**pool**[2] (game) FRENCH *poule* stake (money or something that can be won as part of a bet), hen (possible stake in early times), from LATIN *pullus* young bird.

**poop deck** FRENCH, from LATIN *puppis*.

**poor** FRENCH *povre*, from LATIN *pauper*.

**pop** imitative.

**pope** OLD ENGLISH *papa* father, from GREEK *papas*.

**popinjay** FRENCH *papagal*, from ARABIC *babagha* parrot.

**poplar** FRENCH *poplier*, from LATIN *popularius*.

**poppy** OLD ENGLISH *popæg*, from LATIN *papaver*.

**populace** FRENCH, from LATIN *populus* the people.

**popular** LATIN *populus* the people.

**population** LATIN *populare* live in.

**porcelain** FRENCH *porcelaine* china, from ITALIAN *porcellana*, from LATIN *porcus* pig, because the china was thought to look a bit like a pig's back.

**porch** FRENCH, from LATIN *porticus*, from *porta* a gate.

**porcupine** FRENCH *porc espin* thorny pig, from LATIN *porcus* pig + *spina* thorn.

**pore**[1] (small opening) FRENCH, from LATIN *porus*, from GREEK *poros*.

**pore**[2] (read over) MIDDLE ENGLISH *pouren*.

**porgy** AMERICAN, probably from earlier *pargo*, from SPANISH *pargo*, from LATIN *phagrum*, from GREEK *phagros* sea bream.

**pork** FRENCH *porc* pig, from LATIN *porcus*.

**porpoise** FRENCH *porpeis*, from LATIN *porcus* pig + *piscis* fish.

**porridge** MIDDLE ENGLISH *porrey*, from LATIN *porrata* vegetable soup, from *porrum* vegetable.

**porringer** FRENCH *potager*, from *potage*, from *pot* pot.

**port** OLD ENGLISH, from LATIN *portus* harbor.

**portable** LATIN *portabilis*, from *portare* carry.

**portage** FRENCH *potager*, from *potage*, from *pot* pot.

**portal** FRENCH, from LATIN *portale* like a gate, from *porta* door, gate.

**portcullis** FRENCH *porte colice* sliding gate, from LATIN *porta* gate + *colare* filter (something with spaces in it for things to go through).

**portend** LATIN *portendere* predict.

**portent** LATIN *portentum* sign.

**porter**[1] (baggage carrier) FRENCH *porteur* bearer, from LATIN *portator*, from *portare* carry.

**porter**[2] (doorkeeper) FRENCH *portier* gatekeeper, from LATIN *portarius* doorkeeper, from *porta* gate, door.

**portfolio** ITALIAN *portafoglio* wallet, from LATIN *portare* carry + *folium* sheet of paper.

**portico** ITALIAN, from LATIN *porticus*. See **porch**.

**portion** FRENCH share, from LATIN *portio*.

**portmanteau** FRENCH suitcase, cloak carrier (person who carried the king's cloak), from *porter* carry + *manteau* cloak.

**portrait** FRENCH *portraire* draw. See **portray**.

**portray** FRENCH *portraire*, from LATIN *protrahere*, from *pro-* forth + *trahere* draw.

**pose**[1] (position) FRENCH *poser*, from LATIN *pausare* halt.

**pose**[2] (confuse) FRENCH *aposer* set beside, from LATIN *apponer* place to.

**posh** probably from BRITISH *posh* dandy (a man who is very particular about his clothes).

**position** FRENCH, from LATIN *positio* placing.

**positive** FRENCH, from LATIN *positivus* settled by agreement, from *ponere* place.

**posse** LATIN from *posse comitatus*, literally "the power of the country," in medieval England the body of men a sheriff could call into service to help carry out the law, from *posse* have power.

**possess** FRENCH, from LATIN *possidere*.

**posset** MIDDLE ENGLISH *possot*, origin uncertain.

**possible** LATIN *possibilis*, from *posse* be able.

**post-** LATIN after.

**post**[1] (wood) OLD ENGLISH *post*, from LATIN *postis*.

**post**[2] (soldier's place of duty) FRENCH *poste* station, from ITALIAN *posto*, from LATIN *ponere* place.

**post**[3] (mail) FRENCH *poste*, from ITALIAN *ponere* place, from the early custom of mail being moved by carriers from one relay place to another.

**posterior** LATIN *posterus* following, from *post* after.

**posterity** MIDDLE ENGLISH *posterite*, from LATIN *posterus* following, from *post* after.

**postern** FRENCH *posterne* back door to a fort, from LATIN *posterus* coming after.

**posthumous** LATIN *postumus* lastborn (after the death of the father), from *post-* after + *humare* bury.

**postilion** FRENCH *postillon*, from ITALIAN *postiglione*, from *posta* mail + LATIN *-ilio*.

**post-mortem** LATIN after death.

**postpone** LATIN *postponere*, from *post-* after + *ponere* put.

**postscript** LATIN *postscribere*, from *post-* after + *scribere* write.

**postulate** LATIN *postulare* demand.

**posture** FRENCH situation, from ITALIAN *postura*, from LATIN *positura* position, from *ponere* put.

**pot** OLD ENGLISH *pott* deep container.

**potable** LATIN *potabilis*, from *potare* drink.

**potash** DUTCH *pot* pot + *asch* ash.

**potassium** LATIN *potassa* potash.

**potent** LATIN *potentis*, from *posse* be able, from *potis* able.

**potentate** LATIN *potentatus*, from *potentem* powerful.

**potential** MIDDLE ENGLISH *potenciall*, from LATIN *potentia*. See **potent**.

**pother** Middle English *pudder*, origin unknown.

**potpourri** French *pot pourri* stew, translation from Spanish *olla podrida*, from Latin *olla* pot + *putridus* rotten, probably from food being cooked until it looked "rotten."

**potsy** origin uncertain, possibly from **pot**.

**pottage** French *potage*, from *pot* pot.

**pottery** French *poterie*, from *potier* potter, from Latin *potaria* pottery.

**pouch** French *po(u)che* bag.

**poultice** Latin *pultes* thick, soft food, from *puls*.

**poultry** French *poulet* young chicken, from Latin *pullus* young animal.

**pounce** Middle English *ponson* sharp tool, from French *poinçon*, from Latin *punctio* pierce.

**pound**[1] (beat) Old English *punian* beat.

**pound**[2] (money) Old English *pund* English money, from Latin *pondo* by weight.

**pound**[3] (stray animals) Old English *pund* place fenced in.

**pour** Middle English *pouren*.

**pout** Middle English *pouten*.

**poverty** French *poverte*, from Latin *pauper* poor.

**powder** French *poudre*, from Latin *pulvis* dust.

**power** French *pöer* ability to act, from Latin *potis* able.

**power net** See **power** + **network**.

**powerful** See **power** + **-ful**.

**powwow** Native American shaman, medicine man, from a word meaning to dream.

**practical** Latin *practicus*. See **practice**.

**practice** French *pratiquer*, from Latin, from Greek *practikos* practical, from *prassein* do.

**pragmatic** Latin *pragmaticus* skilled in business, from Greek *pragmatikos*, from *pragma* business, from *prassein* do.

**prairie** French meadow, from Latin *pratum*.

**praise** French *preisier* value, from Latin *pretium* worth.

**prance** Middle English, originally of horses, origin uncertain, perhaps related to Middle English *pranken* show off, from Dutch *pronken* strut, parade.

**prank** Middle English, origin uncertain.

**prate** Dutch *praten* chatter.

**pratfall** Middle English *prat* buttocks + Old English *feallan* drop.

**prattle** German *prateien*.

**pray** French *prier*, from Latin *precari* call upon, from *prex* prayer.

**pre-** Latin *prae-* before.

**preach** French *prechier*, from Latin *praedicare*, from *prae-* before + *dicare* say out loud.

**preamble** French *preambule*, from Latin *praembulus* walking in front, from *prae-* before + *ambulare* walk.

**precarious** Latin *precarius* doubtful, from *prex* prayer.

**precaution** French, from Latin *praecautio*, from *praecavere*, from *prae-* before + *cavere* take care.

**precede** French, from Latin *praecedere*, from *prae-* before + *cedere* go.

**precedent** Latin *praecedere* go before. See **precede**.

**precept** Latin *praecipere* teach, from *prae-* before + *capere* take.

239

**precinct** LATIN *praecinctum* boundary, from *praecingere,* from *prae-* before + *cingere* be around.

**precious** FRENCH *precios,* from LATIN *pretiosus,* from *pretium* a price.

**precipice** FRENCH, from LATIN *praeceps,* from *prae-* before + *caput* a head.

**precipitance** See **precipitate.**

**precipitate** LATIN *praecipitare* throw down, from *praeceps,* from *prae-* before + *caput* a head.

**précis** FRENCH, from LATIN *praecidere.* See **precise.**

**precise** FRENCH *precis,* from LATIN *praecidere* cut off, from *prae-* before + *caedere* cut.

**preclude** LATIN *praecludere,* from *prae-* before + *claudere* close.

**precocious** LATIN *praecox* ripen early, from *prae-* before + *coquere* cook, ripen.

**precursor** LATIN *praecurrere* run ahead.

**predatory** LATIN *praedari* a prey.

**predecessor** FRENCH, from LATIN *prae-* before + *decessor* officer who is retiring, from *decedere,* from *de-* from + *cedere* go.

**predicament** LATIN *praedicamentum,* from *praedicare* say out loud. See **preach.**

**predicate** LATIN *praedicare* say out loud. See preach.

**predict** LATIN *praedicere,* from *prae-* before + *dicere* tell.

**preemption** LATIN *preemere,* from *prae-* before + *emere* buy.

**preen** OLD ENGLISH *proinen.*

**preface** FRENCH introduction to a book, from LATIN *praefatio,* from *prae-* before + *fari* speak.

**prefect** LATIN *praefectus* commander, from *prae-* before + *facere* do, make.

**prefer** FRENCH, from LATIN *praeferre,* from *prae-* before + *ferre* bring.

**prefix** LATIN *praefixum,* from *praefigere* fix in front, from *prae-* before + *figere* fix.

**pregnant** LATIN *praegnans,* from *prae-* before + *gnasci* be born.

**prejudice** FRENCH, from LATIN *praejudicium,* from *prae-* before + *judicium* judgment.

**preliminary** FRENCH *préliminaire,* from LATIN *prae-* before + *limen* threshold (piece of wood underneath the door).

**prelude** FRENCH introduction, from *prae-* before + *ludere* play.

**premier** FRENCH, from LATIN *primarius* chief, from *primus* first.

**premise** LATIN *praemissa,* from *praemittere,* from *prae-* before + *mittere* send.

**premium** LATIN *prae-* before + *emere* take.

**premonition** LATIN *praemonitio* warn in advance, from *praemonere,* from *prae-* before + *monere* warn.

**preordain** See pre- + ordain.

**prepare** LATIN *praeparare,* from *prae-* before + *parare* prepare.

**preposition** LATIN *praepositio,* from *prae-* before + *ponere* place.

**preposterous** LATIN *praeposterus,* from *prae-* before + *posterus* coming after.

**prerogative** LATIN *praerogativus,* from *prae-* before + *rogare* ask.

**presage** LATIN *praesagium,* from *prae-* before + *sagire* become aware of.

**prescribe** LATIN *praescribere,* from *prae-* before + *scribere* write.

**present** FRENCH *presence,* from LATIN *praesentia,* from *prae-* before + *esse* be.

**preserve** MIDDLE ENGLISH keep safe, from FRENCH *preserver*, from LATIN *praeservare* observe beforehand, from *prae* before + *servare* observe, guard.

**preside** LATIN *praesidere*, from *prae-* before + *sedere* sit.

**president** LATIN *praesidens* ruler, from *praesidere*. See **preside**.

**press** FRENCH *presser* crush, from LATIN *premere* press.

**pressure** FRENCH, from LATIN *pressura*, from *premere* press.

**prestige** LATIN *praestigium* trick.

**presume** LATIN *praesumere*, from *prae-* before + *sumere* take.

**pretend** LATIN *praetendere*, from *prae-* before + *tendere* stretch.

**pretense** FRENCH, from LATIN *praetendere*. See **pretend**.

**pretentious** FRENCH *prétentieux*, from LATIN *praetendere*. See **pretend**.

**pretext** LATIN *praetexere* pretend. See **pretend**.

**pretty** OLD ENGLISH *prætt* a trick.

**pretzel** GERMAN *brizilla*.

**prevail** LATIN *praevalere* have greater power, from *prae-* before + *valere* be strong.

**prevalent** LATIN *praevalere*. See **prevail**.

**prevent** LATIN *praevenire*, from *prae-* before + *venire* come.

**previous** LATIN *praevius*, from *prae-* before + *via* a way.

**prey** FRENCH *preie*, from LATIN *praeda* take by force.

**price** FRENCH *pris* value, from LATIN *pretium* value.

**prick** OLD ENGLISH *prica* point.

**pride** OLD ENGLISH *pryte*.

**priest** OLD ENGLISH *preost*, from GREEK *presbyteros*, from *presbys* old, from respect to the elders.

**prig** MIDDLE ENGLISH *prigger* thief, origin uncertain.

**prim** FRENCH, from LATIN *primus* first.

**prima donna** LATIN first lady.

**Primacord** See **primer** + **cord**.

**primal** LATIN *primalis*, from *primus* first.

**primary** LATIN *primarius*, from *primus* first.

**prime** FRENCH, from LATIN *primus* first.

**primer** LATIN *primarius liber* basic book, from *primarius* first in order.

**primeval** LATIN *primaevus*, from *primus* first + *aevum* an age + FRENCH, from LATIN *alis*.

**primitive** FRENCH *primitif*, from LATIN *primitivus* earliest of that kind, from *primus* first.

**primogeniture** LATIN *primus* first + *geniture* produce.

**prince** FRENCH, from LATIN *princeps* leader, from *primus* first + *capere* take.

**principal** FRENCH, from LATIN *principalis* chief, from *princeps*. See **prince**.

**principle** FRENCH, from LATIN *principium*, from *princeps*. See **prince**.

**prink** apparently a variation of **prank**.

**print** FRENCH *preinte* stamp, from *preindre*, from LATIN *premere* bear down on.

**prior** LATIN sooner.

**prism** LATIN *prisma*, from GREEK something sawed, from *priein* saw.

**prison** FRENCH, from LATIN *prensio*, from *prehendere* take.

**prissy** blend of **prim** and **sissy**.

**pristine** Latin *pristinus* former.

**prithee** obsolete form of "I pray thee".

**private** Latin *privatus* belonging to the person and not the state.

**privet**[1] (plant) Middle English *primet*, *primprint*, origin unknown.

**privet**[2] (surgical tool) French *esprouvette*, from *esprouver* try, search out.

**privilege** Latin *privilegium* law for or against a person, from *privus* one's own + *lex* law.

**prize**[1] (reward) Middle English *prise*. See **price**.

**prize**[2] (pry loose) Middle English *prise*, from French *prise* take hold, grasp.

**pro** Latin in favor of.

**pro-** Latin in favor of, for, before, instead of, forward.

**probable** French, from Latin *probare* prove.

**probang** Modern English *provang*, the name given by the inventor, later changed to *probang* to be like the word **probe**.

**probate** Latin *probare*. See **probe**.

**probe** Latin *proba* proof, from *probare* test, from *probus* proper.

**problem** French *probleme*, from Latin *problema*, from Greek *pro-* forward + *ballein* throw.

**proboscis** Latin *proboscis*, from Greek *proboskis* elephant's trunk, from *pro* forward + *boskein* feed, from *boskesthai* graze, be fed.

**proceed** Latin *procedure*, from *pro-* forward + *cedere* go.

**process** French *proces*, from Latin *procedere*. See **proceed**.

**proclaim** French, from Latin *proclamare*, from *pro-* before + *clamare* cry out.

**procrastinate** Latin *procrastinare*, from *pro-* forward + *cras* tomorrow.

**procreate** Latin *procreare*, from *pro-* before + *creare* create.

**proctor** Middle English *procuratour*, from Latin *procurare*, from *pro-* for + *curare* attend to, from *cura* a care.

**procure** French, from Latin *procurare*, from *pro-* for + *curare* attend to, from *cura* a care.

**prod** Middle English poke with a stick, possibly from *brod*, from *brodden* goad, from Old Norse *broddr* shaft, spike.

**prodigal** French, from Latin *prodigalis* wasteful, from *prodigus*, from *pro-* before + *agere* drive.

**prodigious** See **prodigy**.

**prodigy** Latin *prodigium* omen.

**produce** Latin *producere*, from *pro-* forward + *ducere* lead.

**product** Latin *producere*. See **produce**.

**profane** French, from Latin *profanus* not holy, from *pro-* before + *fanum* temple (place to pray).

**profess** Latin *profiteri*, from *pro-* before + *fateri* say openly.

**proficient** Latin *proficere*, from *pro-* forward + *facere* do, make.

**profile** Italian *profilo* side view, from Latin *pro-* before + *filum* thread (like a thin line).

**profit** French advantage, from Latin *profectus*, from *pro-* forward + *facere* do, make.

**profligate** Latin *profligare*, from *pro-* forward + *fligere* drive.

**profound** French *profond* deep, from Latin *profundus*, from *pro-* forward + *fundus* bottom.

242

**profuse** LATIN *profundere*, from *pro-* forth + *fundere* pour.

**prog**[1] (knife) MODERN ENGLISH, origin uncertain, but see **prod**.

**prog**[2] (food) BRITISH, origin unknown (that which is got by progging). See **prog**[3].

**prog**[3] (forage) BRITTISH, origin unknown (to poke about or search for food, etc.). See **prog**[1].

**progenitor** FRENCH *progeniteur*, from LATIN *progenitor*, from *pro-* forth + *gignere* produce.

**prognosis** LATIN, from GREEK *pro-* before + *gignoskein* know.

**program** LATIN *programma*, from GREEK public notice, from *pro-* before + *graphein* write.

**progress** LATIN *progressus*, from *pro-* before + *gradi* step.

**prohibit** LATIN *prohibere* prevent, from *pro-* before + *habere* have.

**project** LATIN *proicere*, from *pro-* before + *jacere* throw.

**prokaryote** FRENCH *procaryote*, from GREEK, from *pro-* before + *karyotos* having nuts, from *karyon* nut.

**proletariat** FRENCH *prolétariat*, from LATIN *proletarius* citizen of the lowest class, from *proles* offspring, progeny.

**proliferate** See **profile**.

**prolific** LATIN *prolifer*, from *proles* children + *ferre* bring.

**prolong** FRENCH, from LATIN *pro-* forth + *longus* long.

**promenade** FRENCH *promener* walk, from LATIN *prominare*, from *pro-* forward + *minare* herd.

**prominent** LATIN *prominere* project, from *pro-* forward + *minere* cause to stick out.

**promise** LATIN *promissum*, from *pro-* before + *mittere* send.

**promontory** LATIN *promonturium*, probably from *prominere* project (throw forward).

**promote** LATIN *promovere*, from *pro-* before + *movere* move.

**prompt** FRENCH, from LATIN *promere*, from *pro-* forth + *emere* take.

**promulgate** LATIN *promulgare*, from *pro-* before + *vulgus* the people.

**prone** MIDDLE ENGLISH, from LATIN *pronus* bent forward, inclined to.

**prong** MIDDLE ENGLISH, from LATIN *pronga* prong, pointed tool.

**pronoun** FRENCH, from LATIN *pronomine* instead of a noun.

**pronounce** FRENCH *prononcier*, from LATIN *pronuntiare* announce, from *nuntius* messenger.

**proof** FRENCH *prueve*, from LATIN *proba*, from *probare* test.

**prop** DUTCH *proppe* a support.

**propaganda** LATIN *propaganda fide prospagate* "tell the people about the faith," from early religious efforts to get more people to come to church.

**propel** LATIN *propellere* push forward, from *pro-* forward + *pellere* drive.

**propensity** LATIN *propendere* hang forward, from *pro-* forward + *pendere* hang.

**proper** FRENCH *propre*, from LATIN *proprius* one's own.

**property** FRENCH *propriete*, from LATIN *proprietas* owner.

**prophecy** FRENCH *profecie*, from LATIN, from GREEK *prophetes*. See **prophet**.

**prophet** LATIN *propheta*, from GREEK *prophetes*, from *pro-* before + *phanai* speak.

**prophylactic** GREEK *prophylaktikos* precautionary, from *prophylassein* keep guard before, from *pro-* before + *phylassein* guard.

**propitiate** LATIN *propitius*, from *pro-* before + *petere* seek.

**propitious** FRENCH *propicius*, from LATIN *propitius*, from *pro-* before + *petere* seek.

**proponent** LATIN *proponere*, from *pro-* before + *ponere* place.

**proportion** FRENCH, from LATIN *proportone*, from *pro-* for + *portio* a part.

**propose** FRENCH *proposer* put forth, from LATIN *proponere*. See **proponent**.

**proprietary** LATIN *proprietas*. See **property**.

**propriety** LATIN *proprietas*. See **property**.

**propulsion** LATIN *propellere*. See **propel**.

**prosaic** LATIN *prosaicus*, from *prosa*. See **prose**.

**proscenium** LATIN *proscaenium*, from GREEK *proskenion* in front of the scenery, from *pro* in front + *skene* stage, tent.

**proscribe** LATIN *proscribere* publish in writing, from *pro-* before + *scribere* write.

**prose** FRENCH, from LATIN *prosaoratio* direct speech.

**prosecute** LATIN *prosequi* go after, from *pro-* before + *sequi* follow.

**prospect** LATIN *prospectus* view, from *pro-* before + *specere* look.

**prosper** LATIN *prosperare* make happy.

**prosthesis** LATIN, from GREEK *pros* to + *tithenai* place.

**prostrate** LATIN *prosternere*, from *pro-* before + *sternere* stretch out.

**protect** LATIN *protegere*, from *pro-* before + *tegere* cover.

**protégé** FRENCH *protéger*, from LATIN. See **protect**.

**protein** GERMAN, from FRENCH, from GREEK *proteios* primary, from *protos* first.

**protest** FRENCH *protester* say in public, from LATIN *protestari*, from *pro-* before + *testari*, from *testis* a witness.

**protocol** FRENCH *protocole* first writing of an important paper, from LATIN, from GREEK *protokollon*, from *protos* first + *kolla* glue, from an early practice of gluing the first sheet (which stated the date and the author's name) to an important piece of writing.

**protoplasm** GERMAN *Protoplasma*, from GREEK *proto-* first + *plasma* something molded.

**protozoa** LATIN, from GREEK *protos* first + *zoia*, from *zoion* animal.

**protract** LATIN *protrahere*, from *pro-* before + *trahere* draw.

**protrude** LATIN *protrudere*, from *pro-* before + *trudere* push forward.

**protuberant** LATIN *protuberantem*, from *protuberare* swell, bulge, from *pro-* forward + *tuber* lump, swelling.

**proud** OLD ENGLISH *prud* value oneself, from FRENCH *prod*, from LATIN *prode*, from *prodesse*, from *pro-* forward + *esse* be.

**prove** FRENCH *prover*, from LATIN *probare* test.

**provender** FRENCH, from LATIN *praebenda* state support to a private person, from *praebere* give.

**proverb** FRENCH, from LATIN *proverbium*, from *pro-* before + *verbum* a word.

**provide** LATIN *providere* look after, from *pro-* before + *videre* see.

**province** FRENCH, from LATIN *provincia* Roman territory.

**provision** FRENCH, from LATIN *provisio.* See **provide.**

**provoke** FRENCH, from LATIN *provocare,* from *pro-* before + *vocare* call, from *vox* voice.

**provost** OLD ENGLISH and FRENCH, from LATIN *propositus,* from *praepositus* chief, from *prae-* before + *ponere* place.

**prow** FRENCH *proue,* from LATIN *prora,* from GREEK *proira.*

**prowess** FRENCH *prouesse,* from *prou* brave. See **proud.**

**prowl** MIDDLE ENGLISH *prollen.*

**proximate** LATIN *proximare* come near, from *proximus* nearest.

**proxy** MIDDLE ENGLISH *procuracle* office of a procurator (in the Roman Empire, an administrator for a district).

**prude** FRENCH *prudefemme* woman who is respected, from LATIN *prode* useful + *femina* woman.

**prudent** FRENCH, from LATIN *prudens* skilled.

**prune**[1] (cut) MIDDLE ENGLISH *prouyne,* from FRENCH *proignier* cut back (vines).

**prune**[2] (fruit) FRENCH *pronne* plum, from LATIN *pruna,* from GREEK *proumnon.*

**pry** MIDDLE ENGLISH *prien.*

**psalm** OLD ENGLISH, from LATIN *psalmus,* from GREEK *psalmodia* song sung to a harp.

**pseudonym** FRENCH, from GREEK *pseudonymon,* from *pseudes* false + *onyma* name.

**pshaw** imitative.

**psychedelic** GREEK *psyche* soul + *delein* make clear to the senses.

**psychiatry** GREEK *psyche* soul + *iatreia* art of healing.

**psycho-** GREEK *psyche* soul.

**psychology** See psycho- + -logy.

**psychometer** See psycho- + meter.

**ptarmigan** SCOTTISH *tarmachan.*

**pterodactyl** LATIN, from GREEK *pteron* wing + *daktylos* a finger.

**puberty** MIDDLE ENGLISH, from FRENCH *puberté,* from LATIN *pubertas,* from *pubes* adult.

**pubescent** LATIN *pubescentia,* from *pubescentem,* from *pubescere* reach puberty, from *pubes* adult.

**public** LATIN *publicus,* from *populus* the people.

**publish** FRENCH *publier* make public, from LATIN *publicare.*

**puce** FRENCH a flea, from the color, from LATIN *pulex* flea.

**pucker** FRENCH *poque.*

**pudding** MIDDLE ENGLISH *puddyng* sausage, from OLD ENGLISH *puduc* swelling.

**puddle** OLD ENGLISH *pudd* a ditch.

**pudgy** BRITISH from *pudge* something that is short and thick.

**pueblo** SPANISH, from LATIN *populus* people.

**puff** OLD ENGLISH *pyff.*

**pug** MIDDLE ENGLISH, origin uncertain.

**pugilism** LATIN *pugil* boxer.

**pugnacious** LATIN *pugnax,* from *pugnare* fight.

**pule** FRENCH *piaule* cheep, chirp, whine.

**pull** OLD ENGLISH *pullian* pluck.

**pulley** FRENCH *po(u)lie,* from GREEK *polos* axis.

**pulmonary** LATIN *pulmo* a lung.

**pulp** LATIN *pulpa* fleshy part.

**pulpit** LATIN *pulpitum* platform.

**pulsate** LATIN *pulsare* beat.

**pulse** FRENCH, from LATIN *pellere* beat.

**pulverize** LATIN *pulverizare* make into dust, from *pulvis* dust.

**pulvino** ITALIAN *pulvino.*

**pummel** See **pommel.**

**pump** DUTCH *pompe* pipe of wood, from SPANISH *bomba.*

**pumpernickel** GERMAN *Pumpernickel* a word for people who aren't agreeable (the bread has a slightly sour taste).

**pumpkin** FRENCH, from LATIN, from GREEK *pepon* ripe.

**pun** MODERN ENGLISH, origin uncertain, perhaps from ITALIAN *puntiglio* trivial objection, from LATIN *punctum* point.

**punch**[1] (hit) MIDDLE ENGLISH *punchen.*

**punch**[2] (drink) HINDI *pac* five, it originally had five ingredients.

**puncheon** FRENCH, from LATIN *pungere* pierce.

**punctilious** ITALIAN *puntiglio* fine point, from LATIN *punctum.*

**punctual** LATIN *punctualis,* from *punctum* point.

**punctuate** LATIN *punctuare,* from *punctum* point.

**puncture** LATIN *pungere* pierce.

**pungent** See **puncture.**

**pungle** SPANISH *póngale* put down, from *poner* put, give.

**punish** FRENCH *punis,* from LATIN *punire.*

**punt**[1] (kick) Rugby football rules, from *punt* strike, from *bunt* butt with the head.

**punt**[2] (boat) OLD ENGLISH, from LATIN *ponto.*

**puny** FRENCH *puîné,* from *puisné* younger, from *puis* afterward + *né* born.

**pupa** LATIN doll.

**pupil** LATIN *pupillus,* from *pupus* boy and *pupa* girl.

**puppet** MIDDLE ENGLISH *popet,* from LATIN *pupa* girl, doll.

**purchase** FRENCH *purchacer,* from LATIN *pro-* before + *captare* try to catch.

**pure** FRENCH *pur,* from LATIN *purus* clean.

**purfle** MIDDLE ENGLISH *purfilen,* from FRENCH *porfiler,* from LATIN *profilare,* from *pro-* forth + *filum* thread.

**purge** FRENCH *purg(i)er* make pure, from LATIN *purgare.*

**Puritan** See **purity.**

**purity** FRENCH *purte,* from LATIN *purus* pure.

**purl** MIDDLE ENGLISH *pirl* twist threads into a cord.

**purloin** FRENCH *purloigner* delay, from LATIN *pur-* for + *loin* far.

**purple** OLD ENGLISH, from LATIN *purpura,* from GREEK *porphyra* shellfish that produces purple dye.

**purpose** FRENCH *purpos,* from LATIN *proponere,* from *pro-* before + *ponere* place.

**purse** OLD ENGLISH *purs,* from LATIN *bursa,* from GREEK *byrsa* skin used to make purses.

**purslane** FRENCH, from LATIN *porcilaca,* from *portulaca.*

**pursue** FRENCH *pursuer,* from LATIN *prosequi,* from *pro-* forth + *sequi* follow.

**pursuivant** FRENCH *poursuir.* See **pursue.**

**purview** FRENCH *purveu,* from LATIN *providere.* See **provide.**

**push** FRENCH *pousser,* from LATIN *pulsare.*

**putrescent** LATIN *putrescere* become rotten, from *putris* rotten.

**putrid** LATIN *putridus,* from *putirere* be rotten.

**putty** FRENCH *potée* potful, from *pot* pot.

**puzzle** MIDDLE ENGLISH *pusle* bewilder, confound; possibly from **pose**[2].

**pylon** GREEK gateway.

**pyogenesis** GREEK *pyon* pus + **genesis**.

**pyometra** GREEK *pyon* pus + *metra* womb.

**pyracantha** LATIN, from GREEK *pyrakantha,* from *pyr-* fire + *akantha* thorn, thorny plant.

**pyramid** MIDDLE ENGLISH, from LATIN *pyramis,* from GREEK *puramis,* origin unknown.

**pyre** LATIN *pyra,* from GREEK *pyra* fire.

**pyrites** LATIN, from GREEK. See **pyre**.

**pyro-** See **pyre**.

**pyrometer** See pyro- + meter.

# Q

**q.v.** Latin *quod vide*.

**quack**[1] (duck sound) imitative.

**quack**[2] (faker) Dutch *quacksalver* one who brags about his medicines, from *quacken* brag + *zalf* salve (greasy medicine for burns, etc.).

**quadrant** Latin *quadrans* fourth part.

**quadri-** Latin *quattuor* four.

**quadrilateral** Latin *quadrilaterus*, from *quottuor* four + *lateralis* from *latus* side.

**quaff** possibly from German *quassen* eat or drink too much.

**quagmire** earlier *quag* marsh + Old Norse *myrr* swamp.

**quail**[1] (bird) Middle English *quayle*, from French *quaille*, from German *quahtala*.

**quail**[2] (cower) Middle English *quail* curdle, from French *coailler*, from Latin *coagulare* coagulate.

**quaint** French *queinte* neat, from Latin *cognitus* known.

**quake** Old English *cwacian* shake.

**qualify** Latin *qualificare*, from *qualis* of what kind + *facere* do, make.

**quality** French *qualité*, from Latin *qualis* of what kind.

**qualm** Old English *cwealm* disaster.

**quandary** possibly from Latin *quando* when.

**quantity** French, from Latin *quantitas* amount.

**quarantine** Italian *quarantina*, from *quaranta* forty (the number of days some foreign ships had to wait before unloading), from Latin *quadraginta*.

**quarrel** French *querele* argument, from Latin *querela*.

**quarry**[1] (stone) French *quarriere*, from Latin *quadraria*, from *quadrus* square.

**quarry**[2] (in hunting) French *cuiree* parts of a dead animal given to dogs after the hunt, from *cuir* skin, from Latin *covium*.

**quart** French *quarte*, from Latin *quartus* fourth.

**quartan** Middle English *quartaine*, from French, from Latin *quartus* fourth (fever supposedly occurring every fourth day).

**quarter** French *quartier*, from Latin *quartus* fourth.

**quartet** French, from Italian *quarto*, from Latin *quartus* fourth.

**quartic** Latin *quartus* fourth + French *-ique*, from Latin *-icus*, from Greek *-ikos*.

**quash** French, from Latin *quassare* shatter, from *quatere* break.

**quaver** MIDDLE ENGLISH *cwafien*.

**quay** FRENCH *cai*.

**queasy** MIDDLE ENGLISH *coysy*, perhaps influenced by FRENCH *queisier*, from *coisier* make uneasy.

**queen** OLD ENGLISH *cwen*.

**queer** MIDDLE ENGLISH, from SCOTTISH, perhaps from GERMAN *queer* oblique, off-center.

**quell** FRENCH *cwellan* kill.

**quench** OLD ENGLISH *acwencan* go out.

**quern** OLD ENGLISH *cweorn*.

**querulous** LATIN *queri* complain.

**query** LATIN *quaerere* look for.

**quest** FRENCH *queste* search, from LATIN *quesita*, from *quaerere* look for.

**question** FRENCH, from LATIN *quaestio* looking for, from *quaerere* ask.

**queue** FRENCH *coue*, from LATIN *cauda* tail.

**quibble** LATIN *quibus* who, which (formerly common in legal papers).

**quiche** FRENCH, from GERMAN *Küche*, from *Kuchen* cake.

**quick** OLD ENGLISH *cwic* alive.

**quiet** FRENCH, from LATIN *quietus* keep quiet, from *quies* rest.

**quill** probably from GERMAN.

**quillon** FRENCH cross-guard of a sword.

**quince** MIDDLE ENGLISH *quyn*, from FRENCH, from LATIN, from GREEK *kydonion*.

**quinine** SPANISH *quina*, bark of the cinchona tree, from QUECHUA *kina* bark.

**quinsy** LATIN *quin(e)sie*, from *quinacia*, from *cynache*, from GREEK *knyanche* sore throat.

**quintal** FRENCH, from ARABIC *quintar*, from LATIN *centenarius* amounting to 100.

**quintic** LATIN *quintus* fifth + FRENCH *-ique*, from LATIN *-icus*, from GREEK *-ikos*.

**quip** possibly from LATIN *quippe* indeed (used to make fun).

**quirk** MIDDLE ENGLISH evasion, perhaps from GERMAN *quer* odd. See **queer**.

**quirl** See **curl**.

**quit** FRENCH *quite*, from LATIN *quietus* at rest.

**quite** MIDDLE ENGLISH completely, from FRENCH freed. See **quit**.

**quittor** MIDDLE ENGLISH *quiture*, from FRENCH *cuiture* act of boiling, from Latin *coctura* boiling liquid, from *coctus*, from *coquere* cook.

**quiver**[1] (shake) imitative.

**quiver**[2] (for arrows) FRENCH *quivre*.

**quiz** possibly from LATIN *quis* what.

**quoit** MIDDLE ENGLISH *coyte* flat stone, quoit, from FRENCH *coilte, coite*, from LATIN *culcita* cushion.

**quonset** *Quonset* Point, Rhode Island, where it was first made.

**quorum** LATIN.

**quota** LATIN share, from *quota pars* how great a part.

**quote** LATIN *quotare*, from *quot* how many.

**quotidian** LATIN *quotidianus* daily, from *quotus* how many, as many as + *dies* day.

**quotient** LATIN *quoties* how often, from *quot* how many.

# R

**rabbi**  LATIN, from GREEK, from HEBREW my master.

**rabble**  MIDDLE ENGLISH pack of animals.

**rabid**  LATIN *rabere* rage.

**rabies**  LATIN madness.

**raccoon**  NATIVE AMERICAN *arakun* scratcher.

**race**[1] (run)  OLD NORSE *ras* running.

**race**[2] (people)  FRENCH, from ITALIAN *razza* kind, possibly from ARABIC *ra's* origin.

**raceme**  LATIN *racemes* cluster of grapes.

**rack**  possibly from DUTCH *rek,* from *recken* stretch.

**racket**[1] (noise)  imitative.

**racket**[2] (frame)  FRENCH *raquette* frame, from *rachette* palm of the hand, from ARABIC *raha.*

**raconteur**  FRENCH *raconter* recount, from *re-* + *aconter,* from *a-* to + *conter* tell.

**racquet**  See **racket**[2].

**radar**  *ra*(dio) *d*(etection) *a*(nd) *r*(anging).

**raddle**  FRENCH *reddalle,* origin uncertain.

**radiant**  LATIN *radiare* send out light, from *radius* a spoke (as of a wheel), or a beam (as of light).

**radiate**  See **radius**.

**radical**  LATIN *radicalis* having roots, from *radix* root.

**radicle**  LATIN *radicula,* from *radix* root.

**radio**  short for **radiotelegraphy**.

**radio-**  LATIN *radius* ray.

**radiotelegraphy**  See **radio-** + **tele-** + **-graphy**.

**radish**  OLD ENGLISH *rædic,* from LATIN *radix* root.

**radium**  LATIN.  See **radius**.

**radius**  LATIN measuring rod, ray.

**raffle**  FRENCH *rafle* game of dice, from GERMAN *raffel* a rake.

**raft**  OLD NORSE *raptr.*

**rafter**  OLD ENGLISH *ræfter.*

**rag**[1] (cloth)  MIDDLE ENGLISH *ragge,* from OLD NORSE *rögg* bit of fur.

**rag**[2] (scold, tease)  slang, of unknown origin.

**ragamuffin**  MIDDLE ENGLISH *raggi* ragged + possibly DUTCH *muffe* mitten.

**rage**  FRENCH, from LATIN *rabies.*

**raglan**  Lord *Raglan,* the British commander in the Crimean war.

**ragwort**  See **rag**[1] + OLD ENGLISH *wyrt* a root.

**raid** MIDDLE ENGLISH *ra(i)de,* from OLD ENGLISH *rad* journey.

**rail** FRENCH, from LATIN *regula* a rule.

**raillery** FRENCH *raillerie,* from *railler,* from LATIN *ragere* yell + FRENCH *-erie,* from LATIN *-aria.*

**raiment** FRENCH *araiement,* from *arayer* array (put in order).

**rain** OLD ENGLISH *regn.*

**raise** OLD NORSE *reisa.*

**rajah** HINDI, from SANSKRIT *rajan* king.

**rake** OLD ENGLISH *raca* tool.

**rale** FRENCH *raler* rattling sound in the throat.

**rally** FRENCH *rallier* put together, from LATIN *re-* again + *alier* join.

**Ramadan** ARABIC *ramadan* the hot month, from *ramada* be hot.

**ramble** MIDDLE ENGLISH *romblen,* from *romen* roam.

**rambunctious** origin uncertain.

**ramekin** FRENCH *ramequin.*

**ramify** FRENCH *ramifier,* from LATIN *ramus* branch + *facere* do, make.

**ramp** FRENCH *rampe* slope, from *ramper* climb.

**rampage** See **ramp** + **age**.

**rampant** FRENCH *ramper* climb.

**rampart** FRENCH *re-* again + *emparer* defend, from LATIN *ante-* before + *parare* prepare.

**ramshackle** See **ransack**.

**ranch:** SPANISH *rancho* small farm, originally group of people eating together.

**rancid** LATIN *rancere* stinking.

**rancor** FRENCH, from LATIN *rancere* stinking.

**random** FRENCH *randon* speed, from *randir* run with force.

**range** FRENCH *ranger* rank, from *renc* a row.

**rank**[1] (order) FRENCH *reng* row.

**rank**[2] (bad smell) OLD ENGLISH *ranc* strong.

**rankle** FRENCH *draoncle,* from LATIN *dracunculus* a sore, from *draco* dragon.

**ransack** OLD NORSE *rann* a house + *sækja* search.

**ransom** FRENCH *raençon,* from LATIN *redemptio,* from *redimere,* from *re-* back + *emere* get.

**rant** DUTCH *ranten.*

**rantipole** possibly from **rant**.

**rap** imitative.

**rapacious** MODERN ENGLISH *rapacity,* from FRENCH *rapacité,* from LATIN *rapacitatem* greediness, from *rapax* grasping, plundering, from *rapere* seize.

**rape** MIDDLE ENGLISH, from LATIN *rapere* take with force.

**rapid** LATIN *rapidus,* from *rapere.* See **rape**.

**rapier** FRENCH *rapière.*

**rapport** FRENCH *rapprocher* bring together, from LATIN *re-* back + *ad-* to + *portare* carry.

**rapscallion** possibly from **rascal**.

**rapt** LATIN *rapere* take with force.

**rapture** See **rapt** + **-ure**.

**rare**[1] (uncommon) LATIN *rarus.*

**rare**[2] (in cooking) OLD ENGLISH *hrer* undercooked.

**rascal** MIDDLE ENGLISH *rascaile* low class people, from FRENCH *rascaille* outcast, rabble.

**rash**[1] (careless) MIDDLE ENGLISH *rasch.*

**rash²** (skin spots) FRENCH *rasche*, from LATIN *rader* scrape.

**rasher** possibly from MIDDLE ENGLISH *rash* cut.

**rasp** FRENCH *rasper*, from GERMAN *raspon* scrape together.

**ratchet** FRENCH *rochet* bobbin, spindle, from ITALIAN *rocchetto* spool, ratchet, from *rocca* distaff.

**rate¹** (amount) FRENCH price, from LATIN *rata*, from *reri* think.

**rate²** (scold) MIDDLE ENGLISH *raten*.

**rather** OLD ENGLISH *hrathor*, from *hræthe* quickly.

**ratify** FRENCH, from LATIN *ratus* rate + *facere* do, make.

**ratio** FRENCH *ration*, from LATIN *ratio* relation.

**ration** FRENCH, from LATIN *ratio*. See **reason**.

**rational** LATIN *rationalis* relating to reason, from *ratio*. See **reason**.

**rattle** MIDDLE ENGLISH *ratelen*, probably imitative.

**rattlepated** See **rattle** + **pate**.

**rattling** See **rattle**.

**raucous** LATIN *raucus*.

**ravage** FRENCH *ravir* carry away, from LATIN *rapere*.

**rave** FRENCH *raver*.

**ravel** DUTCH *ravelen* tangle up.

**ravelin** FRENCH, from ITALIAN *revellino*.

**raven** OLD ENGLISH *hræfn*.

**ravenous** FRENCH *ravineux* violent, from *raviner* destroy.

**ravine** FRENCH, from LATIN *rapina* forceful action.

**ravish** FRENCH *ravir*, from LATIN *rapere* seize.

**raw** OLD ENGLISH *hreaw* not cooked.

**ray¹** (beam) See **radius**.

**ray²** (fish) FRENCH *raie*, from LATIN *raia*.

**raye** FRENCH *rayé*.

**rayon** probably from FRENCH *rayon* beam of light. See **ray¹**.

**raze** FRENCH *raser* shave, from LATIN *radere* scrape.

**razor** FRENCH *rasour*, from *raser*. See **raze**.

**razzle-dazzle** AMERICAN slang.

**re-** LATIN again, back.

**reach** OLD ENGLISH *ræcan* stretch out.

**read** OLD ENGLISH *rædan* understand writing.

**ready** OLD ENGLISH *ræde* prepared.

**real** FRENCH, from LATIN *realis* actual, from *res* thing.

**realm** FRENCH *realme* kingdom, from LATIN *regimen* rule, from *regalis* regal. See **regal**.

**reap** OLD ENGLISH *repan* cut grain.

**rear¹** (back part) FRENCH *arere* backward, from *ad-* to + Germanic *retro* behind.

**rear²** (raise) OLD ENGLISH *ræran* raise.

**reason** FRENCH *raison*, from LATIN *reri* think.

**reaver** OLD ENGLISH *reafere*.

**rebate** FRENCH *rebattre* beat down again, from *re-* again + *abattre* beat down.

**rebel** FRENCH *rebeller* revolt (rise up against the government), from LATIN *rebellare*, from *re-* again + *bellare* make war.

**rebound** FRENCH *rebondir* leap back, from *re-* again + *bondir* leap.

**rebuff** ITALIAN *ribuffo* scolding, from LATIN *re-* back + *buffo* puff (sudden blow of air).

**rebuke** FRENCH *rebuker* turn back, from *re-* again + *buschier* cut wood, from *busche* log.

**recalcitrant** LATIN *recalcitrare* kick back, from *re-* back + *calx* heel.

**recamier** Madame *Récamier* who was portrayed reclining in one in a painting.

**recant** LATIN *recantare* sing again, from *re-* again + *cantare* sing.

**recede** LATIN *recedere*, from *re-* back + *cedere* go.

**receipt** FRENCH *receite* money paid, from LATIN *recepta*, from *recipere*, from *re-* back + *capere* take.

**receive** FRENCH *receivre* accept, from LATIN *recipere*, from *re-* back + *capere* take.

**recent** LATIN *recens* new.

**receptacle** LATIN *receptaculum*. See **receive**.

**reception** FRENCH, from LATIN *recipere*. See **receive**.

**recess** LATIN *recessus* going back.

**recipe** LATIN *recipere*. See **receive**.

**reciprocal** LATIN *reciprocus* returning.

**recite** LATIN *recitare* repeat from memory, from *re-* back + *ciere* wake up.

**reckless** OLD ENGLISH *reccan* care + *-leas*.

**reckon** OLD ENGLISH *(ge)recenian* explain.

**reclaim** FRENCH *reclamer* call back, from LATIN *re-* back + *clamare* call.

**recluse** FRENCH *reclure*, from LATIN *recludere*, from *re-* back + *claudere* shut.

**recognize** LATIN *recogoscere*, from *re-* again + *cognoscere* know.

**recoil** FRENCH *reculer* go back, from LATIN *re-* back + *culus* rump (hind part of an animal).

**recommend** LATIN *recommendare* trust with, from *re-* again + *commendare* trust with.

**recompense** LATIN *recompensare* reward, from *re-* back + *compensare* weigh together.

**reconcile** LATIN *reconciliare*, from *re-* back + *concillium* council.

**reconnoiter** FRENCH *reconnoitre*, from *re-* again + *cognoscere* know.

**record** FRENCH *recorder* remember, from LATIN *recordari*, from *re-* back + *cor* mind.

**recoup** FRENCH *recouper* cut back, from *re-* back + *couper* cut.

**recourse** FRENCH *recours*, from LATIN *recursus* running back. See **re-** + **course**.

**recover** FRENCH *recovrer* get again, from LATIN *recuperare*.

**recreate** LATIN *recreare* restore. See **re-** + **create**.

**recriminate** LATIN *reciminare* accuse someone, from *re-* again + *criminari* accuse.

**recruit** FRENCH *recruter*, from *recroître*, from LATIN *recrescere*, from *re-* again + *crescere* grow.

**rectangle** LATIN *rectangulus*, from *rectus* right + *angulus* angle.

**rectify** LATIN *rectificare*, from *rectus* right + *facere* do, make.

**rectitude** FRENCH, from LATIN *rectus* straight.

**recumbent** LATIN *recumbere*, from *re-* back + *cumbere* lie down.

**recuperate** LATIN *recuperare* recover.

**recur** LATIN *recurrere*, from *re-* back + *currere* run.

**red** OLD ENGLISH *read*.

**reddy** See **red** + *-y*[3].

**redeem** LATIN *redimere*, from *re-* back + *emere* get.

**redolent**  LATIN *redolere,* from *re(d)-* thoroughly + *olere* smell.

**redoubt**  FRENCH, from ITALIAN *ridotto,* from LATIN *reductus,* from *reducere,* from *re-* back + *ducere* lead.

**redoubtable**  FRENCH *redouter* dread, fear, from *re-* an intensifying prefix + *douter* doubt, fear.

**reduce**  LATIN *reducere,* from *re-* back + *ducere* lead.

**redundant**  LATIN *redundare* flow over, from *re(d)-* thoroughly + *undare* rise.

**reed**  OLD ENGLISH *hroed.*

**reef**  DUTCH *rif,* from OLD NORSE *rif* ridge (upper part of something).

**reel**  OLD ENGLISH *hreol* something used for winding silk or thread.

**reeve**  OLD ENGLISH *gerefa.*

**refer**  LATIN *referre,* from *re-* back + *ferre* bring.

**refine**  LATIN *re-* back + *fine* make fine.

**reflect**  LATIN *reflectere,* from *re-* back + *flectere* bend.

**reflex**  LATIN *reflectere.*  See **reflect.**

**reform**  LATIN *reformare.*  See **re- + form.**

**refract**  LATIN *refringere,* from *re-* back + *frangere* break.

**refrain**[1] (hold back) FRENCH *refrener* bridle, from LATIN *refrenare,* from *re-* back + *frenum* bridle.

**refrain**[2] (verse) FRENCH *refraindre* repeat, from LATIN *refringere.*  See **refract.**

**refrigerate**  LATIN *refrigerare,* from *re(d)-* thoroughly + *frigerare* cool, from *frigus* cold.

**refugee**  FRENCH *réfugié,* from LATIN *refugim* refuge (shelter).

**refund**  LATIN *refundere,* from *re-* back + *fundere* pour.

**refuse**  FRENCH *refuser* push back, from LATIN *refundere.*  See **refund.**

**refute**  LATIN *refutare* repel.

**regal**  LATIN *regalis* royal, from *rex* king.

**regale**  FRENCH *régaler* entertain, from FRENCH *gale* something that pleases, from DUTCH *wale* wealth.

**regalia**  See **regal.**

**regard**  FRENCH *regarder,* from *re-* back + *garder* watch over.

**regenerate**  LATIN *regenerare* bring forth.  See **re- + generate.**

**regent**  LATIN *regens* ruler, from *regere* keep straight.

**regimen**  FRENCH, from LATIN, from *regere* rule.

**regiment**  LATIN *regimentus* rule, from *regere.*  See **regimen.**

**region**  LATIN *regio,* from *regere* rule.  See **regal.**

**register**  LATIN *regestum,* from *regerere* record.

**regress**  LATIN *regredi,* from *re-* back + *gradi* go.

**regret**  FRENCH *regreter* mourn.

**regular**  LATIN *regularis* usual, from *regula* rule.

**regulate**  LATIN *regulare* direct.  See **regular.**

**rehabilitate**  LATIN *rehabilitare,* from *re-* again + *habilis* fit.

**rehearse**  FRENCH *rehercier* harrow (plow ground for raising crops) over and over, from *re-* again + *hercer* harrow, from LATIN *hirpex* rake, from *hirpus* wolf, from the way the metal teeth of the harrow look like wolf's teeth.

**reign**  FRENCH *regne* kingdom, from LATIN *regnum.*

**rein**  FRENCH *rene,* from LATIN *retinere,* from *re-* back + *tenere* hold.

**reindeer**  OLD NORSE *hreinn* reindeer.

**reinforce** See **enforce**.

**reiver** See **reaver**.

**reject** LATIN *rejecere*, from *re-* again + *jacere* throw.

**rejoice** FRENCH *rejoir*, from *re-* again + *joir*, from LATIN *gaudere* joy.

**relapse** LATIN *relabi*, from *re-* back + *lapsus* fall.

**relate** LATIN *referre*, from *re-* back + *ferre* bring.

**relative** LATIN *relativus*, from *referre*. See **relate**.

**relax** LATIN *relaxare*, from *re-* back + *laxare* loosen, from *laxus* loose.

**relay** FRENCH *relais* set of fresh horses and dogs for a hunt, from *re-* back + *laier* leave, from LATIN *laxare* loosen.

**release** FRENCH *relaissier* leave behind, from LATIN *relaxare*. See **relax**.

**relegate** LATIN *relegare*, from *re-* back + *legare* send.

**relevant** FRENCH *relever* raise up, from LATIN *relevare*. See **relieve**.

**relic** FRENCH *reliques*, from LATIN *reliquiae* remains.

**relief** FRENCH restore, from *relever*. See **relieve**.

**relieve** FRENCH *relever*, from LATIN *relevare*, from *re-* again + *levare* raise, from *levis* light (not heavy).

**religion** FRENCH, from LATIN *religio*, from *re-* back + *ligare* bind.

**relinquish** FRENCH *relinquir* leave, from LATIN *relinquere*, from *re-* back + *quere* leave.

**relish** FRENCH *reles* remainder, from *relaissier*.

**reluctant** LATIN *reluctari*, from *re-* back + *luctari* struggle.

**rely** FRENCH *relier* bind together, from LATIN *religare*, from *re-* back + *ligare* bind.

**remain** FRENCH *remaindre*, from LATIN *remanere*, from *re-* back + *manere* stay.

**remand** LATIN *remandare*, from *re-* back + *mandare* order.

**remark** FRENCH *remarquer*, from *re-* again + *marquer* mark.

**remedy** LATIN *remedium* medicine.

**remember** FRENCH *remembrer*, from LATIN *rememorari*, from *re-* again + *memor* mindful (keeping something in mind).

**reminiscence** LATIN *reminiscentia*, from *reminisci*, from *re-* again + *memini* remember.

**remiss** See **remit**.

**remit** LATIN *remittere*, from *re-* back + *mittere* send.

**remnant** FRENCH *remanant*, from *remanoir*, from LATIN *remanere*. See **remain**.

**remonstrate** LATIN *remonstrare*, from *re-* again + *monstrare* show.

**remorse** LATIN *remordere*, from *re-* again + *mordere* bite, as if chewing over something in your mind that is worrying you.

**remote** LATIN *removere*. See **re-** + **move**.

**remoulade** FRENCH *rémoulade*.

**remove** FRENCH *remouvoir*, from LATIN *removere* move back. See **re-** + **move**.

**remuda** SPANISH *remudar* change, from LATIN *mutare*.

**remunerate** LATIN *remunerare* repay, from *re-* again + *munus* a gift.

**renaissance** FRENCH rebirth, from *re-* again + *naître*, from LATIN *nasci* be born.

**render** FRENCH *rendre*, from LATIN *reddere*, from *re-* back + *dare* give.

**rendezvous**  FRENCH *se rendre* take yourself to.

**rendition**  FRENCH *rendre*.  See **render**.

**renegade**  SPANISH *renegado* one who denies, from LATIN *re-* again + *negare* deny.

**renege**  LATIN *renegare* deny.  See **renegade**.

**renounce**  FRENCH *renoncer*, from *re-* back + *nuntiare* tell, from *nuntius* messenger.

**renovate**  LATIN *renovare*, from *re-* again + *novare* make new, from *novus* new.

**renown**  FRENCH *renoun*, from LATIN *re-* again + *nomen* name.

**rent**[1] (money)  FRENCH *rente*, from LATIN *rendere* render.

**rent**[2] (torn)  MIDDLE ENGLISH *renten* tear, rend.

**repair**[1] (mend)  LATIN *reparare*, from *re-* again + *parare* prepare.

**repair**[2] (go)  MIDDLE ENGLISH, from FRENCH *repairer*, from *repadrer*, from LATIN *repatriare* return to one's own country.

**reparation**  LATIN *reparationem*, from *reparatus*, from *reparare* restore.

**repeat**  LATIN *repetere*, from *re-* again + *petere* seek.

**repent**  FRENCH *repentir*, from LATIN *re-* again + *paenitere* cause to be sorry.

**repercussion**  See re- + percussion.

**repertoire**  FRENCH list, from LATIN *repertorium*, from *reperire* discover.

**replenish**  FRENCH, from LATIN *replenir*, from *re-* again + *plenus* full.

**replete**  FRENCH, from LATIN *replere*, from *re-* again + *plere* fill.

**reply**  FRENCH *replier* fold back, from LATIN *replicare*, from *re-* back + *placere* fold.

**report**  FRENCH, from LATIN *reportare*, from *re-* back + *portare* carry.

**repose**  FRENCH *reposer* rest, from LATIN *re-* again + *pausare* cause to rest.

**represent**  LATIN *repraesentare*.  See **re-** + **present**.

**repress**  LATIN *reprimere*, from *re-* back + *premere* press.

**reprieve**  MIDDLE ENGLISH *reproven* test again.  See **reprove**.

**reprimand**  FRENCH *réprimande*, from LATIN *reprimere*, from *re-* back + *premere* press.

**reprise**  FRENCH, from LATIN *reprendre* take back.

**reproach**  FRENCH *reprochier* blame, from LATIN *re-* again + *prope* near.

**reprobate**  LATIN *reprobare*, from *re-* again + *probare* test.

**reproduce**  See **re-** + **produce**.

**reprove**  MIDDLE ENGLISH, from FRENCH *reprover* blame, from LATIN *reprobare* disapprove, condemn, from *re-* reversal or opposite of + *probare* prove worthy.

**reptile**  LATIN *reptilis* creeping, from *repere* creep.

**republic**  LATIN *respublica* state, public thing.

**repudiate**  LATIN *repudiare* put away.

**repugnance**  FRENCH, from LATIN *repugnare*, from *re-* back + *pugnare* fight.

**repulse**  LATIN *repellere*, from *re-* back + *pellere* drive.

**reputation**  See repute.

**repute**  FRENCH, from LATIN *reputatio*, from *reputare*, from *re-* again + *putare* think.

**request**  FRENCH *requerre* ask, from LATIN *requirere*.  See **require**.

**require**  LATIN *requirere* ask for, from *re-* again + *quaerere* ask.

**requisite** See **require**.

**requite** See **re-** + **quit**.

**rerebrace** FRENCH *rerebras*, from *rere-* back + *bras* arm.

**rescind** LATIN *rescindere*, from *re-* back + *scindere* cut.

**rescue** FRENCH *rescourre* save, from LATIN *re-* back + *excutere* drive away.

**research** FRENCH *recerche*, from *re-* again + *cerchier* seek.

**resemble** FRENCH *re-* again + *sembler*, from LATIN *simulare*, from *simul* same.

**resent** FRENCH *ressentir*, from LATIN *re-* back + *sentire* feel.

**reserve** LATIN *reservare*, from *re-* back + *servare* hold.

**reservoir** FRENCH, from LATIN *reservare*. See **reserve**.

**reside** LATIN *residere*, from *re-* back + *sedere* sit.

**residue** FRENCH, from LATIN *residere*, from *re-* back + *sedere* sit.

**resign** FRENCH *resigner*, from LATIN *resignare*, from *re-* back + *signare* sign.

**resilient** LATIN *resilire*, from *re-* back + *salire* jump.

**resin** LATIN *resina* sap from trees, from GREEK *rhetine*.

**resist** LATIN *resistere*, from *re-* back + *sistere* set, from *stare* stand.

**resolute** LATIN *resolvere* separate. See **re-** + **solve**.

**resolve** See **re-** + **solve**.

**resonant** LATIN *resonare* sound again.

**resort** FRENCH *resortir*, from *re-* again + *sortir* go out.

**resource** FRENCH *ressource*, from *resourdre*, from *re-* again + *sourdre* spring up, from LATIN *surgere* rise.

**respect** LATIN *respicere*, from *re-* back + *specere* look at.

**respite** FRENCH *respit*, from LATIN *respicere*. See **respect**.

**respond** LATIN *respondere*, from *re-* back + *spondere* pledge.

**responsible** LATIN *respondere*. See **respond**.

**rest**[1] (quiet) OLD ENGLISH *rest* quiet.

**rest**[2] (remainder) FRENCH *reste*, from *rester* remain, from LATIN *restare*, from *re-* back + *stare* stand.

**restaurant** FRENCH *restaurer* restore. See **restore**.

**restitution** FRENCH, from LATIN *restituere* restore, from *re-* again + *statuere* set up.

**restive** FRENCH *restif* stubborn, from *rester* remain. See **rest**[2].

**restore** FRENCH *restorer*, from LATIN *restaurare*, from *re-* again + *staurare* place.

**restrain** FRENCH *restraindre*, from LATIN *restringere*, from *re-* back + *stringere* draw tight.

**restrict** LATIN *restringere*. See **restrain**.

**result** LATIN *resultare* spring back, from *resilire*, from *re-* back + *salire* jump.

**resume** LATIN *resumere*, from *re-* again + *sumere* take.

**résumé** FRENCH *résumer*, from LATIN *resumere*. See **resume**.

**resurrection** LATIN *resurrectio*, from *resurgere* rise again.

**resuscitate** LATIN *rescuscitare*, from *re-* again + *suscitare* revive (bring back to life).

**retail** FRENCH *retaille* cut up, from *re-* again + *tailler* cut, from the idea of selling things in small amounts.

**retain** FRENCH *retenir*, from LATIN *retinere*, from *re-* back + *tenere* hold.

**retaliate** LATIN *retaliare*, from *re-* back + *talio* punishment of the same kind.

**retch** OLD ENGLISH *hræcan* clear the throat.

**reticent** LATIN *reticere*, from *re-* again + *tacere* be silent.

**reticulate** LATIN *reticulatus* having a net-like pattern, from **reticulum**.

**reticule** FRENCH, from LATIN **reticulum**.

**reticulum** LATIN, from *rete* net.

**retinue** FRENCH *retenir*. See **retain**.

**retire** FRENCH *retirer*, from *re-* back + *tirer* draw, pull.

**retort** LATIN *retorquere*, from *re-* back + *torquere* twist back.

**retreat** FRENCH *retraite*, from *retaire*, from LATIN *retrahere*, from *re-* back + *trahere* draw.

**retrieve** FRENCH *retrover*, from *re-* again + *trover* find.

**retrospect** LATIN *retrospicere*, from *retro-* back + *specere* look.

**return** FRENCH *retourner*. See **re-** + **turn**.

**reveal** LATIN *revelare* draw back the veil, from *re-* back + *velum* a veil.

**revel** FRENCH *reveler* make merry, from LATIN *rebellare*. See **rebel**.

**revenge** FRENCH *revengier*, from LATIN *re-* again + *vindicare* avenge (get even for a wrong).

**revenue** FRENCH *revenir* return, from LATIN *revenire*, from *re-* back + *venire* come.

**reverberate** LATIN *re-* again + *verberare* beat, from *verber* a whip.

**revere** LATIN *revereri* respect.

**reverie** FRENCH *rever* wander.

**reverse** FRENCH *revers*, from LATIN *reversus*, from *revertere*. See **revert**.

**revert** FRENCH *revertir*, from LATIN *revertere* turn back, from *re-* back + *vertere* turn.

**review** FRENCH *revue*, from *revoir*, from LATIN *re-* again + *videre* see.

**revise** LATIN *revisere*, from *re-* again + *videre* see.

**revive** LATIN *revivere*, from *re-* again + *vivere* live.

**revoke** LATIN *revocare*, from *re-* back + *vocare* call.

**revolt** FRENCH *révolter*, from ITALIAN *rivoltare*, from LATIN *revolvere*. See **revolve**.

**revolve** LATIN *revolvere*, from *re-* back + *volvere* roll.

**revue** FRENCH.

**reward** FRENCH *rewarder*, from *regarder* look at. See **regard**.

**rhapsody** LATIN *rhapsodia* part of epic (long serious poem), from GREEK *rhapsodia* epic poem, from *rhaptein* stitch together + *oide* song.

**rhetoric** LATIN *rhetorica* art of oratory (formal public speech), from GREEK *rhetorike techne* rhetorical art, from *rhetor* orator.

**rheumatism** LATIN *rheumatismus*, from GREEK *rheumatismos*.

**rhinestone** FRENCH *caillou de Rhin* pebble of the Rhine (a river in Germany), because the gems were first cut and made into stones there.

**rhinoceros** LATIN, from GREEK *rhis* nose + *keras* horn.

**rhizome** LATIN, from GREEK *rhiza* a root.

**rhizopod** See **rhizome** + GREEK *-pod* foot.

**rhododendron** LATIN, from GREEK *rhodon* a rose + *dendron* a tree.

**rhombus** LATIN, from GREEK *rhombos*, from *rhembesthai* spin, whirl.

**rhubarb** FRENCH *rubarbe*, from LATIN *reubarbum*, from GREEK *rheon* rhubarb + *barbaron* foreign.

**rhyme** FRENCH *rime*.

**rhythm** LATIN *rhythmus*, from GREEK *rhythmos* measured time, from *rhein* flow.

**ribbon** FRENCH *riban*.

**rich** MIDDLE ENGLISH, from OLD ENGLISH *rice* wealthy. See **regal**.

**rick** OLD ENGLISH *hreac*.

**rickets** MIDDLE ENGLISH, origin uncertain.

**rickety** See **rickets**.

**rickshaw** See jinrikisha.

**rictus** LATIN open mouth or jaws.

**riddle** OLD ENGLISH *rædels* puzzle.

**ride** OLD ENGLISH *ridan*.

**ridge** OLD ENGLISH *hrycg* back of a man or animal.

**ridicule** FRENCH *riducule*, from LATIN *ridiculum*, from *ridere* laugh.

**rife** OLD ENGLISH *ryfe* more than enough.

**riffle** AMERICAN make choppy water, perhaps from *ruffle* make rough.

**riff-raff** FRENCH *rit et raf* one and all.

**rifle**[1] (gun) FRENCH *rifler* scrape, from GERMAN *riffeln* scratch.

**rifle**[2] (search) FRENCH *rif(f)ler* rob.

**rift** DANISH *rive* tear.

**rig** MIDDLE ENGLISH *riggen*, from SCANDINAVIAN.

**right** OLD ENGLISH *riht* straight.

**righteous** OLD ENGLISH *rihtwis*, from *riht* good + *wis(e)* manner.

**rigid** LATIN *rigidus* stiff.

**rigmarole** MIDDLE ENGLISH *rageman rolle* a long list.

**rigor** FRENCH, from LATIN *rigere* be rigid.

**riksha** See jinrikisha.

**rile** AMERICAN *roil*.

**rim** OLD ENGLISH *rima* border.

**rime** OLD ENGLISH *hrim*.

**rind** OLD ENGLISH.

**ring**[1] (circle) OLD ENGLISH *hring* circle.

**ring**[2] (bell sound) OLD ENGLISH *hringan* clear sound.

**rink** FRENCH *renc* range.

**rinse** FRENCH *raincier* clean with water, from LATIN *recens* fresh.

**riot** FRENCH *riote* argument, from *rihoter*.

**rip** possibly from DUTCH *rippen* tear.

**ripe** OLD ENGLISH ready to be gathered.

**ripple** MODERN ENGLISH ruffle a surface, unknown origin, perhaps from **rip**.

**rise** OLD ENGLISH *risan* go up.

**risible** LATIN *risibilis*, from *ridere* laugh.

**risk** FRENCH *risque* danger, from ITALIAN *risico*, from *riscare* go out where there might be danger.

**risqué** FRENCH *risquer* risk.

**rite** LATIN *ritus* custom.

**ritual** LATIN *ritualis*, from *ritus* religious ceremony.

**rival** LATIN *rivalis* neighbor, using the same stream as another, from *rivus* a brook.

**rive**[1] (stab) OLD NORSE *rifa*.

**rive**[2] (arrive) FRENCH *river*. See **arrive**.

**river** FRENCH *riverre*, from LATIN *riparius*, from *ripa* bank of a stream.

**rivet** FRENCH small rod, from *river* attach.

**rivulet** ITALIAN *rivolo* brook, from LATIN *rivus*.

**roam** MIDDLE ENGLISH *romen*.

**roan** FRENCH, from early Spanish *roano*.

**roar** OLD ENGLISH *rarian*.

**roast** FRENCH *rostir* cook with a fire.

**rob** FRENCH *rob(b)er* steal.

**robe** FRENCH things taken in a robbery. In early times robbers often stole clothes.

**robin** FRENCH diminuitive of *Robert*.

**robot** central European *robota* forced labor, from *rabu* servant.

**robust** LATIN *robustus*, from *robur* oak.

**rock**[1] (stone) MIDDLE ENGLISH *rokke*, from FRENCH *roche*, from LATIN *rocca*.

**rock**[2] (move back and forth) MIDDLE ENGLISH *rocken*, from OLD ENGLISH *roccian*.

**rocket** ITALIAN *rocchetta* a spool, from *rocca* a staff for spinning, from GERMAN.

**rococo** FRENCH *rococo*, from *rocaille* shellwork (referring to the use of shell designs).

**rod** OLD ENGLISH *rodd*.

**rodent** LATIN *rodere* chew to pieces.

**rodeo** SPANISH *rodear* surround, from LATIN *rotare* rotate.

**rogue** MIDDLE ENGLISH beggar, likely from LATIN *rogare* ask or beg

**roil** origin uncertain, probably from FRENCH *rouiller*, from *rouil* mud, rust, from LATIN *robigo* rust.

**roister** FRENCH *rustre* one who brags or cheats, from LATIN *rusticus*, from *rus* the country.

**role** FRENCH *rôle* actor's part, from LATIN *rotula* little wheel. See **roll**.

**roll** FRENCH *roller*, from LATIN *rotula* little wheel, from *rota* wheel.

**romance** FRENCH *romanz* work written in a Romance language (one that came from Latin, such as French, Italian, Spanish) from LATIN *Romanus* relating to Rome.

**romany** GYPSY *romani, romano*, from *rom* man, Gypsy.

**romp** probably from FRENCH *ramper* climb.

**rondo** ITALIAN, from FRENCH *rondeau*, from *rondel* little round.

**rondure** FRENCH *rondeur*.

**ronin** JAPANESE.

**rook**[1] (crow) OLD ENGLISH *hroc*.

**rook**[2] (chess piece) FRENCH *roc*, from ARABIC *rukh*.

**roost** OLD ENGLISH *hrost*.

**root** OLD NORSE *rot*.

**root**[1] (plant part) OLD NORSE *rot*.

**root**[2] (dig) MIDDLE ENGLISH *wroot*, from OLD ENGLISH *wrot, wrotan*.

**rootle** See **root**[2]

**rope** OLD ENGLISH *rap*.

**rosary** LATIN *rosarium* rose garden.

**rose** OLD ENGLISH, from LATIN *rosa*, from GREEK *rhodon* rose.

**rosemary** LATIN *rosmarinus* dew of the sea, from *ros* dew + *marinus*.

**rosette**  FRENCH, from *rose* rose.

**roster**  DUTCH *rooster* a list.

**rostrum**  LATIN beak, from the ancient Roman custom of decorating speaker platforms with the *beaks,* front parts, of captured ships.

**rotary**  LATIN *rota* wheel.

**rotate**  LATIN *rotare* rotate.

**rote**  MIDDLE ENGLISH *bi rote* by heart, origin uncertain.

**rotifer**  LATIN *rotifera,* from *rota* wheel + *-fer* bearing.

**rotogravure**  LATIN *rota* wheel + FRENCH *gravure* engraving.

**rotor**  See **rotate.**

**rotten**  OLD NORSE *rotinn.*

**rotund**  LATIN *rotundus* in a circle.

**rotunda**  ITALIAN, from LATIN.  See **rotund.**

**rough**  OLD ENGLISH *ruh* not smooth.

**roulette**  FRENCH *roele* a small wheel, from LATIN *rota* wheel.

**round**  FRENCH *roont,* from LATIN *rotundus.*

**rouse**  FRENCH, a term used with hawks.

**rout**  FRENCH *route* defeat, from LATIN *rumpere* break (an army).

**route**  FRENCH path, from LATIN *rumpere* break (a path in the forest).

**rove**  possibly from SCOTTISH *rave* wander, stray, from MIDDLE ENGLISH *raven,* probably from OLD NORSE *rafa* wander.

**row**[1] (line)  OLD ENGLISH *raw* line.

**row**[2] (boating)  OLD ENGLISH *rowan* a boat.

**row**[3] (quarrel)  slang, origin unknown.

**rowan**  SCOTTISH *rowan-tree, rountree,* from the root of *red,* in reference to the berries.

**rowdy**  AMERICAN, origin uncertain, probably from **row**[3].

**royal**  FRENCH *roial* regal, from LATIN *regalis,* from *rex* king.

**rubbage**  See **rubbish.**

**rubbish**  MIDDLE ENGLISH, from FRENCH *rubouses,* origin uncertain.

**rubble**  MIDDLE ENGLISH related to **rubbish.**

**rubric**  FRENCH *rubrique,* from LATIN *rubrica* red coloring, from *ruber* red.

**ruche**  FRENCH *ruche* bee hive.

**ruching**  FRENCH *ruche* bee hive, because ruched material resembles it, from LATIN *rusca* bark of a tree (used for making hives.).

**rucksack**  GERMAN *Rucksack* back sack.

**ruddy**  OLD ENGLISH *rudig* reddish.

**rude**  FRENCH, from LATIN *rudis* rough.

**rudiment**  LATIN *rudimentium,* from *rudis* rude.

**rueful**  OLD ENGLISH *hreowan* + *-ful* complete.

**ruff**  See **ruffle.**

**ruffian**  FRENCH *rufyen,* origin uncertain.

**ruffle**  OLD NORSE or GERMAN.

**ruga**  LATIN.

**rugby**  *Rugby,* a boys' school in Britain where the game was first played.

**rugged**  SCANDINAVIAN.

**rugger**  See **rugby.**

**ruin**  FRENCH *ruine,* from LATIN *ruina.*

**rule**  FRENCH *riule* ruler, from LATIN *regula,* from *rugere* lead straight.

**rum** (liquor)  MODERN ENGLISH *rumbullion, rombostion,* origin uncertain.

**rumble**  probably from DUTCH *rommelen.*

**rumbustious**  See **rambunctious**.

**rumen**  Latin esophagus.

**rumenotomy**  See **rumen** + **-tomy**.

**ruminate**  Latin *ruminari* chew, from *rumen* from the mouth to the stomach.

**rummage**  French *arrumage* place (hold) where goods (cargo) are put for transport in a ship, from *a* to + *run* ship's hold, from the lack of order in it.

**rumor**  American spelling. See **rumour**.

**rumour**  French, from Latin *rumorem, rumor* noise, din, common talk.

**rump**  Old Norse *rumpr*.

**run**  Old English *rinnan*.

**rune**  Old English *run* mystery, because writing was a mystery to those who couldn't read and write.

**rung**  Old English *hrung* a stick used for walking.

**runt**  Middle English old or decayed tree stump, origin uncertain.

**rupee**  Hindi *rapya* silver jewelry.

**rupture**  French, from Latin *ruptura* break.

**rural**  French, from Latin *ruralis,* from *rus* the country.

**ruse**  French *ruser* use tricks, from *reüser* escape (by using tricks), from Latin *recusare* refuse.

**rush**  French *reüser* escape.  See **ruse**.

**russet**  French, from Latin *russus* reddish.

**rust**  Old English.

**rustic**  Latin *rusticus,* from *rus* country.

**rustle**  imitative.

**rut**  French *route* way.

**ruthless**  Old English *hreowan* rue (regret) + *-leas*.

**-ry**  See **-ery**.

**rye¹** (grain)  Old English *ryge*.

**rye²** (gypsy)  Gypsy *rai* gentleman.

# S

**Sabbath** LATIN *sabbatum*, from GREEK *sabbaton*, from HEBREW *sabbath* rest.

**Sabbatical** FRENCH *sabbatique*, from LATIN *sabbaticus*, from GREEK *sabbatikos*. See **Sabbath**.

**sabe** See **savvy**.

**saber** FRENCH, from GERMAN *sabel*.

**sable** FRENCH, from RUSSIAN *sobol*.

**sabotage** FRENCH to destroy property, from *saboter* damage, from *sabot* wooden shoe, from the early practice of throwing a wooden shoe at an employer's machines to break them.

**saccharin** LATIN *saccharum* sugar, from GREEK *sakcharon*.

**sachem** NATIVE AMERICAN holy man.

**sachet** FRENCH *sac*, from LATIN *saccus* bag.

**sack**[1] (bag) OLD ENGLISH *sacc*, from LATIN *saccus*, from GREEK *sakkos*.

**sack**[2] (rob) FRENCH, from ITALIAN *sacco,* from LATIN *saccus* bag, from GREEK *sakkos*.

**sacque** imitation of French.

**sacrament** FRENCH *sacrement*, from LATIN *sacramentum,* from *sacer* sacred.

**sacred** MIDDLE ENGLISH *sacren* make holy, from LATIN *sacer*.

**sacrifice** FRENCH, from LATIN *sacrificium*, from *sacer* sacred + *facere* do, make.

**sacrilege** FRENCH, from LATIN *sacrilegus* temple robber, from *sacer* sacred + *legere* take away.

**sacrosanct** LATIN *sacer* sacred + *sanctus* holy.

**sad** OLD ENGLISH *sæd* weary.

**saddle** OLD ENGLISH *sadol*.

**sadism** FRENCH *sadisme* after the marquis de *Sade*, an evil French nobleman in the 18th century.

**safari** ARABIC *safar* journey.

**safe** FRENCH *sauf*, from LATIN *salvus* unharmed.

**saffron** FRENCH *safran*, from ARABIC *za'fardin*.

**sag** MIDDLE ENGLISH *saggen*, probably from SCANDINAVIAN *sagga* move slowly.

**saga** OLD NORSE.

**sagaciate** See **sagacious**.

**sagacious** LATIN *sagacis*, from *sagax* wise.

**sage**[1] (wise) FRENCH, from LATIN *sapere* be wise.

**sage**[2] (plant) MIDDLE ENGLISH *sauge*, from FRENCH *sauge*, from LATIN *salvia*.

**saguaro** SPANISH, from NATIVE AMERICAN name.

**sahib** HINDI, from ARABIC *sahib* master.

**said** See **say.**

**sail** OLD ENGLISH *seg(e)l.*

**saint** FRENCH holy, from LATIN *sanctus.*

**sake** OLD ENGLISH *sacru* conflict.

**sal** LATIN salt.

**sal volatile** LATIN volatile (changes to vapor easily) salt.

**salaam** ARABIC *salam* peace.

**salad** FRENCH *salade* cold vegetable dish, from *sal* salt, from LATIN.

**salamander** LATIN *salamandra,* from GREEK *salamandra.*

**salami** ITALIAN, from LATIN *sal* salt.

**salammoniac** See **sal** + **ammonia.**

**salary** LATIN *salarium* pay, from *sal* salt, from money given to soldiers to buy salt, which at that time was not easy to get.

**sale** OLD ENGLISH, from OLD NORSE *sala.*

**saleratus** LATIN *sal aeratus* salt with air in it.

**salicylate** FRENCH *salicyl,* from LATIN *salic-, salix* willow + *-atus.*

**salient** LATIN *salire* leap.

**saline** FRENCH *salin* salty, from LATIN *sal* salt.

**saliva** LATIN.

**sallender** FRENCH *solandre,* origin uncertain.

**sallow** OLD ENGLISH *salu.*

**sally** FRENCH *saillie,* from LATIN *salire* leap.

**salmon** FRENCH *saumon,* from LATIN *salmo.*

**salmonella** Daniel E. *Salmon,* veterinary surgeon who discovered the bacteria in 1885.

**salon** FRENCH, from ITALIAN *salone* hall, from *sala* hall.

**saloon** FRENCH *salon,* from ITALIAN *sala* a hall.

**salsify** FRENCH *salsifis,* origin uncertain.

**salt** OLD ENGLISH *sealt* the food seasoning.

**saltire** FRENCH *sauteur,* from LATIN *saltatorium.*

**salubrious** LATIN *salubris,* from *salus* health.

**salute** LATIN *salutare* greet, from *salus* health.

**salvage** FRENCH *salver,* from LATIN. See **save.**

**salvation** FRENCH *sauvacion, salvatiun,* from LATIN *salvationem,* from *salvare.* See **save.**

**salve** OLD ENGLISH *sealf.*

**salver** FRENCH *salva* tray, from SPANISH *salva* test food (placed on a tray) for poison, from LATIN *salvare.* See **save.**

**salvia** LATIN.

**salvo** ITALIAN, from LATIN *salve* hail!

**sambur** HINDI *sambar.*

**same** OLD NORSE *samr.*

**sampan** CHINESE *san-pan,* possibly from *san* three + *pan* a plank.

**samphire** FRENCH *herbe de Saint Pierre* St. Peter's herb.

**sample** FRENCH *essample* pattern. See **example.**

**samurai** JAPANESE.

**sanatorium** LATIN *sanatorius* giving health, from *sanus* healthy.

**sanctify** LATIN *santificare* make holy, from *sanctus* holy + *facere* do, make.

**sanctimony** FRENCH, from LATIN *sanctimonia,* from *sanctus* holy.

**sanction** FRENCH, from LATIN *sanctus* holy.

**sanctuary** FRENCH, from LATIN *sanctuarium* holy place.

**sand** OLD ENGLISH.

**sandal** FRENCH *sandale*, from LATIN *sandalium*, from GREEK *sandalion,* from *sandalon* sandal.

**sandwich** a nobleman in 18th century England named *Sandwich* who ate meat between two pieces of bread at the gambling table so he wouldn't have to leave the table for a meal.

**sane** LATIN *sanus* healthy.

**sang-froid** FRENCH *sang froid* cool blood, from *sang* blood + *froid* cold.

**sanguine** FRENCH, from LATIN *sanguineus,* from *sanguis* blood.

**sanitarium** LATIN *sanitas* health.

**sanitary** FRENCH *sanitaire*, from LATIN *sanitas* health.

**sannup** NATIVE AMERICAN *sannop*.

**Sanskrit** SANSKRIT *samskrta* made together.

**Santa Claus** DUTCH *Sant Nikolass*.

**sap** OLD ENGLISH *sæp*.

**sapphire** FRENCH *safir,* from LATIN *sappir,* from GREEK *sappheiros*, from HEBREW *sappir*.

**saprophyte** GREEK *sapros* rotten + *phyton* a plant.

**sarcasm** LATIN *sarcasmos* tease, from GREEK *sarkasmos,* from *sarkazein* tear flesh like dogs, from *sarx* flesh.

**sarcoma** LATIN, from GREEK *sarx* flesh.

**sarcophagus** LATIN special stone (limestone) used for coffins, from GREEK *sarkophagos* flesh-eating stone, from *sarx* flesh + *phagein* eat. The ancient Greeks thought the limestone could eat the flesh of the dead.

**sardine** FRENCH, from LATIN *sarda* kind of fish, probably from GREEK *Sardo* Sardinia.

**sardonic** FRENCH *sardonique*, from LATIN *Sardonicus risus* Sardinian laughter, from GREEK *Sardonios gelos*. A poisonous plant of Sardinia which, when eaten, causes the face muscles to pull in a way that make it look like the person is laughing.

**sarong** MALAY *sarung* sheath, covering.

**sarsaparilla** SPANISH *zarzaparrilla* the plant, from *zarza* bramble + *parra* vine.

**sartorial** LATIN *sartor* tailor.

**sash** ARABIC *shash* muslin.

**sashay** FRENCH *chassé* a gliding dance step.

**sass** See **sassy**.

**sassy** saucy. See **sauce**.

**sastruga** GERMAN, from RUSSIAN *zastrúga* small ridge, furrow, from *zastrugát* plane, smooth, from *strug* plane.

**Satan** LATIN, from GREEK, from HEBREW enemy.

**satchel** FRENCH little bag, from LATIN *saccus* bag. See **sack**[1].

**sateen** See **satin**.

**satellite** FRENCH, from LATIN *satelles* an attendant.

**satiate** LATIN *satiare* satisfy, from *satis* enough.

**satin** FRENCH, from ARABIC *zaituni*, from *Zaitun,* a port in southeastern China where satin was made.

**satire** FRENCH, from LATIN *satira* poem on different subjects.

**satisfaction** LATIN *satisfactio* amends.

**satisfy** FRENCH *satisfier*, from LATIN *satis* enough + *facere* do, make.

**saturate** LATIN *saturare* fill.

**Saturday** OLD ENGLISH *Sæterdæg*, from LATIN *Saturni dies* day of Saturn.

267

**Saturn** OLD ENGLISH *Sætern,* from LATIN *Saturnus* god of agriculture.

**satyr** LATIN *satyrus* a woodland god, from GREEK *satyros,* origin unknown.

**sauce** FRENCH, from LATIN *salsus* salted.

**saucer** FRENCH *saussier,* from *sause.* See **sauce.**

**sauerkraut** GERMAN *sauer* sour + *kraut* cabbage.

**sauna** Finnish bath house.

**saunter** possibly from MIDDLE ENGLISH *santren* muse, be in reverie; origin uncertain.

**sausage** FRENCH *saussiche,* from LATIN *salsicia* seasoned with salt, from *salsus* salted.

**sauté** FRENCH, from LATIN *saltare* dance.

**savage** FRENCH *salvage,* from LATIN *silvaticus* wild, from *silva* wood.

**savanna** SPANISH *zavana,* from NATIVE AMERICAN *zabana.*

**save** FRENCH *sauver,* from LATIN *salvare* make safe, from *salvus* safe.

**savior** FRENCH *sauveor,* from LATIN *salvator,* from *salvus* safe.

**savoir-faire** FRENCH know how to do.

**savor** FRENCH *savour* flavor, from LATIN *sapor* taste.

**savvy** SPANISH *sabe usted* do you know, from *saber* know, from LATIN *sapere* be wise.

**saw** OLD ENGLISH *saga* cutting tool.

**sawyer** See **saw.**

**saxaphone** FRENCH, from Antoine Joseph *Sax,* Belgian instrument maker who developed it.

**saxicolous** LATIN *saxum* a rock + *colere* live.

**saxifrage** FRENCH, from LATIN *saxum* a rock + *frangere* break (the plant grows in rock crevices).

**say** OLD ENGLISH *secgan.*

**scab** OLD NORSE *skabb.*

**scabbard** FRENCH *excaubers* case for a sword.

**scads** AMERICAN large amounts, earlier meant dollars, origin uncertain.

**scaffold** FRENCH *eschaufaud* pieces of wood supporting a platform, from LATIN *ex-* out of + *cata* by, from GREEK *kata* down + *fala* wooden platform.

**scalawag (scallywag)** AMERICAN, perhaps from SCOTTISH *scallag* farm servant, rustic.

**scald** FRENCH *escalder* burn with hot water, from *ex-* out + *calidus* hot.

**scale**[1] (for weight) OLD NORSE *skal.*

**scale**[2] (on skin) FRENCH *escale* shell.

**scale**[3] (music) LATIN *scala* ladder.

**scallop** FRENCH *escalope* shell.

**scalp** MIDDLE ENGLISH, from SCANDINAVIAN.

**scamp** FRENCH *escamper* run away, from LATIN *ex-* out of + *campus* battlefield.

**scampi** ITALIAN *scampo* prawn.

**scan** LATIN *scandere* relating to lines of poetry, from *scandere* climb.

**scandal** LATIN *scandalum* stumbling block, from GREEK *skandalon* trap.

**scant** OLD NORSE *skammr* short.

**scape**[1] (get away) from **escape.**

**scape**[2] (scene) from **landscape.**

**scapula** LATIN *scapulae* shoulders.

**scar** FRENCH *escare* scab, from LATIN *eschara* scab, from GREEK *eschara* scab.

**scarab** FRENCH *scarabeé,* from LATIN *scarabaeus,* from GREEK *karabos* beetle, crayfish.

**scarabae** See **scarab.**

**scarce** FRENCH *escars* not many, from LATIN *excerpere* select.

**scare** OLD NORSE *skirra* frighten.

**scarf** FRENCH *escarpe* a purse hung from the neck, from LATIN *scirpa* pouch, from *scirpus* a water plant used in making baskets.

**scarlet** FRENCH *escarlet,* from LATIN *scarlatum* scarlet cloth, from ARABIC *säqirlat* red dress.

**scarp** ITALIAN *scarpa.*

**scathe** OLD NORSE *skathi* harm.

**scatter** MIDDLE ENGLISH *skateran.*

**scavenger** FRENCH *scawage* a tax collected from foreign merchants, from *escauwer* inspect.

**scenario** ITALIAN, from LATIN *scaena* stage, scene.

**scene** FRENCH, from LATIN *scena* stage, from GREEK *skene* stage.

**scent** MIDDLE ENGLISH *senten,* from FRENCH *sentir* feel, smell, taste, perceive, from LATIN *sentire* feel, sense, perceive.

**scepter** FRENCH *sceptre* royal staff, from LATIN *sceptrum,* from GREEK *skeptron.*

**schedule** FRENCH, from LATIN *schedula* small sheet of paper, from *scheda* strip of papyrus.

**scheme** LATIN *schema* shape, from GREEK *schema.*

**schism** FRENCH *scisme,* from LATIN *schisma* split, from GREEK *schisma.*

**schizophrenia** LATIN, from GREEK *schizein* separate + *phren* the mind.

**schmaltz** YIDDISH *shmalts* melted fat, from GERMAN *smalz,* related to *smelzan* melt.

**schnapps** a kind of Holland gin, from GERMAN *Schnaps* a mouthful, gulp.

**scholar** LATIN *scholaris* about a school, from *schola.* See **school.**

**school** OLD ENGLISH *scol* place of learning, from LATIN *schola,* from GREEK *schole.*

**schooner** MODERN ENGLISH (colonial New England), perhaps from SCOTTISH *scon* send over water, skip stones.

**sciatic** LATIN *sciaticus,* from *ischiadicus,* from GREEK *iskhiadikos,* from *iskhias* pain in the hips, from *iskhion* hip joint.

**science** FRENCH knowledge, from LATIN *scientia.*

**scimitar** ITALIAN *scimitara,* origin uncertain.

**scion** FRENCH *scion.*

**scissors** FRENCH *cisoires* shears, from LATIN *cisorium* cutting tool, from *caedere* cut.

**scoff** possibly from OLD NORSE *skopa.*

**scold** OLD NORSE *skald.*

**scolia** GREEK bent or curved.

**scone** SCOTTISH, from DUTCH *schoonbrot* fine bread.

**scoop** DUTCH *schope* bucket and *schoppe* shovel.

**scope** ITALIAN *scopo* target, from GREEK *skopos.*

**-scope** LATIN *-scopium,* from GREEK *-skopion,* from *skopein* view, examine.

**scorch** MIDDLE ENGLISH, perhaps from OLD NORSE *skorpna* shriveled.

**score** OLD NORSE *skor* count by using marks.

**scorn** MIDDLE ENGLISH, from FRENCH *escarn* make fun of.

**scorpion** FRENCH, from LATIN, from GREEK *skorpios.*

**scoter** origin uncertain.

**scoundrel** MIDDLE ENGLISH *skowndrell,* probably from FRENCH *escoundre,* from LATIN *condere* hide.

**scour**[1] (scrub) DUTCH *schuren* clean, from FRENCH *escurer,* from LATIN *ex-* entirely + *curare* take care of.

**scour**[2] (search) OLD NORSE *skyra* rush in.

**scourge** FRENCH *escorgiee,* from LATIN *excoriare* strip off the hide, from *ex-* from + *corrium* hide.

**scout** FRENCH *escoute* spy, from *escouter* listen, from LATIN *auscultare* listen to.

**scowl** MIDDLE ENGLISH *scoulen,* probably from SCANDINAVIAN.

**scrabble** DUTCH *schrabbelen,* from *schrabben* scrape.

**scramble** possible combination of **scamp(er)** + **scrabble.**

**scrap** OLD NORSE *skrap* scrapings.

**scrape** OLD NORSE *skrapa* scratch.

**scrapple** See **scrap.**

**scratch** probably from MIDDLE ENGLISH *scracche.*

**scrawny** probably from SCANDINAVIAN.

**scream** MIDDLE ENGLISH *screamen,* from OLD ENGLISH *scræman.*

**screech** OLD NORSE *skrækja.*

**screed** OLD ENGLISH *screade.*

**screen** DUTCH *scherm.*

**screw** FRENCH *escroue* the hole in which a screw turns, from LATIN *scrofa* sow, from the threads of a screw looking like the curl of a sow's tail.

**scribble** LATIN *scribillare* write quickly, from *scribere* write.

**scribe** LATIN *scriba* secretary, from *scribere* write.

**scrimp** SCOTTISH, also *skrimp,* origin uncertain.

**scrimshaw** AMERICAN nautical *scrimshander, scrimshonting,* origin uncertain.

**scringe** unknown origin.

**script** FRENCH, from LATIN *scriptum* something written.

**scripture** LATIN *scriptura* writing.

**scrivener** FRENCH, from LATIN *scriba* a writer.

**scroll** FRENCH *eschrowe* strip of parchment.

**scrotum** LATIN.

**scrounge** AMERICAN *scrunge* rummage, perhaps from *scringe* pry about.

**scrub** DUTCH *schrobben* rub.

**scrumple** GERMAN *krumpel.*

**scruple** FRENCH *scrupule,* from LATIN *scrupulus* small sharp stone, from *scrupus,* from being uncomfortable by having a small stone in the shoe.

**scrutiny** LATIN *scrutinium* search, from *scrutari.*

**scry** See **descry.**

**scuba** s(elf) c(ontained) u(nderwater) b(reathing) a(pparatus).

**scud** perhaps from MIDDLE ENGLISH *scut* rabbit, rabbit's tail; origin uncertain.

**scuff** OLD NORSE *skufa* shove.

**scuffle** See **scuff** + **-le.**

**scull** MIDDLE ENGLISH a kind of oar, origin uncertain.

**scullery** FRENCH *escuelerie,* from *escuelle* dish, from LATIN *scutella* tray.

**scullion** See **scullery.**

**sculpture** LATIN *sculptura* a carving.

**scum** DUTCH *scume* foam, froth.

**scupper** MIDDLE ENGLISH, origin uncertain.

**scuppernong** AMERICAN, from a river in North Carolina.

**scurrilous** LATIN *scurrilis* like a buffoon (clown).

**scurry** See **hurry**.

**scurvy** probably from SCANDINAVIAN.

**scutage** MIDDLE ENGLISH from LATIN *scutagium,* from *scutum* shield.

**scutcheon** See **escutcheon**.

**scuttle**[1] (sink a ship) MIDDLE ENGLISH *skottell* opening in a ship's deck, from FRENCH *escoutille,* from SPANISH *escotilla* hatchway.

**scuttle**[2] (run quickly) probably from OLD NORSE *scud.*

**scythe** OLD ENGLISH *sithe,* from LATIN *scindere* cut.

**sea** OLD ENGLISH *sæ.*

**seal**[1] (pledge) FRENCH *seel* formal way to stamp documents to prove they were real, from LATIN *signum* sign.

**seal**[2] (animal) OLD ENGLISH *seolh.*

**seam** OLD ENGLISH.

**sear** OLD ENGLISH *searian,* from *sear* dry.

**search** FRENCH *cenchier,* from LATIN *circare* explore, from *circum* around.

**season** FRENCH *saison* time of the year, from LATIN *satio* time to plant, from *satio* planting.

**seat** OLD NORSE *sæti* chair.

**seaton** LATIN *setonem,* from *seta* silk.

**Seccotine** probably from ITALIAN *secco* dry.

**secede** LATIN *secedere* go away.

**secesh** See **secede**.

**seclude** LATIN *secludere* shut off.

**second** FRENCH, from LATIN *secundus,* from *sequito* follow.

**secret** FRENCH *secre,* from LATIN *secernere* put apart, from *se-* apart + *cernere* separate.

**secretary** LATIN *secretarius* confidential officer, from *secretus.* See **secret**.

**secrete** LATIN *secernere.* See **secret**.

**sect** FRENCH *secte,* from LATIN *secta* school of philosophy (the study of right and wrong).

**section** LATIN *secare* cut.

**sector** LATIN the geometric figure, from *secare* cut.

**secular** FRENCH *seculer,* from LATIN *saecularis* worldly, from *saeculum* age.

**secunda** LATIN *secundus.*

**secure** LATIN *securus,* from *se-* free from + *cura* care.

**sedan** possibly from LATIN *sedere* sit.

**sedate** LATIN *sedare* quiet.

**sedentary** FRENCH *sedentaire,* from LATIN *sedentarius,* from *sedere* sit.

**sedge** OLD ENGLISH *secg.*

**sediment** FRENCH, from LATIN *sedimentus,* from *sedere* sit.

**sedition** FRENCH, from LATIN *seditio,* from *sed* apart + *itio,* from *ire* go.

**seduce** LATIN *seducere,* from *se-* apart + *ducere* lead.

**sedulous** LATIN *se-* apart + *dolo* trickery.

**seed** OLD ENGLISH *sæd.*

**seek** OLD ENGLISH *secan.*

**seethe** OLD ENGLISH *seothan* boil.

**segashuate** See **sagacious**.

**segment** LATIN *segmentum* a piece cut off, from *secare* cut.

**segregate** LATIN *segregare,* from *se* apart + *grex* flock.

**segue** ITALIAN, from LATIN *sequi* follow.

**seine** OLD ENGLISH *segne*, from LATIN, from GREEK *segene*.

**seismic** GREEK *seismos* earthquake, from *seiein* shake.

**seize** FRENCH *seisir*, from LATIN *sacire*.

**seldom** OLD ENGLISH *seldan*.

**select** LATIN *seligere* choose.

**self** OLD ENGLISH *self* own.

**sell** OLD ENGLISH *sellan* hand over for money.

**seltzer** GERMAN *Selters*, the name of the village in Germany where it was first made.

**selvedge** See **self** + **edge**.

**semantics** FRENCH *sémantique*, from GREEK *semantikos*, from *sema* sign.

**semaphore** GREEK *sema* a sign + *phoros*, from *pherein* produce.

**semblance** FRENCH appearance, from *sembler* seem, from LATIN *simulare* make like.

**semi-** LATIN half, partly.

**seminal** FRENCH, from LATIN *seminalis* relating to seed, from *semen* seed.

**seminar** See **seminary**.

**seminary** LATIN *seminarius* of seed, from *semen* a seed.

**Semitic** GERMAN, from LATIN *Semiticus*, from GREEK *Sem*, from HEBREW *Shem* the oldest of Noah's three sons.

**senate** FRENCH *senat*, from LATIN *senatus* the ruling body of ancient Rome, from *senex* old man.

**send** OLD ENGLISH *sendan* cause to go.

**seneschal** FRENCH.

**senile** LATIN *selilis*, from *senex* old.

**senior** LATIN *senex* old.

**sennight** OLD ENGLISH *seofon* seven + *niht* night.

**sense** FRENCH *sens*, from LATIN *sensus* feeling, from *sentire* perceive, feel.

**sensitive** FRENCH, from LATIN *sensitivus*, from *sensus*. See **sense**.

**sensor** See **sensory**.

**sensory** LATIN *sensorium*, from *sensus*. See **sense**.

**sensual** LATIN *sensualis*, from *sensus*. See **sense**.

**sentence** FRENCH opinion, from LATIN *sententia*, from *sentire* feel.

**sententious** LATIN *sententiosus* full of meaning, from *sententia*, from *sentire* feel.

**sentient** LATIN *sentire*. See **sentiment**.

**sentiment** FRENCH *sentement*, from LATIN *sentimentus* opinion, from *sentire* feel.

**sentinel** FRENCH *sentinelle* sentry, from LATIN *sentire* feel.

**sentry** See **sentinel**.

**sepal** FRENCH *sépale*, from LATIN *sepalum*.

**separate** LATIN *separare*, from *se-* apart + *parare* arrange.

**sepia** LATIN kind of fish, from GREEK cause to rot. The liquid from the fish is used in the process of making the color.

**seppuku** JAPANESE, from *setsu fuku*, from CHINESE *qie* cut (with a sword or knife) + *fù* belly.

**September** LATIN *September* seventh month in the early Roman calendar in which March was the first month, from *septem* seven.

**septum** LATIN *saeptum* a fence, from *saepire* hedge in, from *saepes* hedge, fence.

**sepulcher** FRENCH *sepulcre* tomb, from LATIN *sepulcrum*, from *sepelire* bury.

**sequel** FRENCH *sequelle*, from LATIN *sequela* result, from *sequi* follow.

**sequence** LATIN *sequentia* that which follows, from *sequi* follow.

**sequester** LATIN *sequiestrare* remove, from *sequester* trustee (person put in charge of another's property).

**sequin** FRENCH, from ITALIAN *zecchino*, from *zecca* a mint, from ARABIC *sikkah* a stamp.

**sequoia** NATIVE AMERICAN *Sequoya*.

**seraglio** ITALIAN *serraglio* enclosure.

**serape** SPANISH.

**sere** See **sear**.

**serenade** FRENCH, from ITALIAN *serenata*, from LATIN *seremus* clear.

**serene** LATIN *serenus*.

**serf** FRENCH, from LATIN *servus* slave.

**serge** FRENCH, from LATIN *sericus* silken, probably from CHINESE *se* silk.

**sergeant** FRENCH *sergent* officer, from LATIN *servire* be a servant.

**series** LATIN *serere* join together.

**serious** LATIN *seriosus* earnest, from *serius* earnest.

**sermon** LATIN *sermo* speech, serve.

**serpent** LATIN *serpens* creeping thing, from *serpere* creep.

**serrate** LATIN *serratus*, from *serra* a saw.

**serried** FRENCH *serrer* crowd, from LATIN *serare*.

**serum** LATIN watery part of something.

**servant** FRENCH *servir* serve, from LATIN *servire*. See **serve**.

**serve** LATIN *servire* be a slave or servant.

**serviette** FRENCH *servir* serve.

**servile** LATIN *servilis*, from *servus* a slave.

**servitor** FRENCH, from LATIN *servitor*, from *servire* serve.

**servitude** FRENCH, from LATIN *servus* a slave.

**session** LATIN *sessio* meeting, from *sedere* sit.

**set** OLD ENGLISH *settan* place.

**settle** OLD ENGLISH *setl* a seat.

**several** FRENCH separate, from LATIN *separ* different.

**severe** LATIN *severus* strict.

**sew** OLD ENGLISH *siw(i)an* fasten together with thread.

**sewer** FRENCH *esseweur*, from LATIN *ex-* out + *aqua* water.

**sex** LATIN *sexus* either male or female.

**sextant** LATIN *sextans* sixth part, because it has the shape of a sixth of a circle.

**sexton** FRENCH *segrestein*, from LATIN *sacrista*, from *sacer* sacred.

**shabby** OLD ENGLISH *sceabb* itch.

**shack** Origin uncertain, possibly from US slang *shackly* rickety, shaky.

**shackle** OLD ENGLISH *seceacul* fetter (chain put on the feet to slow movement).

**shad** OLD ENGLISH *sceadd*.

**shade** OLD ENGLISH *sceadu* shadow.

**shadow** See shade.

**shaft** OLD ENGLISH *scealf*.

**shah** PERSIAN *kshayathiya* king.

**shake** OLD ENGLISH *sceacan* move quickly.

**shale** OLD ENGLISH *sceulu* a shell.

**shall** OLD ENGLISH *sceal*.

**shallop** FRENCH *chaloupe*, from DUTCH *sloep* sloop (ship).

**shallot** FRENCH *eschalotte*.

**sham** probably from **shame**.

**shaman** RUSSIAN, from TUNGUS *saman* one who knows, probably from SANSKRIT *cramana* monk.

**shamble** MIDDLE ENGLISH *shamel*, from OLD ENGLISH *sc(e)amel* stool, from LATIN *scamnum* bench.

**shame** OLD ENGLISH *sceamu*.

**shampoo** HINDI *champo* press.

**shamrock** IRISH *seamar* clover.

**shank** OLD ENGLISH *sceanca* leg.

**shantung** *Shantung* province in China where the fabric was made.

**shanty** possibly from IRISH *sean toigh* old house.

**shape** OLD ENGLISH *(ge)sceap* a form.

**shard** OLD ENGLISH *sceard*.

**share** OLD ENGLISH *scearu* cutting.

**shark** MIDDLE ENGLISH, origin uncertain.

**sharp** OLD ENGLISH *scearp* fine cutting edge.

**shatter** MIDDLE ENGLISH *schateren* scatter.

**shave** OLD ENGLISH *sceafan* scrape away.

**shawl** PERSIAN *shal*.

**she** OLD ENGLISH *seo*.

**sheaf** OLD ENGLISH *sceaf*.

**shear** OLD ENGLISH *sceran* cut.

**sheath** OLD ENGLISH *sceath, scæth*.

**shed** OLD ENGLISH *sced* shelter.

**sheen** OLD ENGLISH *scene* bright.

**sheer**[1] (thin) OLD NORSE *skærr* shine.

**sheer**[2] (turn away) DUTCH *scheren* move aside, cut.

**sheet** OLD ENGLISH *sceat*.

**sheik** ARABIC *shaikh* old man.

**sheldrake** probably from MIDDLE ENGLISH, from DUTCH *schillede* marked with different colors + *drake* drake.

**shelf** OLD ENGLISH *scylfe* ledge.

**shellac** FRENCH *laque en écialles* lac (substance made from tree sap) in thin plates.

**shelter** OLD ENGLISH *scildtruma* shield soldiers.

**shenanigan** possibly from SPANISH *chanada, charranada* trick, deceit.

**shepherd** OLD ENGLISH *sceaphyrde*, from *sceap* sheep + *hyrde* herdsman.

**sheriff** OLD ENGLISH *scirgerefa* person working for the king in a local area, from *scir* county in Great Britain + *gerefa* officer.

**sherry** MIDDLE ENGLISH *sherris*, from SPANISH *vino de Xeres* wine from Xeres.

**shield** OLD ENGLISH *sceld* piece of armor.

**shift** OLD ENGLISH *sciftan* divide.

**shilling** OLD ENGLISH *scilling*.

**shim** MODERN ENGLISH, origin uncertain.

**shimmer** OLD ENGLISH *scimrian* shine a bit.

**shin** OLD ENGLISH *scinu*.

**shine** OLD ENGLISH *scinan* give out light.

**shingle**[1] (wood) LATIN *scindula* split pieces of wood.

**shingle**[2] (stones) OLD ENGLISH *chyngell*, origin unknown.

**shinny** See **shine**.

**ship** OLD ENGLISH *scip*.

**shirk** possibly from GERMAN *schurke* dishonest person.

**shirr** AMERICAN *shirred*, from *shirr* elastic webbing, origin uncertain.

**shoal** OLD ENGLISH *sceald* shallow.

**shoat** MIDDLE ENGLISH *schote*.

**shock** FRENCH *choc* clash, from *choquer* strike, from DUTCH *schokken* crash.

**shoe** OLD ENGLISH *scoh*.

**shoot** OLD ENGLISH *sceotan* send forth.

**shop** OLD ENGLISH *sceoppa* booth.

**shore** DUTCH *schore* coast.

**short** OLD ENGLISH *sceort* brief.

**should** OLD ENGLISH *sceolde*.

**shoulder** OLD ENGLISH *sculdor*.

**shove** OLD ENGLISH *scufan*.

**shovel** OLD ENGLISH *scofl*.

**show** OLD ENGLISH *sceawian* look.

**shower** OLD ENGLISH *scur*.

**shrew** OLD ENGLISH *screawa*.

**shrewd** MIDDLE ENGLISH *schrewen* curse, from *schrewe* shrew (the animal).

**shriek** OLD NORSE *skrækja* screech.

**shrill** MIDDLE ENGLISH *schrille*.

**shrimp** OLD ENGLISH *scrimman* shrink.

**shrine** OLD ENGLISH *scrin*, from LATIN *scrinium* box.

**shrink** OLD ENGLISH *scrincan*.

**shrive** OLD ENGLISH *scrifan*, from LATIN *scribere* write.

**shrivel** possibly from SCANDINAVIAN.

**shroud** OLD ENGLISH *scrud* clothing.

**shrub** OLD ENGLISH *scrybb*.

**shuck** AMERICAN husk, pod, origin uncertain.

**shudder** MIDDLE ENGLISH *shoddren* tremble with fear, from OLD ENGLISH *scudan* shake.

**shuffle** GERMAN *schuffeln* walk awkwardly.

**shun** OLD ENGLISH *scunian*.

**shut** OLD ENGLISH *scyttan* lock a door.

**shutter** See shut + -er.

**shuttle** OLD ENGLISH *scytel* arrow.

**shy**[1] (afraid) OLD ENGLISH *sceoh*.

**shy**[2] (throw) origin unknown.

**sibilant** LATIN *sibilare* hiss.

**sibling** OLD ENGLISH.

**sibyl** FRENCH *sibile*, from LATIN *Sibylla*, from GREEK name for a prophetess meaning "divine wish."

**sick** OLD ENGLISH *seoc*.

**sickle** OLD ENGLISH *sicol*, from LATIN *secula*, from *secare* cut.

**side** OLD ENGLISH *side*.

**sidle** See side + -ling.

**siege** FRENCH *sege* seat, throne, from LATIN *sedere* sit.

**sierra** SPANISH, from LATIN *serra* a saw.

**siesta** SPANISH, from LATIN *sexta hora* sixth hour, noon.

**sieve** OLD ENGLISH *sife*.

**sift** OLD ENGLISH *siftan*.

**sigh** MIDDLE ENGLISH *sighen*, from OLD ENGLISH *sican*.

**sight** OLD ENGLISH *(ge)siht* something seen.

**sign** FRENCH *signe* mark, from LATIN *signum*.

**signal** FRENCH, from LATIN *signale* sign, from *signum* mark.

**signature** LATIN signing, from *signum* mark.

**signet** FRENCH *signe* a sign.

**significant** LATIN *significantia*. See **signify**.

**signify** FRENCH *signifier*, from LATIN *significare* show by signs, from *signum* mark + *facere* make.

**signor** ITALIAN.

**silent** LATIN *silere* still.

**silesia** GERMAN *Schlesien*, east German province the cloth came from.

**silhouette** Étienne de *Silhouette* (1709–1767), said to be in reference to his unpopular efforts to economize, as silhouettes were less expensive than painted portraits.

**silica** LATIN *silex*.

**silk** OLD ENGLISH *seolc* the material, from GREEK *serikon* the material, from *Seres* the Chinese, who were famous for their silks.

**sill** OLD ENGLISH *syll*.

**silly** OLD ENGLISH *(ge)sælig* happy.

**silo** SPANISH, from LATIN *sirus,* from GREEK *siros.*

**silt** probably from SCANDINAVIAN.

**silver** OLD ENGLISH *seolfer.*

**simian** LATIN *simia* an ape, probably from *simus* flat-nosed, from GREEK.

**similar** FRENCH *similaire* like, from LATIN *similis.*

**simile** LATIN *similis* similar.

**simper** perhaps from SCANDINAVIAN, origin uncertain.

**simple** FRENCH plain, from LATIN *simplex.*

**simulacra** See **simulate**.

**simulacrum** See **simulate**.

**simulate** LATIN *simulare* imitate.

**simultaneous** LATIN *simultas,* from competition, from *simul* at the same time.

**sin** OLD ENGLISH *synn.*

**since** MIDDLE ENGLISH *sinnes,* from OLD ENGLISH *siththan* after.

**sincere** FRENCH, from LATIN *sincerus* clean.

**sinecure** LATIN *beneficium sine cura* benefice (room and board provided to a priest) without also having religious duties, such as the care of souls.

**sinew** OLD ENGLISH *sinu.*

**sing** OLD ENGLISH *singan.*

**singe** FRENCH *sengan.*

**single** FRENCH, from LATIN *singulus* separate, from *singuli* one to each.

**singlet** See **single**.

**singletree** MIDDLE ENGLISH *swingle* a rod + *tre* a tree.

**sinister** MIDDLE ENGLISH, from FRENCH *sinistre*, from LATIN *sinister* left, from the early belief that omens seen on the left side were unlucky.

**sink** OLD ENGLISH *sincan.*

**sinus** LATIN a bent surface.

**sip** OLD ENGLISH *sypian.*

**siphon** FRENCH, from LATIN, from GREEK a tube.

**sir** See **sire**.

**sire** FRENCH a master, from LATIN *senior* older.

**siren** FRENCH, from LATIN *Siren* a sea goddess, from GREEK *Seiren* a sea goddess, part bird and part woman, who sang to sailors to get them to join her in the sea.

**sisal** *Sisal*, port in Yucatan from which the fiber was exported.

**siskin** GERMAN *sisschen*, from *zisec.*

**sissy** AMERICAN *sis* sister.

**sister** OLD NORSE *systir*.

**sit** OLD ENGLISH *sittan*.

**site** LATIN *situs* position.

**situate** LATIN *situare* place, from *situs* position.

**size** MIDDLE ENGLISH *syse* limit, from FRENCH *sise* a set amount.

**sizzle** imitative.

**skate**[1] (ice blade) DUTCH *schaats* a skate, from FRENCH *eschace* stilt.

**skate**[2] (fish) OLD NORSE *skata*.

**skedaddle** AMERICAN Civil War military slang.

**skeet** MODERN ENGLISH, supposed to be an old form of *shoot*, perhaps from OLD NORSE *skotja*.

**skeeter** See **mosquito**.

**skein** FRENCH *escaigne* yarn.

**skeleton** LATIN, from GREEK mummy *skeletas* dried up.

**skelter** See **helter-skelter**.

**skep** OLD NORSE *skeppa*.

**skeptic** GREEK *skeptikos* thoughtful.

**sketch** DUTCH *schets* model, from LATIN *schedium* poem, from GREEK *schedios* done on the spur of the moment.

**skew** FRENCH *eskiuwer* avoid.

**skewer** OLD NORSE *skifa* a slice.

**ski** OLD NORSE *skith* snowshoe.

**skid** probably from OLD NORSE *skith*.

**skidoo** possibly from **skedaddle**.

**skiff** FRENCH *esquif*, from ITALIAN *schifo*.

**skill** OLD NORSE *skil* knowledge.

**skilligalee** origin uncertain.

**skim** FRENCH *escumer* get floating things off a liquid, from *escume* foam.

**skin** OLD NORSE *skinn*.

**skink** FRENCH *scinc*, from LATIN *scincus*, from GREEK *skinkos* lizard.

**skip** probably from SCANDINAVIAN.

**skipple** DUTCH *schepel*.

**skirl** probably from Norwegian *skrylla* scream.

**skirmish** FRENCH *eskimer* fight with a sword.

**skirt** OLD NORSE *skyrta* shirt.

**skit** probably from OLD NORSE *skjota* shoot.

**skive** OLD NORSE *skifa*.

**skivvy** nautical slang, origin unknown.

**skoal** DANISH *skaal* a toast, from OLD NORSE bowl, cup.

**skrike** probably from SCANDINAVIAN.

**skulk** probably from GERMAN *schulken*.

**sky** OLD NORSE cloud.

**slab** MIDDLE ENGLISH *sclabbe*.

**slack** OLD ENGLISH *slæc* lazy.

**slag** GERMAN *slagge*.

**slake** OLD ENGLISH *slacian*.

**slam** probably from SCANDINAVIAN.

**slander** FRENCH *esclandre* disgrace, from LATIN *scandalum* cause of disgrace, from GREEK *skandalon* trap.

**slang** origin unknown.

**slap** GERMAN *slapp*.

**slash** FRENCH *esclachier* break.

**slat** FRENCH *esclat* piece.

**slate** FRENCH *esclat* splinter, from *esclater* split.

**slather** origin uncertain.

**slattern** MIDDLE ENGLISH *slatter* spill or splash awkwardly, waste, origin uncertain.

**slaughter** OLD NORSE *slatr* butcher's seat.

**slave** MIDDLE ENGLISH *Sclavus* one of the Slavic (eastern Europe) people, from GREEK *Sklabos*, which refers to a time in the Middle Ages when a German people made many Slavic people their slaves.

**slay** OLD ENGLISH *slean*.

**sledge** DUTCH *sleedse* sled.

**sleek** See **slick**.

**sleep** OLD ENGLISH *slæpan* be numb (have no feeling).

**sleet** possibly from OLD ENGLISH *slet*.

**sleigh** DUTCH *slee,* from *slede* sled.

**sleight** OLD NORSE *slægth* sly.

**slender** MIDDLE ENGLISH *slendre,* origin unknown.

**slew**[1] (swamp) AMERICAN, from **slough**.

**slew**[2] (swing) nautical *slue,* origin unknown.

**slew**[3] (many) IRISH *sluagh* a host, crowd, multitude.

**slice** FRENCH *esclicier* split.

**slick** OLD ENGLISH *slician* make smooth.

**slide** OLD ENGLISH *slidan* glide.

**slight** DUTCH *slicht* simple.

**slim** DUTCH bad.

**slime** OLD ENGLISH *slim*.

**sling** MIDDLE ENGLISH *slinge(n),* probably from OLD NORSE *slyngva* throw.

**slip**[1] (slide) GERMAN *slippen* glide, from OLD ENGLISH *slupan*.

**slip**[2] (strip) DUTCH *slippe* cut, slit.

**slip**[3] (clay) OLD ENGLISH *slyppe* slime.

**slippery** OLD ENGLISH *slipur*.

**slit** OLD ENGLISH *slitan*.

**slither** OLD ENGLISH *sliderian* slip.

**sliver** OLD ENGLISH *slifan* slice off.

**slob** IRISH *slab* mud, of SCANDINAVIAN origin.

**slobber** MIDDLE ENGLISH, origin uncertain.

**slog**[1] (work) MIDDLE ENGLISH *sluggen*.

**slog**[2] (hit) See **slug**[2].

**slogan** SCOTTISH *sluagh-ghairm* cry for battle, from *sluagh* army + *gairm* shout.

**sloop** DUTCH *sloep*.

**slop** MIDDLE ENGLISH mudhole, from OLD ENGLISH *slypa* a paste.

**slope** OLD ENGLISH *aslupan* slip away.

**slosh** probably from a blend of **slush** and **slop**, origin uncertain.

**sloth** OLD ENGLISH *slaw* slow.

**slouch** OLD NORSE *sllokr* lazy person, from *sloka* droop.

**slough** OLD ENGLISH *sloh* piece of muddy ground.

**sloven** possibly from DUTCH *slof* careless.

**slow** OLD ENGLISH *slaw* dull.

**sludge** MIDDLE ENGLISH *slich* slime.

**slue** See **slew**[2].

**slug**[1] (snail) MIDDLE ENGLISH *slugge* clumsy one, origin uncertain.

**slug**[2] (hit) OLD NORSE *slag*.

**sluggard** MIDDLE ENGLISH *sluggen* be lazy.

**sluice** FRENCH *escluse* floodgate, from LATIN *escludera* shut out.

**slum** AMERICAN *back slum* back alley, from slang for back room, origin unknown.

**slumgullion** AMERICAN slang, probably a made up word.

**slump** probably from GERMAN *slumpen* happen by accident.

**slur** possibly from DUTCH *sleuren* walk in mud.

**slush** origin uncertain, perhaps from SCANDINAVIAN.

**sly** OLD NORSE *slægr* deceiving.

**smack** imitative.

**small** OLD ENGLISH *smæl* narrow.

**smart** OLD ENGLISH *smeortan* be painful.

**smash** See **mash**.

**smear** OLD ENGLISH *smerian*.

**smell** MIDDLE ENGLISH *smellen*.

**smelt**[1] (fish) OLD ENGLISH *smelt* small salmon-like sea fish.

**smelt**[2] (melt) DUTCH *smelten* melt.

**smile** MIDDLE ENGLISH *smilen,* possibly from GERMAN *smilan.*

**smirk** OLD ENGLISH *smearcian* smile.

**smite** OLD ENGLISH *smitan* smear.

**smithereens** IRISH *smiodar* piece.

**smock** OLD ENGLISH *smoc* woman's underclothes.

**smoke** OLD ENGLISH *smoca*.

**smolder** MIDDLE ENGLISH *smoldren*.

**smolt** See **smelt**[1].

**smooch** possibly from German *schmutzen* kiss, smile.

**smooth** OLD ENGLISH *smoth* rough.

**smorgasbord** SWEDISH *smorgasbord* open sandwich table, literally butter-goose table, from *smorgas* bread and butter, from *smor* butter + *gas* goose + *bord* table.

**smother** MIDDLE ENGLISH *smorithren,* from *smorther* thick smoke.

**smouch** See **smooch**.

**smudge** probably from MIDDLE ENGLISH *smogen.*

**smug** probably from GERMAN *smuck* neat.

**smuggle** GERMAN *smuggein.*

**snack** MIDDLE ENGLISH bite or snap (of a dog), probably from DUTCH *snacken* snatch, chatter.

**snaffle** probably from early Dutch *snabbe* bill of a bird.

**snag** possibly from SCANDINAVIAN.

**snail** OLD ENGLISH *snægl.*

**snake** OLD ENGLISH *snaca.*

**snap** DUTCH *snappen* speak quickly.

**snare** OLD ENGLISH *sneare* noose.

**snarl** probably from GERMAN *snarren* rattle.

**snatch** probably from MIDDLE ENGLISH *snakken* take.

**sneak** MIDDLE ENGLISH *sniken* creep, from OLD ENGLISH *snican.*

**sneer** MIDDLE ENGLISH *sneren.*

**sneeze** MIDDLE ENGLISH *finesen,* from OLD ENGLISH *fneosan.*

**snell**[1] (quick) MIDDLE ENGLISH, from OLD ENGLISH, from GERMAN *snel.*

**snell**[2] (fish line) AMERICAN, origin uncertain.

**snib** SCOTTISH.

**snick** imitative.

**snicker** imitative.

**snide** origin unknown, possibly from thieves' slang meaning bad or fake.

**sniff** imitative.

**snifter** imitative

**snig** MIDDLE ENGLISH small eel, origin uncertain.

**snip** DUTCH *snippen* clip.

**snit** AMERICAN, origin uncertain.

**snivel** possibly from OLD ENGLISH *snofl* liquid from the nose.

**snob** OLD NORSE *snapr* lower class person. In the 1800s the word changed to its current meaning.

**snood** OLD ENGLISH *snod*.

**snore** imitative.

**snorkle** GERMAN *Schnorchel*, from navy slang *Schnorchel* nose.

**snort** MIDDLE ENGLISH *snorten*.

**snout** GERMAN and DUTCH *snute*.

**snow** OLD ENGLISH *snaw*.

**snub** OLD NORSE *snubba* scold.

**snuff** DUTCH *snuffen*.

**snuffle** DUTCH *snuffelen* smell out.

**snug** MIDDLE ENGLISH compact, trim (of a ship), perhaps from SCANDINAVIAN.

**so** OLD ENGLISH *swa*.

**soak** OLD ENGLISH *socian*.

**soap** OLD ENGLISH *sape*.

**soar** FRENCH *essorer* throw up in the air, from LATIN *ex-* out of + *aura* breeze, from GREEK *aura*.

**sob** MIDDLE ENGLISH *sobben*.

**sober** FRENCH *sobre* moderate, from LATIN *sobrius* not drunk.

**sobriquet** FRENCH *soubriquet* a chuck under the chin.

**social** FRENCH, from LATIN *socius* companion.

**society** FRENCH *socite*, from LATIN *societas*, from *socius* companion.

**sock** OLD ENGLISH *socc*, from LATIN *soccus* a light, low-heeled shoe.

**sockdolager** AMERICAN *sock* hit hard + made-up ending.

**socket** MIDDLE ENGLISH, from FRENCH *soket* spearhead shaped like a blade for cutting soil.

**sod** probably from DUTCH *sode*.

**soda** MIDDLE ENGLISH alkaline substance, from LATIN for saltwort, a plant from which soda was obtained, probably from ARABIC *suwwad* a saltwort plant.

**sodden** See **seethe**.

**sodium** See **soda**. The element was isolated, from caustic soda.

**sofa** ARABIC *suffah*.

**soft** OLD ENGLISH *softe* gentle.

**soggy** probably from OLD NORSE *sog* sucking.

**soil**[1] (dirt) FRENCH, from LATIN *solum*.

**soil**[2] (stain) FRENCH *sollier* get dirty, from LATIN *suculus* little pig.

**soiree** FRENCH *soir* evening.

**sojourn** FRENCH *sojorner* rest, from LATIN *sub-* under + *diurnus* daily.

**solace** FRENCH *solaz* console (make less sad), from LATIN *solacium*.

**solar** LATIN *solaris* having to do with the sun, from *sol* sun.

**solder** FRENCH *soldure*, from *sou(l)der* fasten together, from LATIN *solidus* firm.

**soldier** FRENCH someone who fights for pay, from *soulde* pay, from LATIN *solidus* a Roman gold coin.

**sole**[1] (bottom) FRENCH *sole* sandal, from LATIN *solea* sole of a sandal, from *solum* foundation, base.

**sole**[2] (only) LATIN *solus* alone.

**solemn** LATIN *sollemnis* yearly, from *sollus* all + *annus* year.

**soleus** LATIN *solea*, sole of a sandal (called such as the soleus muscle is flat.)

**solicitous** LATIN *sollicitus*, from *sollus* whole + *ciere* put in motion.

**solid** LATIN *solidus* firm.

**soliloquy** LATIN *soliloquim* talking to oneself, from *solus* alone + *loqui* speak.

**solitary** LATIN *solitarius* alone.

**solo** ITALIAN alone, from LATIN *solus*.

**solstice** FRENCH, from LATIN *solstitium*, from *sol* sun + *sistere* cause to stand.

**soluble** FRENCH, from LATIN *solubilis*, from *solvere* loosen, dissolve. See **solve**.

**solution** FRENCH *solucion*, from LATIN *solutio* explanation.

**solve** LATIN *solvere* loosen, from *se-* apart + *luere* let go.

**solvent** See **solve**.

**somatic** GREEK *somatikos* of the body, from *soma* body.

**somber** FRENCH *sombre* gloomy, dark, from LATIN *sub-* under + *umbra* shade.

**sombrero** SPANISH *sombra* shade.

**some** OLD ENGLISH *sum*.

**somersault** FRENCH *sombresault* leap, from LATIN *supra* above + *saltus* leap.

**somnolent** FRENCH, from LATIN *somnolentus*, from *somnus* sleep.

**son** OLD ENGLISH *sunu*.

**sonar** so(und) n(avigation) a(nd) r(anging).

**sonata** ITALIAN, from LATIN *sonare* sound.

**song** OLD ENGLISH *sang*.

**sonic** LATIN *sonus* noise.

**sonnet** ITALIAN *suono* sound, from LATIN *sonus* noise.

**sonse** IRISH *sonas* good fortune.

**soon** OLD ENGLISH *sona*.

**soot** OLD ENGLISH *sot*.

**sooth** OLD ENGLISH *soth*.

**soothe** OLD ENGLISH *sothian* prove to be true.

**sophism** LATIN *sophisma* false belief, from GREEK *sophos* clever or wise.

**sophisticate** LATIN *sophisticare* disguise, from GREEK *sophistikos* clever, from Sophists, early Greek teachers of philosophy (the study of right and wrong) and ethics.

**sorcery** FRENCH *sorcerie* magic, taking a chance by drawing lots (things like pieces of pottery used in games of chance), from LATIN *sors* lot.

**sordid** FRENCH, from LATIN *sordes* filth.

**sore** OLD ENGLISH *sar* painful.

**sorghum** ITALIAN *sorgo*.

**sorority** LATIN *sororitas* sisterhood, from *soror* sister.

**sorrel**[1] (color) FRENCH *sor* light brown, from LATIN *saurus*.

**sorrel**[2] (plant) FRENCH *surele*, from *sur* sour, from the taste of its leaves.

**sorrow** OLD ENGLISH *sorg*.

**sort** FRENCH *sortie* manner, from LATIN *sors* kind, from *sortem, sors* lot, condition.

**sortie** FRENCH *sortie* a going out, from *sortir.* See **sort.**

**sot** OLD ENGLISH *sott* stupid person, from FRENCH *sot*, origin uncertain.

**souffle** FRENCH *souffler* blow.

**sough** OLD ENGLISH *swogan* sound.

**soul** OLD ENGLISH *sawol* spiritual part of people.

**sound**[1] (hearing) FRENCH *son*, from LATIN *sonus.*

**sound**[2] (healthy) OLD ENGLISH *(ge)sund.*

**sound**[3] (water channel) OLD ENGLISH *sund.*

**sound**[4] (depth) FRENCH *sonder*, from LATIN *sub-* under + *unda* a wave.

**soup** FRENCH *soupe.*

**sour** OLD ENGLISH *sur.*

**source** FRENCH *sourse* point where a river or stream starts, from *sourdre* rise, from LATIN *surgere.*

**soutache** FRENCH, from HUNGARIAN *szuszak* curl of hair.

**south** OLD ENGLISH *suth.*

**souvenir** FRENCH remember, from LATIN *subvenire* come to mind.

**sovereign** FRENCH *soverain* supreme ruler, from LATIN *super* above.

**soviet** RUSSIAN *sovet* council.

**sow**[1] (pig) OLD ENGLISH *sugu.*

**sow**[2] (plant seed) OLD ENGLISH *sawan.*

**soy** DUTCH *soya*, from JAPANESE *soyu*, from *shoyu*, from CHINESE *shi-yu*, from *shi* fermented soy beans + *yu* oil.

**space** FRENCH *espace* length of place or time, from LATIN *spatium* room.

**spade** OLD ENGLISH *spadu.*

**spaghetti** ITALIAN *spago* small cord.

**spalpeen** IRISH *spailpin.*

**span** OLD ENGLISH *spannen* clasp, fasten, stretch.

**spang**[1] (action) SCOTTISH, with a leap.

**spang**[2] (buckle) See **spangle.**

**spangle** MIDDLE ENGLISH *spang* a clasp, from OLD ENGLISH.

**spaniel** FRENCH *espagnol*, from LATIN *Hispania* Spain.

**spank** imitative.

**spanker** See **spank** + -er.

**spanner** GERMAN.

**spar** OLD NORSE *sperra* beam.

**spar**[1] (pole) MIDDLE ENGLISH *sparre*, from DUTCH.

**spar**[2] (to box) FRENCH *esparer* kick, from ITALIAN *sparare*, from LATIN *ex-* + *parare* ward off, parry.

**spar**[3] (mineral) GERMAN *spar, sper.*

**spare** OLD ENGLISH *sparian* leave unhurt.

**spark** OLD ENGLISH *spearca.*

**sparrow** OLD ENGLISH *spearwa.*

**sparse** LATIN *spargere* scatter.

**spasm** FRENCH *spasme*, from LATIN *spasmus*, from GREEK *spaein* tear.

**spat** imitative.

**spate** MIDDLE ENGLISH, from SCOTTISH sudden flood, origin unknown.

**spatial** LATIN *spatium.*

**spatter** possibly from DUTCH *spatt(en)* splash.

**spatula** Latin broad piece, from Greek *spathe.*

**spavin** French *esparvain.*

**spawn** French *espandre* get rid of.

**speak** Old English *specan* say words.

**spear** Old English *spere.*

**special** French *especial,* from Latin *specialis* particular, from *species* kind.

**species** Latin kind.

**specific** Latin *spectifucus,* from *species.* See species.

**specimen** Latin *specere* see.

**specious** Latin *speciosus* beautiful, from *species* kind.

**speck** Old English *specca.*

**spectacle** French, from Latin *spectaculum* show.

**spectator** Latin see.

**specter (spectre)** French, from Latin *spectrum* appearance, from *spectare* behold.

**spectroscope** See **spectrum** + -scope.

**spectrum** Latin appear.

**speculate** Latin *speculari* view, from *specula* watch tower, from *specere* see.

**speculum** Latin *specere* look.

**speech** Old English *spæc* talk.

**speed** Old English *sped* success.

**spell**[1] (write words) French *espeller* explain.

**spell**[2] (magic) Old English *spell* story.

**spell**[3] (relieve) Old English *spellan.*

**spelunker** Middle English *spelunk* cave, cavern, from French *spelunque,* from Latin *spelunca,* from Greek *spelynx.*

**spencer**[1] (butler) French *espenser, despenser,* from *despencier* dispenser.

**spencer**[2] (in product names) the name *Spencer.*

**spend** Old English *spendan* pay out, from Latin *expendare* pay.

**sperm** French *esperme,* from Latin *sperma,* from Greek seed, from *speirein* sow.

**spew** Old English *speowan.*

**sphagnum** Latin *sphagnos,* a kind of lichen, from Greek *sphagnos* a spiny shrub.

**sphere** French, from Latin *sphera* ball, from Greek *sphaira.*

**sphinx** Latin, from Greek strangler.

**sphygmo-** Greek *sphygmos* the pulse.

**sphygmomanometer** See **sphygmo-** + **manometer.**

**spice** French *espice,* from Latin *species* kind.

**spicule** Latin *speculum,* from *spicule* point.

**spider** Middle English *spithre,* from Old English *spinnan* spin.

**spigot** Middle English, origin uncertain.

**spike** possibly from Dutch nail.

**spill** Old English *spillan* waste.

**spiller**[1] (fish line) Irish, origin uncertain.

**spiller**[2] (fire stick) Middle English *spill* splinter, origin uncertain.

**spin** Old English *spinnan* twist into thread.

**spinach** French *espinache,* from Spanish *espinac,* from Arabic *isbanakh,* from Persian *aspanakh.*

**spindle** Old English *spinnan* spin.

**spine** French *espine,* from Latin *spina* a thorn.

**spinet** French, from Italian *spinetta,* from Giovanni *Spinetti,* inventor of the instrument in the early 1500s.

**spinney** MIDDLE ENGLISH *spenne* thorn hedge, from FRENCH *espinei*, from LATIN *spinetum*, from *spina* thorn.

**spinster** MIDDLE ENGLISH *spinnestere*, woman who spins thread (as an occupation), from *spinnen* spin. In earlier times the *-ster* was added to show a woman's occupation.

**spiracle** MIDDLE ENGLISH, from LATIN *spiraculum*, from *spirare* breathe.

**spiral** LATIN *spiralis* winding, from *spira* coil, from GREEK *speira*.

**spire** OLD ENGLISH *spir* stalk of a plant.

**spirillum** LATIN *spira*. See **spiral**.

**spirit** FRENCH *esprit*, from LATIN *spiritus* breath, life, soul.

**spirochete** LATIN *spirochaeta*, from GREEK *speira* spiral + *chaite* hair.

**spirometer** LATIN *spirare* breathe + GREEK *metron* measure.

**spit** OLD ENGLISH *spitu*.

**spite** See **despite**.

**spittoon** See **spit**.

**splay** MIDDLE ENGLISH *displaten* display.

**spleen** LATIN *splen*, from GREEK.

**splendid** LATIN *splendidus* bright.

**splendor** FRENCH, from LATIN *splendere* shine.

**splice** DUTCH *splissen* join ropes together.

**spline** OLD NORSE *splindra* splinter.

**splint** GERMAN *splinte* metal pin.

**split** DUTCH *splitten*.

**splotch** MODERN ENGLISH, origin uncertain (perhaps a blend of **spot, blot,** and **botch**).

**spoil** FRENCH *espoillier* take by robbing, from LATIN *spolium* things taken by robbing.

**spondulick** GREEK *spondylikos*, from *spondylos* a seashell used as money.

**sponge** OLD ENGLISH, from LATIN, from GREEK *spongia*.

**sponsor** LATIN surety (person who pays the bills of another).

**spontaneous** LATIN *spontaneus* voluntary, from *sponte*.

**spoof** A card game called *Spoof* that includes tricks. It was invented by an English comedian in the late 19th century.

**spook** DUTCH ghost.

**spool** DUTCH *spoele*.

**spoon** OLD ENGLISH *spon* a chip.

**spoor** AFRIKAANS *spor*, from DUTCH.

**spore** LATIN *spora*, from GREEK *spora* seed.

**sport** FRENCH *disporter*, from LATIN *dis-* opposite + *porter* carry, from the idea of leading the attention away from serious things.

**spot** possibly from DUTCH *spotte* stain.

**spouse** FRENCH *espous* bridegroom and *espouse* bride, from LATIN *sponsus* engaged man and *sponsa* engaged woman.

**spout** DUTCH *spouten* spurt.

**sprain** MODERN ENGLISH, origin uncertain.

**sprawl** OLD ENGLISH *sprewlian*.

**spray** possibly from DUTCH *spra(e)yen* sprinkle.

**spread** OLD ENGLISH *sprædan* extend.

**spree** AMERICAN slang, origin uncertain, perhaps from FRENCH *esprit* spirit.

**sprig** MIDDLE ENGLISH *sprigge*.

**sprightly** See **sprite**.

**spring** OLD ENGLISH *springan* grow.

**sprinkle** possibly from DUTCH *sprenkelen*, from *sprenkel* small spot.

**sprint** MIDDLE ENGLISH spring, leap, from OLD NORSE *spretta* jump up.

**sprite** FRENCH *esprit*, from LATIN *spiritus* breath, life, soul.

**sprocket** MODERN ENGLISH, origin uncertain.

**sprout** OLD ENGLISH *sprutan* shoot forth.

**spruce** MIDDLE ENGLISH *Spruce*, Russia, a place where the tree can be found.

**spry** SWEDISH *sprygg* lively.

**spume** FRENCH, from LATIN *spuma* foam.

**spunk** IRISH *sponc* tinder, from LATIN *spongia* sponge.

**spur** OLD ENGLISH *spura*.

**spurious** LATIN *spurius*.

**spurn** OLD ENGLISH *spurnan* kick off, reject, despise.

**spurt** MIDDLE ENGLISH *spirt*, origin uncertain.

**sputter** DUTCH *sputteren*.

**spy** FRENCH *espier* watch with attention.

**squab** MODERN ENGLISH, origin uncertain.

**squad** FRENCH *esquades* small party of soldiers, from LATIN *ex-* out + *quadra* square, referring to the arranging of soldiers into squares.

**squalid** LATIN *squalidus* extremely dirty.

**squall**[1] (storm) MIDDLE ENGLISH, related to SWEDISH *skval*, rushing water.

**squall**[2] (cry) OLD NORSE *skvala*, cry out.

**squalor** LATIN. See **squalid**.

**squamous** LATIN *squamosus* scaly, from *squama* scale.

**squander** MIDDLE ENGLISH, origin uncertain.

**square** FRENCH *esquarrer*, from LATIN *ex-* out + *quadrare* square, from *quadrus* a square, from *quattuor* four.

**squash**[1] (crush) FRENCH *esquasser* break in pieces, from LATIN *ex-* thoroughly + *quatere* shake.

**squash**[2] (vegetable) NATIVE AMERICAN.

**squat** FRENCH *esquatir,* from LATIN *ex-* out + *cogere* force.

**squaw** NATIVE AMERICAN.

**squawk** imitative.

**squeak** OLD NORSE *skvakka* gurgle.

**squeamish** FRENCH *escoimous* shy.

**squeeze** OLD ENGLISH *cwysan* crush.

**squelch** imitative.

**squib** MIDDLE ENGLISH, origin uncertain.

**squid** perhaps from a sailors' variation of **squirt**.

**squiggle** See **squirm** + **wiggle**.

**squint** possibly from MIDDLE ENGLISH *skwyn*.

**squire** FRENCH *esquier*. See **esquire**.

**squirm** imitative.

**squirt** probably from GERMAN and DUTCH *swirtjen*.

**St. Elmo** ITALIAN *Sant'Ermo* St. Erasmus, patron saint of Mediterranean sailors, possibly influenced by GREEK *elene* torch.

**stab** MIDDLE ENGLISH *stabbe*.

**stable** FRENCH *(e)stable* firm, from LATIN *stabilis*, from *stare* stand.

**staccato** ITALIAN separated.

**stack** OLD NORSE *stakkr* haystack.

**stadium** LATIN measure of length about 607 ft (the length of ancient Greek and Roman tracks for athletic events), from GREEK *stadion*.

**staff** OLD ENGLISH *stæf* pole.

**stag** OLD ENGLISH *stagga.*

**stage** FRENCH *estage* floor, from LATIN *stare* stand.

**stagger** OLD NORSE *stakra* push.

**stagnant** LATIN *stagnare,* from *stagnum* swamp.

**staid** See **stay.**

**stain** FRENCH, from LATIN *dis-* from + *tingere* color.

**stair** OLD ENGLISH *stæger.*

**stake** OLD ENGLISH *staca* strong stick.

**stalactite** LATIN *stalactites,* from GREEK *stalaktos* dripping, from *stalassein* trickle.

**stalagmite** LATIN *stalagmites,* from GREEK *stalagmos* a dropping, from *stalagma* a drop, drip, from *stalassein* trickle.

**stale** probably from DUTCH *stel.*

**stalk**[1] (pursue) OLD ENGLISH *bestealcian* go secretly.

**stalk**[2] (stem) OLD ENGLISH *stela* a stalk.

**stall** OLD ENGLISH *steall* place in a stable.

**stalwart** OLD ENGLISH *stælwierthe,* from *stathol* foundation + *wierthe* worth.

**stamen** LATIN, a thread on an upright loom. See **stamina.**

**stamina** LATIN *stamen* thread, from the idea that the warp threads on a loom were the foundation of the fabric. Also, from the idea in mythology that threads spun by the Fates determined the length of the person's life.

**stammel** probably from FRENCH *estamel,* from *estame* woolen thread, from LATIN *stamen* thread.

**stance** FRENCH, from LATIN *stare* stand.

**stanchion** FRENCH *estanchon,* from *estance,* from LATIN *stare* stand.

**stand** OLD ENGLISH *standan* be upright.

**standard** FRENCH *estandart* flag.

**stang** OLD NORSE *stong.*

**stanza** ITALIAN room, from LATIN *stare* stand.

**staple**[1] (produce) FRENCH *estaple* market, from DUTCH *stapel.*

**staple**[2] (metal) OLD ENGLISH *stapol* a post.

**star** OLD ENGLISH *steorra.*

**starboard** OLD ENGLISH. See **steer** + **board** (boats were steered using a paddle on the right side).

**starch** OLD ENGLISH *stearc* stiff.

**stare** OLD ENGLISH *starian.*

**stark** OLD ENGLISH *stearc* severe.

**start** OLD ENGLISH *styrtan.*

**startle** OLD ENGLISH *steartlian* struggle.

**starve** OLD ENGLISH *steorfan* die.

**-stat** GREEK *-states.*

**state** FRENCH *estat,* from LATIN *status* condition, from *stare* stand.

**static** LATIN *staticus,* from GREEK *statikos* causing to stand.

**station** FRENCH, from LATIN *stare* stand.

**statistics** GERMAN *Statistik* science of collecting numerical data, from LATIN *statisticus* having to do with state affairs, from *status* condition, from *stare* stand.

**stator** LATIN, from *stare* stand.

**statue** FRENCH, from LATIN *statua* image, from *stare* stand.

**statuesque** See **statue** + **-esque.**

**status** LATIN condition, from *stare* stand.

**staunch** FRENCH *estanche* watertight, from *estanchier,* from LATIN *stans.* See **stance.**

**stave** MIDDLE ENGLISH plural of **staff.**

**stay** FRENCH *estai,* from *ester* stand, from LATIN *stare.*

**stead** OLD ENGLISH *stede* place.

**steak** OLD NORSE *steik* slice of meat roasted over a fire.

**steal** OLD ENGLISH *stœfan.*

**stealth** MIDDLE ENGLISH *steithe,* from *stelen* steal.

**steam** OLD ENGLISH smoke.

**steed** OLD ENGLISH *steda* stallion.

**steel** OLD ENGLISH *stiele.*

**steep** OLD ENGLISH *steap* high.

**steer** OLD ENGLISH *stieran.*

**stellar** LATIN *stellaris,* from *stella* star.

**stem** OLD NORSE *stemma* dam up.

**stench** OLD ENGLISH *stenc.*

**stencil** FRENCH *estenceler* sparkle, from *stencelle* spark, from LATIN *scintilla.*

**stenography** GREEK *stenos* narrow + *graphia* writing.

**step** OLD ENGLISH *steppan* go on foot.

**stephanotis** GREEK fit for a crown or wreath, from *stephanos* crown.

**steppe** RUSSIAN *step.*

**stereo** GREEK *stereos* hard, firm, solid.

**stereophonic** See **stereo** + **phonic.**

**stereopticon** See **stereo** + **optic.**

**sterile** LATIN *sterilis.*

**stern**[1] (strict) OLD ENGLISH *stirne* severe.

**stern**[2] (ship end) OLD NORSE *stjorn,* from *styra* steer.

**sternal** LATIN *sternalis,* from **sternum.**

**sternum** LATIN, from GREEK *sternon* chest.

**stet** LATIN let it stand.

**stethoscope** GREEK *stethos* chest + LATIN *-scopium,* from GREEK *-skopion,* from *skopein* view, examine.

**stevedore** SPANISH *estivar* put away, from LATIN *stipare* cram.

**stew** FRENCH *estuver* bathe in hot water, from LATIN *ex-* out + GREEK *typhos* steam.

**steward** OLD ENGLISH *stigweard,* from *stig* house + *weard* keeper.

**stick** OLD ENGLISH *sticca.*

**stiff** OLD ENGLISH *stif* rigid.

**stifle**[1] (smother) FRENCH *estouffer.*

**stifle**[2] (leg joint) MIDDLE ENGLISH.

**stigma** LATIN brand (mark with a hot iron), from GREEK.

**stile** OLD ENGLISH *stigan* climb.

**stiletto** ITALIAN *stilo* dagger, from LATIN *stilus.*

**still** OLD ENGLISH *stille.*

**stilt** probably from GERMAN or DUTCH *stelte.*

**stimulate** LATIN *stimulare* prick with a stick.

**sting** OLD ENGLISH *stingan* cut with something pointed.

**stink** OLD ENGLISH *stincan* have an odor.

**stint** OLD ENGLISH *styntan* make dull.

**stipend** LATIN *stipendium* tax, from *stips* wages + *pendere* pay.

**stipulate** LATIN *stipulare* bargain.

**stir** OLD ENGLISH *styrian* move.

**stirrup** OLD ENGLISH *stigrap.*

**stitch** OLD ENGLISH *stice* a puncture.

**stoat** MIDDLE ENGLISH *stote.*

**stock** OLD ENGLISH *stocc* tree trunk.

**stockade** FRENCH *estacade,* from SPANISH *estacada,* from *estaca* stake.

**stoic** LATIN *stoicus,* from GREEK *stoikos,* from *stoa* (roof supported by pillars). The followers of the Greek philosopher Zeno were called Stoics, after the great hall in Athens where he taught.

**stole** LATIN *stola,* from GREEK a garment.

**stolid** LATIN *stolidus* dull.

**stomach** FRENCH *stomeque,* from LATIN *stomachus,* from GREEK *stomachos,* from *stoma* mouth.

**stomacker** See stomach.

**stone** OLD ENGLISH *stan.*

**stool** OLD ENGLISH *stol* seat.

**stoop** OLD ENGLISH *stupian.*

**stop** OLD ENGLISH.

**store** FRENCH *estorer* establish, from LATIN *instaurare* build.

**stork** OLD ENGLISH *storc* stiff, from its stiff-legged walk.

**storm** OLD ENGLISH disturbance.

**story** FRENCH *storie* history, from LATIN *historiea* story of past events, from GREEK *historia* information.

**stoup** MIDDLE ENGLISH *stowpe* bucket, from OLD NORSE *staup.*

**stout** FRENCH *estout* bold.

**stow** OLD ENGLISH a place.

**straddle** OLD ENGLISH *stridan.*

**straggle** probably from MIDDLE ENGLISH *straken* roam.

**straight** MIDDLE ENGLISH *strecchen* stretch out.

**strail** OLD ENGLISH *stræl* blanket, from LATIN *stragula,* from *sternere* lay down, spread.

**strain** FRENCH *estraindre* press tightly, from LATIN *stringere* pull tight.

**strait** FRENCH *estreit* narrow, from LATIN *stringere* pull tight.

**strake** MIDDLE ENGLISH, a line of planking on a boat hull.

**strand** origin uncertain.

**strange** FRENCH *estrange* foreign, from LATIN *extra* outside.

**strangle** FRENCH *estrangler* choke, from LATIN *strangulare,* from GREEK *strangalan* halter.

**stratagem** LATIN, from GREEK *strategema* act of a general, from *stratos* army + *agein* lead.

**strategy** FRENCH, from GREEK *strategia* command, from *strategos* general, from *stratos* army + *agein* lead.

**stratosphere** FRENCH *stratosphère,* from LATIN *stratus* spreading out, from *sternere* spread out + FRENCH, from LATIN *sphera* ball, from GREEK *sphaira.*

**stratum** LATIN something spread out, from *sternere* spread out.

**straw** OLD ENGLISH *streaw.*

**stray** FRENCH *estraier,* from LATIN *estra* beyond + *vagari* wander.

**streak** OLD ENGLISH *strica* mark.

**street** OLD ENGLISH *stræt,* from LATIN *strata via* paved way, from *sternere* spread out.

**strength** OLD ENGLISH *strengthu* power.

**strenuous** LATIN *strenuus* active.

**stress** FRENCH *estrece* narrowness, from LATIN *stringere* draw tight.

**stretch** OLD ENGLISH *streccan.*

**strew** OLD ENGLISH *streowian* scatter.

**strict** LATIN *stringere* draw tight.

**stricture** See **strict**.

**stride** OLD ENGLISH *stridan*.

**strident** LATIN *stridere* say in a rough tone.

**strife** FRENCH *estrif*.

**strike** OLD ENGLISH *strican* go.

**string** OLD ENGLISH *streng*.

**stringent** LATIN *stringere* draw tight.

**strip**[1] (take away) OLD ENGLISH *bestriepan* rob.

**strip**[2] (narrow band) DUTCH *stripe* streak.

**stripe** DUTCH.

**stroboscope** GREEK *strobos* whirl around + LATIN *-scopium*, from GREEK *-skopion*, from *skopein* view, examine.

**stroke** OLD ENGLISH *stracian* strike.

**stroll** probably from GERMAN *strollen*, from *strolchen*, from *Strolch* fortuneteller, vagabond.

**strong** OLD ENGLISH *strang* able.

**structure** LATIN *structura*.

**struggle** MIDDLE ENGLISH *strogelen*, origin uncertain.

**strut** OLD ENGLISH *strutian* stand in a stiff way.

**stubble** FRENCH *estuble* stubble, from LATIN *stupla*, from *stipula* stalk, straw.

**stubborn** origin uncertain.

**stucco** ITALIAN.

**stud**[1] (post) OLD ENGLISH *studu*.

**stud**[2] (breed) OLD ENGLISH *stod*.

**student** FRENCH *estudiant*, from LATIN *studere* study.

**studio** ITALIAN workroom, from LATIN *studium* a study.

**study** FRENCH *estudier*, from LATIN *studere* study.

**stuff** FRENCH *estoffe* material, from LATIN *stup(p)a*, from GREEK *styppe*.

**stultify** LATIN *stultificare* make foolish, from *stultus* foolish + *facere* make.

**stumble** OLD NORSE *stumla*.

**stump** DUTCH *stomp*.

**stun** FRENCH *estoner*, from LATIN *ex-* out + *tonare* thunder.

**stunt**[1] (slow the growth) OLD ENGLISH *stunt* foolish, stupid.

**stunt**[2] (trick) AMERICAN, origin unknown.

**stupefy** LATIN *stupefacere* stun, from *stupere* be amazed + *facere* do, make.

**stupendous** LATIN *stupere*.

**stupid** LATIN *stupidus* dull.

**stupor** LATIN.

**sturdy** FRENCH *estourdir* stunned.

**sturgeon** FRENCH *esturfon*.

**stutter** MIDDLE ENGLISH *stutten*.

**sty** OLD ENGLISH *sti*.

**style** FRENCH pointed writing tool, from LATIN *stilus*.

**stylus** LATIN *stilus* pointed writing tool.

**suave** FRENCH, from LATIN *suavis* agreeable.

**sub-** FRENCH, from LATIN under.

**subdue** FRENCH, from LATIN *subducere* remove.

**subject** FRENCH, from LATIN *subjicere*, from *sub-* under + *jacere* throw.

**subjugate** LATIN *subjugare* make under one's rule, from *sub-* under + *jugum* yoke (wooden collar for a pair of oxen to join them), from an early Roman custom that made defeated soldiers crawl under a yoke to show their defeat.

**subjunctive** LATIN *subjunctivus* serving to join, connecting, from *sub-* under + *jungere* join.

**sublime** LATIN *sublimis*, from *sub-* under + *limen* lintel (horizontal top part of a doorway).

**submarine** See **sub-** + **marine**.

**submerge** LATIN *sub-* under + *mergere* jump into.

**submerse** LATIN *submersus*, from *submergere*. See **submerge**.

**submit** LATIN *submittere*, from *sub-* under + *mittere* send.

**subordinate** LATIN *subordinare* place in a lower order, from *sub-* under + *ordo* order.

**subscribe** LATIN *subscribere*, from *sub-* under + *scribere* write.

**subscript** See **subscribe**.

**subsequent** LATIN *subsequi*, from *sub-* under + *sequi* follow.

**subside** LATIN *subsidere*, from *sub-* under + *sidere* settle.

**subsist** LATIN *subsistere* stand still, from *sub-* under + *sistere* stand up, from *stare* stand.

**substance** FRENCH, from LATIN *substantia*, from *sub-* under + *stare* stand.

**substantive** LATIN *substantia*. See **substance**.

**substitute** LATIN *substituere*, from *sub-* under + *statuere* put.

**subsume** LATIN *subsumere* take under, from *sub-* under + *sumere* take.

**subterfuge** FRENCH *subterfuge*, from LATIN *subterfugium* evasion, from *subterfugere* flee by stealth, from *subter* beneath, secretly + *fugere* flee.

**subtle** FRENCH *soutil* thin, from LATIN *subtilis* thin, from *sub-* under + *tela* web.

**subtract** LATIN *subtrahere*, from *sub-* under + *trahere* draw.

**suburb** LATIN *suburbium*, from *sub-* under + *urbs* city.

**subvert** FRENCH, from LATIN *subversio*, from *subvertere*, from *sub-* under + *vertere* turn.

**succeed** FRENCH *succeder*, from LATIN *succedere* come after, go near to, from *sub-* next to, after + *cedere* go, move.

**success** See **succeed**.

**succinct** LATIN *succingere*, from *sub-* under + *cingere* gird (get ready for action).

**succor** FRENCH, from LATIN *succurrere*, from *sub-* under + *currere* run.

**succulent** LATIN *succulentus*, from *sucus* juice.

**succumb** LATIN *succumbere*, from *sub-* under + *cumbere* lie.

**such** OLD ENGLISH *swelc*.

**suck** OLD ENGLISH *sucan*.

**sucrose** FRENCH *sucre* sugar + chemical suffix *-ose*.

**suction** LATIN *sugere* suck.

**sudden** FRENCH *soudian* quick, from LATIN *subitaneus* hasty, from *sub-* under + *ire* go.

**suds** probably from DUTCH *sudse* marsh water.

**sue** FRENCH *sivre* follow, from LATIN *sequi*.

**suede** FRENCH *Suéde* Sweden, from *gants de Suéde* SWEDISH gloves.

**suet** LATIN *sebum*.

**suffer** FRENCH, from LATIN *sufferre* endure, from *sub-* under + *ferre* bring.

**suffice** FRENCH, from LATIN *sufficere*, from *sub-* under + *facere* do, make.

**sufficient** See **suffice**.

**suffix** LATIN *suffigere*, from *sub-* under + *figere* fix.

**suffocate** LATIN *suffocare* choke, from *sub-* under + *fauces* throat.

**suffrage** LATIN *suffragium*, from *sub-* under + *fragor* loud applause.

**suffuse** LATIN *suffundere* fill, from *sub-* under + *fundere* pour.

**sugar** MIDDLE ENGLISH, from FRENCH *sucre*, from LATIN *succarum*, from ARABIC *sukkar*, from PERSIAN *shakar*, from SANSKRIT *sharkara* candied sugar, originally grit, gravel.

**suggest** LATIN *suggerere* advise.

**suicide** LATIN *sui* self + *caedere* kill.

**suit** FRENCH *suite*, from LATIN *sequi* follow.

**suite** FRENCH.

**sukiyaki** JAPANESE.

**sulfur** LATIN *sulphur*.

**sulky** probably from OLD ENGLISH *solcen* idle.

**sullen** FRENCH *solain* only one, from LATIN *solus* alone.

**sully** FRENCH *souiller* make dirty, soil.

**sulphonamide** LATIN *sulphon*, from *sulphur* + *amide*, from *ammonia* + *-ide*.

**sultry** OLD ENGLISH *sweltan* die.

**sum** LATIN *summa* top, from the early Roman practice of figuring out the problem from the bottom and going upward and placing the sum at the top.

**summary** LATIN *summa* a sum.

**summer** OLD ENGLISH *sumor*.

**summit** FRENCH *somete*, from LATIN *summum* highest.

**summon** FRENCH, from LATIN *summonere* remind secretly, from *sub-* secretly + *monere* warn.

**summons** FRENCH *sononse*.

**sumpter** FRENCH *som(m)etier*, from LATIN *sagma* packsaddle.

**sumptuous** FRENCH *somptueux*, from LATIN *sumptus* expense, from *sumere* take.

**sun** OLD ENGLISH *sunne*.

**sundae** AMERICAN, probably from Sunday, possibly because it was originally a special treat sold on that day.

**Sunday** MIDDLE ENGLISH *sunnenday*, from OLD ENGLISH *sunnandæg*, from LATIN *solis dies* sun's day.

**sundry** OLD ENGLISH *syndrig* separate.

**super-** LATIN beyond, over, above.

**superb** LATIN *superbus* superior, from *super-* above.

**supercilious** LATIN *supercilium* eyebrow, from *super-* above + *cilium* eyelid, from raising the eyebrows to show pride.

**superficial** LATIN *superficialis* surface, from *superficies*, from *super-* above + *facies* face.

**superfluous** LATIN *superfluere*, from *super-* above + *fluere* flow.

**superintendent** See **super-** + **intend**.

**superior** FRENCH, from LATIN higher, from *super-* above.

**superlative** FRENCH, from LATIN *superlativus*, from *super-* above + *ferre* bring.

**supernal** FRENCH, from LATIN *supernus*, from *super-* above.

**superscript** LATIN *superscribere*, from *super-* above + *scribere* write.

**supersede** FRENCH *superceder*, from LATIN *supersedere*, from *super-* above + *sedere* sit.

**superstition** FRENCH, from LATIN *superstitio*, from *super-* over + *stare* stand.

**supervise** LATIN *supervidere* look over, from *super-* over + *videre* see.

**supine** LATIN *supinus*.

**supper** FRENCH *souper*, from *soupe* soup.

**supplant** LATIN *supplantare* trip one's feet, from *sub-* under + *planta* bottom of the foot.

**supple** FRENCH *agile*, from LATIN *supplex* bending under.

**supplement** LATIN *supplementum* supply.

**suppliant** FRENCH *supplier*, from LATIN *supplicare*. See **supplicate**.

**supplicate** LATIN *supplicare* kneel down, from *sub-* under + *plicare* fold.

**supply** FRENCH *soupleier* fill up, from LATIN *supplere*, from *sub-* under + *plere* fill.

**support** FRENCH *supporter* endure, from LATIN *supportare* bring to, from *sub-* under + *portare* carry.

**suppose** FRENCH *supposere* set under, from LATIN *supponere*, from *sub-* under + *ponere* place.

**suppress** LATIN *supprimere* press under, from *sub-* under + *premere* press.

**supreme** LATIN *superus* upper, from *super* above.

**sur-** FRENCH *sur, sour* over, above, beyond, from LATIN *super*.

**surcease** FRENCH *surseoir* stop, from LATIN *supersedere*, from *super-* above + *sedere* sit.

**surcingle** FRENCH *surcengle*, from *sur-* over + *cengle* a girdle, from LATIN *cingulum* girth.

**sure** FRENCH *sur* certain, from LATIN *securus* free from care.

**surf** origin uncertain.

**surface** FRENCH *sur-* above + *face* a face.

**surfeit** FRENCH *sorfaire* overdo, from LATIN *super-* above + *facere* do, make.

**surge** FRENCH *sorgir* rise, from LATIN *surgere*.

**surgery** FRENCH *surgerie*, from LATIN, from GREEK *cheirourgia*, from *cheir* hand + *ergon* work.

**surly** MIDDLE ENGLISH *sirly* lordly, majestic.

**surmise** FRENCH *surmettre* accuse, from LATIN *supermittere*, from *super-* above + *mittere* send.

**surmount** FRENCH *surmonter* rise above, from LATIN *super-* above + *mons* mountain.

**surplus** FRENCH, from LATIN *super-* over + *plus* more.

**surprise** FRENCH, from LATIN *super-* over + *prehendere* take.

**surreal** FRENCH *surréalisme*, from *sur-* beyond + *réalisme* realism.

**surrender** FRENCH *surrendre*, from *sur-* over + *rendre* give back.

**surreptitious** LATIN *surripere*, from *sub-* under + *rapere* take by force.

**surrey** *Surrey*, the county in England where it was first built.

**surrogate** LATIN *surrogare*, from *sub-* in place of + *rogare* elect.

**surround** FRENCH *soronder*, from LATIN *super-* over + *undare* rise, from *unda* a wave.

**surtout** FRENCH *sur* above + *tout* everything.

**survey** FRENCH *surveier* look over, from LATIN *super-* over + *videre* see.

**survive** LATIN *survivre*, from *supervivere*, from *super-* above + *vivere* live.

**susceptible** LATIN *susceptibilis* able to receive, from *suscipere*, from *sub-* under + *capere* take.

**suspect** LATIN *suspicere*, from *sub-* under + *spicere* look.

**suspend** FRENCH *suspendre*, from LATIN *suspendere*, from *sub-* under + *pendere* hang.

**suspense** FRENCH *suspens*, from LATIN *suspendere*. See **suspend**.

**suspicion** FRENCH *sospecon*, from LATIN *suspicere*. See **suspect**.

**sustain** MIDDLE ENGLISH, from FRENCH *sustenir* hold up, from LATIN *sustinere*, from *sub-* under + *tenere* hold.

**susurrant** MIDDLE ENGLISH, from LATIN *susurrare*, from *susurrus* murmur, whisper; imitative origin.

**sutler** DUTCH *soetelen* do dirty work.

**suttee** HINDI *satl* virtuous wife.

**suture** LATIN *suere* sew.

**svelte** FRENCH, from ITALIAN, from LATIN *evellere* pluck out.

**swab** DUTCH *zwabben* splash in water.

**swaddle** OLD ENGLISH *swethel*.

**swagger** probably from SCANDINAVIAN.

**swain** OLD NORSE *sveinn* boy.

**swale** probably from OLD NORSE *svalr* cool.

**swallow**[1] (throat action) OLD ENGLISH *swelgan*.

**swallow**[2] (bird) OLD ENGLISH *swealwe*.

**swamp** MIDDLE ENGLISH *sompe*.

**swan** OLD ENGLISH.

**swank** probably from GERMAN *swanken* sway.

**swarm** OLD ENGLISH *swearm*.

**swarthy** OLD ENGLISH *sweard* a skin.

**swastika** SANSKRIT *svastika*, from *svasti* well-being, luck, from *su-* well + *as-*, from *asti* he is. Originally an ancient cosmic or religious symbol thought to bring good luck.

**swat** possibly from MIDDLE ENGLISH *swap* strike, smite.

**sway** OLD NORSE *sveigja* bend.

**swear** OLD ENGLISH *swerian*.

**sweat** OLD ENGLISH *swætan*.

**sweep** possibly from OLD ENGLISH *swapan*.

**sweet** OLD ENGLISH *swete* pleasing.

**swell** OLD ENGLISH *swellan* increase in size.

**swelter** OLD ENGLISH *sweltan* die.

**swerve** OLD ENGLISH *sweorfan* rub.

**swift** OLD ENGLISH rapid.

**swig** origin unknown.

**swindle** GERMAN *schwindeln* cheat.

**swing** OLD ENGLISH *swingan* rush.

**swish** imitative.

**switch** DUTCH *swijch* branch.

**switchel** origin uncertain.

**swivel** MIDDLE ENGLISH *swyvel*, from OLD ENGLISH *swifan* revolve.

**swoon** MIDDLE ENGLISH *swownen*, from OLD ENGLISH *geswogen*.

**sword** OLD ENGLISH something that destroys.

**sycamore** FRENCH *sicamor*, from LATIN *sycomorus*, from GREEK *sykomoros*.

**sycophant** LATIN, from GREEK *sykophantes*, from *sykon* a fig + *phainein* show.

**syllable** FRENCH *sillabe*, from LATIN *syllaba*, from GREEK *syllabe* that which holds together.

**syllabub** origin uncertain.

**sylvan** LATIN *silva* a woods.

SYMBIOSIS

**symbiosis** LATIN, from GREEK *sumbioun,* from *syn-* together + *bioun* live.

**symbol** LATIN *symbolum* sign, from GREEK *symbolon,* from *syn-* together + *ballein* throw.

**symmetry** FRENCH *symmetrie,* from LATIN *symmetria* proportion, from GREEK *symmetria,* from *syn-* together + *metron* a measure.

**sympathy** LATIN *sympathia* feeling in common, from GREEK *sympatheia,* from *syn-* together + *pathos* feeling.

**symphony** FRENCH *simphonie,* from LATIN *symphonia* agreement of sounds, from GREEK *sympatheia,* from *syn-* together + *phone* sound.

**symposium** LATIN, from GREEK *syn-* together + *posis* drinking.

**symptom** LATIN *symptoma,* from GREEK *symptoma,* from *syn-* together + *piptein* fall.

**synagogue** FRENCH *sinagoge,* from LATIN *synagoga,* from GREEK *synagoge,* from *syn-* together + *agein* bring.

**synapsis** LATIN, from GREEK *syn-* together + *apsis* a joining, from *haptein* join.

**synchronize** GREEK *synchronos,* from *syn-* together + *chronos* time.

**syncopate** LATIN *syncopare* cut short, from *suncope,* from GREEK *syn-* together + *koptein* cut.

**syndicate** FRENCH *syndicat,* from *syndic,* from *syn-* together + *dike* justice.

**syndrome** LATIN, from GREEK *syn-* with + *dramein* run.

**syne** MIDDLE ENGLISH, possibly from OLD NORSE *sioan.*

**synonym** LATIN *synonymum* word having the same meaning as another word, from GREEK *synonymon,* from *syn-* together + *onyma* a name.

**synopsis** LATIN plan, from GREEK *synopsis,* from *syn-* together + *opsis* a seeing.

**synovia** LATIN.

**syntax** FRENCH *syntaxe,* from LATIN, from GREEK *syn-* together + *tassein* arrange.

**synthesis** GREEK *syn-* together + *tihenai* place.

**syphilis** LATIN.

**syringe** LATIN, from GREEK *syringos,* from *syrinx* thin pipe.

**syrup** FRENCH *sirop,* from LATIN, from ARABIC *sharab* a drink.

**system** LATIN *systema* a whole that has several parts, from GREEK *systema,* from *syn-* together + *histanai* set.

**systolic** GREEK *systole* contraction, from *syn-* together + *stellein* put, send.

294

# T

**tab** from tablet. See **table**.

**tabard** FRENCH *tabart*.

**tabernacle** LATIN *tabernaculum* a tent, from *taberna* a hut.

**table** OLD ENGLISH *tabule* board, from LATIN *tabula*.

**tableau** FRENCH picture.

**tablet** See **table**.

**tabloid** FRENCH *tablete* table + GREEK *eidos* form, shape.

**taboo** TONGAN *tabu* forbidden, not allowed.

**tabulate** See **table** + -ate.

**tachometer** GREEK *tachos* speed + *metron* measure.

**tacit** LATIN *tacere* be silent.

**taciturn** LATIN *tacere* be silent.

**tack**[1] (fastener) MIDDLE ENGLISH *tak*, from FRENCH *taque* nail, pin, peg.

**tack**[2] (gear, food) See **tackle**.

**tackle** DUTCH *takel* ship rigging, rope.

**tact** FRENCH, from LATIN *tangere* touch.

**tactics** LATIN *tacticus,* from GREEK *takikos,* from *tassein* arrange.

**tactile** FRENCH, from LATIN *tangere* touch.

**taffeta** FRENCH *taftan* weave.

**taffrail** DUTCH *taffereel,* from *tafel* table, from LATIN *tabula* tablet.

**taffy** origin uncertain, perhaps from *tafia* a liquor distilled from molasses.

**tag** MIDDLE ENGLISH, origin uncertain, related to **tack**[1].

**tail** OLD ENGLISH *tægel*.

**tailor** FRENCH *tailleur* cut, from LATIN *tailiare* split, from *talea* a twig.

**taint** FRENCH *teindre* dye, from LATIN *tingere* wet.

**take** OLD NORSE *taka* grasp.

**talc** FRENCH, from ARABIC *talq*.

**tale** OLD ENGLISH *talu* story.

**talent** OLD ENGLISH *talente,* from LATIN *talentum* sum of money, from GREEK *talanton*.

**talisman** FRENCH *talisman,* from ARABIC *tilsam,* from GREEK *telesma,* from *telein* perform religious rites, from *telos* end.

**talk** MIDDLE ENGLISH *talken* speak, from OLD ENGLISH *talian* account.

**tall** OLD ENGLISH *(ge)tæl* prompt.

**tallow** probably from GERMAN *talg*.

**tally** FRENCH *tallie* score kept on a piece of wood, from LATIN *talea* rod.

**Talmud** HEBREW *talmudh* learning.

**talon** FRENCH, from LATIN *talus* an ankle.

**tamale** SPANISH *tamales,* from NATIVE AMERICAN *tamalli* steamed cornmeal.

**tamarack** NATIVE AMERICAN.

**tambour** FRENCH drum.

**tame** OLD ENGLISH *tam.*

**tam-o-shanter** the title character in a poem by Scottish poet Robert Burns (1759–1796).

**tamper** See **temper**.

**tampion** FRENCH *tampon* stopper.

**tan** FRENCH, from LATIN *tannum.*

**tanager** LATIN *tanagra* named 1758 by the naturalist Linnaeus, from PORTUGUESE, from NATIVE AMERICAN *tangara.*

**tandem** LATIN length.

**tang** OLD NORSE *tangi* spit of land, pointed metal tool.

**tangent** LATIN *tangere* touch.

**tangible** LATIN *tangibilis,* from *tangere* touch.

**tangle** MIDDLE ENGLISH *tagilen* involve in a difficult situation, from SCANDINAVIAN source.

**tank** MODERN ENGLISH, from HINDI *tankh* a reservoir of water, influenced by PORTUGUESE *tanque,* from *estanque* pool.

**tankard** MIDDLE ENGLISH, origin unknown.

**tantalize** LATIN *Tantalus,* from GREEK *Tantalos,* in mythology, a son of Zeus. In the afterlife, as a punishment, he had to stand in water up to his chin under branches full of fruit; both fruit and water withdrew from his reach when he tried to eat or drink.

**tantamount** FRENCH *tant amunter* amount to as much, from *tant* so much, from LATIN *tantus* + *amounter* amount to. See **amount**.

**tantrum** origin uncertain.

**tap**[1] (light hit) FRENCH *taper* hit.

**tap**[2] (faucet) OLD ENGLISH *tæppa.*

**tape** OLD ENGLISH *tæpe* strip of cloth.

**taper** MIDDLE ENGLISH, from OLD ENGLISH *tapor* wax candle (because a candle is generally narrower at one end).

**tapestry** FRENCH *tapisserie* heavy fabric that is decorated, from *tapis* carpet, from GREEK *tapes.*

**tapioca** PORTUGUESE *tapioca,* from NATIVE AMERICAN *tipioca,* from *tipi* residue + *ok* squeeze out (from roots of the cassava plant).

**tapir** NATIVE AMERICAN *tapira.*

**tar** OLD ENGLISH *teoru.*

**tardy** FRENCH *tardif,* from LATIN *tardus* slow.

**target** FRENCH *targuete* small shield, from OLD NORSE *targa* shield.

**tariff** FRENCH *tarif* list of prices, from ARABIC *ta'rir* information.

**tarlatan** FRENCH *tarlatane,* from *tarnatane* thin, stiffly starched muslin from India.

**tarnal** AMERICAN slang. See **eternal**.

**tarnation** AMERICAN *darnation,* from *damnation* influenced by **tarnal**.

**tarnish** FRENCH *ternir* stain.

**taro** MAORI.

**tarot** FRENCH, from ITALIAN *tarocchi,* from ARABIC *taraha* remove.

**tarpaulin** OLD ENGLISH *teru* tar + *pæll* cover.

**tarpon** DUTCH *tarpoen.*

**tarry** probably from FRENCH *targer* delay, from LATIN *tardus* slow.

**tarsier** FRENCH *tarse* ankle, from LATIN *tarsus* ankle (animal so named because of its long ankle bones). See **tarsus**.

**tarsus** LATIN, from GREEK *tarsos*, ankle, flat part (sole) of the foot, originally a flat surface.

**tart**[1] (sour) OLD ENGLISH *teart*.

**tart**[2] (pastry) MIDDLE ENGLISH *tarte*.

**tarweed** OLD ENGLISH *teoru weod*.

**task** LATIN *tasca* tax, from *taxare* put a tax on. See **tax**.

**tassel** FRENCH knob.

**taste** FRENCH *taster* touch, taste.

**tatter** probably from OLD NORSE *töturr* rags.

**tatting** possibly from shortening of GERMAN *frivolitäten* knotted lace used for edging, etc.

**tattle** DUTCH *telen* chatter.

**tattoo** TONGAN *tatau* mark twice.

**taunt** MIDDLE ENGLISH, possibly from FRENCH *tanter* tempt.

**Taurus** MIDDLE ENGLISH, from LATIN bull, the constellation Taurus.

**taut** MIDDLE ENGLISH *toght* tense.

**tavern** FRENCH *taverne*, from LATIN *taberna* hut.

**taw**[1] (marble) origin uncertain, possibly from **tawny**.

**taw**[2] (leather) OLD ENGLISH *tawian* do, make.

**tawdry** fancy laces sold at a fair in Norwich, England called *St. Audrey* laces.

**tawny** FRENCH *tan(n)er* tan, from LATIN *tannare*.

**tax** LATIN *taxare* put a tax on, from *taxare* value.

**taxi cab** abbreviation for *taxi(meter) cab*, from FRENCH *taximéter*, from GERMAN, from LATIN *taxa* a tax + *-meter*, from GREEK *metron* measure + FRENCH *cabriolet* one-horse carriage, from ITALIAN *capriola* leap like a goat, from LATIN *caper* goat, because the carriage bounced like a goat leaping.

**taxidermy** GREEK *taxis* arrangement + *derma* a skin.

**tea** CHINESE *t'e*.

**teach** OLD ENGLISH *tæcan* show.

**teak** PORTUGUESE *teca*, from MALAY *tekka*.

**team** OLD ENGLISH two or more animals harnessed together for work.

**tear**[1] (pull apart) OLD ENGLISH *teran*.

**tear**[2] (from crying) OLD ENGLISH *tear*.

**tease** OLD ENGLISH *tsan* pull.

**teat** FRENCH *tete*.

**technique** FRENCH, from GREEK *technikos* having to do with art and skill, from *techne* art, skill, craft.

**technology** GREEK *technologia* systematic treatment, from *techne* art, skill, craft.

**teddy bear** AMERICAN president Theodore *"Teddy"* Roosevelt.

**tedium** LATIN *taediosus* weary, from *taedium*.

**teepee** NATIVE AMERICAN.

**teeter** possibly from OLD NORSE *titra* tremble.

**teetotal** repeating the first letter of **total**.

**tele-** GREEK *tele-* far off.

**telepathy** See **tele-** + GREEK *-pathia* suffering.

**telephone** See **tele-** + GREEK *-phone* sound.

**telescope** See **tele-** + GREEK *-skopion* examine.

**television** See **tele-** + vision.

**temenos** GREEK *temew* cut off.

**temper** OLD ENGLISH *temprian* regulate, from LATIN *temperare* regulate, from *tempus* a period.

**temperance** See **temper**.

**temperate** LATIN *temperatus* restrained, regulated, from *temperare* moderate, regulate. See **temper**.

**temperature** LATIN *temperatura* measure.

**tempest** FRENCH *tempest(e)* storm, from LATIN *tempestas*, from *tempus* time.

**temple**[1] (building) OLD ENGLISH, from LATIN *templum* space marked out.

**temple**[2] (head) FRENCH, from LATIN *tempora* side of forehead.

**tempo** ITALIAN, from LATIN *tempus* time.

**temporal** LATIN *temporalis* worldly, from *tempus* time.

**temporary** LATIN *tempus* time.

**temporize** FRENCH *temporiser*, from LATIN *tempus* time.

**tempt** FRENCH, from LATIN *temptare* try.

**tenable** FRENCH *tenir* hold, from LATIN *tenere*. See **tenet**.

**tenacious** LATIN *tenax* hold fast, from *tenere*. See **tenet**.

**tenant** FRENCH *tenir* hold, from LATIN *tenere*. See **tenet**.

**tend** FRENCH *tendre* offer, from LATIN *tendere* direct.

**tendency** LATIN *tendere* stretch.

**tender** FRENCH *tendre* gentle, from LATIN *tener* soft.

**tendon** LATIN *tendo*, from GREEK *teinein* stretch.

**tendril** FRENCH *tendrum*, from LATIN *tener* soft.

**tenement** LATIN *tenementum*, from *tenere*.

**tenet** LATIN, from *tenere* hold.

**tennis** probably from FRENCH *tenetz*, from *tenir* hold, from LATIN *tenere*.

**tenon** MIDDLE ENGLISH, from FRENCH *tenir* hold, from FRENCH *tenant*, from LATIN *tenere* hold.

**tense**[1] (tight) LATIN *tendere* stretch.

**tense**[2] (verb form) FRENCH, from LATIN *tempus* time.

**tensile** See **tense**[1] + -ile.

**tent** FRENCH *tente*, from LATIN *tendere* stretch.

**tentacle** LATIN *tentare* touch.

**tentative** LATIN *tentativus*, from *tentare* try.

**tenterhook** MIDDLE ENGLISH *tenter*, from FRENCH *tente*, from LATIN *tendere* stretch + OLD ENGLISH *hoc* bent piece of metal.

**tenure** FRENCH, from LATIN *tenere* hold.

**tepid** LATIN *tepidus*.

**term** FRENCH *terme* limit, from LATIN *terminus*.

**termagant** FRENCH *Tervagant* an imaginary Muslim deity appearing in medieval Christian morality plays.

**terminal** LATIN *terminalis* boundary, from *terminus* limit.

**terminate** LATIN *terminare* end, from *terminus* limit.

**tern** OLD NORSE *therna*.

**terra** LATIN earth.

**terra cotta** ITALIAN baked earth, from LATIN.

**terrace** FRENCH platform, from LATIN *terra* earth.

**terrain** FRENCH, from LATIN *terra* earth.

**terrapin** NATIVE AMERICAN.

**terrarium** LATIN *terra* earth + suffix *-arium*.

**terremote** FRENCH, from LATIN *terre motus* earthquake.

**terrestrial** LATIN *terrestris,* from *terra* earth.

**terret** FRENCH *tour* a turn.

**terrible** FRENCH, from LATIN *terribilis* frightful, from *terrere* frighten.

**terrific** LATIN *terrificus* causing terror, from *terrere* frighten + *ficus,* from *facere* make.

**territory** LATIN *territorium* area, from *terra* land.

**terror** LATIN *terrere* frighten.

**terse** LATIN *tergere* wipe.

**tesseract** GREEK *tesser(es)* four + *aktis* ray.

**test**[1] (exam) MIDDLE ENGLISH small vessel used in testing precious metals, from FRENCH, from LATIN *testum* earthen pot.

**test**[2] (shell) LATIN *testa* piece of burned clay, earthen pot, shell.

**testament** FRENCH, from LATIN *testamentum* last will, from *testari* make a will.

**tester**[1] (one who tests) See **test**[1] + **-er.**

**tester**[2] (bed covering) MIDDLE ENGLISH *testere,* from FRENCH *testiere* headpiece, from *teste* head, from LATIN *testa.* See **test**[2].

**tester**[3] (head armor) See **tester**[2].

**testicle** MIDDLE ENGLISH *testicule,* from LATIN *testiculus,* from *testis.*

**testify** LATIN *testificari,* from *testis* witness + *facere* do, make.

**testimony** LATIN *testis* witness.

**tetanus** LATIN quick tightening of a muscle in the neck, from GREEK *tetanos.*

**tête-à-tête** FRENCH head-to-head.

**tether** OLD NORSE *tjothr.*

**tetrarch** LATIN *tetrarcha,* from GREEK *tetraches,* from *tetra* four + *archos* ruler.

**text** FRENCH *tixte,* from LATIN *textus* wording, from *textus* style, from *texere* weave.

**textile** LATIN *textillis,* from *textus* style, from *texere* weave.

**texture** LATIN *textura* web, from *texere* weave.

**thallophytic** LATIN *Thallophyta,* from GREEK *thallos* green twig + *phyte* plant.

**than** OLD ENGLISH *thanne.*

**thane** OLD ENGLISH *thegen.*

**thank** OLD ENGLISH *thancian* give thanks.

**that** OLD ENGLISH *thæt.*

**thatch** OLD ENGLISH *theccan* cover.

**thaw** OLD ENGLISH *thawian.*

**the** OLD ENGLISH.

**theatre** FRENCH, from LATIN *theatrum* stage, from GREEK *theatron* place for seeing plays.

**theft** OLD ENGLISH *theofth.*

**their** OLD ENGLISH, from OLD NORSE *theirra.*

**theism** GREEK *theos* god + *-ismos.*

**them** OLD ENGLISH, from OLD NORSE *theim.*

**theme** FRENCH, from LATIN *thema* topic, from GREEK *thema* subject, something laid down.

**then** OLD ENGLISH *thænne.*

**thence** MIDDLE ENGLISH *thannes,* from that place, from OLD ENGLISH *thanon.*

**theodolite** LATIN *theodelitus* an instrument for measuring horizontal angles.

**theology** LATIN *theologia* science of religious things, from GREEK *theologia,* from *theos* a god + *-logia* study of.

**theorbo** FRENCH *teorbe.*

**theorem** FRENCH *théorème*, from LATIN *theorema*, from GREEK spectacle, speculation.

**theory** LATIN *theoria*, from GREEK, from *theorein* consider, speculate, look at, from *theoros* spectator, from *thea* a view + *horan* see.

**therapy** LATIN *therapia*, from GREEK *therapeuein* nurse.

**there** OLD ENGLISH *thær*.

**thermo-** GREEK *therme* heat.

**thermogenesis** See **thermo-** + **genesis**.

**thermometer** See **thermo-** + **meter**.

**thermos** GREEK hot.

**thermosphere** See **thermo-** + **sphere**.

**thesis** LATIN, from GREEK a placing, from *tithenai* put.

**thespian** ancient Greek dramatic writer *Thespis,* considered the creator of ancient Greek tragedy.

**thews** MIDDLE ENGLISH *theawes* good qualities, from OLD ENGLISH *theaw* custom.

**they** OLD NORSE *their*.

**thick** OLD ENGLISH *thicce*.

**thicket** MIDDLE ENGLISH, from OLD ENGLISH *thiccet,* from *thicce*.

**thief** OLD ENGLISH *theof*.

**thigh** OLD ENGLISH *theoh*.

**thilke** MIDDLE ENGLISH. See **the** + **ilk**.

**thimble** OLD ENGLISH *thuma* a thumb.

**thin** OLD ENGLISH *thynne*.

**thing** MIDDLE ENGLISH, from OLD ENGLISH *thing*.

**think** OLD ENGLISH *thencan*.

**thiopentone** GREEK *theion* brimstone (sulfur) + *pente* five + *-one* chemical compound.

**this** OLD ENGLISH *thes* (male), *theos* (female), *this* (neither male nor female).

**thistle** OLD ENGLISH *thistle*.

**thole** OLD ENGLISH *tholl*.

**thong** OLD ENGLISH *thwang* narrow strip of leather.

**thorax** LATIN *thorax,* from GREEK *thorax* breastplate, chest.

**thorough** OLD ENGLISH *thuruh*. See **through**.

**thou** OLD ENGLISH *thu*.

**though** OLD ENGLISH *thea* + OLD NORSE *tho*.

**thought** OLD ENGLISH *thoht* idea.

**thow** MIDDLE ENGLISH form of thou.

**thrall** OLD NORSE *thrægll* slave.

**thrash** OLD ENGLISH *therscan* beat.

**thread** OLD ENGLISH *thrægd* thin long cord.

**threaten** OLD ENGLISH *threatnian* force.

**thresh** See **thrash**.

**threshold** OLD ENGLISH *threscold*.

**thrice** MIDDLE ENGLISH *thries*.

**thrift** OLD NORSE having wealth and success.

**thrill** OLD ENGLISH *thyr(e)lian* pass through, from *thyrel* hole, from *thurh* through.

**thrive** OLD NORSE *thrifask,* from *thrifa* take with the hand.

**throat** OLD ENGLISH *throte*.

**throb** MIDDLE ENGLISH *throbben*.

**throe** probably from OLD ENGLISH *thrawu* pain.

**throne** FRENCH, from LATIN, from GREEK *thronos* a seat.

**throng** OLD ENGLISH *(ge)thrang,* from *thringan* crowd.

**throttle** probably from OLD ENGLISH *throte.*

**through** OLD ENGLISH *thurh.*

**throw** OLD ENGLISH *thrawan* twist.

**thrush** OLD ENGLISH *thrysce.*

**thrust** OLD NORSE *thrysta* press.

**thug** HINDI *thag,* perhaps from SANSKRIT *sthaga* cunning, fraudulent.

**thumb** OLD ENGLISH *thuma.*

**thunder** OLD ENGLISH *thunor.*

**Thursday** OLD ENGLISH *Thuresdæg* Thor's (the Old Norse god of thunder) day.

**thus** OLD ENGLISH.

**thwart** OLD NORSE *thvert* across.

**thyme** FRENCH, from LATIN, from GREEK *threin* offer sacrifice.

**tiara** LATIN, from GREEK.

**tibia** LATIN.

**tick**[1] (sound) MIDDLE ENGLISH *tic.*

**tick**[2] (parasite) MIDDLE ENGLISH *teke,* from OLD ENGLISH *ticia.*

**tick**[3] (cover) MIDDLE ENGLISH *tykke,* from LATIN *theca* cover, sheath.

**ticket** FRENCH *etiquet* a little note, from *estiquier* attach. See **etiquette.**

**tickle** MIDDLE ENGLISH *tikelen.*

**tiddlywinks** probably from MODERN ENGLISH *tiddly-wink* small beer shop where such games were played, from *tiddly* a drink.

**tide** OLD ENGLISH *tid* time.

**tidings** OLD ENGLISH *tidung.*

**tidy** MIDDLE ENGLISH in good condition, from *tid* time, from OLD ENGLISH *tid.*

**tie** OLD ENGLISH *tigan.*

**tier** FRENCH *tire* order.

**tierce** FRENCH *terce,* from LATIN *tertiam* third.

**tig tag** See **tag** (the game).

**tiger** MIDDLE ENGLISH *tygre,* from OLD ENGLISH *tiger* from FRENCH *tigre,* from LATIN *tigris,* from GREEK.

**tight** OLD NORSE *thettr* close.

**till**[1] (plow) OLD ENGLISH *tilian.*

**till**[2] (drawer) possibly from MIDDLE ENGLISH *tillen* draw.

**tiller** FRENCH, from LATIN *telarium* roller in a loom, from *tela* a web.

**tilt** MIDDLE ENGLISH *tilten* cause to fall, from OLD ENGLISH *tealt* not steady.

**timber** OLD ENGLISH.

**timbre** FRENCH bell hit with a hammer, from GREEK *tympanon* tympani (large horizontal drum that can be tuned to different sounds).

**time** OLD ENGLISH *tima.*

**timid** LATIN *timidus.*

**timothy** *Timothy* Hanson, who took the seed to the Carolinas around 1720.

**tin** OLD ENGLISH.

**tincture** LATIN *tintura* using dye, from *tinctus* dye.

**tinder** OLD ENGLISH *tynder.*

**tine** OLD ENGLISH *tind.*

**tinge** LATIN *tingere* dye.

**tingle** MIDDLE ENGLISH *tinklen* make light sounds.

**tinker** MIDDLE ENGLISH, possibly from *tink* ring, from the sound tinkers made when mending pots and pans.

**tinkle** imitative.

**tinsel** FRENCH *estincelle,* from *estencele,* from LATIN *scintilla* a spark.

**tint** MODERN ENGLISH *tinct*, from LATIN *tinctus* dying, from *tingere* dye.

**tiny** MIDDLE ENGLISH *tine* a little something.

**-tion** FRENCH, from LATIN *-tionis*.

**tip** MIDDLE ENGLISH *tippe*.

**tippet** MIDDLE ENGLISH, origin uncertain.

**tipple** probably from MIDDLE ENGLISH *tipelar* bar keeper.

**tirade** FRENCH, from ITALIAN *tirata*, from *tirare* fire.

**tire**[1] (needing rest) OLD ENGLISH *tiorian*.

**tire**[2] (rubber) probably from MIDDLE ENGLISH *atir* equipment.

**tissue** FRENCH cloth, from *tistre* weave, from LATIN *texere*.

**titanic** GREEK *Titanikos* Titan, from the Greek myth.

**titanium** LATIN, from GREEK *Titan* a Titan.

**tithe** OLD ENGLISH *teothe* a tenth.

**titillate** LATIN *titillare* tickle.

**title** MIDDLE ENGLISH inscription, heading, from FRENCH, from LATIN *titulus*.

**titter** imitative.

**titular** LATIN *titulus* inscription.

**to** OLD ENGLISH.

**toad** OLD ENGLISH *tade*.

**toady** MODERN ENGLISH *toadeater*, a fake doctor's assistant who pretended to eat poisonous toads and then drank the doctor's cure.

**toast**[1] (heated bread) FRENCH *toster* roast, from LATIN *torrere* make dry using heat.

**toast**[2] (drink) **toast**[1], from flavoring liquor by putting spiced toast in it.

**tobacco** SPANISH *tobaco* the plant.

**toboggan** FRENCH *tabaganne*, from NATIVE AMERICAN *tepaqan* a type of sled for moving things.

**today** OLD ENGLISH *todæg(e)* on this day.

**toe** OLD ENGLISH *ta*.

**toff** FRENCH, probably from LATIN *tufa* helmet decoration.

**toga** LATIN *toga* man's outer clothes worn in ancient Rome.

**together** OLD ENGLISH *togædere* into one gathering.

**toggle** MODERN ENGLISH, nautical, probably from *tog* tug.

**toil** FRENCH *toiller*, from *toeillier* make dirty, from LATIN *tudiculare* stir up, from *tundere* beat.

**toilet** FRENCH *toilette* dressing table, from *toile* cloth, from LATIN *tela* web.

**token** OLD ENGLISH *tac(e)n* symbol.

**tolerate** LATIN *tolerare* put up with.

**toll** OLD ENGLISH tax, from LATIN *telonium* place where taxes were collected, from GREEK *telos* tax.

**tom** the name *Thomas*.

**tomb** FRENCH *tombe* grave, from LATIN *tumba*, from GREEK *tymbos*.

**tome** FRENCH volume, from LATIN *tomus*, from GREEK *tomos*.

**tomorrow** MIDDLE ENGLISH *to morwe*, from OLD ENGLISH *to* to + *morgen* morning.

**tompion** FRENCH *tampon* stopper.

**-tomy** GREEK *temnein* cut.

**ton** OLD ENGLISH *tunne* barrel, its weight when full.

**tone** LATIN *tonus* stretching, from GREEK *tonos* thing stretched.

**tong** OLD ENGLISH *tange, tang.*

**tongue** OLD ENGLISH *tunge.*

**tonic** GREEK *tonikos* of stretching. See **tone.**

**tonight** OLD ENGLISH *toniht* on the night of this day.

**tonneau** FRENCH *tonneau* cask.

**tonsil** LATIN *tonsillae* (plural) tonsils.

**tool** OLD ENGLISH *tol* something to help do work.

**toot** imitative.

**tooth** OLD ENGLISH *toth.*

**top** OLD ENGLISH.

**topgallant** See **top** + **gallant.**

**topic** LATIN, from GREEK *Ta Topika* title of a book about common things, written by the Greek philosopher Aristotle, from *topos* a place.

**topography** LATIN *topographia* description of a place, from GREEK *topographia.* See **topic** + **-graphy.**

**toque** FRENCH cap, from SPANISH *toca,* from Basque *tauka* kind of cap.

**tor** MIDDLE ENGLISH, from OLD ENGLISH *torr.*

**Torah** HEBREW instruction.

**torch** FRENCH *torche* light, made with a bundle of straw that was covered with wax so it would burn, from LATIN *torques* twisted neck chain.

**toreador** SPANISH *toro* bull, from LATIN *taurus.*

**torment** FRENCH torture, from LATIN *tormentum,* from *torquere* twist.

**tornado** SPANISH *tronada* thunderstorm, from LATIN *tornare* thunder.

**torpedo** LATIN numbness, from *torpere* stiff.

**torpid** LATIN *torpidus* numb.

**torque** LATIN *torques* a twisted metal necklace.

**torrent** LATIN *torrens.*

**torrid** LATIN *torridus* needing water.

**torsion** FRENCH *torsion,* from LATIN *torsionem,* from *tortionem* torture, torment, from *tortus,* from *torquere* twist.

**torso** ITALIAN, from LATIN, from GREEK *thyrsos* a stem.

**tortilla** SPANISH *torta* cake.

**tortoise** LATIN *tortuca,* from *torquere* twist, because of the crooked look of a turtle's feet.

**tortuous** LATIN *tortuosus* full of turns, from *torquere* twist.

**torture** FRENCH, from LATIN *tortura,* from *torquere* twist.

**tosh** BRITISH slang, origin uncertain.

**toss** MIDDLE ENGLISH.

**total** FRENCH, from LATIN *totalis* whole, from *totus.*

**tote** unknown origin.

**totem** NATIVE AMERICAN *ototeman* family.

**totter** possibly from DUTCH *touteren* swing.

**touch** FRENCH *touchier* strike.

**tough** OLD ENGLISH *toh* hard to break.

**tour** FRENCH *to(u)r* a turn, from LATIN *tornus* lathe (tool that cuts wood as it turns), from GREEK *tornos.*

**tourmaline** FRENCH.

**tournament** FRENCH *torneiement,* from *torneier* turn around. See **turn.**

**tourniquet** FRENCH *tourner* turn, from LATIN *tornare* turn in a lathe. See **turn.**

**tousle** MIDDLE ENGLISH *tusen* pull.

**tout** OLD ENGLISH *titian* look out.

**tow**[1] (pull) OLD ENGLISH *togian* pull.

303

**tow**[2] (unspun flax) OLD ENGLISH *tow.*

**toward** OLD ENGLISH *toweard.*

**towel** FRENCH *toaille.*

**tower** FRENCH *tour,* from LATIN *turris* high building, from GREEK *tyrsis.*

**town** OLD ENGLISH *tun* village.

**toxaemia** See **toxic** + **anemia.**

**toxic** LATIN *toxicus* poisonous, from *toxicum* poison, from GREEK *toxikon* poison for arrows.

**toxoid** See **toxic** + **-oid.**

**toyon** SPANISH *tollon* the name of the holly.

**trace** FRENCH *tracier* follow a trail, from LATIN *trahere* drag.

**trachea** LATIN, from GREEK *tracheia arteria* rough windpipe.

**track** FRENCH *trac* path.

**tract** LATIN *trahere* draw.

**traction** LATIN *tractio* pull, from *trahere* drag.

**tractor** LATIN that which drags, from *trahere* drag.

**trade** MIDDLE ENGLISH, from GERMAN *trade* track, course, way of life.

**tradition** FRENCH, from LATIN *traditio* handing over.

**traffic** FRENCH *trafique* trade, from ITALIAN *traffico.*

**tragedy** FRENCH *tragedie* serious play with unhappy ending, from LATIN *tradoedia,* from GREEK *tragodia,* from *tragos* goat + *oide* song. The goat may have been the prize for winning a dramatic competition in ancient Greece.

**trail** FRENCH *trailler* tow a boat, from LATIN *tragula* drag with a net.

**train** FRENCH *trainer* drag, from LATIN *trahere* pull.

**traipse** perhaps from FRENCH *trepasser* pass over or beyond, from *trespasser.* See **trespass.**

**trait** FRENCH, from LATIN *trahere* draw.

**traitor** FRENCH, from LATIN *tradere* betray.

**trajectory** LATIN *trajicere,* from *trans-* across + *jacere* throw.

**tram** SCOTTISH iron trucks used in coal mines.

**tramp** GERMAN *trampen* stamp.

**trample** GERMAN *trampen,* stamp, but implying doing such repetitively.

**trance** FRENCH *transe,* from LATIN *transire* die, from *trans-* over + *ire* go.

**tranquil** LATIN *tranquillus.*

**trans-** LATIN across, beyond, over.

**transact** LATIN *transigere,* from *trans-* across + *agere* drive.

**transcend** LATIN *transcendere,* from *trans-* over + *scandere* climb.

**transcribe** LATIN *transcribere,* from *trans-* over + *scribere* write.

**transfer** LATIN *transferre,* from *trans-* across + *ferre* bring.

**transform** LATIN *transformare,* from *trans-* over + *forma* a shape.

**transfuse** LATIN *transundere,* from *trans-* across + *fundere* pour.

**transgress** FRENCH, from LATIN *transgredi,* from *trans-* over + *gradi* step.

**transient** LATIN *transire,* from *trans-* over + *ire* go.

**transistor** LATIN *trans-* across + *sistere* set, from *stare* stand.

**transit** LATIN *transitis,* from *trans-* over + *ire* go.

**translate** See **transfer.**

**translucent** LATIN *translucere,* from *trans-* through + *lucere* shine.

**transmit** LATIN *transmittere,* from *trans-* over + *mittere* send.

**transmute** LATIN *trans-* over + *mutare* change.

**transom** probably from LATIN *transtrum* crossbeam.

**transparent** LATIN *transparere,* from *trans-* across + *parere* appear.

**transpire** FRENCH *transpirer,* from LATIN *trans-* through + *spirare* breathe.

**transport** FRENCH, from LATIN *trans-* over + *portare* carry.

**transpose** FRENCH *transposer,* from LATIN *transponere,* from *trans-* across + *ponere* place.

**transverse** LATIN *transversus,* from *transvertere,* from *trans-* across + *vertere* turn.

**trap** OLD ENGLISH *træppe* something to catch animals.

**trapezium** LATIN *trapezium,* from GREEK *trapezion* small table, from *trapeza* table, from *tra-* four + *peza* foot, edge.

**trapezius** LATIN. See **trapezium.**

**trapezoid** LATIN *trapezoides,* from GREEK *trapezoeides* trapezium-shaped, from *trapeza* table + *-oeides* shaped.

**trash** probably from OLD NORSE *tros.*

**trauma** LATIN, from GREEK.

**travail** FRENCH labor, from LATIN *trepalium* something used to torture, from *tres* three + *palus* stake.

**travel** MIDDLE ENGLISH *travailen* make a journey, originally to labor. See **travail.** The usage probably comes from the difficulty of travel in earlier times.

**traverse** FRENCH *traverser* cross, from LATIN *transversare,* from *transversus,* from *trans-* over + *vertere* turn.

**travesty** FRENCH *travestir* disguise, from LATIN *trans-* across + *vestire* dress.

**travois** See **travail.**

**tray** OLD ENGLISH *treg* wood board.

**treachery** FRENCH *trichier* cheat.

**treacle** FRENCH, from LATIN, from GREEK *theriake* remedy for poisonous bites, from *ther* wild beast.

**tread** OLD ENGLISH *tredan* walk on.

**treadle** OLD ENGLISH *trede* step.

**treason** FRENCH *traison,* from LATIN *tradere* deliver up, from *trans-* over + *dare* give.

**treasure** FRENCH *tresor* precious things, from LATIN *thesaurus* storehouse, from GREEK *thesauros.*

**treat** FRENCH *traitier* drag, from LATIN *trahere* drag.

**treaty** FRENCH *trait(i)e,* from LATIN *tractary* manage.

**treble** FRENCH, from LATIN *triplus.* See **triple.**

**tree** OLD ENGLISH *treow.*

**trek** DUTCH *trekken* draw.

**trellis** FRENCH, from LATIN *trilix* wound three times.

**tremble** FRENCH *trembler* shiver, from LATIN *tremulus* quaking.

**tremendous** LATIN *tremendus,* from *tremere* tremble (shake).

**tremolo** ITALIAN shaking, from LATIN *tremulus.*

**tremor** FRENCH, from LATIN trembling.

**tremulous** LATIN *tremere* tremble.

**trench** FRENCH *trenche,* from LATIN *truncare.*

**trenchant** FRENCH *trenchier* cut.

**trencher** FRENCH *trencheor* tool used for cutting, origin uncertain.

**trend**  OLD ENGLISH *trendan* roll.

**trepidation**  LATIN *trepidatio* alarm.

**trespass**  FRENCH *trespasser* go across, from LATIN *trans-* across + *passus* step.

**tress**  MIDDLE ENGLISH, from FRENCH *tresse*, perhaps from LATIN *trichia* braid, rope, from GREEK *trikhia* rope, from *thrix* hair.

**trestle**  FRENCH *trestel* beam of wood, from LATIN *transtrum* beam that goes across.

**tri-**  LATIN *tres* three, from GREEK *treis*.

**triad**  LATIN *triadis*, from GREEK *triados*, from *treis* three.

**trial**  FRENCH judge in court, from *trier* try.

**triangle**  FRENCH, from LATIN *triangulum*, from *tri-* three + *angulus* corner or angle.

**tribe**  LATIN *tribus* one of the three divisions of the Roman state, perhaps from *tri-* three.

**tribulation**  FRENCH *tribulacion*, from LATIN *tribulationem* affliction, from *tribulare* thresh out grain, from *terere* rub + *-bulum* tool.

**tribune**  LATIN *tribunus* ancient Roman official, from *tribus*.  See **tribe**.

**tributary**  LATIN *tributarius* liable to tax or tribute, from *tributum*.  See **tribute**.

**tribute**  LATIN *tributum* payment, from *tribuere* allot to a tribe, from *tribus*.  See **tribe**.

**trice**  MIDDLE ENGLISH, from DUTCH *trisen* hoist, from *trise* pulley.

**triceps**  LATIN *triceps* three-headed, from **tri-** + *-ceps*, from *caput* head.  So called because the muscle has three origins.

**trick**  FRENCH *trichier* cheat.

**tricorn**  FRENCH *tricorne*, from LATIN *tricornis*, from **tri-** + *cornu* from horn.

**tricot**  FRENCH, from *tricoter* knit, from *trique* a stick, from FRENCH *estriquer* strike.

**trident**  LATIN *tres* three, from GREEK *treis* + *dens* tooth.

**trifle**  FRENCH *trufle* trickery.

**triglyph**  LATIN *triglyphus*, from GREEK *triglyphos*, from **tri-** + *glyphe* carving.

**trigonometry**  LATIN *trigonometria*, from GREEK *trigonon* triangle + *metron* measure.

**trill**  ITALIAN *trillare*, imitative.

**trillion**  FRENCH *tri-* third power + ITALIAN *millione*, from *mille* thousand, from LATIN.

**trilogy**  GREEK *trilogia* group of three sad dramas, from *tri-* three + *logos* story.

**trim**  OLD ENGLISH *trymman* strengthen.

**trinity**  FRENCH *trinite*, from LATIN *trinus* triple.

**trinket**  MODERN ENGLISH, possibly from *trink*, *trick* style of adornment, ornament.

**trio**  LATIN *tres* three.

**trip**  FRENCH *trip(p)er* dance, from DUTCH *trippen* skip.

**tripartite**  LATIN *tripartitus* divided into three parts, from *tri-* three + *partitus*, from *partiri* divide.

**tripe**  ARABIC *tharb* intestines.

**triple**  LATIN *triplus* having three parts, from GREEK *triplous*.

**trireme**  LATIN *triremis*, from *tri-* three + *remus* oar.

**trite**  LATIN *terere* wear away.

**triumph**  FRENCH, from LATIN *triumphus* victory, possibly from GREEK *thriambos* song to the Greek god Bacchus in his honor.

**trivial**  LATIN *trivalis* common, from *trivum* place where three roads meet, from *tri-* three + *via* way.

**trocar** FRENCH *troquart,* from *trois* three + *carre* side, from its triangular shape.

**trocharise** See **trocar.**

**troll**[1] (monster) OLD NORSE.

**troll**[2] (roll) MIDDLE ENGLISH *trollen* wander.

**trolley** See **troll**[2].

**trombone** ITALIAN *tromba* a trumpet, from GERMAN *trumba.*

**tromp** See **tramp.**

**troop** FRENCH *troup* group of persons, from *troupeau* herd, from LATIN *troppus* a flock.

**trophy** FRENCH *trophee* sign of victory, from LATIN, from GREEK *tropaion* stone showing an enemy's defeat, from *trope* defeat.

**-trophy** GREEK *trophia,* from *trephein* feed.

**tropic** LATIN *tropicus* turning of the sun, from GREEK *trope* turning.

**troposphere** FRENCH *troposphère,* from GREEK *tropos* turn, change + *sphaira* sphere.

**troth** OLD ENGLISH *treowth* truth.

**troubadour** FRENCH, from earlier *trobar* compose in verse.

**trouble** FRENCH *trubler* disturb, from LATIN *turba* thick.

**trough** OLD ENGLISH *trog.*

**trounce** MIDDLE ENGLISH harass, origin uncertain.

**trousers** IRISH *triubhas,* possibly from FRENCH *trebus* pants that stop at the knee.

**trousseau** FRENCH *trousse* a bundle.

**trout** OLD ENGLISH *truht,* from FRENCH *truite,* from LATIN *tructa,* from GREEK *troktes* a kind of fish.

**trowel** FRENCH *truele,* from LATIN *truella,* from *trua* ladle.

**truant** MIDDLE ENGLISH shiftless beggar, from FRENCH, related to SCOTTISH *truaghan,* wretched.

**truce** MIDDLE ENGLISH *trewes* temporary peace, from OLD ENGLISH *treow* promise.

**truck** LATIN *trochus* iron hoop, from GREEK *trochos* wheel.

**truculent** LATIN *truculentus* cruel.

**trudge** MODERN ENGLISH, origin uncertain.

**true** OLD ENGLISH *treowe* faithful.

**truffle** FRENCH *trufle,* from *truffe,* from LATIN *tufera.*

**trump** See **triumph.**

**trumpet** FRENCH *trombe.*

**truncate** LATIN *truncatus* cut off, from *truncus* trunk.

**truncheon** MIDDLE ENGLISH *tronchoun,* from FRENCH *tronchon,* from LATIN *truncus* stem, trunk.

**trundle** OLD ENGLISH *trendel* circle, from *trendan* roll.

**trunk** MIDDLE ENGLISH *tronke,* from FRENCH *tronc,* from LATIN *truncus.*

**truss** FRENCH *trousser.*

**trust** OLD NORSE *traust* help.

**truth** OLD ENGLISH *treowth.*

**try** FRENCH *trier* choose.

**tryst** FRENCH *triste* hunting station.

**tub** DUTCH *tubbe.*

**tuba** FRENCH, from LATIN *tuba* trumpet.

**tube** LATIN *tubus* pipe.

**tuber** LATIN a swelling.

**tuberculosis** LATIN *tuberculum,* from *tuber* a swelling.

**Tuesday** OLD ENGLISH *Tiwesdæg* day of *Tiw* (ancient German god of war), from LATIN *dies* day.

**tuft** FRENCH *tufe*, probably from LATIN *tufa* top of helmet.

**tug** MIDDLE ENGLISH *toggen* pull, from OLD ENGLISH *teo(ha)n* pull.

**tuition** FRENCH, from LATIN *tuitio* protection, from *tueri* protect.

**tulip** DUTCH *tulipa*, from FRENCH *tulipe*, from TURKISH *tülbent* turban, from PERSIAN *dulband* turban, from resemblance of the flower to a turban.

**tulle** *Tulle*, the city in France where it was first made.

**tumble** MIDDLE ENGLISH *tumblen* perform as an acrobat, fall, from *tumben* dance, jump, from OLD ENGLISH *tumbian*.

**tumbrel** FRENCH *tomber* fall.

**tumor** LATIN *tumere* swell.

**tump**[1] (mound) BRITISH, origin uncertain.

**tump**[2] (carry) AMERICAN, probably NATIVE AMERICAN origin.

**tumult** LATIN *tumultus*.

**tundra** RUSSIAN.

**tune** See **tone**.

**tungsten** SWEDISH *tungsten*, from *tung* heavy + *sten* stone.

**tunic** FRENCH *tunique*, from LATIN *tunica*.

**tunnel** FRENCH *tonele* shaped like a funnel (tube with a wide mouth).

**turban** FRENCH, from ITALIAN, from TURKISH *tülbent*, from PERSIAN *dulband*.

**turbine** FRENCH, from LATIN *turbo* a whirl.

**turbulent** FRENCH, from LATIN *turbulentus* anxious or disturbed, from *turba* something disturbed.

**tureen** FRENCH *terrine*, from LATIN *terra* earth.

**turf** OLD ENGLISH.

**turkey** from an African bird imported into Europe by way of *Turkey*. The wild American turkey looked similar and came to be called this as well.

**turmoil** perhaps from FRENCH *tremouille* mill hopper, from the hopper's constant motion. (The name *tremouille* for the hopper comes from LATIN *trimodia* vessel containing three measures, from *modius* a Roman dry measure.)

**turn** OLD ENGLISH *turnian* turn around, from LATIN *tornare*, from *tornus* lathe (tool that cuts wood as it turns), from GREEK *tornos*.

**turnip** possibly from **turn**, because of rounded shape.

**turnpike** See **turn** + **pike**[2], from the barriers used to stop travellers for tolls.

**turpitude** FRENCH, from LATIN *turpis* bad.

**turret** FRENCH *tour*. See **tower**.

**turtle** OLD ENGLISH *turtla*.

**tusche** GERMAN, from *tuschen*, from FRENCH *toucher* touch.

**tush**[1] (backside) AMERICAN slang *tochus*, from YIDDISH *tokhes*, from HEBREW *tahat* beneath.

**tush**[2] (tooth) MIDDLE ENGLISH *tusch*. See **tusk**.

**tusk** OLD ENGLISH *tusc*.

**tussle** MIDDLE ENGLISH *tusen* pull.

**tussock** possibly from MIDDLE ENGLISH *tusen* rumple + *ock* little.

**tutelage** LATIN *tutela* protection.

**tutor** LATIN protector.

**tuxedo** *Tuxedo* Park, New York, a vacation place for wealthy families, where the suit first was worn.

**twang** imitative of the sound of a plucked string.

**tweed** See **twill**.

**tweet** imitative.

**tweezers** MODERN ENGLISH, from *tweeze* case for tweezers, from *etwee* a small case, from FRENCH *étui*, from *estuier* keep.

**twig** OLD ENGLISH *twigge*, from *twi-* two, forked.

**twilight** MIDDLE ENGLISH *twi-* two + OLD ENGLISH *leht*, from *leoht*.

**twill** OLD ENGLISH *twilic* woven of double thread, from LATIN *bilix* with a double thread.

**twin** OLD ENGLISH *twinn* double.

**twine** OLD ENGLISH *twin* twisted thread.

**twinge** OLD ENGLISH *twengan* pinch.

**twinkle** OLD ENGLISH *twinclian* sparkle.

**twirl** origin uncertain.

**twist** OLD ENGLISH rope.

**twitch** OLD ENGLISH *twiccian* pluck.

**twitter** imitative.

**tycoon** JAPANESE *taikun* shogun (name of the rulers of Japan during the 11th and 19th centuries), from CHINESE *ta* great + *chün* ruler.

**tyke** OLD NORSE *tik* female dog.

**tympani** LATIN, from GREEK *tympanon* drum.

**tympanites** See **tympani**.

**tympanum** See **tympani**.

**type** LATIN *typus* image, from GREEK *typos* form.

**typhoid** See **typhus** + **-oid**.

**typhoon** CHINESE *tai fung* great wind, from GREEK *typhon* whirlwind.

**typhus** LATIN, from GREEK *typhos* fever.

**typical** LATIN *typicalis,* from *typicus,* from GREEK *tupos* type.

**tyrant** FRENCH, from LATIN, from GREEK *tyrannos.*

# U

**ubiquity** FRENCH *ubiquité,* from LATIN *ubique* everywhere.

**udder** OLD ENGLISH *udr.*

**ugly** OLD NORSE *uggligr* terrible.

**ulcer** FRENCH *ulcere,* from LATIN *ulcus,* from *ulcerare* make sore.

**ulcerate** See **ulcer** + -ate.

**ulna** LATIN elbow.

**ulterior** LATIN.

**ultimate** LATIN *ultimatus* final, from *ultimus* last.

**ultra-** LATIN *ultra* beyond.

**umbel** LATIN *umbella* sun shade, from *umbra* shade.

**umbilical** LATIN *umbilicalis* of the navel, from *umbilicus* navel.

**umbilicus** LATIN.

**umbra** LATIN shade, shadow.

**umbrage** FRENCH shade, from LATIN **umbra**.

**umbrella** ITALIAN *ombrella,* from *onbra,* from LATIN **umbra**.

**umpire** FRENCH *nomper* not even, from LATIN *non* not + *par* even, from the job of the umpire as the odd or third man (someone not on either team) to settle an argument.

**un-** OLD ENGLISH not, opposite or negative of.

**unanimous** LATIN *unanimus,* from *unus* one + *animus* the mind.

**uncle** FRENCH, from LATIN *avunculus* a mother's brother.

**uncouth** OLD ENGLISH *uncuth* strange, from *un-* not + *cuth* known.

**unctuous** LATIN *unctuosus* oily, from *unctus* anoint (put oil on during a ceremony to make holy).

**under** OLD ENGLISH.

**under-** OLD ENGLISH.

**underneath** OLD ENGLISH *underneothan.*

**understand** OLD ENGLISH *understandan* stand under, get the meaning of.

**undine** LATIN *unda* wave.

**undulate** LATIN *undulatus* wavy, from *unda* wave.

**ungulate** LATIN *unguia* a hoof.

**unicorn** LATIN *unicornus,* from *unis* one + *cornu* horn.

**uniform** LATIN *uniformis* having one form, from *unus* one + *forma* form.

**union** FRENCH, from LATIN *unio* unity, from *unus* one.

**unique** FRENCH single, from LATIN *unicus.*

**unison** LATIN *unisonus* having the same sound, from *unus* one + *sonus* sound.

**unit** LATIN *unus* one.

**unite** LATIN *unire* join together, from *unus* one.

**universe** LATIN *universum* the whole world, from *universus* whole, from *unus* one + *versus* turn.

**university** FRENCH, from LATIN *univeritas* the whole, from *universus.* See **universe.**

**until** OLD NORSE *unz.*

**up** OLD ENGLISH *uppe.*

**upbraid** OLD ENGLISH *upbregdan,* from *up-* up + *bregdan* pull.

**upholster** MIDDLE ENGLISH *upholdster* dealer in used goods, from *upholden* repair.

**upright** OLD ENGLISH *upriht* straight up.

**uproar** DUTCH *oproer.*

**uranium** LATIN *Uranus* the planet.

**Uranus** LATIN *Uranus,* from GREEK *Ouranos* heaven. In Greek cosmology, the god who represents the heavens.

**urban** LATIN *urbanus* having to do with a city, from *urbs* city.

**urbane** FRENCH *urbain,* from LATIN *urbanus.* See **urban.**

**urchin** FRENCH *herichon* hedgehog, from LATIN *(h)ericius.*

**-ure** FRENCH, from LATIN *-ura.*

**urea** LATIN, from FRENCH *urée,* from GREEK *ouron* urine.

**uremia** LATIN *uraemia,* from GREEK *ouron* urine + *haima* blood.

**urge** LATIN *urgere* press hard.

**urgent** See **urge.**

**urine** FRENCH, from LATIN *urina.*

**urn** LATIN *urna* pot for holding the ashes of the dead.

**use** FRENCH *user* practice, from LATIN *uti* make use of.

**usher** FRENCH *usser* doorkeeper, from LATIN *ostiarius,* from *ostium* door, from *os* mouth.

**usual** LATIN *usualis* ordinary, from *usus* use.

**usurp** FRENCH, from LATIN *usurpare* get, from *usu* use + *rapere* take by force.

**usury** LATIN *usura,* from *usus* use.

**uterus** LATIN womb, belly.

**utility** LATIN *utilitas,* from *uti* use.

**utmost** OLD ENGLISH *ut(e)mest* most distant, from *ut(e)* out + *-mest* most.

**utopia** LATIN no place, from GREEK *ou* not + *topos* place, from a book written in 1516 by Sir Thomas More called *Utopia,* which was about an imaginary, ideal place.

**utter** DUTCH *uteren* speak.

**uvula** LATIN *uva* a grape.

**uxorious** LATIN *uxor* wife.

# V

**vacant** FRENCH, from LATIN *vacare*. See **vacate**.

**vacate** LATIN *vacare* be empty.

**vacation** LATIN *vacatio* being free from a duty.

**vaccine** LATIN *vaccinus* having to do with cows, from *vacca* cow, from the use of the cowpox virus for vaccination.

**vacillate** LATIN *vacillare* waver.

**vacuole** FRENCH *vacuole*, from LATIN *vacuus* empty.

**vacuous** LATIN *vacuus* empty.

**vacuum** LATIN empty space.

**vagabond** FRENCH, from LATIN *vagabundus* walking about, from *vagari* wander.

**vagary** LATIN *vagari* wander, from *vagus* roving, wandering.

**vagina** LATIN *vagina* sheath, scabbard.

**vagrant** FRENCH *vagarant* wanderer, from LATIN *vagari* wander.

**vague** FRENCH, from LATIN *vagus* wandering.

**vain** FRENCH *vein* worthless, from LATIN *vanus* idle, empty.

**valance** probably from *Valence*, a city in France famous for its fabrics.

**vale** FRENCH, from LATIN *vallis*.

**valediction** LATIN *valedicere*, from *vale* farewell + *dicere* say.

**valence** LATIN *valentia* power, from *valere* be strong.

**valet** FRENCH groom, from *vaslet* young man.

**valiant** FRENCH *vaillant* have worth, from LATIN *valere* be strong.

**valid** FRENCH *valide*, from LATIN *validus* strong.

**valise** FRENCH, from ITALIAN *valigia*.

**valley** FRENCH *valey*, from LATIN *valles*.

**valor** FRENCH *valour*, from LATIN *valor* courage, from *valere* be strong.

**value** FRENCH worth, from LATIN *valere* be strong.

**valve** LATIN *valva* folding door.

**vamp**[1] (of a shoe) MIDDLE ENGLISH *vampe*, from FRENCH *avampié*, from *avant* before + *pié* a foot.

**vamp**[2] (woman) See **vampire**.

**vampire** FRENCH *vampyre*, from GERMAN *Vampir*, from SLAVIC *vampir*.

**vandal** LATIN *Vandalus*, from the name of the early Germanic tribe called Vandals, who invaded and robbed Rome in 455 A.D.

**vane** OLD ENGLISH *fana* a flag.

**vang** DUTCH a catch, from *vangen* catch. Nautical, rope used for steadying a sail.

**vanguard** FRENCH *avant* guard, from LATIN *ante-* before + *garde* guard.

**vanilla** SPANISH *vaina* a pod, from LATIN *vagina* a tube shape.

**vanish** FRENCH *esvanis* disappear, from LATIN *evanexcere,* from *ex-* out of + *vanus* empty.

**vantage** FRENCH *advantage* head start. See **advantage**.

**vapid** LATIN *vapidus.*

**vapor** LATIN steam.

**vaquero** SPANISH *vaca* cow, from LATIN *vacca* cow.

**variable** FRENCH, from LATIN *variabilis* changeable, from *variare* vary.

**varicose** LATIN *varicis,* from *varix.*

**variety** LATIN *varietas* different.

**various** LATIN *varius* changing.

**varlet** FRENCH *vaslet* male servant, attendant for a knight.

**varnish** FRENCH *vernis* the liquid, from LATIN *veronix,* probably from GREEK *Bereniki,* ancient Eastern town where varnish was supposedly first used.

**varsity** from **university**.

**varvel** FRENCH *vervelle,* from LATIN *vertibulum* joint.

**vary** LATIN *variare* change.

**vascular** LATIN *vascularis* pertaining to vessels or tubes, from *vasculum,* from *vas* vessel.

**vase** FRENCH, from LATIN *vas* dish.

**vassal** FRENCH subject, from LATIN *vassallus* servant, from *vassus* servant.

**vast** LATIN *vastus.*

**vat** OLD ENGLISH *fæt.*

**vaudeville** FRENCH comedy, from *Vau de Vire,* a place in Normandy famous for light, merry songs.

**vault** FRENCH *vaute* arch, from LATIN *volvere* roll.

**veal** FRENCH *veel* a calf, from *vedel,* from LATIN *vitellus,* from *vitulus* calf.

**vector** LATIN traveler.

**veer** FRENCH *virer* turn.

**vegetable** LATIN *vegetabilis* able to grow, from *vegetare,* from *vegetus* full of energy.

**vehement** LATIN *vehemens* violent.

**vehicle** LATIN *vehiculum* carriage.

**veil** FRENCH *veil(l)e* cloth covering that hides, from LATIN *velum* cloth.

**vein** FRENCH *veine,* from LATIN *vena* blood vessel.

**velcro** from *Velcro,* a British trademark, the name having been created by the Swiss inventor of the fastener, from FRENCH *velours croché* hooked velvet.

**vellum** MIDDLE ENGLISH *velim,* from FRENCH *velin* parchment made from calfskin, from FRENCH *vel, veel* calf. See **veal**.

**velocipede** FRENCH, from LATIN *velocis,* from *velox* swift + *pes* foot.

**velocity** LATIN *velocitas* quickness.

**velvet** FRENCH *velu,* from LATIN *villus* shaggy hair.

**venal** LATIN *venalis* for sale, from *venum* sale.

**vendue** DUTCH, from FRENCH *vendre* sell.

**veneer** GERMAN *furnieren,* from FRENCH *fournir* provide.

**venerate** LATIN *venerari* worship.

**vengeance** FRENCH *vengeance* revenge, from *venger* avenge (get even for a wrong done), from LATIN *vindicare*.

**venial** FRENCH, from LATIN *venialis,* from *venia* grace.

**venison** FRENCH *veneisum,* from LATIN *venatio* hunting.

**venom** FRENCH *venin* poison, from LATIN *venenum*.

**vent** FRENCH wind, from LATIN *ventus*.

**ventilate** LATIN *ventilare* set in motion, from *ventus* wind.

**ventral** FRENCH *ventral,* from LATIN *ventralis* pertaining to the belly or stomach, from *venter* belly, paunch.

**venture** MIDDLE ENGLISH *aventure*. See **adventure**.

**venue** FRENCH *venir* come, from LATIN *venire*.

**Venus** LATIN.

**veracity** LATIN *veracitas* truthfulness, from *verax* truthful.

**veranda** HINDI *varanda,* probably from PORTUGUESE *veranda* railing.

**verb** FRENCH *verbe,* from LATIN *verbum* word.

**verbatim** LATIN *verbum* word.

**verbena** LATIN.

**verbose** LATIN *verbosus* full of words, from *verbum* word.

**verdant** FRENCH *verdioer,* from LATIN *viridis* green.

**verderer** FRENCH *verd,* from LATIN *viridis* green.

**verdict** FRENCH *verdit* true saying, from LATIN *verus* true + *dictum* saying.

**verdigris** FRENCH *vertegrez,* from *vert de Grece* green of Greece, from LATIN *viridis* green + *de-* of + *Graecia* Greece.

**verge** FRENCH rod, from LATIN *virga*.

**verify** FRENCH *verifier* examine to make sure it is correct, from LATIN *verus* true + *facere* do, make.

**veritable** FRENCH, from LATIN *veritas* truth.

**vermillion** FRENCH *vermeil* bright-red.

**vermin** FRENCH *vermine* insects, from LATIN *vermis* worm.

**vermis** LATIN worm.

**vernacular** LATIN *vernaculus* native, from *verna* slave born in the master's house.

**vernal** LATIN *vervus,* from *ver* spring.

**vernier** Paul *Vernier,* a 17th century French mathematician.

**verrucos** LATIN *verruca* wart.

**versatile** LATIN turning round, from *vertere* turn.

**verse** OLD ENGLISH *fers* line of poetry, from LATIN *vertere* turn.

**versificator** LATIN, from *versificare* versify.

**version** LATIN *versio* translation, from *vertere* turn.

**versus** LATIN *vertere* turn.

**vertebra** LATIN a joint, from *vertere* turn.

**vertex** LATIN top of the head.

**vertical** LATIN *verticalis* upright, from *vertex* highest point.

**vertiginous** FRENCH *vertigineux,* from LATIN *vertiginosus* suffering from dizziness. See **vertigo**.

**vertigo** LATIN, from *vertere* turn.

**very** FRENCH *vrai,* from LATIN *verus* true.

**vespers** FRENCH *vespres*, from LATIN *vespera* evening.

**vessel** FRENCH, from LATIN *vas*.

**vest** FRENCH *veste* short jacket, from ITALIAN, from LATIN *vestis*.

**vestibule** LATIN *vestibulum* entrance hall.

**vestige** FRENCH footprint, from LATIN *vestigium*.

**vestment** FRENCH, from LATIN *vestimentum*, from *vestire* clothe.

**vestry** probably from FRENCH *vestairie* place for keeping clothes for religious ceremonies, from LATIN *vestiarium* wardrobe (clothing for a person or situation), from *vestis* clothing.

**vetch** FRENCH, from LATIN *vicia*.

**veteran** LATIN *veteranus* experienced soldier, from *vetus* old.

**veterinary** LATIN *veterinarius* relating to beasts of burden (animals used for carrying things).

**veto** LATIN "I forbid", from the officials of ancient Rome when they disagreed with a suggestion brought before the ruling body.

**vex** FRENCH, from LATIN *vexare* stir up.

**via** LATIN a way.

**viable** FRENCH *vie* life, from LATIN *vita*.

**viaduct** LATIN *via* road + -*duct*, from *ductus*, from *ducere* lead.

**vial** FRENCH, from GREEK *phiale* shallow cup.

**vibrant** LATIN *vibrare* shake.

**vicar** LATIN *vicarius* substituted, from *vicis* change.

**vicarious** LATIN *vicis* change.

**vice** FRENCH fault, from LATIN *vitium*.

**vice versa** LATIN *vice* in place of, from *vicis* change + *versa* turn about.

**viceroy** FRENCH *vice*- in the place of another + *roy* king, from LATIN *rex*.

**vicinity** LATIN *vicinus* of the same village, from *vicus* village.

**vicious** LATIN *vitiosus* full of faults, from *vitium*. See **vice**.

**vicissitude** FRENCH, from LATIN *vicissitudo*, from *vicis* a turn.

**victim** LATIN *victima* animal offered for sacrifice.

**victor** LATIN *victere* conquer.

**victual** FRENCH *vitaille* supply of food, from LATIN *victualia*, from *victus* food.

**video** LATIN I see.

**vie** FRENCH *envier* challenge, from LATIN *invitare*.

**view** FRENCH *vewe* eyes, from *veoir* see, from LATIN *videre*.

**viga** SPANISH beam.

**vigil** FRENCH *vigile* staying awake on the night before a holy day, from LATIN *vigilia* watching.

**vigilant** LATIN *vigilare* watch.

**vigilante** SPANISH *vigilante* watchful, from LATIN *vigilans*. See **vigilant**.

**vignette** FRENCH little vine, ornamental border that has vines. See **vine**.

**vigor** FRENCH *vigour* strength, from LATIN *vigor* activity.

**viking** OLD NORSE *vikingr*.

**vile** FRENCH *vil* cheap, from LATIN *vilis*.

**vilify** LATIN *vilificare* make have little value, from *vilis* cheap + *facere* do, make.

**village** FRENCH small group of houses of peasants, from LATIN *villa* farm.

**villain** FRENCH *vilain* peasant, from LATIN *villanus* farm servant, from *villa* farm.

**villein** See **villain.**

**vim** LATIN, from *vis* energy.

**vindicate** LATIN *vindicare* avenge (get even for a wrong done).

**vindictive** LATIN *vindicta* revenge. See **vindicate** + **-ive.**

**vine** FRENCH, from LATIN *vinum* wine.

**vinegar** FRENCH *vinaigre* sour wine, from LATIN *vinum* wine + *acer* sharp.

**vintage** MIDDLE ENGLISH *vendage* gathering grapes, from LATIN *vindemia*, from *vinum* wine + *demere* take away.

**vinyl** MODERN ENGLISH *polyvinyl*, from *vinyl* as a chemical derived from alcohol, from LATIN *vinum* wine.

**viol** FRENCH *viole*, from *viula*, from LATIN *vitula.*

**violate** LATIN *violare* injure, dishonor.

**violence** FRENCH, from LATIN *violentia* much force.

**violin** ITALIAN *viola* viol (early stringed instrument, usually played with a bow).

**viper** LATIN *vipera* snake.

**virago** OLD ENGLISH, from LATIN a manlike or heroic woman, from *vir* a man.

**vireo** LATIN *vireo* green bird, from *virere* be green.

**virgin** FRENCH *virgine* maiden (girl who is not married), from LATIN *virgo.*

**viridian** LATIN *viridis* green.

**virtual** See **virtue.**

**virtue** MIDDLE ENGLISH *vertu*, from FRENCH, from LATIN *virtus* manliness, from *vir* man.

**virus** LATIN poison.

**visage** FRENCH *vis*, from LATIN *visus* look.

**viscount** FRENCH *visconte*, from LATIN *vice* in place of + *comes* companion.

**vise** FRENCH *vis* screw, from LATIN *vitis* vine, which tends to wind around things.

**visible** LATIN *visibilis* can be seen, from *videre* see.

**vision** LATIN *visio* sight.

**visit** LATIN *visitare* go to see.

**visor** FRENCH *viser* visor of a helmet, from *vis* face. See **visage.**

**vista** ITALIAN, from LATIN *videre* see.

**vital** LATIN *vitalis* having to do with life, from *vita* life.

**vitamin** LATIN *vita* life + *amine*, because they were thought to contain amino acids.

**vitiate** LATIN *vitiare* spoil.

**vituperate** LATIN *vitrium* a fault + *parare* prepare.

**vivacious** LATIN *viviax* lively.

**vivandier** FRENCH, from LATIN *vivenda*, from *vivere* live.

**vivid** LATIN *vividus* full of life, from *vivus* alive.

**vivisection** LATIN *vivus* alive + *secare* cut.

**vixen** MIDDLE ENGLISH *fixen*, from OLD ENGLISH *fyxe* a female fox.

**vocabulary** LATIN *vocabularium* list of words, from *vocabulum.*

**vocal** LATIN *vocalis*, from *vox* sound.

**vocation** LATIN *vocatio* invitation.

**vociferate** LATIN *vociferari* cry out, from *vox* sound + *ferre* bring.

**vogue** FRENCH fashion, from *voguer* move along, row, from GERMAN.

**voice** FRENCH *vois* sound, from LATIN *vox.*

**void** FRENCH *voide* imply, from LATIN *vacare* be empty.

**volatile** LATIN *volare* fly.

**volcano** ITALIAN, from LATIN *Vulcanus* Vulcan, the Roman god of fire.

**vole** MODERN ENGLISH *volemouse*, probably from OLD NORSE *völlr* field.

**volition** FRENCH, from LATIN *volitio*, from *velle* will.

**volley** FRENCH *volee*, from LATIN *volare* fly.

**volly** FRENCH *volee* flight, from *voler* fly, from LATIN *volare*.

**volt** Allessandro *Volta* (1745–1827), Italian scientist and inventor.

**voluble** FRENCH, from LATIN *volubilis*, from *volere* roll.

**volume** FRENCH book, from LATIN *volumen* roll of writing, from *volvere* roll.

**voluntary** LATIN *voluntarius* willing, from *volantas* will.

**volunteer** FRENCH *volontaire* one who offers to do something on his own, from LATIN *voluntarius* willing.

**voluptuous** LATIN *voluptas* pleasure.

**voodoo** FRENCH *voudou*, from AFRICAN *vodu* spirit.

**voracious** LATIN *voracis*, from *vorare* devour (eat up hungrily).

**vortex** LATIN *vertere* turn.

**votary** LATIN *vovere* vow + *-arius, -aria, -arium*.

**vote** LATIN *votum* wish.

**vouch** FRENCH *voucher* claim, from LATIN *vocare* call.

**vow** FRENCH *veu* promise made to a god, from LATIN *votum*.

**vowel** FRENCH, from LATIN *vocalis littera* vocal letter, from *vox* voice.

**voyage** FRENCH *voiage* way, from LATIN *viaticum* money or food for a journey.

**vulgar** LATIN *vulgaris* common, having to do with large numbers (masses) of people, from *vulgus* the masses.

**vulnerable** LATIN *vulnerabilis* a wounding, from *vulnus* wound.

**vulture** LATIN *vultur*.

# W

**wad** LATIN *wadda,* from ARABIC *bata'in* lining inside clothes.

**waddle** See **wade**.

**wade** OLD ENGLISH *waden* go.

**wadi** ARABIC.

**wafer** FRENCH *waufre,* from DUTCH *wafel.*

**waft** GERMAN, from DUTCH *wachten* guard, the original sense meaning "carried by water," the way an escort ship would accompany another.

**wag** MIDDLE ENGLISH *waggen* shake, from OLD ENGLISH *wagian* sway.

**wage** FRENCH pledge.

**wagon** DUTCH *wagen* cart with wheels used for carrying heavy loads.

**waif** FRENCH *gayf,* of SCANDINAVIAN origin.

**wail** OLD NORSE *væla,* from *væ* woe.

**wain** OLD ENGLISH *wægn* wheeled vehicle.

**waist** OLD ENGLISH *weaxan* grow.

**wait** FRENCH *waiter* watch.

**waive** FRENCH *wehver,* from OLD NORSE *veifa* keep changing.

**wake** OLD ENGLISH *wacian.*

**walk** OLD ENGLISH *wealcan* move about.

**wall** OLD ENGLISH *weall,* from LATIN *valum* side of a building built for protection, from *vallus* a stake.

**wallet** MIDDLE ENGLISH *walet,* origin uncertain.

**wallop** OLD NORSE *waloper* gallop.

**wallow** OLD ENGLISH *wealwian* roll about.

**walnut** OLD ENGLISH *wealh* foreign + *hnutu* a nut.

**waltz** GERMAN *walzen* dance about.

**wan** OLD ENGLISH *wann* dark.

**wander** OLD ENGLISH *wandrian.*

**wane** OLD ENGLISH *wanian* fade.

**wang**[1] (plow part) See **wing**.

**wang**[2] (tooth) OLD ENGLISH cheek.

**want** OLD NORSE *vanta.*

**wanton** MIDDLE ENGLISH *wantowen* not having discipline, from OLD ENGLISH *wan* not having + *teon* educate.

**wapatoo** NATIVE AMERICAN *wapatowa* white mushroom.

**war** FRENCH *werre* fighting, from GERMAN *werra* disagreement.

**warble** OLD NORSE *werbler.*

**ward** OLD ENGLISH *weard* keep guard.

**warden** MIDDLE ENGLISH guard, from FRENCH *wardein*.

**wardrobe** FRENCH *warderobe* place to keep clothes, from *warder* guard + *robe* clothing.

**ware** OLD ENGLISH *waru* goods.

**warm** OLD ENGLISH *wearm*.

**warn** OLD ENGLISH *warnian* take notice of.

**warp** OLD ENGLISH *weorpan* throw.

**warrant** FRENCH *warant* protection.

**warren** FRENCH *warir* keep safe.

**wary** OLD ENGLISH *wær* aware.

**was** OLD ENGLISH *wæs*.

**wash** OLD ENGLISH *wæscan*.

**waste** FRENCH *waster* destroy totally, from LATIN *vastare* make empty.

**wastel** FRENCH, from LATIN *wastellum*.

**watch** OLD ENGLISH *wæccan* be awake.

**water** OLD ENGLISH *wæter*.

**watt** James *Watt* (1736–1819), Scottish inventor.

**wattle** OLD ENGLISH *watel* twigs woven in.

**wave** OLD ENGLISH *wafian*.

**waver** MIDDLE ENGLISH *waven* wave.

**wax**[1] (beeswax) OLD ENGLISH *weax*.

**wax**[2] (increase) OLD ENGLISH *weaxan* increase.

**wax-chandler** MIDDLE ENGLISH *chaundeler*, from FRENCH *chandelier*, from LATIN *candella* a candle.

**way** OLD ENGLISH *weg* path.

**weak** OLD NORSE *veikr*.

**weal** OLD ENGLISH *walu*.

**wealth** OLD ENGLISH *wela*.

**wean** OLD ENGLISH *wenian*.

**weapon** OLD ENGLISH *wæpen*.

**wear** OLD ENGLISH *wearian*.

**weary** OLD ENGLISH *werig*.

**weasel** OLD ENGLISH *wesle*.

**weather** OLD ENGLISH *weder* wind.

**weave** OLD ENGLISH *wefan* make cloth by threading.

**web** OLD ENGLISH *webb* woven cloth.

**wedding** OLD ENGLISH *weddung*.

**wedge** OLD ENGLISH *wecg*.

**wedlock** OLD ENGLISH *wedlac* marriage vow, from *wedd* promise + *lac* activity.

**Wednesday** OLD ENGLISH *Wodnesdæg* Woden's Day. Woden was the chief god of the ancient Germanic people.

**weed** OLD ENGLISH *weod*.

**week** OLD ENGLISH *wice*.

**weep** OLD ENGLISH *wepan*.

**weevil** OLD ENGLISH *wifel*.

**weft** OLD ENGLISH *wefta*, from *wefan* weave.

**weigh** OLD ENGLISH *wegan* carry.

**weir** OLD ENGLISH *wer*.

**weird** MIDDLE ENGLISH *wyrde* fate, from OLD ENGLISH *wyrd*.

**welcome** OLD NORSE *velkominn*, from *vel* well + *koma* come.

**weld** OLD ENGLISH *wellan* boil.

**welfare** MIDDLE ENGLISH good fortune, from *wel faren* fare well, from OLD ENGLISH *wel faran*.

**well**[1] (good) OLD ENGLISH *wel* properly.

**well**[2] (hole) OLD ENGLISH *wella*.

**wellington** Arthur, first duke of *Wellington* in England (1769–1852), who first wore the boots.

**welt** MIDDLE ENGLISH *welte*.

**welter** DUTCH *welteren*.

**wench** MIDDLE ENGLISH *wenche* female servant, from OLD ENGLISH *wencel*.

**wend** OLD ENGLISH *wendan* go.

**wentletrap** DUTCH *wenteltrap* winding stair, spiral shell, from GERMAN *wendeltreppe*.

**were** OLD ENGLISH *wæron*.

**werewolf** OLD ENGLISH *werewulf*, from *wer* man + *wulf* wolf.

**wergeld** OLD ENGLISH, from *wer* man + *geld* yield.

**west** OLD ENGLISH.

**wester** OLD ENGLISH *westra* west, from OLD NORSE *verstri*.

**wet** OLD ENGLISH *moist*.

**whack** imitative.

**wharf** OLD ENGLISH *hwearf*.

**what** OLD ENGLISH *hwæt*.

**wheedle** possibly from GERMAN *wedeln* wag the tail.

**wheel** OLD ENGLISH *hweol* circle turning around a rod.

**wheeze** OLD NORSE *hvæsa* hiss.

**whelk** OLD ENGLISH *weoloc*, origin uncertain.

**whelm** MIDDLE ENGLISH *whelmen* turn upside down, from OLD ENGLISH *-hwelfan* cover over.

**whelp** OLD ENGLISH *hwelp*.

**when** OLD ENGLISH *hwienne*.

**whence** OLD ENGLISH *hwanan*.

**where** OLD ENGLISH *hwær*.

**whet** OLD ENGLISH *hwettan* sharpen.

**whether** OLD ENGLISH *hwæther*.

**which** OLD ENGLISH *hwilc*.

**whicker** imitative.

**whiff** imitative.

**Whig** *Whiggamore*, Scottish Presbyterians who marched on a city in Scotland in 1648, from *whig*, from a sound to get horses to move, from *mare* a horse.

**whim** MIDDLE ENGLISH *whim-wham* fanciful object, origin unknown.

**whimper** MIDDLE ENGLISH, possibly from GERMAN *wimmern*.

**whimsey** probably from *whim-wham*. See **whim**.

**whine** OLD ENGLISH *hwinan*.

**whinny** See **whine**.

**whip** DUTCH *wippen* swing.

**whippoorwill** imitative.

**whir** MIDDLE ENGLISH *quirre*, of SCANDINAVIAN origin.

**whirl** OLD NORSE *hvirfla* turn about.

**whisk** MIDDLE ENGLISH *wysk* fast sweeping movement, of SCANDINAVIAN origin.

**whiskey**[1] (liquor) IRISH *usquebaugh*, from *uisce* water + *beathadh* life.

**whiskey**[2] (carriage) GERMAN *wisken* move quickly.

**whisper** OLD ENGLISH *hwisprian*.

**whist** MIDDLE ENGLISH *whisk*, perhaps influenced by MIDDLE ENGLISH *whist* silent. See **whisk**.

**whistle** OLD ENGLISH *hwistlian* make a hissing sound.

**whittle** OLD ENGLISH *thwitan* cut.

**who** OLD ENGLISH *hwa.*

**whole** OLD ENGLISH *hal* not divided into parts.

**whoop** imitative.

**whopper** MIDDLE ENGLISH *whop* beat, origin uncertain.

**whorl** probably from **whirl**.

**whortleberry** BRITISH *hurtleberry,* from OLD ENGLISH *horte.*

**wick** OLD ENGLISH *weoce.*

**wicked** MIDDLE ENGLISH *wikke* evil, from OLD ENGLISH *wicce* witch.

**wicker** DANISH *vigger* branch of willow.

**wicket** FRENCH *wiket.*

**wide** OLD ENGLISH *wid.*

**widow** OLD ENGLISH *widuwe.*

**wield** OLD ENGLISH *wieldan* control.

**wiener** GERMAN *Wiener Wurst* Viennese sausage.

**wife** OLD ENGLISH *wif.*

**wig** MODERN ENGLISH, from *periwig,* from *perwyke,* from FRENCH *perruque.*

**wiggle** MIDDLE ENGLISH *wegelen,* from GERMAN *wiggelen.*

**wight** MIDDLE ENGLISH, from OLD ENGLISH *wiht* creature, being, thing.

**wig-wag** BRITISH *wig* move + *wag,* from OLD ENGLISH *wegan* move.

**wild** OLD ENGLISH *wilde.*

**wildebeest** AFRIKAANS wild beast.

**wilderness** OLD ENGLISH *wildeoren* wild, from *wilde* wild + *deor* animal.

**wile** OLD ENGLISH *wigle* magic.

**will**[1] (going to) OLD ENGLISH *willan* be willing.

**will**[2] (choice) OLD ENGLISH *willa* desire.

**willow** OLD ENGLISH *welig.*

**willy-nilly** MODERN ENGLISH *will I, nill I* I am willing, I am unwilling, from OLD ENGLISH *nyllan.*

**wilt** MODERN ENGLISH, probably from MIDDLE ENGLISH *welk* dry up.

**wimple** OLD ENGLISH *wimpel.*

**win** OLD ENGLISH *winnan* fight.

**wince** FRENCH *guenchir* turn aside.

**winch** OLD ENGLISH *wince.*

**wind**[1] (air) OLD ENGLISH.

**wind**[2] (turn) OLD ENGLISH *windan* turn.

**windle** See **wind**[2] + **-le**.

**window** OLD NORSE *vindauga,* from *viondr* wind + *auga* eye.

**wing** OLD NORSE *vægr* bird's wing.

**wink** OLD ENGLISH *wincian* close one's eyes.

**winker** See **wink**.

**winnow** OLD ENGLISH *wind-wian* let air go through grain to separate it from its dry covering, from *wind.*

**winsome** OLD ENGLISH *wynsum* pleasant, from *wynn* pleasure + *-sum* -like.

**winter** OLD ENGLISH.

**winze** See **wind**[2].

**wipe** OLD ENGLISH *wipian.*

**wire** OLD ENGLISH *wir.*

**wise** OLD ENGLISH *wis.*

**wish** OLD ENGLISH *wyscan* want.

**wisp** MIDDLE ENGLISH.

**wistful** OLD ENGLISH *wyscan* want.

**wit** OLD ENGLISH mind.

**witch** OLD ENGLISH *wicce*, feminine form of *wicca* sorcerer.

**witch hazel** MIDDLE ENGLISH *wyche hazel*, from *wyche*, from OLD ENGLISH *wice* having pliant branches.

**with** OLD ENGLISH.

**withe** OLD ENGLISH *withthe*.

**wither** MIDDLE ENGLISH *widderal* get smaller, from *wederan* let out in the weather, from OLD ENGLISH *weder*. See **weather**.

**withers** MIDDLE ENGLISH *wither* resistance, from OLD ENGLISH *withre*, from *wither* against.

**withy** OLD ENGLISH.

**witness** OLD ENGLISH *witnes* evidence. See **wit**.

**wizard** MIDDLE ENGLISH *ywsard* wise person, from OLD ENGLISH *wis*. See **wise**.

**wizen** OLD ENGLISH *wisnian, weosnian* shrivel.

**wobble** GERMAN *wabblen* move without being steady.

**woe** OLD ENGLISH *wa*.

**wok** CHINESE.

**wolf** OLD ENGLISH *wulf*.

**wolfsbane** English translation of LATIN *lycoctonum*, from GREEK *lykotonon*, from *lykos* wolf + *kteinein* kill.

**woman** OLD ENGLISH *wifman*.

**womb** MIDDLE ENGLISH *wombe*, from OLD ENGLISH *wamb* belly.

**wonder** OLD ENGLISH *wundor* miracle.

**wont** MIDDLE ENGLISH *wonen*, from OLD ENGLISH *wunian*.

**woo** OLD ENGLISH *wogian*.

**woodbine** OLD ENGLISH *wudubinde*.

**woof**[1] (cloth) OLD ENGLISH *owef*, from *o-* on + *wefan* weave.

**woof**[2] (dog bark) echoic.

**woosle** See **ousel**.

**woozy** See **ooze**.

**word** OLD ENGLISH news.

**work** OLD ENGLISH *weorc*.

**world** OLD ENGLISH *weorold*.

**worry** OLD ENGLISH *wyrgan* strangle.

**worse** OLD ENGLISH *wyrsa*.

**worship** OLD ENGLISH *weorthscipe* respect.

**worsted** MIDDLE ENGLISH *Worstead*, from OLD ENGLISH *Wurthestede* town in England where the cloth was originally made.

**worth** OLD ENGLISH *weorth*.

**would** See **will**[1].

**wound** OLD ENGLISH *wund*.

**wrack** OLD ENGLISH *wræc* misery.

**wraith** OLD NORSE *vartha* guard.

**wrangle** MIDDLE ENGLISH *wringen* squeeze.

**wrap** MIDDLE ENGLISH *wrappen*.

**wrath** OLD ENGLISH *wræththu*.

**wreak** OLD ENGLISH *wrecan* avenge.

**wreath** OLD ENGLISH *writha*.

**wreathe** OLD ENGLISH *writhan* wrap around.

**wreck** FRENCH *wrec* shipwreck, from SCANDINAVIAN.

**wren** OLD ENGLISH *wrenna*.

**wrench** OLD ENGLISH *wrencan* twist.

**wrest** OLD ENGLISH *wræsten* turn.

**wretch** OLD ENGLISH *wrecca*.

**wriggle** GERMAN *wriggeln*.

**wright** OLD ENGLISH *wyrcan* work.

**wring** OLD ENGLISH *wringan* squeeze.

**wrinkle** MIDDLE ENGLISH *wringled* twisted, from OLD ENGLISH *gewrinclod* crooked.

**writ** See **write**.

**write** OLD ENGLISH *writan*.

**writhe** OLD ENGLISH *writhan* wrap around.

**wrong** OLD ENGLISH *wrang* not just, from OLD NORSE *rangr* crooked.

**wroth** OLD ENGLISH *wrath*.

**wrought** See **work**.

**wry** MIDDLE ENGLISH *wrien* twist, from OLD ENGLISH *wrigian* move.

**wurst** GERMAN *Wurst* sausage.

**wych-elm** OLD ENGLISH *wice* tree with branches that bend easily + *elm*.

# X

**xanthophyll** FRENCH *xanthophylle,* from GREEK *canqos* yellow + *phyllon* leaf.

**xebec** FRENCH *chébec,* from ITALIAN *sciabecco,* from ARABIC *shabbak* a small warship.

**xylophone** GREEK *xylon* wood + *phone* voice, sound.

# Y

**-y**[1] (little) MIDDLE ENGLISH *-y, -i, -ie*.

**-y**[2] (full of) MIDDLE ENGLISH *-y, -ie*, from OLD ENGLISH *-ig*.

**-y**[3] (kind) MIDDLE ENGLISH *-ie*, from FRENCH, from LATIN *-ia*.

**-y**[4] (action) MIDDLE ENGLISH *-ie*, from FRENCH, from LATIN *-ium*.

**yacht** DUTCH *jachtschip* ship that chases.

**yam** SPANISH *igname*.

**yammer** OLD ENGLISH *geomerian*, from lament, from *geomor* sorrowful.

**yank** SCOTTISH, origin uncertain.

**Yankee** DUTCH, possibly from *Janke* Little John, from *Jan* John. Used by the early settlers in New York to refer to English settlers in Connecticut.

**yap** imitative.

**yard**[1] (ground enclosed) OLD ENGLISH *geard* something enclosed.

**yard**[2] (measure) OLD ENGLISH *gierd* staff (stick).

**yarn** OLD ENGLISH *gearn*.

**yaw** OLD NORSE *jaga* move or swing back and forth.

**yawn** OLD ENGLISH *geonian* open the mouth wide.

**yawp** MIDDLE ENGLISH *yolpen*.

**year** OLD ENGLISH *gear*.

**yearn** OLD ENGLISH *giernan*.

**yellow** OLD ENGLISH *geolu*.

**yeoman** MIDDLE ENGLISH *yeman*, probably from contraction of *yengman* young man.

**yes** OLD ENGLISH *gese*.

**yet** OLD ENGLISH *giet(a)* still.

**yew** OLD ENGLISH *iw*.

**yield** OLD ENGLISH *gieldan* give in return.

**yodel** GERMAN *jodeln*.

**yoga** SANSKRIT union.

**yogurt** TURKISH *yoghurt*, from *yog* intensify.

**yoke** OLD ENGLISH *geoc*.

**yokel** perhaps from GERMAN *Jokel*, "little Jakob" a derogatory name for a farmer.

**yolk** OLD ENGLISH *geolca*.

**yon** OLD ENGLISH *geon* that.

**yonder** MIDDLE ENGLISH *yond*, from OLD ENGLISH *geond*.

**yore** OLD ENGLISH *geara* of years.

**you**  OLD ENGLISH *eow.*

**young**  OLD ENGLISH *geong* fresh.

**your**  OLD ENGLISH *eower.*

**youth**  OLD ENGLISH *geoguth* being young.

**yowl**  OLD NORSE *gaula.*

**yo-yo**  a trademark name, originally probably from the name of the toy in the language of the PHILLIPPINES, where it originated.

**yucca**  SPANISH *yuca.*

**yule**  OLD ENGLISH *geol.*

**yurt**  RUSSIAN *yurta.*

# Z

**zaftig**  GERMAN *saftig* juicy.

**zany**  ITALIAN *zanni* clown.

**zeal**  LATIN *zelus* strong feeling, from GREEK *zelos.*

**zenith**  LATIN *cenith* highest point of the sky, from ARABIC *sami* way.

**zephyr**  LATIN, from GREEK *zephyros.*

**zero**  ITALIAN nothing, from ARABIC *çifr* empty.

**zest**  FRENCH *zeste* orange or lemon peel used as a flavoring, from GREEK *zesti* warm, hot.

**zester**  See **zest.**

**zetetic**  GREEK *zhthtikos,* from *zhtew* inquire.

**zig-zag**  FRENCH having sharp turns in alternating directions.

**zinc**  GERMAN *Zink,* from *Zinke* prong, point, from *zint* a point, jag.

**zip**  imitative.

**zither**  GERMAN, from LATIN, from GREEK *kithara* a stringed instrument.

**zodiac**  LATIN *zoidion,* from GREEK *zoidiakos* circle of figures.

**zoetrope**  GREEK *zoe* life + *trope* turn.

**zombie**  AFRICAN.

**zone**  LATIN *zona* belt, from GREEK *zone.*

**zoo**  *Zoological Gardens* (of the London Zoological Society).

**zoology**  GREEK *zoion* animal + *-logia* study of.

**zoom**  imitative.

**zucchini**  ITALIAN *zucca* a gourd (vegetable).

# APPENDIX

# List of Languages

Here is a list of the languages referenced in the derivations in this dictionary. Below some are sub-category languages that are not used in this dictionary, but which you may run into in other dictionaries.

Explanations of all these languages can be found in the following glossary.

African

Afrikaans

American English (American)

Amharic

Arabic

Australian Aboriginal

British English (British)

Chinese

Danish
    Old Danish

Dutch
    Middle Dutch

Egyptian

Eskimo
    Greenland Eskimo

Finnish

Frankish

French
    Old French
    Anglo-French
    Norman French
    Middle French
    Canadian French
    Louisiana French
    Swiss French

German
    Old High German
    Middle High German
    High German
    Middle Low German
    Low German
    Old Saxon

Greek

Gypsy

Hebrew

Hindi

Hungarian

Icelandic

Irish (Gaelic)
    Old Irish
    Irish English (Anglo-Irish)

Italian
    Old Italian

Japanese

Latin
    Vulgar Latin
    Late Latin
    Medieval Latin
    Modern Latin

Malay

Maori

Middle English

Modern English

Native American
    North American Indian
    Arawakan
    Aztec Indian
    Brazilian Indian
    Canadian Indian
    Nahuatl
    Taino

Norwegian

Old English

Old Norse

Pashto

Persian
    Old Persian

Portuguese

Quechua

Romanian

Russian

Sanskrit

Scandinavian

Scottish
    Scots
    Scottish Gaelic
    Scottish English

Slavic

Spanish
    American Spanish
    Mexican Spanish

Swedish

Tamil

Thai

Tongan

Tungus

Turkish

Welsh

Yiddish

Arctic Ocean

Eskimo

Eskimo

Icelandic

English

Native
American

Native
American

North
Pacific Ocean

English

Native
American

Native
American

Native
American

North
Atlantic Ocean

See map on
next page

Native
American

Native
American

Afric

Native
American

La

South
Pacific Ocean

Spanish

Native
American

Native
American

Portuguese

Native
American

South
Atlantic Ocean

Quechua

Native
American

# Language Map

The maps here and on the next
page show the general locations
of the languages referenced in
this dictionary. (It does not show
all world languages.) Those in
smaller font are older languages
no longer in broad use.

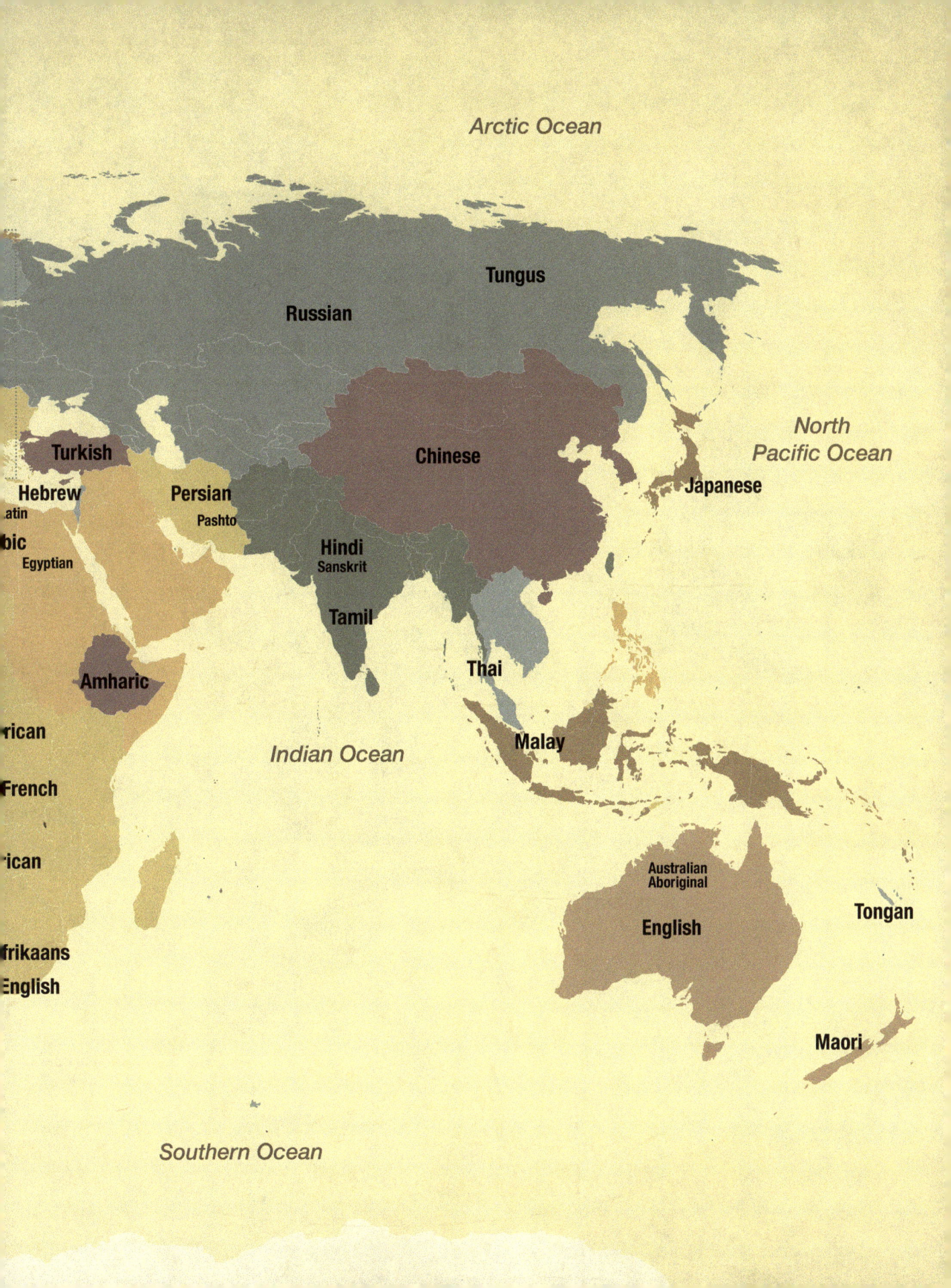

Arctic Ocean

Tungus

Russian

North
Pacific Ocean

Turkish

Chinese

Japanese

Hebrew

Persian

Latin

Pashto

bic

Egyptian

Hindi

Sanskrit

Tamil

Amharic

Thai

rican

Indian Ocean

Malay

French

ican

Australian
Aboriginal

Tongan

frikaans

English

English

Maori

Southern Ocean

Norwegian

Old Norse

Finnish

Swedish

Old Norse

Scottish

Danish

Old Norse

Irish

British
English

S l a v i c

Welsh

Old English
Middle English

Dutch

German

Frankish

Y i d d i s h

French

G y p s y

Hungarian

Roman

Latin

Latin

S l a v i

Latin

Latin

Italian

Portuguese

Spanish

Latin

Greek

# Glossary

**African** a group of native languages, a number of which remain the primary language spoken in large parts of the continent.

**Afrikaans** one of 11 official languages of South Africa, developed by 17$^{th}$ century Dutch settlers to the area. Today it is spoken by about 7 million South Africans, the majority of them people of color. While it borrowed quite a few African words, it is primarily a form of Dutch.

**American** (or **American English**) the English spoken and written in the United States. *French fries* is an American English term while the British call these *chips*. An American parks a car in a *parking lot* while the British term is *car park*. American English is part of Modern English, but it is distinctly American.

**American Indian** See **North American Indian**.

**American Spanish** the Spanish spoken in North America. It includes, for example, Mexican Spanish, Puerto Rican Spanish and the Spanish spoken in parts of the United States like California, New Mexico, Arizona and Texas.

**Amharic** the language of the African country of Ethiopia.

**Ancient Greek** the language spoken by the people of Greece starting around 3000 BCE. Between 700 BCE and 500 CE it spread and was widely spoken throughout the Mediterranean area. Today it is the world's oldest recorded language still in use. Many words in English and other languages have their roots in Ancient Greek. Examples of words acquired from Greek are *democracy* (from *demos* people + *kratos* power) and *planet* (meaning "wanderer," as the Greeks saw planets as wandering stars.)

**Angles** (AN GULZ) a people from parts of what we now call Denmark and Germany who invaded Britain about 450 CE. Their spoken language, mixed with Saxon, became Anglo-Saxon, the earliest version of English. The name "England" comes from Old English *Engla land*, meaning "land of the Angles."

**Anglo-French** same as **Anglo-Norman**.

**Anglo-Irish** the version of English spoken in Ireland. It is also known as Irish English.

**Anglo-Norman** a version of Norman French spoken by the ruling class in England from 1066 to about 1450 CE. This ruling class consisted of Normans, people from other areas of France and some Anglo-Saxons. Anglo-Norman was the language used in the king's court, in courts of law, literature, schools and universities, and trade. Many Anglo-Norman words became part of English. *Apprentisse* (apprentice), *grammeire* (book learning) and *were* (war) are examples of Anglo-Norman words.

**Anglo-Saxon** See **Old English**.

**Arabic** the language spoken throughout the Arab world, which includes the Middle East and most of northern Africa. Spoken by more than 200 million people, it is the official language of more than 20 countries. Arabic was first written down in the 4$^{th}$ century CE. It is written and read from right to left.

**Arawakan** (AR UH WOK UN) a large family of native languages of South and Central America, including the Caribbean.

**Australian Aboriginal** a group of over 250 languages spoken by the native (aboriginal) people of Australia before English was established there during the 1800s. Only a few of these native languages survive today.

Examples of Native Australian words are *wallawani* (hello), *billabong* (lake), and *yakka* (hard work).

**Aztec, Aztec Indian, Aztecan** See **Nahuatl.**

**BCE** an abbreviation for *Before Common Era.* BCE following a date means it was that many years before the Common Era which starts in year 1 with the birth of Christ.

**back-formation** forming a new word by removing things that look like prefixes or suffixes. So the word *looks like* it is the base of another word, but it was really formed *from* that word. For example, *peddle* is a back-formation of the word *peddler* because the word *peddler* came into existence before *peddle.*

**blend** a word formed by combining parts of other words. *Smog* is a blend made by combining *smoke* and *fog. Brunch* is a blend made from *breakfast* and *lunch.*

**Brazilian Indian** Tupinambá (TOO PIN NAM BAH), an extinct Native American language of Brazil's Tupinambá or Tupi people.

**Britons** the ancient inhabitants of Britain.

**Canadian Indian** a group of about 70 Native American languages of Canada. In Canada, Native Americans are generally referred to as First People or Native Canadians.

**British** (or **British English**) the English spoken and written in the United Kingdom. Some of its vocabulary is different from the English spoken in other places. Americans, for example, open the *hood* of their cars while in Britain they open the *bonnet.* British English is part of Modern English, but it is distinctly British.

**CE** an abbreviation for *Common Era,* it begins with the birth of Christ, which is designated as Year 1.

**Celtic** (KEL TIC) a group of mostly extinct languages named for the Celtic people who controlled much of Europe from about 800 to 50 BCE. Celtic is still spoken in a few places, mainly Wales, Ireland and Scotland.

**cf.** short for Latin *confer,* which means "compare." In a derivation, cf. directs one to consider other information as well and points to where it can be found.

**Chinese** a group of similar languages spoken by the people of China. While somewhat different from one another, they share a common system of writing, one in which each word has its own symbol. About 1.2 billion people speak a variety of Chinese. Some examples of Chinese words are *shu* (book), *mao* (cat) and *shengri* (birthday.) Note that these are written using the English alphabet and would look very different written in Chinese.

**colloquial** found in informal, conversational speech or writing. From Latin *colloquium* conversation.

**Danish** (or **Modern Danish**) the language spoken today by the people of Denmark. It is descended from *Old Norse.* Examples of Danish words are *dansk* (Danish), *tak* (thank you) and *posthus* (post office.)

**derivation** a brief explanation of where a word comes from. In addition to a word's origin, a derivation may also give some history that shows how it evolved into its current form.

**dialect** a form of a particular language used by a specific area or group. It can differ in pronunciation, grammar, or vocabulary from the regular language. An example would be a Southern dialect where people might say "you all" or "y'all" instead of "you," or "hold your horses!" instead of "stop!"

**diminutive (dim.)** a word or name with an added beginning or ending that indicates smallness or, occasionally, affection or familiarity. The words *droplet, minivan, kitty, duckling* and *kitchenette* are all diminutives.

**Dutch** the language of the Netherlands where it is spoken by about 30 million people. Dutch is closely related to both English and German. All three are descended from the same parent language. Examples of Dutch words are *goedenmorgan* (good morning), *honderd* (one hundred) and *bedankt* (thank you.)

**echoic** See **imitative**.

**Egyptian** (or **ancient Egyptian**) an extinct language that was spoken in Egypt throughout several different periods, from roughly 3000 BCE to 1600 CE. It was one of the first written languages. Around 640 CE, Egypt was conquered by the Arabs and the use of Arabic spread. Around 1600 Arabic became its official language, so today Egyptians speak a variety of Arabic.

**Englisc** (ANG LISH) the Old English (Anglo-Saxon) name for the culture and language brought to Britain by the invading Angles and Saxons. The earliest form of English, Englisc developed and changed over a period of several hundred years, from about 450 to 1100 CE, gradually becoming what we now refer to as Middle English.

**Eskimo** a family of Native American languages spoken in Alaska, parts of Canada and Greenland. The two main Eskimo languages are Yupik and Inuit. Examples of Eskimo words are *akiak* (brave), *denilgi* (moose) and *qimmig* (dog.)

**Finnish** one of two official languages of Finland (the other being Swedish.) It is related to Hungarian. Although sometimes Finland is thought of as a Scandinavian country, its language is very different from the Scandinavian languages used in Denmark, Norway and Sweden. Some examples of Finnish words are *kiitos* (thank you), *hyvää huomenta* (good morning), *anteeksi* (sorry) and *kyllä* (yes.)

**Frankish** language of the Franks, one of the Germanic tribes who conquered the Roman territory of Gaul (now France) about 400 CE. France gets its name from the Franks.

**French** the language spoken in France and 28 other countries around the world. It originated around 700 CE and is mostly based on Latin. Nearly half the words in the French vocabulary are identical or similar to English words, for example *chef, salade* and *omelette*. Other examples of French words are *adieu* (good-bye), *avoir* (have), *autre* (other) and *faire* (make or do.)

**Gaelic** See **Irish**.

**German** the language spoken today in Germany, Austria and parts of Switzerland. It originated around 750 CE and is closely related to English and Dutch, as they all share the same parent language. Examples of German words are *Deutsch* (the German language), *Jahr* (yar) meaning year and *Morgen* (morning). (Nouns are always capitalized in written German.)

**Germanic** a group of languages widely spoken around Europe starting at the beginning of the Common Era by tribes we now refer to as Germanic. The Angles and the Saxons were Germanic tribes, and their languages were from the Germanic group. English, German, Dutch and the Scandinavian languages of Norwegian, Danish and Swedish are all descended from Germanic languages.

**Greenland Eskimo** (more commonly called **Greenlandic**) the native Eskimo language spoken by about 60,000 people in Greenland. (See **Eskimo**.) Examples of Greenlandic are the words *qanik* (snow in the air), *unnugu* (tonight) and *immuk* (milk.)

**Greek** See **Ancient Greek**.

**Gypsy** (or **Romani**) a group of languages spoken by the Romani or Gypsy people. Originally from India, the Romani mostly live in Europe. They are unique in that they have a culture and a history, but no country. Examples of Romani words are *chauv* (child), *mush* (man), *shav* (run) and *yog* (fire.) (Note: the term Gypsy is sometimes considered derogatory but is usually the most commonly recognized name for the Romani people.)

**Hebrew** Modern Hebrew is the official language of the country of Israel in the Middle East. The name *Hebrew* derives from the name for the people of ancient Israel. Ancient Hebrew was spoken from about 1000 BCE until 400 CE and is the language of the Old Testament (the first section of *The Bible*). It is a Semitic language, which means it is one of several related languages spoken throughout the Middle East and parts of Africa. Arabic is probably the best-known Semitic language. Some examples of Hebrew words are *shalom* (peace), *imma* (mommy) and *ivrit* (the modern Hebrew language.)

**High German** the standard version of spoken and written German. It is the language used in central and southern Germany, Austria and parts of Switzerland. The term "high" comes from the fact that the central and southern parts of Germany are covered with hills and mountains, so they are "higher" than the northern part of the country. (compare Low German)

**Hindi** the language spoken in the northern part of India. It is one of the most commonly spoken languages in the world. Much of Hindi comes from Sanskrit. Some examples of Hindi words are *namaste* (good-bye), *danyavāda* (thank you) and *hān* (yes).

**Hungarian** called *Magyar* in Hungarian, is the national language of Hungary in Eastern Europe. It is related to Finnish, and has borrowed a number of words from German, Slavic and Turkish. Examples of Hungarian words are *ma* (today), *holnap* (tomorrow), *kicsi* (small) and *nevet* (laugh.)

**imitative** words that are created in imitation of a sound. The word *hiss,* for example, is a close imitation of the sound a snake makes.

The word *clang* imitates the sound of metal hitting metal, as in a ringing bell.

**Icelandic** the national language of Iceland. Descended from Old Norse, written Icelandic has not changed much in the last thousand years. Some examples of Icelandic words are *epli* (apple), *steinn* (stone), *bók* (book) and *hús* (house).

**Indo-European** a language spoken by ancient settlers of the eastern part of Europe about 3000 BCE. About 2500 BCE these settlers began spreading out into other parts of the world. Some went towards what is now India, some into what is now Greece and Turkey, and some into Europe. The name that has been given to these people, and their language, is Indo-European. This is because they settled in areas from India to Europe. In places where they settled, the Indo-European language became a foundation for a number of modern languages, such as German, English, Italian, French, Spanish and Russian. Now, about half the world's people speak a language descended from Indo-European.

**Irish** (also known as **Gaelic**) the traditional language of Ireland, spoken by most Irish until the 1700s when English began to take over. Some examples of Irish words are *im* (butter), *uisce* (water), *bui* (yellow) and *feoil* (meat).

**Irish English** the English language as it is spoken in Ireland today. It is also called Anglo-Irish.

**Italian** the language spoken in Italy. It is the language still the most like Latin, from which it is descended. Some examples of Italian words are *ciao* (hello or goodbye), *felicita* (happiness) and *amore* (love).

**Jamaican** a language spoken by the people of Jamaica, which they call Patois. It is based in English with some African words mixed in. Even though English is the official language of Jamaica, most Jamaicans speak Patois. Example words are *bredda* (brother), *fren'* (friend) and *cyar* (car.)

**Japanese** the national language of Japan, spoken by roughly 130 million people. An Asian language that has been around since roughly 700 CE, it has a number of words borrowed from Chinese. Some examples of Japanese words are *Nihon* (Japan), *ashita* (tomorrow), *gakkou* (school) and *susshin* (hometown).

**Late Latin** a form of Latin spoken and written by administrators and educated citizens during the last part of the Roman Empire from about 200 to 600 CE.

**Latin** a language that was spoken, beginning about 700 BCE, by an ancient people who lived in Italy. They inhabited an area they called Latium, close to what we now know as Rome. Gradually their tongue, Latin, became the main language of Italy. As the Roman Empire expanded, Latin spread. The Latin spoken before the days of the Roman Empire is called "Old Latin." Latin as it was spoken and written by the literate class (educated writers, poets, historians and so on) in the days of the Roman Empire is called "Classical Latin" and this is what is usually referred to as simply Latin. The everyday speech of the same period is often called "Vulgar Latin."

**Louisiana French** versions of French that are mainly spoken in southern parts of the state of Louisiana. It has words from French as well as English, Native American, Spanish and African. *Padna* (friend), *beaucoup* (a lot), and *Tante* (aunt).

**Low German** the version of German spoken in the lower, flatter coastal lands found in the northern part of Germany. (compare High German)

**Malay** a language spoken by roughly 300 million people across Indonesia and Malaysia, Singapore and parts of Thailand and the Philippines. English has a number of words that have come from Malay, words like *gong*, *gecko* and *ketchup*. Some common Malay words are *membaca* (read), *gambar* (picture), *haiwan* (animal) and *kerja* (work).

**Maori** (MAO ree) a native language of New Zealand and one of three official languages of the country. Examples of Maori words are *haka* (a Maori dance), *moana* (sea), *tamariki* (children) and *aroha* (love).

**Medieval** (MID ee vul) **period** (or **Middle Ages**) occurred in Europe from about 470 to 1450 CE, beginning with the defeat of the Roman Empire. Invading tribes from Northern Europe caused great destruction, and much of the learning and art of early Greece and Rome was lost to western Europe for centuries. The term *medieval* comes from Latin *medium* middle and *aevum* age.

**Medieval Latin** the form of Latin in use during the Middle Ages, from about 600 to 1500 CE. It was the language of the Roman Catholic Church. (In the Middle Ages nearly all inhabitants of western Europe were followers of this religion.) It was also the language of learning, and the first books printed in Europe were in Medieval Latin.

**Mexican Spanish** the Spanish spoken in Mexico and parts of the United States. Spanish was originally carried to Mexico in the 1500s by the Spanish conquistadores, and there it gradually mixed with words from Native American languages of the area. An example of a Mexican Spanish word is *guacamole* from Native American *ahuacatl* (avocado) + *mōlli* (sauce). Other examples are *macho* (manly), *bronco* (not tamed, wild) and *chicle* (gum, also originally Native American.)

**Middle** in the history of a language, describes the period between the **Old** or earliest version of the language and its **Modern** or most current version. For example, Middle English was spoken between Old English (450 to 1100 CE) and Modern English (1550 CE forward).

**Middle Dutch** the version of Dutch spoken in the Netherlands from about 1100 to 1500 CE.

**Middle English** the language spoken in England from 1100 to 1550 CE.

**Middle French** the language spoken in France from approximately 1250 to 1500 CE.

**Middle High German** the version of German used in the mountainous southern area of Germany from about 1100 to 1500 CE.

**Middle Low German** the version of German used in the lowlands of Germany from about 1100 to 1500 CE.

**Modern** in the history of a language, refers to its most recent version, the one currently in use.

**Modern English** English as it has been spoken and written from about 1550 until the present. When books first began to be printed in the 1400s, agreement had to be reached as to what written English should look like. The spelling, writing and grammar that was decided on at that time continues, for the most part, to this day.

**Modern Latin** (or **New Latin**) the version of Latin in use from about 1500 on. Latin was revived during the Renaissance, and most of the original scientific works written at that time were in Modern (New) Latin. An example is Galileo's 1610 work *Siderius Nuncias* (Starry Message) describing the first scientific observations made with a telescope. Much of our scientific vocabulary is Modern Latin. For example, the names of all the bones of the body, the scientific name for the crow (*corvus),* and the bumblebee (*bombus),* are all Modern Latin.

**Nahuatl** (NAH wah tul) the Native American language of the Aztec people, whose empire flourished from about 1300 to 1500 in what is now Mexico. Versions of Nahuatl are still spoken in about half the Mexican states. Here are some examples of Nahuatl words: *coyotl* (coyote), *āhuacatl* (avocado) and *tomatl* (tomato).

**Native American** a large group of languages that includes all the native and first people languages of North, Central, and South America, including Canada, the Caribbean, Alaska and Greenland. Before Europeans arrived, there were thousands of native languages spoken throughout the Americas. Several had systems of writing. Sometimes settlers learned native languages. At other times, they ignored or suppressed them in favor of their own. By the 1800s, English, French, Spanish, Dutch and Portuguese had become the main languages of the Americas. Many Native American words have been absorbed into English. (For examples of some Native American languages see **Brazilian Indian, Arawakan, Eskimo, Greenland Eskimo, Nahuatl, Taino, Quechua.**)

**nautical** from the speech of sailors.

**Nordic** See **Scandinavia, Scandinavian.**

**Norman** (or **Norman French**) a variety of French spoken in Normandy, where William the Conqueror came from. When he and his Norman army invaded England, they brought the Norman language. It mixed with some Anglo-Saxon and eventually became the variety of French spoken in England. (See **Anglo-Norman.**) Norman is still spoken in parts of Normandy. Examples of Norman words are *creire* (believe), *feis* (time) and *gaumbe* (leg).

**Norman invasion** the Normans were from Normandy, a region of France across the channel from Britain. In 1066, under the leadership of William of Normandy (also known as William the Conqueror), they defeated the English army. William became king and the Normans became the ruling class of England.

**Norse** the Norse people, also called Norsemen, or Vikings. *Norse* meant *north* in their language, which we call Old Norse. Norsemen came from what is now Denmark, Norway and Sweden. They invaded the northern parts of England beginning around 800 CE. See **Old Norse**.

**North American Indian** the large group of Native American languages of the United States (including Alaska), Canada, Mexico and Greenland. Examples of North American Indian languages are Navajo, Cherokee, Seneca, Oneida, Nahuatl, Eskimo and Greenland Eskimo.

**Norwegian** a main language spoken and written in Norway where it is an official language, along with Swedish and Danish. Norwegian is descended from Old Norse. Examples of Norwegian words are *vann* (water), *navn* (name), *verdensrommet* (outer space), and *blad* (leaf).

**obsolete (obs.)** words that are no longer actively used in the spoken and written versions of a language.

**Old** used to designate the earliest written version of a language. For example, Old English is the name given to the earliest version of English.

**Old Danish** a version of Old Norse, used from about 800 to 1500 CE. The Danish language used today (Modern Danish) is descended from this particular form of Old Norse.

**Old English** (or **Anglo-Saxon**) the language spoken in Britain between 450 and 1100 CE. Brought from Europe by the invading Angle and Saxon tribes, it was the first English to be spoken. A fairly simple but lively and descriptive language, it had a lot of short, punchy words, thousands of which we still use. *Bridd* (bird), *fox, cild* (child) and *hamor* (hammer) are examples.

**Old French** the earliest version of French, spoken from about 1000–1400 CE.

**Old High German** the earliest version of German in use in the mountainous southern area of Germany from about 700 to 1100 CE.

**Old Irish** (or **Old Gaelic**) the earliest form of Irish, used from roughly 600 to 900 CE. Examples of Old Irish words are *son* (sound), *long* (ship), *derc* (dierk) hole and *marb* (dead),

**Old Italian** the earliest version of Italian, spoken from about 1000 until the mid-1500s CE.

**Old Latin** (or **Early Latin**) the earliest version of Latin, spoken until about 75 BCE. See **Latin**.

**Old Low German** (or **Old Saxon**) the earliest version of German spoken in the low, flat coastal area of northern Germany up to about 1100 CE. Old Low German and Old Saxon are two names used for the same language.

**Old Norman French** the French language spoken in Normandy around the time of the Norman invasion. See **Norman invasion**.

**Old Norse** the language spoken by the people of Scandinavia (now Norway, Sweden, Denmark and Iceland) from about 600 to 1400 CE. Old Norse was the language of the Vikings. Modern Norwegian, Swedish, Danish and Icelandic are all descended from it. As the Vikings took over parts of northern England, a number of Old Norse words were borrowed into Old English. Some examples of Old Norse words are *geta* (get), *taka* (take), *vanta* (want) and *hvirfla* (whirl).

**Old Persian** the earliest version of the Persian language, used up until about 300 BCE. See **Persian**.

**Old Saxon** See **Old Low German, Saxon**.

**Pashto** the language of the people of Afghanistan. Examples of Pashto words are *zel* (one hundred), *angresi* (English) and *manana* (thank you).

**Persian** known to those who speak it as **Fārsī** (FAR see), Persian is the official language of Iran, Afghanistan and some other surrounding areas. It gets its name from ancient Persia which we know today as Iran. Some examples of Persian words are *salam* (hello), *parande*

(bird), *bozorg* (big) and *barg* (leaf). Note that these example words are written using the English alphabet, which makes them look very different than they would if written in Persian.

**Phoenicians** ancient traders who lived across the Mediterranean from the Greeks. They had an early alphabet that the Greeks used as a basis for theirs.

**Portuguese** the official language of Portugal, Brazil and several African countries. One of the most commonly spoken languages in the world, it has about 340 million speakers. Some examples of Portuguese words are *ano* (year), *rir* (laugh), *minuto* (minute) and *bonito* (beautiful).

**Quechua** (KETCH WUH) a family of related native languages spoken by about 9 million people in the Andean mountains of Peru, Ecuador, Colombia, Bolivia, Chile and Argentina. Quechua originated in Peru around 500 BCE and today is the most widely spoken surviving native language of the western hemisphere. The words *llama* and *puma* come to English from Quechua. Other Quechuan words are *yaku* (water), *wasi* (home), *pachu* (earth) and *killa* (moon).

**Renaissance** a period of the 15th and 16th centuries marked by a revival in western Europe of Greek and Latin learning. A person of the Renaissance was considered educated if they knew how to read and write Latin and Greek, resulting in many Greek and Latin words entering English.

**Romance languages** the languages descended from Vulgar Latin, the everyday language spoken during the days of the Roman Empire. We get the term "romance" from the Vulgar Latin word *romanice,* which meant "in the Roman tongue." The most widely spoken of the Romance languages are Spanish, Portuguese, French, Italian and Romanian.

**Romani** See Gypsy.

**Romanian** a language spoken by about 25 million people in Romania, a country in the Balkan Peninsula. It is descended from Vulgar Latin. Some examples of Romanian are *Salut* (hello), *la multi ani* (happy birthday) and *unu, doi, trei* (one, two, three.)

**root** a word or part of a word used as a base for making other words, and which has no added parts. The word "certain" is a root found in the words *uncertain* and *certainly.*

**Russian** the language spoken in Russia and some of its surrounding areas. One of the most widely spoken languages in Europe, it has its own alphabet. Some words that have traveled from Russian into English are *cosmonaut* and *mammoth.* Some examples of Russian words (written using the English alphabet) are *preevyet* (hello), *zvat* (call) and *peet* (drink).

**Sanskrit** an ancient language of India, dating back to about 1500 BCE, or even earlier. It is the language of Hinduism and the parent of a number of languages now spoken in India.

**Saxon** the name given to the language spoken by the ancient Saxon tribes, some of whom invaded Britain and some of whom remained in part of what is now Germany. Those that remained in Germany are sometimes referred to as Old Saxons, while those that invaded Britain came to be known as Anglo-Saxons.

**Scandinavia** the region of northern Europe that includes Denmark, Norway and Sweden. Because they have cultures similar to those countries, Finland and Iceland are often referred to as part of Scandinavia. The larger group, including Finland and Iceland, are properly referred to as the Nordic countries.

**Scandinavian** (also called **Nordic**) not to be confused with the Nordic countries, a group of similar languages, all descended from Old Norse, consisting of Danish, Swedish, Norwegian and Icelandic. The languages are similar enough that speakers of Danish,

Swedish and Norwegian can generally understand one another.

**Scots** the native language of the southern lowland parts of Scotland.

**Scottish** (or **Scottish English**) is the version of Modern English spoken in Scotland.

**Scottish Gaelic** a native language spoken in the northern parts of Scotland (the Highlands) starting around 1200 CE. It developed from Irish Gaelic but today it is a distinctly separate language.

**Semitic** (SUH MIT IK) refers to several related languages spoken throughout the Middle East and parts of Africa. Arabic is the most widely spoken Semitic language.

**slang** used to describe informal or very informal language, more often spoken than written. Examples of American slang are *no worries, chill out, slay,* and *epic!*

**Slavic** a group of languages spoken in most of the central and eastern parts of Europe, a number of the Balkan countries, and parts of Asia. They include languages like those spoken in Russia, Ukraine, Poland, Croatia, Bulgaria, Slovakia and the Czech Republic.

**Spanish** a language that originated in what is now Spain. Descended from Vulgar Latin, it arrived to the Americas in the late 1400s. It is now most widely spoken throughout the Americas. Examples of Spanish words are *chica, chico* (girl, boy), *amigo* (friend), *nuevo* (new) and *feliz* (happy.)

**Swedish** the Scandinavian language spoken in Sweden. It is descended from Old Norse. Some examples of Swedish words are *tack* (thank you), *komma* (come), *vatten* (water) and *Svenska* (Swedish).

**Swiss French** a version of French spoken in Switzerland that is quite similar to the French spoken in France. The main languages spoken in Switzerland are Swiss forms of French, German and Italian.

**Taino** a Native American language spoken by the Taino people who lived throughout much of the Caribbean. When Columbus and the Spanish arrived in the New World, it was the Taino they met first. Some examples of Taino words are *inaru* (woman), *canoa* (canoe), *hamaca* (hammock), *huracan* (hurricane), *guey* (sun) and *ni* (water.)

**Tamil** a language spoken by the Tamil people of southern India and Sri Lanka. It is an ancient language over two thousand years old, yet is still spoken by roughly 75 million people. It has its own alphabet. Examples of Tamil words (written using the English alphabet) are *talai* (head), *itayam* (heart), *kai* (hand) and *vitu* (house).

**Thai** the national language of Thailand. Thai has its own alphabet. Examples of Thai words (written using the English alphabet) are *sawa dee* (hello), *ahan* (food), *hong* (room) and *nam* (water.)

**Tongan** the national language of the Kingdom of Tonga, a group of islands in the South Pacific partway between Australia and the United States, and part of Oceania. Some examples of Tongan words are *taha* (one), *tohi* (book), *faiako* (teacher) and *liuaki* (goodbye.)

**Tungus** (or **Tungusic**) a family of native languages still spoken by about 75,000 people in eastern Siberia and Manchuria.

**Turkish** a language spoken in Turkey, Greece, Cyprus and other nearby countries. Until 1928, Turkish was written with the Arabic alphabet, but it is now written using the same alphabet used for English. Some examples of Turkish words are *türk* (Turkish), *merhaba* (hello), *mutluluk* (happiness), *evet* (yes) and *güle güle* (goodbye.)

**ultimately (ult.)** means the point beyond which further investigation in a word's origins is not possible.

**US** a designation used in some dictionaries for variations and additions to English developed in the United States.

**variant (var.)** a different spelling, pronunciation, or form of the same word.

**vernacular** the everyday language spoken by a people in a particular region, often considered informal, not broadly accepted or used.

**Vikings** a seafaring people from what we now call Sweden, Norway and Denmark, the Vikings were excellent craftsmen and traders as well as raiders. From about 800–1000 CE they invaded and settled in northern Britain and other areas of Europe. The language they spoke was Old Norse, and a number of Viking words are still part of the English we speak today.

**Vulgar Latin** meaning "common speech," Vulgar Latin was the everyday Latin spoken by the various inhabitants of the Roman Empire, which included the common folk of many Roman provinces and members of the Roman Army. Latin *vulgaris* meant "common, everyday." A number of European languages are descended from Vulgar Latin.

**Welsh** the native language of Wales, descended from the language of the ancient Britons who left Britain after the Angles and Saxons invaded. It is spoken today by about twenty percent of the Welsh people, while a form of English called "Welsh English" is spoken there as well. Some examples of Welsh: *Cymraeg* (the Welsh language), *dyn* (human being), *plentyn* (child), *anifail* (animal), *aderyn* (bird) and *deilen* (leaf.)

**word family** a group of words with the same root. In some dictionaries a derivation is provided at the root word and is not then repeated for every word in the family.

**Yiddish** a vernacular language based on German that has been spoken by Jewish people for centuries, most particularly in areas of central and eastern Europe and Russia. The literal meaning of Yiddish is "Jewish," and it was called that for a period. It includes words from Hebrew, Slavic, German and other European languages. It is still spoken in a number of Jewish communities today. Examples of Yiddish words are *klutz* (a clumsy person), *kvetch* (complain), *nosh* (snack), *punim* (face) and *spiel* (a long speech or tale).

# HERONBOOKS

If you like the *Derivation Dictionary,* we invite you to explore our wide selection of books and learning materials for students of all ages at heronbooks.com.

## Using the Dictionary Workbooks 1 & 2

Fun exploring dictionaries
Ages 6-8

## Animal Kingdom book & flash cards

The beauty and wonder of animals
Ages 7-9

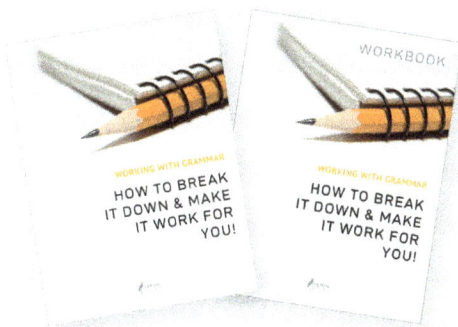

## Working with Grammar & Workbook

Grammar made simple
Ages 13 and up

## Math Essentials Finding & Filling the Gaps

Math repair through simple algebra
Ages 13 and up

www.ingramcontent.com/pod-product-compliance
Lightning Source LLC
Chambersburg PA
CBHW050350110426

42812CB00008B/2428